Southern Slavery and the Law, 1619–1860

STUDIES IN LEGAL HISTORY

Published by the University of North Carolina Press
in association with the American Society for Legal History

Thomas A. Green and Hendrik Hartog, editors

Thomas D. Morris

Southern Slavery and the Law, 1619–1860

The University of North Carolina Press

Chapel Hill and London

Publication of this work was made possible in part through a grant from
the Division of Research Programs of the National Endowment for the
Humanities, an independent federal agency whose mission is to award
grants to support education, scholarship, media programming, libraries,
and museums in order to bring the results of cultural activities to a broad,
general public.

The paper in this book meets the guidelines for permanence and
durability of the Committee on Production Guidelines for Book
Longevity of the Council on Library Resources.

Library of Congress Cataloging-in-Publication Data
Morris, Thomas D., 1938–
Southern slavery and the law, 1619–1860 / by Thomas D. Morris.
p.   cm.—(Studies in legal history)
Includes bibliographical references and index.
ISBN 0-8078-2238-8 (cloth : alk. paper)
1. Slavery—Law and legislation—Southern States—History.
2. Slavery—Southern States—History. I. Title. II. Series.
KF482.M67   1996
342.73′087—dc20   95-6565
[347.30287]   CIP

Parts of this work have been published elsewhere and are used here with
permission. Chapter 2 appeared as " 'Villeinage . . . as It Existed in
England, Reflects but Little Light on Our Subject': The Problem of the
Sources of Southern Slave Law" in the *American Journal of Legal History*
32 (April 1988): 95–137. A portion of Chapter 6 appeared as " 'Society Is
Not Marked by Punctuality in the Payment of Debts': The Chattel
Mortgages of Slaves" in *Ambivalent Legacy: A Legal History of the South*,
edited by David J. Bodenhamer and James W. Ely Jr. (Jackson: University
Press of Mississippi, 1984), 147–70. Chapter 10 appeared as "Slaves and the
Rules of Evidence in Criminal Trials" in the *Chicago-Kent Law Review* 68
(1992): 1209–40. Finally, Chapter 17 appeared as " 'As If the Injury Was
Effected by the Natural Elements of Air or Fire': Slave Wrongs and the
Liability of Masters" in *Law and Society Review* 16 (1981–82): 569–99.

00   99   98   97   96   5   4   3   2   1

For Sally

Contents

PART IV
Manumission

Acknowledgments

My obligations have mounted during the course of this work, which has gone on for about fifteen years. I regret that my effort to acknowledge the help of people individually falls far short because there have been so many.

One group I wish to thank collectively consists of the numerous workers in the state archives, various manuscript collections, and county courthouses throughout the South. Uniformly, they were helpful and courteous. Without their efforts this study could never have included the information about local practice. Because I worked in the local records of all the slaveholding states (with the exception of Delaware), the list of my obligations is so lengthy that I cannot name all the people. I can only hope that they will accept my gratitude. One or two examples must suffice to illustrate their help. During the better part of a morning a county employee in the courthouse in Nachitoches, Louisiana, and I clambered about an old courthouse building soon to be torn down. We sought (without success, in this case) some criminal records in an attic of the building where documents were scattered around, unorganized, and mildewed. In Hayneville, Alabama, the county clerk drove my wife and me to an old garage where the nineteenth-century records were kept and gave us unrestricted access to all the material we could find amid the school desks and old engines. Such stories could be multiplied endlessly.

I shall always cherish the enthusiasm of the staffs of the state archives, county records, and manuscript collections—especially when they realized that I was a Northerner rummaging about in one of the ugliest aspects of Southern history. In addition to these people, the staffs of the University of Washington Law Library, the Law Library at the Northwestern College of Law at Lewis and Clark College, and the interlibrary loan office at Portland State University provided access to the vital published legal materials.

Southern hospitality is so renowned that it seems to exist in a mythical world. But it is a fact, and oddly enough it even appeared among people living in the South who were not born Southerners. Among the Southerners and transplanted Northerners who made our trip to the region so pleasant were Paul Finkelman, then living in Austin, Texas; Ronald Labbé in Lafayette, Louisiana; James Ely Jr. in Nashville; Coburn and Mona Freer in Athens, Georgia; John and "Boots" Basil in Columbia, South Carolina; Mart Stewart in Atlanta; Virginia and Pat Patterson in Richmond; and Walter Evans and Becky Berg in Washington, D.C. Outside the South Cliff and Betty Kroeber made our stay in southern California, where I worked in the Huntington Library, a real treat.

The responses of scholars have been a source of real pleasure, even when they have been less than gentle (sometimes these comments have been the most important and have saved me from the kind of mistakes that leave long-lasting embarrassment). An anonymous reader of one of the chapters deserves to be singled out because he found a gaffe that was almost good enough to send to the *New Yorker* when it published howlers. I am relieved that that one of mine did not live to see the light of day. My critics, however, have been of more value than that. The following have read and commented on chapters or portions of this study: Eugene Genovese, Joel Grossman, Kermit Hall, Peter Hoffer, Stewart Macaulay, A. E. Keir Nash, Christopher Tomlins, and a number of readers who must remain anonymous (although I think I can guess who they might be).

Two scholars must be singled out for their unlimited professional support and their critical acumen. Stanley Engerman and Paul Finkelman read the entire manuscript for the University of North Carolina Press; they made numerous suggestions for improvement of the arguments and the organization of the material and raised important interpretive questions. Both colleagues deserve the highest praise I can offer. They not only read the whole thing, they read revisions of parts and gave them the same critical attention. They especially deserve my warmest appreciation because there are points (occasionally significant ones) where we read the record in different ways. Their support, despite our disparate views, is evidence of the best the community of scholars can offer. I will be forever indebted to Thomas Green, the general editor of the series in legal history. Tom read the manuscript in three different versions. Whatever clarity of argument and organization this volume possesses owes as much to Tom Green as to anyone else. His continuous, warm, and sometimes witty support have made the book possible. Of course, like all the other scholars who have forced me to sharpen my ideas, he bears no blame for any failings that may be present. I did not always accept suggested changes, and perhaps that was unwise. What stylistic crudities and obscure passages remained after their suggestions were then open to the copyediting of Stevie Champion, who worked to clean up the prose and helped with the presentation of the arguments. The final result owes a great deal to her efforts.

I have saved the most important acknowledgment for the end. I cannot express how much I owe my wife, Sally Scholz. Not only has she been a constant support (only she knows how much), she has been a sharp critic of the project over its lifetime and worked as a researcher on a number of occasions, especially on our trip through the South. She gathered a great deal of the information used, particularly the material on criminal trials involving slaves. The dedication of this book to Sally is a truly inadequate tribute, but I offer it with love.

Southern Slavery and the Law, 1619–1860

Introduction

By 1860–61 Southern slaveowners had chosen a course that would end in the death of over half a million people and the freeing of several million more. Toward the end of the slaughter the Federal secretary of war, Edwin M. Stanton, and the Union general William Tecumseh Sherman asked a group of black ministers to define slavery, the root cause of secession and war. Garrison Frazier, one of those ministers, replied with a commonsense definition—slavery was "receiving by irresistible power the work of another man, and not by his consent."[1] Proslavery Southerners occasionally tried to explain slavery as well. Almost thirty years before Frazier met the Federal officers, William Harper of South Carolina wrote in his "Memoir on Slavery": "If I should venture on a definition, I should say that where a man is compelled to labor at the will of another, and to give him much the greater portion of the product of his labor, there *Slavery* exists; and it is immaterial by what sort of compulsion the will of the laborer is subdued."[2]

A decade later, in 1848, the compiler of the laws of Mississippi mentioned a crucial element of Southern slavery left out by Frazier and Harper, race; he referred to slavery as the "Institution of African Service." Four years after that Alabama's lawmakers tried to compose a more formal definition: "the state or condition of negro or African slavery is established by law in this State; conferring on the master property in and the right to the time, labor, and services of the slave, and to enforce obedience on the part of the slave to all his lawful commands."[3] The statement that slavery existed by law was correct and stood in direct opposition to the claims of abolitionists like William Goodell, who asserted in his *American Slave Code* (1853) that slave law was not really law at all: "in speaking . . . of the 'legal relation,' of the 'laws' of slavery and of slave 'owners,' we must not be understood to concede the 'legality' of such 'laws,' or the reality of such 'ownership,' in the proper meaning of those terms. The 'law of sin and death' is not obligatory law."[4]

Frazier bitingly expressed a reality in the lives of Southern slaves, but he did not get it all, anymore than did Harper, the Mississippi codifier, or the Alabama lawmakers. Their emphasis was on the slave as a human being (the reference of Alabama's lawmakers to property was to a property claim in labor and in that sense was not too different from a claim to the labor of a wage worker or an indentured servant).[5] The law gave permission to slaveowners to govern their slaves in order to compel their productive labor. Eugene Genovese called this a "system of complementary plantation law" resting on the authority of the master[6]—that is, it complemented the public law that governed slaves through police laws. But public law also set limits on the violence slaveowners were permitted.

The permission to use force against slaves was secured as well by the claim that the slave was property. Such a claim involved a legally backed right to use the "property" in certain ways. It also involved rights to transfer the slave to someone else, and to name someone to succeed to the ownership on the death of the owner. The notion of the person as property is so ethically repugnant that even scholars who mention the slave as a "thing" often drop it in order to get on to the ways law governed the slave as a person. Alan Watson, one of the most insightful modern writers on slave law (especially Roman slave law), provides an example. He wrote that a "slave might also be treated as a thing . . . and be the object of a legacy." "Little need be said about this subject," he added, "since it is very much an ordinary part of the law of succession and reveals nothing important about slavery."[7]

The slave as an object of property claims, however, is very much a part of the relationship between slavery and law. This is often overlooked for several reasons: property law is not specific to slaves; people naturally think in terms of slaves as human beings as it is hard even to conceive of a person as a thing, and people assume that there is some discrete collection of laws that we can identify as specific to slaves and that we can call *the law of slavery*. Nonetheless, the fact remains that the slave as property is central to any consideration of the relationship between slavery and law. And because that is so, the first major division of this book will examine such subjects as the slave as real or chattel property, the rules by which people succeeded to the ownership of slaves on the death of the owner, and the doctrines used when slaves were transferred to others (as in sales, mortgages, and the hiring of slave labor). Still, as the Alabama lawmakers claimed, slaves at law were human beings who labored and who owed obedience to the commands of their owners. Because slaves were "thinking property," as Aristotle described them,[8] tensions existed. The slaves' humanity even conditioned or altered the application of legal rules of property that were not specific to them. But it was as human beings subject to the protection of the law, as well as to its commands and the commands of their owners, that the slaves' humanity was most evident. This was especially true when a slave was dealt with as a victim or a perpetrator of crime or misbehavior. The problems created will be considered in the chapters that make up the second major division of this book. This law included rules about whites and free blacks, as well as slaves. Among the most prominent that concerned all three groups were measures that controlled both consensual interracial sexual relationships and interracial sexual violence. In the end, however, it all came to bear on the slaves. The final section of the book is concerned with emancipation— that is, with the authority of the owner to end all property claims in the slave.

A portion of the law involving slaves is found in statutes, but a great deal of it is not. Nonstatutory law included the body of doctrine worked out by judges applying ideas found in common law legal sources (such treatises as *Coke on Littleton* [1628], Blackstone's *Commentaries on the Laws of England* [1765–69], Powell on contracts [1790], and Hawkins on crime [1724–26]).[9] Both statutory and nonstatutory legal doctrines also included policy judgments that involved nonlegal matters. These included concerns that grew out of class relationships among whites, a racist commitment to keep people of color subordinate to whites, market demands and theories of political economy, and even evangelical Christianity. By the mid-nineteenth century policy increasingly covered issues that arose out of the festering sectional struggles with the free communities of the North.

The interrelationship between slavery and law, however, was more than policies found in statutes and judge-made legal doctrines—the law was practice as well as doctrine. In order to grasp the law as practice at the local level, I examined the records of over fifty Southern counties. I have tried to capture the rich texture and variety with as diverse a sample as the extant records permit. There is material from urban communities like Savannah, Richmond, and Natchez (older communities and newer ones); from older rural counties with large slave populations, like Westmoreland County, Virginia; and from counties with smaller numbers of slaves, such as Spartanburg District, South Carolina, and Harrison County, Texas.

Ira Berlin has warned against the creation of "an essentially static vision of slave culture" because of a focus on one period, especially the nineteenth century, when slavery had undergone significant change from the colonial world. By the nineteenth century, to use the felicitous phrase of Willie Lee Rose, there had occurred a "domestication of domestic slavery."[10] If we focus our attention on the later years of slavery, we violate Berlin's injunction to be mindful of "time, space, and the evolution of Afro-American society."[11] The same can be said of Southern legal culture: some of the finest work to date is limited by its focus on the nineteenth century. To understand the transformation of Southern legal culture insofar as it concerned slavery, we must broaden our vision to include the colonial world. Therefore I have integrated judicial doctrine developed in the highest courts of the Southern colonies and states, legislative policies that emerged over time, and the actual practice of the law at the county and municipal levels throughout the region that made up the slave states on the eve of the Civil War.

To give texture to this comprehensive study it is important to place it in the broader historical context of New World slavery. "Plantation slavery," Elizabeth Fox-Genovese and Eugene Genovese have written, "arose in the Americas as part of the process of international capitalist development."[12] But it appeared in different forms from Brazil, through the Caribbean, and into the North American continent, and it coexisted with a variety of slave systems around the world. The South was one variation on the theme of social and legal transformation that went along with the spread of slavery and capitalism during the seventeenth through nineteenth centuries. Within the South, in turn, there were variations among the differing slave societies that depended on several variables, such as the time of settlement, the demographics of the slave population, and the climate and the crops produced.

Slavery began in the English colonial settlement of Virginia as early as 1619, when the settlers traded for twenty blacks brought by a Dutch man-of-war. The number of slaves in Virginia, however, was small until the end of the seventeenth century, when the settlers turned from white indentured servants to slaves to labor on the plantations. Thereafter the numbers grew rapidly. From 1708 to 1750, according to Edmund Morgan, "Virginia recorded the entry of 38,418 slaves into the colony" largely to work in the tobacco fields. By the end of the century, at the time of the first Federal census, there were 292,627 slaves in Virginia.[13] Slavery was the source of labor for Maryland's tobacco planters as well. But Maryland's slave population was never as large as Virginia's. Although there were as many as 111,502 slaves as late as 1810, their number declined as Maryland turned toward commercial activities and cereal production.[14] Life changed for slaves throughout the region. Allan Kulikoff has shown that sex ratios came closer to parity in the Chesapeake Bay colonies by the mid-eighteenth century so that slaves came to live more commonly in family units.[15] Slavery also surfaced in Delaware during the seventeenth century, but it did not flourish—in 1790 there were fewer than 9,000 slaves.[16]

Slavery appeared with the settlement during the late seventeenth century of the area that later was separated into North and South Carolina. Rice planted in the swampy coastal region was the most valuable crop in South Carolina as early as the eighteenth century and one of the most valuable Southern commodities until the spread of cotton in the nineteenth century.[17] By the end of the eighteenth century there were about 107,000 slaves in South Carolina and 100,000 in North Carolina.[18] Georgia's settlers originally accepted the decision of the trustees to keep slavery out, but by 1750 the pressures to introduce it overwhelmed the earlier intention. At the end of the eighteenth century there were approximately 30,000 slaves in Georgia. The greatest period of growth in the slave population of that state occurred after 1830. By 1850 Georgia and South Carolina each had over 380,000 and were surpassed only by Virginia with more than 470,000.[19] All of these slave societies were cushioned along the Atlantic coast.

The first settlements away from the coast appeared toward the end of the eighteenth century. Kentucky (with significant investments in hemp plantations) and Tennessee (where cotton became a leading crop) were created as slave states out of the states of Virginia and North Carolina. Kentucky entered the Union in 1792 and Tennessee in 1796. Neither had large slave populations at the close of the eighteenth century (there were about 12,400 slaves in Kentucky and 3,400 in Tennessee). By 1850 each state had slave populations of over 200,000.[20]

The cotton kingdom spread through the Deep South after the War of 1812 as Mississippi and Alabama entered the Union, but development was not always immediate even though many Southerners from the older seaboard South succumbed to "Alabama fever," the desire to move on and acquire a fresh start on fresh land. One of the richest cotton-producing areas of the whole region, the Mississippi Delta counties running from Vicksburg north to Memphis, was a plantation frontier as late as midcentury with a boisterous, sparse white population and unsettled conditions in which people still hunted bears and cougars while they wrested wealth from the rich alluvial soil.[21] In 1810 Mississippi and Alabama had small slave populations that hardly exceeded those of Tennessee and Kentucky of twenty years earlier. By 1850 these Deep South states had been largely, but not completely, transformed into prosperous communities with the material trappings of conspicuous wealth and over 300,000 slaves apiece.[22] Arkansas and Missouri (where Kentuckians had introduced the hemp industry, which provided a lot of the rope and bagging needed by cotton planters) entered the Union at the end of the War of 1812 as well.[23] Slavery did not expand as rapidly there as in the Deep South: as late as 1830 there were only 25,000 slaves in Missouri and 4,500 in Arkansas.[24]

During the 1820s Florida entered the Union as a territory, and later became a state, but slavery did not expand quickly. It had only about 15,000 slaves in 1830 and one of the smallest slave communities on the eve of the Civil War.[25] The last slave state to enter was Texas, where slavery had been established during the 1830s and 1840s, only a couple of decades before the outbreak of the Civil War. There were approximately 58,000 slaves in Texas as of 1850, and most of them were concentrated in the eastern counties.[26]

Louisiana, settled early in the eighteenth century by the French, was a special case. As Gwendolyn Midlo Hall noted: "French Louisiana cannot be accurately described as a plantation society. It never really developed a viable, self-sustaining economy . . . [it] was not a prosperous slave plantation society producing valuable export staples." There were about 4,700 slaves by 1746. Things began to change after 1769 with the accession of the Spanish to power in the region. "Louisiana was Spain's most heavily subsidized colony," Hall observed,[27] and by the nineteenth century it had become a major slave market and sugar as well as cotton producer of the United States: from about 34,000 slaves in the 1810 census the population grew to nearly 245,000 slaves by 1850.[28]

There were significant changes in economic structure throughout the South during the nineteenth century. The cotton kingdom spread into upland South Carolina, for instance, and with the decline in the profitability of tobacco many Chesapeake planters shifted to the production of wheat. Substantial consequences accompanied the shift, as Barbara Jeanne Fields observed for Maryland: "the retreat of tobacco and the advance of cereal agriculture in the longer-settled regions of the state . . . diminished the need for a fixed labor force."[29] Alexis de Tocqueville was so impressed with this change that he argued (incorrectly, as it turned out) that with the decline in tobacco profits Virginians and Marylanders were on the verge of abandoning slavery.[30]

Both slavery and Southern legal culture were also affected during the nineteenth century by the introduction of railroads and industry regionwide. Industrial development in the South lagged far behind the North, of course, but it was fairly significant.[31] Nonetheless, capital invested in the South remained overwhelmingly committed to slaves in particular and to land. As late as 1860, according to Roger Ransom and Richard Sutch, the value of slaves was almost 60 percent of all agricultural wealth in the cotton states of South Carolina, Georgia, Alabama,

Mississippi, and Louisiana. Land and buildings amounted to less than one-third of the value of agricultural wealth.[32] Gavin Wright summarized the point neatly: "In the antebellum South, wealth and wealth accumulation meant slaves, and land was distinctly secondary. This was not just the perspective of a few giant planters. The owner of as few as three slaves had a larger investment in human beings than the average nonslaveholder had in all other forms of wealth put together."[33] Notwithstanding, the region was becoming more complex economically as the Civil War approached and railroad mileage began to increase and a few factories appeared. All of these changes gave rise to new legal questions and a variety of legal responses as people tried to adapt slavery to economic structures being transformed by the pressures of international capitalism.

It was an adapted English legal culture that upheld this complex social and economic order based on human bondage. Because most of the states of the American South built their laws bearing on slaves on an English legal heritage, I shall refer to technical rules of English law at a number of points in this book. Legal specialists will be completely familiar with the rules and the structure of the system, but, because I hope this study will be of value to nonlegal specialists, it should provide a brief introduction to prominent features of the inherited system. Specialists, no doubt, will want to skip over the next few pages.

At the heart of the private side of seventeenth- and eighteenth-century common law was the writ system. A writ was a document issued from a court commencing a civil suit. This was the primary use of the writ and the one to which I refer in what follows. The system of common law writs evolved and expanded over time as the king's officials responded to novel kinds of complaints. Each type of writ was known by a particular name and possessed a number of technical features. The most important "forms of action" in the laws of slavery were detinue, trespass, debt, case,[34] trover, and assumpsit. Detinue can serve as an example of the way the action worked in general and of the fact that particular ideas were associated with each of the actions. The defendant in detinue was charged with an "unjust detainer," not an unlawful taking. The most important feature of the action was that "the defendant when worsted is always allowed the option of surrendering the goods or paying assessed damages. The reasons of this may perhaps be found partly in the perishable character of medieval moveables, and the consequent feeling that the court could not accept the task of restoring them to their owners, and partly in the idea that all things had a 'legal price' which, if the plaintiff gets, is enough for him."[35]

The original writs commenced suits and required litigants to adhere to certain formalities; often they delineated the nature of the remedy (a person might be compelled to pay damages for his conduct, or relinquish property, or he might have the option as in detinue). Each of the writs required elaborate forms of pleading—statement of the complaint, response, and so forth. According to a

number of legal historians, common law thought about rights, duties, and remedies was tied to the specific forms of action. As Frederic William Maitland, perhaps
the leading student of the system, put it, "each procedural pigeon-hole contains its
own substantive law."[36] People did not think in terms of general categories, such as
contract or property or torts.[37] By the nineteenth century patience with the extreme technicality and artificiality of the common law (fictions abounded—something had to be done "with force and violence" to give a court jurisdiction even
though there had been none) had grown thin.[38] Indeed, the system had long been
under increasing criticism. Even Sir William Blackstone, who exalted the common
law, wrote this about the system in the mid-eighteenth century: "we inherit an old
Gothic castle, erected in the days of chivalry, but fitted up for a modern inhabitant.
The moated ramparts, the embattled towers, and the trophied halls, are magnifi-
cent and venerable, but useless. The inferior apartments, now converted into
rooms of convenience, are chearful [*sic*] and commodious, though their approaches are winding and difficult."[39] By the late eighteenth and early nineteenth
centuries the common law was slowly coming to be reorganized around the general categories with which we are familiar. Nonetheless, the common law writ
system continued to coexist with these newer ways of thinking about law down to
the end of slavery in the South.

This system was supplemented by a "parallel" law of equity, a body of rules and
remedies derived from the court of chancery. The history of equity involves a
complex and long-standing jurisdictional struggle between the court of chancery
and the common law courts, that is, the courts of King's Bench, common pleas,
and exchequer. Henry Home, Lord Kames, one of the greatest of Scotland's
eighteenth-century jurists, pointed out the general sweep: "equity, in its proper
sense, comprehends every matter of law that by the common law is left without
remedy."[40] That meant a great deal, for equitable jurisdiction covered a wide range
of substantive matters. In contract, for instance, one might look to equitable relief
for the rescission or reformation of the contract on grounds of mistake, fraud,
duress, or accident. Equity also provided forms of relief unavailable at common
law, such as an injunction or a decree for specific performance of a contract
(whereby a party was commanded to perform what he or she had promised rather
than pay damages for nonperformance).[41]

Together common law and equity made up a complex legal system that rested on
precedent, tradition, and custom: understandably, it was not without its critics. As
early as the seventeenth century Sir Francis Bacon, in *De Augmentis Scientiarum*,
argued for an intrusive use of legislation to achieve the "reconstruction of the law"
and remove the ambiguity, obscurity, and technicality of the common law.[42] Nonetheless, it was not until the nineteenth century that the English and Americans
turned increasingly to the use of statutes to achieve clarity and predictability in the
law.[43] Generally, the above remarks apply to the private side of the law.

Categorization of wrongs into criminal and civil in English law was the result of
a knotty history, and some of the earlier distinctions would confuse modern

readers. As English legal historian Theodore F. T. Plucknett put it about the English law of the Middle Ages, people "were more intent on doing what had to be done, than on classifying the ways of doing it."[44] Nevertheless, by the time of the English settlements in North America it was common to deal with "crime" under the subject of the "pleas of the Crown" (Sir Edward Coke's Third *Institute* [1644] bears that title, as do the works of Sir Matthew Hale and Sir William Hawkins later).[45] The pleas of the Crown concerned the procedural and substantive rules whereby the king's courts dealt with certain forms of misbehavior—including what we would consider serious criminal conduct like homicide, theft, arson, and rape. They were "pleas of the Crown," according to Blackstone, "because the king, in whom centers the majesty of the whole community, is supposed by the law to be the person injured by every infraction of the public rights of that community."[46] As S. F. C. Milsom, another English legal scholar, observed, "the criminal law grew from the methods evolved by the crown for prosecuting pleas of the crown at its own suit."[47] But he also noted that legal change in criminal law was more often by legislation than in other parts of the English legal heritage. Consequently, treatises on pleas of the Crown often involved procedural and substantive law that emerged from the king's courts and from statutes. I rely on these treatises often in the second part of this book when examining the legal context in which Southerners developed their criminal law involving slaves.

There are two exceptions to these general remarks—the legal systems of Texas and Louisiana. It will be important to remember that the legal system of Texas was influenced by Spanish law on the civil side. As Chief Justice Abner Lipscomb of Texas informed Judge Joseph Henry Lumpkin of Georgia in 1853, "our System of Jurisprudence is a very peculiar One," but he preferred it to the "ancient system" of the common law which was filled with "evils."[48] Louisiana's legal order was a tangled blend of French and Spanish concepts and, after 1803, of some aspects of the English legal tradition. Although Louisiana was acquired by the United States in 1803, its legal structure was not changed completely. The rules and procedures of English criminal law largely supplanted the civil law of the French and Spanish, but the law relating to succession to property and transfers and uses of property remained that of the continental civil law.[49]

In recent years there have been a number of thoughtful efforts to identify what A. E. Keir Nash called the "driving explanations" of the rules and the changes in the law as it affected slaves. For some scholars the most important factor in any explanation is race, whereas for others it is class relationships, or the needs of capitalism, or even an internal dynamic in legal thought. There is much to be said for the prominence given each of these by scholars, but if presented as *the* explanation of the adoption of legal rules the emphasis can be misleading. Morton Horwitz recently bemoaned the "new cult of complexity" that has replaced the "admirable generalizing and simplifying goals of nineteenth-century modes of explanation."[50] But "multi-factored complexity" (which Horwitz adopted despite his misgivings) is precisely what is needed to understand the history of the relationship between law and slavery in the American South. The weight of the various factors differed depending on time, place, and subject. My hope is that I have integrated and built upon the insights and the debates of those who have advanced the various explanations for the adoption of the legal rules affecting slaves.

For some writers the strongest explanatory factor is race. Watson, for instance, described Southern slavery as the "paradigm case of racist slavery." Fox-Genovese and Genovese, on the other side, have urged us to avoid the misleading "tendency to study southern law primarily, indeed often exclusively, as 'the law of slavery' or as 'Negro law.' "[51] Despite the wisdom of this caution, we should not lose sight of the importance of race. And most writers have emphasized race to some degree. An excellent example is the influential 1946 work of Frank Tannenbaum, *Slave and Citizen: The Negro in the Americas*, comparing slavery in the English and non-English New World slave societies. The English, he believed, were the most racist. They created a closed system based on race that could be destroyed in the end only by violence because they made the emancipation of people of color all but impossible. Tannenbaum's brief work, influenced by the horrors of the Holocaust, raised crucial questions—"those that trouble our own day. They are questions of freedom, liberty, justice, law, and morality." The questions "all . . . revolve about the place of man in the world and the relation of men to each other." Slavery, he noted, "was not merely a legal relation: it was also a moral one." Tannenbaum was especially concerned with social change and believed that slavery had an important lesson to teach: "wherever the law accepted the doctrine of moral personality of the slave and made possible the gradual achievement of freedom implicit in such a doctrine, the slave system was abolished peacefully. Where the slave was denied recognition as a moral person and was therefore considered incapable of freedom, the abolition of slavery was accomplished by force—that is, by revolution."[52] Ever since Tannenbaum's volume appeared there has been a notable debate about the degree to which Southern law accepted the moral personality of slaves.[53]

One of the strongest efforts to place race at the center of any study of slave law, and to deny that Southerners gave much recognition to the humanity of the slave, has been that of A. Leon Higginbotham Jr. In his 1978 study, *In the Matter of Color: Race and the American Legal Process: The Colonial Period*, he tried to show "how the American legal process was able to set its conscience aside and, by pragmatic toadying to economic 'needs,' rationalize a regression of human rights for blacks." But he did not overlook nonracial causes either: it was the "demand of the marketplace" that reduced blacks to rightless persons. The result was the "legal cannibalism" of whites and the "dehumanization" of blacks at law.[54] More recently he and Anne F. Jacobs put forward ten "basic, underlying precepts" that permeated the law of slavery, the first three running as follows:

1. *Inferiority*: Presume, preserve, protect, and defend the ideal of the superiority of whites and the inferiority of blacks.

2. *Property*: Define the slave as the master's property, disregard the humanity of the slave except when it serves the master's interest, and deny slaves the fruits of their labor.

3. *Powerlessness*: Keep blacks—whether slave or free—as powerless as possible so that they will be submissive and dependent in every respect, not only to the master, but to whites in general. To assure powerlessness, subject blacks to a secondary system of justice with lesser rights and protections and greater punishments than for whites.[55]

The debate about the relationship between racism and slavery remains unsettled, however. Whatever position one takes, no one would quarrel with George Fredrickson's observation that "demoting other people from the ranks of humanity on grounds of race or ethnicity, and treating them accordingly, is a sin of unique and horrendous character." It is not necessary, on the other hand, to agree with him that we gain much by arguing that this injustice surpasses the "injustices of class in modern capitalist societies." Nor need we agree that racism was the "child of slavery."[56] Others have contended that racism preexisted slavery and provided a fertile soil for white enslavers. Winthrop Jordan, for instance, in *White Over Black: American Attitudes toward the Negro, 1550–1812* (1968), maintained that "blackness" was loaded with special negative meanings for the English. Moreover, blacks were not Christians: "heathenism was treated not so much as a specifically religious defect but as one manifestation of a general refusal to measure up to proper standards, as a failure to be English or even civilized."[57] The English, in short, were predisposed to view Africans as inferior to themselves, and in the end they used racial differences to justify slavery in their possessions. This is a view I favor. Slavery, then, reinforced racist perceptions.

The precise relationship between race and legal notions also remains unsettled, even for those who emphasize the role of race. Although he called Southern slavery the "paradigm case of racist slavery," Watson looked to legal culture for an explanation of legal developments. Slavery was a racist institution in Latin America, but "the law remained nonracist in its rules" because it was based on Roman law, and that law was the "paradigm case of nonracist slavery." The English, on the other hand, had no direct experience with slavery, and so they created a legal system "*de novo*" based on race. Watson nonetheless argued that the real driving force in the law is internal: that is, "lawyers thinking about law, not societal conditions . . . determines the shape of legal change in developed legal systems."[58]

Mark Tushnet adopted a different perspective toward the relationship between Southern law and race. Southern judges sought to find an "ordering principle" for slave law, and one of the possibilities was race. But it failed to provide the principle, in Tushnet's view, because of the existence of free blacks. "To transform the society into one in which race was unequivocally coextensive with slavery," he wrote,

"manumission would have to have been eliminated . . . [but] eliminating manumission would have required that the master class accept the propriety of social
control over their individual choices." A. E. Keir Nash saw Southern judges caught
up in a struggle between "unresolved dichotomies"—"the rule of law versus the
supremacy of whites over blacks, and the black man as human versus the black
man as property." William W. Fisher III, as a final example, correctly pointed out
that among the crucial issues for an understanding of the law of slavery was the
"changing ways white Southerners conceived of and sought to justify their social
world." For Fisher, that depended on the ways they answered three questions—
"What are Negroes like? Why is slavery just? How should an honorable and moral
person live?"[59] My own view on the general role of race in the law of slavery is
explained in the first chapter of this book. Its influence on the rulings of particular
judges and in the adoption of particular legal rules is developed throughout the
volume.

The relationship between Southern law and capitalism has been another thorny
problem for scholars. Stanley Elkins, in *Slavery: A Problem in American Institutional and Intellectual Life* (1959), concluded that unchallenged capitalism rather
than race provides the real explanation for the laws of slavery. There was nothing
in the American South—not the church and not the state—to stop "unmitigated
capitalism from becoming unmitigated slavery." One of his basic conclusions was
that "the master must have absolute power over the slave's body, and the law was
developing in such a way as to give it to him at every crucial point."[60]

Although I disagree with this conclusion, I agree completely that capitalist
culture was a vital component of the laws applied to slaves. But what is capitalism?
Some scholars see the treatment of labor as a commodity to be traded in a market
as one of the most significant defining characteristics of capitalism. Central to the
emergence of what C. B. Macpherson has called "possessive individualism" was the
notion that one had a property in one's own labor and could alienate that labor.[61]
The social world of which this was a part was one in which autonomous individuals traded goods (which could include their labor) in a market in which each
party to the transaction was free. The reality was different, of course, as Robert
Steinfeld has shown: "The property that masters had enjoyed for centuries in the
labor of their servants . . . began to be reimagined as the product of a voluntary
transaction struck between two separate and autonomous individuals, one of
whom traded away to the other the property in his labor for wages or other
compensation." The result was new social relations "based on personal freedom,"
but, as Patrick Atiyah noted, it was an illusion.[62] Some of the legal rules applied to
slaves came from this illusory world in which workers were not truly free precisely
because of their degraded and dependent position in society.

Other scholars add the perception of property as a key to understanding the
capitalist societies of the seventeenth through nineteenth centuries. Fox-Genovese
and Genovese argue that "the extension of capitalist development within a country
or a region depended upon a free market in labor-power and upon absolute

property—in short, upon the maximum mobility of capital, land, and labor." Capitalism was incomplete, James Oakes added, "until 'absolute' property rights had fully replaced the feudal system, in which customary rights to the use of land were held 'conditionally' by serf, lord, and ultimately the king."[63]

Franklin Knight suggests that the essence of capitalism was the "pervasive *mentality* that the accumulation of profit for private purposes represents a worthwhile end in itself." There is a similar emphasis in Robert Fogel and Stanley Engerman's *Time on the Cross: The Economics of American Negro Slavery* (1989).[64] Capitalism was all of these things—a set of values about "free labor," markets, profits, and property. My own use of the notion differs from these scholars only in that I think it bears emphasis that "absolute" property is not necessary for capitalism to flourish. Absolute property may be the goal, but it has never been attained and need not be.

Legal ideas and instruments supported capitalism as well as channeled some of its impulses or bent to accommodate them as far as slaves were concerned. This complex relationship was further complicated in the Anglo-American world of the seventeenth through nineteenth centuries by a struggle between different social conceptions. Republicanism was one pole in the struggle. Property, in a republican society, was not simply a means to make money, it was a "means of anchoring the individual in the structure of power and virtue and liberating him to practice these activities. In this classical political tradition men realized their fullest potential in politics, in serving the public good and protecting the constitution." The alternative vision was of the "natural harmony of autonomous individuals freely exerting themselves to take care of their own interests while expanding the range of free exchange and free inquiry."[65] Liberal capitalism, which emerged by the nineteenth century, was the result of that vision when joined with the newer perceptions of absolute or nearly absolute property. Republicanism and liberalism engaged Southern slaveowners of the nineteenth century as they did those Americans living in the free states of the North.

Elkins's conception of "unmitigated capitalism" at the center of legal change in the South is most compatible with the view that holds that the South was essentially a region that accepted liberal capitalism. Tushnet, a Marxist legal scholar, sees the South in a different way. Following Genovese,[66] he argues that the South was a hierarchical society that differed in important ways from the capitalist world with which it coexisted. Furthermore, he contends, Southerners tried to create an autonomous body of slave law that was separate from bourgeois law. Tushnet relies on a model of law that emphasized a failed quest for formally rational principles:

> The emergence of a law of slavery, distinct from a law of crimes, torts, and contracts where slaves were involved, was facilitated by the increasing codification of the law, especially the criminal law, because the theory of the common law adopted by Southern courts made it possible for them to accept lines between slaves and whites, when drawn by legislatures, that would have seemed arbitrary if drawn by courts. Codification can be seen as a manifesta-

tion of the process labeled "formal rationality" by Max Weber, the product of the cognitive and institutional inability of judges to process the always increasing number of cases that had to be accommodated in a precedent system.[67]

Common law judges, Tushnet noted, reasoned by analogy from one situation to another, and the possible analogies in nonslave common law decisions were almost open-ended. The very style of common law thought, in other words, created problems for judges who tried to create an autonomous law of slavery. The "inevitable openness of reasoning by analogy" was one serious limitation on judges, but even more crucial was the "structural incompatibility of a 'law of slavery' in a slave society."[68] In the end codification could not provide the answer either.

A slave society, Tushnet pointed out, was based on devolution of authority to the masters on the plantations. Moreover, the relationship between masters and slaves was a total relationship that covered virtually everything that made up human contact. Slave society was not a capitalist society. But the South existed in a capitalist world, and the legal heritage was of a bourgeois or market-driven world. Property, in a bourgeois world, was defined in terms of money. Law in such a world was filled with rules that reflected that particular view of property—for example, contract rules that provided money damages for breaches of contractual agreements because the property exchanged was interchangeable with other property and measurable in money. But such bourgeois rules, defined by market relationships alone, did not fit the master-slave relations of a plantation slave society. Ultimately, Tushnet argued, "categorization attempted to confine slave law to the slave setting, but the enterprise was incompatible with the logic of slavery, which entirely denied the relevance of law to that setting." Slave law, as Fox-Genovese and Genovese put it, took into account the master-slave relationship and therefore resisted "the normal bourgeois effort to reduce all forms of property, especially slaves, to the common denominator of money." As long as Southern judges used the norms of a bourgeois legal order in their search for an autonomous slave law, they were doomed to fail, in Tushnet's view, because of the basic incompatibility of slave society and bourgeois law.[69]

Although there is much to be learned from Tushnet's approach, I do not believe that his analytic model captures the messy and often complex attempts of Southern judges to deal with the problems created by "thinking property." There is a too rigid reliance on the notion that lawmakers sought a formally rational and discrete body of law limited to slaves. Codification was not important until the nineteenth century, and even then it was only one strand in a complex legal culture. Judges applied property rules that were nonspecific to slaves without much effort to create property rules that were limited to them, and there is little statutory evidence that they tried to create such a discrete body of slave law, either (Tushnet emphasized that codification appeared especially in the criminal law). Still, there is force in the belief that many rules of law that emerged from the seventeenth through nineteenth centuries were not very congenial to a hierarchical society that rested on the bondage of people of color. In that sense there is much to be said for the view that there was a "structural incompatibility" between slave society and the rules of law built around the market relationships that were central to capitalism.

No matter what explanatory model scholars have used, they all recognize that the South was a world under considerable stress by the mid-nineteenth century. Southerners, under severe attack especially after 1830 from militant abolitionists, defended themselves with the theory of a social order based on the subordination and obedience of "inferior" people of color. Mary Boykin Chesnut, one of the most brilliant diarists of the Old South, pointed out a serious error of Northerners. "They expected an African to work and behave as a white man," she wrote, "we do not. . . . People can't love things dirty, ugly, and repulsive, simply because they ought to do so."[70] This was a social world resting on the "work" of "repulsive" people and shored up by a complex body of law that applied to slaves. But it was a social order filled with contradictory impulses, some of which grew out of the humanness of those in bondage and some out of the fact that Southern slavery coexisted with capitalism and evangelical Christianity. It was also under assault from those outside the South who found slavery to be against the word of God as well as incompatible with nineteenth-century capitalism. A striking representative of that view was the abolitionist Goodell, who had denied that slave law was really law. The way to end the horrors of the immoral system of Southern slavery was this: "Let those who need the labor of the colored people employ them for honest wages, and leave off living by plunder. This is God's own remedy for slavery."[71]

There were, then, numerous pressures, and the future in the mid-nineteenth century was open-textured. It contained many possibilities, and some were awful from the standpoint of some of the more insightful slaveowners. John C. Calhoun, one of the greatest proslavery statesmen and a man who shared Mary Chesnut's view that Northerners just did not understand, captured as well as any the anxiety about the future:

> It is to us a vital question. It involves not only our liberty, but, what is greater (if to freemen anything can be), existence itself. The relation which now exists between the two races in the slave-holding States has existed for two centuries. It has grown with our growth, and strengthened with our strength. It has entered into and modified all our institutions, civil and political. None other can be substituted. We will not, we cannot, permit it to be destroyed. . . . Come what will, should it cost every drop of blood and every cent of property, we must defend ourselves; and if compelled, we would stand justified by all laws, human and divine . . . we would act under an imperious necessity. There would be to us but one alternative,—to triumph or perish as a people.[72]

I

Sources: Racial and Legal

1

The Function of Race in Southern Slave Law

The Institution of African Service

Code of Mississippi (1848)

"These two words, *Negro* and *Slave*," the Reverend Morgan Godwyn wrote in 1680, had "by custom grown Homogeneous and convertible; even as *Negro* and *Christian, Englishman* and *Heathen*, are by the like corrupt Custom and Partiality made Opposites."[1] A century later Thomas Jefferson wrote of the "elegant symmetry of form" of whites and the "strong and disagreeable odor" of blacks. Blacks were "much inferior" in intellect, and their "griefs are transient." Jefferson believed that blacks, "whether originally a distinct race, or made distinct by time and circumstances, are inferior to the whites in the endowments both of body and mind."[2]

Long before, Aristotle had written that some were "natural slaves."[3] There was a profound debate held in Valladolid, Spain, in 1550–51 between Juan Gines de Sepulveda and Bartolomé de Las Casas about whether Amerindians were such natural slaves. As inferiors, Sepulveda claimed, they needed "to be placed under the authority of civilized and virtuous princes or nations, so that they may learn . . . worthier customs and a more civilized way of life." Las Casas also accepted the Aristotelian notion but believed that Indians were more accomplished than did Sepulveda. As an alternative he suggested, only to later recant, that Africans rather than Indians ought to be enslaved.[4]

Especially striking in early observations about Africans were whites' views on the sexuality of the males. Oliver Goldsmith argued that the African's "penis was longer and much wider" than the white's. This was a "scientific" commonplace by the end of the eighteenth century.[5] Obsession among whites with the size of the penis has figured prominently in often testy racial relationships, but it is only one element in a larger scientific predisposition to categorize groups of people in terms of physical characteristics. This was linked in Western thought with the notion of a "Great Chain of Being."[6] Life was part of a chain that ascended from the lowest to the highest order. Such a view, together with the Aristotelian notion of the natural slave and—finally—the perversion of the so-called curse of Ham in Christianity,[7] raised and answered the crucial question for Southern whites, at least by the nineteenth century: which "race" of people were "natural slaves"?

An illustration of the answer is in T. R. R. Cobb's 1858 study of the law of slavery in the South. Cobb explored the "nature" of "negroes" to show that they were natural slaves. He concluded that

> this inquiry into the physical, mental, and moral development of the negro race, seems to point them clearly, as peculiarly fitted for a laborious class. Their physical frame is capable of great and long-continued exertion. Their mental capacity renders them incapable of successful self-development, and yet adapts them for the direction of a wiser race. Their moral character renders them happy, peaceful, contented, and cheerful in a status that would break the spirit and destroy the energies of the Caucasian or the native American.[8]

Still, slavery and racism were not inevitably joined. Most societies enslaved people of the same race.[9] Watson has claimed that "Roman law is the paradigm case for nonracist slavery." Nonetheless, in the New World the relationship between slavery and racial difference was close. Early in this century U. B. Phillips contended that slavery was a form of racial control. Harry Hoetink, on the other hand, later argued that "it is not the peculiar institution of slavery per se which lies at the root of race relations. . . . In retrospect, slavery is nothing but a temporary arrangement, brought about by temporary economic conjunctures." Arnold Sio has maintained that this view puts us in danger of explaining away the "very facts of slavery." He agreed with Carl Degler that "the status of the slave and a dark skin always went together." Genovese focused on slavery as a class system; nonetheless, he accepted the importance of race. As he put it, "slavery in the Americas had a racial basis and therefore must be understood, not simply as a class question, but as a class question with a profound racial dimension, which can only be understood as the particular product of each slaveholding regime. A class analysis, in short, is not enough and can only serve as the basis for a much more complex analysis." Fredrickson took issue with the notion that slavery was paternalistic. Yet he stated that slavery was a system that "fused class and race elements." But, he concluded, "a stable class hierarchy could only exist in the presence of inherent racial differences between leisured and laboring classes, such as those said to exist between black and white in the southern states. Attempts to have servile work done by biological equals, namely whites, was a prescription for class conflict and revolution."[10]

According to Watson, "since it was only in English America that a slave law grew up *de novo* with slavery based on race, that law ought to be the paradigm case for racist slavery."[11] No one would claim that Southern slavery lacked a "profound racial dimension," so it is surprising that few scholars have examined the role of race in *legal* thought. Tushnet is a major exception. Southern courts, he contended, needed to "define and thereby restrict slave law" in order to create an "autonomous" law of slavery. One of the most obvious classifying devices was race. Ultimately, however, "the slave-law/black-law equation failed as a general ordering principle." One possible reason there was only an "incomplete acceptance of race" was that it was not always easy to draw lines "when it mattered." Miscegenation and manumission created problems for drawing racial lines. A. Leon Higginbotham Jr. also considered the role of race in the legal process, especially during the colonial period. Because manumission was not frequent then, he did not have to deal with the classification problem presented by a large number of free persons of color, many of mixed race. He tended to lump people under the rubric "black" and argued, for instance, that the difference between black and white spared whites any guilt over the "legal cannibalism" of blacks.[12] A different view is that of A. E. Keir Nash, whose work focused on the nineteenth century. He concluded that one of the unresolved tensions in Southern law was the "black man as human versus the black man as property."[13] Whether race failed as an "ordering" principle or how the tensions might have been mediated or resolved cannot be answered until we have a clear understanding of exactly what job race was intended to do in Southern legal thought.

Indian Slavery

Who could be enslaved? In English America "blacks" could, but not "whites." Not all persons were unmixed African or all English, however, and what of the Amerindians?

Brutishness was common in the English world of the seventeenth century, and this was reflected in the responses to the problem of the Amerindians. Here there was no finespun Aristotelianism as at Valladolid. After the massacre of whites on Good Friday 1622, white Virginians turned with savagery against the Indians. One settler suggested that the Indians might "now most justly be compelled to servitude and drudgery, and supply the roome of men that labour, whereby even the meanest of the plantation may imploy themselves more entirely in their Arts and Occupations, which are more generous whilest Savages performe their inferiour workes of digging in mynes, and the like." Others preferred killing to enslavement.[14] For still others, enslavement was a prelude to sale into the Caribbean. South Carolinians were adept at disposing of enslaved hostile Indians outside the province, as they did with the Tuscarora and Yemassee in the early eighteenth century, and in Louisiana the French used the same technique to dispose of the Natchez.[15]

Nonetheless, the experience with Indian slavery was not deep. The earliest relevant Virginia statute, March 1654/5, provided that Indian children could become servants to whites in order to be educated and Christianized. They would be "servants for such terme as shall be agreed on" by the parent and the master. This was indentured servitude,[16] not slavery. Three years later a law was adopted that held that service due from an Indian child to be educated could not be assigned to someone else, and the child would be free at age twenty-five. Another law of that year made it a crime for anyone to buy an Indian from an Englishman. Some English had "corrupted" some Indians to bring them the children of other Indians "to the greate scandall of Christianitie and of the English nation."[17]

Ambiguity remained. In 1670 the burgesses responded to a dispute about the status of Indians "taken in warr by any other nation" and sold to the English by holding that only those "servants not being christians imported into this colony by shipping shalbe slaves for their lives." Children who came by land would be servants until they were thirty, and adults would serve for twelve years. Indians sold to the English, of course, would come by land whereas Africans would come by sea. Another law of that year did treat Indians and Africans similarly. They could not buy a white servant, even if they themselves were free and Christianized, but they could own "any of their owne nation." One of the strongest early statements of the right to enslave Indians was in a law of June 1676 of the Baconian rebels. It said that "all Indians taken in warr be held and accounted slaves dureing life." In 1679, after the collapse of the Baconian uprising, the burgesses provided that any Indian taken in war "shalbe free purchase to the souldier takeing the same."[18]

Although Indian slavery existed in English colonies, the numbers were not large. In Henrico County, Virginia, for instance, thirty-three Indian children were brought before the county court to have their ages adjudged, from April 1683 to April 1684. Outside Henrico the figures were even lower. In Northumberland County there were two Indian and three black children whose ages were adjudged in the two-year period after 1682, and in York there were four Indian and twelve black children.[19] By a law of 1682 the ages of a young "negroe, or other slave" would be settled by a court for the purpose of the payment of tithes.[20]

The number of enslaved Indians in South Carolina may have been larger. In 1708, for example, a census reported the following figures for the colony as a whole: 120 white servants, 3,960 free whites, 4,100 black slaves, and 1,400 Indian slaves. Indian slavery declined in South Carolina after 1719. The supply dried up after the Tuscarora War of 1711–13 and the Yemassee War of 1715–17.[21] In North Carolina Indian slaves were also mentioned on occasion. Seth Sothell, a governor of the province, disposed of these properties in his will: "A Negro Nantell and his wife[,] a Negro Named Charles[,] and [an] Indian Woman named Dinah and her Child an Indian Boy."[22]

Even though marginal, Indian slavery did exist. As late as 1853 the abolitionist Goodell asserted that "the *native Indians* have also been enslaved, and *their* descendants are still in slavery."[23] In the early nineteenth century the Virginia Court of Appeals concluded in *Hudgins v. Wrights* that it was lawful to enslave Indians only down to 1691, when a law was passed on free trade between the Indians and the white colonists. Thereafter, the only Indians who could be slaves were those descended from a female who was enslaved lawfully before that date.[24] In South Carolina John Belton O'Neall noted in 1848 that "all negroes and Indians (free Indians in amity with this Government, negroes, mulattoes and mestizoes, who now are free, excepted . . .), were slaves," but added that the "race of slave Indians . . . is extinct."[25]

A special problem was presented by the enslavement of Indians in Louisiana before its acquisition by the United States in 1803. The difficulty appeared in *Seville v. Chretien* (1817). In the 1760s an Indian trader at Opelousas sold an Indian woman to Chretien. Seville was a child of the Indian woman. One of the grounds on which freedom was claimed was that under Spanish law Indians could not be lawfully enslaved. The response contended that the case should be decided under French law, and it allowed the enslavement of Indians. When the Spanish took control of Louisiana in 1769, they discovered that the French had been holding Indians as slaves. Alejandro O'Reilly, the Spanish governor, confirmed the titles until the pleasure of the Spanish monarch was made known. It never was. As late as 1794 Baron de Carondelet, the governor, ordered two Indian slaves to return to their owners. Seville remained a slave.[26] This was a belated victory for Sepulveda, but doubtless he would have been less content with the 1834 decision of the Missouri Supreme Court in *Marguerite v. Chouteau*.[27]

This case also turned on a claim under Louisiana law before the American acquisition. Judge George Tompkins rejected the argument that where there was no positive law *against* slavery, persons "already reduced to that state may be held in it." It required a positive enactment to justify enslavement, custom was not enough.[28] Such a sanguine view was too much for Judge Robert Wash. In dissent he claimed that slavery did not rest on municipal law, and Lord Chief Justice William Mansfield's claim in the landmark English case of *Somerset* that it must was pure tosh.[29] "To say that nature, enlightened humanity and the pure principles of christianity, cry out against slavery," Wash wrote, "is to talk not only without authority, but directly in the face of authority. . . . It is out and out, from beginning to end, a pure question of power." What the "despot or the despotic will of the majority . . . decrees or permits, becomes the law of the land."[30] Despite such legal disputes, as far as Amerindians were concerned enslavement figured as only a marginal danger in the ruthless, bloody relationship with whites. Death rather than slavery was the more common prospect.

Presumptions and Definitions

Most slaves in North America were Africans or persons who had African ancestors. That led to a significant principle of American slave law. As Cobb put it, "the black color of the race raises the presumption of slavery."[31] With one notable exception the general presumption based on "blackness" was a commonplace of Southern law by the nineteenth century. The exception was Delaware. *State v. Dillahunt* (1840) involved a black witness in a murder trial who was objected to because it had not been proved that she was free. The court ruled her competent. It admitted that earlier in Delaware "the fact of the existence of the negro race in a state of bondage to the whites, and a large majority of that color being slaves, was considered sufficiently strong . . . to introduce a legal presumption that a colored person is *prima facie* a slave." That had changed. Of the 20,000 "persons of color" in Delaware in 1840, fully 17,000 were free and 3,000 were slaves. There was no longer any reason to "presume slavery from color."[32]

Despite this exception Cobb was correct. However, he added that the presumption is "extended, in most of the States, to mulattoes or persons of mixed blood, casting upon them the onus of proving a free *maternal* ancestor." His textual support for this was that "in Virginia and Kentucky, one-fourth negro blood presumes slavery, less than that, freedom." This one-fourth rule, he claimed, was adopted in other states as well.[33] Cobb was careless. What he did was to extend a rebuttable legal presumption of slavery that arose from "blackness" to a larger category of people and link it to a statutory rule that defined a mulatto. They were not the same. They did involve the problem of legal categorization, and this, perhaps, was the reason for the mistake.

Exactly how did Southern whites categorize people at law and for what purposes? It may seem odd but the only effort to define a "negro" in statutory law was in the Virginia code of 1849. The whole section was this: "Every person who has one-fourth part or more of negro blood shall be deemed a mulatto, and the word 'negro' in any other section of this, or in any future statute, shall be construed to mean mulatto as well as negro." There were other efforts to provide descriptions of a "negro" in legal sources, but not in statutes. Cobb, for instance, wrote that "the black color alone does not constitute the negro, nor does the fact of a residence and origin in Africa . . . : the negro race is marked by a black complexion, crisped or woolly hair, compressed cranium, and a flat nose. The projection of the lower parts of the face and the thick lips evidently approximate it to the monkey tribe." O'Neall observed that the "term negro is confined to slave Africans, (the ancient Berbers) and their descendants. It does not embrace the free inhabitants of Africa, such as the Egyptians, Moors, or the negro Asiatics, such as the Lascars."[34]

Some Southern legislators did try to define "mulattoes." The Spanish word *mulatto* came into English usage about 1600, but there was no *legal* definition in Virginia until 1705.[35] For over half a century Virginians dealt with miscegenation without any formal legal definition to categorize the offspring.

Mulatto (derived from the Spanish word for a mule) was used to refer to a person with one white parent and one black. When colonial Virginians finally defined a mulatto in a legal text, they departed from the original idea. The Virginians' effort appeared in 1705 at the end of "An act declaring who shall not bear office in this country." This law did not create a legal presumption of slavery based on race; rather, it was an attempt to define who would enjoy all the rights and powers of free men and women and who would not. It was blatantly racist, of course, but it had nothing to do with slavery. The definition itself was odd: "the child of an Indian and the child, grand child, or great grand child, of a negro shall be deemed, accounted, held and taken to be a mulatto."[36] The law defined as a mulatto a person born to a white and an Indian, an Indian and a black, a white and a black, or several other combinations covered outside the English slave societies by words such as quadroon or octoroon. Virginia's law, in other words, defined as a mulatto the offspring of any racially mixed couple no matter what the racial types.

Virginians, of course, had dealt with interracial sexual relationships before the adoption of this curious definition. Hugh Davis's case is but the earliest recorded example. In 1630 he was "soundly whipt" before a number of blacks and whites for "defiling his body in lying with a negro."[37] The first statute on interracial sexual relationships, however, was not adopted for another thirty-two years. The law of 1662 was introduced because "doubts have arrisen whether children got by any Englishman upon a negro woman should be slave or ffree."[38] The principle applied was that the status of the child derived from its mother. By using this rule the legislators closed off the possibility of an innovative racial solution. They could have adopted the Chinese rule that all children born to mixed couples would take the status of the most degraded parent.[39] Race could have been a reasonably firm "ordering" principle of Southern slave law. But the Virginians left a large gap. What about the status of a child born to a white woman by a black father, especially a slave father? In 1679 Susanna Barnes was ordered to serve an additional two years in Charles City County because she had had a "Bastard child being a Mulatto."[40] Nothing was recorded about the child. The void was filled by a law of 1691. It provided that any free Englishwoman who had a bastard by "any negro or mulatto" would be fined. If she could not pay the fine, she was to serve five years as an indentured servant. Her child would be bound out as a servant until age thirty. In 1705 the age was raised to thirty-one; this law included an explanation: it was because the child was an "abominable mixture and spurious issue." The burgesses added another layer in 1723. Any child born to a "female mullatto, or indian" who was bound to serve for the thirty or thirty-one years would also serve that woman's master. The time of service would be the same as the mother's. By 1765 the ages of service were dropped to twenty-one for males and eighteen for females because it was considered "an unreasonable severity" to make them serve until the age of thirty-one.[41] By the nineteenth century enforced servitude of children born to a free white woman by a slave father dropped out of the records. During the colonial period it was different. In Charles City County, for instance, Joseph Barham, a bastard "begot by a negro on the body of a white woman," was bound out in 1744 according to the law.[42]

Virginia's final effort to define a mulatto was an influential statute copied in other jurisdictions. The 1785 law provided that "every person who shall have one-fourth part or more of negro blood, shall . . . be deemed a mulatto." Outside of colonial Virginia, Maryland and North Carolina also tried to define a mulatto. North Carolina developed a couple of definitions but, according to Jordan, "pushed the taint of Negro ancestry from one-eighth to one-sixteenth." South Carolina, Georgia, and Delaware did not produce statutory definitions: it was a matter of observation in those jurisdictions. In 1715 Maryland initiated the thirty-one-year servitude rule for mulattoes born to white women, and North Carolina adopted it in 1741.[43]

Racial prejudice, of course, ran deep, but there was ambivalence as many people crossed the line.[44] Some of these interracial sexual relationships rested on affection, but far too many of them were based on the property claim of masters to control the reproduction capacities of slaves and on a claim to "use" their slaves as they wished. This was one of the ugliest forms of exploitation resting on the notion that the person was property. Robert Newsome of Callaway County, Missouri, represented an extreme expression of that claim. He bought a young girl, Celia, for the purpose of sexual exploitation, and in the end both paid with their lives: during the 1850s Celia killed Newsome and was executed by hanging. This was a rare example of an exploited slave woman reacting against the ongoing sexual violence of her owner. One of the issues at stake, according to Melton McLaurin, was that of "who controlled sexual access to female slaves." Although those whites who ended in court (but not so much as victims like Newsome) were lower-class people, it bears emphasis that it was not they alone who crossed the line. William Byrd of Westover, for instance, admitted that he had "played the fool with Sally," one of his slaves. In the nineteenth century there are numerous well-known illustrations. James Henry Hammond, the proslavery apologist, fathered a son by one of his slaves. And there is this famous remark of Mary Boykin Chesnut: "Like the patriarchs of old our men live all in one house with their wives and their concubines, and the mulattoes one sees in every family exactly resemble the white children—and every lady tells you who is the father of all the mulatto children in everybody's household, but those in her own she seems to think drop from the clouds, or pretends so to think."[45]

The patriarchs rarely paid a legal price for their randy conduct, however. One never comes across a person of the position of a Byrd, a Hammond, or a Chesnut in court because of interracial sexual relationships. In fact, aside from an occasional case like that of Hugh Davis or a divorce action, there is scant evidence that adult white males were held legally responsible. Sexism was another layer in Southern patriarchal societies. Most whites who suffered for consensual interracial sexual relationships were women and their children. A typical entry in the colonial records was the action involving "Mallatto Jane" in 1740 in Prince Georges County, Maryland. She was ordered to serve seven years, and her "mulatto" bastard was bound out for thirty-one years.[46]

By the end of the colonial period whites clearly no longer felt comfortable with the enforced servitude of mixed-race children born to free women. This was because of an increasing humanitarian sensibility by the end of the eighteenth century, the collapse of the institution of indentured servitude, and a "promulatto bias" that emerged by the nineteenth century.[47] Cobb provided an illustration of the latter in his *Historical Sketch of Slavery* when he discussed the lack of chastity in female slaves and the "corresponding immorality in the white males." An important cause, in his view, was that the "negress knows that the offspring of such intercourse, the mulatto, having greater intelligence, and being indeed a superior race, has a better opportunity of enjoying the privileges of domestics; in other words, *is elevated* by the mixture of blood."[48]

However extensive the hopes of the "negress," the fact is that most racially mixed people remained slaves, because most interracial sexual relationships were between white males and slave women. But not all mixed-race people were slaves—both because of emancipation and because some miscegenous relationships were between white women and slave men. This raised questions about status. What happened when someone claimed to be free and someone else claimed them as a slave? This is where the crucial legal presumption came into play. One of the most forceful statements of the presumption was that of O'Neall of South Carolina. He observed that "color is prima facie evidence, that the party bearing the color of a negro, mulatto or mestizo, is a slave." There are several things to note about this presumption. First of all, it bore no direct or necessary relationship to the one-fourth definition used to identify a mulatto, despite Cobb's inference.[49] Second, it was a rule of evidence and could be rebutted. Finally, though widely used it was not universal.

It was vital to adopt some presumption or other whenever there was a question about a person's status. This occurred with the spread of manumission in the late eighteenth century as slavery came under increasing condemnation. According to the census for 1790, there were over 12,000 free persons of color in Virginia, over 8,000 in Maryland, nearly 5,000 in North Carolina, 1,800 in South Carolina, and 400 in Georgia.[50] In a society based on the ownership of nonwhite slaves it was inevitable that the existence of a large number of free nonwhites would raise crucial legal problems involving status. One of the first such cases was *Gobu v. Gobu* (1802), tried in North Carolina. Judge John Louis Taylor accepted the legal "presumption of every black person being a slave." This was because "the negroes originally brought to this country were slaves." He did not adopt the presumption as O'Neall later described it. The presumption in North Carolina was that every *black* person was a slave. According to Taylor, the "doctrine of presuming against liberty" had not been pressed before in cases involving "persons of mixed blood, or to those of any color between the two extremes of black and white." This meant that no presumption of slavery arose from a color other than black. The reason was that people of color from mixed backgrounds "may have descended from Indians in both lines, or at least in the maternal; they may have descended from a white parent in the maternal line or from mulatto parents originally free, in all which cases the offspring, following the condition of the mother, is entitled to freedom. Considering how many probabilities there are in favor of the liberty of these persons, they ought not to be deprived of it upon mere presumption." North Carolina's judges generally adhered to this norm. In the civil contract case, *Nichols v. Bell* (1853), for instance, Chief Justice Frederick Nash wrote: "let the presumption rest upon the African color; that is a decided mark: but to carry it into shades, would lead us into darkness, doubt and uncertainty, for they are as various as the admixture of blood between the races, and against the rule that presumptions are always in favor of liberty."[51]

Virginia's judges also wrestled with the problem. *Hudgins v. Wrights* (1806) involved a claim of descent from an Indian. The members of the court did not confine themselves to that claim. St. George Tucker's view was that one who was "*evidently white*" was presumed free, and the burden of proof of slavery rested on the person claiming him or her as a slave. The problem was one of observation. "Nature," he declared, "has stampt upon the African and his descendants two characteristic marks, besides the difference of complexion, which often remain visible long after the characteristic distinction of color either disappears or becomes doubtful." Color was not a sufficient standard by itself. The two characteristics were a "flat nose and woolly head of hair. The latter of these characteristics disappears the last of all: and so strong an ingredient in the African constitution is this latter character, that it predominates uniformly where the party is in equal degree descended from parents of different complexions, whether white or Indian." So "pointed" was the distinction between blacks and Indians, he concluded, that a "man might as easily mistake the glossy, jetty cloathing of an American bear for the wool of a black sheep, as the hair of an American Indian for that of an African, or the descendant of an African."[52] Tucker treated the problem as one of observation, not legal definition. He did not mention the one-fourth rule that appeared in the Virginia statute.

Was Cobb altogether wrong about the one-fourth rule? In two jurisdictions, Kentucky and Arkansas, the link between the one-fourth rule and the legal presumption was made or discussed. Kentucky's Supreme Court did so in *Gentry v. McMinnis* in 1835. Whenever there was a question of liberty or slavery in Virginia, under whose law the case was to be decided, "a black or mulatto complexion is *prima facie* evidence that the person of such color is a slave." Chief Justice George Robertson concluded that "being a mulatto, or having at least one fourth of African blood, has been held, in Virginia and in Kentucky, to be presumptive evidence of being a slave."[53] However, he cited no case other than *Hudgins*, and nowhere in the Virginia case did a judge mention the one-fourth rule.

A bizarre development occurred in the Arkansas cases. These cases were not representative of Southern legal thought,[54] but they presented an additional and extreme way Southern judges might deal with the problem of the presumption arising from color. Chief Justice Elbert H. English delivered the opinion in *Daniel v. Guy* (1857). He admitted that in a strict sense a mulatto was a person born to parents one of whom was white and the other black. But the word *mulatto* was to be viewed in a nontechnical way in the state law. In Arkansas persons less than quadroons could lawfully be held in slavery. If a slave woman were a quadroon and she had a child by a white, the child, much less than one-fourth black, would be a slave by virtue of the maxim, *partus sequitur ventrem*.[55]

English then marched with waving banners at the head of his parade of horribles. He noted that in Arkansas "mulattoes" could not be witnesses against whites, but if the word was limited to those one-fourth or above, slaves less than one-fourth could testify against whites, even against their master. The person might be entitled to the writ of habeas corpus and might even be allowed to marry a white. Despite the statutory definition, English arrived at this conclusion: "they meant to embrace in the term *mulatto*, persons belonging to the *negro race*, who are of an intermixture of white and negro blood, without regard to grades." This is the "one-drop" rule that apparently existed in the South after the end of slavery, but it is the only instance of it I have seen before 1865.[56]

The evidentiary conclusion in *Daniel*, nonetheless, went back to observation, not legal definition. If it "manifestly" appeared that a person suing for freedom was a "negro," the presumption was that he was a slave; if it appeared that he was white, the presumption was reversed; and "if it be doubtful," there was "no basis for legal presumption, one way or the other." The benefit of the doubt went to the person claiming freedom because "courts should be careful that a person of the white race be not deprived of his liberty."[57]

It is difficult to find much coherence in the Arkansas court's approach, as *Gary v. Stevenson* (1858) shows. Dr. Brown testified that he had examined Thomas Gary, the complainant. He "could discover no trace of the negro blood in his eyes, nose, mouth or jaw—his hair is smooth and of sandy complexion, perfectly straight and flat, with no indications of the crisp or negro curl: his eyes blue, his jaws thin, his nose slim and long." Among the "experts" only Dr. Dibbrell raised a question. He believed that Gary might possess a small amount of Negro blood; not more than a sixteenth, "perhaps not so much, would not positively swear he had any at all, so vague are the signs of the admixture of the negro race, in one so remotely removed from the African blood by crossing with the white." Dibbrell summarized his observations as follows: his "hair is sandy and straight, brows white, features regular as in the white race, eyes grey and clear, upper lip rather thicker than in the white race—temperament sanguine." Dibbrell testified that he knew that Gary had been held as a slave and that his mother, later emancipated, had been also. The mother was of a "very light complexion." The judgment of the court was that "it is to be observed that the complainant does not allege . . . that he is a free person, otherwise than that he is a white person, born of a white person." Judge Christopher C. Scott, for the court, held that "whether he belonged to the white, or the negro race, we think the preponderance of the testimony is, that he belongs to the latter." There is nothing in the opinion itself to account for this astonishing conclusion. The headnote may contain the explanation. It was that when there was a doubt from one's personal appearance, evidence that the person's mother was a lawfully held slave would "repel any presumption in his favor that he was entitled to freedom." Gary's mother had been held as a slave and emancipated. She had not contested her bondage. Her son, therefore, was a slave, and because white people should not be deprived of their liberty, Gary must be a "negro."[58]

Generally speaking, the presumption of freedom based on whiteness was rarely rebutted by evidence of status, and the presumption of slavery based on color was not reduced to a one-drop rule. For Louisiana, for example, with its large cultured free black and mulatto community, the presumption was the same as in *Gobu*. In *Adelle v. Beauregard* (1810) the court relied on the North Carolina decision. It held that blacks were presumed slaves but that "persons of color" were not.[59]

Judges in South Carolina broadened the presumption. In *State v. Scott* (1829) a defendant convicted in the court of general sessions of trading with a slave claimed that that court lacked jurisdiction because he was a mulatto and should have been tried in an ad hoc magistrate freeholders' court. Judge, later Chancellor, David Johnson held that it was a question of fact to be determined by a jury. Nevertheless, he tried to provide guidance. "We know," he wrote, "that nature has clothed her children in all the variety which can exist between European fairness and the African black; and although color would in general be a safe guide in determining genealogy, yet in this country where all the shades are so mixed up and blended together, it is not an infallible criterion." What would amount to proper evidence was a matter of great difficulty, he believed. "When the color is distinctly marked, that of itself would furnish a presumption of the class to which the individual belonged." "In a doubtful case, common reputation," Johnson reasoned, "which is always admissible in the deduction of pedigree, would serve as a guide. But these, as mere presumptions, must yield to positive proof." Reputation rather than simple observation would do the job.[60]

Two years later Chancellor William Harper considered two cases involving the competency of witnesses who were objected to on the ground that they were mulattoes. "It would be dangerous and cruel to subject" to the statutory disqualification "persons bearing all the features of a white, on account of some remote admixture of negro blood; nor has the term mulatto, or person of colour, I believe, been popularly attributed to such a person." He added: "where there is a distinct and visible admixture of negro blood, the person is to be denominated a mulatto, or person of colour," and that was a question for the triers of fact. They possessed the evidence of "inspection" and "reputation." Nonetheless, Harper was not satisfied and turned to Louisiana for a standard. There a descendant of a white and a quadroon was to be considered white. Harper urged the South Carolina legislature to adopt this rule, and in one of the cases before him he held that the witness was a quadroon and so a "mulatto, or person of color." Harper judicially employed the one-fourth rule, but the legislature did not. In 1848 O'Neall summarized the position in South Carolina. A mulatto, he wrote, was the "issue of the white and the negro. When the mulatto ceases and a party bearing some slight taint of the African blood, ranks as white, is a question for the solution of a Jury." He noted that "no specific rule, as to the quantity of negro blood . . . has ever been adopted." "Between 1/4 and 1/8 seems fairly to be debateable ground. When the blood is reduced to, or below 1/8, the Jury ought always to find the party *white*. When the blood is 1/4 or more African, the Jury must find the party a mulatto."[61]

There was some truth in Cobb's assertion even though it was misleading. There was a tendency to run together what had been a legal definition of a mulatto and a legal presumption of slavery based on color, at least to the extent that Southerners specified who *could* be a slave. The inclination was to define a quadroon as a mulatto and a mulatto as a Negro. The one-drop rule in Arkansas and the reverse presumption in Delaware were quixotic exceptions to the general trend. One way to determine whether a person fell into the category of possible slave was observation. It was probably the most crucial. There is no reason to conclude that race failed as an "ordering principle." One of the legal jobs of race was to decide who could be a slave and who could not. Outside the law of slavery it dictated the rights of free persons. As far as slavery was concerned, in the widest sense a white could not be a slave, a person of color could be, a black presumptively was, and those who fell between a white and a quadroon might be, but the evidentiary presumption of liberty was in their favor. The standard was not precise and in individual cases might be absurd, but it was not so incoherent as to amount to a legal failure.

Racial Relations at Law

The first problem was to define people by race, although that did not identify them as free or slave. Once a racial definition was made, and once a person was determined to be a slave or a free person of color, the question became the allowable relationship between whites and nonwhites, and between free persons of color and slaves. In other New World slave societies the problem was handled in a number of ways, but often whites tried to make allies of free persons of color even while limiting their rights. Jamaican whites, for instance, allowed free persons of color selected rights and tried to coopt them precisely because the number of whites was small on the island in comparison to the number of nonwhites, free and slave. Whites in Jamaica needed the support of free nonwhites, but the precise relationships could be complex. Hoetink has shown that there were crucial differences between the Dutch plantation colony of Surinam and the Dutch commercial colony of Curaçao in terms of the alliances whites made and the rights they allowed the various elements in the free colored community.[62] The policy choice in the South was to avoid any alliance with the free nonwhites and to place severe restrictions upon them, even to the point of exclusion from the state.[63] They would be on one side of a rigid color line. What remained to be defined was the allowable relationship between the slave and the free nonwhite who lived on the same side of the color line. One way was to try to keep them separated, and the other was to press them closer together.

An extreme example of the first way, and one of the only ones, was a North Carolina law of the 1830s. Free blacks who married or lived as husband or wife with a slave would be punished.[64] Insofar as the law included a *marriage* between a slave and a free black, it was an absurdity. Slaves lacked the necessary "will" to enter into a marriage contract, and slave jurisdictions universally refused to recognize any slave marriage.[65] Cohabitation was different. In any event, the law was enforced. There were a number of indictments in New Hanover and Northampton Counties against free blacks in the 1850s and in 1860–61, for example.[66] Mariah Sweat, a nineteen-year-old mulatto, pled guilty to cohabiting with a slave in 1860. Several others indicted also were mulattoes.[67]

A touchier issue concerned the right of free blacks to own slaves. In some jurisdictions the right was affirmed, and in others it was denied. In cases in the Carolinas in 1833, for instance, the right of free blacks to own slaves was upheld. In *State v. Edmund, (a slave)*, Judge Thomas Ruffin observed that in North Carolina "a free man of colour may own . . . lands and personal property, including slaves." Free blacks could own slaves, but they could not live with them as spouses. North Carolina's legislators ended the absurdity in 1861, when they passed a law denying the right of any free black to own a slave. In South Carolina no such law was ever enacted. In *Cline v. Caldwell* (1833), Judge O'Neall noted that as "free persons" they could own slaves without restrictions.[68]

Free black owners of slaves throughout the South were often owners of their own kin whom they could not free because of legal restraints, but some were involved in what Luther Porter Jackson called "holding of the commercial type." There were such people in Virginia, South Carolina, and Louisiana, for example. Among them were Marie Thereze Coincoin of the Cane River settlement in Louisiana and William Ellison of South Carolina. Both had been slaves.[69]

Some states, on the other side, denied the right of free persons of color to own slaves. By a statute of 1818 Georgia prohibited such ownership: "No free person of color within this State . . . shall be permitted to purchase or acquire . . . any slave or slaves." How far this prohibition extended was debated in *Bryan v. Walton* (1856). Judge Lumpkin refused to include within the concept, a "free person of color," anyone with the slightest black ancestry. The court would not endorse the doctrine "that if a person has any negro blood, he is disabled from conveying slaves. . . . we should say that to put him under such a disability, he must have one-eighth of African blood in his veins." A person with less than one-eighth black ancestry would not be a person of color under Georgia law. Once a free person was defined as a person of color, however, he or she could not own a slave.[70]

Adjudications in Missouri, Arkansas, and Delaware also dealt with the problem. Missouri's Judge William Scott, in *Davis v. Evans* (1853), argued that "a negro, under our laws, cannot hold slaves. It is against their policy, and in its tendency is subversive of all the police laws for the government of slaves." Judges Hamilton R. Gamble and John F. Ryland did not agree "that a free negro may not legally hold slaves."[71]

The Delaware and Arkansas judgments are more significant because they rested squarely on a perception of the master-slave relationship. The result in *Tindal v. Hudson* (Delaware, 1838) was less generous to free blacks than one would imagine in view of the decision two years later that color did not raise a presumption of slavery. If free blacks could own slaves, a "dangerous species of slavery hitherto unknown" would be allowed. The free black was "almost as helpless and dependant on the white race as the slave himself." The master-slave relationship meant that in exchange for obedience and labor the master provided protection, but free blacks could not do so. "Neither usages, policy, nor the necessary relations of master and slave," the Delaware court observed, "will permit free negroes in this state to hold slaves."[72]

A more fulsome racist defense of the position that free blacks could not own slaves appeared in *Ewell v. Tidwell* (Arkansas, 1859). "The ownership of slaves by free negroes," the Arkansas court began, "is directly opposed to the principles upon which slavery exists among us." It was an institution that had

> its foundation in an *inferiority of race*. There is a striking difference between the *black* and *white* man, in intellect, feelings and principles. In the order of providence, the former was made inferior to the latter; and hence the bondage of the one to the other. . . . The bondage of one negro to another, has not this solid foundation to rest upon. The free negro finds in the slave his brother in blood, in color, feelings, education and principle. He has but few civil rights, nor can have consistent with the good order of society; . . . civilly and morally disqualified to extend protection, and exercise dominion over the slave.[73]

Both Arkansas and Delaware judges agreed that one duty of a master was protection, and free blacks, who lived under numerous legal disabilities, could not provide it. This legal duty emerged in the South by the late eighteenth century. Such issues did not arise in the colonial world, and many nineteenth-century judges who discussed the duty in some connections overlooked its relevance in the case of the right of free blacks to own slaves.

Voluntary Enslavement

Enslavement took a psychological toll,[74] and it created debased images of the victims in the minds of the enslavers. As Thomas R. Dew put it in his influential proslavery work, the "blacks have *now* [emphasis added] all the habits and feelings of slaves, the whites have those of masters." Dew made no distinction between blacks who were free and those who were slaves; in fact, he was at pains to argue that freedom for blacks was a failure.[75] Nonetheless, it took over twenty years of agitation and debate before Southern whites reached an obvious conclusion. If blacks were "natural slaves," then a free black was a contradiction and all blacks should be slaves. One of the more forceful expressions of this was by George Fitzhugh of Virginia: "What Shall be Done with the Free Negroes?" he asked. "A free negro! Why, the very term seems an absurdity. It is our daily boast, and experience verifies it, that the Anglo-Saxons of America are the only people in the world fitted for freedom. The negro's is not human freedom, but the wild and vicious license of the fox, the wolf or the hawk."[76] Many Southern jurisdictions moved to protect themselves from such infectious vermin by exclusion laws. The most extreme was the law of Arkansas providing that any free black who remained in the state after January 1, 1860, either would be allowed to choose a master or would be sold into slavery. Although the law was postponed and never actually went into effect, the free blacks of the state, wisely, left.[77]

An alternative, *voluntary* enslavement, was adopted by seven Southern states from 1857 to the outbreak of the Civil War. Two others approved it by means of special acts of the legislature in individual cases. Alabama, Florida, Louisiana, Maryland, Tennessee, Texas, and Virginia passed general laws allowing free persons of color to enslave themselves. South Carolina and Georgia permitted that alternative in special legislation.[78]

An initial premise involving the sale of oneself was that a person possessed a property right in himself that he might alienate. The question is whether or not a person was conceived to have a property right in himself in every aspect of the self, or whether he merely possessed a property right in his labor or, as Marx put it, his "labour power." In the view of Stephen Innes, "few questions were so compelling to Englishmen in the early modern era as the ownership of one's 'owne labour.' " Locke, however, did not limit his consideration of the problem of self-ownership to labor. "Every man has a property in his own person," he wrote, and "this nobody has any right to but himself." This became the foundation of his labor theory of value. But could a man alienate himself and thereby become a slave? "A man not having the power of his own life cannot by compact, or his own consent, enslave himself to anyone, nor put himself under the absolute arbitrary power of another to take away his life when he pleases." Jeremy Waldron reconciled Locke's arguments by suggesting that the *life* of a man is the possession of his creator, therefore he cannot alienate himself. He can still have a property interest in his labor alone.[79]

Rousseau was less certain. "To say that a man gives himself gratuitously, is to say what is absurd and inconceivable; such an act is null and illegitimate, from the mere fact that he who does it is out of his mind." And "to renounce liberty is to renounce being a man . . . such a renunciation is incompatible with man's nature." Despite this Rousseau conceded the possibility of self-alienation: "A man who becomes the slave of another does not give himself; he sells himself, at the least for his subsistence." Kant, a leading proponent of the so-called will theory of contract, adopted a different position. "No one," he claimed, "can bind himself by a contract to the kind of dependency through which he ceases to be a person, for he can make a contract only insofar as he is a person." Hegel, another proponent of the will theory, showed more sensitivity to history than Kant. He understood that it was possible for a man to alienate his personality by voluntarily enslaving himself. Marx's discussion of the alienation of labor power has been especially influential. According to him, "the exchange of commodities of itself implies no other relations of dependence than those which result from its own nature. On this assumption, labour power can appear upon the market as a commodity, only if, and so far as, its possessor, the individual whose labour power it is, offers it for sale, or sells it, as a commodity. In order that he may be able to do this, he must have it at his disposal, must be untrammelled owner of his capacity for labour, i.e., of his person." In Marx's view, workers and moneybags met in the market. The relationship between labor and capital was a market relationship. "The continuance of this relation," he maintained, "demands that the owner of the labour power should sell it only for a definite period, for if he were to sell it rump and stump, once for all, he would be selling himself, converting himself from a free man into a slave, from an owner of a commodity into a commodity." But was it possible for a man to sell himself "rump and stump"? Of course it was, but not in a liberal capitalist society, a point emphasized by Genovese. After his remark about turning oneself into a commodity, Marx wrote, almost pleadingly, that "he must constantly look upon his labour power as his own property, his own commodity, and this he can only do by placing it at the disposal of the buyer temporarily, for a definite period of time. By this means alone can he avoid renouncing his rights of ownership over it." Macpherson has followed this analysis in his study of "possessive individualism." The centerpiece of a mature market society was that "each individual's capacity to labour is his own property and is alienable." The unrestrained market society regarded the parties to a labor contract as equals and held that a man did have a property interest in his labor that he could alienate. But the line of thought represented by Locke and Kant held that one could not alienate one's entire being by voluntarily enslaving oneself. Rousseau, Hegel, and Marx believed that it was *possible* to sell oneself "rump and stump," but to do so was to destroy oneself. They never said that it was legally or logically impossible, however much they found the prospect abominable and incompatible with a liberal society.[80]

Within legal thought, two poles were Blackstone and Adam Smith. Blackstone admitted that a man could sell himself to another, but within sharp limits. "This, if only meant of contracts to serve or work for another, is very just: but when applied to *strict slavery* [emphasis added] . . . is also impossible." The reason it was impossible was because a sale "implies a price, a *quid pro quo*, an equivalent given to the seller in lieu of what he transfers to the buyer: but what equivalent can be given for life, and liberty, both of which (in absolute slavery) are held to be in the master's disposal?" Smith, one of the leading intellectual progenitors of liberal market capitalism, included among the ways of enslavement "a sort of voluntary slavery when an indigent citizen sells himself to be the slave of another person."[81]

Self-sale occasionally was defended on grounds of humanity, as an alternative to starvation before the emergence of the welfare state. This was the case in Russia.[82] Did anyone see it that way in the South? To a degree, yes. One of the first actual cases of self-sale I found fit such a perception in the civil law state of Louisiana. The "contract" was made well before the voluntary enslavement law of the 1850s, for it was recorded in the St. Landry Parish conveyance book on July 18, 1818, as an "indenture of servitude." By the terms of the agreement, signed by William Brown and Daniel Ferguson, Ferguson paid $840 to a woman in Rapides Parish to release from his indenture "a free negro man named William Brown, of the State of New York." In exchange Brown bound himself to Ferguson "to serve him as a slave from the day of the date of these presents until the full end and term of fifty years, during all which time the said William Brown shall well and faithfully serve his said master, his heirs, etc. and that honestly and obediently in all things, as a good and faithful servant ought to do." Ferguson, for his part, agreed to "find & provide for the said William Brown sufficient meat, cloathing, &c. suitable for a slave."[83] It is absurd to suggest that because there was a time limit in this contract Brown was not a slave. But if the element of time is not crucial to a definition of slavery, the argument of Marx needs refinement. It can be saved by focusing on the notion of the alienation of labor power. If a person alienated more than that, for whatever length of time, that person could be a slave.

"Is there any good reason," Fitzhugh asked, "why men should not be allowed to sell their liberty? Is it wise, politic or humane, to prevent the man, who sees his family starving around him, from hiring himself so as to bind his person, even for a day, a week, or a month, to save himself and family from death?" But it was especially important to enslave the free blacks. It was "our right and our duty" to "re-consign him to the only condition for which he is suited."[84]

Slavery, according to Oakes, was "by definition, the negation of whatever principles defined freedom in any given society." In liberal societies it meant the "denial of rights,"[85] for liberty was viewed as the possession of life, liberty, and the right to property.[86] The right to possess property included the right to alienate property. If liberty was property this meant that one could alienate one's liberty. This is close to the definition given by A. E. Samuel in his study of manumission in ancient Greece. "Legal freedom in Greece," he wrote, "is essentially a concept of property. The sole meaning of freedom is that a man has jurisdiction over his property and family, and the concept of manumission is the concept of change of property; a man no longer is property, but has it."[87] From this vantage point liberty could be a property right in oneself. But this was not the perception of liberal capitalism. The right to alienate one's labor in a labor market, for a time, was one thing, but the right to give up one's liberty completely was something else. The voluntary enslavement laws rested on a basic departure from the ideology of nineteenth-century America and Western Europe. But they did so in an incoherent way because they were framed in the language of nineteenth-century contractarian notions. They rested on the idea that one could contract oneself into slavery, which is incoherent according to the basic concepts of liberal capitalist thought.

Southern white racial perceptions finally led people to confront the logic of their proslavery racism, but at the expense of a coherent commitment to the principles of liberal capitalism, principles Southerners also embraced to some degree. If blacks were natural slaves and liberty could be bartered for a price, then it made good sense to provide that blacks could alienate their freedom and become slaves. More and more states did. There were some variations, especially in the rules concerning the children of black women who chose slavery. In Louisiana, children under ten became slaves along with their mothers; in Maryland, children under five followed their mothers, whereas those over five were to be bound out. Moreover, the laws did not always provide that "all the incidents" of slavery would attach to the people who enslaved themselves. In some states, for instance, a person could not be liable for the debts of the person to whom he or she became property.[88]

Some people did avail themselves of these laws, even though the number was not large. On one point my view of these self-enslavements differs from Berlin, who is one of the only scholars to have studied these laws. He claimed that it was decrepit old people who sold themselves, but it was more complex. Henry Reed, for example, petitioned to become the slave of Sidney Alderman in Jackson County, Florida, in 1864 because he was "tired of liberty & its ills & inconveniences." He was fourteen years old.[89]

There are twenty-nine requests covering the state of Virginia to 1861. In one of them Margarett Price petitioned for enslavement in the circuit court of the city of Richmond in 1859, after having been emancipated by will earlier. When she asked to become the slave of John H. Tyler, the motive was obvious: Tyler owned her father.[90] Filial devotion was doubtless Margarett Price's motivation for going into slavery, but the cases of Elmira Mathews in Georgia and Lucy Andrews in South Carolina were more common.

Elmira Mathews was authorized to become the slave of John J. Doherty by a private law of Georgia in December 1861. She was to be "subject to all the incidents of slavery," whereas, on his part, the "sole consideration for which voluntary enslavement . . . shall be the obligation thereby incurred by her master of feeding, clothing and protecting her."[91] Georgia's lawmakers viewed the process in the context of known legal categories. In this case it was the doctrine of "consideration" in contract law.

Lucy Andrews's case in Lancaster District, South Carolina, was poignant. She was sixteen "and (the mother of an infant child) being a Descendant, of a white woman, and her Father a Slave: . . . she is dissatisfied with her present condition, being compelled to go about from place to place, to seek employment for her support, and not permitted to stay at any place more than a week or two, at a time, no one caring about employing her." She realized that she had to support a family and could not do it and then added in her petition that "she sees, and knows, to her own sorrow, and regret, that Slaves are far more happy, and enjoy themselves far better, than she does, in her present isolated condition of freedom; and are well treated and cared for by their masters, whilst she is going about from place to place." Naturally enough she ritualistically repeated the refrain whites doubtless wished to hear: she "prefers Slavery to freedom in her present condition."[92]

"Race" was doing its primary legal job as Southern whites inched ever closer to the point from which they had departed. Having helped create a complex racial society by the end of the eighteenth century by their own sexual conduct, they worked to simplify it into black and white, as it had been in the early seventeenth century. Having defined most persons of mixed racial heritage as capable of enslavement, and having blended such people from quadroons to pure blacks under the term *Negro*, they needed only to reach the logical conclusion and come full circle to Godwyn's notion of 1680 that these two words, "*Negro* and *Slave*," had become "convertible."[93]

2

The Sources of Southern Slave Law

Villeinage . . . as it existed in England, reflects but little

light on our subject.

State v. Boon (North Carolina, 1801)

"The civil law," George Stroud wrote in 1827 in his influential abolitionist attack on Southern law, ". . . is generally referred to in the slaveholding states, as containing the true principles of the institution."[1] He summarized the essential principles, using John Taylor's *Elements of the Civil Law,* a work first published in 1754/5.[2] What followed was a grim portrait of the complete dehumanization of human beings as slaves. Before the collapse of the Roman Empire, Stroud admitted, "several important changes had been introduced favourable to the slaves." He outlined some of these, such as the notion that the killing of a slave was punishable and the rule added by Hadrian that "cruel treatment towards slaves" was prohibited.[3] Stroud's conclusion was that it would "be found, upon a close comparison, that the condition of the slave, in our slave-holding states . . . is but little— if in any respect—better than was that of the Roman slave under the civil law."[4] He did not indicate whether he had in mind ancient slavery before or after amelioration.

Some twentieth-century scholars have made similar comparisons. Arnold Sio concluded that Roman and American slave laws were very close.[5] Similarity is important, but it does not necessarily signify influence. It can mean that certain generalizations about social relationships will hold true without regard to different historical experiences.[6] The existence of such generalizations, however, does not indicate that one slave society has been a direct influence on another.[7]

Were the principles of Southern slave law derived from legal systems other than that of England? Some Southern jurists before the Civil War made the same connection between ancient slavery and Southern law as did the abolitionists.[8] On the other hand, Henry St. George Tucker, a nineteenth-century Virginia jurist and son of St. George Tucker, disagreed: "What was more natural than a tacit acquiescence by every individual in the authority of the laws to which they had always been accustomed." "We can scarcely presume," he concluded, "that any but enthusiasts would adopt a jurisprudence entirely foreign to their habits instead of the institutions of their fathers."[9]

Scholars are not wholly agreed. Watson and Jonathan Bush have argued that the colonial law of slavery grew up largely outside any direct English influence because English colonial policy rested on delegating law-making authority to local assemblies. Watson puts it as follows: "In the English colonies, the basic laws were those made by the colonists in the colonies. Slavery as a social institution was accepted in the English colonies without legal authorization. Thus, in the early days in the colonies overall, there were slaves but no law of slavery. The law came into being bit by bit, either by statute or by judicial precedent, sometimes based on what people did."[10] Bush has shown that through a theory of "tacit delegation" of lawmaking to the colonies, English constitutional policy "allowed *all the colonies* a private space in which planters and merchants could deploy slave labor with little oversight from England."[11] From his viewpoint, what resulted was that nothing "remotely like a jurisprudence of slavery emerged in the English colonial world"— instead, "only one body of significant slave law existed in the English colonies: the incomplete and analytically inadequate colonial statutes."[12] Bradley Nicholson, on the other hand, argues that "early American slave law was based on English legal traditions, mostly outside the common law, rather than created in the colonies out of whole cloth." The legal traditions he focused on were the "often brutal police law—outside the common law—for society's lower strata."[13] What were the actual sources of the legal rules and principles of slavery in the American South? Part of the answer depends on whether the concern is with the laws used to police slaves as persons and part on whether it is the slave as the object of property claims. Watson and Bush are correct about the fact that the English constitutional theory of empire rested, as far as slavery is concerned, on a notion of the "tacit delegation" of law-making authority (the laws, however, were subject to approval or disallowance by English authorities residing in England). Moreover, there is no doubt that English law did not provide direct rules for the policing of slaves. But it is also true, as Nicholson notes, that there are ample precedents in English legal traditions for the governance of lower-class people, precedents that were easily adapted to slaves in the colonies. It is also true that some of the colonial police regulations were responses of slaveowners to particular problems in the colonies that had no parallel in England. But none of this concerns the slave as property, so the answers are incomplete. To finish the picture it is necessary to plumb deeper for the sources of law, including but not limited to those laws that governed the slave as person.

The Colonial South

The origins of Southern laws on slavery lie deep in seventeenth-century Virginia. John Rolfe wrote about the introduction of blacks into English North America in 1619: "About the last of August came in a dutch man of warre that sold us twenty Negars."[14] The status of the early blacks brought to Virginia has been a problematic historical question. James Curtis Ballagh took the view that they were not dealt with as slaves, but rather as indentured servants. The standing of the blacks deteriorated during the course of the seventeenth century and especially after 1660. This thesis has been widely accepted. One forceful expression of this view has been that of Oscar and Mary Handlin. They noted that "slavery had no meaning in law" and that Virginians lacked a "previous conception of slavery as a legal status within which the Negro" could be placed.[15] For them the condition of chattel slavery "emerged" by the late seventeenth century. Jordan, to take a final example, suggested that the status of the early blacks was not clear until about the 1640s, but by that time some were treated as slaves rather than as indentured servants.[16]

An important and parallel debate among legal scholars concerns the status of the common law in seventeenth-century Virginia. Warren Billings, for instance, has argued for the general adherence to the common law, whereas David Konig has contended that a "swift and discretionary justice unbound by common law" had a deep and persistent impact on Virginia's legal culture. His view was that Virginians relied on a "harsh and discretionary justice" in order to control a "disorderly class of free husbandmen as well as servile laborers." This was done before they turned to large numbers of black slaves. By the end of the century the ways blacks were treated would derive from this tradition of ruthless treatment of lower-class whites. Dales Laws, in turn, derived from the martial law England used when it pacified the "hinterlands in the North and West, and colonized its frontier in Ireland."[17] Wilcomb Washburne suggested that the "concept of 'the common law' as a principle operative in the legal culture of seventeenth-century Virginia . . . should be abandoned." It obscures the fact that although Virginians tried "to follow English law as best they could," they had to make adjustments to their peculiar needs. Moreover, focus on the common law can obscure the "really significant legal evolution in the seventeenth century," which was "one altering the fundamental assumptions underlying colonial life." The transformation was captured in the emergence of "a love of self as the higher law (rather than God or King)." With the rise of market capitalism the interest of the individual rather than of society became the central assumption.[18]

The status of the common law in early Virginia, then, is no less problematic than that of the blacks. This makes it very difficult to talk about the origins or sources of a law of slavery. Nevertheless, there are pieces of evidence that must be considered, even if with diffidence.

One thing is reasonably clear, and that is that blacks as early as the 1620s, whatever their precise legal status, were viewed as separate from whites. Alden Vaughan found that for blacks listed in the census of 1624 "none is accorded a last name and almost half are recorded with no name at all." He also noted that when Governor George Yeardley wrote his will in 1627, he placed the blacks in a category separate from servants. He left to his heirs "goode debts, chattels, servants, negars, cattle or any other thing.[19]

A case from the 1620s, however, is ambiguous. On September 19, 1625, the general court ordered that "the negro y^t cam in wth Capt. *Jones*" was to remain with Lady Yeardley "till further order be taken for him" and that he was allowed what amounted to wages for his service while he stayed with her. And in October of that year the court ordered that "ye negro caled by the name of *brase* shall belonge to S^r *ffrancis Wyatt* Gou^{r}nor &c., As his servant" despite an alleged sale from Captain Jones to another man.[20] There is nothing here to show that Brase was considered a slave or an indentured servant.

The evidence from the 1620s, in short, is so shadowy that it is not possible to prove that blacks were regarded as slaves or indentured servants. There is some evidence, however, that they were placed in a different category from ordinary servants, even if it was not a precise "legal category."

Perhaps the most important thing about the Hugh Davis case of 1630 involving interracial sex (see Chapter 1) is that nothing is said about any punishment given to the woman.[21] Ten years later Robert Sweet was ordered to "do penance in church according to laws of England, for getting a negroe woman with child and the woman whipt."[22] The first Virginia statute on bastardy was adopted in 1657/8 so presumably English law covered the Sweet case. The Elizabethan statute on bastardy called for a punishment for both mother and father but did not specify what that was. According to Blackstone, "a corporal punishment was intended."[23] Sweet appears to have been dealt with under English ecclesiastical law, even though it was not clearly in force in Virginia. On the other hand, the woman was sentenced under the English statute. A probable reason for the difference was that the black woman was not a Christian. The earlier case is a little more puzzling. Davis and the black woman were guilty of fornication, not bastardy. But only the punishment of Davis is recorded, not the woman's. In England fornication was an "offense" handled by ecclesiastical courts, but there were no such courts in Virginia. After 1642/3 churchwardens were expressly authorized to deal with the "high & foule offences of adultery, whoredome or fornication." Hugh Davis received a punishment by order of the civil authorities, but the more interesting question is this: why did the woman receive no punishment at all?[24]

By the 1640s the evidence begins to mount that blacks were often considered slaves.[25] In Accomack-Northampton County on the eastern shore Nathaniell Littleton, "Comaunder" and so-called Gentleman Justice (justice of the peace),[26] acknowledged in June 1640 that a "negro viz. John Negro of Anne my wife" had been sold to Garrett Andrewes for 1,200 pounds of tobacco and that he gave up any claims to John. Two years later Thomas Jacob, a seaman from County of Kent, England, gave "my negro Woman Susan" to Mrs. Bridgett Seaverne, the wife of John Seaverne of Accomack "in the County of Virginia Chirurgion And her Little Sonne John Seaverne." Susan was given to them "and their heyres and Assignes Freely forever." The inventory taken across the bay in York County of the estate of William Stafford in the spring of 1644 was more conclusive. His estate included such things as four "draught Steeres" and "one feather bed & furniture," the total value of which was 2,800 pounds of tobacco. Also listed were a number of blacks.

Anthony was valued at 2,700 pounds of tobacco, as was Michael. There were two black women, listed at 2,500 pounds of tobacco, and four children: a four-year-old girl, Mary, valued at 700 pounds; a three-year-old girl, Elizabeth, valued at 400 pounds; "one negroe boy," one year old, valued at 400 pounds; and a "negroe boy," "2 weekes old," valued at 200 pounds. An even stronger illustration is included in the inventory of William Burdett's estate, recorded in 1643. Mary Vaughan, "have-ing Eleaven monthes to serve," was valued at 400 pounds of tobacco; Caine, "the negro, very anncient," at 3,000 pounds; and "one negro girle about 8 yeares old," at 2,000.[27] Clearly these were slaves and not indentured servants. It would make little sense to place a market value on a two-week-old child as an indentured servant, for instance, or to value an "anncient" black well above a white servant with just under a year to serve. Moreover, the matter-of-fact manner of the entry and the market valuation of all of these blacks suggest that the appraisers were working with familiar concepts, not something that had suddenly or subtly emerged by the 1640s. If this inference is correct, it indicates that blacks were treated as slaves and separate from white indentured servants from the outset. This is not to imply a rigidified color line or to dispute the thesis of T. H. Breen and Stephen Innes that "not until the end of the seventeenth century was there an inexorable hardening of racial lines."[28] The story of Anthony Johnson, a black who acquired property and became the owner of slaves in his own right, is strong presumptive evidence.[29]

The question here is not the nature and sources of racial attitudes;[30] rather, it is the treatment of blacks as slaves at law and the sources of that law. There is sufficient evidence to suggest that blacks were treated as slaves at a very early time. But information revealing the precise sources of the legal notions that defined slavery is simply not present. We are forced to engage in speculation. I can see no reason to assume that the early settlers were recalling ancient slavery or Roman slave law. Nor are there grounds for believing that these settlers were thinking in terms of European civil law. If colonial Virginians possessed little developed knowledge of their own legal system, it is unlikely that they would have had much understanding of the rules of the civil law systems of continental Europe or of Roman law. I have found no references to the civil law in any court cases or in the statutes from seventeenth-century Virginia. A couple of cases from the eighteenth century discuss civil law (although not the Roman law of slavery). One of these, which rested on the work of the French civilian, Jean Domat,[31] involved an argu-ment based on the civil law of implied warranties in the sale of a slave.[32] The case, decided in 1736, is important, but it hardly helps us grasp the origins of slave law a century earlier, and it is not the kind of thing that people like Stroud had in mind.

The Handlins argued that the English did not have a "previous conception of slavery as a legal status." One problem with this view is that it rests on the er-roneous idea that slavery had to have some precise legal contours. Many people hold that lifetime servitude is key to a definition of slavery, but that has not always been the case. The English themselves, for instance, provided for the enslavement of vagrants in 1547. The law stipulated that the master of a slave could "cawse the saide Slave to worke by beating, cheyninge or otherwise in such worke and Labor how vyle so ever it be." Masters could also lease, sell, or bequeath their slaves like "any other movable goodes or catelles," and they could put iron rings on a slave's neck and legs. Despite all of this, such persons could be held as slaves for only two years.[33] This harsh law was repealed after only two years, but the point remains: the English were quite capable of conceptualizing human beings as slaves, if we do not hold too confined a perception of the status of slavery.

That does not mean that there are no critical elements. Although some question the emphasis, I believe that there is great force to Sir Moses Finley's notion that the essence of slavery "is the totality of powerlessness in principle, and for that the idea of property is juristically the key—hence the term 'chattel slave.' "[34] If we bear this in mind, some of the mystery of early slavery tends to disappear. Blacks were viewed as slaves, and that meant that they were viewed as property. It is simple common sense to assume that colonial Englishmen would apply English notions and rules of property law to slaves. The common law of England, as well as the emerging rules of equity and statutes that covered gifts, or sales, or inheritances of personal property, in other words, could also cover the situations discussed above. English law was not always clear or wholly isolated from civil law. English law was undergoing transformation during these years. The point is that it was English law that provided the legal categories into which blacks as property could be placed. There was no need to adopt statutes to cover this; the common law of property already did, and it allowed wide authority to those who possessed property to use it as they pleased. Consider, for example, the remark of J. H. Baker: "the common law took the strict view that no estates could be created in chattels, because it was contrary to the nature of ownership that the owner for the time being should not be able to do what he liked with the chattel, including its destruction." He noted that estates came to be recognized, but more important is the fact that when applied to chattel slaves, the owners' virtually unlimited power over chattel property could easily create a "right" in the master comparable to that given to ancient slaveowners before amelioration.[35]

What has diverted our attention is something fundamental, and that is the way historians have tended to regard the notion of a "law of slavery." Far too often we have fallen into the trap of assuming that statutes on slavery were designed to control black slaves as human beings. What is missing from this analysis is precisely Finley's notion that "juristically" the idea of "property" is the key to the definition of slavery. The laws adopted to control slaves as human beings generally come much later in the seventeenth century, and they have been ably summarized by a number of scholars. Although statutes are certainly important, they are not the only source of legal rules and principles; in fact, they were not the source of most of the basic rules of property law that were constructed by the courts.[36] Historians, then, have often spoken with some eloquence but not always with the right voice, and this has obscured the fact that when we search for the origins of the law of slavery, we ought not to overlook *English* property law. A particular legal principle, however, has been used to show that it was the civil law to which Virginians turned. This is the principle, *partus sequitur ventrem*. Crudely translated, it means that the status of the child derives from its mother. The normal common law rule on status was that it derived from the father. There is no doubt that the rule *partus sequitur ventrem* was of importance in the legal history of slavery. Stroud referred to it as the "genuine and *degrading*" principle of slavery because it "places the slave upon a level with *brute* animals."[37] This maxim, he added, prevailed in all of the slave states. It is vital, therefore, to understand it.

Partus Sequitur Ventrem

The first statutory provision on status was adopted in Virginia in 1662: "all children borne in this country shalbe held bond or free only according to the condition of the mother."[38] Billings concluded that Virginians searched the common law for precedents to deal with mulattoes but found none. "So," he argued, "they ransacked their knowledge of the civil law and discovered a useful definition of status (*partus sequitur ventrem*)." The one supporting citation for this conclusion was Henry Swinburne's *Brief Treatise of Testaments and Last Willes* (1590).[39]

The phrase appeared in Swinburne's discussion of those who lacked the capacity to make wills. He began with the observation: "Of all men which be destitute of libertie or freedom, the slave is in greatest subiectio, for a slave is that person which is in servitude or bondage to an other, even against nature." He possessed nothing, and "even his children also are infected with the Leprosie of his fathers bondage."[40] The condition of the child, in other words, followed that of the father, not the mother. It was not in his discussion of slaves that he used the Latin maxim, however. And if Swinburne was the source, it is difficult to understand why the Virginians deviated from the common law rule on status because Swinburne himself applied the common law to slaves.

He proceeded as follows: by the civil law, "the wife being a free woman, the children are likewise free, *Quia partus sequitur ventrem*; in so much that if the mother be free . . . that child shall be free, notwithstandinge the bondage of the father: Yet it is otherwise by the laws of the realme, for the childe dooth follow the state & condition of the father, and therefore in England the father being a bondman, the child shal be in bondage, without distinction whether the mother be bond or free: So that the childe be begotten or borne in lawfull matrimonye."[41] The latter was an important point for Swinburne. "A bastarde," he wrote, "shall not be bound though the father were a bond-slave, because the lawe dooth not acknowledge any father in this case, for by the lawe a bastard is sometimes called, *filius nullius*, the sonne of no man: sometimes *filius vulgi*, the sonne of every man."[42]

Swinburne did not treat *partus sequitur ventrem* as a degrading principle that reduced human beings to the level of beasts, as Stroud argued. He used the civil law axiom as a contrast to the notion that a child was infected with the "Leprosie of his fathers bondage." He treated it as though it were a principle of freedom, not slavery.

Still another possible source that might be derived from Swinburne's treatise is the law on bastardy. In his treatment Swinburne made this the one major exception to the rule that status derived from the father. Because there is no evidence that English colonials ever viewed slaves as capable of "lawfull matrimonye," any child a slave woman bore would fall under English bastardy law, and status there followed the mother. I do not claim that this was the source of the 1662 statute, only that it is one strong possibility.[43] The law of 1662, incidentally, did not contain the Latin phrase, nor did any other Southern statute to the end of slavery in 1865. If that Latin phrase found its way into English law through treatises like Swinburne's, and from there to the colonies, it would have been necessary to cut the phrase loose from the reasoning and the treatise.

The law of 1662, in any event, was adopted because of uncertainty. This uncertainty is evident in some of the earlier legal records. In 1652 a Virginia planter sold a ten-year-old black girl "with her Issue and produce duringe her (or either of them) for their Life tyme" and "their Successors forever." This is obviously a case where children followed the mother, and there was no statute to affirm the point.[44] But in 1655/6 Elizabeth Key was found by the county court to have been the child of a slave woman by a man named Thomas Key. He had been fined, according to law, "for getting his Negro woman with Childe which said Negro was the Mother of the said Molletto." Elizabeth claimed her freedom on the basis of her birth while she was also claimed as a slave. This case went to the Virginia assembly, which turned it back to the county court for reconsideration because no one appeared before the burgesses to speak against her petition for freedom. Despite the inconclusive result, the assembly report showed that the burgesses believed Elizabeth was entitled to freedom. Christianization was one possible ground. But another was this: "by the Comon Law the Child of a Woman slave begott by a freeman ought to bee free." The end result was that Elizabeth Key was declared free in Northumberland County, and then she married the attorney who had represented her.[45]

Clearly, there was uncertainty about the status of persons born of miscegeneous relationships. The law of 1662 settled it. Why was the particular rule adopted? There is no special reason to believe that the English of the seventeenth century would have been squeamish about separating a child from its mother. If the English rule—that status followed the father—was used, the white men who crossed the color line, however shadowy it might be, would then be liable for raising the child. In the absence of the father, the county might have taken care of such children and recovered its expenses from the labor of the child when it grew up. Heavy fines and the liability for raising a child could have been a deterrent to fornication between white men and slave women just as well as adopting the rule that status derived from the mother, if that was what the burgesses were concerned about. But the record in Elizabeth Key's case just six years before the rule was adopted ought to make us pause. She was unquestionably a mulatto, and yet not only was she declared free, but also she married her white attorney without any apparent sanctions. Still, there is no doubt that white Virginian lawmakers were concerned about race mixing.[46]

Race was a factor, but it did not necessarily determine the outcome. Rather, the key rests in the concern for the property rights of the slaveowner. According to English law on chattel property, the increase of that property belonged naturally to the owner of the property. As Blackstone put the matter about the mid-eighteenth century, "Of all tame and domestic animals, the brood belongs to the owner of the dam or mother; the English law agreeing with the civil, that '*partus sequitur ventrem*' in the brute creation, though for the most part in the human species it disallows the maxim."[47] Blackstone, at this point in his work, treated the Latin phrase not as a rule that determined the status of someone, but as a rule that determined the ownership of something.

English law provided ample doctrines to explain the law of 1662 without reference to the civil law or even the phrase *partus sequitur ventrem*. If the burgesses were thinking of the mulatto as a person, the law of bastardy would hold that the child followed the mother, which is what the statute provided. If they were thinking of the mulatto in terms of property rights, chattel property law required that the increase go to the owner of the mother, and, in essence, that is also what the law stated.

The difficulties are compounded when we look at other colonies. A year after the burgesses adopted their law, Maryland's legislators introduced one that provided that "all children born of any negro or other slave, shall be slaves as their fathers were for the term of their lives."[48] Stroud did mention this law and said that once it was repealed at the turn of the century, the situation was cleared up.[49] In 1715 Maryland lawmakers determined that all "negroes and other slaves" and children born "of such negroes and slaves, shall be slaves during their natural lives." Because the language was not related to gender, this provision did not answer the question about status. That has to be culled from an analysis of another section. In order to stop "unnatural and inordinate copulations," it was stipulated that children born to free white women by black males would be indentured servants until they became thirty-one.[50] It did not matter whether the father were free or slave, he only had to be black. The inference, however, is that a child born to a white free woman, even by a black slave, would not be a slave. If one were concerned about status, it appears that a child followed that of its mother but Marylanders were so appalled by interracial sexual relations that they required the harsh sanction of thirty-one-year servitude for the offspring. Virginians had done the same. None of this suggests a civil law origin of the rule that status followed the mother rather than the father. And it certainly does not indicate that seventeenth-century English colonials were thinking in terms of the Roman law of slavery. Moreover, there is no reason to believe that slavery was any less "degrading"—as

Stroud's argument implies—in Maryland than in Virginia during the century, despite their different rules for determining status.

South of the Chesapeake the law was even murkier. North Carolina adopted its major slave code in 1741. It did not then, or at any other time, introduce a statute on the status of mulattoes.[51] South Carolina's first provision on the matter was in a law of 1712. It stated that "all negroes, mulatoes, mustizoes or Indians, which at any time heretofore have been sold, or now are held or taken to be, or hereafter shall be bought and sold for slaves, are hereby declared slaves; and they, and their children, are hereby made and declared slaves, to all intents and purposes." South Carolinians did not adopt either the common law or the civil law rule on status. The statute of 1712 was not gender specific, and there was no thirty-one-year law to cover children born to white women by slave fathers. What this law provided was that the status of the child followed the most degraded position of its two parents. Nearly all miscegenation thus led to slavery for the offspring.[52] Unfortunately, there is no evidence of any source on which South Carolinians drew to reach this result. Although there have been slave systems in which this rule was used,[53] we cannot say that the lawmakers of 1712 were familiar with them. The probability is that they simply made a policy choice based on a deep racism, rather than on a conscious effort to derive a legal rule from some known body of law. In any event, this was not changed until the code of 1740 provided that children "shall follow the condition of the mother."[54] Whether South Carolinians consciously selected the civil law rule or followed the lead of Virginia is not clear. In fact, why they changed their legal rule at all is unanswerable. By 1770 Georgia, the last of the English continental settlements, had adopted not only slavery but also the legal code of South Carolina.[55]

Before I move beyond the colonial South, a few more words need to be said about the assertion that the source of slave law was the civil law in general and the Roman law of slavery in particular. It is difficult to imagine exactly what the first point is intended to convey, for there was not merely one civil law: complex legal systems throughout Europe fell under that rubric. Which law, or even which legal principle, is meant? In one of the classic comparative studies of slavery, *Slave and Citizen*, Tannenbaum contrasted the brutal, dehumanizing legal system of the English colonies with what he believed to be the more humane legal code of Latin America, which in turn was based on the medieval Spanish code, *Las Siete Partidas*.[56] But that code was part of a civil law system that had integrated slavery within it. Nonetheless, there is no doubt that those who saw or still see the Southern law of slavery as grounded in civil law principles were not thinking of this body of law.

If we turn to Roman slave law, moreover, there are serious difficulties. Aside from the problem of defining that law at any given period, it is hard to discern precisely what is meant by the comparison. One of the more famous rules of the Roman law concerned the *peculium*, property held by a slave. "If much in Roman law and life can be said to dehumanize the slave," Watson has written, "the peculium did much to humanize him." There was no limit to the amount of property a slave could acquire, nor were there limits on the kind of property. Slaves could "hold slaves, even many slaves, of their own." Furthermore, slaves could be educated; some were very knowledgeable indeed, and some were "high-income earners."[57] There was nothing in Southern slave law to match this. Some Roman law rules, such as the *Senatus Consultum Silanianum*, which required that if a master was murdered by a slave, all the slaves "who lived under the same roof are to be subjected to torture and then condemned to death," were never adopted.[58] Precisely, then, what rules of the civil law or the Roman law of slavery provided sources for rules of law in the South?

A final piece of evidence from the pre-Revolutionary years to consider is Blackstone's discussion of the principle *partus sequitur ventrem*. In the reference cited earlier he treated it largely as a rule to determine the ownership of the increase of personal property, and here the common and civil law agreed. But he also mentioned the maxim when he discussed villenage. "The children of villeins," he wrote, "followed the condition of the father, being free if he was free, and villein if he was villein; contrary to the maxim of the civil law, that *partus sequitur ventrem*." "But," Blackstone continued, "no bastard could be born a villein, because of another maxim of our law, he is *nullius filius*; and as he can *gain* nothing by inheritance, it were hard he should *lose* his natural freedom by it." In the case of bastardy, then, as was true in Swinburne's treatise, the civil law maxim worked to affirm freedom. Equally important, however, is the fact that Blackstone treated the Latin phrase as though it covered both status and the ownership of the increase of personal property. Blackstone, who was trained as a civilian and was writing a treatise in that tradition but on the subject of the English common law,[59] had squeezed together a rule of status and a rule of property under the same Latin phrase. That phrase need not cover both, but intellectual sloppiness has often had an impact on the development of legal doctrine.[60]

Post-Revolutionary advancements in the use of the principle that the status of a child followed the mother also show some confusion as to the source of the norm. There were, first of all, a few statutory developments, but they do not clarify matters. The first change occurred in Virginia. It was provided that no one could be a slave in that state except those who were so on October 17, 1785, "and the descendants of the females of them." Kentucky adopted this law in 1798, complete with the October date. For the remainder of the Southern states the statutory history is as follows: Mississippi in 1822 embraced the phrase "and the descendants of the females of them" from the Virginia law, and Florida did the same in 1828. Finally, Louisiana, a civil law state, introduced this language in its civil code of 1825: "Children born of a mother then in a state of slavery, whether married or not, follow the condition of their mother."[61] Nearly one-half of the Southern states, in other words, made no provision in their black codes to affirm the notion that the condition of the child followed the mother or to adopt expressly the civil law phrase, *partus sequitur ventrem*. This does not mean, of course, that the other states did not use that norm. They did through judicial rulings, but the source for that norm could just as well have been the common law doctrine, which agreed with the civil law, that to the owner of property belongs the increase. The use of this principle, in other words, does not show that Southern slave law was based on the civil law and certainly does not show that it was based on the Roman law of slavery.

There is a complication, however. Among the states that did not adopt statutes were those that had been influenced by civil law traditions, especially Spanish ones. We cannot overlook the possible source of the rule in the civil law traditions in a state like Texas,[62] not to mention the obvious direct link in Louisiana, which overwhelmingly relied on civil law rules.[63] Still, this hardly establishes the civil law as the source of *partus sequitur ventrem* for those states or for colonies whose traditions were otherwise predominately based on English common law.

The principle did play a role in nineteenth-century appellate cases. One was referred to by Judge Ruffin of North Carolina as the leading case in American jurisprudence on the status of children of women who were to be freed in the future.[64] Judge John Green, of Virginia, who wrote the lead opinion in *Maria v. Surbaugh* (1824), believed that before 1662 slaves "were held as absolute property, and the children of female slaves were held to be slaves, without doubt, until the question was raised, (probably in reference to the English law of *villenage* . . .) whether the child of a freeman by a female slave was bond or free." By virtue of the law of 1662, "the rule which had before prevailed, was adopted; a rule conforming to the civil law as to slaves, and contradicting the rule of the common law as to *villeins*."[65] Reasoning such as this surely reinforced the impression left by a reading of Blackstone.

Francis Taliaferro Brooke took a different approach. He admitted that the rule involved was a "rule, probably adopted from the civil law." "Probably adopted," is not a phrase to suggest great confidence in the conclusion, but this mattered little. Neither he nor any other jurist was all that concerned with historical accuracy.[66] The rule was firmly in place, and that was sufficient. But Brooke proceeded to discuss the matter in a way that has been overlooked. "The rule *partus sequitur ventrem*," he wrote, "is a rule of *property*, not of *liberty*, applicable to questions of property decided by this Court, and has no application to the question now to be decided." If, then, it was not the Latin maxim that applied, what did? According to Brooke, it was the rule that the condition of a child, whether bond or free, derived from the mother.[67]

By the 1820s, however, he was an aberration. Jurists wasted no time on the distinction he made. Moreover, they spent little time on historical questions about the "sources of law." The child of a female slave entitled to future freedom, Ruffin wrote in *Mayho v. Sears* (1842), must be a slave. This followed "conclusively from the maxim, *partus sequitur ventrem* which, we believed, has been universally adopted in this country." He took comfort in the fact that the principle was universal throughout the South, but he did not mention that no statute in his own state affirmed it. He also took some comfort, if not pride, in finding that it "pervaded also that Code, which was at one time the law of nearly all the civilized world, the civil law of Rome, in the dominions of which nation the class of slaves was more numerous than it has ever been in almost all other countries."[68] What had begun as a principle to determine status had been fused with a notion to decide the ownership of the increase of chattel property and had been identified, by the nineteenth century, not just with a civil law source but with the Roman law of slavery.

This was precisely what Stroud and Goodell had alleged and condemned. Southern legalists were hardly conceding that the abolitionist publicists were correct. This is obvious from one of the last discussions of the maxim by a proslavery writer, Cobb of Georgia. On one side Cobb treated the question as one involving status. He then shifted to consider it as one of property; depending on his purposes he pulled out that element from the general concept, *partus sequitur ventrem*, that best met the objective. When he treated the maxim as one involving property questions, he noted that "from the principles of justice, the offspring, the increase of the womb, belongs to the master of the womb." Cobb shifted when he discussed status. He drafted one of the longest footnotes in his treatise in order to directly answer Stroud. In Cobb's view *partus sequitur ventrem* was really neutral. Some principle was necessary to determine the status of persons in disputed cases, and the one adopted was no more "degrading" than the opposite standard. Although it meant that some people were doomed to be slaves, it also meant that others would be free.[69]

The Roman Law in Appellate Cases

Southern judges, however, did not discuss the Roman law as the source of legal principles solely when they confronted questions of status. An early example is the case of *Guardian of Sally, a Negro, v. Beaty* (1792) in South Carolina. It involved a slave woman who had been allowed out to hire and who had accumulated a sum of money with which she bought not her own, but the freedom of a young black woman. Could such a purchase stand in the face of a claim by the putative owner of the young woman that she remained a slave despite the sale? His counsel argued that the common law had no bearing on the case. It "did not contemplate a system of slavery: consequently, none of its rules could reach this case fully." But, he added, the "*civil* law did." By that law the "property acquired by a slave went to the master."[70]

The attorney on the other side argued that "the tremendous power of life and death which the *Romans* . . . exercised on their slaves did not exist in South Carolina," and if there were exceptions to the notion that the civil law prevailed, there could well be others. The situation before the court was unique, he contended, and should be determined by "general principles of justice" and not the civil law.[71] The South Carolina court, without reference to any source of law, agreed.[72] One counsel, then, had argued that the law of slavery was governed by the civil law, and he lost the case.

The next South Carolina case, *Bynum v. Bostick* (1812), went the other way. It involved a trust created to free a slave. "The condition of slaves in this country," Chancellor Henry William DeSaussure began, "is analogous to that of the slaves of the ancients, the Greeks and Romans, and not that of the villeins of feudal times. They are generally speaking not considered as persons, but as things . . . all our statute regulations follow the principles of the civil law in relation to slaves, except in a few cases, wherein the manners of modern times, softened by the benign principles of christianity, could not tolerate the severity of the Roman regulations."[73] This case is a direct illustration of a jurist who tied Southern slave law to that of the Romans. DeSaussure's summary, however, was quite general, and he added the Greeks. He did not give any examples of statutes that followed principles of Roman law, but undoubtedly he was thinking in terms of absolute power and of the authority that goes with the ownership of property. We are now much closer to the real point. But it is of some significance that other South Carolina judges later chose other sources for the legal principles used in cases involving slaves.[74]

Another early case in which a jurist used "Romanist premises," and relied on "Continental doctrine,"[75] was *State v. Boon* (North Carolina, 1801). The action involved the killing of a slave, and Judge John Hall argued that slaves were outside the common law. From what source did he derive his ghastly picture of the relationship between slaves and the law? His analysis rested on the notion of a "pure state of slavery," which meant complete rightlessness in the slave and absolute power in the master. His references were to Blackstone's *Commentaries* and Montesquieu's *Spirit of the Laws.* Blackstone, in turn, took his characterizations directly from Montesquieu, so that the latter is the source for Hall's argument.[76] Montesquieu did not focus solely on Roman slavery, although he did discuss it. His sweep was broader and included references to Greek slavery, Germanic slavery, and Muscovite and Islamic bondage, for instance. His hostility to absolute power was profound, and it was that that he primarily wanted to express. He was far less concerned with precise legal rules, and he did not mention, for example, *partus sequitur ventrem.*[77] Judge Hall took the same approach. He referred to the "pure state of slavery," but he did not discuss legal principles as such. In addition, he never cited any legal treatise, not even Taylor's *Elements.*[78] His analysis derived, even though turned on its head, more from an Enlightenment condemnation of slavery than it did from "Romanist jurisprudence" directly.

By the 1820s there was little in Southern appellate cases on which to rest a claim that the civil law or Roman slave law provided the basic legal principles of Southern slave law. An 1823 North Carolina case, *State v. Reed*, hardly changed that. This also involved the killing of a slave, and Hall simply referred to his opinion in *Boon*, which, incidentally, had not been joined by the other members of that earlier court. Chief Justice Leonard Henderson,[79] in the 1823 case, argued that it was the common law, modified by statutes, that determined the court's ruling. He added:

"with me it has no weight to show that, by the laws of ancient Rome or modern Turkey, an absolute power is given to the master over the life of his slave. I answer, these are not the laws of our country, nor the model from which they were taken."[80]

Two years earlier, in *State v. Jones*, the Mississippi Supreme Court had also rejected the analogy. Counsel for the defendant, accused of killing a slave, had relied heavily on the analogy and on Hall's opinion in *Boon*. Judge Joshua D. Clarke, for the court, held that Hall had "based his conclusions . . . upon erroneous principles, by considering the laws of Rome applicable here." He excoriated the notion that it was lawful or excusable for an owner to kill a slave. Such a legal principle would "be worthy [of] the age of Draco or Caligula."[81] The court used the supposed analogy as a foil against which to project an image of a more benign American law of slavery.

Another significant case was *Bryan v. Walton* (1853), brought in Georgia. Judge Lumpkin began with an express rejection of any analogy to English villenage:

> How different the circumstances of the villain, from the slave of the Southern States. His *status* resembles much more strikingly the slavery of the ancient Republics. Their slaves, like ours, had no name, but what their masters gave them. They could take nothing by purchase or descent; they could have no heirs; they could make no will or contract of any kind. The fruits of their labor and industry belonged to their masters. They could neither plead nor be impleaded; and were utterly excluded from all civil concerns. They were incapable of marriage. The laws of adultery did not apply to them. They might be sold or mortgaged. *Partus sequitur ventrem*, was the rule indiscriminately applied to slaves and cattle.[82]

Lumpkin's source was Taylor's *Elements*. Had he stopped here his opinion could be used with force by those who believe that the link between ancient slave law and the law of the South was firm and direct. But he did not. In his next sentence he added that the summary he had just given "was not only the civil law, but the law of the Jews, Phoenicians, Carthagenians, Egyptians and Greeks, and all other nations, tongues and peoples."[83] Clearly, the idea that the social order he believed in rested on universal features and structures was far more important to Lumpkin than any identification of precise "sources of law."

A final case is *George, (a slave), v. State* (1859), which involved the alleged rape of a slave by another slave in Mississippi. Judge William L. Harris,[84] a strong proslavery apologist, cited an earlier New York ruling that the "state of slavery in this country compares with that existing under roman law."[85] He did admit that some cases had gone the other way, but these he characterized as "founded mainly upon unmeaning twaddle, in which some humane judges and law writers have indulged, as to the influence of the 'natural law,' 'civilization and Christian enlightenment,' in amending . . . the rigor of the common law, and on a supposed analogy between villanage in England and slavery here." The fact was, he believed, that it was almost universally held that slavery "as it exists in this country, was unknown to the common law of England," and therefore the rules of that law did not provide the source of rules in Mississippi. The provisions of the common law were "inapplicable to injuries inflicted on the slave here."[86]

These, then, were some of the leading cases in which Southern jurists tried to identify the civil law, or Roman law, or ancient law in general as the source or sources of Southern slave law. Southern jurists, as well as abolitionists, were not interested in careful historical reconstruction, or in showing that a particular legal principle derived from the civil law or the Roman law of slavery. The purpose, in short, was more political than legal. Abolitionists pointed to ancient slavery and the civil law in order to construct an image of "pure slavery" that rested on unrestrained or absolute power. They did this with no more or less care than did Southern jurists, some of whom accepted that image in order to contrast it with the social and legal system they knew.

But what of those, like Hall and DeSaussure early in the nineteenth century or Harris and Lumpkin by the middle, who did not contrast ancient and American slavery but could see no difference between them. Were they admitting that the abolitionists were correct, that slaves were outside the protection of the common law and had no rights or legal identity? Were they acknowledging the complete dehumanization of the blacks among them as far as the law was concerned? At one level the answer is that they were, but we need to be careful. Hall, one of the first to make the connection with "pure slavery," may well have been appalled by it more than some later jurists, for instance.[87] For those judges who considered the question after the 1830s, when Northern abolitionism heated up, the politics of law had become more open. For them the point was to uphold their social order by tying it to universal human experience, and one way to do that was to tie it to the ancient world. But when they did so, they were caught by their own political purposes into accepting a system that made them uncomfortable. The way they tried to escape the problem created by their political use of legal history was to suggest that the viciousness had been removed either by the law (i.e., statutes) or by practice. Chancellor DeSaussure pointed to both potential escape routes. He mentioned ameliorative statutes, and he noted that trusts for the benefit of slaves had often been allowed to take affect *sub silentio*. It was only when jurists turned to the law that unfortunately harsh rules came into play.[88]

Villenage and Southern Slave Laws

Although most Southern judges rejected any analogy between English villenage and black slavery, there were some exceptions. Whether they relied on the analogy or repudiated it, the two main sources of information were Blackstone's *Commentaries* and, even more crucial, Coke's commentaries on Littleton's treatise on tenures.[89] Hall, for instance, used the latter in his opinion in the Boon case in 1801. "Villeinage," he concluded, "as it existed in England, reflects but little light on our subject; it had, attached to it, certain rights, that were unknown to a pure state of slavery." Masters did not possess absolute power, and villeins could go to court and sue persons other than their masters.[90] Jurists like DeSaussure did not waste the time to discuss the precise rights of villeins. They simply said that there was nothing analogous. Harris in the 1859 rape case in Mississippi even missed a chance to seal his point with a direct quotation from Coke on Littleton: according to Coke, a villein "that is ravished by her Lord may have an Appeal of Rape against him."[91] Certainly no one argued that a black slave woman could do that.

Perhaps the most complete negation of the possible analogy came in two Georgia Supreme Court opinions in the 1850s, *Neal v. Farmer* (1851) and *Bryan v. Walton* (1853). In *Neal*, a civil action for damages for killing a slave, Judge Eugenius Nisbet ruled that "*African slavery* does not, and never did exist in England." No analogy whatever to villenage would hold, and therefore the killing of a slave was "not an offence against the law—of course the Common Law."[92] In *Bryan*, Lumpkin was equally emphatic: "any analogy drawn from the villeinage of the feudal times is utterly fallacious as to the investigation. A villain . . . might acquire any kind of property, real or personal; and he might freely dispose thereof, unless prevented by the entry and seizure of the lord; he might sue all manner of actions against any other than his lord; in the capacity of executor, he might even sue his lord. In a word, where his lord was not concerned, a villain was a freeman in all his dealings."[93]

A less complete but still interesting rejection of villenage as a source of law was in the first case I found in which it was mentioned, *Spicer Adm'r. Ex'r. of Stone v. Pope & al* (Virginia, 1736). It involved the construction of a will in which slaves, including those born in the future, were distributed among the heirs. The opinion was that a devise to a person not yet conceived could be valid under the common law, but that the devise of a thing not yet in existence could not. "It is [a] known Rule that a bare Possibility cannot be devised." This rule was applied because there were no others relevant: "cases in point cannot be expected there being no Slaves in England. The Case of Villains comes the nearest to Slaves but I find nothing concerning them as to this Matter."[94] The court then applied the rule derived from English property law.

A major exception came in 1829 in *Fields v. State* (Tennessee), which concerned the murder of a slave by a third party. Judge Robert Whyte argued forcefully that the common law did apply to slaves. Though admitting that "pure and proper slavery" (which he defined in terms of the power of life and death) did not exist in England, Whyte stated that "a species of slavery or servitude existed there from the earliest times; the subjects of it were not styled slaves but villains; and their state and circumstances much resembled that of our slaves, at the present day." His primary contention was that the common law protected the person of the villein even while it "noticed and sanctioned" the "harsh characteristics of the villains condition." It protected him against the "atrocious injuries of his lord; for he might not kill or maim him, and for these he shall be indicted at the suit of the king." The critical point followed: "this short review of the condition of villains at the common law, exhibits a strong resemblance to the condition of our slaves: the principal features of both are the same, and differing only in some *minutiae*, which do not require to be noticed. Why then do not the principles of the common law apply, as far as the state or condition is similar, the one to the other?"[95] Slaves were compared to villeins in order to bring them within the protections of the common law. This analogy was used to achieve a legal and not a political result. Its purpose was quite the opposite of that of most jurists who applied the Roman law, such as Harris, who referred to this Tennessee case when he condemned the "unmeaning twaddle" of humane jurists.

A final case of note is *Willis v. Jolliffe*, a South Carolina dispute decided in 1860 that involved an out-of-state emancipation. The opinion that included a discussion of villenage was that of Chancellor F. H. Wardlaw on circuit and not the opinion of the court of appeals. Wardlaw was no opponent of slavery. At one point he declared: "it may be safely affirmed that slavery is not contrary to the divine law promulgated in the Holy Scriptures. It was sanctioned and regulated under the Mosaic dispensation."[96] From here he embraced Blackstone's condemnation of "pure slavery," which, Wardlaw believed, not only never existed in England but also did not "ever subsist in South Carolina." But there was serfdom. "Villeinage . . . in England," Wardlaw maintained, "is identical with slavery in South Carolina, in many respects, differing mainly as to the civil remedies of serf and slave on the master; and this sort of villeinage was adopted by our Act of 1712." He then quoted Francis Hargrave's antislavery argument in the classic English slavery case, *Somerset*.[97] According to Hargrave, at least, "the condition of a villein had most of the incidents of slavery in general. His service was indeterminate, and such as his lord thought fit to require. He knew not in the evening what he was to do in the morning; he was bound to do whatever he was commanded; he was liable to beating, imprisonment, and every other chastisement his lord might prescribe, except killing and maiming." Wardlaw included other characteristics, such as being subject to sale, and then concluded that all of this was "an apt description of our slaves."[98]

Why a proslavery judge like Wardlaw should make the favorable comparison he did is not clear. Nothing in his opinion suggests that he was attempting to ameliorate the condition of the slaves, as was true of Whyte in Tennessee. It is probable that his purpose was political and not truly legal. By grounding South Carolina slavery firmly in Anglo-American experience, as well as providing a biblical justification, he not only would give a firm foundation for the master-slave relationship, but he also would undercut abolitionists who charged that it was a vicious and brutal system as well.

An earlier proslavery South Carolina chancellor, Harper,[99] on the other side in *Fable v. Brown* (1835), had flatly rejected any analogy to English villenage. What made his analysis different was that he did not grasp the civil law, or the Roman law of slavery either. Even though he conceded that the civil law was an "enlightened and admirable" system of jurisprudence, he felt constrained to add that "it is not our law, nor have our Courts any authority to declare it so." Yet, he added, "a great portion of our law was derived from that source," and it was appropriate whenever "our law is obscure or doubtful" to turn to the civil law for guidance. But Harper was not through. There was a source of principles that Southern legalists had overlooked. The "true state of the slave," he believed, "must be ascertained by reference to the disabilities of an alien enemy, in which light the heathen were anciently regarded."[100] What it might have lacked in legal specificity Harper's opinion made up for by the reference to a justification for slavery that had deep roots. Both Locke and Hobbes, for instance, had explained slavery as having its origins in captivity during a time of war.[101] It was rare, however, for a Southern jurist to discuss the "disabilities" of slaves in terms of those of "alien enemies."[102]

The attempt, then, to find an analogy between American slavery and English villenage produced as much of a homemade quality as did the search in the ruins of ancient slavery. Most judges simply rejected it. The rights villeins possessed were clearly different from those of American slaves. Those judges who rejected the reference to villenage placed weight on the differing civil conditions of villeins and slaves, rather than on the lack of protection from unlawful violence. When the latter question was presented, one jurist, Whyte, grasped the analogy in order to bring slaves within a cranny of the common law, whereas another, Harris, rejected it.

For the most part, the effort to analogize the two social orders was not a success. It is difficult to find in English villenage much of a "source of law" for Southern slavery. The primary source for Southern judges was *Coke on Littleton*, and surely it is doubtful that even Whyte would have argued that black slaves could go into court and sue someone other than their master, or that they had property rights that could be protected at law, or that a female slave could bring a successful legal complaint against her owner for sexual assault or abuse. These were hardly "minutiae."

Hebraic Slavery as a Source of Law

There is no question whatever that many nineteenth-century Southerners placed a great deal of faith in the religious defense of slavery. But proslavery apologists faced certain difficulties when they dealt with Hebraic slavery.[103] Some, like Albert T. Bledsoe, described that ancient slave system as fairly benign when compared to the slavery that existed under Roman law. Bledsoe tried to link Southern slavery with slavery among the Hebrews. But he did not suggest that Hebraic slavery provided rules of law followed in the South. Other writers used this ancient slave system as a contrast to American slavery rather than as a source of it. Daniel Hundley, for example, condemned the slavery found in Exodus, where slaves could be killed by their masters; if they languished for a day or two before their death the master would not be punished, "for he is his money," as the Bible had it.[104]

The question, however, is not the use of Hebraic slavery by proslavery apologists, but rather the possible use of it as a source of law. It is useful to begin with

Cobb's treatise. Genovese has ably summarized the main points. Cobb tried hard to use the various biblical passages to justify a "multi-level system of subordination based on patriarchal principles."[105] Moreover, he attempted to demonstrate that biblical texts affirmed the racial basis of slavery. He also used them to describe what he called "pure slaves" who were subjected to "rigorous treatment."[106]

When we plumb beyond the ideological purposes Cobb had in mind to pin down any supposed biblical sources of law, the treatment becomes quite sparse. There is a section entitled "Slavery Viewed in the Light of Revelation," but it is a proslavery apologia and not a discussion of legal rules or principles. Outside of that chapter, Cobb cited biblical texts on only two occasions. One was to show that the principle of *partus sequitur ventrem* was the rule under Hebraic slavery, and the other was to provide a sharp contrast to the "qualified" slavery of the South. It was the same section of Exodus cited by Hundley. The only point directly followed in the South, then, was that caught in the Latinism, but even then the connection to Hebraic slavery was diluted. It was a principle, Cobb insisted, that was "almost universal among those nations recognizing slavery."[107]

In the broadest sense it can be argued that Southern judges turned to the Bible to find a foundation for the argument that slaves owed a duty of obedience to their masters,[108] which was the same point made by a number of proslavery apologists. But it was rare that a jurist directly cited the "laws" of Hebraic slavery. One example is Judge William A. G. Dade in *Commonwealth v. Richard Turner*, a Virginia case decided in 1827. The proceeding concerned an indictment against a slaveowner for a cruel beating of his slave. In his discussion of this indictment Dade explored the sources of Virginia's laws on slavery. He expressly rejected villenage and concluded that the colonial slave law was grounded in the "few and vague rules" found in the Bible and in the Roman civil law. He gave no supporting citation for this reasoning, and he did not identify the rules he had in mind. It is doubtful that he was thinking of Exodus 21, for instance, where it is provided that if a servant should say he loved his master, the master could present him before the judges and "bore his ear through with an aul; and he shall serve him forever."[109] It is also noteworthy that Dade linked Hebraic and Roman slavery, so that Hebraic slavery standing alone amounted to little.

If villenage was not much of a direct source of law and Hebraic slavery was even less important, and, finally, if the civil law borrowings were significant but limited, where are we to look for the basic sources of Southern slave law? The answer was given by Judge William Brockenbrough in a dissent from Dade's judgment in *Turner*. Why would Virginians, he asked, resort "to these strange laws, when they had one which they brought with them from the Mother Country, with which they were familiar, and which might be easily adapted to all the varying relations of their society?"[110] The core of American slave law was the common law of England, as well as the equitable principles used in English chancery courts. We miss this because we have not paid enough attention to the fact that it was indeed the property element in the slave that was "juristically" significant.

Laws were changing through statutes and adjudications, but the core body of legal principles to which Southerners turned when they fashioned their law of slavery was English. This should occasion little surprise, as all legal systems are sufficiently plastic to provide rules and principles that can be used to uphold systems of oppression.

The abolitionist reference to the civil law as the source of the basic rules of Southern slave law was meant to provide the foundation for a condemnation of oppression, of absolute power, and of an unethical social order. Southerners, on the other side, tried to defend their social system by showing its universality. One way to do that was to identify it in terms of legal principles as well as social relationships with the widest range of human experiences, not just English traditions. But no matter how they might squirm or shuffle, no matter how much they tried to show that the harshness of slavery was mitigated in the South, they could not escape the fact that one of the essential "incidents" of slavery was that the slave was an object of property rights, he or she was a "thing."

II

Slaves as Property

3

Slaves as Property—Chattels
Personal or Realty, and Did It Matter?

The slave is to be regarded as a thing . . .
GEORGE STROUD, *Sketch of the Laws* (1827)

After the Civil War judges often referred to the "badges and incidents of slavery" when confronted with claims of denial of equal protection of the law. Stroud, in 1827, wrote that the "cardinal principle of slavery—that the slave is to be regarded as a thing,—is an article of property,—a chattel personal,—obtains as undoubted law in all of these states."[1] An influential scholarly formulation has been that of Finley: the "idea of property is juristically the key—hence the term 'chattel slave.' "[2] Others have been skeptical of the effort to define slavery in terms of property rights in humans. Orlando Patterson, for instance, believes that it leads to confusion because there are numerous human relationships that involve property claims in others that fall short of slavery. At most we should remember, as Finley did, that slaves were a "*subcategory* of human proprietary objects."[3] There is nothing wrong with this caveat, but it does not relieve us of the problem of unraveling what it meant to claim property rights in humans in a slave society.

What did it mean to claim a property right in a "thing" in the Anglo-American legal world? "A legal right," Oliver Wendell Holmes Jr. observed, "is nothing but a permission to exercise certain natural powers, and upon certain conditions to obtain protection, restitution, or compensation by the aid of public force." Within mature legal systems the liberal conception of ownership includes the "right (liberty) of using as one wishes, the right to exclude others, the power of alienating and an immunity from expropriation." These are the "cardinal features of the institution" of ownership.[4]

Could they extend to human beings? Abolitionists denied that there could be property rights in humans,[5] whereas proslavery writers scoffed at such a claim. Fitzhugh, for one, responded: "We think we can dispose of this objection to domestic slavery in a very few words. Man is a social and gregarious animal, and all such animals hold property in each other."[6] But exactly what was it that was "owned" when a person made a claim that he or she "owned" a human being as a slave? The abolitionist Goodell was emphatic: "this claim of property in slaves, both in theory and in practice, as defined by legislation and jurisprudence, as defended by theologians and as sanctioned by ecclesiastical bodies, as carried out into every-day practice by the pious and the profane, is manifestly and notoriously a claim, not only to the bodies and the physical energies of the slave, but also to his immortal soul, his human intelligence, his moral powers, and even (in the case of a pious slave) to his Christian graces and virtues."[7] One proof for Goodell was that the "body of the slave without his soul would be a dead carcass of no value."[8]

Others were less certain. Francis Lieber, onetime professor at the University of South Carolina,[9] stated: "Properly speaking . . . the slave himself is not property but his labour is. Property involves the idea of a free disposal over the thing owned, or, as the ancient civilians expressed it, the exclusive right of use and abuse . . . we possess no such right over the slave and have never claimed it. We own the labour of the slave and this cannot be done without keeping the person performing the labour, thus owned, in bondage." But, he continued, "at the same time the slave remains a person. Slavery is an institution of property so far as the labour is concerned, but it is also an institution which established a *status*, that is a certain personal condition. The two are indissolubly united, but they are nevertheless two different things, and from this very fact arises all the difficulty attending this institution."[10] E. N. Elliott, in the introduction to his 1860 collection of some of the leading proslavery writings, wrote similarly: "slavery is the duty and obligation of the slave to labor for the mutual benefit of both master and slave, under a warrant to the slave of protection, and a comfortable subsistence, under all circumstances. The person of the slave is not property, no matter what the fictions of the law may say; but the right to his labor is property, and may be transferred like any other property, or as the right to the services of a minor or an apprentice may be transferred."[11] Bledsoe agreed that a man could not be owned like a horse or a tree. A man could only be "required to perform . . . the work of a man. The right to such work is all the ownership which any one man can rightfully have in another; and this is all which any slaveholder of the South needs to claim." "We lay no claim to the soul of the slave," he observed, ". . . only a right to the labor and lawful obedience of the slave."[12]

As slavery was increasingly and passionately condemned during the nineteenth century, proslavery apologetics tried to narrow the claim to property rights in slaves to a claim to their labor, and this was joined with a claim to obedience.[13] But slaves as property were closer to the description of Blackstone that the owner of property was allowed "not the immediate *use* only, but the very *substance* of the thing to be used."[14] More than simply the labor of the slave was claimed as a property right, but, in nonlegal discourse, the more the system came under attack the more Southern whites defended their system and the less they seemed to claim. In the end proslavery apologists tried to disarm their abolitionist assailants with a description of their social order as a rather ordinary patriarchal labor system. It was more than that, as Southern whites, as a legal proposition, claimed "property with souls."

Stroud's formulation, however, needs some refinement because for some purposes in some jurisdictions slaves were claimed as real property and not as chattels personal. Some have suggested that there is moral as well as legal significance in this. Because of the importance of this claim, this chapter examines the categorization of slaves as realty as a legal problem and the possible moral implications. Slaves as "chattel," which they were for most purposes most of the time, is considered more fully in later chapters.

There are two basic forms of property, realty and personalty. In the Anglo-American legal world of the seventeenth and eighteenth centuries land and perishable property were viewed in different ways and were governed by different rules. Real property had always been at the center of the legal order of England, whereas "the common law took the strict view that no estates could be created in chattels, because it was contrary to the nature of ownership that the owner for the time being should not be able to do what he liked with the chattel, including its destruction."[15] With the spread of market capitalism and the rise in the value of personal property (such as stocks), the rules involving realty and personalty moved closer to one another.

A good summary of the differences within English law in the earlier years was that of Attorney General John Randolph of Virginia in 1768:

> The natural property of land is, that it is fixed and permanent: its legal properties, that it shall descend to heirs in various manners; shall be subject to widows' dowers, shall not be liable to execution; cannot be aliened but by writing; shall give its proprietor a right of voting at elections: cannot be demanded but by action real, &c. Again the natural properties of personal estate are, that it is moveable and perishable: its legal properties that it shall be distributed among the next of kin equally; shall be liable to execution; may be aliened without writing; shall not give a right to vote; must be demanded by action personal, &c.[16]

Still, personal property was rising in estimation, and slavery was part of this intellectual transformation. An illustration of the impact of slavery is an 1827 South Carolina equity case, *Dunlap v. Crawford*. As other forms of property rose in value, the court argued, the distinction between real and personal property began to break down. By 1827, it concluded, "That distinction which once existed between real and personal property has been gradually lost sight of, and it very often happens that a testator is more concerned about the disposition of his personal than of his real property. How then is it to be expected that ordinary men should suppose that more formality was required in disposing of an hundred acres of pine land, than in disposing of two or three prime negroes?"[17]

Such, however, had not always been the view, and landed property held pride of place. How slaves would be categorized could be important to the slaves and would be to widows, heirs, legatees, debtors, and creditors. Would slaves be defined as realty or as chattels? Given the mobility and the humanity of slaves, the answer may seem obvious, but it is not, even though scholars normally refer to slaves as "chattels personal." In Virginia from 1705 to 1792 slaves were defined as real estate for some purposes.[18] South Carolina tried to characterize slaves as real estate in 1690, when it followed the Barbadian code, but this was disallowed by the English Privy Council.[19] In Louisiana slaves were designated as "immoveables," although sometimes the phrase "real estate" was used. They were defined as realty for some purposes in Kentucky from 1798 to 1852 and in Arkansas from 1840 to 1843. But that does not end the list. Some judges analogized slaves to land and adopted rules reflecting that correspondence.[20] For one reason or another rules of real property law were applied to slaves in some instances in over one-third of the jurisdictions that made up the slave South.

In the view of some abolitionists and a few later scholars, there was potential significance in this. In 1853 Goodell included a piece of whimsy in his vitriolic broadside: "under the old feudal system, the estate, consisting of soil and serfs, was kept together by the law of primogeniture, entailing it to the eldest son, in perpetuity. The repeal of that law has been justly regarded as a step in the march of human progress; but if the 'peculiar' institution of slavery is to remain, humanity might, perhaps, invoke its re-enactment, as it might prevent the separation of slave families, or rather, permit their existence." When slaves were deemed real estate rather than chattels personal, he argued, a "tenure" was created that "would attach the slave to the soil."[21]

Ballagh agreed. "Had the conception of realty been made complete," he wrote, "it would have tended to modify for the better the condition of the slave . . . by restricting alienation, particularly devise."[22] Eugene Sirmans adopted a similar position in his study of the legal status of slaves in colonial South Carolina. As "freehold property," he claimed,

> the Negro enjoyed a higher legal status than he did as a chattel, because free- hold was a higher form of property than chattel. Freehold property was at- tached to a landed estate and could not be moved; its holder legally had a right only to its use and not absolute ownership. Freehold slavery thus implied that a master had a right to the slave's services rather than to the slave himself. On the other hand, chattels were defined as the owner's personal belongings which he could dispose of as he pleased. In short, freehold slavery attached the slave to the land . . . while chattel slavery attached him to a master.[23]

On the other side, David Brion Davis took issue with Sirmans about the "moral significance of slaves being defined as freehold property," and he denied that defining a slave as "realty" implied that an owner had a right only to the "services of his slave and not to the slave himself."[24]

Goodell, Ballagh, and Sirmans maintained that status improved with the legal definition. This is incorrect. R. H. Graveson observed that in Roman law the concept of "status" was used "for the entire position of an individual regarded as a legal person, the . . . elements of the conception being liberty, citizenship and family rights." In Roman law a slave, at least in early times, had no "status." The notion of status in the common law was not the same. It was not the "normal" citizen who had status, but persons who had fewer rights or "who enjoy capacities greater than those of the normal person." In early English law status was linked with "estate." A person's status depended on "his legal estate and tenure in English land." The history of the concept in the common law was of the gradual separation of the ideas of "status" and "tenure or estate."[25]

The definition of a slave—a thing—as a chattel personal or as realty defined, if anything, the status of the owner and not the slave. Different rights, powers, or incapacities attached to the owner by virtue of the legal fiction. As an object of property rights, a slave had no *legal* interest in whether he or she was defined as a chattel personal or a piece of real estate as far as *status* was concerned. The status of the slave as a legal personality was something else, it was nonfree. Defining slaves as realty might or might not have had an affect on their lives or their treatment, but it had nothing to do with their status. What it did concern, for example, would be the rules that would apply to them if their owner died without a will.

Personalty and realty are legal constructions, divisions of the notion of "mine and thine." The significant question is not whether the slave was considered realty or a chattel as much as it was what precise incidents attached. As St. George Tucker presciently observed in a summary of the laws of Virginia:

> the incidents to real and personal property, respectively, are merely creatures of the *juris positivi*, or ordinary rules of law concerning them; and may be altered and changed to suit the circumstances, convenience, interest and advantages of society. . . . Thus in England it might be for the benefit of commerce to consider a lease for a thousand years, in lands, as a mere chattel; and in Virginia it might have been equally for the advantage of agriculture to consider the slave who cultivated the land as real estate.[26]

An example of the flexibility of the law was a proposal made by O'Neall in 1848 for a reform in the slave law of South Carolina. He suggested an important change in the "incidents" attached to the ownership of slaves. The "continual change of the relation of master and slave, with the consequent rending of family ties among them," disturbed him and led him to the view "that if by law, they were annexed to the freeholds of their owners, and when sold for partition . . . they should be sold with the freehold, and not otherwise—it might be a wise and wholesome change in the law."[27] Such a position did not find much favor in the nineteenth-century South, however, and political economists, such as Louisa McCord and J. D. B. De Bow, leading proponents of a laissez-faire market, expressly rejected the idea that slaves should be attached to the soil or be exempt from sale for payment of debts.[28]

Slaves as Realty in Eighteenth-Century Virginia

Earlier, in the eighteenth century, people were willing to place more restraints around the alienation of slaves by regarding them as realty, but it was not in order to preserve slave families or even to preserve the remnants of feudalism as much as it was to assure a labor force for the commercial plantations of the South and the power of some of the patriarchal families. Actually, the first English effort to define slaves as realty was a 1668 law of Barbados. It was passed to clear up uncertainty about who was to take slaves in cases of intestacy.[29] The options were to allow slaves to go immediately to the heirs designated by law, which was the rule in the case of land, or to allow them to be considered assets in the hands of executors and administrators for paying off debts and so forth, which was the rule in the case of chattels personal. Moreover, widows had claims to land that they did not have to chattels. The law held slaves to be "estates real, and not chattels, and shall descend unto the heir or widow of any person dying." This was to assure that heirs and widows would not have "bare lands without negroes to manure the same."[30] But there were provisos. A person could sell a slave without having to record the sale (sales of realty had to be recorded), and the law did not apply to merchants, factors, or agents bringing slaves to Barbados for sale. Such imported slaves were chattels until sold.[31] It was an ingenious compromise between the economic needs and claims of planters and their families on one side and merchants on the other.[32]

The Virginia law of 1705 followed the Barbadian. Slaves were "real estate" and descended as such.[33] The exemption in cases of merchants, factors, and agents was included. There were other provisos as well. Slaves were liable to be seized for the payment of debts "as other chattels or personal estate may be." And they would go as chattels to executors and administrators rather than directly to the widow or heir.[34] A slave, moreover, could be recovered, if unlawfully detained, by a personal action rather than an action for the recovery of real property. If a person died intestate and left a number of children, the slaves would be valued, after the dower was set apart, and the value divided among the children. The money was to be paid by the heir who received the slaves.[35] Slaves were treated as chattels personal for some purposes and as real estate for others. The primary objective was to assure that those who received the land of a slaveowner would also receive the slaves necessary to work the land.

Confusion abounded, so the burgesses adopted an explanatory statute in 1727. It is imperative to remember that the notion of property in Anglo-American law is a notion captured by the so-called bundle of rights.[36] Property is not really a "thing," it is a collection of rights to a thing, and a collection can be divided. The highest property right a person could possess under English law was a "fee simple." People who possessed this right could convey the property by will or deed to whomever they wished. The "fee" was the totality of all the rights to property in land. As Holmes elegantly put it, every "fee is a distinct *persona*, a distinct *hereditas*, or inheritance."[37] The fee could be "divided lengthwise, so to speak, among persons interested in the same way at the same time: it may also be cut across into successive interests, to be enjoyed one after another. In technical language, it may be divided into a particular estate and remainders. But they are still all parts of the same fee, and the same fiction still governs them."[38] Of the lesser estates the most important to understand in colonial Virginia law is the fee tail.

An entailed estate could be either general or special. The general entail involved a devise of lands to one and the "*heirs of his body begotten.*" All of his children could take in the appropriate order, no matter how many times a testator was married. The special entail limited the devise to certain heirs of the donee's body, as male heirs or the children of a first wife only. As a fee was an estate of inheritance, there had to be some word or words suggesting perpetuity, such as "heirs." Without this there would be no inheritance, and one might be dealing with property that was consumable or perishable; a fee was neither.[39]

A foundation for the entail was the thirteenth-century English statute *de donis conditionalibus*. That statute upheld entails on the notion that the intention of the testator ought to prevail and could alter the otherwise normal course of inheritance fixed by law. The will of the testator could determine the disposition of his property after his death even though that meant constraining the will of those to whom he devised or bequeathed his property.[40] By the time slavery was established in the English continental colonies, ways had been constructed to get around entails. It was possible to diminish an entail: this was to "dock" it. It was also possible to put an end to the entail, which was to "bar" it.

The point of the entail was to assure that landed property descended in a unit and thereby secure the property and the authority of the family. As Samuel Johnson observed in the eighteenth century, "entails are good, because it is good to preserve in a country, series of men, whom the people are accustomed to look up to as their leaders." Living in a society marked by the activities of merchant capital, however, he was quick to add: "I am for leaving a quantity of land in commerce, to excite industry, and keep money in the country; for, if no land were to be bought in the country, there would be no encouragement to acquire wealth, because a family could not be founded there."[41]

By virtue of the law of 1727 Virginia slaveowners were authorized to entail slaves as well as land, and the affect would be to "annex such slave or slaves to the freehold and inheritance." But the burgesses chose not to destroy the "credit of the country" by removal of entailed slaves from the fund creditors could reach. Slaves possessed by tenants in tail could be seized and sold under executions to satisfy lawful debts. However, executors and administrators could sell slaves only to satisfy the debts of the decedent where the personal estate was insufficient to pay the debts. And those slaves entailed and possessed by a husband in right of his wife could not be seized to satisfy his debts.[42] There were numerous other provisions in the 1727 law, but these were the most important and the ones that gave rise to litigation.

C. Ray Keim, a leading student of primogeniture and entail in colonial Virginia, concluded that entails of land were not widespread. But, he added, the question of entailing slaves remained to be studied.[43] It still does, but as a modest contribution to that end, as well as to an understanding of the laws making slaves realty, I examined the 215 wills probated in York County between 1715 and 1760 and the efforts to dock entails by legislative act. Of the 215 wills, only 3 provided for special entails of slaves by limiting the succession to male heirs. The first was in 1718. James Burwell, a prominent planter, gave nineteen slaves to his son Nathaniel and the "heirs males of his body lawfully issuing." If there were none, then the slaves went to the next male heir of Burwell, with the oldest male always to be preferred (this was the principle of primogeniture). Twenty years later Joseph Mountfort gave land and a couple of slaves to each of his sons and the male heirs. Mountfort entailed his slaves, but he did not resort to primogeniture. Finally, in 1748 one of the wealthiest York County planters, Philip Lightfoot, entailed land and slaves to his three sons, William, John, and Armistead. Each son received a plantation and sixty slaves and to the "Heirs Male of his Body." Like Mountfort, Lightfoot did not follow the rule of primogeniture.[44]

What happened to the entailed estate of Armistead Lightfoot was typical of what occurred when land and slaves were entailed. By a legislative act of 1769 the entailed estate was docked. Among the lands given to John Lightfoot, Armistead's brother, had been 6,588 acres in Brunswick County. Because he died without male heirs, the land went to Armistead. But the slaves who had been annexed to the Brunswick lands had been seized and sold for the payment of Armistead's debts. His lands in Goochland, also entailed, were more valuable than those in Brunswick, and the act noted that it would be advantageous to the support of the family to dock the upper 2,800 acres of the 6,588 acres in Brunswick and vest them in trustees and be sold by them. The trustees would then put the money in the purchase of slaves to be settled on the Goochland plantation. The trustees allowed the use of the slaves for life to Armistead, then his wife received one-third of the slaves, and then they went to Armistead's heirs, a general entail.[45]

A variation of a docked special entail involved Lewis Burwell's will, probated in 1710. Burwell devised lands to a son, also named Lewis. Young Lewis successfully docked the entail in the 1730s. The reason he did so was that the acres in King William County were far away, and he had "laid out great sums of money, in building a mansion-house, and other out-houses, and in making gardens, and other considerable improvements, upon part of the . . . land [in York and James City]; intending the same for the seat of the eldest son of the family." Patriarchalism had its privileges, and the result was that the acres in King William were transformed by legislative action into a fee simple estate. Acres in Isle of Wight County and land in York and James City Counties were transformed into a special entail to Lewis and his male heirs. Also, twenty-one named slaves were annexed to the entailed land with the stipulation that they "shall forever go" with the land.[46]

The Burwell family was also involved in an important case involving the entailing of slaves, *Burwell et ux. v. Johnson et ux.* (1762). One claim was that slaves could not be entailed under the act of 1705. The general court dismissed this bill in 1758, and the case then went on appeal to the king in council. There is no report of the privy council decision, but it appears that the council upheld the notion that slaves were entailable under the 1705 law.[47]

For the most part the practice of special entails to male heirs was limited to a handful of patriarchs. In addition to such special entails, thirty-three wills in the York County sample bequeathed slaves to a person and the "heirs of the body," and a handful more referred to "heirs lawfully begotten," a phrase often deemed equivalent to "heirs of the body."[48] The overwhelming majority of York County slaveowners, in other words, did not entail slaves.

By 1748 the burgesses adopted a statute that provided that thereafter slaves would be chattels personal. This law was disallowed in 1751.[49] The burgesses wanted to reenact the disallowed law, but the reasons did not impress the crusty Landon Carter. They were the "most Specious and Partial that can be imagined, running all upon the transitory Nature of Slaves and those Clauses in the Old Law that for the sake of trade etc." The majority would not budge. Carter petulantly confided to his diary that "I could discover the securing an Estate was the only motive with some."[50] This remark came with ill grace, for Carter had one of the largest and most beautiful Georgian estates in Virginia. What offended the patriarchal Carter was men caught up in the acquisitive spirit of market capitalism.

The response to the disallowance, the "humble address and representation of the council, and burgesses" of Virginia, began with a simple assertion: "Slaves are in their nature personal estate, and not real." Instead of defining slaves as realty for some purposes, personalty for others, and "both" in still other cases, they should be "reduced . . . to their natural condition."[51] Part of the trouble was that the tenant in tail "overstocked the plantations, and often the tenant was the proprietor of fee simple land, much fitter for cultivation than his intailed lands, where he could work his slaves to a much greater advantage." It was also common to remove entailed slaves to other counties beyond where the entail was recorded, creating serious problems for "purchasers, strangers, and creditors." Entailed slaves were mixed in with those held in fee simple, and because of the "uncertainty of distinguishing one from another, after several generations . . . and none of them having surnames," purchasers and creditors were deceived and had difficulty collecting debts. The law also "lessened the credit of the country; it being dangerous for the merchants of Great Britain to trust possessors of many slaves, for fear the slaves might be intailed." "And should credit be destroyed," the burgesses admitted, "in a trading country, as ours may be properly called, the consequence might be fatal."[52] Despite the appeal to the acquisitive instincts of British merchant capitalists, the law remained disallowed.

Sixteen years later, in *Blackwell v. Wilkinson*, the general court confronted an elaborate argument over a critical issue involving entails. Between 1705 and 1727 slaves had been entailed without being annexed to land. Were such entails lawful? Randolph, the attorney general, argued that they were. Although the burgesses could not change the "natural properties" of slaves, they could engage in the "transmutation of properties" at law. The words in the 1705 act were general. Slaves were real estate, and the exceptions did not prevent people from entailing slaves and did not require that they be annexed to land. Randolph concluded his argument with an attempt to outflank any effort to suggest that his line of reasoning proved too much: "I annex this restriction to it," he noted, "that the subject should be of distinguished value." George Wythe, on the other side, argued that things entailable besides land "concerns lands, is annexed to, exercisable in, or issuing from lands," and slaves could not be so described. "Slaves are transitory and changeable both in the time and place of their existence, and difficult to be traced to the root from which they sprang."[53]

There was one formidable obstacle in Wythe's path, *Burwell*. He tried to work his way around it by noting that the lands entailed were devised in the same clause and by the same words as were the slaves, and it was always held that "things annexed to lands might be entailed." But the general policy of the law was against perpetuities, and the entail in this case was an attempt to introduce a perpetuity. It was a fine lawyerly argument. Eight members of the court ruled that "slaves could never be entailed unless annexed to lands." Three members—William Byrd II, Landon Carter, and Robert Burwell—dissented.[54]

A major legal issue involving slaves as realty concerned the seizure of slaves for debts. One of the first extant cases that dealt with slaves as realty (*Tucker v. Sweney*, 1730) raised this question: Could slaves born after the death of the debtor be taken to satisfy the judgment against him? The court ruled that they could. "Negroes notwithstanding the Act making them Real Estate," it stated, "remain in the Hands of the Ex'ors by that Act as Chatels and as such do vest in them for payment of Debts so that in this Case they are considered no otherwise than Horses or Cattle." Missing was any discussion of the rule in the 1727 law that executors were to try to pay all debts out of the personal property before slaves were touched.[55]

Two years later, in *Goddin v. Morris*, the court did consider that problem. The case asked, when a personal estate along with several slaves was sufficient to pay debts, and a creditor served an execution judgment against the executor that was levied on some of the slaves, and the executor redeemed the slaves by paying less than the market value for them, was the property the executor's or did it belong to the heir at law? The court ruled the latter. Anything less would defeat the "Policy of the Law of this Country in preserving Slaves for the Benefit of Heirs."[56]

For the most part Virginians treated slaves as realty for very limited purposes, and even when defined as real estate they existed in a cluster of legal boxes. By virtue of the law of 1727 they were protected more than chattels personal and less than real estate when there were debts. And as early as 1705 slaves were defined as real estate in order to grant dower rights to widows and settle the line of succession when persons died without leaving a will. Moreover, the definition of slaves as real estate opened the way for them to be entailed. It was not all that common, however, and was largely confined to the great planters of the colony whose patriarchalism coexisted in tension with the spread of market capitalist values.

In the end the entail gave way. The entail was the device of a feudal society, and Virginia was rather a "trading country." This does not mean that people did not continue to place restraints on the alienation of slaves. They did, but not in the same sense as the strict entail, and they did not annex them to the land. Moreover, after 1792 slaves in Virginia did not go to an heir designated by the law but were distributed as other personalty. The law of that year was simple: "all negro and mulatto slaves . . . shall be held, taken and adjudged to be personal estate."[57] Jefferson was pleased. In his *Notes on the State of Virginia*, he extolled the changes in the legal system. Among the most important was "to make slaves distributable among the next of kin, as other moveables."[58] This change would be of no benefit to the slaves, of course. But defining them as real estate had not been of much benefit to the slaves of masters who died with wills, either.

Slaves as "Realty" in Kentucky

Kentuckians adopted a law based on the earlier Virginia laws six years after Virginians redefined slaves as chattels.[59] Most of the qualifications, such as liability for debts and the use of personal actions, were retained. But there could be no fee tail in Kentucky, although a person could annex a slave to the land so that the slave could not be devised or sold separately.

Despite the statute, not many if any Kentuckians annexed slaves to land. The largest number of cases concerned the liability of slaves to be sold to pay the debts of a decedent. Because of the liability Chief Justice George M. Bibb ruled in *Cox v. Ex'r. of Robertson* (1809) that although slaves were real estate for many purposes, they were also "assets in the hands of the executors." Executors of wills had an "absolute right to the possession" of the slaves and could sell them. Moreover, the purchaser need not show that the debts of the testator required the sale. They would be chattels until the debts were liquidated. Bibb's ruling also considered the notion that slaves were to be sold only if the other personal property was insufficient. He was at pains to secure creditors rather than the rights of heirs to particular slaves. For the person or persons entitled to the slave under the will the only redress would be a suit for money against the executor. They could assure possession of the slaves if they secured the executor that "they will refund their proportions of any debts or demands which may afterward appear against the decedent."[60]

A variation of the problem appeared in *Grimes v. Grimes' Devisees* (1812). Could a person bring an action for a slave without showing that the executor had assented to their taking the slave? The agreement of an executor normally was required. Chief Justice John Boyle noted that if a chattel was devised, the devisee could have no remedy without showing consent. The legal right to chattels was in the executor. The rule for real estate differed. A testator who devised his landed estate immediately passed it to the devisee on the death of the testator. The devisee could take land without assent. An act of 1800 provided that "slaves, so far as respects last wills and testaments, shall hereafter . . . be held and deemed as real estate, and shall pass by the last will and testament of persons possessed thereof, in the same manner, and under the same regulations, as landed property." Boyle ruled that this law was so clear that no doubt remained. Assent was not necessary: legal title immediately vested in the devisee.[61] It is difficult to see how *Grimes* and *Cox* can be reconciled. Bibb treated slaves as assets in the hands of the executor. Boyle treated slaves as real estate that immediately vested in the devisee without the agreement of the executor.

By a law of 1798 land in Kentucky was made liable to seizure and sale for the payment of debts, and this pitted land and slaves against each other. In *Faris v. Banton* (1831) the executor recovered a judgment against three men, William T. and John Banton and William Faris, on an obligation executed by them to the testator. A tract of land of John Banton was seized and sold. The principal was William T. Banton, and John Banton and Faris were the sureties. The lower court quashed the seizure and sale of John Banton's land. The claim by Banton was that Faris had more than enough personal property (one slave had been seized and sold), and before the land of Banton was seized and sold the personal property of Faris should have been. The duty of the sheriff was to "make the amount of the execution in his hands, first out of the personal estate of the defendant, therein, if he can; if not, out of the slaves; and, if there be none, or not sufficient to raise the amount, that then the land is to be sold." The court ruled, however, that the land could be seized and sold on the ground that the sheriff had no duty to exhaust the personal property of all defendants when there were several before he could touch the land of any one.[62]

The law allowed persons to consent to the seizure and sale of land in preference to the seizure and sale of their slaves. The land of John Banton had been seized because Faris directed it so that he could protect his slaves. Judge Joseph R. Underwood held that land was protected in preference to slaves, but owners could choose to protect their slaves. It was, however, the individual owner of slaves alone who could protect them by surrendering his own land, not that of a codefendant. Banton's counsel had attempted to show that land was held in such high regard, and was so vital to "strengthen our republican form of government," that the law should be read to mean that all the property (chattels, slaves, and land) were to be a total fund, and that the land was always to be the last touched if there were sufficient chattels or slaves in the common fund.[63] The court declined to treat land as that sacred.

A particularly significant case involving the liability of a slave for debts was *Caleb v. Field and Others* (1840). James Quertermus devised his slaves to his wife with the authority to dispose of them at her death. By her will she emancipated Caleb. After her death Caleb was sold under an execution obtained by John Murphy. The court held that Caleb was a free man, but with the "contingent liability to be subjected to the satisfaction of any *bona fide* debt due by his deceased master." The court in *Caleb* held that a slave "emancipated by will, is not assets in the hands of the executor, but that the title to freedom passes to the beneficiary immediately." The only way the reservation to creditors of the emancipator could be enforced was in a proceeding in which the person freed would be entitled to defend his rights, and he should "never be disfranchised for an instant, unless the debt of the pursuing creditor can not be otherwise made, nor to a greater extent than the payment of it should render necessary."[64]

This was sharpened in *Snead v. David* (1840), which arose on an action of trespass to claim freedom under a will. The slave was sold under an apprehension that the real and personal property of the testator would be insufficient to pay all debts. The bill of sale noted that if the estate was sufficient, the purchase money would be returned and the slave David would go back to the executors, who would then free him. The estate was, however, insufficient. Judge Thomas A. Marshall, for the court, found in favor of David, although he remained vulnerable.[65]

The fact was that there was no real distinction between the effect of a will that emancipated slaves and one that devised them to be held as property. In either event the slaves passed as lands passed, and that kept them out of the reach of executors. Slaves passed, Marshall held, like lands directly by force of the will, but they did not have to be in the same "condition, state or quality" at the end of the passage as at the beginning. The person was said "to pass by the will from a state of slavery to a state of freedom." Marshall continued:

> But it is really the title in the slave that shall pass by will, as the title in land passes by will. And what is the title to a slave? Undoubtedly, it is such dominion, or right of dominion, as the laws allow one man to have over the services, the powers and the faculties of another. By the act of emancipation, whether by deed or will, or in whatever form, this right is lost by the master, and acquired by the slave; who thenceforth, by reason of this acquired right, becomes his own master, the proprietor of himself, and thus a free man. . . . If he is emancipated by will, the title passes to him by the will. And, at all events, it passes out of the former owner, which is sufficient whether it be extinguished without vesting in the slave, or by so vesting. For, if it passes from the testator as land, it never can come to his executor.

The executor could not possess persons as assets. A devisee of slaves who was liable for a testator's debts could protect the slaves by paying their value to the creditor, and, Marshall held, persons emancipated by a will could protect themselves the same way. The creditor, finally, had a right to the value of the emancipated persons, but not to their person or services, and this "value" he could obtain only by appropriate proceedings. Since 1800 those proceedings were through the intervention of equity.[66]

This all changed in 1852, when Kentucky made slaves chattels personal. It was then provided that "slaves shall not be sold by the personal representative, unless, for the want of other assets, it be necessary to pay the debts of the decedent."[67] Slaves were assets, although preferred ones.

Slaves as Realty in Arkansas and Louisiana

The experience in Arkansas under its 1840 law was shallow. Slaves were defined as real estate and would descend as it descended. This law was repealed after only three years.[68] The only occasion an Arkansas court had to consider it was in *Gullett & Wife v. Lamberton* (1845), which concerned the proper form of action to recover possession of slaves. The court noted that the law of 1840 defined slaves as realty and that "it was beyond the power of the legislature to change their nature, which was never designed to be done, but it was only designed to change their mode of descent and the title by which they should be held." Moreover, it would be absurd to strip owners of the use of the forms of action used to recover personal property. Judge Williamson S. Oldham held that detinue, a personal—not real—action, was appropriate despite the definition of slaves as real estate.[69]

Louisiana was different, as the civil law did not expressly provide that slaves would be considered real estate. *Las Siete Partidas*, the basis of the Spanish slave code, was influential in Louisiana,[70] but it contained no such definition, and there was none listed by L. Lislet Moreau and Henry Carleton in their work, *The Laws of Las Siete Partidas Which Are Still in Force in the State of Louisiana* (1820). The earlier French *code noir* had expressly defined slaves as movable property. The change in Louisiana came in laws adopted in 1770, as Hans Baade has shown. These were modifications introduced by the Spanish governors. They were mortgage and conveyance ordinances and made slaves immovables for the purposes of sale and mortgage (the civil law phrase is hypothecation).[71] Following the transfer of authority to the United States, Louisiana adopted a slave code in 1806. By that *code noir* it was provided that "Slaves shall always be reputed and considered real estates, shall be, as such, subject to be mortgaged, according to the rules prescribed by law, and they shall be seized and sold as real estate."[72] But Chief Justice George Eustis claimed in *Girard et al. v. City of New Orleans et al.* (1847) that "slaves are in no sense real estate; they are considered as immoveables."[73]

The distinction between movables and immovables derived from Roman law. But it concerned matters of secondary importance, such as the period of prescription (the time one must possess a thing before his or her title was perfected), the system of marriage portions, and the law of thefts. In French private law the distinction remained and, apparently, was considered more significant. The right of disposal of movables was much greater than that of immovables. The reasoning was similar to that which applied in the early common law to chattels personal: they were perishable and of relatively little value. Because movables were of short duration, they could not be mortgaged in the civil law, they could be confiscated whereas immovables could not, and the patterns and rules of succession to movables and immovables differed. The one quality often cited to distinguish the two was mobility, but that was not necessarily the most important element. As Jean Brissaud put it, "Immoveables are things which are everlasting and which produce annual income; perpetuity and the production of issues characterize immoveables even more than the important fact of immobility; it is these two qualities which make up their value, whereas moveables are perishable and do not bring in anything."[74]

Hopefully, these distinctions will help remove the confusion. Slaves, because of their relative permanence and because of their value, would be more like an immovable than a movable. When the United States took possession of Louisiana, different legal traditions, rules, concepts, and language intermixed.[75] The *statute* used the common law phrase to cover the rules first put into Louisiana law by the Spanish in 1770. The Spanish, however, had used the word "immoveables" rather than "real estate." Eustis's remark in *Girard* retained the older civil law notion, despite the statutory language.

The real problem, however, was the same as that in the common law systems. What incidents attached to the forms of property? The statute of 1806 was unambiguous about one incident, the liability to mortgage. But defining slaves as immovables did not mean that all of the rules applied to immovables, or to realty, would attach. A good illustration is the problem of prescription.[76] According to the Louisiana code, the "time necessary to prescribe for property is different, whether the property is immoveable, slaves or moveable." Slaves were treated as different from either immovables or movables for the purpose of acquiring title by possession.[77]

Although Louisiana defined slaves as immovables or real estate throughout the period from 1770 to 1865, there is surprisingly little case law. An early illustration was *Harper v. Destrehan* (1824). The plaintiff recovered a female slave who had been stolen and purchased by the defendant at a public auction. The lower court ruled that the plaintiff recover the slave, but he must pay the price of the slave to the defendant. The basis of the lower court ruling was the civil code's provision that in cases of movables prescription would apply after three years unless the movables were stolen. Judge Alexander Porter disposed of this claim quickly: slaves were not movables but immovables. Moreover, the reasoning of the rule in the civil code could not apply to "this kind of property. It does not pass by delivery, but by writing, and the purchaser should look to title, and not to possession, as evidence of ownership."[78] The common law notion that possession raised a presumption of ownership of chattels did not apply when slaves were not viewed that way, as was the case in civil law Louisiana.

It was not that clear, however. The problem in *Monday v. Wilson et al.* (1832), for instance, regarded the failure to record a deed in the parish where the slaves were located. They were on a plantation in St. Helena Parish, but the deed was recorded in East Feliciana Parish. By a law of 1810 such recordings involving immovable property would be without affect against third persons unless they appeared in the parish where the immovables were located. This would seem to apply, but Judge George Matthews ruled that it did not. Even though slaves were immovable property "in some respects," they were not in all. "Being in their nature moveables, considered as things, and being semorentes considered as men, they cannot strictly speaking be held to be immoveables situated in any particular parish of the state."[79] Therefore, the recording law did not apply.

A final prominent case was *Girard et al. v. City of New Orleans et al.* (1847). Land and slaves were part of the succession of Stephen Girard, a wealthy merchant capitalist of Philadelphia. The plaintiffs were his heirs at law. In his last will Girard left a plantation and slaves in Ouachita Parish to the city of New Orleans. The use of the plantation and slaves went to Henry Bry for twenty years as long as Bry survived that long. Then the land, plantation, slaves, and other personal property were to be sold by the city and the proceeds used to promote the health and prosperity of the people of New Orleans. In construing this will, Chief Justice Eustis observed that "there is no attempt made to attach, by a condition, the slaves to the land, or to render it obligatory that they should be employed on it, and in no other way." In any event, the slaves became insubordinate, and Bry, who thought they burned their cabins, "removed the hands from the place." Were the slaves owned by the city, or did they descend to the heirs at law? The heirs relied on a law of 1805 that allowed the city to hold, convey, and use real estate provided it was within the city limits. If slaves were real estate, the city could not own them. This was the point of Eustis's remark quoted before. Slaves were not real estate, they were immovables by law, and the restriction in the 1805 act did not apply. The slaves belonged to the city, not to the heirs at law.[80]

The effect on slaves of being defined as immovables in Louisiana was hardly to keep them attached to plantations, or in family units, or as a community. Such a definition there had no more moral impact than it did in colonial Virginia. It scarcely aided the slaves of Robert McCausland in West Feliciana Parish, for instance. After his death the court ordered a judicial partition of his slaves. The slaves were divided into two lots, and the heirs drew the lots from slips of paper marked Lot 1 and Lot 2. As of May 1, 1851, the lots were these:

Lot 1

William Henry (Jinney's infant)
Harkless, aged 9 months (Peggy's infant)
Evans, aged 10 months (infant of Long Milly)
Huldah (Salva's infant)
Big Jim (Carpenter)
Scott (Maria's infant)—born since the taking of the inventory to Red Maria
Lucy, aged 34 years (not healthy)
Ben Brown (blacksmith), aged 45
Judy (wife of Ben Brown), aged 40
Judy (his wife, dirt eater [the "his" was a slave named Jack])

Eliza (his wife: Bob)
Levy (Eliza's son)

Lot 2

Red Maria (and child)
Kent'y Jane (his wife [the "his" was John Millen])
Polly (dirt eater)
Andrew, aged 2 months (infant of Polly)
Harrison (dirt eater)
Abram (carpenter)
Henry (a runaway), aged 30
Chaney, aged 19 (and child)
Ben Wright (driver)
Jacob (dirt eater)
Kentucky William (dirt eater)[81]

Still other slaves were community property,[82] and before the division was completed another batch, from the separate estate of Robert McCausland, was added to Lot 2. In the division of this estate slaves clearly were separated. Scott, for example, was born between May 1851 and January 1852 when the lots were drawn. His mother was Red Maria. She was in Lot 2 and he was in Lot 1. There is some bitter irony in this situation. As early as 1806 it was unlawful in Louisiana to sell a child under the age of ten separately from its mother. But this applied to sales, not judicial partitions of estates on the death of an owner. Definition as an immovable scarcely helped slaves such as Red Maria and Scott. Nor, for that matter, was it useful to the heirs at law of Stephen Girard. In fact, the statutory definition of a slave as a chattel personal, or as realty, or as an immovable did next to nothing to benefit the slave. These were not moral categories, they were legal categories.

Judicial Rulings

Aside from statutory definitions of slaves, Southern judges, on occasion, analogized slaves to land and applied real property rules to slaves. The most extensive experience was in South Carolina. In *Helton v. Caston* (1831) O'Neall considered an action of trespass brought by the owner of a slave against the hirer for a cruel beating. The hirer argued that this should be a nonsuit because the owner could not compel such an action unless he had possession of the slave. The case, in other words, involved problems with the concept of possession at common law, and the corresponding correct common law pleading. O'Neall admitted that if the right of possession were in reversion, the action could not be trespass, it had to be case. The rules of personal property law did not include the notion of any reserved property interest. However, O'Neall reasoned, "all analogies of the law in relation to land sustain it fully." One illustration was leases of land. He argued that "there is in England no case where the question could arise in relation to personal property; but in this State, where slaves are a more valuable part of our property, than even land, where they approach nearer to its fixedness and certainty, than any other personal property, and where the hiring of them is analogous to the renting of land, it would seem that it is but reasonable and right to transfer the principles applicable to leases of lands, to contracts for the hire of slaves."[83] A right of possession could be reserved, and trespass was an appropriate remedy. His analogical approach led him to modify the normal common law rules that applied to chattels when the chattels involved were slaves.

O'Neall continued to press his analogical approach six years later in *Tennent v. Dendy* (1837). This was an action of trespass brought against the captain of a patrol for whipping a slave unlawfully. At the time of the whipping the slave was in the possession of a hirer. Relying on *Helton*, O'Neall argued that "slaves, although chattels personal, cannot in every respect be treated by the rules which apply to and govern personal estate." They were also human beings, and even as property they were not exactly like other personal property. O'Neall, in fact, "always thought there was more analogy to slaves in the rules of law applicable to land, than was to be found in the law of personalty." Here he held that by "analogy of an easement, the owner may, notwithstanding the hiring, recover in this form of action."[84]

When we recall that Judge O'Neall proposed to change the rules of law in order to keep slave families together as much as possible, it becomes clear that he wished to preserve a patriarchal society based on a stable gentry, one that took its duties to slaves seriously. But in seeking this by conflating the rules of real and personal property, O'Neall was in danger of contributing to the deflation of the concept of land that many considered so central to republicanism.[85] With the spread of industrial capitalism in the North, the nearly sacred perception of land was under pressure.[86] Yet the potential was there for the same thing to happen in the South because of the high value placed on slaves and the tendency in some places to blend the rules of real and personal property law where slaves were concerned.

A circuit decree given by Chancellor George W. Dargan of South Carolina in 1850 is a good illustration. *Hull v. Hull* involved the rule to be applied when both real and personal property were available to pay off the debts of a testator. The commissioner in equity had ruled that the debts had to be paid by the money received from the sale of the specific legacy (the grant of slaves to a daughter) before the devise of land (which had gone to a son) could be touched.[87]

The rule, Dargan noted, arose under feudalism when "landed estate constituted the predominant element in the social and political organization. And hence, we can hardly be surprised at the vast importance that was attached to its possession. The aggregate of the personal property then, embraced but a small portion of the wealth of the nation, while the few goods and chattels, that were possessed by the humbler classes, were insecure, and liable to be snatched away by the lawless, marauding barons." With the growth of capitalism, however, personalty (such as rents and income) increased in value in England, but the distinction between real and personal property remained intact. The reason, according to Dargan, was social. The "privileged classes form a barrier, that interposes between the throne, and popular encroachments and republican tendencies." The landed aristocracy of England was "appreciated by the middle classes, and by all the friends of peace, order and stability." It was essential to prevent the sort of bloody upheaval that rocked France at the end of the eighteenth century. "Volcanic and pent up fires," he wrote, "smoulder beneath the venerable pile; the waves of popular discontent dash madly round the foundations. Take away the barrier, from which the surge is made to recoil; remove the weight by which the popular upheaval is repressed, and the flood and the earthquake would do their work in an instant; and this proud and powerful monarchy, in all its colossal proportions, would be swept away at once and forever." Rules of property, for all their dryness, were vital. But in South Carolina the same rules were not needed. "Our law of descent," Dargan continued, "is adapted not to aristocratic, but to republican forms of society. Its policy is rather to pull down, than to build up and sustain, great and overgrown estates." This was grand theory, but it did not resolve the legal issue before him. On that point he ruled that real and personal property should abate *pro rata*. Each fund should be used, and the devise of land should not be protected. "Lands have not here that adventitious value, which for causes we have investigated, obtains in the parent country. They are not more valuable than personal property; than negroes, for example. Indeed, the latter, if facility of converting them into cash, at an established marketable value, may be considered a test, are the most desirable of the two."[88]

Chancellor Dargan represented one tendency in Southern legal discourse, but it was only that. His circuit decree was modified on appeal. Chancellor Job Johnstone ruled for the court that "in the administration of the assets of a testator . . . the personal estate is liable for the payment of debts, before resort to the realty." Land should be favored over "mere chattels." "Is nothing due to sentiment? Is the home of one's ancestors," he queried, "the place of one's nativity, with which all the recollections of childhood are associated, to be put on a footing with vulgar chattels?"[89] Johnstone clung to an older republican tradition, but it was a tradition that was under stress in the South, as it was in the North. In the South the pressure was created by the high market value placed on slaves.

A sanguine view of the tension between the value placed on land and on slaves appeared in a late Florida case. In *McLeod v. Dell* (1861) the question arose whether or not slaves could pass by a nuncupative will (an oral will dictated in one's last illness). The rule of the common law was that land could not pass in this fashion. The court concluded that slaves could not pass by a nuncupative will any more than land could. Slaves, Chief Justice Charles H. DuPont argued, were taken "out of the category common to personalty, and . . . [placed] in close juxtaposition with land." The motive of the legislators (Florida passed a statute on wills in 1828), in fact, was "to place that species of property upon an equal footing with realty."

DuPont's reasoning demonstrates the influence of proslavery thought even on technical legal points. Florida's legislators wanted to withdraw slaves from the "class of personalty to which they belong for ordinary purposes" because "the growth and progress of the 'peculiar institution' in the Southern States, has inspired sentiments which impart to that particular species of property even a greater degree of permanence than is accorded to realty. It is the cherished subject of inheritance, and a man under the stress of adverse circumstances will strip himself of every other species of property, even the old 'homestead' the scene of his early childhood, before he will consent to part with his slaves." DuPont added that "a feeling of benevolence prompts him to maintain the integrity of the partriarchal relation, by transmitting them to the care and protection of the surviving family."[90]

Ultimately, of course, whatever rules were applied by statutes or judicial rulings to slaves, what was crucial was dominion. For this purpose the concept of property, the notion of a person as a "thing," was obviously the central "incident" in slavery. Whether the person was defined as a chattel or as realty had no real moral dimension, and it did not raise the status of the slave. What it did do was determine what particular legal and equitable rules, what precise "incidents" of property law, would be used by judges and chancellors. Of greatest importance was the set of rules relating to the law of inheritance. There, as elsewhere, the general trend was toward assuring an early alienability in the market, despite decisions like that of the 1861 Florida court.

4

Slavery and the Law of Successions

Born to a slave inheritance.

WILLIAM GOODELL, *American Slave Code* (1853)

"Every one is familiar," Goodell wrote, with the claim that one was said to have been " 'born to a slave inheritance,' or 'born a slaveholder.' These phrases occur in almost every plea for the blamelessness of the slaveholder, and for the 'innocency of the legal relation.' " Goodell was not impressed with the excuse. "This feature of the 'legal relation,' " he continued, "will be found . . . to embody one of the most foul and damning features of the whole system—the feature of self-perpetuity—of self-transmission to the future."[1] He was correct to highlight succession law as it involved the validation and perpetuation of a social order. It also concerned moral choices (such as between the right of inheritance and the right of bequest).[2] From the seventeenth century through the 1770s the rules of succession in the common law world were under increasing pressure to favor easier alienation of property. Nonetheless, the old rules were not completely rejected during that period. By the end of the eighteenth century and into the nineteenth they began to break down or were overthrown under the pressures of capitalism and a liberal property law.

By the end of the eighteenth century, for instance, the entail was abolished. But when entails fell into disfavor, new categories, or old ones used in new ways, were embraced by those who sought the same ends as had been achieved by the entail. Richard Ely noted that one purpose of the trust, an equitable category, was to function as a substitute for the old entail.[3] The entail and its functional equivalents rested on a communitarian or familial notion of property rather than on a liberal conception of property.

During the nineteenth century a "liberal property law" occupied a powerful place in American legal thought. Gregory S. Alexander, a legal scholar, isolated two prominent characteristics of such a view of private property; "first, it promotes individual freedom of disposition as the basic mechanism of allocation. Second, it exhibits a strong preference for a fully consolidated form of property interest." A consolidation of property interests meant that those who favored a liberal property law tried to "concentrate in a single legal entity . . . the relevant rights, privileges, and powers for possessing, using, and transferring discrete assets."[4] This was the legal expression of a social order in which basic social relationships were overwhelmingly determined by market relationships. Such a conception of property and property rights was not congenial to efforts to restrain the disposition of property represented by the entail and its functional equivalents. These different views coexisted in tension within Anglo-American law in general, and they coexisted in the law of slavery.

To understand how it worked under the law of slavery, one must bear in mind that there were two ways to succeed to property under the common law, and each contained different rules restraining alienation. One was by *descent*, whereby title to property was acquired by right of representation as the heir at law, without any act of one's own. This concerned the succession to property of those who died without wills, the intestate succession. The other mode covered the succession to property through wills.

Intestate Succession

Under the common law land descended to a designated "heir at law." The rules derived from the world of feudalism.[5] The pattern of descent for chattels differed, but because slaves were defined as real estate on occasion, it is important to understand both sets of rules.

A number of canons of descent for land existed by the seventeenth and eighteenth centuries. One was that inheritances "lineally descend to the issue of the person last actually seised . . . but shall never lineally ascend."[6] In civil law Louisiana property could go in ascent to parents as well as in descent to children. By the end of the eighteenth century the major change in the rules on the distribution of land of intestates was the abolition of the rule of primogeniture and the substitution of the notion of partible inheritance.[7]

The rules on the disposition of the personal property of intestates were set in the English Statute of Distributions of 1670. Among the leading provisions were these: one-third of the estate would go to the widow, the residue in equal portions to the children, or if they were dead to their representatives. If there were no children, one-half of the property would go to the widow and one-half to the "next of kindred in equal degree and their representatives" and so on.[8] Most of the Southern jurisdictions followed the English statute. One exception was Virginia.

One year after the adoption of the English statute Virginia's burgesses dealt with the problem of dividing slaves among the children of a decedent. The existing law on intestates had provided that sheep, cattle, and horses should be delivered in kind to orphans when they came of age. Some wanted to add slaves to the list, but there was the "difficulty of procureing negroes in kind as alsoe the value and hazard of their lives." Because of this it was not possible to find men who would "engage themselves to deliver negroes of equall ages if the specificall negroes should dye, or become by age or accident unserviceable." The humanity of the blacks meant that they were not essentially interchangeable like cattle. The result was that the county courts were authorized to have the slaves appraised and either sold or "preserved in kind" as the court felt best would preserve or improve the estate of the children.[9] Thirty-four years later the burgesses adopted the law that made slaves descend to heirs of intestates in the same way land descended. This lasted until 1792. Thus for eighty-seven years slaves in Virginia would descend to the eldest son and so forth. When the law was changed to define slaves as chattels, the rule that was first set down in 1671 was used; if it was not possible to make a distribution in kind "on account of the nature of the property," the courts could order a sale and the distribution of the money. There could be an objective value attached to slaves, but there could also be a subjective value. The law allowed any claimant of the slaves to show cause why there should be no sale.[10] Virginia's approach was not widely followed.

Partitions of slaves of intestates occurred all over the South, and they were among the most wrenching, lonely experiences for the slaves. O'Neall, for one, was disturbed enough to suggest a reform. He proposed that when slaves were "sold for partition . . . they should be sold with the freehold." It was rare, however, that any Southern state placed restraints on partitions. One exception was a Georgia law of 1854 that prohibited executors or administrators from selling children under the age of five apart from their mothers. They were to be placed together "in one of the parts into which the estate to which they belong, is to be divided." This would apply to administration of intestate estates, as well as divisions under wills. But there was a proviso: "unless such division cannot in any wise be affected without such separation."[11] The right of inheritance outweighed even this minimal effort to limit the horrors that slaves lived with because of partible inheritance. One way to alter the course of successions in spite of rules about partible inheritance was by will.

Testate Successions

The descent of lands to an heir in England "could not be interfered with by will . . . whereas it was sinful not to execute a will of personal property."[12] But there were ways around this restraint. The statute De Donis allowed landowners to entail their land. One of the primary rules was that the intention of a testator ought to prevail. This clearly meant that the will or intention of a landowner would be allowed to modify the normal course of descent. But it did not wholly overturn the direction of an inheritance; it did not give a landowner complete power to alienate the land anyway he saw fit. He could always bequeath his personal property, although early in the history of the common law there were the rules about the *reasonable* part to the wife and children. By the seventeenth to eighteenth centuries owners of personal property could bequeath all of that property to whoever they wanted.[13] In civil law Louisiana the idea that the testator could not completely disinherit was retained in the notion of the fixed or forced heirship. Persons who were designated by the law as normally meriting a portion of the estate could not be disinherited unless they had been deemed "unworthy" in a court action. The Louisiana civil code of 1825 listed unworthy acts as failures of duty toward the deceased.[14]

Some Common Law Restraints on the Disposition of Property by the Eighteenth Century

In addition to the entail (examined in the last chapter), those who wished to tie up property utilized remainders and executory devises to control "future interests." There were two types of estates, those in possession and those in expectancy. An estate in expectancy embraced remainders and executory interests.[15] "An estate" that was in remainder, wrote Blackstone, was one "to take effect and be enjoyed after another estate" ends. One point that must be kept clear is that there could be no remainder that followed a fee simple absolute for the obvious reason that nothing remained. The entire estate was possessed by the person who held it in fee simple. Where a remainder did exist, it could be either a vested or a contingent remainder. A vested remainder was one in which a present interest "passes to the party, though to be enjoyed *in futuro*." It was an estate that was fixed and in a particular individual and would be enjoyed after a "particular estate" ended. A particular estate meant a life estate or one for years. A contingent remainder was one in which no present interest vested but rested on a future event that might not happen.[16]

The executory devise existed in opposition to the basic rules about carving up estates. A creation of courts sympathetic to restraints upon alienation, it existed when a fee, or an estate less than a fee, was established or "limited" after a fee. Conceptually, the executory devise was odd. The normal rule was that once the whole estate had been given in fee, there was nothing left to devise. But that was not the case here. This was an indulgence to the will, the intention, of someone who shortly would be dead. Occasionally, moreover, testators resorted to equitable concepts such as the "trust," whereby title was given to one person for the benefit of another.

Entails, remainders, executory devises, and trusts were all ways to tie up property. They were a means to keep power in families and to withstand the pressures of the market and of an emerging liberal property law. One expression of the latter was the idea that the common law abhorred perpetuities, that is, a suspension of the power of alienation for a lengthy period of time.[17] There was a steady struggle to undermine perpetuities. Two rules are especially important: the rule in Shelley's case and the rule against perpetuities.

The rule in Shelley's case was that if a person was granted an estate less than a fee simple and then the estate was to go to his heirs, the heirs took nothing and the person who got the life estate took the whole. This was based on the notion that "the ancestor, during his life, beareth in himself all his heirs."[18] The word "heirs" enlarged a life estate to a fee simple so that the property could be alienated earlier.

The problem with a testator using the word "heirs" only was that it might mean that the property must go in perpetuity until there were no more heirs, and that might be a hundred years or more. Historically, however, the rule had been used only to reach cases involving life estates and not executory devises. English jurists, moreover, were not totally hostile to restraints upon alienation. By the seventeenth century they had formulated a compromise that allowed people to restrain alienation but not forever. This was the rule against perpetuities.[19] This rule could apply to executory devises or contingent remainders. According to Blackstone, the contingency on which these estates rested must occur within a reasonable time: "for courts of justice will not indulge even wills, so as to create a perpetuity, which the law abhors: because by perpetuities . . . estates are made incapable of answering those ends, of social commerce, and providing for the sudden contingencies of private life, for which property was at first established. The utmost length that has been hitherto allowed, for the contingency of an executory devise . . . is that of a life or lives in being, and one and twenty years afterwards."[20] The last sentence contains the modern rule against perpetuities. It was a rule that allowed them within limits.

All of these modes of tying up property, as well as the rules for breaking them down, found expression in the laws concerning claims to slaves, as people continued to try to protect the interests of their families through the control of succession to slave property even during the nineteenth century as a "liberal property law" emerged. In order to open up an inquiry into that history I consulted, in addition to the appellate cases and the relevant statutory changes, samples of probated wills. From the colonial period I used the 215 wills from York County discussed earlier. For the nineteenth century I reviewed over 200 wills probated in Fairfield District and Spartanburg District in South Carolina. I also looked at a sample from Saline County, Missouri, and have drawn on the work of others who have examined wills in Missouri and Virginia,[21] as well as scattered wills of well-known Southerners from outside the selected sample counties in order to give still more flavor to tentative, impressionistic conclusions. There are in the sample a little over 600 wills. The intention was to focus particularly on probated wills from areas of the South that had fairly large numbers of slaves during both the colonial period and the nineteenth century, but not a disproportionate number such as along the Sea Islands of South Carolina and Georgia, nor a minuscule number such as might be found in the mountains of western Virginia. I make no claim, of course, to a persuasive mathematical sample. My desire is to make a reasonable, if modest beginning that others, hopefully, will pursue.

Remainders and Executory Devises
of Slaves in Practice

Under the common law devices such as remainders had originally applied to land. Since slaves were most often defined as chattels personal, a question of some significance was this: could there be a remainder in a chattel? The old view was that there could not because there were no estates in chattels. Moreover, there was a maxim of the law that a gift of a chattel for an hour is a gift forever.[22] There is limited evidence to show, however, that the old rule had broken down by the eighteenth century. In *Edmonds v. Hughs* (Virginia, 1730), a case that arose on a will of 1695, the court ruled in favor of a remainder in slaves. Use of the slaves had been given to the spouse with a remainder over to the son. An English precedent held that "where personal Chattels are devised for a Limitted [*sic*] time it shall be Intended the use of them only, and not the Devise of the Thing itself, and therefore allowed the Rem'r over to be good."[23] The Virginia judges followed this lead.

By the nineteenth century there was only an occasional reference to the earlier law, and a remainder over was good. In Arkansas Judge David Walker noted in *Maulding et al. v. Scott et al.* (1852) that the common law rule had been relaxed and the current rule was that "whether the gift be of the thing itself for life, or only of the use of the thing, a limitation over to a subsequent devisee after the decease of the first taker, will be supported."[24] But it was suspect and the intention had to be clearly expressed. Because estates could exist in chattels and remainders would be upheld, the rule in Shelley's case could apply to life estates in slaves. It was in fact adopted in numerous Southern jurisdictions in cases involving remainders in slaves, even when not defined as realty.

In *Ham v. Ham* (1837) Judge Joseph J. Daniel of North Carolina held that the rule in Shelley's case applied to chattels personal. Mrs. Ham's estate in the slaves, therefore, was enlarged from a life estate to an absolute fee. Ten years later the Georgia Supreme Court, in *Robinson v. McDonald*, applied the rule in Shelley's case in a suit involving an executory bequest of slaves.[25] A full discussion occurred in a Tennessee case of 1836, *Polk v. Faris*. "It is a rule or canon of property," according to Judge William B. Reese, "which, so far from being at war with the genius of our institutions, or with the liberal and commercial spirit of the age . . . seems to be in perfect harmony with both. . . . It is owing, perhaps, to this circumstance that the rule—a gothic column found among the remains of feudality—has been preserved in all its strength to aid in sustaining the fabric of the modern social system."[26]

Remainders were valid, if executed properly, as they are today. As far as slaves were concerned, one of the most common forms was the grant of a life estate to a wife, and then the slaves would be given to specific children or simply divided among them. The rule in Shelley's case would not enlarge such a vested remainder. The only time it did was when a testator created a life estate and then gave the remainder to her "heirs" after the death of the wife. This occurred infrequently, however. Most testators had some sense of the problem and gave the remainder to some specific person. The contingent remainder was even less common. It appeared only in a handful of cases in the colonial York County sample, for instance. Every case involved a bequest of slaves to a female. Often the contingency was the marriage of the decedent's wife.[27] In addition to remainders in slaves, an occasional testator resorted to the executory devise.[28] But by the nineteenth century executory devises were viewed with considerable hostility by some and barely tolerated by others as more and more judges absorbed the values of liberal capitalism.

In *Robinson v. McDonald* (Georgia, 1847) the testator gave slaves to his son and his heirs, but if he died single without a "lawful heir of his body," the slaves would be divided among three of his brothers. Counsel contended that the limitation over to the three sons was good as an executory devise. Judge Hiram Warner noted that the bequest did not create a life estate with a contingent remainder in the three brothers because there "was no *particular* estate to support such remainder." But it was not a good executory bequest, either. Under the common law the limitation over had to be confined to a stated period. Warner referred to the time in the rule against perpetuities. Language was vital. If the testator failed to use the right words that showed his intention to comply with the rule, then the will would be taken as resting on an "indefinite" failure of issue and would be void for remoteness. In this case the testator failed. He did not say "if Robert died without a lawful heir living at the time of his death, or within the time set in the rule against perpetuities." Warner wrapped himself in the mantle of republicanism. The rule against perpetuities, he wrote,

> best comports with the genius of our institutions and the habits of our people, which requires executory devises and bequests to be strictly confined within the limits prescribed thereby; for it is a species of entailed estate, to the extent of the authorized period of limitations, which the people of Georgia have not been disposed to encourage. . . . Chancellor Kent says, "entailments are recommended in monarchical governments, as a protection to the power and influence of the landed aristocracy; but such a policy has no application to republican establishments, where wealth does not form a permanent distinction, and under which every individual of every family has his equal rights, and is equally invited by the genius of the institutions, to depend upon his *own merit and exertions*."

In addition, as noted, Warner adopted the rule in Shelley's case as well. He also threw in the 1821 Georgia statute on conveyances. It provided that words that would create an entail would in Georgia vest an absolute fee simple. The slaves were the property of Robert McDonald, and his brothers got nothing.[29]

In *Jordan v. Roach* (Mississippi, 1856) counsel made impassioned arguments against executory devises and entails in general. Benjamin Roach Sr. gave land and thirty slaves to his sister and her heirs forever, but if she should die without issue or her surviving children died before they reached twenty-one, the estate would go to the other children of Roach Sr. His sister married German Jordan. She died, and her two children died shortly thereafter before they were twenty-one. Roach's children claimed as beneficiaries of the executory bequest, whereas Jordan claimed that it was unlawful and his deceased wife had the absolute property, which vested in him as the husband.[30]

Counsel for Jordan directly attacked executory devises. All noted that they were a species of entail and one of the worst. W. T. Withers, for instance, stated that the executory devise went "much further towards creating perpetuities, and imposing restraints on alienation of property than did estates tail."[31] The reason was that an estate tail could be barred easily, whereas the only limit on an executory devise was the rule against perpetuities, which allowed them up to a point.

A conveyance statute of 1822 was critical to the resolution of the case. That law converted an entailed estate into a fee simple, but it also included a compromise. As Chief Justice Cotesworth Smith observed, the legislature "thought, and thought wisely, that the right of alienation might, consistently with sound policy, be suspended for a limited period of time." It was set at a life or lives in being. It did not include "plus twenty-one years." This was not strictly the rule against perpetuities, but, according to Smith, that did not matter because the English common law was not completely incorporated into Mississippi jurisprudence. The regulation of inheritances and bequests was within the power of the legislature. The purpose of the 1822 law was "by converting fees tail into fees simple, to withdraw the restraints upon the alienation of property imposed by the system of entailments, and to render the property of the community subservient to the purposes of the community." It was to "prevent inequality in the condition of families, which would most likely be produced by that means."[32]

Trusts in Practice

By the nineteenth century trusts were of increasing importance in the jurisprudence of slavery. I found only four in the colonial York County sample,[33] but there were thirty in a sample of wills probated in Fairfield District later. By the 1800s the trust was often a device to protect the property from being seized for debts. Many times it was used to safeguard the property of a married daughter from liability for the debts of an improvident husband. Suzanne Lebsock has found that such trusts were widespread in nineteenth-century Petersburg, Virginia. By her count more than one thousand slaves were held as the "separate, relatively secure property of married women." They were "more likely to be spared chattel slavery's loneliest ordeal—the public auction, the trader, the sale to who-knew-where."[34]

Within Fairfield District Lebsock's generalization holds, with one qualification. The trust devise was not used solely to protect a property interest of married women. Trusts created by wills in Fairfield were used nearly as often to secure property for males as for females. Rachel Griffin was particularly fond of the trust. In her 1845 will she gave one slave to her executors for the use of her son for life, and then the executors held the slave in trust for the use of the grandson for life. Finally, she left two more in trust for the daughter of Margaret Davis. Possibly one of the more pathetic trusts was that in Jane Williamson's will, probated on November 13, 1865. She gave her executor money to use his judgment to buy one or more slaves for the use of her granddaughter. Williamson died unreconciled to the fact that the social world she knew had been consumed in the Civil War.[35]

Trusts, executory bequests, remainders, and entails were all efforts to limit the power of someone to alienate property. All ran counter to a full-blown liberal property law. The evidence from the samples suggests that only in the years before the Revolution was the entail used to try to perpetuate the power and wealth of an aristocratic, landed, slaveowning elite. After that the restraints upon alienation could be designed to keep property in a family, but the number of slaves involved was so small that it is hard to argue that this was an effort to maintain the power of an elite: often only one or two slaves were concerned and rarely more than half a dozen. When such restrained bequests were brought before Southern judges, moreover, they often met with disfavor. A major exception was the trust created to protect the slaves of a married woman from seizure and sale because of the debts owed by her husband.

The Question of "Increase"

Special legal and equitable problems arose when the person bequeathed was a woman. If a slaveowner made a will in which he bequeathed a female slave along with her "increase," did this include all of her children? Did it include only those born after the will was made? Did it include only those born after the death of the testator? Could a testator bequeath children who were not yet born? If the bequest was of a life estate with a remainder over, to whom did the "increase" belong?

The question, could a slaveowner bequeath slaves not yet born, was argued in a 1738 Virginia case, *Giles v. Mallicotte*. The issue counsel confronted was whether the "Devise of a Negro Child in the Mother's Belly be good tho' the Child is not born till after the Testator's death." Counsel agreed that remote possibilities were not devisable, but he argued that there was a difference between a near and a remote possibility. In fact, he did not believe in "carrying Devises of this Sort any further than where the Child is actually in the Mother's Belly It would be very inconvenient to allow a Devise of the 2. 3. or 4. Child that shall be born for Reasons that are very obvious." He did not provide the reasons. This case was compromised so that there was no decision, and the issue was never raised again in colonial Virginia's higher courts.[36]

Slaveowners behaved as though they could bequeath unborn children. In York County there are a handful of wills in which females and their "increase" or "future increase" were bequeathed.[37] A small number expressly devised particular children. In 1733 William Trotter gave five slaves to his wife for life, including the slave Judy, with the provision that if Judy had a child it would go to a grandson.[38]

Such practices, although not common, persisted into the nineteenth century. Among the wills probated in Fairfield District, Robert Hamilton's, in 1842, provided—after a number of bequests of slaves—that "if any of the above named negro girls have a daughter the first born is to go to Sarah McCreight." And in *Nelson v. Nelson* (North Carolina, 1849) Judge Ruffin admitted, with some distaste, that a slaveowner could, "by plain words," give the female to one person and her first or second child or all of her children to someone else. The case involved the bequest of a slave woman Leah, and any increase would be equally divided among three daughters. The court ruled that this applied only to children Leah had in the lifetime of the testator and held that afterborn children went with Leah. If there had been "plain words" to the contrary, they would have been respected, but there were not, and Ruffin argued that "it is most unnatural that the testator should have intended, on the one hand, that the infants should be immediately taken from the mother, and not reasonable, on the other hand, that the owner of the mother should be obliged to keep the children for the other owners until it should be fit to separate them from the mother."[39] It would make no sense to bequeath a slave absolutely and then expect the owner to pay the expenses of the pregnant slave "and yet give away two-thirds of the offspring—almost the only profit of such slaves— which she may have in the course of her whole life. It would destroy the value of the gift, and, in effect, render the negro inalienable."[40] Unfair burdens on the owner and the demands of commerce precluded giving the mother to one and any of her increase to another absent "plain words." In any event, it was rare for owners to make such express bequests of unborn children. Usually, if increase was mentioned at all it was linked to the female: it was "Leah and her increase" or her "future increase." This does not mean, of course, that females and their children were not separated as a result of wills. It was common to bequeath a female to one's wife for life, along with her increase, only to provide that at the death of the wife the woman and her children were to be divided among the children of the testator.[41]

The two cases in which the problem of increase arose most often were first, the ownership of the children of a slave held by a life tenant, and second, the owner-ship of children born after the making of a will but before the death of the testator. In Maryland and Delaware the basic rule was that the children of a slave owned by a life tenant were the property of the life tenant. Everywhere else the rule was that the increase belonged not to the life tenant but to the one entitled to what was left, that is, the remainder. The analysis in Maryland and Delaware was similar. Daniel Dulany summarized the reasoning of the court in *Scott v. Dobson* (Maryland, 1752) as follows: "1. That the issue ought to go to the person to whom the use was limited; otherwise, having no interest worth regarding, he might not take care of the issue. That it would only be a reasonable satisfaction for the expenses of maintenance, and for the time lost by the parent. 2. That when the use is given, a bounty at all events is intended; but instead of a benefit, if the issue should go over there might be a loss." In *Smith v. Milman* (1839) Delaware's Chief Justice John M. Clayton reached the same conclusion. "He who supports the child of the slave in infancy," he argued, "ought to be justly remunerated for his expense and trouble by its services, and the expectation that he will be so remunerated, will insure greater care and attention to the wants of the child."[42] Humanity required that the children of a female slave belong to the life tenant. But it was a humanity stood on its head. The problem was that this could separate mothers and children if the life tenant chose to dispose of them other than to the person entitled to the mother (the common law phrase was the "remainderman").

By 1850 the Maryland Supreme Court showed signs that humanity might require a different rule. *Holmes v. Mitchell* involved a trust for the benefit of the testator's aunt and uncle who were to receive the income, and at their deaths the slaves would go to their children. The uncle, as if tenant, asked for the children of the slaves. The court ruled against him:

> To separate the issue from the mother involves the necessity of determining at what age this may be done. The infant cannot be torn from its mother and sold or transferred to the complainant. No one would buy, and humanity would cry out against it. There would have then to be a periodical partition, or sale, after first determining at what age the offspring could with propriety or without shocking the public sensibility, be separated from the mother. . . . I cannot think . . . that the reasons which have influenced the courts to give to the legatee for life or for a term, the after-born issue, apply to a case where a mass of property is left in trust as here . . . the title to the issue . . . will pass with their parents to those who are entitled in remainder upon the termination of the life estates.[43]

Three years later this equity case was again before the Maryland court. This time the court divided two to two over whether the word "income" included the "increase" of slaves. Judges William Hallam Tuck and John Thomson Mason argued that the word did not mean "increase." No court, Tuck wrote, had ever held the word "income" to "be synonymous, in law, with the issue of slaves." If they ruled otherwise they would defeat the benevolent intentions of the testator, who not only had intended to keep his slaves together, but also "he appears to have had a peculiar regard for his negroes. Some he sets free and provides for." Chief Justice John Carroll LeGrand and Judge John Bowers Eccleston reached a different conclusion. For them the word "income" was as broad as the words "use" and "profits." "The loss of service of the mother," they reasoned, "with the expenses attendant upon her confinement, and the cost of maintaining the children, are such an interference with . . . the *use* or *profits* of the mother, as will make the children pass, as part of the *use* or *profits*. If so, why should they not pass as income?" Because the court divided evenly, the lower chancery court ruling against the claim of the uncle remained intact, but it is clear that some judges were uncomfortable.[44]

Elsewhere the problem did not arise in this way because the common rule was that the afterborn children went to the remainderman. It did not matter whether they were referred to as "increase" or "profits" or "income." Occasionally this rule was defended on the grounds of humanity, but often it was just noted as a rule of property. In North Carolina, for instance, the rule was settled in the 1780s in *Tims v. Potter*. In contrast to the reasoning used in Maryland, the court noted that "as to the children being an incumbrance on the life estate . . . people are generally of a different opinion, as to thinking a breeding wench a loss." By 1825 Chief Justice Taylor commented that "it has now become a fixed rule of property that the increase of slaves, born during the life of the legatee for life, belong to the ulterior legatee, who is the absolute owner." The basic rule was defended on more humane grounds in an 1819 Kentucky case, *Murphy v. Riggs*. It is "a long and well settled rule," Judge John Rowan wrote, "that the children of a female slave, born during the tenancy for life, shall go with their mother, to the claimant in remainder. This rule has, also, its sanction in some of the strongest and tenderest feelings of our nature. The mother is not, by its operation, torn from her infant child, nor is the sucking child torn from the breast of its mother." But humanity had its limits. After paying tribute to the humaneness of the rule, he applied a different standard to separate one of the children from the mother. It was that a will had effect only at the death of the testator, and therefore any "increase" born before his death remained part of the estate and did not pass with the mother. In *Murphy* this meant that Absalom became the property of someone other than the owner of his mother. But Absalom was not a "sucking child."[45]

The rule that a will took effect only on the death of a testator was almost universally applied in the case of the "increase" of females. The common approach was that employed in *Powell v. Cook* (North Carolina, 1834). The "increase" born before the death of the testator belonged to the executor of the estate for the purpose of paying debts, or for distribution to the heirs, rather than to the legatee for life.[46]

The sole exception to such cases was *Gayle v. Cunningham*, decided in South Carolina in 1824. In the lead opinion, Chancellor DeSaussure admitted that the rule as to increase between a life tenant and a remainderman was settled in favor of the remainderman, but in *Gayle* the problem concerned children born during the life of the testator after he made his will. DeSaussure applied the rule *partus sequitur ventrem* to the case.[47] No other court did. To him the maxim meant that the issue of a female slave bequeathed "would go with the mother, to the legatee." But it was policy, not the force of the legal maxim, that carried the day. "Now the legatee," DeSaussure wrote, "of a female slave risks every consequence of breeding and child-birth, and should therefore be entitled to the issue. The original foundation of property was derived from labor bestowed on it, whereby its value was created or augmented. The issue of a female slave would often be valueless but for her exertions and sufferings, all of which are at the risk of her master or owner. . . . Those who incur the risk are reasonably entitled to the gain." But there was more to it than that. "Humanity obviously dictates that the children should follow their mothers," DeSaussure argued, "a contrary decision would separate even sucking infants; for in most cases of legacies, the children would be young." "Such a separation," he continued, "would be revolting. . . . Sound policy, as well as humanity, requires that everything should be done to reconcile these unhappy beings to their lot, by keeping mothers and children together. By cherishing their domestic ties, you have an additional and powerful hold on their feelings and security for their good conduct." "As a question of property," he concluded, "it is unimportant how the rule is settled, for it will operate alike on all." Chancellor Theodore Gaillard dissented; he held that the basic common law rule should apply and that the maxim *partus sequitur ventrem* did not. "The children of a female slave are slaves," he reasoned, "and belong to the owner of the mother, as the increase of any other female animal belongs to him who owns her. As the testator owned the female slave, the children she had after he made his will were his, and he might have disposed of them to whom he pleased."[48] By 1837 this legal rule was applied and *Gayle* was overruled in *Seibels v. Whatley* (1837). Even concern for "sucking" children could give way before a fidelity to legal rules.

Dower and Widows' Thirds

Widows were not heirs or successors at law, but they were taken into account. It was a maxim of the common law that law favored life, liberty, and dower. Dower was a right possessed by a widow to one-third of the *real property*. She took a life estate, however, so that her power over the property was limited. On the other hand, dower property was not subject to seizure for the payment of debts.[49] The widow also had a right to one-third of the personal property of her husband in cases of intestacy.

Sometime between 1692 and 1718 Maryland passed a law that tried to settle the problem of successions. As far as personal property, including slaves, was concerned, the law followed the English Statute of Distributions. The widow got her "thirds." When there was a will there was a problem. Men had bequeathed "a considerable part of their Personal Estates," intending it as in full of the "thirds." The problem was that the wives not only claimed what was bequeathed "but have further claimed their part of the remaining Estate." Therefore the widow was required to elect between her "thirds" and the specific bequest, and whichever choice she made stood as a bar to any claim to the other property. If she failed to elect, then she would have "a full Third part of the Clear Personal Estate of her Deceased Husband besides her Dower of his Real Estate."[50] Because a widow could obtain a third of the personal estate, which in Maryland would include the slaves, by doing nothing she could defeat a niggardly bequest of less than that. She was entitled to such a portion.

The last point was also true in Virginia. A law of 1673 gave a widow a life estate in one-third of the real property of the estate and one-third of the "personall estate" if there were one or two children; if there were more than two children, however, the widow and the children would divide the personal property equally. Because slaves were not defined as realty until 1705 they would fall under the provision on personal estate, but the phrase used is that this was part of the dower right of the widow. Unlike Maryland's law, the law of Virginia fused dower and thirds. But like Maryland's law, the law of Virginia rested on the premise that the testator could not disinherit his wife. The law concluded, "the husband . . . hath it in his power to devise more to his wife then what is above determined, but not lesse."[51] How did testators dispose of slaves as far as wives were concerned? The York County sample shows that where it is possible to determine whether a testator gave his widow more or less than one-third of the slaves of the estate for life, the vast majority gave more.[52] Of course, the bequest was occasionally *in terrorem*. This was probably the intention behind the will of James Shields in 1727. He gave all of his slaves to his wife during widowhood, but if she remarried she was to receive only one-third of them.[53]

The story in nineteenth-century South Carolina, a state in which widows did not have dower rights in slaves, was similar. In Fairfield District over forty wills expressly provided widows more than a one-third life estate. Either they gave more slaves, more power, or both. Isaac Arledge Sr., in 1847, left his widow five slaves "in fee simple, to her and her heirs forever." William Watt, who owned fifty-one slaves in 1850, gave his widow twenty-four slaves in his will the next year.[54]

Whether widows received dower slaves or one-third of the personalty under a statute of distribution, the fact is that security for the widow could mean disruption among the slaves. One well-known example of the possibility is the estate of George Washington. Washington's will of 1799 provided freedom for his slaves on the death of his wife Martha. But not all of the slaves he possessed belonged to him. As he put it in his will:

> Upon the decease (of) my wife, it is my Will and desire th(at) all the Slaves which I hold in (*my*) *own right*, shall receive their free(dom.) To emancipate them during (her)life, would, tho' earnestly wish(ed by) me, be attended with such insu(perab)le difficulties on account of thei[r interm(ixture) by Marriages with the (Dow)er Negroes, as to excite the most pa(i)nful sensations, if not disagreabl(e c)onsequences from the latter, while (both) descriptions are in the occupancy (of) the same Proprietor; it not being (in) my power, under the tenure by whic(h t)he Dower Negros are held, to man(umi)it them.

At that time Washington owned 124 slaves and there were 153 dower slaves. Within a year of his death Martha had freed all of the slaves, but not altogether because of humanity. According to Abigail Adams, Martha Washington told her that "she did not feel as though her life was safe in their hands, many of whom would be told that it was their interest to get rid of her. She therefore was advised to set them all free at the close of the year." She also claimed to be "distressed" about the many slaves who would be going into the world "adrift" and without "horse, home, or friend."[55]

Two illustrations of the way the rule on thirds worked on a day-to-day basis come from the records of the Orphans Court in Somerset County, Maryland, in the mid-1830s. When Joseph B. Brinkley died in 1836 he owned twelve slaves. He left a widow and five children. Of the twelve slaves the widow took five, not four. It was not the number of slaves that was relevant, it was their value. The five accounted for one-third of the total value of the twelve slaves. Seven children, rang-ing in ages from eight to eighteen, were divided up among five other owners. A much larger slave community was broken up the next year when the estate of George A. Dashiell was settled. The total value of the forty slaves divided among Dashiell's children was $11,190. Sixteen were under ten years old. Unfortunately, the record does not show how this group of slaves was divided among the children. The total value of the slaves taken by the widow was $5,550. It included sixteen slaves. Five of the sixteen were eleven or younger. The eleven-year-old was "infirm & sickly," and Lidy, aged sixty-six, was without any value at all "& Insane."[56]

Dower rights did not always work to the disadvantage of slaves, however. In a Missouri case, *Herndon v. Herndon's Adm'rs.* (1858), the question was whether the children born to a slave that was possessed by the wife as her dower remained as part of the decedent's estate, or whether they went with the mother. According to Judge William Napton, the children went with the mother to the widow. Napton linked dower with the property brought to the marriage by the widow, which would be similar to dowry. Conceptually, there was nothing quixotic about that. Blackstone, for instance, noted that dower "among the Romans signified the mar-riage portion, which the wife brought to her husband." Napton added the rule that the issue of females followed the condition of the mother and went to a remainder-man if she held a life estate. He concluded: "A difference has thus been adopted between slaves and other property, founded upon motives of humanity, and hav-ing regard to the moral as well as legal relations between master and slave. This distinction is so well understood, not merely by the profession, but so generally recognized and acted on by the community at large, that it is no violent presump-tion to suppose that the legislature intended . . . to embrace the increase of slaves, as well as the slaves themselves, as property coming by the marriage."[57]

That humanity only went so far was evident in *Fitzhugh v. Foote*, a Virginia dower case decided by the court of appeals in 1801. Margaret Fitzhugh married John Thornton Fitzhugh two years after the death of her husband. Dower, in land and slaves, was assigned to her after her marriage, but it appeared to be in excess of thirds. Her two sons by her deceased husband brought suit to set aside the assign-ment of dower to their mother. The court displayed some sensitivity to the slaves, but it also showed the limits of that sensitivity. It began with the assertion that the mother was entitled to dower in the slaves, and that there might have been some excess. "That an equal division of slaves, in number or value," the judges noted, "is not always possible, and sometimes improper, when it cannot be exactly done without separating infant children from their mothers, which humanity forbids, and will not be countenanced in a Court of Equity: so, that a compensation for excess must, in such cases, be made and received in money." A new division should not be made in this case because of a small excess to the widow; this was especially so because of the lapse of time (the original assignment had been made in 1780) and because the whole of the dower slaves, with their increase, would go to the sons on the death of their mother in any event. The court did not simply order the mother and husband to compensate the sons with cash. It directed that the commissioner in equity was to see whether the excess could be "rectified by a delivery of one or more of the dower slaves"; if so, they were to be delivered along with the profits.[58] Only if it could not be done in this way was the commissioner to require compensation in money. The order did not match the rhetoric. Nonetheless, the language of the court did limit the inquiry of the commissioner. Presumably, rectification was not to be done by the separation of *young* children from their mothers. If so, equity courts sometimes achieved through decrees what was achieved by statutes elsewhere.

In some jurisdictions there were clearly dower rights in slaves, whereas in others the claims were of widows' thirds. This could be changed by statute. By and large, a statutory foundation for a claim to dower was critical, otherwise the common law limitation to a dower claim to land only would apply. One case in which a statute was central arose in Arkansas in 1844. In *Hill's Adm'rs. v. Mitchell* the court ruled that there could be a claim to dower in slaves. Judge Thomas J. Lacy, for the majority, held that a state law of 1838 created a dower right in slaves. In Arkansas slaves were not defined as realty until 1840.[59]

No matter who was entitled to the slaves of a decedent—whether it be a widow, a designated heir, or a beneficiary of the will of the former owner—there was always a danger that the slaves would be split up because of the indebtedness of the estate. But some lawmakers and judges tried to limit this danger through judgments in cases involving increase or in rules on partitions, for instance. Policy choices in an increasingly commercialized society dominated by market relationships did clash with a lingering patriarchalism and an occasional recognition of the human claims of slaves, especially mothers and young children.

Liability for Debts Due

Slaves remained liable to sale for the payment of the debts of decedents whether they died with or without a will. Testators could alter or affect this to some extent, but it did not happen often. In the colonial York County sample less than ten wills called for the sale of slaves to pay debts. A handful of wills provided that slaves were to be hired out to pay debts, but not sold.[60] Later in Fairfield District the story was much the same. Only a handful of testators directed the sale of slaves to pay debts. Most tried to shield the beneficiaries of their wills from having slaves seized, and a small number instructed that slaves were to be hired out until the debts were paid. Of over six hundred wills studied, less than twenty provided for the sale of any slaves to pay debts.[61]

This left the bulk of the slaves exposed to the relevant legal rules if their former masters were in debt at the time of their deaths. The most tragic situations involved the liability of slaves for debts even though a will had granted them freedom. Even when the tragedy did not reach that level, the seizure and sale of slaves could rend families and slave communities. This was one further danger added to the separations that occurred when testators made specific bequests, or the law ordered a partition of an intestate's estate, or dower in slaves was set apart.

Some jurisdictions tried to reduce the danger to the legatees and heirs of indebted slaveowners. Some even suggested concern for the slaves themselves. Possibly one of the most radical proposals surfaced in 1853 in the Alabama legislature. A bill was introduced to exempt slaves from sale under execution. According to the *Southern Cultivator*, there was much to recommend the bill. Those who favored it contended that "the institution of slavery will thereby be fortified, as inducements are held out to each citizen to become a slave owner; . . . the relations of master and slave will thereby assume a more kind and affectionate character."[62]

The normal rule of the common law was that personal property was the fund from which debts were to be paid. Until the eighteenth century land could not be seized and sold. When it was allowed, the rule was that the first or primary fund remained the chattels.[63] There were a number of different statutory approaches to adjusting these rules.

The Chesapeake colonies in the early eighteenth century created a threefold categorization of property. Land was not seized, but slaves were separated from other personal property and made a semiprotected category.[64] In 1805 Georgia's legislators added another element as well as the slaves themselves, their labor. "No administrator shall be allowed to sell any slave or slaves belonging to the estate . . . but where the other personal estate, together with the hire of such slave or slaves for twelve months, shall be insufficient to discharge the debts due by the estate." The year before Georgia had made real property and personal property of intestates "altogether of the same nature, and [put the property] upon the same footing."[65] By its civil code of 1808 Louisiana required executors to sell all "perishable goods" except those specifically bequeathed. "If such perishable goods" were insufficient, the executors or administrators would "sell the other personal estate disposing of the slaves last, until the debts and legacies be all paid having regard to the specific legacies."[66]

In other states the rules were changed to allow the seizure and sale of land as well as chattels, but the personal property, which included slaves, remained the first fund. In such states the twofold categorization remained. Examples here would be laws in Tennessee and North Carolina. Tennessee made all the debtors' property "assets" liable for the satisfaction of debts but provided that the personalty was to be exhausted first, and North Carolina made real estate liable to seizure but expressly required that the personal estate be the first fund.[67]

Whatever the variations slaves were always liable to sale for debts due, even when they were defined as real estate. In *Tucker v. Sweney* (Virginia, 1730), the court acknowledged that slaves were real estate, but for purposes of debts they were as other chattels. In *Goddin v. Morris* (Virginia, 1732), the court acknowledged that they were in a special category and the other personal property was to be sold first, and that if that had not been done, the heir was entitled to recover the slaves.[68]

Even in those jurisdictions where slaves were not placed in special categories, courts occasionally treated them differently from other chattels. In *Holderness v. Palmer* (North Carolina, 1858), the testator had made specific bequests of slaves and directed them to be kept on the land. However, the estate was more indebted than thought and the executor sold land rather than slaves. Judge William Battle upheld the sale. "An exigency had occurred," he wrote, "not provided for by the testator; for he no more expected the slaves, which he had specifically bequeathed, would be sold, than that the land would be disposed of. Had the slaves been sold instead of the land, they could not have been kept together on the home tract, and thus the testator's will would have been disappointed as much as it was by the sale of the land." The existence of the will was crucial: it allowed Battle to develop an analysis that would be impossible in the absence of an expression of the "intention" of the decedent. "Is it certain," Battle asked, "that he did not act for the best in selling the land? Does it any where appear, that the increase of the slaves, notwithstanding the death of some of them, and the rise in value of the others, did not make them to be worth as much to the legatees when they received them, as the land would have been worth, had that been kept?"[69] The undergirding of classic republicanism, the ownership of land, was giving way a bit not so much to the humanity of the slaves per se, but to their value in the market.

A different perception emerged in *Alexander v. Worthington* (Maryland, 1854). The testator had made specific bequests of slaves, and the land had descended to the heir. The court framed the issues as follows: "1st. Whether a specific legacy or land descended is first applicable in payment of debts. 2nd. Whether the specific legatee of a chattel of peculiar value, as a household slave, has an equity to restrain the executor, who is also the heir at law, from applying that chattel to the payment of debts for the purpose of protecting his inheritance, the creditors being passive and content to take the payment out of either fund?" The court held that land descended was the first fund rather than personal estate specifically bequeathed. The answer to the second question was yes, precisely because of the special value of a favored slave. The court said nothing about a field hand who might be unknown to the legatee. The special facts in this case accounted for the result. They were that certain slaves had been bequeathed to the widow with the express desire that they not be sold for the payment of debts, and these slaves were "cherished by the widow during her lifetime, and manumitted by her last will." The court suggested that it would be unconscionable to permit the heirs to sell "the negroes into ceaseless bondage in foreign climes" to pay debts chargeable against descended land, especially when the creditors' only concern was to be paid regardless of the fund. To allow this, the court concluded, "would seem to be an act of injustice of which a court composed of slave-holders, residing in a slave-holding State, could not possibly be guilty."[70]

Despite the reform efforts, and despite such cracks in the legal rules about liability for the payment of debts, the fact is that most of the time courts ruled that slaves as personal chattels were *assets* in the hands of executors. That meant that they were a fund out of which debts were to be paid, and that they did not go to the legatees in the will until the executor assented.

In Kentucky even this was muddled. In *Logan v. Withers* (1830) Judge Richard A. Buckner held that because slaves were realty, "the legal title to them is immediately transferred to the devisee, and he may lawfully take possession of them without the assent of the executor." Slaves, moreover, "are not assets in the hands of the executor." But a series of other cases suggested otherwise and became the foundation for the judgment in *Anderson v. Irvine* (1845). That line of cases held that slaves were assets. The judges in *Anderson* ruled that an heir "does not, by the death of the ancestor and by descent merely, acquire a complete title, but . . . he acquires it . . . [by the] assent of the administrator; . . . slaves are . . . assets in his hands."[71]

It is obvious that the death of a master could create a deep trauma among the slaves. Separation from loved ones was likely either because of the master's concern for the welfare of his own family, or their demand that they had a right of inheritance, or simply the legal rules of succession. But it could be a moment of expectation for favored slaves.

Inheritances and the "Humanity" of Slaves

Even while they made dispositions of their human property, some slaveowners did take the humanity of their slaves into account. These were decent people but there were limits to their decency. Few provided for the wholesale emancipation of their slaves. This is illustrated by the 1840 will of David Harrison of Fairfield District. Harrison left sixty-seven slaves to his brother, but he added that his executors were to allow Penny and her two children and Margaret and her two children the privilege of free persons, and "when they get grown or before if convenient be carried to a free State and be emancipated and be given something to live on."[72] Of the sample wills, almost none freed all of the slaves owned by the testator. Benevolence rarely ever wholly defeated the claims of heirs or legatees of a deceased slaveowner, and it was not intended to.

Much more common than freeing a slave or slaves were provisions that took into account the humanity of the slaves but fell short of granting freedom. James Madison, who agonized for some time and even implied on occasion that he might free his slaves at his death, included only the following clause in his will (and this was not completely honored after he died): "I give and bequeath my ownership in the negroes and people of colour held by me to my dear wife, but it is my desire that none of them should be sold without his or her consent, or in case of their misbehaviour; except that infant children may be sold with their parent who consents for them to be sold with him or her, and who consents to be sold." Twenty years later David Johnson, a onetime member of the South Carolina Supreme Court and former governor of the state, provided that the bulk of his slaves were to be divided among his heirs and in kind, if possible, so that they would stay within the family. If a sale was necessary, however, it was authorized, "but in no Event are mothers of young Slaves to be separated from their children under Twelve years of age."[73] These were among some of the more humane provisions in wills. Of the sample wills in Virginia and South Carolina, about 10 percent recognized the slaves as human beings.

Rarely, a testator did mention those who were or might not be faithful. Madison's will, for instance, had said that slaves were not to be sold without their consent "or in case of their misbehavior."[74] George Brewton, in 1815 in Spartanburg District, provided that "if any of the above negroes which is left to my wife during her lifetime should prove refractory that they be sold by my Executors." John Rosborough of Fairfield District in 1840 gave his executors the authority to sell slaves if any of them did not "serve peaceably and willingly."[75] In successions sanctions could be held over the heads of slaves who resisted their enslavement or did not serve peacefully.

The majority of the testators who tried to do something for faithful slaves allowed them to choose their masters upon sales or to choose which of the testators' children they would live with. Or those testators instructed their executors to sell only to humane masters or tried, occasionally, to prevent the separation of families.

Other than those who freed slaves, testators who allowed slaves the choice of masters came the closest to recognizing their humanity in that they acknowledged a will, however constrained, in the slave. Only one master in the colonial sample, Charles Wise, did this. In his will of 1740 he provided that George was to be sold "having the liberty of choosing his master." Only one will studied for Spartanburg District allowed this. The will of Cassandra Farrow, probated in 1859, directed her executors to sell the slaves "to those they may wish to live with, at private sale if practicable." Possibly as revealing as any of these documents was the 1861 will of Edward Winning of Saline County, Missouri. He desired that his slaves were to be sold privately and allowed to "choose their new homes, and if it could be done to be kept in the family." However, there were two caveats. This was to be done only "if they should behave well and do their duty as they formerly have done." If, he concluded, the slaves became "unmanageable and disobedient," they were to be hired out or sold as the executor thought best.[76]

A number of Fairfield masters also permitted slaves the choice of masters, either among the possible legatees or among those who might purchase from the estate. In most of these cases the right to choose, as far as possible, was not granted to all of the slaves owned. For instance, John Rosborough made a number of bequests of slaves without this provision. He gave the privilege only to "old Jude." And in 1854 Nathan Cook provided that "old negro woman Molly" was to reside with which of his children she preferred. As of 1850 Cook owned forty-five slaves.[77]

Although the overwhelming majority of wills divided the slaves owned by the testator, thus breaking up a coherent group, and many of them separated some of the "increase" of a female slave from their mother, testators, at times, tried to keep some family members together. However, such efforts did not appear until the wills of the nineteenth century. A possible explanation lies in the transformation of ideas about human feelings and sensitivities, as well as about the family, as Jan Lewis found in Jefferson's Virginia. As she put it, "the nineteenth century awakened feeling and gave it form." This spilled over into a more sensitive view, at least of a few people, of the human relationships among the slaves, or at least of some of them. In Spartanburg District Martha Golightly (1860) expressly tried to keep a family intact. She began by stating that she did "especially desire that my negroes be not sold." They were to be put in lots, but often, Golightly realized, this might separate people. She, therefore, provided that David and his wife Phyllis and their infant child were to be put in one lot.[78] In Saline County Peyton Nowlin added in his 1837 will that Davy and Miley "who live together as husband and wife, be not separated unless they should consent." And Edward Winning, in 1861, urged that Harry and Hannah be sold as a couple even if a lower price were taken for them. Finally, an occasional master in Fairfield tried to keep people together. William Chapman in 1841, after making a number of bequests of slaves, willed that two couples, including "Dave and old Milly," were to be sold together, and the purchasers had to enter into bond not to separate the husbands and wives.[79] In sum, only seven out of about six hundred testators expressly tried to assure that slaves would be kept together.

Most testators who took into account the humanity or personality of the slaves did so only because of faithfulness. Moreover, the overwhelming majority of the small number that even went this far did not do so at any significant cost to those entitled to inherit. This is not to suggest that this was not done. The cases in which testators emancipated large numbers of slaves attest to that. But there is little evidence that slaveowners' taking into account the humanness of the slaves led them to question the rightness of the slave system within which they lived, especially to raise questions so serious that the result was to disinherit potential heirs and thereby impoverish the family. When they considered humanness they did so in very limited ways. They occasionally rewarded the subordinate, faithful slave, and they occasionally provided for possible sanctions against the unfaithful. Last wills and testaments did not reflect doubts about bondage, but, rather, an affirmation of it, as well as a sensitivity to the "right of inheritance," even though some judges favored unburdening property so that it might flow more readily in the market. Although a liberal property law abhorred perpetuities, the perpetuation of the whole social order based on the ownership of human beings was a very different question. Even in the late eighteenth century, when slavery was under attack and the law of successions was undergoing change, in theory and in practice that law still clearly legitimized and assured human bondage.

5

Contract Law in the Sale and Mortgaging of Slaves

Sold, transferred, or pawned as goods, or personal estate,

for goods they were.

WILLIAM GOODELL, *American Slave Code* (1853)

A frightening "incident" of bondage was that slaves were "at all times liable to be sold absolutely."[1] They also could be used as collateral, or their labor might be transferred in a hire contract. The danger increased by the turn into the nineteenth century with the spread of liberal capitalism. Debt and the allocation of market risks were crucial elements in the emergence of capitalism. The central legal concept was "contract."

A contract is a promise that the law will enforce. "Contracts and promises are essentially risk-allocation devises" and came with an "advanced level of economic development." But not all promises were enforceable. "Consideration" was a crucial doctrine. The notion was that "the promisee must give something in exchange for the promise that is either a detriment to himself or a benefit to the promisor."[2]

These ideas evolved. During much of the seventeenth and eighteenth centuries there was no body of law known as "contract law," and there were many unsettled questions. For instance, because it was not always clear what had been promised, would the law ever assume certain things that had not been mentioned in the bargain? An old paternalistic notion, uncongenial to the full laissez-faire freedom of contract doctrine of the nineteenth century, was that "a sound price implies a sound commodity." The emerging idea was caught in John Joseph Powell's comment in his late-eighteenth-century treatise on contracts: "it is the consent of parties alone, that fixes the just price of any thing. . . . Therefore a man is obliged in conscience to perform a contract which he has entered into, although it is a hard one."[3]

One crucial earlier development had been the creation of the common law writ of assumpsit,[4] which was used to hold people accountable for the nonperformance of assumed obligations. While the "contract" was emerging, various forms of

contracting, such as mortgages and bailments, were singled out for separate consideration. It was no coincidence that the first major English treatises on contracts
in general, and on bailments and mortgages in particular, appeared in the last two
decades of the eighteenth century.[5] After the turn into the nineteenth century these
substantive categories were of increasing importance in the law of slavery as well.
Because of the confusion and complexity surrounding the bailment, the hiring of
slaves, that subject is treated separately.

While substantive contract law was transformed so was remedial law. At law
breaches of contract were enforced by damages. Equity, however, used the remedy
of specific performance whereby the party would be compelled to perform what
he or she had promised.[6] Morton Horwitz has argued that "the moment at which
courts focus on expectation damages rather than restitution or specific performance to give a remedy for nondelivery is precisely the time at which contract law
begins to separate from property."[7] He placed that time around 1790.

Finally, within a free enterprise system of exchanges a crucial additional notion
was that people enter the market as equals, they bargain, and they accept the
consequences of that bargain. There was no room for legal paternalism. Market
relationships were one-dimensional, and, in the perfect model, such things as
social power or weakness were insignificant in determining the nature or binding
quality of a contract. A splendid illustration, as far as slavery is concerned, is the
conversation between Tom's owner and the trader in *Uncle Tom's Cabin*: " 'Haley,'
said Mr. Shelby, 'I hope you'll remember that you promised, on your honor, you
wouldn't sell Tom, without knowing what sort of hands he's going into.' 'Why,
you've just done it sir,' said the trader. 'Circumstances, you well know, *obliged* me,'
said Shelby, haughtily." The horrid reply of Haley was this: " 'Wal, you know, they
may 'blige *me* too,' said the trader.' "[8]

Michael Tadman has argued persuasively that it was extremely rare for slave
traders or slaveowners disposing of slaves to show any grasp of the indecency of the
sale of people; they closed their eyes to what the abolitionist Stroud called the
"pang agonizing beyond description." The same can be said of Southern judges.
Thomas Russell has shown that we have too often overlooked the role of the courts
in the initial sale of slaves. In South Carolina the "courts were at the center of the
domestic slave trade. At sheriffs', probate, and equity court sales, court officials and
agents of law conducted 50% of the antebellum sales of slaves."[9] But it was not just
local officials involved in an execution or probate sale who closed their eyes to the
inhumanity of selling people. It was appellate judges as well.

Most often the market overwhelmed sentiment, and judges behaved as though
the object in the sale mattered not at all. Consider, for instance, the judgment of
the Alabama Supreme Court in *Thomason v. Dill* (1857). The case was an action on
a promissory note of $800 for the purchase of Ellick. The defense was that the
buyer did not take immediate possession of the slave, and that the seller later
wanted to rescind the sale but the buyer refused. The seller had kept Ellick for a
time and informed the buyer that if he insisted on taking the slave, he must

provide some security. The buyer had a note drafted with two sureties. Judge George W. Stone's judgment for the court was that a promise without consideration was not binding, but that a promise could be a "good consideration to support a promise," which was sound contract doctrine. Moreover, parties could modify or rescind a contract by mutual agreement even though the original sale amounted to an executed contract that passed the title to the buyer and secured payment of the purchase money to the seller. What was buried was the reason for the failure of the promises. One reason the seller wanted to rescind the sale was that his wife asked him to and when Ellick came in from the field and was told he had been sold, he "commenced crying, and begged plaintiff to rescind the trade." But the reason for voiding the contract was not so decent as this implies. When the new note was delivered to the seller with the demand that Ellick be turned over, the seller replied that "he could not deliver the negro, because he was dead, but that witness could have his body or his bones, if he desired them." Ellick had killed himself.[10]

The humanity of slaves was not always ignored, and there were opportunities for judges to adapt contract law to take into account the fact that the objects involved were human beings, not milch cows. This occurred in the law of warranties and in remedial law. However, this element in the business law of slavery emerged in the older, established slave societies rather than the more rough-and-ready commercial communities of the expanding South.

Warranty Law

The maxim that a "sound price implies a sound commodity" was not a part of English common law; the true English doctrine was *caveat emptor*. Atiyah observed that *caveat emptor* "seems to have gained a foothold in the law with the growing commercial freedom of enterprise in the seventeenth century." There was no common law tradition of "protection of the buyer against shoddy or defective goods." A basic reason is that "few goods would have cost enough to justify a suit in the courts of common law." Still, an "older tradition" protected victims of an "unfair bargain" if what was purchased turned out to be worthless. But this tradition was not strong even in the seventeenth century, and by the eighteenth it had largely collapsed.[11] Where it remained of some force was in equity.

A protective paternalism persisted in continental civil law. Domat, for instance, observed that sales could be annulled, or the price could be reduced if the commodity sold had such defects "which render the things altogether unfit for the use for which they are bought and sold" or diminish the use in such a way that a buyer, had he known of the defects, "would have either not bought them at all, or at least not given so great a price for them."[12] Were such doctrines employed in the sale of slaves?

Waddill v. Chamberlayne (Virginia, 1735) is the only relevant extant case from pre-Revolutionary times. What exists is the argument of the counsel for the defendant and the decision of the court. Clearly, this is too weak a foundation to determine basic doctrine during the colonial period, but it remains a striking case. The plaintiff charged that the defendant had "fraudulently and deceitfully Sold to him a Slave for a great Price 25£. knowing the said Slave at the Time and for a long Time before laboured under an incurable Disease not discovered by the Plt. and was of no value." The action was an "Action upon the Case in Nature of Deceit," not assumpsit. Intention would be crucial, whereas an implied warranty of soundness might arise regardless of the intention of the seller if the action were assumpsit.[13]

The argument of counsel, however, turned not on intentions but on larger questions of policy and morality. The "Charge here is no more than selling a Thing of Small Value for a great Price and not discovering the Defects." Counsel even admitted that the conduct might be inconsistent with "natural Justice" but added that it was "tolerated by the universal Consent of Mankind where buying and selling is used." The law protected buyers in that they had the right to insist on an express warranty and could have an action if there were a breach of this warranty. No action could be maintained if a person sold a horse that was diseased or lame, and "where is the difference between a Horse and a Slave as to this Matter?" Nonetheless, he was uneasy, as it could appear that he was "arguing in Favour of Fraud," and the alternative view might "gain popular applause and raise a High Idea of the Orator's Integrity." But "the Laws of Society and Civil Government," he contended, "are not founded upon the strict Rules of natural Justice."[14]

The wrong to an individual must be overlooked in the interest of the "Good of the Majority." A person could protect himself after all, and if he did not he suffered "through his own Folly and Negligence and the Law is not to be blamed." If the action before the court was sustained, counsel warned, "every Vendor of Slaves imported will be subject to the same[.] It frequently happens that there are Distempers among their Slaves but the Seller does not think himself obliged to publish this to the World Nor is it thought criminal even to use arts to conceal it."[15]

The judgment was for the plaintiff. Was the court adopting the notion that a sound price in the sale of something of such value as slaves did raise an implied warranty of soundness? Or was the court acting on the assumption that it was dealing with a case of deceit? It is difficult to say because the remedy is not recorded. We do not know whether the contract was annulled, the price was reduced, or damages were awarded. One thing is clear. The losing counsel adopted the notions of the dominant capitalist and individualist ethic that controlled Anglo-American contract law in the nineteenth century. But he was the losing counsel. At best he was a harbinger.

The contest in *Waddill* represented a wider struggle during the eighteenth century between those who tried to ensure that the law did not stray too far from "natural justice" and those who viewed it as an instrument to promote economic activities. Another dimension of this contest was the struggle between "the protective paternalism of the eighteenth century" and the "individualism of the new order." "Natural justice" and a "protective paternalism" are not linked inevitably, but the tendency to relate the two in the eighteenth century was strong, as was the view that individualism required that people accept the consequences of their own conduct without the intervention of the state.[16] These divergent views can be found scattered throughout the legal and ethical treatises of the late eighteenth century, when the intellectual struggle became acute.

William Paley, in *The Principles of Moral and Political Philosophy*, for instance, noted that "the rule of justice, which wants with most anxiety to be inculcated in the making of bargains, is, that the seller is bound in conscience to disclose the faults of what he offers to sale." He did not argue that implied warranties were part of the law. Rather, he maintained that the primary security for purchasers was the integrity of the seller. The market protected buyers. The general rule, for Paley, was an expectation approach to contracts: "*Whatever is expected by one side, and known to be so expected by the other, is to be deemed a part or condition of the contract.*"[17]

There is little doubt that by the end of the eighteenth century the dominant view was *caveat emptor*. Lord Chief Justice Mansfield expressly rejected the idea that a sound price implied a sound commodity, and his rejection "met with general approval in England as well as in most of the United States."[18] During the 1790s, however, there appeared to be signs of life in the older tradition. Richard Wooddeson published *A Systematical View of the Laws of England* in 1792. According to him, the "unconscientious maxim" of *caveat emptor* was "now exploded, and a more reasonable principle has succeeded, that a fair price implies a warranty." Powell argued that contracts respecting private property were to be determined by the "principles of natural or civil equity." Robert Joseph Pothier, a leading French civilian whose work appeared in North Carolina in 1802, observed that a warranty meant that when a fair price was offered for something, it was implicit that the thing sold was sound. This was but part of a much broader notion that "in a moral light, we ought to view as contrary to good faith every thing that deviates, in the least, from the most exact and scrupulous sincerity. Mere dissimulation as to what concerns the thing, which is the object of the contract and which the party with whom I contract has an interest to know, is contrary to good faith. For since we are commanded to love our neighbour as ourselves, it cannot be permitted us to conceal from him, what we would not wish should be from us, were we in his place."[19] A profound debate was going on about the nature of law and its relationship to "natural justice" and the needs of society.

It was within this heady intellectual environment that South Carolina's judges decided *Timrod v. Shoolbred* (1793). The day after he was sold, Stepney broke out with smallpox and in a short time died. The defendant offered to pay for Stepney's wife and child if the plaintiff would deduct the price of Stepney or else rescind the contract. The plaintiff sued for the whole price. Counsel for the defendant alleged that the rule of law in South Carolina was that "soundness of price amounted to a warranty of soundness of goods, and that the juries . . . were bound, in justice and common honesty, to support and maintain this doctrine; otherwise, innumerable frauds might be practised by one citizen on another." Counsel on the other side argued that the only warranties that derived from a sound price were that the thing sold was of the description given and that the seller had title. There would be complete uncertainty if a seller were made liable to answer for every indisposition of blacks.[20]

The judges, Aedanus Burke and Elihu Bay, believed that "in every contract all imaginable fairness ought to be observed, especially in the sale of negroes, which are a valuable species of property in this country." The conclusion was that "selling for a sound price, raises, in law, a warranty of the soundness of the thing sold; and if it turns out otherwise, it is a good ground for the action of *assumpsit*, to recover back the money paid."[21] The judges had expanded the common law action to include the maxim that was part of civil law thought. But the maxim was not confined to actions brought on assumpsit.

Two years later Judges Thomas Waties and Bay decided *Rouple v. M'Carty* (1795). This arose on a special action on the case for selling an unsound slave. The problem was that the evidence was unclear as to whether the unsoundness was the result "of disease before or after the sale." This time the judges were more skeptical because "these kind of actions had become very frequent of late." Moreover, juries had been rescinding sales rather than "making a reasonable abatement in the price so as to do justice to both parties, without setting aside a bargain." They cautioned juries "not to slide too easily into a practice that really rendered almost all sales uncertain." The norm of *Rouple* was that in doubtful cases it was "better to support contracts, than to vitiate, or set them aside."[22]

By the 1820s judges in South Carolina began to refine the rules concerning the doctrine of implied warranty of soundness. In *Smith v. M'Call*, for instance, the court dealt with one of the more problematic issues posed by the doctrine: what was covered by the concept of soundness. In that case the court decided that no implied warranty of the moral qualities of a slave arose from the sale or the price paid.[23]

By the 1840s the rule that an implied warranty of soundness flowed from a sound price was openly questioned. In *Porcher ads. Caldwell* (1842) Judge Josiah J. Evans raised doubts about the propriety of the doctrine. In the case before the court the purchaser had taken a warranty of title. Evans held that the fact that he did not also take one of soundness raised a "fair argument" that the seller did not intend to warrant soundness. This was not a conclusive argument, however: it was one more circumstance for a jury to consider.[24]

A revealing case was that of *Watson v. Boatwright* (1845). There was a discount in the price because the parties agreed that the slave Harriet was suffering from a venereal disease. In fact she was not, but she had an "incurable disease of the heart." The seller claimed that there was no implied warranty because a full price had not been paid. Judge Andrew Pickens Butler relied on the ideas of liberal capitalism: "The design and tendency of some of our late cases have been to require parties to rely more upon the terms of their own contracts, than upon the general principles of law. When men make contracts, and have fair opportunities of consulting their own prudence and judgment, there is no reason why they would not abide by them; leaving the law to afford its relief in cases where injury has resulted from bad faith, wilful deceit, or a clear misunderstanding of the parties." This did not, Butler added, "affect the general doctrine, that when property is sold without qualification and for a full price, the law will raise an implied warranty of soundness."[25]

During the early 1840s another set of cases limited the doctrine. In *Rodrigues ads. Habersham* the court dealt with a case of a slave woman, Hannah, who had incurable uterine cancer. The purchaser sued to recover the price paid. Through Judge Evans the court ruled against him because the defendant had refused to give a warranty, "and he who buys after such notice, must take the thing purchased subject to the rule of *caveat emptor*."[26] The sellers of slaves only had to refuse to warrant as a general practice in order to defeat the legal presumption.

One final limit that emerged in the 1840s was to restrict implied warranties to cases involving the sale of slaves. In 1843, in *Evans v. Dendy*, Evans rejected the attempt to apply the doctrine to land sales.[27] One year later F. H. Wardlaw, in *Rupart v. Dunn*, went further, which threw even Evans into dissent, along with O'Neall. This was a land case, but the ethic adopted would affect slave sales as well. In Wardlaw's view:

> Where the buyer examines for himself and has the means of forming his own judgment, he cannot be permitted to resist the obligation of his contract, because the seller did not disclose what he himself might have discovered, and what a prudent man would have discovered. He cannot complain because in the trial of judgment and contest of puffing and cheating which has resulted in a bargain, the seller, making no misrepresentation of matters peculiarly within his knowledge, and using no unfair artifices, has taken care of one side and left the other to the buyer.[28]

Liberal capitalism, in its harsher form, could hardly have been expressed so unabashedly. The older tradition, even in the sale of slaves, could not have stood much longer in the face of such a battering. There was irony in the fact that in England and in some Northern jurisdictions there was beginning to be a softening in the support for the doctrine of *caveat emptor*, a development that Evans himself wrote about in *Rodrigues*.[29]

South Carolina was nearly but not wholly alone in the use of implied warranties in slave sales. Four years after the decision in *Timrod* North Carolina's judges adopted the rule in *Galbraith v. Whyte* (1797). "Every man is bound to be honest," the court observed, and if an unsound horse was sold for the full price, an action of assumpsit would lie. By the 1840s, however, there were signs that the doctrine was in trouble in North Carolina. In *Foggart v. Blackweller* (1844) Judge Nash noted that "as it respects the value or soundness of the article sold, the law implies no warranty." And in 1858, in *Brown v. Gray*, Chief Justice Richmond Pearson began his opinion with this observation: "in the sale of a chattel, the rule of our law is *caveat emptor*, and if the thing be unsound, to entitle the purchaser to maintain an action, he must prove, either, a warranty of soundness, or a deceit." This was a tort action for deceit in the sale of a slave, not an assumpsit, but Pearson did not confine his remark.[30]

North Carolina and South Carolina were the only common law states in the nineteenth century that intervened to protect the purchasers of slaves through implied warranties. Yet even in those two states the old doctrine that rested on the moral perception that fairness was an ingredient in contractual relations was severely damaged by the spread of liberal capitalist ideas by the 1840s.

There were other issues associated with warranty law. A number of judges confronted the obvious question, what was "unsoundness"? This forced them to deal with slaves not as interchangeable, but as unique persons. Diseases of the body were one thing, but what about the "moral qualities" and the mental soundness of slaves? In *Smith v. M'Call* (1821) Abraham Nott of South Carolina held that a sound price/sound commodity principle had never extended to the "moral qualities of a slave." Such a quality, he reasoned, "depends so much upon the treatment he receives, the opportunities he has to commit crimes, and the temptation to which he is exposed, that we can form but a very imperfect opinion of it, abstracted from those considerations. A vice which would render him worthless in one situation, would scarcely impair his value in another."[31] There was a relationship between vices and value, and that was the point.

Did a general warranty of soundness include mental as opposed to physical soundness? One of the first cases that dealt with this subject, *Caldwell v. Wallace* (1833), arose in Alabama. Judge John M. Taylor held that a general warranty did include mental soundness, although he did not offer a definition. He wrote that "the best lexicographers give the word 'person,' as meaning the whole man . . . it is a term used to contradistinguish rational from irrational creatures, and thus applied, seems to refer peculiarly to the mind."[32] Clearly, the humanness of the slaves had an impact on the rules applied in warranties in their sale.

The question of mental soundness rather than moral character occurred far more often in the common law courts. One of the first attempts to grapple with this issue was made in North Carolina in *Sloan v. Williford* (1843). The standard set by Judge Ruffin was that "if the slave, though not actually an idiot, be so weak in understanding and possess so dim a reason as to be unable to comprehend the ordinary labors of a slave, and perform them with the expertness that is common with that uneducated class of persons, his mind must be deemed unsound within the meaning of the warranty. If, for want of competent sense, he cannot discharge the ordinary duties of our slave population, he is of no value to the purchaser, who ought, therefore, to have redress upon his warranty." Eight years later Judge Pearson, in *Simpson v. McKay*, held that a general warranty included the mind: "the value of a slave depends as much, if not more, upon his having sense enough to do the work ordinarily done by slaves as upon the soundness of his body."[33] The norm in North Carolina was the ability to do the "ordinary duties" of a slave.

An important series of cases in Tennessee began with *Belew v. Clark* in 1844. The seller of the six-year-old girl in *Belew* told the buyer that she was of an "obstinate, mulish, sullen temper, but that she was of sound mind so far as he knew." She seemed worse than that to the purchaser. Judge William Turley, for the court, declared that "the want of intellect must be of such a character as disqualifies from the performance of the ordinary duties of life, and renders the person afflicted therewith an irresponsible agent." Two years later Judge Nathan Green affirmed but refined the *Belew* standard because another rule would be "too uncertain." It was no longer the "ordinary duties of life," it was some if not all of the duties required of slaves. The boy in the case, he held, could well be fit "for the ordinary services of a field hand," even though he might be incompetent to manage horses. In Texas, in *Nations v. Jones* (1857), the problem was the degree of idiocy. The purchaser had been told that the boy was not bright, and he said that that was the kind of person he wanted. He later alleged that the boy was worse than not bright. The court ruled against him. The boy, as to "his mental qualities," wrote Judge John Hemphill, "was just such a boy as the defendant wished. . . . He desired to have a chuckle-headed fool, that had just enough sense to do what he was told." Moreover, there was no proof of "absolute idiocy." Men could contract for what they wished, and "mental soundness" was anything short of total idiocy.[34]

What if the issue was insanity, not idiocy? In an Arkansas case, *Pyeatt v. Spencer* (1842), the court, without resort to contemporary theories of madness, held that the seller was not liable because the slave was not insane. Although it showed no subtle grasp of psychological phenomena, the court did touch on a cruel reality. "It is with pain and sensibility," it said, "that the court feels itself constrained to remark, that whatever seeming wildness and aberration of mind might be perceived in the slave, it is but reasonable to suppose, was caused by grief, and the excessive cruelty of her owner."[35] But cruelty held no consequences for the seller when it came to the sale of this distraught woman. The market had little tolerance for such considerations.

A different situation existed in civil law Louisiana, where the sale of unsound slaves came within the rules of the civil code. One action was *quanti minoris*, a proceeding to reduce the price of a thing because of some defect. The more frequent response was "redhibition," which canceled the sale. It was among the most common sources of appeals to the state supreme court in cases involving slaves before the Civil War. There were 166 actions to cancel sales because of diseased slaves.[36]

Latent defects that the purchaser did not know about gave rise to the redhibitory action. The code divided latent defects into two categories: "vices of body, and vices of character." The physical "vices" were, in turn, divided in two, absolute and relative. The absolute vice gave rise to redhibition without doubt. This list included only three things—leprosy, epilepsy, and madness. It is little wonder that there were numerous actions based on claims that a slave suffered from epilepsy. Comprising the relative vices were all the transgressions of the body that made a slave useless or inconvenient. "The vices of character," the code provided, "are confined to the cases in which it is proved that the slave has committed a capital crime; or, that he is addicted to theft; or, that he is in the habit of running away. The slave shall be considered as being in the habit of running away, when he shall have absented himself from his master's house twice for several days, or once for more than a month." The inclusion of "madness" in this category was rooted in nineteenth-century scientific thought, whereas the "vice" of being a runner rested on a perception of proper social relations. Slaves owed a duty of obedience, and those who fled displayed a basic character defect.[37]

Louisiana's nineteenth-century code on redhibition followed the Code Napoleon.[38] However, redhibition was long known to civil law jurisdictions, and in numerous cases the sale of slaves was canceled, or prices were discounted in eighteenth-century Louisiana, as well. One of the earliest entries in the French records was a petition of recovery decided on October 18, 1726. Antoine Augrere had purchased a slave from a Mr. Melik for 600 francs "not knowing that the negro was epileptic." The judgment was that Melik "be cited to take back the negro, and to meet costs and other charges."[39]

It was fairly common for slave sellers to conceal defects and take their chances. Many of the sales of Bernard Kendig, for example, ended in the state supreme court. At the same time, in many recorded sales sellers would warrant the body or title only, or they might refuse to warrant at all. Sometimes sellers expressly disclosed defects in slaves, and then buyers took them at their own risk. Three examples will illustrate the use of what the supreme court, in *Berret v. Adams* (1855), referred to as "the customary stipulations." On March 28, 1824, in the sale of thirty-nine slaves and a plantation on Bayou Sara by Benjamin Ballard to Bennett Barrow, all the slaves were warranted sound except for "Harry an invalid." In St. Landry Parish in April 1817 David Glenn sold Jack to John Lyons and "warrants him free from all the diseases termed redhibitory in law." On the other hand, Louaillier Freres sold "Bombora, aged about thirty years, native of Africa" to Jacques Charlot in January 1818 with the caveat, "it being well understood that the slave so described . . . is a drunkard and has many other vices and is sold . . . with all his good and bad qualities."[40]

A frequent problem brought to the court, at least by the 1850s, was presented by the purchaser of a slave who, even after discovering that the slave suffered from some disease, did not care for the slave, or even seek a rescission of the contract, until the disease had gone so far as to cause the death or uselessness of the slave. Then the buyer either sought a rescission or tried to defend against the seller's action for the price by pleading that the sale was tainted by the unknown defect. This situation was so common that it cluttered the dockets in the mid-1850s.[41] *Roussel v. Phipps*, for example, was an action *quanti minoris* to deduct $800 from the price of the slave Adeline, who had died. The problem was that Roussel, when apprised of her diseased lungs, still had her "employed in cooking and in field work." He had been told by the physician that her condition was too far gone to do much for her, but he kept her working anyway. In Judge Alexander M. Buchanan's view, Roussel had a duty either to return the slave or to provide medical care. He did neither and had to bear the loss.[42]

Then there was the question of mental capacity or illness. But what is madness to one may be eccentricity to another. The phrases used in the nineteenth-century Louisiana code were "madness" or "insanity" and "idiocy" or "imbecility." In *Berret v. Adams* (1855) the court dealt with the former, but it had no difficulty. The slave Nelson had been acquitted of having assaulted his master with an ax and having bitten him. He was acquitted on the ground of insanity. The court was a little less firm two years later in *McCay v. Chambliss* when it considered the problem of idiocy. Here the judges confronted an earlier case, *Briant v. Marsh* (1841), in which the court had waffled. *Briant* involved two fugitives, one of whom was described as "so deficient in intellect as to be nearly useless." "It is very difficult, if not impossible," Judge Rice Garland wrote, "to fix a standard of intellect by which slaves are to be judged." For that reason the court felt that it should not extend cases of the "relative vices" very far: "Madness is an absolute redhibitory vice, and actual idiocy may perhaps be so considered." But Garland added that the defect of idiocy would be apparent and thus would be brought within the exemption in the code that protected sellers of defective goods if the defect was observable. The court in *McCay* relied on this last point. If the slave "had so little mind or sense as to be utterly worthless, it appears to us that it must have been apparent to an ordinary observer at the date of the sale."[43]

Judith Schafer, our leading student of these cases, concluded that "despite an entirely different legal heritage, the Louisiana *Civil Code* and the state's statute law protected the slave buyer in much the same spirit as the other slave importing states, although it operated in a way which was unique to Louisiana."[44] This is true in general, but buyers were not always favored. They, as well as sellers, were held to the terms of sale. This happened if they did not offer to return the "defective" slave in time or provide appropriate medical care, for instance. Moreover, if the records of sales in parishes such as St. Landry, West Feliciana, and Natchitoches are a fair sample, most sellers of slaves were careful about the grant of warranties. There were few cases of rescissions there.[45] A different perspective, of course, can be gained from a close examination of the experiences in major trading centers, such as New Orleans. One conclusion is that "the large number of redhibition-illness cases indicates that owners, slave dealers, and auctioneers knowingly sold unwell slaves in at least some instances to offset the financial loss of a slave with a serious or terminal illness."[46] This is doubtless true, but it was not necessarily the norm outside of the major centers. Until we know much more, this will be conjectural.

Slave sellers in Louisiana had to behave with some circumspection for fear of bearing the loss of ill slaves, even though they did not knowingly conceal the disease. Elsewhere, in the absence of unquestionable cheating, the rule was *caveat emptor*.

The purchase of Mary Ann by a Mr. P. Harsh in Davidson County, Tennessee, was more common than the experiences of buyers and sellers in Louisiana or South Carolina. This case never went beyond the circuit court, and I use it here precisely because of its commonness. Harsh purchased Mary Ann in a court-ordered sale. Two or three days after the sale he said that he was dissatisfied because she was unsound. The court agreed that she was but, "not being satisfied there was any fraud or misrepresentation upon said Harsh," denied him any relief.[47] Nineteenth-century Southern judges, overall, either adopted the legal norms in the emerging Anglo-American law of contract, or, if still steeped in an older tradition, they faced increasing pressure to change. Liberal capitalism had made deep inroads into the older legal traditions in the years just before the Civil War.

Damages and Specific Performance

Anthony Kronman made the point that "fundamental to economic theory" was the notion that "all goods are ultimately commensurable." If this were true, the idea that a court should order the delivery of a specific good (the rule of specific performance) because it is "unique" collapses because the concept of "uniqueness" has no meaning. Such notions were a formidable barrier to taking the individual personalities of slaves into much account in remedial law. But, according to Tushnet, Southern judges "rather quickly developed the rule that courts would direct the transfer of slaves rather than the payment of damages, without regard to the peculiar characteristics of the particular slaves." He claimed that Southern courts tended to begin with the requirement of "uniqueness" before they would resort to specific performance rather than damages, but they usually ended by "treating all slaves alike." Although this allowed "state intervention in transactions between masters, it minimized the intrusion on master-slave relations, by eliminating detailed inquiry into individual relations."[48]

What were the rules available to Southern courts? There were the common law remedies and rules, and there were equitable remedies and rules. Two common law actions were trover and detinue. Trover was an action to recover damages rather than the specific property, whereas detinue was an action to recover the specific property, although it had generally fallen into disuse by the early nineteenth century. Were these actions adequate or were they not? This was an important question because an "adequacy test" had been developed to mediate the struggle for power between the common law and equity courts. The rule was that "equity would stay its hand if the remedy of an award of damages at law was 'adequate.'" And "to this test was added the gloss that damages were ordinarily adequate—a gloss encouraged by the philosophy of free enterprise with its confidence that a market economy ought to enable the injured party to arrange a substitute transaction."[49]

Judges rarely discussed these actions, despite their frequent use. There were cases in South Carolina and Virginia. Chancellor Johnson, in an 1841 South Carolina case, observed that "when called to the bar, in 1803, I found it the almost universal practice of the law Judges to recommend to the juries, in actions of trover, for slaves, to find for the plaintiff a greater sum than their value, with the alternative, that the plaintiff should release the damages, on the defendant's delivering up the slaves." "The juries," he added, "entered into the spirit of it with so much zeal, that it was not unusual to find damages to an amount of double the value, or more, to make it the interest of the defendant to deliver them up."[50] Law judges used the common law remedy of trover to compel a specific delivery of particular slaves. This practice was halted in *M'Dowell ads. Murdock* (1818). The lower court had instructed the jury that in an action of trover for slaves, it might find in the alternative without regard to the actual market value of the slaves. The damages might be set at a sum "as would compel the defendant to deliver it up." Judge Abraham Nott held that if the actual market value of the slave had been the alternative to delivery, there would be no harm. But to depart from that value to force a delivery was "not supportable on any principle of law."[51] A potentially promising legal remedy had been cut off by a rigid adherence to proper common law pleading and the weight of the notion that slaves, like other objects, had an objective market value.

Virginia's judges tried something different. Judge John J. Allen, in *Martin v. Martin* (1842), began with a discussion of detinue. It was little used in England, he admitted, but it was different in Virginia. "The importance of slave property has led to the revival of the action with us," he wrote, and "it has become a convenient and valuable remedy. The damages recovered in an action of *trover*, the substitute for *detinue* in *England*, would furnish no adequate remedy in respect to this species of property; for, owing to the attachment springing up between master and slave, no damages would compensate for the loss."[52]

When legal remedies were seen as inadequate, judges, if they possessed an equitable jurisdiction, could turn to the equitable remedy of specific performance. It was precisely the two states that explored the possibilities of using trover and/or detinue that had the deepest experience with specific performance. One of the earliest South Carolina cases was *Brown v. Gilliland* (1813). Money damages were inadequate in all cases because land was considered "unique" in English law. This is important because the only reason Chancellor DeSaussure gave for granting relief in *Brown* was that "I am inclined to think that there are good reasons for including negro slaves, (which in some of the states are considered as real estate . . .) among those chattels relative to which this Court might decree a specific execution of contracts."[53]

There was a struggle going on between law and equity in South Carolina, however. Judge Charles J. Colcock, in *Rees v. Parish* (1825), a decade after *Brown* represented the other side of the struggle. The slaves in question were claimed by the children of John Rees under the will of their grandfather. The defendants claimed that they purchased the slaves for a fair and full price. The plaintiffs sought a specific performance of the terms of the will, but the lower chancery court dismissed the bill for want of jurisdiction. Colcock affirmed the decree. The "full value of the negroes, with a reasonable compensation for their labors" was an adequate remedy, he said.[54] Colcock had another opportunity to explain his views on the remedial issue the following year. *Farley v. Farley* (1826) involved a bill for the specific performance of a sale of a number of slaves. For a unanimous court he declined to bring slaves under the rule of "uniqueness." For Colcock slaves were essentially interchangeable, and "substitutional relief" (i.e., damages) rather than specific relief was more than adequate.[55]

The break in this pattern came in 1835, when Chancellor William Harper affirmed a decree of specific performance issued by Chancellor DeSaussure in *Sarter v. Gordon*. Some of the slaves had been raised by a Mrs. Sims, but they were all sold at a sheriff's sale. The purchaser agreed to sell them back if the Sims family would pay what he paid plus compensation for his trouble. They agreed and then turned to equity to obtain a specific performance of that contract.[56]

Harper based his ruling on his perception of the master-slave relationship:

> Suppose the case, which I have known of a slave accustomed to wait on a deaf and dumb person, and from long habit able to communicate ideas with him. This would add nothing to his market value, though rendering him inestimable to his owner. . . . A slave may have been the nurse . . . or may have saved the life of one of . . . [the] family . . . what mockery . . . to tell the master that he might have full compensation by damages for the loss of the slave? And unless there be something very perverse in the disposition of the master of the slave, in every instance where a slave has been reared in a family, there exists a mutual attachment. . . . The tie of master and slave is one of the most intimate relations of society.

There was an exception. If the "purchaser contracted for the slaves as merchandise to sell again . . . complete justice might be done by a compensation in damages." Only when the market intruded would there be no case for specific performance.[57]

Harper again affirmed a decree for the specific performance of a contract for slaves in *Horry v. Glover* (1837), two years after *Sarter*. It was enough that a man's slave had come into the possession of someone who refused to deliver him up, or if he had contracted for specific slaves. Any other norm would lead to serious difficulties. For instance, if a uniqueness standard were really required, "will you go into evidence of the slave's character and qualities to determine whether they are such as give him a peculiar value to the feelings of his owner, or to have formed a probable inducement to the purchaser in making a contract for him?" This would be far too intrusive and would "afford room for great looseness of discretion." As in *Sarter*, there was an exception. If someone had contracted for "slaves generally, with no view to any particular individuals, or they were contracted for as merchandize, to sell again, the remedy is at law."[58]

There was uncertainty despite these decisions. It was settled in 1841 with *Young v. Burton* in the court of errors. Speaking for the court, Chancellor Johnson noted that the "only remedy which a Law court can afford" is an "equivalent in money; and the inadequacy of such a remedy, in numerous instances, is too palpable to require illustration. It is equally clear, that it is at war with the great principles of natural right; a conventional substitute for what is demanded by good faith and fair dealing."[59] The South Carolinians did not feel wholly at ease with the implications of the market.

Chancellor Johnson placed considerable weight on the humanness of slaves:

> Can you go into the market, daily, and buy one like him, as you might a bale of goods, or a flock of sheep? No. They are not to be found daily in the market. Perhaps you might be able to buy one of the same sex, age, color, height and weight, but they must differ in the moral qualities of honesty, fidelity, obedience, and industry; in intellectual qualities of intelligence and ignorance; in physical qualities of strength and weakness, health and disease; in acquired qualities, derived from instruction, in dexterity in performing the particular labor you wish to assign him. . . . When one goes into market to purchase a slave, or a number of them, his selection is determined by the best evidence he can obtain in reference to these qualities. And why should he not have them in specie?

Moreover, there were ties that united masters and slaves. As Johnson put it: "tell the people of this State that a stranger may enter upon you, and carry off your female slave, the mother of a dozen children, otherwise the humblest of your gang; that he may select from them the most valuable, and drive them all off en masse, and that at law your only remedy is damages, estimated at their marketable value, and I know nothing of their feeling and opinions, if they would not arm themselves, and prepare to oppose force to force."[60] It was rousing rhetoric, of course, emphasizing such qualities as "fidelity, obedience and industry." Ironically, when he came to write his own will, the best Johnson could do was to provide for a division of his slaves, in kind if possible, but if a sale were necessary, children under twelve were not to be sold apart from their mothers.[61] There were limits to the ties that bind. Nonetheless, it was a strong opinion, and the lone dissent was written by Benjamin F. Dunkin, who preferred to follow *Rees* and *Farley* rather than *Sarter* and *Horry*. The decrees in the latter two cases could have been affirmed, but without the abandonment of the norm of uniqueness. All that was needed, Dunkin believed, was some specification of the peculiar circumstances that made the slaves unique.[62] But by 1841 specific performance would be awarded in South Carolina because of the nature of slave property, without any requirement that the special qualities of a slave be alleged.

A similar conclusion was reached in a line of Virginia injunction cases that began with *Wilson and Trent v. Butler* (1813). Trustees obtained an injunction against the seizure and sale of slaves who had been conveyed in trust. The slaves seized were "family slaves" who were to be hired out for the support of a married woman. The hire they brought in would far exceed any interest received on the purchase money, even though their actual value at law might be recovered. A sale would defeat the purpose of the trust. Chancellor Spencer Roane accepted this argument and ruled that the injunction was appropriate.[63]

The next significant case was *Allen v. Freeland* (1825). Allen bought a number of slaves for $1,209. Freeland had levied an execution on two of the slaves. He had obtained a judgment against Wright, the man who sold the slaves to Allen. Allen claimed to be a bona fide purchaser, whereas Freeland maintained that it was a fraudulent purchase designed to conceal Wright's true assets. The question was whether or not the injunction that had been issued to prohibit an execution sale was properly dissolved. Judge Dabney Carr wanted to affirm the dissolution: "No sacrifice of feeling, no considerations of humanity, are involved. These are not family slaves, but strangers to the plaintiff,—brought from a distance, and casually purchased at a public sale; no statement that they were peculiarly valuable . . . or that the plaintiff bought them cheap, and would be injured by the loss of his bargain." "He has paid no money," Carr continued, "and never can be forced to pay a cent, if he does not hold the slaves. The money which he intended to vest in this way, he has had the use of; and could now vest it much more advantageously, in the same kind of property."[64]

Tushnet believed that Carr considered slaves to be interchangeable. Carr was clearly appalled at fraudulent conduct, and he was no supporter of equity. In the same year that *Allen* was decided, he wrote in another slave case, *Bowyer v. Creigh*, that "this interference of equity, has grown to be a crying evil among us . . . and has become the common resort for fraudulently covering the property of debtors." Despite his concern about fraudulent debtors and equity, Carr did leave the way open to a decree of specific performance in a proper case. This could include "family slaves." Moreover, he acknowledged that a slave could have a unique value for "character, qualities, or skill in . . . [a] trade or handicraft." Slaves were not totally interchangeable.[65]

Judge John Green noted in *Allen* that equity normally would not decree the specific execution of a contract for chattels personal "because damages are, in such cases, a perfect compensation." But "slaves are a peculiar species of property. They have moral qualities, and confidence and attachment grow up between master and slave; the value of which cannot be estimated by a jury." The problem was, what standard would be used? "I should be inclined to think," Green wrote, "that slaves ought, *prima facie*, to be considered as of peculiar value to their owners, and not properly a subject for adequate compensation in damages . . . but that this presumption may be repelled, as in the case of a person purchasing slaves for the avowed purpose of selling them again."[66] The case before the court did not involve special attachment, however, so the injunction was properly dissolved.

Allen ought to be placed next to *Bowyer v. Creigh* (1825). In *Bowyer* James Caldwell had purchased from William Bowyer his interest in White Sulphur

Springs. A few years later, in 1820, when he was deeply in debt and knew that there would be judgments against him, Caldwell executed a deed of trust to John Caldwell for the security of his debt to Bowyer. The trust deed included slaves. The judgments were obtained and executions levied on some of the property. An injunction stopped the sale, but upon a hearing on a charge that the trust deed was fraudulent, the injunction was dissolved.[67] This was the situation when the case reached the court of appeals.

Carr, writing for a *unanimous* court, was disgusted with the abuse of equity powers used to shield debtors. The injunction cases, he noted, were based on the same grounds as those involving specific performance of contracts and therefore were within the discretion of the court when there was no adequate remedy at law. From this analytic viewpoint "it must be obvious to every one, that various causes may exist, to give slaves a value in the eye of the master, which no estimated damages could reach. The slave may have been raised by him, and may possess moral qualities, which, to his master, render him invaluable. He may have saved the life of the master, or some one of his family, and thus have gained with them a value above money and above price. When any case of this kind is addressed to a Court of Equity, it will interfere." But it never intervened in cases involving a mere "incumbrancer." The dissolution was upheld.[68]

Tushnet's evaluation of *Bowyer* was that "Carr seemed to get agreement on his nonuniqueness position."[69] This can be misleading, although I assume that Tushnet was referring to most slaves, not the special one. It would be odd if he were able to get unanimous agreement on a "nonuniqueness" position in the same year *Allen* emphasized "uniqueness." The Virginia judges in this case, rather, held firmly to a uniqueness standard and even spelled out some of the circumstances that might lead to it, but it had to be uniqueness.

This precise problem was confronted by the Virginia judges three years later in *Randolph v. Randolph* (1828). According to Carr, a crucial question had never been answered by the court: whether slaves "from their *nature merely*" were such property that equity would intervene to preserve it and give it to its true owner, rather than allow a damages remedy at law. They were not. There must be some unique quality, and equity could be used to preserve "the slave to his master *in such cases*." But, Carr added, he would restrict it to those. "We must all agree," he observed, "that there are many cases, in which a slave has no peculiar value with his owner; some, among the large slave-holders, where he is not even personally known; or he may be vicious or worthless."[70]

Judge Green admitted that there could be inconvenience no matter what the court decided, but for him slaves "ought, *prima facie*" to be considered as property of a special kind by its nature. Slaves "have moral qualities, which make them, in some instances, peculiarly valuable to their owners; but which could not be the subject of enquiry in each particular case, without great inconvenience and uncertainty." As he had in *Allen*, Green said that the presumption could be overturned.

This would apply to slaves owned by slave traders or in a case where slaves were sold for debts and the question was between a creditor claiming on a specific lien and one claiming under an execution judgment.[71]

One of the more interesting judgments was that of John Coalter. He argued that not only were the "affections and predilections" and the money interest of the master involved. The master "owes a *duty* to the slave, as well as the slave does to the master, and which he ought to perform; the duty of protection from a violent seizure and sale, which may terminate in the destruction of his happiness, and in breaking asunder all his family ties and connexions."[72] Grounding an equitable jurisdiction in the reciprocal relationships of masters and slaves, and placing these on the ground of duty, was a striking position.

This line of cases involved injunctions to stay execution sales. And even though it was occasionally mentioned that this power rested on the same principle as the equitable remedy of the specific performance of a contract ("uniqueness"), it was not until 1856 that the Virginia Court of Appeals considered the specific relief. Judge Richard Moncure wrote for all in *Summers v. Bean* except Green B. Samuels, who dissented without opinion. Moncure began his presentation with an English case, *Pearne v. Lisle* (1749). "As to the merits," Lord Hardwicke had ruled, "a specific delivery of the negroes is prayed; but that is not necessary, others are as good." This case, Moncure contended, was not binding. Hardwicke was, of course, correct that slaves were property, but, Moncure noted, he failed to add that they were also human beings.[73]

Were slaves "in their very nature" a form of property for which no adequate remedy at law could exist for a breach of a contract to sell and deliver them? They were, and the same principle should apply as to real estate, and a specific performance should be awarded. "Slaves are not only property but rational beings; and are generally acquired with reference to their moral and intellectual qualities. Therefore damages at law, which are measured by the ordinary market value of the subject, will not generally afford adequate compensation for the breach of a contract for the sale of slaves."[74] Moncure concluded that equity could order the specific performance of a contract of sale even though there was no allegation in the bill or proof that the slaves were of any peculiar value.

According to Tushnet, the position adopted in Virginia was "repeated throughout the South." His major supporting case was from Mississippi. In *McRea v. Walker* (1840) Judge James F. Trotter overturned a lower chancery court's decision dismissing a bill for the specific delivery of a "negro girl named Mary." Mary had been sold with the complete knowledge of the title of the complainant. Trotter recognized that the facts would sustain an action of trover or detinue for the slave, but "the complainant has averred that this is a family slave, and that no compensation in damages merely would be an adequate relief." "Family slaves," he concluded, "have been decreed to be specifically delivered up. This is an indulgence which has long been extended to the claims of attachment which may have grown up between the slave and his owner." "Long" may be a relative term, but in this instance it is misleading. The only authorities cited by Trotter were the Virginia cases beginning with the 1825 decision in *Allen*. He mentioned no precedents from Mississippi or from any other jurisdiction. Three years later, in *Sevier v. Ross*, the court granted an injunction against the seizure and sale of slaves already sold by the debtor. As Chancellor Robert H. Buckner put it, "the importance which has been attached to slave property, in the slave-holding states," justified equitable intervention "even without any allegation of peculiar . . . value."[75]

The course pursued in Alabama and Georgia was different. Judge Reuben Safford of Alabama was particularly strict in *Baker v. Rowan* (1832). "We freely concede," he wrote, "that slave property is, in general, distinguishable from other chattels, in this respect; that family slaves, to which owners are attached, should be preserved in specie, by the interposition of Chancery, rather than leave the party to seek reparation in damages." The critical point was that there must be some peculiar value. Moreover, the emphasis was on "family slaves," not field hands. In the case before the court the bill "describes the property in general terms, as family slaves . . . but the circumstances which would create peculiar value or attachment, are not stated with sufficient precision; nor is even the existence of particular attachment alleged." Eight years later, in *Hardeman v. Sims*, the court noted that although equity might order the delivery of specific slaves, it had to be a case of more than simply "family slaves."[76]

Tushnet's conclusion from this set of cases was that the "courts started by requiring some special relationship but ended, except in Alabama and Georgia, by treating all slaves alike."[77] This meant not that they were interchangeable, but that all were unique. One problem with this conclusion is that about half of the slave states never considered the issue. Modern contract law, not the paternalism of specific performance, dominated the sale of slaves in the more bumptious commercial states in the West. Moreover, the line of cases Tushnet examined only began in the teens of the nineteenth century. For nearly two hundred years the peculiar nature of slaves, "property" with the quality of humanity, meant next to nothing insofar as contractual relationships that would be enforced at law or equity were concerned. The specific performance of a contract because of the peculiar nature of slaves, for example, was not even considered in an appellate case in Virginia until 1856, and Virginia's experience was deeper than most. The humanity of the slaves did have some impact on emerging contract law as far as the problem of damages or specific performance was concerned, but it was not especially meaningful. And it did come up in the warranty cases. These cases show that judges, on occasion and in special circumstances, did adopt a subjective theory of value when the objects transferred were slaves. But just as often they used an objective theory, and in most instances they showed no understanding of the "pang agonizing." Rather, when they incorporated the humanity of the slaves into the substantive and remedial law of contracts, it was to protect the interests of slave consumers—sellers and masters.

Mortgage Contracts

The same was true of the mortgaging of slaves. Debt is central to a mature market society, and here was another point where "humanity" and the commercialization in slave law became intermeshed. It was also an area where the paternalistic rules fashioned by equity clashed with the emerging rules of contract law fashioned in law courts more sympathetic to the individualism at the heart of the will theory of contract. Perhaps a good way to illustrate the tension would be to juxtapose a remark of Chief Justice John Marshall for the U.S. Supreme Court with one from Judge Brooke of Virginia. The problem was to distinguish a conditional sale from a genuine mortgage. According to Marshall, speaking in 1812, "to deny the power of two individuals, capable of acting for themselves, to make a contract for the purchase and sale of lands defeasible by the payment of money at a future day, or, in other words, to make a sale with a reservation to the vendor of a right to repurchase the same land at a fixed price and at a specified time, would be to transfer to the Court of Chancery, in a considerable degree, the guardianship of adults as well as of infants." In an 1839 Virginia case, on the other side, Judge Brooke argued that the transaction before him was a mortgage of slaves and not a conditional sale because the "borrower," to use his phrase, "might in some sense be said to be the slave of the lender."[78]

Although mortgages were originally the creation of law, equity asserted a role, and by the 1800s the supervision of mortgage transactions was one of its major functions. As early as the 1600s, the general rule was that the creditor got the legal title to the property, the debtor usually retained possession, and the creditor's right would be reconveyed to the debtor if he paid on time. If he did not, he lost the property forever. But equity created an "equity of redemption" that gave a debtor the right to redeem his land whenever he could, even after failure to pay on time. By the end of the 1700s equity set a twenty-year limit in order to discourage stale claims. While debtors were given this vital equitable right, creditors received a remedy as well—the right of foreclosure. They could go into equity to force the debtor to pay or forever lose the equity of redemption. Those involved in commercial investment, however, did not consider this a happy solution. Members of the business community would avoid court actions if at all possible. The horrors described in Charles Dickens's mordant story of the equity case of *Jarndyce v. Jarndyce* in *Bleak House* are ample testimony of the reason they avoided equity in particular. By the end of the eighteenth century, conveyancers often inserted a clause in mortgage contracts giving the creditor the right to seize and sell the property upon failure to pay on time. Such a clause bypassed the cumbersome foreclosure process.[79]

By the late 1700s all of this applied only to transactions involving land; there was no body of *chattel* mortgage law. Chancellor James Kent, in his *Commentaries on American Law*, cited only one English chancery case in which personal property was a proper subject for mortgage, and that case was decided after 1800. Judge

Henderson, in *Falls v. Torrence* (North Carolina, 1826), said that nothing could be learned from English decisions, "personal property not being the subject of mortgage." Six years later, in *Overton v. Bigelow* (Tennessee, 1832), Judge Whyte, relying solely on Kent, stated that "Negroes may be the subject of mortgage, as well as real estate."[80]

By the 1800s English law had been transformed. Powell, a critical figure in the rise of the will theory of contract, wrote in his *Treatise on the Law of Mortgages* (1799) that "every thing which may be considered as property . . . may be the subject of a mortgage." Chattels had risen in importance even before the late 1700s with the spread of a market society. Personal property no longer meant simply items like linen or jewels. It now included such things as stocks. This change in the way people thought about chattels played a role in the rise of capitalism. The precise relationship between the ownership of slaves and this process is not clear, but a reasonable conjecture would be that it was close. Slaves, after all, always had been viewed as of much more value (and social importance) than bedsheets or stock animals. If this interpretation is accurate, slavery played a critical part in the emergence of market capitalism.[81] It performed a major role in the change in legal thought about property, and it preceded the spread of national commodities markets.

In any case Southern courts, when they had to say precisely what it was that was created when a slave was mortgaged, adopted one of two theories: the legal estate or the lien. Under the first theory, the creditor held a legal estate whereas the estate of the debtor was entirely equitable. A mortgage was seen as a conveyance of legal title to property as it was in the case of land. The alternative theory was that a mortgage was not really a conveyance and did not confer an estate upon the creditor but merely created a lien on the property of the debtor.

Maryland, one of the most commercial Southern states, was the strongest legal theory state. South Carolina's equity court, on the other side, held in 1847 that, although a creditor might in some sense be the "legal owner," he was not considered in equity "as in any manner . . . the owner of the slaves." Georgia also maintained that title was in the mortgagor (the debtor). Other states and judges wobbled. In Alabama one judge ruled that the debtor was the legal owner against all persons except the mortgagee and that the mortgage created a mere chattel interest. Another contended that the creditor became the absolute legal owner upon failure to pay.[82]

Conditional sales, whose history is clouded in obscurity, were woven into the story of chattel mortgages. Conditional sales, which in the form of the installment contract or purchase on time have become one of the foundations of our modern credit economy, were defined during the 1700s as sales with the seller holding the right to repurchase the property at a particular time.[83] If he did not, he lost all claim. The purchaser took possession from the outset. Equity courts did not look with favor upon such sales because the seller might in fact be a person in severe economic difficulty who was forced to sell his property for a price well below its real value. The problem was that the debtor, economically weak, would be unlikely to be able to repurchase at all and would then lose his property for a price well below the market value. To protect people against such oppressive contracts, equity courts acted on the assumption that if a transaction was unclear (whether it was a mortgage or a conditional sale), they would rule it a mortgage.[84] This rule, and the fear of the conditional sale, came before the introduction of national commodities markets, which transformed the functions and theory of these contracts.

One more legal instrument played a role in the law of chattel mortgages. The trust deed was a transfer of property to trustees, who held the entire estate (legal and equitable), to carry out the purposes of the trust—this could include the power to sell the property for the benefit of creditors or to receive rents and profits to be applied to the liquidation of debts. Although there is an enormous body of chattel mortgage case law, slaveowners often used trust deeds as the "fundamental equivalent" of mortgages. They were quite common in Mississippi and Alabama, for example. In Alabama the courts referred to the trust deed as a "virtual mortgage" so that these two categories collapsed into one another.[85]

Because the line between mortgages and trust deeds was often wiped out, the greatest difficulty faced by Southern courts was whether a contract was a conditional sale or a chattel mortgage. It is in these cases that we can see the conflict between the old equitable paternalism and the emerging will theory of contract.

The analytic problem was that the language in a contract was not always helpful. All courts, therefore, tried to cut through the inartfully drawn contract (a frequent problem in the nineteenth-century South) to the intention of the parties. In a major exception to accepted common law procedure, equity had long held that it was proper to admit oral testimony to explain a contract. Although some judges were not happy with this equitable rule, most accepted it. The most hostile was the commercially oriented state of Maryland. In *Watkins v. Stockett's Adm'r.* (1820), the court held that "parol evidence is inadmissible to vary or contradict the clear, certain, and unequivocal import of a written instrument." Other courts ruled that even an absolute sale could be a mortgage in fact, and oral testimony would be admitted to show that the parties understood the transaction that way.[86] One of the strongest statements, however, came from another commercially oriented state, Louisiana. In *Boner v. Mahle* (1848) Judge Thomas Slidell fell back on the civil code and rejected the references to English equity. Louisiana policy, he noted, "prefers that cases of individual hardship should sometimes occur, rather than the daily transactions of the people and their titles to immoveable property, should be exposed to the uncertainty which would result from permitting written contracts to be questioned upon oral testimony."[87]

What a court might do with oral testimony—whether it would lean toward equitable paternalism or market individualism—was largely a result of the ideology of particular judges. Whichever way they leaned, nevertheless, analysis would be built upon what one judge called the "indicia of a mortgage."[88]

One apparently clear measure was that there had to be a debt for the contract to be a mortgage. A mortgage, by definition, was a security for a debt due. But at a time when the conditional sale was gaining legitimacy, even this got muddled. The reason was that the debt could be the price or the balance of the price paid for a slave.[89] Despite such a collapse of legal notions into one another, courts heroically went ahead with the attempt to distinguish the two transactions.

One of the norms most often used was whether or not a difference of some magnitude existed between the price paid for the slave and the actual market value. If the money the seller received was far below the market value of the slave, a strong presumption would arise that the court was dealing with a mortgage and not a conditional sale. Even this, however, was not as objective as it might appear. The price criterion was a remnant of the older "just price" concept, but this notion was losing its force. Just price, Powell had observed in his 1790 work on the law of contracts, was to be found in the consent of the parties. Equity, nevertheless, continued to use the price standard. In their supervisory role, judges could transform what in fact had been oppressive sales into mortgages. Their "guardianship of adults" would continue, and they would preserve the notion of a just price by requiring an adequate price as a measure of a sale. This was less than solid because the notion of objective value outside the consent of parties was collapsing.

The North Carolina court observed in 1840, for instance, that what was needed was a "gross disproportion." The next year this was given more form: a price of one-half or less of the market value would be "gross." The inadequacy of the price standard had emerged at least as early as 1798 in Virginia, but the North Carolina cases of the early 1840s appear to be the first that tried to define what was "inadequate." What this would be for most judges would depend on their sense of the fairness of a given transaction. In the North Carolina case, for example, the slave was valued at the current market rate of $400 but sold for $311. The court saw this simply as a good deal for the purchaser and ruled that it was a conditional sale. In 1857 Judge Nash suggested that the experience of business people would be a proper aid: the circumstances of the "sale" had to be such as "to the apprehension of men versed in business, and judicial minds, are incompatible with the idea of an absolute purchase, and leaves no fair doubt that a security only was intended."[90]

The collapse of the idea of just price and the flabbiness of its equitable reflection, the inadequacy standard, left the way open for the development of a general law of contract based on the will theory. Still, in the case of slave mortgaging this was not complete: many Southern judges were not as eager as Nash to embrace the market. Despite its fuzzy contours, the inadequacy norm still found a place in slave mortgage cases down to the Civil War. The tension between equitable paternalism and market individualism was also reflected in cases concerned with the recording of slave sales and mortgages, problems of possession, and the equity of redemption, among others.[91]

The recording of slave sales and mortgages was required by statute throughout the South, but what was the effect of a registry? Judge Ruffin of North Carolina ruled that it was an essential element in a valid mortgage. Other judges held that if a third party knew of a mortgage, even if it was not recorded, that was enough.[92] One of the most revealing discussions came in a Louisiana case of 1857, *Johnson v. Bloodworth*. Judge Henry M. Spofford for the majority argued that "registry laws are artificial rules, the creatures only of positive legislation. As they tend to multiply forms in the transmission of property, and to restrict the natural right of man to do what he will with his own, they have seldom, if ever, been extended by judicial construction to cases not within their plain and obvious intendment." A third person, the court held, who accepted a mortgage from a "naked possessor without a recorded title" only to find himself ousted by a superior title "has only himself to blame." Chief Justice Edwin T. Merrick dissented. "The policy of our law," he wrote, "has always been to place property directly in commerce, and protect the possessor in good faith in his title and property. . . . The sanctioning of the principles contended for would render insecure the most important interests, and would . . . fill with alarm the holders of mortgage securities and the owners of real estate, slaves and moveables."[93]

As this case suggests, possession was often a problem in mortgage disputes. Possession was *always* transferred in a conditional sale, but in a mortgage it might not be. The form the problem took most often involved the question of fraud against third persons. Was it a fraud if the mortgagor retained possession of a slave before a debt became due? Was it a fraud if he retained it after the due date? Registry laws did not resolve the issue.

The most striking discussion of possession came in South Carolina. In 1835 the court held that "it is the common understanding and practice of the country that possession shall not be taken till condition broken." Aside from the fact that this was not the common practice everywhere (Texas is a notable exception), the court said nothing about the more crucial issue of possession after default.[94] In 1839 the court conceded that possession was normally an appropriate measure of title. The case of slaves, however, was different because in South Carolina slaves "partake more of the nature of realty"; mortgages of slaves thus fell more under the rules of real property than did other chattels, and possession was not a measure of title to real estate.[95] Analytically, this left the way clear for a rule that possession after default did not amount to fraud. The decision came in 1844. Judge Edward Frost noted that

the presumption of fraud from possession by a mortgagor after condition broken, would be arbitrary, because contrary to almost universal experience. The habits of society are not distinguished by such punctuality in the payment of debts, or such rigor in enforcing the rights of creditors, as to justify any such presumption from the default of the debtor, or forbearance of the creditor. Mortgages commonly remain unsatisfied for a longer or shorter time after the debts secured by them have become payable; and investments are sometimes permanently so continued.

This was a different world from that inhabited by the pettifoggers and money pinchers portrayed by Dickens. It was all too much for Wardlaw who, dissenting alone, argued that possession after breach without notice of the mortgage was a fraud on subsequent creditors.[96]

Possession in the creditor created its own analytic problems. As early as 1791 the Virginia court affirmed that a mortgagee in possession after failure to pay was valid. Nevertheless, the court believed that creditors often would not take possession because debtors had their equity of redemption. Up to twenty years after failure to repay the loan, a creditor who took possession would have the expense of raising and "improving" the property of someone else. This happened so often that the mortgagee's claim of presumption of title after a long possession did not impress the court.[97]

The North Carolina court in 1830 also believed that creditors would not want possession because they would be subjected to an accounting. Ruffin added that debtors would not want to part with their property. He concluded that "no mortgagee or mortgagor ever yet made a contract, upon which the possession was to change immediately, unless it were the veriest grinding bargain that could be driven with a distressed man, who had no way to turn."[98] Yet in many cases in Southern courts possession was transferred even before default. Were these actually conditional sales transformed by the courts into mortgages? There can be no answer to this, but it should be clear that possession (before or after default) was not an inflexible measure of a fraud or of the existence of a mortgage or conditional sale. The remarks about possession, nonetheless, suggest that equitable paternalism persisted, however weakly, alongside a spreading market individualism.

These rules governing mortgages, of course, were adaptations of English legal and equitable traditions. There was possibly no feature more important than the equity of redemption. No one openly argued that this equitable right ought to be abolished, but there was severe pressure on the length of time allowed debtors to redeem their slaves. Down to the 1820s the old twenty-year rule held firm. Fissures then began to appear. During that decade, for example, the Virginia court held that a suit brought thirteen years after failure to repay was really too late.[99]

Creditors increasingly began to plead statute-of-limitations bars to the assertion of the right to redeem. Tennessee refused to accept the argument that the legal three-year limit in personal property actions could be pleaded in an equity court. Missouri went the other way and held that the statutory bar did apply. This was necessary to "preserve property, and promote the peace and welfare of the people." More curiously, the court held that it was unclear whether redemption would even be allowed, whether it could be foreclosed in equity, or whether "when the time is passed, the estate in a chattel is indefeasible." Missouri simply had no firm body of chattel mortgage law as late as this 1834 case. Unrestrained by any equitable tradition, the court accepted the statutory bar and added that, in its judgment, poverty was not a sufficient excuse for a suit's delay. Missouri's hostility was extreme, but the equity of redemption rarely escaped even in more sensitive courts. Kentucky and Arkansas, for instance, judicially set up a five-year limit if the possession of the creditor was "adverse," that is, if the creditor refused to admit the existence of a mortgage.[100]

Several states modified the time to redeem by statute. In Georgia it was four years, and in Alabama (by analogy to the limit in the legal action of debt) it was set at six. The most rigorous arrangement was in North Carolina. In an 1826 case Judge Henderson upheld the twenty-year period, but the legislature immediately set a ten-year limit. In 1829 there was a severe drop in the price of slaves, and the next year the legislature imposed a two-year statutory limit on the equity of redemption.[101]

During the 1850s several cases that involved the 1830 scheme reached the state's highest court. In 1851 Judge Ruffin noted that "the period of two years seems to be short, and, it may be feared, will not unfrequently operate severely on the necessitous people, who are compelled to mortgage slaves." Nevertheless, that was the law, and the plaintiff's case came within it so that the court could provide no relief. Judge Pearson, in a later case, suggested that the rule could be hard but "we cannot help it—*six lex ita scripta est.*" Ruffin and Pearson, generally sensitive to the "necessitous," were not happy with the rule. The same was not true of Judge Nash. He wrote that the delay in the case before him (eight years) was "unreasonable" because the mortgagor "might lie by any length of time at his pleasure, according to the maxim in equity, once a mortgage always a mortgage, a maxim which in its operation as applied to female slaves, has often been attended with disastrous consequences to mortgagees." The distance between the Virginia court of 1791 and Nash could not have been greater.[102]

Social relationships among whites, then, could be seen by a judge like Nash in terms of market relationships, but others continued to regard them as a more complete human relationship based on relative social position. Ruffin, for example, ruled in 1859 that the transaction before him was a mortgage. To arrive at this conclusion he took into account the relative positions of the parties to the contract. The debtor in the case was needy, illiterate, and "in the power of the other party." Probably the most outrageous case in the appellate records is *Esham v. Lamar* (Kentucky, 1849). A Maryland couple migrated to Kentucky with a slave girl they owned. When they arrived, they found themselves without money for even the basic necessities. A former Maryland neighbor persuaded them to "sell" the girl to him for twenty-five dollars. The court declared the transaction to be a mortgage and gave the couple the right to redeem their slave. Time and again Southern judges found a debtor to be a needy person or, to use one of their favorite words, "necessitous."[103]

The recognition of a social hierarchy, not just market calculations, did play a role in the way judges dealt with contracts to mortgage or sell slaves. A paternalistic social system grounded in the ownership of human beings did find expression in the courts that would protect whites, in some cases at least, from being dealt with as though they were as powerless as slaves. Such a worldview, however, lived in uneasy alliance with a market individualism that was seeping into the cases involving contracts for the transfer of slaves.

Cobb ended his study of the law of slavery in 1859 as follows: "[having] concluded our view of the negro slave as a person, we shall hereafter consider of those rules of law to which as property he is subject. In that investigation we shall find that his nature as a man, and his consequent power of volition and locomotion, introduce important variations in those rules which regulate property in general."[104] The promised study never materialized. Still, some cases support his conclusion.

Fugitive slaves placed a severe strain on the slave system of the South, as well as on the Union as a whole. The courts occasionally had to deal with this dilemma even in mortgage cases. In *Webb and Foster v. Patterson* (Tennessee, 1846), Judge Nathan Green noted that equity would not usually rescind a contract because of the suppression of truth "in relation to the moral character of a slave." A mortgage was different because the parties "are to account with each other." When a slaveowner knew his slave to be prone to flight and he concealed the fact, the court ruled, the person who took the slave as security would not bear the expenses of recovery. *Keas v. Yewell* (Kentucky, 1834) is even more revealing. A creditor tried to foreclose the equity of redemption but failed because the slave had run away. "The casualty," Judge Samuel S. Nicholas wrote, "by which the slave was lost, is a peril incident to the very nature of such property; and therefore in contracts or covenants concerning such property, the peril should never be presumed to have been intended to be guarded against, unless so expressly stipulated." The creditor bore the loss.[105]

Kentucky, Maryland, and Louisiana addressed the question of whether or not a mortgagee had the right to hold the issue of mortgaged slaves as security. In every case the courts rested their decision on the principle of *partus sequitur ventrem.* Louisiana's court reinforced this principle with a reference to the code that prohibited the sale of children under ten away from their mothers. Maryland's court grounded its ruling in the legal theory of mortgages: because the mortgagee was the legal owner, he was entitled to the offspring. The court ended the case, *Evans v. Merriken* (1836), with this observation: "We will only remark in conclusion, that we are happy to find that in this instance, the law of the land, and the law of nature, so far from being at variance, are in perfect harmony; and that whilst on the one hand, full and ample justice will be administered to the honest creditor, the claims and feelings of nature will not be violated on the other."[106] This decision represents a rejection of neither commercialism nor slavery, and it is not one to support the Cobb thesis—no rule of law was adjusted to the humanity of the slave. But it does show the ambivalence that could exist because of a social system built upon property rights in human beings.

Nevertheless, the humanity of the slave sometimes did skew a decision, and here is where Cobb might have found some support. Judge Reese of Tennessee, for instance, ruled the contract before him in *Ballard v. Jones and Ingram* (1846) to be a mortgage, not a conditional sale, because "the slave was one of peculiar value, worth not less than $1,000; he had been brought up from infancy with the complainant, who was a young man, and they were reciprocally attached to each other." This could backfire, however, as it did in *Harrison v. Lee* (Kentucky, 1822). The court there found a conditional sale because the evidence showed that the debtor's supposed unwillingness to part with the slave "is rebutted, by proving that Sam, by an act of rebellion, had given him great offence, which induced him to declare he would sell him, and that he should remain no longer on his premises."[107]

Chancellor Harper, in *Bryan v. Robert* (South Carolina, 1847), explored another dimension of this situation. A bill for the specific performance of a contract could not be upheld in the case of a mortgagee of slaves. "He is not supposed to know anything of the peculiar qualities of the slaves," Harper wrote, "except that he might form an estimate of the market values of such slaves, and certainly not to have the same attachment, or knowledge of their character and qualifications, as the owner, who has been in possession of them, and has been deprived of it."[108]

Courts, then, did recognize the communalism in the world built by masters and slaves, but in instances of chattel mortgage it was usually limited to the special circumstances of favored slaves. A notable case that perhaps points to a wider understanding was *Flowers v. Sproul et al.* (Kentucky, 1819). The court ruled that the intention of the parties should be decided "as well from the subject matter of the contract" as from other circumstances. The problem was the equity of redemption, which was unfair and injurious to the fortune and prospects of the mortgagee and his family. But a ruling that the contract was a mortgage (with the right to redeem) would also be devastating to the subjects of the contract,

> as slaves, though property, are intelligent and sympathetic beings; they interchange sentiments, mingle sympathies, and reciprocate, with their possessor and the members of his family, all the social regards and kind attentions which endear the members of the human family to each other, and bind them in the social state. The agonies of feeling, as well on the part of the slaves as of their possessors, inseparable from a sudden disruption of those social relations, ought not to be lightly regarded by the judge who, after the lapse of many years from its date, is called upon to decide whether a contract for slaves be a contract of mortgage or conditional sale.[109]

The irony is that the equitable paternalism of the Kentucky court in *Flowers* pointed to the same legal result as the market individualism of other judges, such as Nash in North Carolina: the validation of the conditional sale.

Despite such gestures toward the humanity of slaves, it should never be forgotten that, where the subject matter of mortgages was property rights in people, we are dealing with a legal history filled with human misery. Buried within all the legal discussions about possession, adequacy of price, and equity of redemption could be broken slave families. In this form of contract it must be put in the conditional, because slaves could live and die without ever knowing that they had been mort-gaged. Nonetheless, it takes only a casual reading of a random selection of cases to see the blunted morality. Case after case refers to a thirteen-year-old girl, a ten-year-old boy, or other minors. One case will have to stand as a symbol. Thirty years after *Flowers*, the Kentucky court decided *Lee v. Fellowes & Co.* It ruled that sales of mortgaged property under execution could not be sold in gross as they had been in this case. A sale in gross (that is, of all the slaves together) would, of course, preserve the family and personal relations of those involved. But in the court's view, "a sale in gross would be often detrimental to the best interests of debtor and creditor." It therefore upheld a lower court decree disregarding the earlier sale in gross and ordered a new sale of the slaves individually.[110]

After referring to the collapse of equitable doctrines in the early 1800s, Horwitz concluded that "in one of the greatest triumphs of form over substance common law judges during the nineteenth century . . . began to treat these transactions as conditional sales, thus entirely freeing this economic relationship from regulatory and paternalistic equitable mortgage doctrines."[111] The story of the mortgaging of slaves, however, is not a clear example of the rise of formalism. Equitable maxims, such as "if there is doubt the court will find a mortgage," did persist, although the use of them began to sound rather hollow by the 1850s. It is true, nevertheless, that market notions controlled the way some Southern judges dealt with "these trans-actions." It is also true that chattel mortgage law was so confused that the bound-aries between mortgages, trust deeds, and conditional sales were often fuzzy. Be-cause the weight of traditional legal thought was none too heavy, the way was open for the commercialization of slavery, at least in the area of mortgage relation-ships.[112] There is no necessary antipathy between slavery and commercialism, nor is there a necessary correspondence; the relationship can be close and congenial, or it can be distant and tense.

What a complete triumph of market ideas in the Southern courts might have meant for the social and moral order of the South we can never know, for it did not occur. Instead of prolonged intellectual transformation, that order collapsed in violence. In any event, the morality of keeping promises was especially strong in mid-nineteenth-century American legal thought, even if the contract was quite lopsided. Such a notion, however, stood against moral values peculiar to a com-munal society resting on property rights in people. At its best, the latter moral order could come out in communalism, as in the *Flowers* case, or in the concern of judges to protect the "necessitous" from being reduced to the powerlessness of the slave.

Less often, as the war approached, did the courts choose to sit as guardians of adults. Increasingly, regardless of the form of the contract (whether an absolute or conditional sale or a mortgage), the terms of the contract represented the law of the contract. Liberal capitalism, though never wholly victorious, had made deep inroads into the rules of law governing the contractual relationships of whites when the subject of the contract was a slave. Less and less did judges fashion their rules because of the peculiar nature of the "property," but even then it was impossible to completely avoid it, as the warranty and specific performance cases show. It was also impossible to wholly avoid in the case of the slave hireling.

6

The Slave Hireling Contract
and the Law

No hirer of a Negro understands himself . . .

bound to deliver him at *all* events.

Harris v. Nicholas (Virginia, 1817)

Estimates of the number of slave hires during the nineteenth century vary from 5 to 15 percent of the total annual slave population. Hiring obviously "was not a minor or inconsequential feature of slavery." There is no evidence of widespread slave hiring in colonial America, however. The percentages were on the rise in the last years before the Civil War as ownership of slaves became increasingly difficult for nonslaveholders with the sharp rise in slave prices. Roger Shugg suggested that many nonslaveholders could not even hire slaves during that period. This point was affirmed by John Shlotterbeck, who noted that "hiring extra hands at harvest was expensive and often impossible." Still, hiring persisted. As Kenneth Stampp put it, "small farmers who could not afford to buy slaves were well represented in the 'hiring-day' crowds." Slave hires, as Robert Fogel and Stanley Engerman argued, put to rest the notion that "the ownership of men was incompatible with the shifting labor requirements of capitalist society."[1] But there was an important difference between slave hires and the "commodification" of free labor by its sale in a market, and it was reflected in the law that applied to the two different exchanges. Even though the reduction of free labor to a commodity to be sold in a market reduced the position of the free worker, it was not to the same level as the slave. Master-servant law governed the relationship between employers and free workers. A slave hire was more like the rental of a thing and was not governed by master-servant law.

The Law of Bailments

Prior to the 1830s Southern judges searched for possible common analogies that would cover the legal issues in cases of slave hires. From the 1830s forward nearly all Southern courts treated them as a species of the law of bailment, a category of property law. The first English treatise on the law of bailments, Sir William Jones's *An Essay on the Law of Bailments*, did not appear until 1781. And the first American treatise on the subject, Joseph Story's *Commentaries on the Law of Bailments*, was published in 1832. Before Jones's essay the law of bailment was skimpy.[2]

Most scholars attribute the development of bailment law to the decision of Chief Justice John Holt in *Coggs v. Bernard* in the early eighteenth century. Atiyah used this legal development to illustrate his point that eighteenth-century lawyers were "striving after the notion of a fair exchange, a fair bargain." In bailment law the idea was that the "extent of a bailee's liability should correspond with the purposes of the bailment, and therefore, to some extent at least with the extent of the benefit he took under it." This concept, Atiyah argued, was found in *Coggs* and in the 1781 treatise of Jones. Sir William Holdsworth used the law of bailment to illustrate the transformation in the law that came with the notion of the "idea of negligence as a foundation of civil liability." The earlier idea that a bailee was under an "absolute liability to redeliver to his bailor" was modified to excuse a bailee "for failure to redeliver to his bailor occasioned by no fault of his own." Bailments were linked to the growth of the action of assumpsit. This allowed people to see bailments in contractual terms; it permitted bailees and bailors to modify the "older law as to the rights and duties of bailees" by their own agreement and by "the growth of rules of law relating to particular contracts of bailment."[3]

Although such judgments have much to recommend them, they can be misleading in that they suggest well-developed law back to the early eighteenth century. In fact, the common law of bailments was pretty thin even after *Coggs*. Blackstone had only two entries under "bailment" in his index, for instance. Jones was particularly puzzled by Blackstone's limited treatment. On the vital question of liability for negligence, he wrote this about Blackstone's approach: "on the great question of *responsibility for neglect*, he speaks so loosely and indeterminately, that no fixed ideas can be collected from his words." Instead of relying on the very minimal treatment in the common law alone, Jones turned to civil law sources. His conclusion was that in a contract of hire, it would be beyond the "bounds of justice" if a bailee "were made answerable for the loss of it *without his fault*." The real point was this: "*When the contract is reciprocally beneficial to both parties*, the obligation hangs in an even balance; and there can be no reason to recede from the standard [the standard was diligence]; nothing more, therefore, ought in that case to be required than *ordinary diligence*, and the bailee should be responsible for no more than *ordinary neglect*." Holt had held that "if goods are let out for a *reward*, the *hirer* is bound to the *utmost* diligence such as the *most diligent father of a family* uses."[4]

Story did not rely on Jones, but on civil law treatises, especially the work of Domat and Pothier. The first sentence of his *Commentaries* suggests the orientation: "the Law of Bailments lies at the foundation of many commercial contracts, and therefore is entitled to receive a distinct and independent consideration."[5] By the time his son, William Wetmore Story, published *A Treatise on the Law of Contracts Not under Seal* in 1844, bailments included five types of transactions: "1.

Deposits; 2. Mandate; 3. Loan for use; 4. Pledge or Pawn; 5. Hiring." The fifth category covered slave hires. But it is critical to understand that hiring included two distinct types. One was the hiring of a thing, a *locatio rei*, and the other was the hiring of labor and services, a *locatio operis*. Jones's description of this fifth category is useful: "1. *Locatio rei*, by which the hirer gains the temporary use of *the thing*, or, 2. *Locatio operis faciendi*, when *work* and *labour*, or *care* and *pains*, are to be performed or bestowed on the thing delivered, or 3. *Locatio operis mercium vehendarum*, when goods are bailed for the purpose of being *carried* from place to place, either to a *public* carrier, or to *private* person."[6] Contracts made between owners of slaves and captains of steamboats to transport the slaves from one place to another would be a bailment. But that is not my concern here. Rather, it is the hiring of slaves to work for another person.

Early Legal Practice

Among the earliest influential cases were two in Virginia. The first, *George v. Elliott* (1806), produced the decision of Chancellor Creed Taylor in the superior court of chancery for the Richmond District. In this case Elliott let a slave to George for the year 1802. The slave became sick and died in June. Should George be allowed a credit for the amount of the hire from the time of the slave's death to the end of the year? "The court understands the rule to be," Taylor wrote, "where one hires a slave for a year, that if the slave be *sick*, or *run away*, the tenant must pay the hire; but if the slave *die without any fault in the tenant*, the *owner*, and not the *tenant*, should lose the hire from the death of the slave, unless otherwise agreed upon." The "act of God," Taylor held, "falls on the *owner*, on whom it must have fallen if the slave had not been hired; from which time it would be unreasonable to allow the owner hire—Hire!—for what?—for a dead negro!"[7] There was no discussion of the law of bailment.

The second Virginia case, *Harris v. Nicholas* (1817), involved a construction of a covenant to hire. Wilson Cary Nicholas, a U.S. congressman, had entered into an agreement with Frederick Harris. He promised to pay $280 for the hire for the year of four slaves, "who are to be returned well cloathed on or before the 25th of December." Nicholas delivered Joe to John Patterson to work on Patterson's plantation. The overseer beat the slave to death, and Harris sued Nicholas.[8]

There were a number of arguments recorded, and most of them turned on the nature of the covenant Nicholas had made. "No hirer of a Negro understands himself," one counsel argued, "as bound to deliver him at *all* events. In this case the Covenant is not, that the Slave shall be returned, but that he shall be *well cloathed when* returned." He also contended that "if there had been a Covenant, to restore the negro in good health, the covenantor would have been an Insurer; but his is not such a Covenant." William Wirt, on the other side, argued that there was an express covenant to return Joe. At the end of his argument he made one of the first references to the law of bailment. "Hiring," he noted, citing Jones's treatise, "is one species of *bailment*. If the property be destroyed by the misconduct of the person, to whom it is hired, or of his servant, the master is liable." This was not Wirt's primary argument. As he concluded, "our suit . . . [is] *upon his express Covenant.*"[9]

Roane, for the court, held that the custom in Virginia was that slave hirers were not insurers against all contingencies. Although the lives of slaves hired out had been insured through policies issued by private companies in the nineteenth century, the practice was extremely rare until the last few decades before the Civil War. In any case, slave hirers were not considered as insurers by the mere fact of the contract of hire. Moreover, Nicholas could not be held liable for the overseer's wrong, which was a "wilful and unauthorized trespass."[10] This was a point where the basic rule of liability in master-servant law was embedded in the law involving contracts of bailment.

The same year *Harris* was settled, the Tennessee Supreme Court decided *Hicks v. Parham, Ex'r.* (1817). In *Hicks* the slave died, from no fault of the hirer, within one month of the hire. The claim of the hirer was that "the consideration has failed" with the death of the slave. Tennessee's judges declined to follow the lead of Virginia's. In fact, they noted that they could find no principled difference between the loss by the death of a slave and one occasioned by flight or sickness. They chose to make slave hirers insurers. They did so on the basis of an analogy to a contract of sale, not the law of bailment. Consideration would fail only if the vendor failed to transfer the "thing contracted for" to the purchaser. But if he did transfer it and the thing was "determined by a contingency to which it is naturally subject," that was part of the contract and was "calculated on, and provided against, in fixing the price at the time of the purchase. And just so much is to be presumed to have been deducted from the price as would purchase an insurance against it, and it is either given to an insurer, or the purchaser keeps it, and becomes his own insurer." The judges buttressed their reasoning by an analogy to the leasing of a house. The tenant was the owner for the time of his lease, and he must bear the loss. It followed, the judges contended, "by parity of reasoning, that neither is the temporary owner of a slave exempt from paying the price of his hire, in case the slave die within the year."[11] The Tennessee judges, in sum, relied on rules derived from contracts of sale and leases of land rather than bailments to impose a much wider liability on the hirer of slaves than existed under the rule in *George*.

An early Kentucky case also imposed a significant duty on hirers. In *Redding v. Hall* (1809), the problem concerned a claim for a credit for the amount a hirer had paid a physician to attend a sick slave woman he had hired for the year. If the owner had agreed to provide a proportional abatement in the hire contract in case of sickness or death, there would be no question that the hirer was entitled, but, on the basis of analogous English cases involving rent, the court ruled that the hirer was not entitled here. It concluded that the party "by his own contract" had created a duty he was bound to fulfill. The English cases turned on the notion that "the tenant takes the property subject to every casualty."[12]

Having done this much Judge Boyle finally turned to the law of bailment. "As a bailee to whom the slave was delivered upon the contract of hire, he was bound upon principles of moral right as well as of law, to pay proper attention to the health of the slave." Morality and law imposed duties on the hirer. A "culpable negligence" would make him not only liable for the hire, but also "liable for the value of the slave." Considerations of humanity were pertinent to the case, and what the court intended to do was create a motive of self-interest in hirers to care for the health of slaves and to "treat the slave humanely." The "mere feelings of humanity," Boyle concluded, "we have too much reason to believe in many instances of this sort are too weak to stimulate to active virtue."[13]

Fifteen years later Judge Henry Minor for the Alabama Supreme Court, in *Outlaw and McClellan v. Cook* (1824), followed the reasoning in *Redding*. Hirers were held liable for the entire amount when a slave became disabled from an "accidental wound." As Minor put it, "in actions on contracts for the rent of houses, &c., or for the hire of slaves . . . the loss of the house by fire, or of the labour of the slave by sickness, or his running away during the term, does not discharge the tenant or hirer from the payment of any part of the sum agreed to be paid on such consideration." The "tenant or hirer" took the property during the term subject to the same risks as if "he was the purchaser of the fee simple."[14] Minor did not refer to bailments. Many of these early judges, in other words, were groping for appropriate legal rules and categories.

This remained true as late as 1831, when the South Carolina appeals court decided *Helton v. Caston*. The issue was the appropriate common law remedy. If the owner "reserves a right in his property" trespass would lie, said Judge O'Neall. This would not be the case if the analysis was based solely on the rules of bailment law, but O'Neall held that trespass would lie on the basis of an analogy to leases of land. The point, which was ancillary to this opinion, was that once a bailee became a wrongdoer by destroying or damaging the thing he had hired, the bailment was at an end and basically possession reverted to the owner.[15] The next year Story published his treatise on the law of bailment, and thereafter Southern judges generally followed the rules set down in that treatise. Analogies derived from landlord-tenant law largely disappeared.

Still, the old analogy did appear on occasion, such as in *Perkins v. Reed* (Missouri, 1843). The court rejected the analogy because it would not accept the implications about liability that followed from an analogy to land. The hirer, the court observed, "could not have the same absolute control over the hired negro that a lessee of a house has over that inanimate property." Absolute control was something the Missouri judges would not concede. They adopted the same approach in treating the liability of masters for the civil wrongs of their slaves. In this instance they contained the power of hirers in the interest of owners.[16] The earlier analogies to landlord-tenant law tended to be used to impose duties on hirers and affirm the interests of the owners as a matter of "humanity and policy." What was happening was that liability was lessened through the concept of negligence, and that favored entrepreneurial activities and a labor market in slaves.

The Powers and Rights of Hirers

"The hirer and possessor of a slave," Judge Ruffin wrote in *State v. Mann* (1829), "in relation to both rights and duties, is, for the time being, the owner." But consider the position of the Tennessee judges in *James v. Carper* (1857). "We wholly dissent," they wrote, "from the conclusion . . . that upon a contract of hiring . . . the right of the owner is, by mere implication of law, delegated to the hirer of the slave. A more startling proposition to the slaveowner can scarcely be conceived. . . . One of the great dangers to the owners of slaves is the recklessness and wanton disregard, on the part of hirers, of the safety of the slave and the interests of the owners."[17]

What rights and powers and what liabilities were created by the contract of hiring? Some judges tended to allocate liabilities and risks on the basis of the price paid by the hirer. They tended to see the contract as "entire," that is, all the terms and liabilities were contained in the contract itself, and no additional duties could be imposed by courts. For them, the price paid included calculations of the various risks involved in the use of slave labor.

A classic contractual analysis was *Harrison v. Murrell* (Kentucky, 1827). The slave died, from no fault of the hirer, before the end of the hire, and the ultimate owner sued for the entire hire. Judge William Owsley, for the court, denied relief to the hirer. "The uncertainty of the negro's life was equally well known to both Harrison and Murrell, when the contract for the hire was entered into between them," he wrote, "and with that knowledge, it was competent for them to contract in the way most acceptable to themselves, and when fairly made, the court possesses no power to alter or change the import of their contract."[18]

A similar analysis was adopted in Mississippi and Georgia. In *Harmon v. Fleming* (1852), the Mississippi court held that "as the defendant did not stipulate for an abatement of price in the event of . . . death, we do not think he has any legal right to demand" it. Judge Lumpkin, in *Lennard v. Boynton* (1852), held the hirer liable for the full hire as "he hired the negro for the year, *unconditionally*. He must comply with his engagement. The uncertainty of the negro's life was equally well known to both Boynton and Lennard, when the contract for the hire was entered into between them. They were capable of making their own agreement, and in the way most acceptable to themselves. What power has any Court to modify or change their contract?" Lumpkin buttressed this contractual analysis with an appeal to humanity: "Humanity to this dependant . . . class . . . requires, that we should remove from the hirer . . . all temptation to neglect them . . . or to expose them to situations of unusual peril."[19]

In 1860 Georgia's legislators adopted a new civil code. The codifier was T. R. R. Cobb, Lumpkin's son-in-law. One of the provisions was this: "If a slave dies during the time for which he is hired, and from no fault or neglect of the hirer—the onus to prove which is on the hirer—he is bound only for hire to the time of his death."[20] David Langum used this condition to suggest that a simple analysis based on social or economic pressures was not adequate to explain the change. Fortuity and intellect must be considered, at least in analyzing "short run" changes in the law. In this case "self-conscious, legalistic, lawyer-like ideas" were important, and "legal change may be generated by the purposeful role of individual intellect." He suggested that Cobb may have made the change because he felt it was more equitable. One additional reason, Langum noted, may have been the availability of insurance. The problem is that this would still require a policy choice as to which party would be the insurer. Langum's points are weighty, but we should not dismiss too quickly the notion that social pressures may have played a role. Some people in Milledgeville denounced Lumpkin's opinion because it was "signally oppressive to the poorer classes of our citizens—the large majority—who are compelled to hire servants."[21]

A contractual analysis, however, did not require the result reached by Lumpkin. In *Dudgean v. Teass* (Missouri, 1846), the court ruled that abatement in the case of nonfault in the death of a slave, an "act of God," "appears most conformable to the principles of natural justice, and is not inconsistent with any settled rules of law regulating contracts, in relation to this species of property." The fact that Texas derived a great deal of its noncriminal law from a civil law tradition was important in a case from that state, *Townsend v. Hill* (1857). "On the question whether the hirer of a slave for a year is entitled to an abatement of the price in case of the death of the slave before the expiration of the term," Judge Royall Tyler Wheeler wrote, "the authorities are divided. Those which follow the civil law, without exception, doubtless, maintain the affirmative." And the Texas court chose to do so as well: "Surely the failure to stipulate against the consequences of an event which neither of the parties anticipated, ought not to preclude the hirer from having the contract apportioned, according to the dictates of natural justice."[22] Markets and natural justice operated on different principles in Texas.

Finally, the court in Arkansas reduced to rubble one of the underpinnings of the decisions in states like Kentucky and Georgia, the notion of an "entire" contract closed to further judicial modification:

> The doctrine of entire contracts, as it formerly prevailed, has been much softened and relaxed in modern times, and we are clearly of opinion that the principles of equity have been greatly advanced by such relaxation. It is not only unjust that the hirer should be held bound for the hire accruing after the death of the negro, but it is not in accordance with the understanding of the parties to the contract. Suppose, for example, that a party should hire a negro, for a year, for the sum of one hundred and fifty dollars, and that he should die the next day after the contract was made: would it not be flatly absurd, as well as shocking to our sense of justice and propriety, to hold that he would be liable for the full amount stipulated for the year?[23]

What about the loss of a hired slave by flight, not death? In *Singleton v. Carroll* (1830), the Kentucky court held against liability when a person was prevented from returning the slave "by an event over which it was . . . impossible for them to have any control." Courts in Arkansas and Georgia rejected the Kentucky approach. In Arkansas, in *Alston v. Balls and Adams* (1852), the court held that the flight of a slave differed from the death of a slave: "It is true that there was a risk to run. The slave might abscond. And so, upon a covenant to deliver stock, or to pasture a horse and return him, the cattle or the horse might escape and never be reclaimed. All these casualties are incident to such undertakings; and if the party contracting was unwilling to run the risk or hazard attending them, he should have excepted them in his contract." The hirer was under a duty to control the slave and return him. In Georgia, Judge Ebenezer Starnes reached a similar conclusion in *Curry v. Gaulden* (1855). He admitted that flight might be an "incident" of this peculiar species of property, but flight was not "inevitable." The hirer had a duty to control in such a case, but "it is not necessary to assume, that bolts and bars or chains would be necessary, in order to ensure the detention of the slave." For Starnes "good treatment would, in most cases, do it quite as effectually." Implicit in such cases, and explicit in some, was the question of the power and duty of slave hirers to control the slave. Southern judges adopted divergent views. According to *Mann* in North Carolina, hirers must possess "the same extent of authority" as the owner. And the *Helton* decision in South Carolina held that the hirer had the right to the services of the slave, but, in order to secure it, he had only the right of "moderate correction."[24]

It should be remembered, however, that *Mann* was a criminal action, and Ruffin had said that the owner of a slave would have a civil action against a hirer if the slave received a permanent injury. The standard he would employ appeared in *Jones v. Glass* (1852). Nash, for the court, admitted that "whipping or chastising" a slave hired was a "lawful" act, but, he added, "to the extent of compelling him to work." "But in the correction it was his duty to do it properly; that is, in a proper manner and with a proper instrument." Ruffin wrote a concurrence. He agreed that the hirer was liable when he inflicted a permanent injury by an "unreasonable and dangerous blow" with a deadly weapon "instead of resorting only to such moderate and usual correction as would have reduced the slave to subordination and been of good example to other slaves."[25]

Yet some measure of power was crucial. Although it placed restraints on the "mere bailee," the Kentucky court left hirers with a measure of power. In *Craig's Adm'r. v. Lee* (1853), the court said that the ultimate owner had the authority "to secure obedience, submission and service of his slave, and to enforce the same by the administration of such chastisement and correction as may be reasonably required for that purpose." He could not be cruel or inhuman. The "mere bailee" could be civilly liable, even though there was no one to whom the ultimate owner would be. The grounds of liability, however, were essentially similar. One ground of liability in the hirer was "inhuman treatment in the form of immoderate chastisement."[26]

Duties by "Implication"

Contractual rights and duties involving hired slaves were not always defined by the words of the contract. Often all that might be written was that so-and-so hired a named slave for a certain sum for the year. Within the contractual action of assumpsit courts held persons liable not just for *malfeasance,* but for *nonfeasance* of presumed or implied duties.[27] The duties implicit in contracts for the hiring of slaves could involve important questions such as an implicit duty to control the slaves, as, for example, in the case of runaways. Another implicit duty was the duty to provide proper medical care and allocation of the loss in case of a failure to do so. Whose duty was it to provide such care? I have seen no discussion from the colonial period.

This question came up in late cases in Georgia and Alabama, for instance. In the leading Georgia case, *Latimer v. Alexander* (1853), a slave who was hired to work in a hotel was exposed to smallpox. The hirer called Dr. Alexander without consulting the ultimate owner of the slave. Dr. Alexander sued the owner for his services. The supreme court ruled that the owner "had by the contract of hiring, lost all control over the slave." The hirer was liable for the medical expenses, but that was because of the contract, not "ownership" as such. Three years later, in *Brooks v. Cook* (1856), Lumpkin interpreted *Latimer* to mean that a hirer was bound to provide "all necessary attendance and nursing to his sick hired slave" unless there was a special contract that placed that duty on the owner.[28] The 1860 civil code, however, modified this at the same time it overruled *Lennard.* The code provided that "the master . . . is responsible for physician's bills, unless the necessity for medical treatment arose from the fault or neglect of the hirer."[29]

A striking set of cases were heard in Alabama. In *Hogan v. Carr & Anderson* (1844), the hirer's defense was that the slaveowner had taken a slave out of his possession five months before the end of the period of hire. The plaintiff offered to prove that the hirer, Carr, had mistreated the slave so badly that he was unable to work and required rest and medical attention. The physicians who examined the slave had been called in by both the plaintiff and the defendant and in Carr's presence had noted that to continue work he would be "at the extreme hazard of one of his legs, and, perhaps, of his life." Carr refused to provide medical assistance and vowed that he would continue to work him. The trial judge held that the contract was entire, and when the owner took the slave back, he terminated the contract and was entitled to nothing. This was overturned by the state supreme court in an opinion by Judge John J. Ormond. According to him, "the hirer . . . impliedly stipulates, that he will treat the slave humanely, and provide for his necessary wants."[30]

Six years later, in *Sims & Jones v. Knox* (1850), the court refined the *Hogan* rule. Here the hire contract stated the price and time and that the hirer would provide clothes and board. During the year William became very sick with a "brain fever," and his owners sent for a physician, who sued the hirer for medical services. Chief

Justice Edward S. Dargan held that a slave hirer was responsible for medical services "where no agreement to the contrary is made." The question was whether such an agreement existed. "If the contract of hiring had contained no stipulations, except the time for which the slave was hired, and the price agreed to be paid," Dargan wrote, "then it is clear that the law would have implied the obligation on the part of the hirer. . . . But this contract expressly provides, that Knox should furnish clothes and board. Why express some of the implied obligations and omit others?"[31]

Five years after that a new set of Alabama judges considered another case involving the duty to provide medical assistance. A railroad company hired Allen as a laborer on the road, but it used him to work as an ox driver hauling logs to the defendant's steam mill near Selma and later at a steam mill in Perry County. By November Allen was sick and was sent back on a night that was "cold, damp and inclement"; within a few days he died of "dropsy of the chest." The jury in the lower court held the company liable because of its negligence. "The law," Judge Samuel Rice observed, however, "does not make it the duty of the hirer, under a contract general in its terms, to call a physician on every occasion when the slave is manifestly sick and the hirer does not know what is the matter with him." His only legal duty was to exercise "that diligence and care which the generality of mankind use . . . in relation to their own slaves."[32]

In 1857, in one of the decisions involving a case before the court on two previous occasions, *Wilkinson v. Moseley* (Alabama, 1850, 1854), Judge Stone acknowledged that the earlier standard did not provide a clear line. He tried to give it more substance. Adeline had been hired by the defendant under a contract providing that if she became sick, the hirer would take "due and proper care" and would "bestow upon . . . [her] proper care, medical treatment and attention." She did become sick, but instead of calling in a physician the overseer of the subhirer treated her with a bleeding and mustard plasters. At the time she was pregnant, and she had chills and fever. She died within a few days. The hirer paid the full hire, but the plaintiff sued for her full value. One defense offered but rejected by the trial court was that "prudent planters generally did not call in a physician to attend their negroes, unless in dangerous cases." The Alabama Supreme Court overruled the trial court. "We apprehend that no certain and fixed rule could be laid down, for the treatment of all diseases, even of the same name." Doctors disagreed, and so did the "generality of mankind." But clearly the judges believed that slaveowners and hirers had the right to administer medicine and therefore the "right to determine when a case is, and when it is not, a plain one." The planter or overseer, however, had to possess such "reasonable knowledge and experience of the disease he treats, as are possessed by the generality of mankind." To require more than contemporary customary conduct would be too demanding. Stone seemed uneasy because he added that "we are unwilling to expose the property hired to stupid and reckless empiricism" so that the custom of treating slaves on the plantation would be no defense if the treatment were "palpably improper."[33] To one slushy standard he had added another. In any event, the requirement that medical attention be provided was one of the general duties some judges held was an implied assumpsit in slave hire contracts.

Wrongdoers

Prudence was not enough to shield hirers from liability if they were wrongdoers. Persons who altered the contract of hire placed themselves in the wrong and were held to a strict liability. As Jones put it in 1781, "A *borrower* and a *hirer* are answerable in *all events* if they . . . *use* them [the things borrowed or hired] *differently* from their agreement."[34] When this happened plaintiffs often brought an action of trover for a wrongful conversion. The question of negligence was not relevant.

In *Mullen v. Ensley* (Tennessee, 1847), a bailee under a general hire contract used a slave in blasting rock in the construction of a turnpike. While doing so the slave "was blown up"; one of his eyes was put out and one of his hands severely injured. Judge Turley framed the problem as follows: was blasting rock "an ordinary and usual employment, such as men of ordinary discretion and prudence would usually be willing to engage their own slaves in"? The answer was no: hirers who used slaves in that way were guilty of a conversion and liable for the full value of the slave. Another example is the case of *The Mayor and Council of Columbus v. Howard* (Georgia, 1849). Braden had been hired to the city of Columbus in 1844 to help repair and clean the streets. Instead of that he was put to work on a precipitous bank at the mouth of the city sewer. The bank collapsed and Braden was killed. This was the basis of a count in case. A second count was in trover for an unlawful conversion of Braden. Judge Lumpkin upheld the jury verdict of $800 for the loss of Braden. The first question was whether the lower court judge had been correct in refusing to strike the count in trover. Lumpkin was one of those jurists who had scant patience with the technicalities of common law pleading. "Whatever of good sense they [the rules of pleading] contained should be preserved; their subtlety and prolixity should be abandoned." The crucial issue ultimately was liability. The law was that the hirer had "an implied obligation not only to use the thing, be it servant or horse, or any thing else, with due care and moderation, but also not to apply it to any other use than that for which it was hired." On this count alone the city of Columbus was liable for Braden's death.[35]

There was also the count in case, and that action required a showing of negligence. In bailment contracts, Lumpkin observed, being contracts for mutual benefit, the hirer was liable for "ordinary diligence" only. For Lumpkin, in the case before him, this turned on the nature of slaves: "The want of discretion in our slave population is notorious. They need a higher degree of intelligence than their own, not only to direct their labor, but likewise to protect them from the consequences of their own improvidence." Because the city of Columbus had failed to provide such guidance and protection, it was guilty of "gross negligence," and the judgment on the count in case, as well as trover, was valid.[36]

Southern appellate records are full of cases involving claims against hirers for deviations in the use of slaves from that stipulated in the hire contract. A frequent problem concerned the use of slaves in some place other than that agreed upon. In *Collins v. Hutchins* (Georgia, 1857), the slave had been hired to work on the South-Western Railroad in the counties of Houston, Macon, Sumter, and so forth for the year 1853. He was used in Burke County, however, and that was not on the list. In June he was sent home sick, and he died in July. Judge Charles J. McDonald, writing for the court, held that "if a negro is hired to work in a particular place, and the hirer removes him to a different place without the consent of the owner, it is such a departure from the contract, as, if a loss ensues, makes the hirer liable. The contract of the parties . . . is the law of the parties." The lower court had refused to charge that the defendant was not liable because the slave had died from his own "imprudence while under his master's control." Despite the warning of the physician, he had eaten peaches and watermelons, and, in the opinion of that physician, this deviation from a prescribed diet did him in. McDonald sustained the lower court's ruling. "A negro is an intelligent human being, having the power of thought and volition," he wrote, "and capable of ministering to the cravings of his appetite, and providing for their gratification, but does not generally have judgment to direct him in what is proper for him, or prudence and self-denial to restrain him from the use of what is injurious." This might suggest that a hirer would be liable because of a failure to direct the slave in what was proper. But McDonald did not adopt that approach. A slave "can not be shut up and controlled and managed as a horse or a cow, but from the necessity of the case, must be left, under orders for the best, with power, if he disobeys, to do wrong." Nonetheless, liability did attach in this case because the railroad had used the slave in a county not listed in the contract.[37]

Negligence

One of the more important issues was liability for injuries to hired slaves. One form concerned liability that attached to hirers when slaves were injured because of the negligence of the hirers themselves. The other form was liability for on-the-job injuries suffered because of the negligence of the slaves' coworkers.

Sir William Jones derived liability initially from the duty in all bailments to restore the thing bailed, but the duty could not be absolute. The "bounds of justice" would be passed if it were. The "omission of that care *which every prudent man takes of his own property*, is the determinate point of negligence." When contracts were mutually beneficial, as were hire contracts, the norm was "*ordinary diligence*" and a bailee was liable only for "*ordinary neglect.*" That, in turn, was the "*want* of that diligence which the *generality of mankind use in their own concerns,* that is, of *ordinary care.*" Gross neglect, on the other hand, was nearly identical with fraud, in Jones's view, although American commentators tended to consider that too harsh. Jones's definition was "the *omission* of that care *which even inatten-*

tive and thoughtless men never fail to take of their own property: this fault they justly hold a violation of *good faith*."[38] When contracts were mutually beneficial, bailees would be answerable either for gross or ordinary neglect. Bailment law, unless altered by the terms of the particular contract, required hirers or bailees to use the thing hired as prudent people.

It was not the universal approach before the 1830s. Prior to that time hirers were sometimes held to a strict accountability for the loss or injuries suffered on the basis of analogies derived from landlord-tenant law. One of the earliest references to the more generous standard was in a North Carolina case of 1814, *Williams v. Holcombe*. In that action a sixteen-year-old slave was burned to death in a fire in a still house. During the trial in the lower court the judge charged the jury that the hirer was not bound for the full hire "if he used ordinary care and attention, such as a prudent man would afford to his own property." The jury found for the defendant, and this charge was not discussed in the subsequent appellate case.[39]

Appellate records are devoid of discussions of the diligence/negligence issue until about the 1840s. Strict liability was common earlier. Most cases from the late 1840s to the outbreak of the Civil War were actions of case in which negligence was a crucial element in the analysis. Many of them turned on the perceptions judges held of slaves, and that in turn implicated their views of the duties of masters.

One of the earliest of these was *Swigert v. Graham* (1847) in Kentucky. Edmund had been hired by the plaintiff to work on the defendant's steamboat on the Kentucky River in 1844. Edmund was drowned, and his owner was sued for his value because he was lost as a result of the "carelessness, negligence, unskillfulness, misdirection and mismanagement" of the owners. Chief Justice Thomas A. Marshall noted that the case turned not simply on the "general principles applicable to the case of bailment on hire" in relation to animals or inanimate property. "Ordinary diligence" had to be seen in terms of the subject of the contract. What might be gross neglect in relation to one species of property could be extraordinary care in relation to another. The hired slave was a unique property. A slave,

> being ordinarily capable, not only of voluntary motion by which he performs various services, but also of observation, experience, knowledge and skill, and being in a plain case at least, as capable of taking care of his own safety as the hirer or owner himself, and presumably, as much disposed to do it, from his possession of these qualities, with habits and disposition of obedience implied in his condition, and on which the hirer has a right to rely, he may be expected to understand and perform many, and indeed most of his duties by order or direction more or less general, without constant supervision or physical control, and may be relied on, unless under extraordinary circumstances, for taking care of his own safety without particular instructions on that subject, and *a fortiori*, without being watched, or followed, or led to keep him from running unnecessarily into danger.

The crucial problem became the particular circumstances of the case. Marshall held that hirers must protect a slave as a prudent man would if he exposed him to extraordinary hazards. One fatal error in the lower court judgment was to require not only "ordinary care" but also "good management" of Edmund. The law did not compel the latter.[40]

The diligence of a "prudent man" often appeared as the standard. A variation, the "humane master," cropped up in Tennessee in *Lunsford and Davie v. Baynham* (1849). A hired slave came down with bronchitis and died about a month after the onset of the illness. Shortly before his death, he was seen in ragged clothes on a wet, cold day. Judge Robert J. McKinney was anything but happy with the circumstances of the case:

> Putting aside all considerations of what was due to the slave himself as a rational being, shutting out all the sympathies of our nature on the score of his privations and sufferings, and looking only to the legal rights of the owner, in the property of the slave, we think no jury could have hesitated for a moment to find the verdict rendered in this cause. The necessary protection of the rights of the master, all other considerations out of view, demands that the hirer of a slave should be taught to understand that more is required of him than to exact from the slave the greatest amount of service. . . . The law, as administered at this day, in most of the slave States, rigidly exacts from the hirer an observance of the duties of humanity, and that measure of care and attention to the comfort and welfare of the slave, that a master, of a just and humane sense of duty, would feel it incumbent upon him to exercise in the treatment of his own servant.

The standard here was the master who acted out of a "just and humane sense of duty."[41]

A cluster of cases from Georgia and North Carolina provide a useful profile of some of the ways judges considered the problem of negligence. The opening case in North Carolina is *Heathcock v. Pennington* (1850). The hirer employed a slave under twelve to drive a horse attached to a whim to a gold mine. He drove the whim to the mine at about nine at night and was told to continue through the night under the directions of a nineteen-year-old. The night was cold, and the slave boy was allowed to warm himself at a fire about 2½ feet from a mine shaft 160 feet deep. Called to get the horse the boy "being drowsy, in attempting to go to his horse fell into the pit and was killed." The defendant offered in evidence that he employed one of his own slaves in the same way, as well as his own son. The court charged that the defendant was liable to exercise ordinary care toward the slave, and that the use of his son was not relevant to his duty to the hired slave. The jury found for the hirer.[42]

According to Ruffin, upholding the judgment, the want of due care was not established. "Ordinary care is that degree of it which in the same circumstances a person of ordinary prudence would take of the particular thing were it his own." A slave, moreover, "being a moral and intelligent being, is usually as capable of self-preservation as other persons. Hence, the same constant oversight and control are not requisite for his preservation as for that of a lifeless thing, or of an irrational animal." Nonetheless, having discussed "ordinary care" Ruffin shifted his analysis to gross negligence. "But admit that the boy would not have met with the fate he did but for going to the fire," he observed, "or if the fire had been in a different situation, yet it cannot be deemed gross negligence not to forbid the boy to go to the fire where it was, or not to have one in a different situation." Ruffin exonerated the defendant: "But with common bodily vigor and ordinary intelligence the boy was capable, after the repose of the day, of doing his business on the surface of the ground for the night, though near the shaft, without any probable hazard of getting into it; and, in the same degree, the vigilance of the defendant over his safety might be relaxed without exposing him to the imputation of negligence, much less gross negligence."[43] Other judges did not use the notion of gross negligence. Ruffin raised the stakes for slaveowners.

Two years later the North Carolina court considered *Jones v. Glass* (1852). In this case Willie was hired to work in a mine, and in the process of "correcting" him the overseer hit him in the head with a large piece of wood. Willie was temporarily paralyzed by the savage blow, and his master sued for damages. The hirer tried to escape liability on the ground that the injury did not result from negligence but from a clear trespass. The North Carolina judges held the hirer liable on the ground of *respondeat superior*. The correction in the course of the employment to compel work was appropriate. "But in the correction," Chief Justice Nash wrote, "it was his duty to do it properly. . . . If he was negligent or guilty of a want of care . . . he is answerable for the permanent injury resulting to the boy." Judge Ruffin concurred. This case was beyond the standard of "ordinary prudence" required in bailment law. It was an "unreasonable and dangerous blow."[44]

Five years later the court decided *Couch v. Jones* (1857). Calvin was killed by a stone during a blasting of rocks. Judge Battle stated that the definition of the norm, "ordinary prudence," "does not fix a standard by which any thing like an approach to mathematical exactness and certainty can be attained." Nevertheless, "necessity requires some rule." The crucial consideration turned on the nature of slaves. He concluded that a slave "is to be considered an intelligent being, with a strong instinct of self-preservation, and capable of using the proper means for keeping out of, or escaping from, scenes of danger." The defendants were excused from liability.[45]

Chief Justice Pearson dissented. Each case was unique, and Pearson admitted that he was not satisfied with *Heathcock* even though he had not filed a dissent at the time. It was an opinion in which the words *ordinary* and *gross* were confounded. His analysis of Ruffin's evaluation was this:

He uses the word "gross" as applicable to the degree of neglect, in that case, four times, and concludes that the defendant was not, under the circum-

stances, "exposed to the imputation of negligence, *much less gross negligence.*"
Yet, that case, is used as a guide for arriving at a conclusion in this, and this,
will be used as fixing the principle, that if one gives a general order, although
he knows that the party has been in the habit of disobeying it, and has no
reason to believe that he will obey it on the particular occasion, he may screen
himself, under such general order, from a liability to which his negligence
would otherwise expose him. Against such a principle, I feel called on to enter
my dissent.[46]

Pearson believed that the overseer had the duty to control the slave Calvin more
effectively under the circumstances.

The Georgia case of *Gorman v. Campbell* (1853) is a fitting contrast to the North
Carolina line of cases. London had been hired as a steamboat hand to work on the
Ocmulgee and Altamaha Rivers. The captain and the white hands aboard were
clearing logs to open a passage when London "engaged in the work of his own
accord, and worked for about half an hour, in the presence and sight of the captain
without anything being said to him." It was not customary to use slaves in that work
"unless under circumstances of urgent necessity." When the log London was working on was about to give way, the captain yelled to him to stop and get off. London
jumped to another, but it was loose and floated down the river with London aboard.
His hat fell off, and in trying to retrieve it he fell in and was drowned. The judge in
the lower court charged the jury that the defendant was not liable if London
engaged in the work of his "own free will, and the Captain forbid him to do it, the
defendant was not liable, because the owner of the boat and its officers, are not
required to keep the negro in chains, which he must do if he were responsible for
any act of his, however trivial, while on the boat, if it would end disastrously." Judge
Lumpkin held that the defendant had the duty to "exercise proper care in the
supervision of the slave." The question, of course, was what that required. The hirer,
Lumpkin wrote, "not only *may* use coercion even to chains, if necessary, for the
protection of the property from peril, but it is his duty to do so." The court's
conclusion, the reverse of that in North Carolina, followed from the nature of
slaves. "Humanity to the slave," Lumpkin believed, "as well as a proper regard for
the interest of the owner, alike demand that the rules of law, regulating this contract
should not be relaxed. We must enforce the obligations which this contract imposes, by making it the interest of all who employ slaves, to watch over their lives
and safety. Their improvidence demands it. They are incapable of self-preservation,
either in danger or in disease."[47] Such racist perceptions also played a part in the way
Lumpkin viewed injuries that slaves received while working with others.

The Problem of the Slave as a Fellow Servant

Several scholars have considered the emergence of the fellow servant rule in
nineteenth-century American law and attempts to apply the rule in the case of

slaves. This rule, which appeared in the 1840s, exempted employers from liability for injuries suffered by workers because of the negligence of fellow employees. The notion, especially well developed in the landmark Massachusetts case of *Farwell v. Boston & Worcester Railroad* (1842), held that workers had contracted implicitly to accept the ordinary risks of employment, and they assumed the liability for such injuries when they bargained with their employers.[48] This was a departure from the normal common law rule of *respondeat superior*, which held a person liable for the acts of others if he was in some way responsible for those acts. *Respondeat superior* in master-servant cases was a "hybrid of tort and contract law, providing a plaintiff a cause of action in tort against an employer because of the employer's contractual relationship with the tortfeasor." Legal scholars have generally argued that this notion was in disfavor by the early nineteenth century precisely because it did not rest on the idea that liability must hinge on fault.[49] It was a form of vicarious liability. It was also a notion based on a social relationship of subordination and superordination and thus existed in tension with an emerging nineteenth-century liberalism. Timothy Walker, for instance, in his *Introduction to American Law*, acknowledged that the use of words like "master" and "servant" could be embarrassing; it did "not sound very harmoniously to republican ears." He suggested that "employer" and "employee" be used instead. He also preferred to treat the relationship as one created by contract. But since "custom" put the relationship under the category of "personal relations" rather than "contract," he would continue to treat it that way. Nonetheless, it is evident that there was tension between an older social order based on status and a newer one rooted in contract.[50]

The problem of the on-the-job injury by a worker because of the negligence of a fellow worker could rest on the principle of either *respondeat superior* or contract. Lemuel Shaw, for the Massachusetts court, argued that the first did not apply because it only concerned injuries or wrongs done to strangers, persons not in "privity" to the master. What remained was contract, and liability here could rest only on an express or an implied contract. Shaw declined to imply some duty in the master that grew out of the social relationship between master and servant. Both parties contracted from points of abstract legal equality. The parties to the contract allocated the risks created by the contract in the agreement itself, and to burden the master with some implicit duty to provide for the safety of the worker would undermine and alter the expectations of the parties to the contract.[51] Thus, the fellow servant rule appeared. One of the most significant problems involved in the common employment situation was that of liability for the wrongs committed by someone else. In 1691, in *Boson v. Sandford*, John Holt took the position that "whoever employs another is answerable for him, and undertakes for his care to all that make use of him."[52] In Tapping Reeve's influential 1816 treatise on master-servant law, the concept appeared that a "master at his peril, employ servants who are skilful and careful." This was part of the eighteenth-century law of agency. However, the concept of agency as a separate legal category had not broken free from other legal categories. "As late as Blackstone," Holmes noted, "agents appear under the general head of servants, and the first precedents cited for the peculiar law of agents were cases of master and servant."[53] By the nineteenth century this had changed, and in 1839 Joseph Story published a separate treatise, *Commentaries on the Law of Agency.*

Agency law, if Holmes was correct, was buried within the confines of master-servant law of the eighteenth century, and master-servant law, as it appeared in Blackstone, was itself not extensively developed, at least not in the sense of nineteenth-century notions. There was no discussion, for instance, of the problem of common employment or on-the-job injuries. Master-servant law did not really deal with modern industrial labor, but rather with such relationships as master craftsmen, journeymen, and apprentices. The fact that factory labor was largely a development of the nineteenth century explains why injuries caused by the negligence of fellow workers did not engage either English or American judges until the 1830s. Sean Wilentz, a prominent American labor historian, has traced the transformation of workers in New York from incipient craftsmen learning a trade they hoped to enter as independent artisans to increasingly dependent wage laborers.[54]

One additional aspect of vicarious liability that needs to be kept in mind is its place in bailment law. Frederick Wertheim correctly noted that the fellow servant rule "was purely a product of the relationship between master and servant." In the preceding sentence he had stated that "slaves were property, accordingly, slave hirings were governed by the law of bailments, which is unrelated to the law of master and servant." This is an important insight, but one element needs polishing. Although slave hires were treated as bailment contracts and the fellow servant rule was a product of master-servant relationships, it would be an error to think that there was no connection between the principles of bailment law and master-servant law. The main point of contact was precisely the notion of vicarious liability. As Jones put it in his 1781 treatise on bailments, "the negligence of a *servant*, acting *by his master's express or implied order*, is the negligence of the *master*." This was an axiom that flowed "from natural reason, good morals, and sound policy."[55]

Could any of this apply to a hired slave who was injured because of the negligence of a coworker? Slave hires had posed some conceptual problems for judges, but by the 1830s they were routinely treated not on the basis of analogies to leases of lands, for example, but as a species of bailment. There are points in bailments law that need to be kept clear in analyzing the ways Southern judges could have used that law to assign liability in cases of injuries to hired slaves caused by the negligence of people with whom they worked. It is important to remember the two essential forms of bailment of hire (aside from a hiring to carry someone from one place to another): the hire of a thing and the hire of service or labor. Most commentators treat the latter as a contract with someone to perform some labor on personal property delivered to him or her. It is the delivery of the property for a purpose that makes the contractual arrangement a bailment.[56] The common example was the delivery of cloth to a taylor to make clothing. The craftsman was bound to exercise skill in working the cloth and was liable for unskillfulness or "ordinary negligence" if damage resulted to the property. If the craftsman allowed an apprentice to work on the cloth and the apprentice did it negligently, the rule was that the craftsman was liable. In such a case master-servant law and bailment law would overlap. There is no reason to believe, however, that anyone would see much of an analogy between this class of bailment contracts and the hiring of a slave. Even though a slave was property, the bailment of a slave was not for the purpose of having the bailee "work" on the slave. It was to use the labor of the slave. Incidentally, there was one notable exception, but I have never seen it in a legal forum. That was the case of the deposit of a slave with a slave breaker, as was done with Frederick Douglass.[57] Nonetheless, in most instances it would take a large intellectual leap to turn a bailment for hire for a slave's services into a simple master-servant contract. As long as the hiring of a slave was treated as the bailment of a thing, it would be difficult to treat the *thing* as a potential coworker or fellow servant.

There was still the problem of allocating risks and liabilities. Many commentators have been sidetracked by the discussion of "negligence." The reason is twofold and interrelated. The first element is that it is too easy to forget that slave hire cases were analyzed in terms of bailment law by the time the fellow servant doctrine was introduced. The second is that many slave cases involving the applicability of the fellow servant rule consider the problems of slaves as persons. This has led some to regard these cases outside the context of ordinary bailment law, but that is misleading. In the context of bailment law, discussions of the slave's humanity can be seen, at least sometimes, as linked not to the applicability of the fellow servant rule (could a slave be a fellow servant who might complain or walk away?), but to the issue of what constituted negligence in the free coworker. Because a slave was a human being the question naturally arose, how far did the duty of the free coworker to control the slave extend, especially one with direct authority over the slave, before failure to control amounted to negligence?

Most of the dispute among scholars has focused on the analyses of two cases, *Scudder v. Woodbridge* (Georgia, 1846) and *Ponton v. Wilmington & Weldon Railroad Co.* (North Carolina, 1858). Both originated as tort actions, but the results were markedly different. In *Scudder* the facts were that Ned, a carpenter, had been hired to make a trip from Savannah to St. Mary's. During the journey Ned was drowned when he got entangled in a waterwheel trying to help free the boat. Woodbridge sued Scudder as the owner of the boat for the loss caused by the "carelessness and mismanagement of the captain of the boat, who was employed by the owner." Judge William B. Fleming charged the jury that Scudder was liable if the slave was lost because of the want of skill or negligence of those employed on the boat, the *Ivanhoe*. The jury found for the slaveowner.[58]

The reasoning of counsel and the judgment of the court, given by Lumpkin, are not always clear. At no point in his argument for the boat owner did counsel mention that the person killed was a slave. Most of his presentation was a summary of cases involving free persons and a discussion of policy with no reference to the status of the worker, whether free or slave. The only mention of Ned was this: "in this case no negligence has been proven on the part of the plaintiff's agent, save that of the defendant's own boy, who was killed. He was told not to go into the wheel-house; and again, to come out of it. He did wrong in going into a place of danger, and then not coming out when ordered." Counsel tried two lines of defense. One was that the fellow servant rule ought to apply and excuse Scudder. Liability for the negligence of "servants" or "agents" applied only to injuries to strangers, and that was not the slave in this case. The second point was that the only negligence involved was that of the victim. Counsel on the other side denied the applicability of the fellow servant rule on two grounds. One was that the position of a slave was not like that of a free worker: "complain they dare not, and leave they cannot." But the second ground was the "main objection." It was that the cases establishing the fellow servant rule involved injuries to persons, and this one concerned a fatal injury to property. "No one can doubt," he continued, "if I hire my servant to another, he is bound to take ordinary care of him, and he is responsible if he does not take such care, by employing incompetent agents to superintend the common employment. It is a case of bailment." He was also appalled at the notion that the owner had to turn to a coworker, especially given the facts of the case. "Are we to be insulted," he asked, "by being told to resort to a remedy against the black fireman! who is not responsible *civiliter*, and ought not to be responsible when placed, perhaps against his will, in a position which he has no science to fill?"[59]

Lumpkin did not produce a model of clarity. He did accept the fellow servant rule insofar as "*free white agents*" were concerned. What followed is less plain. Interest to the "owner, and humanity to the slave" forbade application of the rule to slaves "*ex necessitate rei.*" He followed this with an extensive commentary on the position of slaves to show that "they have nothing to do but silently serve out their appointed time, and take their lot in the mean while in submitting to whatever risks and dangers are incident to the employment."[60]

This is clear enough, but the final paragraph is less so. "A large portion of the employees at the South," he began, "are either slaves or free persons of color, wholly irresponsible, *civiliter*, for their neglect or malfeasance." The engineer of the *Ivanhoe* was a free black. Why a free black could not be held civilly liable, at least in theory, is not at all understandable. Perhaps the problem for Lumpkin rested on the social position of free blacks as much as anything, as he applied the fellow servant rule to free whites only. He concluded:

> The *restriction of this rule is indispensable to the welfare of the slave.* In almost every occupation, requiring combined effort, the employer necessarily in-trusts it to a variety of agents. Many of those are destitute of principle, and bankrupt in fortune. Once let it be promulgated that the owner of negroes hired to the numerous navigation, railroad, mining and manufacturing com-

panies which dot the whole country, and are rapidly increasing—I repeat, that for any injury done to this species of property, let it be understood and settled that the *employer* is not liable, but that the owner must look for compensation to the *co-servant* who occasioned the mischief, and I hesitate not to affirm, that the life of no *hired* slave would be safe.

Lumpkin, in other words, followed the argument of the counsel for the slave-owner. Whether he meant to treat the case as a bailment (he did not use the phrase) is not clear. If he viewed the case as a matter of bailment, as counsel had argued, it is difficult to see how he could regard the hiring of a slave as creating the slave an "agent" of the hirer in any sense of the notion of agency. "*Free white agents*" were a separate category in his analysis. Nonetheless, Lumpkin did refer to the destitute "agent" as a "*co-servant*." Did this imply that he was thinking of slaves and free blacks as coservants in a legal sense? We do not know.[61]

A number of scholars have commented on *Scudder*. Tushnet argued that Lumpkin followed a tort rather than a contract analysis because it "promoted vigilance and reduced the costs of superintendence." Moreover, the problem of "humanity to the slave" precluded Lumpkin from seeing that a contract rationale might protect the slave and the owner by "increasing the rental price or by demanding that the hirer act as an insurer." Others have agreed with some of his observations, but not all. Paul Finkelman is the most forceful in rejecting the notion that Lumpkin could have been concerned about humanity to slaves as persons. Moreover, and correctly I believe, he emphasized the racist element in Lumpkin's approach. The case was not simply one of slave versus free, it was black versus white. This last is a point that Wertheim, in an otherwise fine analysis, missed. He suggested that Lumpkin had applied the fellow servant rule only to "free workers" without noting that it was to "*free white workers.*"[62]

Quite different perceptions emerge from an analysis of the other most frequently examined case of the slave as fellow servant, *Ponton v. Wilmington & Weldon Railroad Co.* (North Carolina, 1858). An action was brought for the value of a slave killed because of the negligence of a railroad employee. A freight train and a passenger train collided at night near Joyner's Station, North Carolina. The freight train, on which the slave was employed as a brakeman, had left the main track and entered a turnout. Another employee at Joyner's Station was supposed to adjust the switches, but he failed to do so, and the passenger train entered the turnout where it crashed into the freight train and crushed the slave.[63]

"The distinction was put," Judge Ruffin observed, "upon the difference between a hired freeman and a slave, the former being competent to make what terms he chooses in his contract and to leave the service, if dangerous, at his will, while the latter, by the hiring, becomes the property, temporarily, of the hirer, with no will of his own and is beyond the control of the owner." It was a distinction that Ruffin considered unsound. Had the person to benefit by the recovery been a slave it might have been, but the action was for the benefit of the owner. And, according to

Ruffin, the master had the power "by stipulations in the contract, to provide for the responsibility of the bailee for exposing the slave to extraordinary risks, or for his liability to the owner for all losses arising from any cause."[64]

Counsel for the owner of the slave had relied on *Jones v. Glass*, but Ruffin distinguished the cases:

> But that was not the case of fellow-servants, in the ordinary sense of the term. It is true that the overseer and the slave were both serving the same person, but in very different capacities; the slave, there, not only worked with the overseer, but under him, as the superintendent and agent of the master to control and punish the slave, and thus, in a peculiar degree, representing the master in his authority over the hired slave; and, therefore, upon the common principle of bailments the master was responsible to the owner for the injury done to the slave by the overseer while in the service of the employer, as he would have been had the injury resulted from the act of the hirer himself.

Was the case before the court one in which the slave was a fellow servant in the "ordinary sense of the term"? This can be teased out of the opinion by Ruffin. His primary analysis was not in terms of master-servant relationships. It was a contractual analysis based on the bailment of the slave to the railroad company. But that was the employment of property; it was the bailment of a *thing* and not a bailment for services or labor in the sense of a *locatio operis*. Because that was so, it is difficult to see how he could have logically applied the fellow servant rule. He began his opinion with an examination of the English case, *Priestly v. Fowler*. The principle point there was that the servant "undertakes, as between him and his master, to run all the ordinary risks of the service, which includes the risk of the negligence of a fellow-servant, acting in the discharge of his duty as servant of the common master; but while the servant undertakes those risks he has a right to require that the master shall take reasonable care to protect him by associating him only with persons of ordinary skill and care." By the end of his opinion Ruffin had come full circle. He noted that the action in *Ponton* could not be maintained, "as there was no want of ordinary care on the part of the company to provide a competent number of persons, fit, or supposed to be fit, to discharge the duties, by the neglect of which the injury arose."[65] What Ruffin had done was to give more content to the notion of ordinary care or diligence in the law of bailment of slaves by bringing into it the rule associated with the fellow servant rule, that is, that the only clear duty of the employer was to engage fit persons. At no point did he directly say that a slave was actually the fellow servant of a free person. It is just as reasonable to read *Ponton* as one of the ordinary bailment of a thing, a slave, as it is to see it as a case of master-servant law.

This has not been the normal analysis. Finkelman, for instance, was puzzled by Ruffin's failure to really examine the applicability of the fellow servant rule to slaves. "He did not delve into the master-slave relationship as other judges had.

Instead, he simply boldly asserted that this case did not involve the slave *per se*, and thus there was no fellow-servant question at all." Finkelman continued: "in *Ponton* Ruffin essentially applied the fellow servant rule, not to the slave, but to the master. In effect, the master became the fellow servant of the railroad. The master could have demanded greater protection in the contract, but he did not."[66] However, this overlooks the fact that the contract in question was not a contract between a master and a prospective servant. It was a bailment contract for the use of a thing.

Tushnet argued that Ruffin dropped the mixed tort-contract analysis used by Judge Shaw in *Farwell* in favor of a contractual analysis alone. One of Tushnet's reasons for saying this was very basic. It was that to provide sufficient superintendence to assure safety in the workplace, employees had to have the right to leave the workplace or notify the employer. "But in a slave setting," Tushnet contended, "that kind of communication posed difficulties." A tort rationale, then, was inappropriate in such a setting, and what remained was a highly commercialized legal rule that paid scant attention to the "sentiment" of the masters. At no point, however, did Tushnet quite say that Ruffin applied or did not apply the fellow servant rule. He stated that Ruffin's analysis differed from Shaw's because he dropped the tort rationale.[67]

Wertheim's interpretation is far closer to Ruffin's intent, but even here the analysis is misleading. First of all, Wertheim asserted that Ruffin did apply the fellow servant rule, whereas I would suggest that he either did not do so or else it is very ambiguous whether or not he did. Wertheim argued that Ruffin intended to force slaveowners to protect themselves contractually rather than creating a "rule of law that distinguished slaves from free men when they were working side by side." It would be "singular," Ruffin had maintained, if a rule were adopted that allowed a slaveowner to recover damages for injuries to his slave when the slave, if he were free, could not recover under the same circumstances. "This argument overlooked," Wertheim countered, "the interstitial nature of bailment law, which had for years provided remedies for slave owners where contracts had been silent. In other words, it was rather late to suggest that the same law had to apply to slaves and to freemen." This is an important insight, but Wertheim did not develop the full implications in terms of understanding *Ponton*. Ruffin did not really overlook bailment law at all. Throughout his earlier work on cases dealing with the hiring of slaves, he had always been one of the few judges especially favorable to hirers, and he had always analyzed the cases in terms of bailment law. He did the same in *Ponton*, and to do so he used the notion of diligence required of employers associated with the fellow servant rule to cut into or explain the fairly strict liability imposed[17] when slaves were hired and used in particularly hazardous jobs. He did not actually treat the case as one of master-servant law.[68]

What is confusing is Ruffin's treatment of *Jones*. In that case the owner was held liable for injuries caused by the overseer. That situation, Ruffin noted, was "not the case of fellow-servants, in the ordinary sense of the term." The relationship between slave and overseer was not that of coemployees even though they were "serving the same person." The problem there was the relationship between the overseer and the slave, and it was not one of equality. But, surely, Ruffin did not intend to suggest that the slave and the free worker on a railroad were on a level of equality? At no point did he do that. His direct reference to the negligent switchman was this: "it results from the principles thus established that the present action cannot be maintained, as there was no want of ordinary care on the part of the company to provide a competent number of persons, fit, or supposed to be fit, to discharge the duties, by the neglect of which the injury arose. There was a man at the switch, or rather for it, who failed of due diligence and caused the damage."[69] In this summary there is no mention whatever of the fact that the injury or the damage was to a person, much less that it was to a coworker, or a coservant, or a slave. The relationship between the slave and the switchman was not relevant to Ruffin's analysis. It is therefore perfectly reasonable to view Ruffin's approach in *Ponton* in the context of bailment law generally and in the context of his own earlier efforts to define the duties and liabilities of hirers of slaves.

One of the crucial questions finessed in *Ponton* was whether a slave could be a coemployee or fellow servant at all. The problem was directly confronted in a Florida case, *Forsyth and Simpson v. Perry* (1853). A slave had drowned trying to carry out an order given him by the mate of the steamboat on which both were employed. Judge Albert G. Semmes saw the law of agency as dispositive. He cited Story's treatise on the subject regarding the point that *respondeat superior* held principals liable to third persons for the "misfeasances, negligences and torts of his agent." The critical qualification had been that liability was to third persons, but not to "different agents." But was the slave an agent, and did the fellow servant rule apply? The rule did not apply because of the relationship between the slaveowner and the bailee and because of the position of the slave. The owner was not in the employment of the steamboat operators, and he was not their agent. Nor was the slave. "The doctrine of agency," Semmes reasoned, is "founded upon reciprocal duties. The slave has none of these. The fact of his being a slave, places him beyond the operation of this law." "Unlike white persons," he continued, "the slave does not, upon entering into the service of another, voluntarily incur the risks and dangers incident to such service. He has no power to guard against them by refusing to incur the peril, or by leaving the service of his employer. He is but a passive instrument in the hands of those under whose control he is placed."[70] The judgment was straightforward:

> In all relations, and in all matters, except as to crimes, the slave is regarded by our law as *property*; and being so considered, the case before us is governed by the law of bailments. The contract of hire in this case, constituting a bailment of the property, and it being reciprocally beneficial to both parties, something more than mere *good faith*, on the part of the bailee, is requisite. The owners of the boat were bound to take ordinary care of the slave, and failing to do so, through their agent, they are responsible for the consequences.[71]

The very nature of slaves and the treatment of slave hires as forms of bailment led to the obvious conclusion. The rules of bailment law applied, and a slave could never be considered the agent of an employer. This was a much clearer formulation of the issues than appeared in either *Scudder* or *Ponton*.

The fact is that it was relatively easy to deal with risk allocation in cases involving the hiring of slaves to work alongside free workers whose negligence might lead to injury to the slave and loss to the master. It would be treated within the contours of a contract of bailment of a thing. Slaves were not free; they could not contract, they could not complain, and they could not walk away. They could not be an "agent" for the purposes of allocating risk, and consequently the fellow servant rule did not apply. This was fully consistent with the notion that the older concept of vicarious liability, *respondeat superior*, did apply and an employer of a slave was liable to the owner if the slave was injured because of the negligence of a free worker. There was obviously no equality of position or status between a free worker, an "agent," and a slave. The labor market in slaves simply produced different legal rules from the free labor market: older legal notions applied.

Essentially the same point emerged three years later in a Kentucky case, *Louisville and Nashville Railroad Co. v. Yandell* (1856). Henry, who had been hired to the railroad to connect cars to the locomotive and attend the brake at the front of the car closest to the engine, had lost most of one leg in an accident caused by the carelessness of another railroad employee. Judge B. Mills Crenshaw for the court held that Henry and the other worker, Craig, were not fellow servants in the sense of ordinary employer-employee law: "A slave may not, with impunity, remind and urge a free white person, who is a co-employee, to a discharge of his duties, or reprimand him for his carelessness and neglect; nor may he, with impunity, desert his post at discretion when danger is impending, nor quit his employment on account of the unskillfulness, bad management, inattention, or neglect of others of the crew." The slave must "stand to his post, though destruction of life or limb may never be so imminent. He is fettered by the stern bonds of slavery—necessity is upon him, and he must hold on to his employment." Despite their humanity, in other words, slaves could not be coworkers with free men. Because they could not, the fellow servant rule had no application, and the case had to be determined by the "well-known principles" used in "the bailment or hiring of slaves."[72]

Two other states also rejected the use of the fellow servant rule: Louisiana in *Howes v. Steamer Red Chief* and South Carolina in *White v. Smith*, both in 1860. The facts in *Howes* were that Tom drowned as the result of an accident while moving freight from one vessel to another moored beside it along Canal Street in New Orleans. Judge Albert Duffel began his analysis with a reference to the force of the *respondeat superior* rule, and he rested not on the code, which was normal in Louisiana jurisprudence, but on Story's treatise on agency. Duffel concluded that the fellow servant rule did not apply. The basic reason was the nature of the contract of hiring. In Louisiana jurisprudence, he noted, there were two forms of hiring, the hiring of a thing and the "letting out of labor or industry." But the latter did not apply to slaves; it was a "contract by which a free person hires his own time and services." Duffel's was essentially a contractual analysis based on the ordinary rules of bailment as well as the master-slave relationship:

> As there could not, from the nature of the case, exist a privity of contract between the slave of the plaintiff and the defendants, it follows that the relations of the slave Tom and the free servants, towards the defendants, and vice versa, were not the same, and must, by the force of the case, be governed by different rules, for it is apparent, that the reasons for the exception made in favor of the master against the action of his servants, can not here be invoked, in as much as the slave is bound to risk his safety in the service of his master, cannot decline any service, still less leave the service, but is wholly, absolutely, and unreservedly under the absolute control, nay caprice of his master.

The free workers aboard the *Red Steamer* were agents of the employer, and the employer therefore was liable to indemnify the slaveowner for the loss of Tom.[73]

Finally, the South Carolina court joined the throng in 1860 in the *White* case. But before that the problem of the fellow servant rule had been considered in *Murray v. South Carolina Railroad Co.* (1841). The case did not involve slaves, but Judge O'Neall in his dissent from the majority's adoption of the fellow servant rule considered the possible application. O'Neall believed that the ordinary master-servant law should apply, and that meant that the employer would be liable for injuries that resulted from the negligence of his employee. The central point for O'Neall was the relationship between the employees. One of the most crucial questions in the fellow servant cases was the precise relationship of the workers to one another. For O'Neall, the facts in *Murray* did not involve workers who were coequals. Rather, an employee was injured while under the supervision of another employee. They were coservants, to be sure, but not equal. One was in command, and that person stood in the place of the employer. The rule O'Neall wanted to apply was the rule of prudence used in the hiring of goods—in other words, he wished to use the norm of a bailment of hire of things to define the liability of the hire of free persons for labor. There was some confusion here, of course, inasmuch as O'Neall was treating the hiring of persons as both a matter of master-servant law and the law of bailment of services. Agency law and labor law were intertwined in his analysis. In any event, the important question for him was this: "Is more favor to be bestowed on a man's goods than on his person?" The answer could be found by "inquiring if the plaintiff, instead of himself, had hired his negro man to the defendants as second fireman, and he had lost his leg by the carelessness of the engineer." The point at issue was, "would not the defendants have been liable?" They would, he noted, or "one section of the law of bailments would be repealed by the Court of Errors. There can be no difference in the law, as applicable to the white man or the slave, in a contract of hiring. Both are capable of self-preservation, and both are capable of wrong and right action; and in the capacity of fireman, both are under the orders of the engineer, and must look to him for safety."[74] O'Neall's fusion of bailment law and labor law was unique among Southern judges. He treated the white free worker in paternalistic terms, not as "equal."

The facts in *White* were that Charles was killed when he fell between a moving railroad car and a platform. A coemployee, Jackson, had yelled to the slaves on the platform to board the slowly moving train, and Charles had responded. The slaves were under Jackson's authority. F. H. Wardlaw, for the court, simply held that Charles and Jackson were "not employed together." *Murray*, he concluded, "was not intended to make a slave such a representative of the master in work done by the slave in common with other hirelings, as to constitute the master a co-employee with the hirelings." Wardlaw did not even consider the possibility that the slave could be an agent of the common employer. He cast the question in the form of the slave's possible representation of the master. It was an odd construction, but it was as far as he went on this point. Still, he did acknowledge that the slave was "a man, wilful and intelligent, and capable of defeating all proper care on the part of those who have him in charge." In short, the bailee of slaves would not be liable for "their loss, where it is the result of their own heady misconduct or negligence."[75] Here there was no strict liability based on the notion of absolute control, nor was there any argument that the bailee or hirer of a slave had the kind of duty to control that Lumpkin imposed in Georgia.

No Southern jurist, in sum, applied the fellow servant rule to the case of hired slaves. Whether Ruffin did or intended to perhaps is an open question. What is clear enough is that all of the judges analyzed the problem in terms of the law of bailments of things, and that they expressly rejected the notion of agency in slaves. How they might decide a particular case, of course, and the standard they might employ to find negligence differed widely. Usually it depended on the individual judge's perception of slaves on one side and the power and duties of masters on the other. Lumpkin represented one pole: the duty to control irresponsible, ignorant blacks was acute. Other judges placed greater weight on the responsibility of slaves to preserve themselves even while emphasizing that "complain they dare not, leave they can not."

III

Slaves as Persons

7

Southern Law and the
Homicides of Slaves

The evil is not that laws are wanting, but that they

cannot be enforced.

GEORGE STROUD, *Sketch of the Laws* (1827)

"Killing a slave," wrote Frederick Douglass, "or any colored person, in Talbot County, Maryland, is not treated as a crime, either by the courts or the community."[1] Goodell claimed that he was unable "to ascertain a single instance in which a slave owner has been convicted or even prosecuted for the murder of his own slave."[2] Evidence from slaveowners supports these impressions. On February 19, 1849, for example, Thomas B. Chaplin of coastal South Carolina recorded a ghastly case. He had sat that day on an inquest jury looking into the death of Roger. Roger, a "complete cripple," because of "impertinence" had been "placed in an open outhouse, the wind blowing through a hundred cracks, his clothes wet to the waist, without a single blanket & in freezing weather, with his back against a partition, shackles on his wrists, & chained to a bolt in the floor and a chain around *his neck*, the chain passing through the partition behind him, & fastened on the other side." The next morning he was found "dead, *choked, strangled*, frozen to death, *murdered*. The verdict of the jury, was that Roger came to his death by choking by a chain put around his neck by his master—*having slipped from the position in which he was placed*." Chaplin was dutifully outraged, but no criminal action was brought.[3]

One of the most important issues in the lives of slaves and masters alike was the degree of power of governance (which meant the use of force) society left in the hands of slaveowners. A related, but different concern in a slave society resting on race was that of the authority society granted third parties to use violence against a slave. The starkest questions arose when the slave died as a result of the force used. Slaveowners, of course, possessed the right, even the duty, to punish and control their slaves on their plantations. This was the system Eugene Genovese called the "complementary system of justice" to that of the public forum. But there were limits even for owners, and there were limits on how far society would indulge the violence of third parties. To what extent, then, was the power of whites, owners, and third parties, restrained—were the lives of slaves under the protection of the law?

One West Indian planter declared that slaves there were not under the protection of English common law.[4] Was this also true in the South? It depended on time and place. It depended on who the killer was, as well as on local values, attitudes, and fears. It depended, finally, on whether the redress sought was criminal or civil and on legal notions. In the case of slaveowners civil remedies were of no use, whereas they would be in cases of third parties (including overseers and hirers as well as those with no direct claim to the services of the slave)—a subject I have set aside for the next chapter. This chapter focuses on criminal remedies for the homicides of slaves whether committed by masters, overseers, hirers, or third parties. Given the importance of the master-slave relationship, however, the heaviest emphasis will be on the authority or power granted masters.

Early English Homicide Law

The English law of homicide incorporated a number of crucial notions: among them were justification, excuse, and mitigation. "In the case of 'justification,'" according to H. L. A. Hart, an English legal philosopher, "what is done is regarded as something which the law does not condemn, or even welcomes," such as killing in self-defense. In the case of excuse what was done was "deplored," but the results were "unintentional" because of coercion, insanity, and so on. Mitigation, the third notion, concerned the amount of punishment and not the question of guilt or innocence. Conviction and punishment remained, but there might have been a "good reason for administering a less severe penalty." Mitigation could be either formal or informal. The latter occurred when a maximum penalty was set and the judge was given discretion to set a lesser one if the circumstances warranted it. Mitigation was formal when the "mitigating factor" always put the offense "into a separate category carrying a lower maximum penalty." The most prominent example was the notion of "provocation" in homicide cases, which reduced the crime from murder to manslaughter.[5]

Murder, Coke wrote in the early seventeenth century, "is when a man of sound memory, and of the age of discretion, unlawfully killeth within any County of the Realm any reasonable creature *in rerum natura* under the kings peace, with malice fore-thought, either expressed by the party, or implied by law."[6] Later Coke observed that "there is no difference between murder, & manslaughter, but that the one is upon malice forethought, and the other upon a sudden occasion: and therefore is called Chance-medley."[7]

Another possibility was killing by misadventure or misfortune. According to Michael Dalton, in *The Countrey Justice*, a widely used treatise on justices of the peace in colonial Virginia, this was "when any person doing of a lawfull thing, without any evill intent, happenth to kill a man." His examples were these: "As if a Scholemaster, in reasonable manner beating his scholler, for correction only: or a man correcting his child, or servant in reasonable manner; and the scholler, childe, or servant happen to die thereof, this is homicide by misadventure."[8] Those with authority in a hierarchical social order had the right and the duty to "correct" their charges.

Dalton's definitions of murder and manslaughter were similar to those of Coke. Dalton added the following point, which was buried deep within his discussion not of manslaughter but of homicide by misadventure: "but if a man doing of an unlawfull act, though without any evill intent, and he happenth, by chance, to kill a man, this is felonie, *viz.* manslaughter at the least, if not murder, in regard the thing hee was doing, was unlawfull."[9] Conceptually, it was possible to view a fatal correction of a servant that was not "reasonable" as unlawful and thus manslaughter if it was done without an evil intention; otherwise it might be murder. But Dalton did not put it this way—he separated the remarks by several paragraphs, and his examples of "unlawful" do not indicate that he made this connection.[10] The ideas associated with the common law of manslaughter during the seventeenth century were not modern.

An important step came in the early eighteenth century with Sir William Hawkins's work, *A Treatise of the Pleas of the Crown.* Manslaughter was a homicide without malice; it was "such killing as happens either on a sudden Quarrel" or "in the Commission of an unlawful Act, without any deliberate intention of doing any Mischief at all." In a section on homicides by misadventure, he stated: "yet if such Persons in their Correction be so barbarous as to exceed all Bounds of Moderation, and thereby cause the Party's Death, they are guilty of Manslaughter at the least; and if they make use of an Instrument improper for Correction, and apparently indangering the Party's Life, as an iron Bar, or Sword, &c. or kick him to the Ground, and then stamp on his Belly and kill him, they are guilty of Murder."[11] What was implicit but separated in Dalton was clarified and joined in Hawkins.

Unless modified by statute, or unless people believed that the common law did not apply to those in bondage, these were the legal concepts that would frame the responses of Southern whites to the killing of slaves before the Revolution.

Colonial Statutes

One of the first statutes on slavery was a Virginia law of 1669. Its title, "An act about the casuall killing of slaves," is arresting. The lawmakers began with an obvious problem. Slaves could not be punished by the extension of their time in servitude so that their "obstinacy" could only be suppressed by violence. The law provided that if slaves resisted their master or anyone correcting them on the order of the master and "by the extremity of coercion" should "chance to die," the death would not be considered a felony. Rather, the master or other person lawfully administering the correction would be acquitted "since it cannot be presumed that prepensed malice (which alone makes murder felony) should induce any man to destroy his own estate."[12]

This law did not concern third parties who killed slaves, even slaves who might be "insolent" to them. Moreover, manslaughter was omitted. Slaveowners would not view a "correction" as a "Chancemedley" that occurred when two fought on a sudden and one died. It is little wonder that the Virginia burgesses would be loath to prosecute a slaveowner for murder if he killed a slave when the slave was in the act of resistance. To do so could undermine the master-slave relationship. What was left, if Dalton's categories were influential, was to regard the death as a homicide by misadventure or to excuse the death altogether. The burgesses chose to excuse it. Legal notions helped predetermine their choice, a choice based on a firm determination to break the "obstinacy" of slaves and to assure a docile workforce. In 1705 the disparate parts of the emerging slave code were brought together. If anyone with authority correcting a slave killed him "in such correction, it shall not be accounted felony," and the killer would be freed "as if such accident had never happened."[13]

In 1723 the burgesses adopted the last law on the subject before the Revolution. The law provided that there would be no punishment or prosecution if a slave died "by reason of any stroke or blow given, during his or her correction." Owners now could punish to the point of killing a slave even if the punishment was for picking trash tobacco rather than resisting authority. The protection of the common law was removed, but not totally. There could still be a murder indictment if one lawful and credible witness would swear on oath that the homicide resulted "wilfully, maliciously, or designedly."[14] The last part of the law stated that any provocation by a slave to any person would excuse his killing.[15] Under the common law as it had developed by the early eighteenth century, it ought to have been manslaughter and possibly murder if someone exceeded "all Bounds of Moderation, and thereby cause the Party's Death" during a "correction." By 1723 Virginians rejected that.

Neither Maryland nor Delaware made statutory changes in the English common law of homicide. It was not until 1773 that North Carolina enacted a statute on the killing of slaves. This was vetoed because of procedural problems, but a similar bill was accepted the next year. It punished the willful murder of a slave, but only with imprisonment for one year, and if the killer was not the master, he was to pay the owner the value of the slave.[16]

South Carolina, like Virginia, made some important changes in the English law. In 1690 the legislators provided that there would be no legal consequence if a slave died because of punishment from "the owner for running away or other offence." However, "if any one out of wilfulness, wantoness, or bloody mindedness, shall kill a slave," he would be jailed for three months and had to pay the owner of the slave 50 pounds. "Wantoness" and "bloody mindedness" were not terms found in leading English legal treatises. There was no capital murder of slaves in South Carolina.

By 1740, following the Stono Rebellion, the law on slave homicides took the form it would have until 1821.[17] The provision began on a high note: "cruelty is not only highly unbecoming those who profess themselves christians, but is odious in the eyes of all men who have any sense of virtue or humanity." What followed was a modification in the punishments of the common law. Any person who murdered a slave would be fined 700 pounds current money and barred from holding public office. Also, "if any person shall, on a sudden heat or passion, or by undue correction," kill a slave, he should be fined 350 pounds current money.[18]

When the trustees of Georgia considered the introduction of slavery into that colony in the 1740s, they determined that any owner who "wilfully and maliciously Murders Dismembers or Cruelly and Barbarously uses a Negro" would be dealt with under the normal common law rules. As late as 1770, when Georgians adopted the bulk of the South Carolina code of 1740, there were no modifications of the common law.[19]

These were the colonial statutory schemes. Both Virginia and South Carolina made significant changes early, but their laws were different by the mid-eighteenth century. No free person could be executed for killing a slave in South Carolina no matter how grotesque or unjustified the killing might have been. Virginia, on the other hand, left open the possibility—however remote—that anyone, even a slave-owner, could be executed for the homicide of a slave.

Regrettably, the extant records from the colonial period are too sparse to allow more than an impressionistic reconstruction of actual practice. Still, it is worth-while to try to grasp some of the texture so that we can begin to recapture the level of power people conceded to slaveowners and the circumstances, if any, under which they would consider punishing people, including owners, for killing slaves.

Slave Homicides in the Colonial South

During the 1680s the Reverend Samuel Gray of Middlesex County, Virginia, re-ported an "unfortunate accident" to his slave Jack. Jack had been beaten to death. When he reported the incident to authorities, Gray observed that it was "an unfortunate Chance which I would not Should have happened *in my family* for three times his price." That was the end of the matter.[20]

Because of political concerns Frances Wilson was not as lucky. In January 1713/4 Andrew Woodley, a justice of the peace and coroner in Isle of Wight County, met with John Clayton, soon to become the attorney general of Virginia.[21] Woodley informed Clayton that he had heard that Frances Wilson "was suspected to be Guilty of whipping one of her Husbands Slaves to death." Woodley had the body exhumed, an inquest jury returned a judgment, and Woodley sent the report to Williamsburg.[22]

What followed Clayton's return to Williamsburg was a crisis between Governor Alexander Spotswood and the council, as well as the only full-scale trial before 1775 of an owner of a slave for a homicide in colonial Virginia. In the end Clayton felt compelled to explain the case to the Board of Trade in defending the administration against accusations in "a paper" dated February 7, 1715/6. The administration was charged "with Partiality, Injustice, & Destroying the End of Government, In Commanding the Attorney Generall to prosecute a Woman contrary to Law, for the Death of her Slave under a very moderate correction, & cleared both by the Jury's Inquest, & County Court."[23]

The inquest jury finding of November 26, 1713, was that "by hard useage she [the slave Rose] is come to her death & we finding no mortall wound but only stripes." This jury rendered a guarded verdict. It did not say who had inflicted the beating, and it did not find a homicide. Clayton was not satisfied. He told the governor that "it being my opinion, that no Subject has power over the Life of his Slave, . . . , I thought the person suspected to have been the Cause of the death of the sd Slave ought to undergo a Tryall." Clayton proposed that the governor instruct him to write to the county court to inquire into the matter and prosecute according to law. Spotswood did so on February 18, 1713/4.[24]

A month later the county court heard the evidence of Mary Lupo against Frances Wilson. This examination was certified to Clayton, "But the sd Court still declined" to sit. The tenacious Clayton issued a summons to Lupo to appear in April 1714 in Williamsburg before the general court, which consisted of the governor and the royal council.[25]

After Lupo's appearance Clayton "drew an Inditement against the sd Frances Wilson for the murder of the sd Slave." He delivered the indictment to the "Grand Jury in Court," and on the evidence the grand jury found a true bill. It determined that "with a certain Cord" Frances Wilson did "tye & bind" Rose and with a "certain stick" gave to the back part of her body "forty mortal strokes each of the length of three inches & of the breadth of half an inch." From this treatment the grand jurors believed that Rose "then & there instantly dyed." Perhaps this jury was swayed by Governor Spotswood, who informed the Board of Trade that "untill your Lord'ps condemn it, I will dare stand to my Charge given to a Grand Jury here, vizt: that in this Dominion no Master has such a Sovereign Power over his Slave as not /to/be liable to be called to an Account whenever he kills him; that at the same time, the Slave is the Master's Property he is likewise the King's Subject, and that the King may lawfully bring to Tryal all Persons here, without exception, who shall be suspected to have destroyed the Life of his Subject."[26] Following this indictment Clayton had the general court order Wilson to appear in Williamsburg at the October Term, 1714. She appeared, pled not guilty, and was acquitted.

There is substance to the condemnations by scholars,[27] but they do not completely capture the complexity and significance of the trial. After Wilson's plea of not guilty, Samuel Seldon appeared for her and argued that she should not be "molested for the killing the sd Slave." Unhappily, this is all we know. A possible line of argument was that he contended that Rose died as a result of a lawful and moderate correction. The general court ruled that "She ought to be tryed on the sd

Inditement." The law went against Wilson—she was required to stand trial for the murder of her slave, precisely the point Clayton had urged before the governor.[28]

The governor, attorney general, grand jury, and a majority of the council then all agreed that Frances Wilson should stand trial for the murder of her slave. To that extent they agreed that a slave *might* be within the "kings peace." Nevertheless, given the facts and the rules of the common law on deaths by misadventure, or under "moderate correction," the death of Rose did not present the strongest argument. It is hard to avoid the notion that Clayton grabbed the case in order to assert the authority of the Crown and the common law over the planters of Virginia. Frances Wilson was tried within a political context, without which she probably would not have been indicted.

By the mid-eighteenth century the number of slave homicides increased, but most of the alleged killers were overseers or persons without authority over slaves, rather than masters. Some of the defendants were even executed, but not often.[29] In 1729 Andrew Byrn, an overseer, was tried for murder because he had whipped to death a slave under his authority. He was found guilty by a jury and sentenced to hang. The council petitioned the governor, Sir William Gooch, to reprieve him. His pardon was recommended on the ground that he had not intended to cause death. The slave had been a notorious runaway, and Byrn, "transported with anger," had given him "immoderate correction." Governor Gooch appealed to England for a pardon because "the executing of him for this offense may make the slaves very insolent and give them an occasion to condemn their Masters & Overseers, which may be of dangerous Consequence in a Country where the Negroes are so numerous and make the most valuable part of Peoples Estates."[30]

Fourteen years later William Lee, another overseer, was held for killing Will, a slave of Thomas Barber. The events leading to the indictment began on May 2, 1743. Will was a captured runaway. The morning after his return "Barber tied him up and Whipt him a Considerable time" and then sent for Lee, who, under Barber's orders, whipped him some more with a "catt of Nine tails and Cowskin whip." In all he received about two hundred lashes that day. Will throughout the whipping, according to the witness, "behaved himself Very Sullenly and stubbornly" and refused the pleas of "standersby to Submit and beg his Masters Pardon."[31]

The next day Will refused to take his jacket off when demanded by Lee. The overseer hit him with a switch, Will tried to escape, and when caught Lee kicked him in the mouth, stripped him, whipped him again, and then "Washed him in Brine." Barber testified that he ordered Lee to take Will to the smith's and have him "Ironed" to prevent his running away again. When Lee returned late at night, he told Barber's wife that he had had to beat Will five times as much as before in order to get him to the smith's. By the sixth of May the slave was complaining of pain in his stomach and shoulders, and by the tenth he was dead. On this testimony the case was certified for trial in Williamsburg.[32]

Four years later, in Lancaster County, Hannah Crump was ordered taken into custody by the sheriff after a coroner's inquest led to a charge that she had murdered Jenny, a slave belonging to her husband. She was discharged.[33] In 1752 in Westmoreland County William Cox was as fortunate. The evidence was not sufficient to send him on for trial for the "murther of his negro Boy Spencer."[34]

On March 31, 1762, Sarah Scott of Prince William County hit her husband's slave, Davy, twice in the head with a "walking cane or stick." Davy went to a nearby log house where he shortly died. From that point a tangled and suspicious case began to develop. There were charges that Scott's husband, a man of local influence, resorted to intimidation "by various means & unjustifiable methods" to cover up the case. One inquest juror said that no juror had more than a "small Dram of Brandy" before hearing the witnesses.[35] The coroner testified that he and the jury believed that Davy died as the result of an "accidental stroke . . . without any Intention of killing." The judgment of the inquest jury was "accidental Homicide."[36]

In the 1750s William Pitman made numerous appearances before the court in King George County. On the first occasion he and his children, Sarah and Isaac, were the plaintiffs in a civil suit. The case was dismissed, but it was only the beginning of a series of adverse actions.[37] On April 21, 1775, sixteen years after he first appeared in the records, the *Virginia Gazette*—in the sole account of the incident—noted that William Pitman had "justly incurred the penalties of the law" for the murder of his slave. The newspaper editorialized that his story ought "to be a warning to others to treat their slaves with moderation, and not give way to unruly passions, that may bring them to an ignominious death, and involve their families in their unhappy fate." Pitman had been "in liquor" and in the "heat of passion" when he "tied his poor negro boy by the neck and heels, beat him most cruelly with a large grape vine, and then stamped him to death." The witnesses against William Pitman were his son and daughter.[38] Pitman was a brutish, contentious man whose own children would not accept quietly his homicidal violence toward a slave.

Had Goodell gone deeper into Southern records he might have found such cases, but that does not mean that his perception was without force. In 1773 an anonymous writer excoriated a certain "R. M." from Amelia County. "R. M." allegedly had been "for several Years, wantonly, cruelly, and inhumanly" dripping with the "Blood of his miserable Slaves." The writer charged that in the preceding summer "R. M." had brutally beaten one of his slave women. She had fled and when caught and returned to him, he "not fully satiated with the Blood of her Brethren, tied her up and tortured her to Death." The author then queried: "Were a Stranger to come here, and be told that the Perpetrator of such Deeds remains unpunished, would he not suppose that there did not exist a Law for bringing the Murderer to Justice?" But, the writer noted, there was a law of Virginia "making the wilful Murder of Negroes a capital crime, and Blood to go for Blood."[39] R. M. was never tried as was William Pitman. A tentative identification of the man by Philip J. Schwarz suggests one possible reason. If R. M. was Robert Munford Sr., he was a powerful local figure who had served as a burgess for Amelia Country from 1767 to 1771.[40]

An even more sinister reason R. M. escaped might have been that those who controlled the strings of power in Amelia County were moved less by Munford's power, or by corruption, than by the view condemned in a stirring charge to a grand jury in North Carolina in 1771 by Chief Justice Martin Howard. Howard was upset by a recent instance where a white had been indicted for the murder of a slave, but the grand jury had returned a no bill. He thought that the jurors had acted on the belief "THAT IT IS NOT MURDER FOR A WHITE MAN TO KILL A NEGRO SLAVE." This was unacceptable. "Excepting the fruits of his labour, which belong to the master," Howard declared, "a slave retains all the rights of subjects under civil government that are NATURALLY UNALIENABLE: Of this kind is self-defence, and personal safety from violence. No one has a right to take away his life without being punished for it." If, he concluded, "a negro slave is a reasonable creature, it must be murder in any one that shall feloniously slay him."[41]

Throughout the period some colonists, but not all, had been able to persuade themselves of this. The experience in Maryland, although thin, suggests that in the absence of a statute modifying the common law, people were reluctant to deal with the killers of slaves. I have found only one case where a person might have been tried for the homicide of a slave in that colony. In July 1696 Ann Smith, "Spinster," was "indicted Tryed and Convicted for murthering a Negro Boy." Because most blacks were slaves, it is likely that the victim was a slave. Despite the conviction, however, Ann Smith was not executed. The court added, "Reprieved, but that the thing be kept private . . . untill She has made her Speach at the place of Execution, understanding She has Something which burthens her Conscience to discover, which she deferrs till then."[42]

As in Virginia, more cases occurred in Maryland by the mid-eighteenth century, but in Maryland none ended in trials. In March 1761 the *Maryland Gazette* referred to an incident in Prince Georges County where an overseer beat a slave to death but there was no indictment. The paper commented: "*What a pity it is, that* INHUMANITY *should be a necessary ingredient in the composition of a* GOOD OVERSEER." Then in April 1762 the *Gazette* noted that the escaped overseer of the slaves of Nicholas Dorsey gave one of them "under his Care, such an unmerciful and barbarous Flagellation" that the slave died.[43]

The story from South Carolina is similar in one respect. The number of cases rose by the few decades before the outbreak of the Revolution. Because of the statutory changes, no one could be executed in South Carolina, so it is not surprising that there were trials in that colony. Between 1768 and 1770 the colonial press noted four convictions for the homicide of slaves. The results in the trials of Robert Hunter, Daniel Price, George Roberts, and Gilbert Campbell were identical. All were fined 350 pounds after they were found guilty of killing slaves in "sudden heat and passion."[44]

What is remarkable is that anyone was tried and punished for the homicide of a slave, either their own or someone else's. The colonial world was a cruel world. In the 1760s, for instance, the *Maryland Gazette* complained about bodies floating in the bay around Annapolis. Dead seamen were being thrown overboard and contaminating the harbor.[45] Earlier, the *South Carolina Gazette* had described the suicide of Charles Lowndes in that colony. "After having shav'd and dress'd himself," the article noted, "he laid down on the Ground, with a loaden Pistol in each Hand, he put one close to his temple and blew out his Brains, which were found at a little Distance all in one heap, his Scull being split in two."[46]

Two of the more famous diaries from colonial Virginia show similar hard-boiled attitudes toward suffering and death. William Byrd II's diary for 1709–12 is filled with the stultifying presence of sickness and death. On January 24, 1710, he recorded, "I had my father's grave opened to see him but he was so wasted there was not anything to be distinguished. I ate fish for dinner. In the afternoon the company went away and I took a walk about the plantation. I said my prayers . . . I had good health, good thoughts, and good humor, thanks be to God Almighty." The diary kept by Byrd's onetime son-in-law, Landon Carter of Sabine Hall, in the last decades before the Revolution is also revealing. His slaves, for example, were frequently the victims of disease. Page after page refers to vomits, purges, bleedings, worms, bile, and death.[47]

As for "cruelty," both diaries are replete with evidence of severe whippings. In the spring of 1712 Byrd had two fights with his wife over the punishment of household slaves. The following scene speaks for itself: "My wife caused Prue to be whipped violently notwithstanding I desired not, which provoked me to have Anaka whipped likewise who had deserved it much more, on which my wife flew into such a passion that she hoped she would be revenged of me." However, in the evening Byrd and his wife were reconciled, and he "gave her a flourish in token of it." About a month before Byrd had had another quarrel over the correction of Jenny. His wife was "beating her with tongs."[48]

Carter thought he avoided such barbarism. His diary reveals much evidence of his paternalistic concern for his slaves. Yet in January 1757 he became so frustrated by his "lazy threshers" that he "ordered them Correction which they took three days running." His exasperation with two of his slaves who drove some cattle through a marsh where they got mired down and died led to this observation: "When people can do this notwithstanding they have a plain level main road to be sure correction can never be called severity."[49]

As long as such harsh views about death and suffering were not softened, it would take extraordinary brutality or some special circumstances (such as the political objectives of Clayton and Spotswood to control the planters) to bring the killer of a slave before the courts. But by the late colonial period certain events tended to change attitudes. One of these was the growth of distinct Afro-American communities. Sex ratios were coming closer to parity, and slave families were developing.[50] Slavery was becoming "domesticated," and the blacks themselves seemed less "outlandish" and more human to the whites. Moreover, and of critical significance, enlightenment humanism, liberal capitalism, and evangelicalism, with their greater emphasis on the ultimate importance and dignity of the individual, were spreading at the same time. In Southside Virginia, for instance, the Meherrin Baptists openly opposed cruelty in the whipping of slaves and even tried to discipline a member in 1772 for mistreating his slaves. This was a far cry from the accommodationism of early Anglicanism in Virginia when Commissary James Blair spent as much time ensuring that the clergy became slaveowners in order to influence other slaveowners as he did ministering to the slaves or working to ameliorate their lot. During the 1760s and 1770s Quakers moved against slavery within the fellowship, and evangelicals in general began to raise questions about it. The capitulation of the Methodists to the proslavery position came after the Revolution, not before.[51]

The late colonial world was filled with tension and uncertainty about the institution of slavery in general and the treatment of the slaves in particular. It was a climate, despite the harshness of that world, in which it became more and more possible to try and punish whites for killing slaves. The only early indictment, though arising in part because of the political needs of the royal administrators, clearly stated the basic principle. While masters possessed considerable power, Spotswood contended, slaves were still within the king's peace. The record shows that colonials were ambivalent about that. Still, some people were fined for killing slaves in "sudden heat and passion" in South Carolina, although there is no evidence that they were owners, and a small number of people were executed for the homicides of slaves in Virginia. Others faced trials or at least preliminary examinations. Slaves were not always killed with impunity. One legal problem, however, was whether slaves came under the protection of the common law, or whether they were protected only when there were statutes. Chief Justice Howard in North Carolina argued that they were protected by the common law, but whether other jurists in that colony agreed is not at all clear. Nor, except for people like Clayton and Spotswood, is it clear for Virginia. The indictments and executions there may have been under the Virginia statutory scheme, and the fines in South Carolina surely were under the 1740 statute. There were no apparent indictments or trials in Maryland or Delaware. No extant records show whether Georgia ever tried a white for the homicide of a slave in the colonial period.

Slavery, of course, was a violent social order and the colonial world harsh. Slaves were sometimes killed without any legal consequences for the killer, but not always, and not only overseers, hirers, or poor whites faced trial. On rare occasions masters themselves were tried or faced preliminary examinations, and in at least one instance a master was executed for the murder of his slave.

Post-Revolutionary Constitutional and Legal Changes

After the Revolution a growing "humanitarian sensibility" led to changes in parts of the law of homicide when applied to slaves. People were moved by a regard for the individual,[52] and they were increasingly sensitive to human suffering. One form this took was the drive to eliminate corporal punishment for sailors;[53] another was the campaign against capital punishment.[54] It also spilled over into a greater regard for the lives of slaves. State after state, whether through constitutions, judicial decisions, or statutes, extended greater legal security to slaves. Whether the practice followed theory is another question.

Four states included a provision in their constitutions. Georgia's constitution of 1798 provided: "Any person who shall maliciously dismember or deprive a slave of life shall suffer such punishment as would be inflicted in case the like offence had been committed on a free white person, and on the like proof, except in case of insurrection by such slave, and unless such death should happen by accident in giving such slave moderate correction."[55] Excusing the death of slaves who died under a "moderate correction" has been castigated by scholars.[56] It was, however, deeply rooted in the common law of homicide when applied to those in positions of subordination, such as wives, children, and servants. Infamous it was, unique to slaves it was not.

Following Georgia's model were Alabama, largely settled by Georgians, in 1819;[57] Missouri, in 1820; and Texas, where Alabamians had some influence (for instance, a chief justice of Alabama, Lipscomb, moved to Texas and became the chief justice of Texas),[58] in 1845. But there were some differences. Alabama's constitution used Georgia's language but omitted the reference to "moderate correction." Missouri did not mention insurrection or moderate correction, and Texas adopted the provision of Alabama.

Notable statutory changes in the late eighteenth century occurred in Virginia, North Carolina, and Tennessee. In 1788 Virginia repealed the law of 1723;[59] thereafter those persons indicted for the murder of a slave and convicted of manslaughter could be punished. In 1791 North Carolina made the willful killing of a slave a murder, unless the slave was killed in resisting or he died under a moderate correction. The homicide was to be punished the same as if the victim were white. The reason was that the 1774 law on the killing of a slave "however wanton, cruel and deliberate, is only punishable in the first instance by imprisonment and paying the value thereof to the owner; which distinction of criminality between the murder of a white person and one who is equally an human creature, but merely of a different complexion, is disgraceful to humanity and degrading in the highest degree to the laws and principles of a free, christian and enlightened country."[60] In 1799 Tennessee adopted a law similar to North Carolina's. The law did not apply to the killing of "any slave in the act of resistance to his lawful owner or master, or any slave dying under moderate correction."[61]

When Louisiana adopted its black code in 1806, it provided that anyone willfully killing his or her own slave or the slave of another would be tried and condemned in accordance with the laws of the territory. After that law there came a spate of statutes between 1816 and the late 1820s, at the outset of the social upheaval known as the Age of Reform. Georgia's law of 1816 provided that "in all cases the killing

[of] . . . a slave or person of color shall be put upon the same footing of criminality as the killing [of] . . . a white man or citizen." Yet it was justifiable homicide to kill a slave in revolt or one who resisted a legal arrest. A year later North Carolina declared that killing a slave "shall partake of the same degree of guilt, when accompanied with the like circumstances, that homicide does at common law." South Carolina made the murder of a slave a capital crime in 1821. Killing a slave in "sudden heat and passion" was punishable by a $500 fine and six months in jail.[62] Alabama provided two degrees of murder of slaves. First-degree murder was equivalent to a murder at common law. Second-degree murder occurred if anyone "having the right to correct such slave or slaves, shall cause the death of the slave by . . . barbarous or inhuman whipping or beating, or by any other cruel or inhuman treatment, although without intention to kill, or shall cause the death of any such slave or slaves by the use of an instrument in its nature calculated to produce death, though without intention to kill."[63]

Whatever the variations the trend was clear. Unless slaves resisted or died under a moderate correction for some misconduct, their killing usually would be placed on a level with the homicide of whites. This brought slaves within the protection of the law while it accommodated the law to the subordinate status of the slave. It also meant that the "good slave" of Seneca and St. Paul would receive a measure of legal protection,[64] whereas the recalcitrant one would receive less or none at all. It was a partial amelioration that represented an attempt to legitimize the social order by "rewarding" obedience from the lower order. Even this, however, had some opposition. The old attitudes reflected in the South Carolina law of 1740 or the Virginia laws, for instance, were not completely gone. In 1829 some of the leading planters of Christ Church Parish just outside of Charleston petitioned the legislature to repeal the law of 1821. Prior to that year "the slaves of this part of South Carolina were in every respect more obedient and better servants, and infinitely more trust-worthy and faithful than they have been subsequently." Despite the claim of those who supported the law that their motives were ones of "great humanity," these planters charged that they were not really "practical Southern Planters, otherwise they would have foreseen that the law would be useless, and even hurtful to those whom it professes to protect." According to them, the persons who adopted the law were not even "Southern Legislators, for if they had been, they would have known that *changing the nature of the penalties in the case of negroes*—that inflicting the punishment of death on a white man for killing a slave, *who is a property, instead of exacting a fine for the loss of that property,* was placing the white inhabitants on a footing which would not be admitted by Juries of our countrymen, and hence that the penalty would never be inflicted in any case however enormous."[65] Kenneth Stampp quoted a South Carolina jury foreman whose views were compatible: he "would not convict the defendant, or any other white person, of murdering a slave."[66]

According to the Christ Church Parish planters, however, the law of 1821 was worse than ineffectual. Its real effect was to "produce upon the part of the negro, such acts of violence, as call immediate vengeance down upon him." The law impressed upon the minds of the slaves "that they are now on a different footing as regards their owners and the whites, from what they formerly were, a footing approaching nearer to a state of emancipation from their authority, and of course to a state of unrestrained liberty and licentiousness." This could change only with a repeal of the law of 1821 and the adoption of one declaring any slave absent thirty days "from his work without his owners permission" to be an outlaw who could be killed.[67] By the nineteenth century such attitudes were rarely expressed openly, and the plea of the planters fell on deaf ears. Despite the statutes, of course, the real test was in their implementation.

Appellate Practice

One of the first significant cases was *State v. Boon* (North Carolina, 1801). Boon was indicted under the 1791 law but escaped punishment because of ambiguities in that law. An argument for the state was that the willful and malicious killing of a slave was a common law murder and did not come only under the terms of the 1791 law. According to Judge Hall, English common law was of little use because slavery did not exist in England. Pure slavery was a social condition in which "an absolute power is given to the master, over the life and fortune of the slave." Hall noted that the power of masters could be restrained and they could be punished for killing, but this was the result only of positive law, by which he meant statutes.[68]

Two of the remaining three judges, Samuel Johnston and John Louis Taylor, disagreed. Johnston argued that the murder of a slave was the same as the murder of a white person under the right circumstances. It was, in fact, more despicable. It was a "crime of the most atrocious and barbarous nature. . . . It is an evidence of a most depraved and cruel disposition, to murder one, so much in your power, that he is incapable of making resistance, even in his own defense."[69] "A slave," Taylor wrote, "is a reasonable creature; may be within the peace; and is under the protection of the State." He presented a natural law alternative to Hall's positivism. "Upon what foundation can the claim of a master to an absolute dominion over the life of his slave, be rested?" he asked. "The authority for it, is not to be found in the law of nature, for that will authorize a man to take away the life of another, only from the unavoidable necessity of saving his own; and of this code, the cardinal duty is, to abstain from injury, and do all the good we can. It is not the necessary consequence of the state of slavery, for that may exist without it; and its natural inconveniences ought not to be aggravated by an evil, at which reason, religion, humanity and policy equally revolt."[70] Nonetheless, Boon escaped because the law of 1791 said that the same punishment would be inflicted for killing a slave or a free man. The problem was that punishments varied depending on whether the killing was malicious or had been the result of provocation, for instance. The statute left too much discretion to the courts.[71]

In *State v. Reed* (1823) the North Carolina court again considered the applicability of the common law. Reed had been found guilty on an indictment that had concluded not with the statute but "at common law." Hall dissented from the affirmation of his conviction. Chief Justice Taylor went the other way. He argued that "there was no necessity to conclude the indictment against the form of the statute, for a law of paramount obligation to the statute was violated by the offense—the common law, founded upon the law of nature, and confirmed by revelation."[72]

Judge Henderson wrote an elaborate opinion. A slave, he began, is a "human being. . . . But it is said that, being property, he is not within the protection of the law, and therefore the law regards not the manner of his death; that the owner alone is interested and the State no more concerned, independently of the acts of the Legislature on that subject, than in the death of a horse." If, however, a slave was a reasonable "creature within the protection of the law," the killing of a slave could be common law murder. To discern whether the slave was within that protection, Henderson analyzed the master-slave relationship in North Carolina. "With the services and labors of the slave the law has nothing to do," he reasoned; "they are the master's by the law; the government and control of them belong exclusively to him. . . . in establishing slavery, then, the law vested in the master the absolute and uncontrolled right to the services of the slave, and the means of enforcing those services follow as necessary consequences; nor will the law weigh with the most scrupulous nicety his acts in relation thereto."[73] Nonetheless, the "life of a slave being no ways necessary to be placed in the power of the owner for the full enjoyment of his services, the law takes care of that." The notion that the life of the slave was at the disposal of a master was "abhorrent to the hearts of all those who have felt the influence of the mild precepts of Christianity."[74]

The supreme court of Mississippi faced a different analytic problem in *State v. Jones* (1821) because there was no statute in that state. The question was stark: could murder "be committed on a slave" in Mississippi? Slaves, under Mississippi law, were "reasonable and accountable beings," according to Judge Clarke. They were because they were themselves prosecuted when they committed homicides. "It would be a stigma," Clarke continued, "upon the character of the state, and a reproach to the administration of justice, if the life of a slave could be taken with impunity, or if he could be murdered in cold-blood, without subjecting the offender to the highest penalty known to the criminal jurisprudence of the country." There was no positive law giving the master, or a stranger, power over the life of the slave. "The taking away the life of a reasonable creature, under the king's peace, with malice aforethought, express or implied, is murder at common law. Is not the slave a reasonable creature, is he not a human being, and the meaning of this phrase reasonable creature is a human being, for the killing a lunatic, an idiot, or even a child unborn, is murder, as much as the killing a philosopher, and has not the slave as much reason as a lunatic, an idiot, or an unborn child."[75] Isaac Jones was sentenced to hang on July 27, 1821.

The question also came up in Tennessee in 1829 in *Fields v. State*. Counsel for

Fields argued that the case should be governed by the law of nations and the statutes. By the law of nations, masters possessed "an absolute and unlimited power over the life and fortune of the slave." The statutes, he argued, only created one kind of homicide when the victim was a slave, and that was murder. Judge Whyte, however, upheld a manslaughter conviction on the ground that the common law did apply. Judge Jacob Peck was impassioned: "I have been taught that christianity is part of the law of the land. The four gospels upon the clerk's table admonish me it is so every time they are used in administering oaths. If the mild precepts of christianity have had the effect to ameliorate the condition of this order of people, is it expected that we must recede from the improvement obtained, retire more into the dark, and become in government partly christian and partly pagan because we own pagans or savages for our property?" And, he concluded, "that law which says thou shalt not kill, protects the slave; and he is within its very letter. Law, reason, christianity and common humanity, all point out one way."[76] The Texas Supreme Court, relying heavily on *Fields*, held in *Chandler v. State* (1847) that under the common law it was manslaughter to feloniously kill a slave without malice. It added that "the only matter of surprise is that it should ever have been doubted."[77]

A discordant note was struck in an 1848 South Carolina case, *State v. Fleming*. The majority of the court held that there was no common law of homicide that concerned the killing of slaves. Judges O'Neall and John Smith Richardson believed that, until the passage of the statutes, there was an applicable common law.[78]

Because the overwhelming majority of convictions that reached appellate courts were for killings less than murder, the issues of "provocation" and the authority to chastise loomed large. One of the first cases was *State v. Weaver* (North Carolina, 1798). In his jury charge Judge John Haywood, later a judge in Tennessee, said that it would be justifiable homicide if after a slave resisted the commands of a master and the master then tried to force obedience, the slave again resisted and the master killed him. It would be neither murder nor manslaughter. This charge, which led to an acquittal, directly followed the 1791 statute.[79]

North Carolina modified the law to cover manslaughter in 1817. The law was tested the same year in *State v. Walker*. John Walker, a man near sixty and later pardoned by the governor, was convicted of murdering a slave. The slave was a runaway whom Walker had agreed to take back to his owner. The slave was tied, but about six miles away from where he was captured, he fell down; he had not eaten in days. At that point Walker "stepped up to him and kicked him on the hinder part of the neck with violence, and immediately kicked him on the side of the head with violence, which last kick turned his face from the ground so that the side of the head lay on the ground." Walker then put the slave on a horse and informed a witness to the event that "the scoundrel is holding his breath." When the body was examined, the neck was dislocated and one of the eyes "destroyed." There was also a dent in one of the temples. On these facts the judge charged the jury that the case was one either of murder or of no offense. It was not manslaughter. There had been no provocation. Defense counsel focused on the questions of correction and provocation. Walker, he argued, "had the right to inflict upon the negro such correction as was necessary to make him proceed on the road home," and the jury should have been allowed to decide whether the treatment was an immoderate correction. Counsel suggested, moreover, that there was a potential provocation that would reduce the offense as well. The provocation was the perceived deceitfulness of the slave in falling down! The court held simply that it was not a case of manslaughter on the evidence, and that it was proper for the trial judge to so charge.[80]

Three years later the court decided *State v. Tackett* (1820). The dead slave had lived on a lot in Raleigh with his free black wife. The defendant was a journeyman carpenter who lived at the home of the owner of the lot. Daniel, the slave, and Tackett, the defendant, had had arguments in the past about Daniel's wife; some said that Daniel had threatened to kill Tackett if he did not leave his wife alone. Tackett offered to prove that Daniel was a "turbulent man, and that he was insolent and impudent to white people." The court refused unless the defense proved that Daniel had been insolent to Tackett. The jury brought in a verdict of murder, and Tackett was sentenced to die.[81]

There was an evidentiary problem, according to Chief Justice Taylor. There was no direct evidence as to the "immediate provocation," and this was crucial because the type of homicide depended on it. According to Taylor, the provocation need not be the same in cases where slaves and whites were killed. The difference would be defined "by the common law of the country—a system which adapts itself to the habits, institutions and actual condition of the citizens." It followed that "it exists in the nature of things that, where slavery prevails, the relation between a white man and a slave differs from that which subsists between free persons; and every individual in the community feels and understands that the homicide of a slave may be extenuated by acts which would not produce a legal provocation if done by a white person." Never mind that Taylor ignored the *free* black community, the critical problem that remained was to find some contours of "legal provocation." But he admitted the impossibility. Still, the "sense and feelings of jurors, and the grave discretion of courts, can never be at a loss in estimating their force as they arise, and applying them to each particular case, with a due regard to the rights respectively belonging to the slave and white man—to the just claims of humanity, and to the supreme law, the safety of the citizens."[82] Local prejudices would define the law much as they do under modern obscenity rules.

Nearly two decades later the North Carolina Supreme Court had advanced little beyond *Tackett*. John Hoover's slave Mira died after a series of "brutal and barbarous whippings, scourgings and privations" that lasted over several months, including the latter stages of her pregnancy and after her delivery. According to Hoover, who was not supported by his white neighbors, the reasons were that Mira was impudent, had attempted to poison the family, attempted to burn some buildings, and was a thief.[83]

Judge Ruffin admitted that a master could correct his slave, and that the degree must, in general, "be left to his own judgment and humanity, and cannot be judicially questioned." Nonetheless, the authority to correct was not absolute: "He must not kill." There were circumstances that might mitigate the offense: "If death unhappily ensue from the master's chastisement of his slave, inflicted apparently with a good intent, for reformation for example, and with no purpose to take life, or to put it in jeopardy, the law would doubtless tenderly regard every circumstance which, judging from the conduct generally of masters towards slaves, might reasonably be supposed to have hurried the party into excess." That was not the case here. Hoover's acts "do not belong to a state of civilization."[84] Ruffin held that the trial court had been generous in even allowing provocation to be considered. Even if there had been provocation, it would be no excuse "because however flagrant the provocation, the acts of the prisoner were not perpetrated in sudden heat of blood, but must have flowed from a settled and malignant pleasure in inflicting pain, or a settled and malignant insensibility to human suffering." Ruffin made his point with a litany of Hoover's acts: "He beat her with clubs, iron chains, and other deadly weapons, time after time; burnt her, inflicted stripes over and often, with scourges, which literally excoriated her whole body; forced her out to work in inclement seasons, without being duly clad; provided for her insufficient food; exacted labor beyond her strength, and wantonly beat her because she could not comply with his requisitions."[85] Such brutish conduct breached the customary code of conduct accepted by slaveowners toward slaves in the nineteenth century. The use of force to maintain the subordination of slaves was one thing, but this was beyond the pale.

The same thing could be said of the sickening conduct of Simeon Souther, in Virginia, who was convicted of second-degree murder and sentenced to five years in prison. He appealed on the ground that if a slave died from a correction, no matter how excessive or cruel, the offense could only be manslaughter unless it were proved that he intended to kill. Under the common law of Virginia it had been held that a man could not be indicted for the cruel punishment of his slaves, and this meant that a beating for the purpose of correction was lawful. This reduced the offense to manslaughter when the slave died. The Virginia General Court was sufficiently appalled by Souther's conduct that it did not accept this reasoning. The evidence showed that Sam got drunk and Souther, to chastise him, did the following: "after the tieing, whipping, cobbing, striking, beating, knocking, kicking, stamping, wounding, bruising, lacerating, burning, washing, and torturing . . . the prisoner untied the deceased from the tree, in such way as to throw him with violence to the ground, and he then and there did knock, kick, stamp, and beat the deceased upon his head, temples, and various parts of his body."[86] He then put a rope around his neck, fastened to a bed post, "thereby strangling, choking and suffocating the deceased."[87]

Judge Richard H. Field suggested that Souther was guilty of murder. He admitted that slaveowners in Virginia had the authority to punish and the law would not intervene: "It is the policy of the law in respect to the relation of master and slave, and for the sake of securing proper subordination and obedience on the part of the slave, to protect the master from prosecution in all such cases, even if the whipping and punishment be malicious, cruel and excessive." But the master still acted at his peril. If the slave died, the "principles of the common law in relation to homicide" applied, and under those principles Hoover was guilty of murder.[88]

A much different line of cases emerged in South Carolina, largely because of statutory language. The appellant in *State v. Raines* (1826) had been charged with murder, and there was a second count of killing "on sudden heat and passion." The jury found him guilty of manslaughter. There had been resistance by the deceased, a fugitive, and Raines beat him to death.[89] Judge Colcock ruled that there could be no manslaughter of a slave under South Carolina law. The existing law of 1740 had modified the common law and left three kinds of homicides: murder, killing in sudden heat and passion, and a homicide that followed an undue correction. Manslaughter actually embraced the latter two but was different. Manslaughter at common law, Colcock argued, was an offense that occurred "between men standing on equal footing in society." It was as though there had been no development whatever in the law since the seventeenth century, when two "Gentlemen" armed to the teeth confronted one another on an English highway. In any case, Colcock concluded that all that was left by the law of 1821 was a murder or a killing in "sudden heat and passion." The "undue correction" homicide was omitted, and the verdict had to be either one of the offenses left by the law of 1821. That did not include manslaughter.[90]

In *State v. Gaffney* (1839) the court, in an opinion by Judge Baylies J. Earle, undercut *Raines*. A killing by undue correction was an offense under South Carolina law. He also noted that a conviction for a homicide in sudden heat and passion was similar to manslaughter: in each case there was a killing, no malice, and no sufficient excuse. In 1848, in *State v. Fleming*, the court held that a killing by undue correction was conceptually covered by the killing-in-sudden-heat-and-passion language of the 1821 law.[91] The South Carolina court, finally, confronted a defense similar to that of Souther in Virginia. In *State v. Motley* (1854) three men ran down a runaway slave, Joe, and treated him in a "cruel and barbarous" way that led to his death. Their defense was that the death was in pursuit of a lawful purpose, apprehending a runaway, so that it should have been a killing "on sudden heat and passion," not murder. The court held that the conduct of the prisoners "affords an exhibition of a wicked purpose and gross recklessness of human life, rarely met with."[92] The peculiar circumstances of *Motley*, like those of *Hoover* and *Souther*, disgusted the judges enough to affirm convictions.

Local Practice

A. E. Keir Nash has suggested that if we dig deeply enough, these appellate cases may be but the tip of an iceberg.[93] Were there a large number of nonappealed cases brought against whites for the homicide of slaves after the Revolution in the lower court records? In 1827, for example, Delaware held an inquest into the death of the slave Ador. Nicholas A. Bell, his owner, said that he beat the slave for refusing to work as she had been told. The condition of Ador was disgusting. Her "wounds ulcerated on her back . . . the smell was offensive, one on her rump had living animals (or maggots) in it before her death." Still, there is no evidence of an indictment or a conviction in this case.[94]

The same was not true in the action brought against Warner Taylor and Thomas Huff in Granville County, North Carolina, in 1825. Huff was acquitted, but Taylor was convicted of manslaughter, granted benefit of clergy, and "burnt in the brawn of the left hand." Taylor himself initiated the inquiry when he wrote to the local authorities. "I had this a negro man," he stated, "who made an attempt to run away, he was caught & tied at the end of the row, & remained in that situation not more than two hours, when my negroes reached that and he was found, as was supposed fainted, an attempt was made to bleed him & water through [sic] on him to bring him to, but proved ineffectual, he is dead & I wish you to come & hold an Inquest immediately to prevent misrepresentations." Unfortunately for Taylor, the evidence showed that he had beaten the slave to death, but apparently the jury believed that he had not intended to kill so that the offense was manslaughter. Peter died under an immoderate correction.[95]

From Virginia I found thirteen examples of the homicide of slaves by whites after the Revolution that at least reached the stage of a preliminary examination before a county court. Almost half of those cases came from Westmoreland County, two from Lunenburg County in the Southside (and they were related), one from Orange County, and four from the city of Petersburg. Five of the thirteen cases involved indictments against masters for the homicide of their own slaves. Four of the five were certified for trial in the superior court.[96]

There were also a number of cases from South Carolina. Between 1834 and 1860 Laurens County drew up six indictments. One of those was struck off, two ended in not guilty verdicts, and three led to guilty judgments. Of the guilty verdicts, two were for manslaughter and the third, against Drury Cheek in 1835, was on two counts of murder. In Marlborough District from 1852 to 1866 there were four cases: one was struck off, one produced a no true bill, in one a nolle prosequi (nol pro) was entered, and in the last, against Lewis A. J. Stubbs in 1852, the defendant was found guilty of murder. In the mid-1820s there were three indictments in two years in Fairfield District. One of them—the case of Guy Raines—produced a verdict of guilty of manslaughter.[97]

Many other Southern communities produced few or no criminal cases at all, or when they did the results were closer to what we might expect. Bennett Barrow noted a case in 1839 in the Florida Parishes of Louisiana. "Went to Town," he wrote, "man tried for Whipping a negro to Death. trial will continue till to morrow— deserves death—Cleared!" In Lowndes County, Alabama, Malachi Warren faced two charges. In the first, that of cruel and unusual punishment, he was accused of putting "divers iron rods and bands" around Dick's belly, chest, and neck—all held together by an iron rod up and down the slave's back. It was also alleged that Dick was "bruised wounded and cut." The verdict was not guilty. The next charge repeated those facts but added that the punishment lasted for ten days (November 1–10, 1842) and Dick died. Warren was charged with murder but was again acquitted by the jury in Hayneville. Theodore H. Davis did not even face a trial in Mercer County, Kentucky, in the early 1850s for shooting Jack in the face. The evidence was that Jack, who was known as a "violent fellow," and Davis were working in a garden at the time of the shooting. Jack, with a rake in his hands, threatened to beat Davis's brains out; according to Davis, "I was obliged to do what I did to save my life." A nol pro was entered in the case.[98]

A different, but probably not atypical result occurred in Lowndes County, Mississippi. James Paul was not brought to trial because he fled and was never caught. The inquest into the death of Aaron, Paul's slave, was that he "came to his death by maltreatment." Aaron was a runaway who when caught was ironed, including an iron gag in his mouth, and whipped. Paul then left. When he returned he and his brother discovered that Aaron was dead. The body was taken to a log heap and burned. A neighbor suspected that the bones were Aaron's and that Paul was responsible.[99]

It is not an inspiring record. Almost all homicides of slaves, from the colonial period to the end of slavery, ended in acquittals, or at most in verdicts of manslaughter, which meant that there had been some legal provocation from the slave. There were also killings that never led to criminal actions. Still, in theory some protection for the lives of slaves existed because people could be punished for their homicides. Occasionally they were. To that limited extent the law mediated or controlled some of the violence created by a social relationship based on the violent control of labor power in a biracial society.

But the master-slave relationship was so delicate that it was intruded upon only in extreme or unusual circumstances. Those circumstances could be quite indeterminate and imprecise. They could include the political objectives of a Clayton and Spotswood in Virginia, and they could include community hostility to a particularly contentious individual like Pitman or community repugnance at the savagery of a Souther. One thing is clear: the community had the power necessary, however ambiguous that might be, to ensure that people of color who were in bondage behaved with deference. But this was sometimes balanced against the humanity of the enslaved. In a formal legal sense the balance was struck through the use of the notions of provocation and mitigation, as well as "moderate correction." Less technically it was done through the jury's expression of the "conscience" of the community. Yet in the end, even after amelioration, those who resisted bondage would be less under the king's peace than those who did not.

8

Law and the Abuse of Slaves

They don't all cruellize slaves.

Lydia Maria Child, *Fact & Fiction* (1846)

"Wrapt in its own congenial, midnight darkness,"[1] the plantation was the place most masters and slaves struggled to define their relationship, although less as the Civil War approached and more slaves were hired out to railroads and factories.[2] Punishment was central to that relationship. There was a coherent purpose in punishment: it was one procedure used to "degrade and undermine" the humanity of the slave and "so distinguish him from human beings who are not property."[3] At the same time, there were limits on the amount or type of violence that society would accept. In addition to the potential social and religious limits on violence, there were the limits of the legal order. But as Daniel Flanigan notes: "it was in the protection of blacks from crime rather than the treatment of black offenders that the criminal law of slavery failed most miserably."[4] One difficulty was to provide some legal definition of such terms as "inhumanity" or "cruel treatment" or "cruel punishment." To limit the power of slaveowners was always difficult, and it was not at all irrational to treat the violence they used against their slaves as if it were outside the legal order, as a noncrime. Vicious such a policy choice would be, but it would be logical. At the same time, it would be logical to try to place some limits on the cruel treatment of slaves precisely because cruelty threatened the delicate balance in the reciprocal obligations.[5] Another way to express this is through Jean Paul Sartre's notion that obedience, even if obtained by constraint and force, could be used as an argument to support legitimacy.[6] If slaves would be more obedient with decent treatment than with brutality, it would make sense to affirm the legitimacy of the system by an amelioration of the condition of the slaves by restraining the power of masters. If not, amelioration would be more dangerous than it was worth.

The actual degree to which the legal system restrained the power of masters and protected slaves from abuse has been a matter of dispute. Rose suggested that by the third decade of the nineteenth century the state had intervened to reduce the suffering that had marked the colonial period. She contended that it is ahistorical to overlook the "evolutionary nature of all institutions" and argue that "there could be no improvement in the physical or moral condition of victims of so barbarous an institution."[7] Andrew Fede has seen the matter differently. "A fixed principle of slave law," he maintained, "granted masters the unlimited right to abuse their slaves to any extreme of brutality and wantonness as long as the slave survived." The legal changes that "appeared to protect slaves from violent white abuse" in fact served a "legitimizing purpose." The laws actually "decriminalized" violence to the extent that it was thought a "necessary" or "ordinary" incident of slavery.[8]

Statutes Restraining Masters

During the colonial period South Carolina and Georgia adopted statutes to restrain the nonfatal violence of masters. Virginia, North Carolina, Maryland, and Delaware did not. Later, in several jurisdictions, cruel masters in theory faced the loss of their slaves. In 1860 Maryland provided that a slave whose master was convicted of abuse on three occasions, a remnant of a 1715 law on indentured servants, would become free. Much earlier, Louisiana had provided that if a master was convicted of cruel treatment, the judge could order the slave sold at public auction "in order to place him out of the reach of the power which his master has abused." Alabama's 1819 constitution, followed in 1845 by Texas's, authorized the legislature to enact a law requiring the sale of abused slaves "for the benefit of the owner or owner." Neither state, however, adopted such legislation. Kentucky did in 1830. If a jury determined that a slaveowner had treated a slave cruelly so as to "endanger the life or limb of such slave, or materially to affect his health, or shall not supply his slave with sufficient wholesome food and raiment, such slave shall be taken and sold for the benefit of the owner."[9] Because the slaves were sold for the owners' benefit, even cruelty had its rewards. Nevertheless, slaves had a chance to escape the clutches of the more inhumane masters.

Most jurisdictions, however, adopted laws, if at all, to punish masters criminally for cruelty or inhumanity. There were two types of laws: one specific and one general. Examples of the first type would be statutes of South Carolina and Louisiana. The South Carolina law of 1740, established in the wake of the Stono Rebellion and adopted by Louisiana in 1806, showed the perception of "humanity" held by the mid-eighteenth-century South Carolina legislators. The law provided for a fine of up to 100 pounds if a person cut out the tongue, put out the eye, castrated, or did "cruelly scald, burn, or deprive any slave of any limb or member." It also imposed a fine for other cruel punishments, with some important exceptions. The phrase was "any other cruel punishments other than." The punishments allowed were "whipping or beating with a horsewhip, cowskin, switch or small stick" or putting on irons, or confining or imprisoning the slave.[10] Whipping, no matter how long or bloody, would not be criminal if done with acceptable instruments unless the slave died, and then only under certain circumstances. It was a compromise between humanity and Christian values, on one side, and the power of masters, on the other. Although whipping with horsewhips, for instance, might be a "cruel punishment," it was considered necessary.

There was, however, a serious evidentiary problem. Slaves could not testify against their masters. The problem was admitted to be serious because the plantations in South Carolina were widely separated, and "many cruelties may be committed on slaves, because no white person may be present to give evidence of the same." This difficulty was dealt with by reversing what is today a benchmark of Anglo-American criminal justice—the presumption of innocence. The rule was that the white in charge of a slave who had been abused would be presumed guilty of the offense. But the presumption of guilt would be nullified by the owner's oath. He or she would be discharged unless two white witnesses offered "clear proof" of the owner's guilt.[11]

In 1853 the Fairfield grand jury recommended the adoption of a new law because "informal complaints have been made of ill treatment of slaves by their owners which cannot be corrected by the present law."[12] It was not until 1858 that a new law was introduced. It provided that masters could be fined and jailed at the discretion of the sessions court for the "cruel and unusual punishment" of their slaves. There was a proviso: nothing in the statute would "prevent the owner or person having charge of any slave from inflicting on such slave such punishment as may be necessary for the good government of the owner."[13] Georgians modified their code in 1816. Masters could be indicted for the "unnecessary and excessive whipping" of their slaves. And in 1851 Georgia amended the law to expressly include "overseers" and to add this language: "beating, cutting or wounding, or by cruelly and unnecessarily biting or tearing with dogs."[14]

Louisiana, when under Spanish control, adopted a law to restrain the authority of masters. The 1783 statute noted that "the slave is entirely subject to the will of his master, who may correct and chastise him, though not with unusual rigor, nor so as to maim, or mutilate him, or to expose him to the danger of loss of life, or to cause his death."[15] This remained as article 173 of the civil code of 1838. In 1806, as mentioned, Louisiana passed legislation based on the South Carolina law of 1740.[16]

The remaining states that enacted protective legislation approved a more general statute. There was one anomalous law. North Carolina, which never adopted a protective measure, did establish a regulation in 1796 that denied compensation to the owners of slaves executed for crimes if the slaves had not been adequately fed, clothed, and treated with the "humanity consistent with his or her situation."[17] This was a recognition that masters who treated slaves cruelly bore some responsibility to the rest of society for the crimes that sprang from desperation and illtreatment. It was an indirect incentive to treat slaves with some semblance of decency. Hierarchy did entail duties.

An example of a law in the second, nonspecific category was that of Alabama. Its 1852 code required a master to "treat his slave with humanity" and demanded that he not "inflict upon him any cruel punishment." It was sufficient in an indictment to say that the "defendant did inflict on a slave any cruel punishment" or "that he treated such slave with inhumanity, without specifying in what such inhumanity consists, and the jurors are the judges of what constitutes cruel punishment."[18] Parochialism suffused the Alabama code. The legislators made a policy choice to avoid specificity. Cruelty wore a human face, William Blake had written, but the crags and crannies, the wrinkles of that face would be sketched by locality.

Were these laws of any real significance in protecting slaves from cruel treatment by masters? The answer is very infrequently, but on occasion. A small number of nonappealed cases and an even smaller number of appellate cases arose under these statutes. There were no cases from the colonial or early national periods. Virtually every action occurred after the 1820s, despite the existence of laws such as South Carolina's of 1740, Georgia's of 1750 and 1816, or Louisiana's and Mississippi's of 1806. All of the cases that rested on statutes were in the Deep South.[19]

South Carolina, with its early statutory scheme, produced a feeble record. The only lower court case in the sample used was in Laurens County in 1847. John Wait was indicted before the grand jury, but it returned a no bill.[20] At the appellate level there were two cases, but neither of them involved masters, even though the legal analyses could have applied to them. "The *criminal* offence of assault and battery," O'Neall wrote in *State v. Maner* (1834), "cannot at common law be committed on the person of a slave." "There can be no offence against the State for a mere beating of a slave unaccompanied by any circumstances of cruelty or an attempt to kill, and murder. The peace of the State is not thereby broken; for a slave is not *generally* regarded as legally capable of being within the peace of the State."[21] The second case, against John Wilson in 1840, arose under the 1740 law. Wilson, who was drunk and thought that he had stumbled across an Indian, beat the slave over the head with a pistol. Richard Gantt, on appeal of the conviction, upheld the charge to the jury by the lower court judge. It was that the "punishment inflicted on the slave need not be of the same grade of cruelty with those particularized in the statute." What was important to Judge Gantt was the fact that the beating was of "an unoffending and unresisting slave" who was disabled "to perform service for his master, and subjecting the master to the expense of a physician's attendance."[22] This case, like *Maner*, did not involve a cruel master, but it did show that cruelty, as a legal concept, was supple. Given the paucity of cases, however, this was largely a theoretical question.

The same can be said for Georgia. There was no appellate construction of the statutes of Georgia, and I have found only one nonappealed action—a perjury case against a man who charged an owner with cruel punishment. There was truth in the remark of William Gaston of the North Carolina Supreme Court: "A cruel master is a term of opprobrium which would be as bitterly resented and is as carefully avoided as that of a dishonest tradesman or of a drunken mechanic."[23]

Elsewhere the record is equally uninspiring or ambivalent. Of the five nonappealed cases in Alabama, only one produced a guilty verdict. William Samuel was fined $100 in Chambers County in 1850 for the cruel punishment of his slave.[24] There were two appellate cases, and both were remanded. In the first, *Turnipseed v.*

State (1844), the defendant was found guilty of inflicting cruel and unusual punishment on his slave Rachel. Chief Justice Henry W. Collier gave the statute a peculiar reading. There were two separate offenses, cruel punishment and unusual punishment. The law was "merely intended to make the enactment sufficiently broad to embrace a high offence against good morals, no matter under what circumstances committed." But that left courts no more guidance than if there had been no statute at all. Cruel punishment did not have to be unusual—a fact that would come as no surprise to a slave. Punishment, he reasoned, could be both cruel and unusual, as when a slave was punished "in a manner offensive to modesty, decency and the recognized proprieties of social life" even though no bodily pain was inflicted.[25] Collier saw cruelty in what offended the sense of propriety of whites. But the real problem was that the indictment did not "declare with particularity" what elements of the offense Turnipseed was to defend against. Collier wrung his hands in regret that he had to overturn the conviction, but "we must hold the scales of justice in equipoise, and however odious the offence, we must admeasure right to every one according to law."[26] Eight years later, when the legislature adopted a new law, parochialism replaced the view of the Alabama court that required particularity.[27]

There were no appellate cases in either Texas or Florida, but a number of cases were brought against people for cruelty, mistreatment of a slave, or cruel and unusual punishment. During the 1850s, for instance, a number of men were indicted in Harrison County, Texas.[28] Louisiana, which had both civil and criminal protective statutes, provides a more interesting story. In a unique civil case, *Markham v. Close* (1831), Markham had petitioned the district judge to order a slave, Augustin, removed from his master's possession and sold. The reason was that the owner "had cruelly beat and maltreated" the slave. Close, the owner, defended himself on the ground that Augustin was a runaway and was chastised with a whip as allowed by law. The testimony suggested a savage whipping of a sullen runaway ("the weather being warm, the wounds smelled badly"). The jury found against Close, but the Louisiana Supreme Court overturned the judgment on the ground that the statute required a criminal conviction before an order to sell, and there had been no criminal action.[29] The black code of 1856 changed the rule when it allowed the court and jury hearing a criminal indictment for maltreatment "whether they convict or not, to decree the sale of the slave at public auction."[30]

In 1849 the first case based on the law of 1806 reached the Louisiana Supreme Court. *State v. Morris* turned on the provision that allowed owners to clear themselves upon oath. Judge George Rogers King held that the oath could not be conclusive. It was one more piece of evidence to rebut the statutory presumption of guilt, a presumption "founded upon the relation of master and slave, and the power of the former to maltreat the latter secretly and without the possibility in many instances, of otherwise establishing his guilt." The oath of the owner could not block the state, otherwise a master might succeed in escaping punishment even if the proof were incontrovertible. The judgment against Morris for cruelty to his slave was upheld.[31]

The Louisiana lower court record is ambivalent, as two cases from St. Landry Parish illustrate. Sometime during 1843 Elizabeth Rabassa "with stick, stones, hot irons and knives did cruelly beat, bruise, burn, wound, and ill-treat" her slave Martha. Her defense was that Martha had been whipped severely for theft before she got her, and that she was "of bad character, vicious and uncontrollable." Rabassa claimed that the whipping she had given Martha was "as house keepers generally chastise their servants but never cruelly." The hirers had used violence "in order to keep her under proper restraint." There was a mistrial in May 1843, and Rabassa posted a bond to appear in December. She did not appear, and in August 1844 an execution was issued against her property for the bond and costs.[32] Felonise Israel Lapointe was charged in 1850 in the second case. She allegedly did "cruelly mutilate, beat, ill treat and [inflict] other punishments" on the slave. There is no disposition recorded in this case, and the only other thing we know is that the slave was a seven-year-old girl.[33] William Rawley, on the other hand, was acquitted of a charge of cruel punishment in 1845 in West Feliciana Parish.[34]

Finally, in Mississippi the lower court record is fuller whereas the appellate record is thin. In 1856 the Mississippi high court heard *Scott v. State*, which turned on the claim that as a mere "overseer" the defendant did not come under the terms of the statute. Chief Justice Smith brusquely disposed of the argument. An "overseer" had the "right to command the obedience, and, of course, is entitled to the services of the slave placed under his charge." The notion that the legislature intended to limit the statutory coverage to those "beneficially interested in" or who "own the labor" of the slave was "wholly without foundation."[35]

Mississippi had more cases at the county level than other states. Despite the fact that the provision for punishing cruelty had been on the books since 1806, however, all of the cases I found came after 1847.[36] Although the cases in Lowndes County often did not go to trial, the fact remains that a fair number of indictments were brought. There is no reason to assume that Lowndes County was an especially brutal place. It did, on the other hand, enjoy a reputation as one of the more accomplished legal communities in the state of Mississippi. Possibly a high regard for the rule of law may have played some role in the number of indictments produced in that county.[37] The fact that the cases tend to cluster around certain years suggests that Lowndes had a zealous set of county officials rather than an unusual amount of violence and cruelty. It is probable that various counties scattered throughout the South would produce patterns similar to Lowndes, whereas many others would be devoid of indictments because the residents believed that what a slaveowner did with his or her slave was no business of theirs.

Reliance on statutes defining cruelty or providing for its punishment, however, was not the only way masters might be restrained by law. There were limits on violence allowed superiors in the common law. Would the common law apply in cases involving masters and slaves?

Common Law

There were significant adjudications in Virginia and North Carolina. The first was in the Virginia Court of Appeals in 1824. Richard Booth was found guilty in a special verdict of the cruel and inhuman beating of the slave he had hired. The verdict was subject to a ruling of the court on two questions: first, "Can the Defendant be indicted and punished for the excessive, cruel and inhuman infliction of stripes on the slave *Bob*, while in his possession . . . no permanent injury having resulted to the said slave . . . ?," and second, whether the defendant could be punished under the indictment brought in this action, which charged the cruel and inhuman beating. Judge Richard Parker focused on the second question, which he interpreted this way: Could Booth be found guilty of assaulting a slave held "by himself as an hireling, that is, upon his own slave for the time being"? He could not because the indictment nowhere noted the relationship of the parties, and it failed "to shew that it is the *excess* of the punishment which is complained of, and not, that the right to punish at all, is questioned." This, said Parker, was the rule of master-apprentice law, and there was no reason to depart from it in this case. The offense was different from an unlawful assault on the slave of another. The assault on one's own slave "becomes unlawful by subsequent excess and inhumanity," and if this was what the indictment meant to deal with, it should have done so. The court, according to Parker, did not have to resolve the first question, which "involves a grave and serious, as well as delicate enquiry into the rights and duties of slaveholders, and the condition of their slaves." Nonetheless, by analogizing the master-slave relationship to the master-apprentice relationship at common law, the inference was that it was possible to bring a common law indictment against a slaveowner for a cruel punishment. An assault on one's own slave, Parker had said, "becomes unlawful by subsequent excess and inhumanity." He addressed in part the very question he disclaimed answering. Yet he did avoid the problem of defining "cruelty" or "inhumanity."[38]

Three years later, in *Commonwealth v. Richard Turner* (1827), the Virginia court did a volte-face when it probed into the "rights and duties of slave-holders." Courts, Judge Dade argued, were to determine "not what may be expedient, or morally, or politically right in relation to this matter, but what *is the law*." He was aware that courts in England and in Virginia had "long exercised a control over offences *contra bonos mores*." But were current notions about the treatment of slaves sufficiently clear to justify upholding this indictment? Dade's view was that courts ought not to take on themselves a "latitude of jurisdiction . . . which could not be exercised without an alarming encroachment upon the liberty of the subject or citizen." A broad assertion of power would be "inquisitorial: a power to be exercised, not within the limits of a long line of established precedents, but to be deduced . . . from a course of reasoning upon a subject admitting as much diversity of opinion, as much subtlety and refinement, as any other whatsoever."[39] There were no judicial standards or legal norms, and there was no social consensus.

Dade continued his excursus with a discussion of the nature of the common law. Transformations were "slow and imperceptible: so that society may easily conform itself to the law. When great changes take place in the social order, a stronger hand, that of the Legislature, must be applied." Dade then turned to the statutes. "After the passage of the act of 1669, and until the year 1788, there certainly could have been no pretence for maintaining such prosecutions as these." From 1788 on the life of the slave was protected, and statutes against maiming did apply. But the common law and statute law never did "protect the slave against minor injuries from the hand of the master." This was disingenuous. Turner was not indicted for inflicting "minor injuries" on Emanuel. He was indicted because he did "violently, cruelly, immoderately, and excessively beat, scourge and whip" his slave. Once he trivialized the problem, Dade tried to recapture some moral authority with the remark that it was "to be deplored that an offence so odious and revolting as this, should exist to the reproach of humanity."[40] His analysis then lurched back to the beginning to reinforce the point. The "only remaining pretext" to sustain the indictment "would be the ductile and flexible character of the common law, which moulds itself to the changing condition of human society." But Dade had begun with a very conservative view of judicial power. If there was to be any change in the law to uphold the "new idea" that it was appropriate to indict masters for cruelty to slaves, such amelioration must come from the legislature.[41]

Brockenbrough was uneasy. He had recently sustained an indictment of precisely the kind at issue. Even though the common law did not recognize slavery, it did have well-established rules for the "relations of superior and inferior." After 1788 the common law was revived and "again extended its aegis over the slave to protect him from all inhuman torture." Moreover, society itself was in no danger: "When it is recollected, that our Courts and Juries are composed of men who, for the most part, are masters, I cannot conceive that any injury can accrue to the rights and interests of that class of the community." Self-interest and humanity were blended. "With respect to the slaves, whilst kindness and humane treatment are calculated to render them contented and happy," he asked, "is there no danger that oppression and tyranny, against which there is no redress, may drive them to despair?"[42] Amelioration could assure contentedness among slaves, whereas brutality would endanger the domination of the masters. Romanist reasoning, on the other hand, rested on the notion that desperation, not contentedness, was the normal condition of slaves, and they must be kept in subordination by force. There was surely a point to both perceptions. A slave, as Sartre put it, "who is deeply rebellious, and conscious of the injustice of his condition, may obey either cynically and out of mere prudence or, possibly, in the expectation of a revolt which he will join." But "a given slave may be reconciled to his fate . . . he may regard the master's authority as legitimate, that is to say, he may almost unconsciously betray his fellow-slaves."[43] These were incompatible social perceptions that the law could not mediate very well.

Two years after the decision in *Turner* the North Carolina Supreme Court decided *State v. Mann*, a case often discussed by scholars.[44] John Mann had been found guilty in Chowan County in 1829 of an assault and battery on Lydia, a slave he had hired. Lydia was being punished for some "small offense" when she fled. Mann ordered her to stop, she refused, and he shot her. The jury charge from Judge Joseph Daniel was that if the jurors believed that this was "cruel and unwarrantable, and disproportionate to the offense," then Mann was guilty, "as he had only a special property in the slave."[45] Because North Carolina had no protective statute, this case rested on the authority of courts to uphold indictments of slaveowners for a common law assault and battery or cruelty as an offense *contra bonos mores*.

Briefly, the North Carolina Supreme Court overturned the conviction on the ground that a master was not subject to an indictment for a battery committed on his own slave. The reason the case was momentous, however, was found in the notion developed in Ruffin's opinion that "inherent in the relation of master and slave" was the fact that "the power of the master must be absolute to render the submission of the slave perfect." This led Harriet Beecher Stowe, in 1853 in her *Key to Uncle Tom's Cabin*, to praise Ruffin for "that noble scorn of dissimulation, that straightforward determination not to call a bad thing by a good name." "No one can read this decision," she wrote, "so fine and clear in expression, so dignified and solemn in its earnestness, and so dreadful in its results, without feeling at once deep respect for the man and horror for the system."[46] Most scholars have followed this judgment, but the opinion is not all that clear and free of dissimulation.

Toward the start of the most quoted section, Judge Ruffin made a remark that is usually overlooked. "The established habits and uniform practice of the country," he wrote, ". . . is the best evidence of the portion of power deemed by the whole community requisite to the preservation of the master's dominion." I will reserve comment on this until the line of analysis usually discussed is included. Of slavery, he wrote:

> The end is the profit of the master, his security and the public safety; the subject, one doomed in his own person and his posterity, to live without knowledge and without the capacity to make anything his own, and to toil that another may reap the fruits. What moral considerations shall be addressed to such a being to convince him what it is impossible but that the most stupid must feel and know can never be true—that he is thus to labor upon a principle of natural duty, or for the sake of his own personal happiness, such services can only be expected from one who has no will of his own; who surrenders his will in implicit obedience to that of another. Such obedience is the consequence only of uncontrolled authority over the body. There is nothing else which can operate to produce the effect. The power of the master must be absolute to render the submission of the slave perfect.

At the end of the paragraph Ruffin argued that such a hard discipline "belongs to the state of slavery. They cannot be disunited without abrogating at once the rights of the master and absolving the slave from his subjection." Violence, he concluded, "is inherent in the relation of master and slave."[47]

Did Ruffin truly believe the master must have absolute dominion over the body of the slave? Were there no limits? The following remarks are illuminating. "The protection already afforded by several statutes," Ruffin noted, "that all-powerful motive, the private interest of the owner, the benevolences towards each other, seated in the hearts of those who have been born and bred together, the frowns and deep execrations of the community upon the barbarian who is guilty of excessive and brutal cruelty to his unprotected slave, all combined, have produced a mildness of treatment and attention to the comforts of the unfortunate class of slaves, greatly mitigating the rigors of servitude and ameliorating the condition of the slaves." Suddenly, Ruffin sounded like Brockenbrough. He was still drawing on the theme twenty-six years later in an address to the state Agricultural Society of North Carolina. In that apologia Ruffin conceded that slavery "is not a pure and unmixed good. Nor is anything human. There are instances of cruel and devilish masters, and of turbulent and refractory slaves, who cannot be controlled and brought into subjection but by extraordinary severity." Such cases, however, he believed to be "exceptions." "Great severity in masters is as much opposed to the usages of our people as to the sentiment of the age, and, indeed, to the interest of the master. Moderation in the punishment of dependents is founded in nature; and unjust, excessive, and barbarous cruelty is not to be presumed, but quite the contrary." Self-interest dictated "humane treatment," but even that did not end the security for the slave: "Often born on the same plantation, and bred together, they have a perfect knowledge of each other, and a mutual attachment. Protection and provision are the offices of the master, and in return the slave yields devoted obedience and fidelity of service." Now good slaves obeyed because they were protected and cared for, not because they were subject to the absolute power of their masters.[48]

In an unpublished piece Judge Gaston of North Carolina spoke with the same voice. "It is difficult to imagine a state of slavery to exist more mitigated than that which prevails in North Carolina," he wrote. "Slavery is regarded as an evil not to be removed, but as susceptible of mitigation. The Laws are continually contributing to this result—but public opinion and enlightened self interest contribute far more efficaciously." One basic reason for the mildness of slavery in North Carolina, he contended, was because slaves were "distributed in small numbers thro' the community." A harsher discipline, he conceded, was necessary on large plantations, but there were fewer of those in North Carolina than in any other "atlantic state."[49]

If Ruffin believed all this as well, as he seemed to, how much power was necessary to preserve slavery in his view? It is here that it is useful to return to the quotation noted earlier. Wherever the limits on the authority of masters might be would be determined, said Ruffin, by the "established habits and uniform practice of the country." Such standards would determine the "portion of power deemed by the whole community requisite to the preservation of the master's dominion." But if this was true (and he also included state statutes), what had happened to the notion that the power of the master *must* be absolute? Did it mean that slavery was crumbling, that the rights of masters were being "abrogated" and the "duties of the slave" ended? Not in Ruffin's view. In his 1855 speech he eulogized slavery and even suggested that if slaveowners ended their dominion over the slaves, "their fate would soon be that of our native savages or the enfranchised blacks of the West Indies, the miserable victims of idleness, want, drunkenness, and other debaucheries." Slaves were saved from becoming a debased peasantry, a standard proslavery argument that often focused on the poverty in Haiti after the successful slave insurrection on the island. Slavery, then, was not "a blot upon our laws, not a stain on our morals, nor a blight upon our land." In fact, Ruffin embraced a "harmony of interest" doctrine: "where slavery exists labor and capital never come in conflict, because they are in the same hands, and operate in harmony."[50]

One way to reduce the tensions in the earlier *Mann* opinion is to view it as moving along on dissimilar planes: the one abstract, the other grounded in a view of historical experience and concrete social relations. What Ruffin did in the often-quoted section was to create an abstract model, an image of the total or perfect slave. The actual dominion of masters over slaves in North Carolina deviated from this model because of statutes, public opinion, and the self-interest and benevolence of masters. Absolute power would create the "slave perfect," but a slave system would continue to exist without the perfect slave. Because Ruffin included public opinion among the chief restraints on the power of masters, he introduced a parochialism of time and place into the determination of the precise portion of power needed to maintain dominion.

Ruffin further confused the issue when he looked into the future. "The same causes are operating," he wrote in *Mann*, "and will continue to operate with increased action until the disparity in numbers between the whites and blacks shall have rendered the latter in no degree dangerous to the former, when the police now existing may be further relaxed."[51] The absolute authority over the body was less essential if the demographics of black slavery were less threatening to whites.

Ruffin's view of the role of courts introduced a final dimension. Judges, he declared, must "recognize the full dominion of the owner over the slave," but he added "except where the exercise of it is forbidden by statute." Ruffin's position on judicial authority was restrained. "We cannot allow the right of the master to be brought into the discussion in the courts of justice. The slave, to remain a slave, must be made sensible that there is no appeal from his master; that his power is in no instance usurped; but is conferred by the laws of man at least, if not by the law of God." Legitimacy might not derive wholly from the obedience of slaves, but it did derive in part from the laws of their masters. For a Southern judge to ignore this would be to ignore how high the stakes really were:

The danger would be great indeed if the tribunals of justice should be called on to graduate the punishment appropriate to every temper and every dereliction of menial duty. No man can anticipate the many and aggravated provocations of the master which the slave would be constantly stimulated by his own passions or the instigation of others to give; or the consequent wrath of the master, prompting him to bloody vengeance upon the turbulent traitor—a vengeance generally practiced with impunity by reason of its privacy. The Court, therefore, disclaims the power of changing the relation in which these parts of our people stand to each other.[52]

A final appellate case was *Worley v. State*, heard in Tennessee in 1850. Judge A. W. O. Totten described Gabriel Worley as an older man who was "remarkable for his kindness and humanity towards his slaves." One of them, Josiah, however, was "turbulent, insolent and ungovernable." Worley decided to reform him. He and his son tied Josiah and cut off his testicles. Was Josiah's castration unlawful? If it was not, it would have to be based on a claim of absolute power over a slave. "We utterly repudiate the idea," Totten wrote, "of any such power and dominion of the master over the slave, as would authorize him thus to maim his slave for the purpose of moral reform. Such doctrine would violate the moral sense and humanity of the present age." Totten was developing an argument based on the power of courts to deal with offenses *contra bonos mores*. But the decision did not rest wholly on this common law ground because there was a statute in Tennessee that punished the unlawful and malicious castration "of another." This law was not part of the slave code, and Worley's counsel argued that a slave was not included because offenses committed by slaves were dealt with elsewhere in the code. The court disagreed.[53]

There was, then, no appellate case that upheld the indictment and conviction of masters for cruelty to their slaves if the indictment rested solely on a common law foundation. Little evidence exists that law, either statutory or common law, amounted to much protection for slaves against the nonfatal abuse inflicted on them by their masters. They had a much better chance turning to their common churches.[54] The question must remain open, of course, whether practice might have caught up with the theoretical protections afforded by the statutes and whether all Southern jurisdictions would have adopted them in time.

"Civil Rights" of Slaves

Cruel punishments were not the only forms of abuse slaves suffered, and security from direct physical violence was not the only form of security provided by law, at least in theory. In some states slaves were granted a limited range of civil rights, even though they could not enforce them at law through any act of their own and could not testify against whites even if violations of those rights ended in court. It is a tenuous right indeed if people cannot vindicate themselves in a court, and even those rights granted slaves were not always unadulterated with other considerations, such as the safety of society. Even the notion that they possessed some civil rights doubtless sounds strange, but that is because of a linguistic obscurantism. The oddity exists because we too often confound the notions of civil liberties and civil rights. Slaves were denied civil liberties without a doubt. As T. R. R. Cobb put it, "the right of personal liberty in the slaves is utterly inconsistent with the idea of slavery."[55]

Civil rights were not the same as civil liberties, however. The former were often linked to what Patterson describes as civic freedom as opposed to personal freedom. They were an element of participation in a society, not what is sometimes called "negative liberty" or the freedom to do what one wished to do. The notion of unconstraint, in Quentin Skinner's view, "has underpinned the entire development of modern contractarian political thought." But negative liberty does not exhaust the notion of "rights." Civil rights are not an element of negative liberty, they are akin to welfare rights.[56] By the eighteenth century, however, the two ideas were confounded in English legal writing. In the process an important distinction was obscured. It was a linguistic confusion that reflected the collapse of a feudal social order and the emergence of one based on individualism in a market capitalist economy.

The word *liberty* involved freedom, and by the eighteenth century it was taken to mean freedom from unlawful restraints. It rested on individualism and free will. The word *right* need not imply freedom. Civil rights could easily exist in a paternalistic social order. The confusion of the two concepts, liberty and right, can be seen in Blackstone. He began his section on the "rights of persons" by noting that the "absolute rights of man" was the "natural liberty of mankind." "This natural liberty," he wrote, "consists properly in a power of acting as one thinks fit, without any restraint or control." When people entered society, they had to part with some of these natural rights in order to obtain order and security. The rights that were left, in Blackstone's view, comprised "civil liberty, which is that of a member of society" and "is no other than natural liberty so far restrained by human laws (and no farther) as is necessary and expedient for the general advantage of the public." Those rights he placed under three headings: "The right of personal security, the right of personal liberty, and the right of private property." It is here that the obscurantism appears. Blackstone lumped civil liberties and civil rights; he fused the individualist notion of a right to "act as one thinks fit" with an ambivalent notion of "personal security." One of the benefits of entering society was to obtain security from violence. But, Blackstone continued, "there is no man so indigent or wretched, but he may demand a supply sufficient for all the necessities of life from the more opulent part of the community, by means of the several statutes enacted for the relief of the poor." A demand for that which is necessary to sustain life is a civil right, not a civil liberty. A sense of social responsibility implicit in the English poor laws, as ghastly as they were, was not wholly consistent with a full-blown civil libertarianism. The Benthamite liberals of early nineteenth-century England understood that, and they tried to remove the inconsistency by attacking the poor laws.[57] Gone was the idea of a civil right as understood in the feudal order of the Middle Ages, or as it existed in Blackstone, or as it would resurface in twentieth-century America's welfare state, however attenuated.

It was not completely gone from the paternalistic social order of the nineteenth-century South. A pale reflection can be found in a few statutes and cases that required masters to properly feed or clothe slaves or punished them when they did not. Judge O'Neall was not engaging in obfuscation when he entitled one of the sections of his digest of the slave law, "Slaves, Their Civil Rights, Liabilities, and Disabilities."[58]

As early as 1740 masters could be fined in South Carolina for failing to provide sufficient clothing and food for their slaves. O'Neall regretfully noted that although the law was wise and humane, he was forced to admit "*that there is in such a State as ours,* great occasion for the enforcement of such a law, *accompanied by severe penalties.*" One problem was that the penalty was too light. His only concrete suggestions, however, were that the law should be read to the grand juries, which should be charged with inquiring into any violations of the legal duty of masters, and every master reported should be instantly indicted.[59]

The only South Carolina appellate case that involved this problem was *State v. Bowen* (1849). Bowen had been found guilty of neglecting and refusing to provide adequate food or clothing for his slaves. The slaves' feet were described as frostbitten and sore. Judge Frost, for the court, upheld the conviction of Bowen, but his analysis did not focus on the notion that slaves possessed rights. "Instances do sometimes, though rarely, occur," he wrote, in "which it is necessary to interfere in behalf of the slave against the avarice of his master. In such cases the law should interpose its authority. It is due to public sentiment, and is necessary to protect property from the depredation of famishing slaves."[60]

South Carolina was alone on this matter until the last decade before the Civil War, when a number of states adopted statutes. A typical example was Alabama's law of 1852. The critical provision was this: "The master . . . must provide him with a sufficiency of healthy food and necessary clothing; cause him to be properly attended during sickness, and provide for his necessary wants in old age." In 1862, in Lowndes County, Randall Cheek was indicted under this law for "not feeding certain slaves." The case was continued until Cheek's death in 1864 abated it. In 1853 Erasmus Murdoch was found guilty of failing to provide for an aged slave in Chambers County. In the same county Samuel Callahan was indicted in 1857 for not feeding his slaves. When he did not appear for his trial, his bond was ordered forfeited. The next year Lettberry Sherrall was fined for failing to feed his slaves.[61] Cases also arose in Mississippi under a similar law passed in 1857. Peter Nelson, for instance, was indicted in Lowndes County both for cruel punishment and for neglecting to provide the slave adequate clothing. In 1858 Joseph W. Field and George Hairston were indicted for inhumanity in not supplying "necessary provisions & food." Field owned sixty slaves, and Hairston owned sixty-four slaves in 1850.[62]

Similar laws were adopted in Kentucky in 1852 and in Louisiana in 1856, although I found no cases relating to them. By far the most intriguing law was the one enacted by Georgia in 1852. This law went straight to the heart of a master's prerogatives. It is difficult to imagine how it might have been enforced. The law punished owners who failed to provide adequate food and clothing, but it also prohibited "requiring greater labor from such slave or slaves, than he, she or they are able to perform." The closest any jurisdiction had come to such a law before was by restricting the number of hours a slave could be worked. In its 1740 code South Carolina had limited the hours to a maximum of fifteen in any twenty-four-hour period. Georgia's law went further.[63]

All amelioration was a calculated risk. It was not so much of a risk in the view of the Methodist clergyman, Francis Asbury, who confided to his journal in 1809: "would not an *amelioration* in the condition and treatment of slaves have produced more practical good to the poor Africans, than any attempt at their *emancipation*?" There was a danger, however, as John Codman Hurd noted in the 1850s in *The Law of Freedom and Bondage*: "every recognition of rights in the slave, independent of the will of the owner or master which is made by the state to which he is subject, diminishes in some degree the essence of that slavery by changing it into a relation between legal persons."[64]

The law was not the only thing that intruded on the prerogatives of masters. The claims of nonowners to "punish" a slave did so as well and raised some serious problems for Southern whites.

Third-Party Violence against Slaves

In 1827 Stroud observed that "submission is required of the slave not to the will of his master only, but to the will of all other white persons." This was a logical assertion about a hierarchical racial society; was it true? Stroud's evidence was the statutes that punished slaves who lifted their hand against whites. On the other side were laws that provided criminal or civil remedies for third-party abuse of slaves. Goodell scoffed at both civil and criminal actions against those who abused or killed slaves belonging to others. The real purpose of criminal sanctions, he believed, was to "prevent 'damage' to the slaveholder," not to protect the slave. The civil actions for damages were more terrible. They certified and sanctioned the "degradation to the condition of a brute."[65]

A number of statutes adopted in the colonial period, and copied widely thereafter, restricted the violence a person could inflict on the slave of another. These laws allowed at the same time that they limited the right of owners of land or a plantation to whip a slave who was on their property unlawfully. The Maryland law of 1723, for instance, permitted an owner to whip a strange slave up to thirty-nine lashes if he refused to leave after being asked to do so. The model statute for other jurisdictions, however, was the Virginia law of 1748. It allowed the owner of the plantation to give a slave ten lashes if he was on the land without written permission from his owner or had not been sent on some lawful business.[66]

When slaves were off plantations, some jurisdictions expressly authorized "any white person" to stop them, and if they refused to submit to questioning, it was lawful for the white to correct them. Such laws were adopted in South Carolina in 1740, Georgia in 1770, and Louisiana in 1806. But Louisiana made one significant modification, and in doing so it revealed an important element in the making of slave laws—the class relationships among whites. In its law, not "any white person" was allowed to whip, only a "freeholder." Lower-class or propertyless whites were given no authority to whip. Generally, the problem of slaves unlawfully out and about was handled by patrols. Patrols were made up of all able-bodied males in a county, whether slaveowners or not. People had a legal duty to arm themselves and ride around the county to police the slaves. But their legal authority to whip was limited. The Florida law of 1846 was typical. Patrollers were permitted to inflict a "moderate whipping" of up to twenty lashes on slaves outside plantations without a ticket or without a white person present. All of these laws expressly authorizing third parties to whip a slave included limits. Violence against slaves by such persons—whether the owners of plantations, members of patrols, or just "any white person"—that went beyond those limits could lead to some legal sanction, civil or criminal. The Florida law provided that if the patrol beat or bruised a slave who was "quietly and peaceably" on the plantation, it would be subject to a fine of $50 to be recovered by a common law action of debt, as well as to a trespass action for damages. More often, however, statutory provisions on third-party abuse were separate and very general. The Alabama law of 1852 stipulated that any unauthorized person who committed an assault and battery on a slave "without just cause or excuse, to be determined by the jury, is guilty of a misdemeanor."[67]

Although it is true, as Fede suggested, that statutory criminalization of third-party batteries of slaves came from the teens forward, it is also true that criminal actions were brought against third parties who abused slaves earlier. We lose sight of this only because we tend to rely on statutes too much. People could face a common law indictment. In 1725 in Princess Anne County, Virginia, for instance, an information was filed against James Nimmo for assaulting a mulatto slave woman. This was a criminal, not a civil, action. The case was dismissed after Nimmo admitted his guilt and there was a "mutuall promise or agreement of good neighbourhood for the time to come." In 1761 Ziperus Degge underwent a preliminary examination on a criminal charge of "maiming and wounding a negro boy named Isaac belonging to William Flynt." There are also examples from Maryland. In March 1735 a grand jury presentment was brought against Josiah Coleman for assaulting Will, the slave of Benjamin Tasker, one of the more powerful men in the colony. Thirty years later, in Talbot County, William Wales and James Wrightston had to enter recognizances to appear to answer a criminal charge of assault and battery on Ceasar, the slave of Jonathan Harrison. These were common law indictments.[68]

The *Maner* decision in South Carolina was on the other side of this issue. In *Maner* Judge O'Neall had ruled that "the *criminal* offence of assault and battery cannot at common law be committed on the person of a slave. For ... generally, he is a mere chattel personal, and his right of personal protection belongs to his master, who can maintain an action of trespass for the battery of his slave."[69] In states that followed this approach there could be no criminal action against a third party for assault and battery on a slave in the absence of a statute.[70]

A different analysis emerged in North Carolina in *State v. Hale* (1823). Judge Daniel ruled that the striking of a slave by itself was not indictable. This was overruled on appeal. In reaching his conclusion, Chief Justice Taylor resorted to "general principles, from reasonings founded on the common law, adapted to the existing condition and circumstances of our society." Courts were free to adapt the law to keep up "with the march of benignant policy and provident humanity." Moreover, an unredressed assault and battery offends and disturbs "that social order which it is the primary object of the law to maintain." A slave, of course, is "tamed into subservience to his master's will" and will quietly accept chastisement from him because he "knows the extent of the dominion assumed over him, and that the law ratifies the claim." More likely, what he knew was the viciousness and ubiquitousness of the whip, not the law. If a stranger usurp the authority, however, "nature is disposed to assert her rights and to prompt the slave to a resistance." Further, "a wanton injury committed on a slave is a great provocation to the owner, awakens his resentment, and has a direct tendency to a breach of the peace by inciting him to seek immediate vengeance." If a person "has received an injury, real or imaginary, from a slave," he should not "carve out his own justice, for the law has made ample and summary provision for the punishment of all trivial offenses committed by slaves." This law, Taylor concluded, "while it excludes the necessity of private vengeance, would seem to forbid its legality, since it effectually protects all persons from the insolence of slaves, even where their masters are unwilling to correct them upon complaint being made."[71] An indictment would hold because of legalism along with a Christian regard for the well-being of all persons regardless of station.

Taylor had other concerns. "These offenses," he believed, "are usually committed by men of dissolute habits, hanging loose upon society, who, being repelled from association with well disposed citizens, take refuge in the company of colored persons and slaves, whom they deprave by their example, embolden by their familiarity, and then beat, under the expectation that a slave dare not resent a blow from a white man." Taylor's towering contempt for lower-class whites who associated with slaves was unconcealed. Nor was his concern for the property interests of slaveowners a secret. "If such offenses," he wrote, "may be committed with impunity the public peace will not only be rendered extremely insecure, but the value of slave property must be much impaired, for the offenders can seldom make any reparation in damages."[72] A civil remedy against slave abusers was not enough precisely because it was ineffectual against lower-class whites.

Yet the fact remained, they were white. Although a criminal action was good, "at the same time it is undeniable that such offense must be considered with a view to the actual condition of society, and the difference between a white man and a slave, securing the first from injury and insult and the other from needless violence and outrage." Numerous circumstances that "would not constitute a legal provocation . . . committed by one white man on another would justify it if committed on a slave, provided the battery were not excessive." "It is impossible," Taylor admitted, "to draw the line with precision . . . the circumstances must be judged of by the court and jury with a due regard to the habits and feelings of society."[73]

When the battery of the slave occurred without cause or sufficient provocation, it was indictable. North Carolina's judges emphasized the problem of provocation, whereas South Carolina's only allowed for indictments that rested on the vicious-ness of the assault or the intention to kill. One focus was on the conduct of the slave, the other on the conduct of the white. The difference may have occurred because the South Carolina judges had a statutory basis for their analysis, whereas the North Carolina judges did not. For the latter the case had to be analyzed in terms of the common law. "The common law," Taylor wrote, "has often been called into efficient operation, for the punishment of public cruelty inflicted upon animals, for needless and wanton barbarity exercised even by masters upon their slaves, and for various violations of decency, morals and comfort. Reason and analogy seem to require that a human being, although the subject of property, should be so far protected as the public might be injured through him."[74] There is no extant evidence to support the claim that in North Carolina the common law had been used to punish masters for "needless and wanton barbarity" inflicted on their slaves.

In 1860, in *Commonwealth v. Lee and Bledsoe*, the Kentucky Supreme Court faced the same problem that had earlier separated the courts in the Carolinas. Because there was no statute in Kentucky, the case had to be decided by "general principles," the views of other judges, and "reasonings founded upon legal rules, and adapted to the peculiar institution of slavery." The court cited both *Maner* and *Hale* and ruled that *Hale* was the more congenial. "The master's authority over the slave is complete to secure to him obedience and submission to his will," Judge Belvard J. Peters wrote, "and for the minor offense, such as insults to others, he can punish the slave himself, or permit the offended party to inflict such as the offense deserves; but if the master should refuse, the law affords the party a remedy, to which . . . it is his duty to appeal."[75] These are some of the cases at the appellate level that dealt with the issue of common law criminal indictments against third parties. Often the policy choice depended on the judges' perception of the power and authority of masters or on their attitudes toward lower-class whites. The choices were not uniform.

A few appellate cases arose on statutes. The first were *Commonwealth v. Dolly Chapple* (1811) and *Commonwealth v. Carver* (1827) in Virginia. Both involved indictments brought against whites under general mayhem laws rather than laws framed to deal with slaves alone. The question was whether a slave came under those laws. Dolly Chapple was found guilty of the malicious stabbing of a slave. Her ground of appeal was that there was no offense chargeable because the victim was a slave and the defendant a white. One of the sanctions in the law was a fine, three-fourths of which would go to the victim, and slaves could not take property. Therefore, they were not covered by the law. Moreover, the law allowed the victim to be a competent witness, and slaves could not testify against whites. The court rejected the arguments. Even though slaves could not take property, the prisoner could not be shielded from punishment. The incapacity to take applied to married women as well, and no one believed that the law did not punish offenses against married women. The second reason was brushed aside with the observation that it meant to make competent witnesses only those who otherwise would be excluded on the ground of an interest in the fine.[76] It did not make competent witnesses of those who were incompetent for other reasons, such as slaves. The word *person* in the general statute did include slaves, unless there were words of exclusion.

The next action fell under the mayhem statute of 1819.[77] William Carver was indicted for shooting the slave of another person. The case came up because the presiding judge indicated that he disagreed with *Chapple*. He wanted to know whether he was bound by a decision of the higher court. Brockenbrough ruled that he was. There was no reason, he believed,

> arising from the relative situation of master and slave, why a free person should not be punished as a felon for maiming a slave. Whatever power our laws may give to a master over his slave, it is important for the interest of the former, as for the safety of the latter, that a *stranger* should not be permitted to exercise an unrestrained and lawless authority over him. It is for the benefit of the master, and consoling to his feelings, that a third person should be restrained under the pains and penalties of felony, from maiming and disabling his slave.[78]

A Texas case, *Nix v. State* (1855), turned on similar reasoning. The defendant was indicted and found guilty of assaulting the slave of another. The indictment was framed on a general statute rather than the law on cruelty to slaves. Judge Royall Wheeler held that Nix was punishable. The cruelty law was designed to restrain those with authority over slaves, and the defendant had none. He had neither "authority, provocation or excuse" when he attacked Lucy McRea, a slave. Slaves were included, Wheeler argued, in the word "persons" in the Texas criminal code. "The interest of the master, as well as the dictates of humanity," finally, "require that they should be within the protection of the law."[79]

In South Carolina one decision was based on the law of 1740, and two were based on a statute adopted in 1841. In the first case, *State v. Wilson* (1840), Gantt had concluded that the law of 1740 did not punish only those precise forms of cruelty mentioned but reached any "unauthorized cruelty." The next year South Carolina's lawmakers provided another legal peg. They made it an indictable offense to unlawfully whip a slave without sufficient provocation. The first appellate case that arose under this statute was *State v. Boozer* (1850). A patrol had whipped a number of owners' slaves who had gathered, with permission, for a quilting. By all accounts the slaves were orderly, and those from neighboring plantations had tickets to be there. The patrollers' defense was that, as members of a patrol, they had the authority to break up an unlawful assembly and whip the slaves. Judge Thomas Jefferson Withers, for the court, held that the innocuous quilting was hardly an unlawful assembly. In fact, he felt that it would be sad if the law prohibited masters from allowing a slave the "humble virtues that may be consistent with his condition." Withers showed considerable deference for slave-owners. "A judicious freedom of administration of our police law for the lower order," he wrote, "must always have respect to the confidence which the law reposes in the discretion of the master." The convictions stood.[80]

Boozer was followed by *State v. Harlan* (1852). William Harlan, at the request of his sister, had whipped a slave from the calves of his legs to his shoulders between 200 and 300 stripes. The slave had gone to the sister's house in Columbia one night, was ordered off the place, and left "hooping and hallooing." He later returned and pretended to be lost, which frightened the sister. He was ordered off again and subsequently was whipped by Harlan. A number of white witnesses testified that they thought the whipping to be a severe one, whereas others considered it a "light whipping." For the latter group, doubtless, no whipping would be indictable. Judge O'Neall presided over the trial and sent up the following report:

> The case went to the jury, who were told that the whipping of the negro was without legal authority. No one had the right to whip the slave of another, unless the law authorized it to be done. That in this case, if the proof satisfied them that the defendant had reasonable provocation . . . it might excuse him. That to solve this question, they must, as slave owners, put themselves in the defendant's place, and if then they could say, they would have done as he did, they might acquit the defendant. They were told, if the whipping was unreasonable, totally disproportioned to the offence, then I thought the defendant would be guilty.[81]

O'Neall made no effort to reconcile his remark that no one had a right to whip the slave of another without legal authorization or legal provocation with his view in *Maner* that the slave was not within the peace of the state, and a simple battery of a slave was not indictable. But the one rested on a statute and the other on the common law.

Judge David Wardlaw wrote for the court, which included O'Neall. The law of 1841 was interpreted to mean that the beating of someone else's slave was indictable. A beating without provocation could be justified, however, such as one inflicted by a patrol or by a constable executing a lawful sentence. Unjustifiability was defined to mean "unlawfully." "It must moreover be without the excuse of sufficient provocation." "A reasonable proportion between the whipping and the provocation is implied by the word 'sufficient,'" Wardlaw observed, "and of this proportion there can be no standard but the opinion of the jury, formed with just regard to the usages of the community and the circumstances of the particular case." Although a person might not have a "right" to whip a slave, he could be excused if he did so in the face of some provocation. This was consistent with a much earlier ruling in a civil case, *Witsell v. Earnest* (1818), in which Judge Colcock had ruled that "the peace of society, and the safety of individuals required that slaves should be subjected to the authority and control of all freemen, when not under the immediate authority of their masters." "And," he had continued, "while it is conceded, that this is necessary, it is equally obvious, that both principle and policy require, that their lives should be protected from the attacks of the violent and unthinking part of the community."[82]

It was not until the years after the War of 1812 that Southern appellate courts dealt with this problem, and, in general, the pattern of criminal indictments against third persons in lower courts is similar, although there are earlier examples as mentioned before. In my sample there were nearly 140 cases.[83] The overwhelming majority were after 1820. Of those found guilty, almost all received fines ranging from one cent to $150. Most involved fines of $10 or less, and few were given jail sentences. Most of the cases came from the last two decades before the Civil War.[84]

Some illustrations provide impressions of the diversity of cases and the significance of localism in the enforcement of the law. One jurisdiction to highlight is Savannah, where there were thirty-nine cases.[85] No other city studied (Richmond, Nashville, Natchez, or Petersburg, for instance) produced a similar record. It is possible that Baltimore, Charleston, or New Orleans would do so; these were major port towns with boisterous, transient populations of sailors.

A full and revealing record comes from Maury County, Tennessee. It shows as well as any that we should never lose sight of the personal element in the administration of the law. In 1833 Edmund Dillahunty, as attorney for the state, prosecuted Archibald Gilchrist for whipping another man's slave. The result was a guilty verdict and a fine of $25. The fine was not as severe as some in Savannah, but it was above the mean and clearly above the majority levied. But this case had deeper roots. Two years earlier the slaveowner had unsuccessfully sued Gilchrist for trespass in ejectment. Three days after Dillahunty successfully prosecuted Gilchrist for whipping the slave, the owner accused Gilchrist of assault with intent to kill. This case ended in a not guilty verdict a year later.[86] There was a lot of violence and hostility between these two men, and the situation aroused the ire of Dillahunty and the court. The total context rather than the violence to the slave standing alone accounts for the result.

By the 1840s Edmund Dillahunty was the judge of the court in Maury County and showed no interest in imposing severe penalties on anyone found guilty of unlawfully beating someone else's slave. It was Dillahunty who in 1845 fined James Douglas a total of one cent plus costs after a jury found him guilty of assault and battery on a slave.[87] Perhaps Dillahunty now believed that third-party whites possessed a right to correct slaves regardless of the claims of owners or that a "wanton" beating equaled one without the slightest provocation from the slave. Possibly he felt that in order to maintain class hegemony, slaveowners had to allow others to occasionally whip an insolent slave. And perhaps he never thought about it.

The case of John Bolton in Maury County shows us the underside of Southern society. In 1852 Bolton admitted that he had wantonly beaten another person's slave. He was fined $5 plus costs. The same day he pled guilty to "open & notorious lewdness" and was fined another $5. Bolton could not pay so a schedule of his effects was taken. He took the oath of insolvency and was discharged from custody. Four years later he was indicted again for wantonly beating another's slave. He was bailed but found guilty in a trial in 1857 and fined one cent plus costs. In 1859 he was again indicted. This time it was a case of malicious shooting, but not of a slave. John Bolton was a very violent poor white. In two cases of wantonly beating slaves in which guilt was established he ended paying one penny plus costs. A contrast is the case of Alfred E. Jones in Savannah. He was sentenced to a large fine, $150, and to thirty days in jail. He may have upset the judge because he fought his conviction. Jones unsuccessfully moved for a new trial.[88]

Approximately one-half of the cases went to trial; of those, about 31 percent ended in guilty verdicts or pleas and 20 percent in not guilty verdicts. The results in the remainder are unclear.[89] Did slaveowners use the threat of prosecution to warn others to keep their hands off their property? Poor whites like John Bolton had to be reminded of their station but not punished too often or too harshly, lest they become discontented and possibly even align themselves with the blacks. This accords far more rationality to the process than it deserves. Most of these cases were concentrated within a short period of time and scattered about the South. Masters may have had every expectation of convictions. Courts and juries, however, responded in unpredictable ways. They might have reacted against a defendant, such as the pugnacious Alfred Jones in Savannah, or they might have cared little, despite the law, if a white whipped a slave, even a mean-spirited white like John Bolton. We should not impose too much coherence on this ambivalent record. About all that can be said is that slaveowners did use criminal indictments against third parties on occasion and with increasing frequency after about 1820.

Often enough, however, masters bypassed criminal actions in order to sue for damages because of the beating or killing of slaves. Civil actions for damages frequently occurred when owners sued those who had hired the slave. There were also important cases where masters sued third parties who possessed no colorable authority over the slave. A number of issues confronted the courts when masters sued for damages against third parties. Sometimes they were quite technical, such as which form of action was correct, or whether a civil complaint was merged in the felony, which was the common law rule. It did not apply to misdemeanors.

Sometimes the issue tended to take on a larger significance, as in the question of the social relationship between whites in general, slaveowners, and slaves when slaves behaved insolently.

An opening question was whether there was any remedy available to masters. It was not until the judgment in White v. Chambers in 1796 that this issue was settled in South Carolina. Kentucky's lawmakers felt it necessary to adopt a law in 1816 that authorized the owner of a slave to bring an action of trespass against any person who "shall hereafter whip, strike, or otherwise abuse the slave of another, without the consent of the owner of such slave." There was a proviso: "nothing in this act . . . shall be construed to prevent any person or persons from inflicting such punishments on slaves as the laws now in force permit."[90]

Unfortunately, it is impossible to know whether civil actions for damages for the abuse of slaves were routine because the nature of the court records precludes that. Those records normally would only note that A had sued B in case, or trespass, or trover, or whatever, but the facts behind the suit are not mentioned. A rare exception is Bernard v. Alsop, heard in King George County, Virginia, between 1802 and 1804. The case began as a trespass action in March 1802. William Bernard charged Ritchie Alsop with "whiping, beating and wounding" Bernard's slave "so that his life was greatly despaired of"; because of the beating the plaintiff lost the slave's service for five days. The defense was that Alsop possessed a right to chastise the slave because the slave was a trespasser on the land of John Skinker. Alsop was Skinker's overseer and at his command had caught the slave and did "moderately chastise" him for his trespass. Bernard countered that Alsop made the assault without just cause. A jury returned a verdict for Alsop. On motion of Bernard's counsel, the verdict was set aside and a new trial was ordered for a later term. The case was continued the next year, and it ended in 1804 when the parties reached an agreement out of court.[91]

One jurisdiction in which civil actions for damages against third-party abuse of slaves did pose some legal difficulties was South Carolina. One problem concerned whether case or trespass vi et armis would lie. Case would be used to recover damages for wrongs not committed with force, or if force was used the injury must be consequential and not immediate. Trespass lay to recover damages for wrongs committed with force, and the injury was immediate. A variant was trespass per quod servitium amisit. This was an action by a master for the loss of service when someone beat a servant. The servant, by the common law, in turn had his or her own action of trespass vi et armis.[92]

The opening case in the South Carolina sequence was White v. Chambers (1796). The question was whether case would lie when a master's slave had been beaten. The defendant admitted that the per quod servitium amisit could lie "for the loss of his [the slave's] labour, but not for any violence offered to his person; for it is this loss of labour, which alone entitled the master to his right of action." And White had declared "for the personal injury done to his slave, and not for the loss of his services." Chambers also contended that a master could not maintain case for violence against a servant because a personal action could be maintained only by the party suffering the injury. The defendant moved from a technical legal argument to a profoundly important social one. He took a position that doubtless would receive the support of many whites and raise the fears of others. The slave had been insolent, and "it was necessary that the freemen of *Carolina* should, at all times and in all places, possess a power to check them, whenever they were disposed to be forward or unmannerly, and to chastise them for insolent language whenever it was offered by them. And unless this speedy and summary mode of redress was allowed, this class of people could never be kept in order and due subordination." White countered that the defendant's argument would place the slaves "at the mercy of every violent or vindictive man who might choose to give vent to his brutal resentments against this class of people." A great deal rested on this civil action. White continued with an admission that slaves could bring no action, but that only meant that a master had an "additional obligation" to afford them protection. There must be some way to provide a remedy when slaves who were obeying their master's orders were abused by a third party, he concluded.[93]

The court held that the action on the case "ought to be supported . . . even if there had been no precedent to warrant it." It grounded the right to bring case for an injury to a slave on the responsibility masters owed to slaves: "He [the slave] is bound to obey his [the master's] orders and injunctions, and as obedience and protection seem in the nature of things, to be reciprocal duties, he is bound in return to protect his slave from personal injuries, which can only be done in a *peaceable manner* by suit at law." Compensation for the loss of labor, the remedy by the *per quod* action, was not adequate. The court believed that it was necessary to adapt the law. "Because very often an injury offered to a slave, in the execution of his master's commands, is a direct injury to the master who gave the orders, or an affront offered to his authority, which would too often lead on to quarrels and bloodshed, if some adequate remedy was not provided for this kind of injury offered to a slave."[94]

The court also had something to say about Chamber's claim of his right to chastise an insolent slave: "The best rule would be, in all cases where a slave behaved amiss, or with rudeness or incivility to a free white man, to complain to the master, or other person having the charge of such offending slave, who, if he was actuated by curtesy and civility to his neighbour, would on such application, give him the necessary satisfaction for every insult or piece of improper conduct which a slave had offered." This was necessary to preserve good order and the prerogatives of the masters. If it was insufficient, then instead of beating the slave the offended white should appeal to a magistrate to secure satisfaction "according to the nature and circumstances of the case."[95] The classic republican sense of community was blended with the need to maintain the subordination of the slaves and the system further validated by a proper respect by third parties for the master and the law. Whites, as a general rule, did not possess a legal "right" to whip a slave for insolence.

Twenty-five years after the *Chambers* decision the South Carolina court turned in a different direction. There was no opinion recorded in *Goodard v. Wagner* (1821). The headnote reads simply: "Trespass *vi et armis* is the proper action for beating plaintiff's slave." Three years later, in *Carsten v. Murray* (1824), the court gave the reasons. Judge Johnson held that the beating was the result of immediate force and the injury proceeded immediately from the defendant:

> An argument in support of the motion [for case] has been drawn from a supposed analogy in the relation of master and servant in England, where the remedy for an injury done through the person of the servant is case, and that of master and slave in this country; but it will not hold good. In England, the master has no immediate and direct interest in the person of the servant, and consequently can only be mediately or consequentially affected, by an injury done to him; but in this country, the master's property in the slave, is as absolute as in any other article of property. Force committed on a slave is, therefore, an immediate injury to the master.

Johnson circumvented *Chambers* with the suggestion that the problem there was not what the proper remedy might be but whether any action at all would lie for such an injury.[96]

The court returned to the claim of a "right" to whip another's slave in 1841. In *Grimké v. Houseman* the defendant "undertook, by unauthorized violence, to redress the grievance of his own slave." He "pursued the plaintiff's servant and beat her in her own house." Judge Butler was offended: "Common courtesy required that he should have complained to the plaintiff . . . before he took redress in his own hands. The great object of the law is to give security to the enjoyment of property, free from an illegal interference with it against the consent of the owner."[97] The action of trespass therefore was good, and the jury should have found for the plaintiff which it had not done.

In 1839 the legislature supplemented the common law actions and provided another remedy for masters. There would be a $50 penalty for any one who whipped a slave who had a ticket to be lawfully off the plantation. In addition, the owner of the slave was allowed to bring his trespass action.[98]

This summary process was involved in another 1841 case, *Caldwell ads. Langford*, in which the court construed the words "beat and abuse" in the statute. O'Neall, for a unanimous court, held that "any unlawful whipping of a slave, is a beating and abusing" within the meaning of the statute. If the slaves had been disorderly, a different situation obtained. In *Caldwell*, they had tickets and were behaving in an orderly fashion at a store in Newberry. If they had not been, O'Neall noted, the defendants "would have been protected, under the general authority which devolves on all white men, of correcting slaves who may so offend."[99] This admission, of course, was vital. It was the position the court rejected in 1796 in *Chambers*, and it is difficult to square with Butler's remark in *Grimké* the same year *Caldwell* was

decided. Judges were working for results, and they produced doctrinal inconsistency and occasionally incoherence.

Another legal issue in civil actions came into play when a slave had not been
simply beaten but had been killed. The question was whether the civil action was
"merged" in the felony, that is, could the owner of a slave have a civil action before
there was a criminal trial for the homicide? Generally speaking, the courts ruled,
following *Smith v. Weaver*, a North Carolina decision of the 1790s, that the civil act
was not barred altogether, but that it was suspended.[100]

Finally, an important question in these cases was the proper measure of damages. In 1827, in *Richardson v. Dukes*, the South Carolina court granted a new trial
on the matter of damages. The defendant had found two slaves stealing potatoes
and shot and killed one of them. The evidence was that the victim "was a negro of
bad character." The jury found for the plaintiff but set the damages at one dollar.
According to Judge Nott, that was not sufficient. Even though the slave was "of bad
character," he was still entitled to the protection of the law "and his owner to the
value of his services." Still, the slave's character might be taken into account in the
"mitigation of damages." But, the court hastened to add, "it was no justification.
The jury were not at liberty, therefore, to let the defendant off with merely nominal
damages." Nott concluded: "The verdicts of juries, though always well intended,
are often the result of momentary feeling, and the tenure of property would be
very precarious, if it were to depend upon such hasty and fleeting impressions."[101]

Another example is *Wilson v. Fancher* (Tennessee, 1858). This was a striking civil
case that shows we often miss rich veins when we focus too much on criminal
actions or the policing of slaves. Technically this was an action on the case to
recover damages for killing a slave of the plaintiff named Austin. The jury found
one penny damages for the plaintiff. There is no doubt why. The lower court
allowed evidence of Austin's character, and what it showed was that Austin was in
jail on charges of rape and murder. He was taken from the jail and lynched. Some
members of the lynch mob, in fact, had made a written contract. Some agreed to
"stand by each other" by a "written agreement," and others, "without having
signed it, moved by concert to the jail, broke down the door, took out the negro,
and hung him till he was dead."[102]

Judge Robert L. Caruthers expressed his outrage. "There is neither valor nor
patriotism in deeds like these . . . courts and juries, public officers and citizens,
should set their faces like flint against popular outbreaks and mobs, in all their
forms." Such an outburst needs to be placed alongside the tepid responses to the
mob executions in Mississippi in 1835. An insurrection scare led to the violence,
but there was no judicial and little political reaction to the lynchings. Scholars have
suggested that this episode is evidence of the use of mob violence to affirm values
and to help solidify a sense of community. Judges like Caruthers, on the other side,
were fearful that lynch law exacted too high a price, the corrosion of the whole
notion of a rule of law.[103]

But the rule of law has often meant a regard for property rights, and that is the way it appeared in *Wilson*. What was the proper measure of damages in such cases? The value of the slave should be "determined from age, appearance, health, and, with all these, what he would sell for in the market" without taking into account the charges against him. This case, Caruthers believed, was a proper one for exemplary and vindictive damages. The reason was simple: "it was a deliberate, premeditated, and violent destruction of the plaintiff's property, in disregard of both the civil and criminal laws of the State, of most evil example." He did not demand that those responsible be brought before the courts for a criminal trial, but he did conclude that the civil verdict under review was a "mockery of justice."[104]

A slightly different analytic foundation for a claim of vindictive damages was developed by Ormond in Alabama in *Wheat v. Croom* (1845). The reason was the character of slaves. "The slave, although property," he wrote, "is also a moral agent, a sentient being. As such, he is capable of mental, as well as corporal suffering, and for this, as well as for the evil example, vindictive damages, may be given." The humanity of the slave was of little value to him, it but increased his value to his master. The more deferential he was, the more value he had.[105]

In some states slaves were to be submissive to all whites, who possessed a general authority to chastise or correct them when they were not. In others this was not so. In 1831, in *Sublet v. Walker*, for instance, the Kentucky Supreme Court ruled that "even if the slave had injured or offended the defendant . . . he had no legal right to beat her, with force and arms, as he did, without the plaintiff's consent." And in Alabama, in *Townsend v. Jeffries' Adm'r.* (1854), the court ruled that "no person has the right to inflict chastisement on his neighbor's slave, without the consent of the owner, unless such authority is given him by statute." Yet Southern judges had some difficulty reconciling the rights of masters and the claims of the rest of society, especially that part of it that rarely washed. Despite the rhetorical flourishes, the focus of these legal developments was seldom on the need to protect slaves as human beings from being abused. There were protestations to the contrary, of course, such as those of South Carolina's Judge O'Neall, who contended that the laws were designed to "protect slaves, who dare not raise their own hands in defence, against burtal violence." But, he tellingly concluded, they were also to "teach men, who are wholly irresponsible in property, to keep their hands off the property of other people."[106] To some small extent the law also was used to stay the hands of those who owned that property.

9

Jurisdiction and Process in
the Trials of Slaves

The worst system which could be devised.

JOHN BELTON O'NEALL, *Negro Law of South Carolina* (1848)

"Trial of slaves upon criminal accusations," wrote Stroud, "is in most of the slave states different from that which is observed in respect to free white persons; and the difference is injurious to the slave and inconsistent with the rights of humanity."[1] Stroud's condemnation rested on the idea that process matters. Before they were punished by public authorities slaves would be judged, and the processes followed in judging them tell us a great deal about slave law. Process guides and constrains judging, and judging itself is a complex jurisprudential problem. Law in the Western legal tradition, outside its application to slaves, has often been analyzed in terms of styles of judging. Patrick Atiyah and Robert Summers, for instance, compared the styles of judging of English and American judges. They found that the former had "throughout history shown anxiety lest the effect of legal prohibitions should be weakened by equitable modifications designed to show mercy or compassion (or even justice) to those who have committed prohibited acts." English judges, they concluded, tended to a much "greater use of formal rules" than did American judges, who saw a legal rule not as a clear and formal command, but as a guide at most. American judges were more likely to go outside a formal rule to examine substantive considerations of justice. Much earlier, Weber had identified two characteristics of lawmaking: a "formal rationality" in which "only unambiguous general characteristics of the facts are taken into account" and what he called "*Khadi*-justice," which followed not rules of "formal rationality" but widely held ethical, social, or religious values embedded in a "substantively rational law."[2] These, of course, are analytic models, but they can help us frame some questions about the nature of the trials of slaves. Did the judging of slaves tend toward formal rationality or toward an open reliance on widely held community values about race and about the subordination of those in bondage? The latter view is more congenial and is in accord with the judgment of abolitionists like Stroud. The intuition is sound enough, but the history of the procedural side of the criminal law of slavery is more ambiguous than the intuition allows. Concern about the property interests of the owners of accused slaves and, even occasionally, concern about fair treatment of the slaves themselves, as well as fidelity to a notion of a rule of law, complicated the history. Generally, the trend was toward the introduction of more formality as time passed. Monumental difficulties remained, however, such as the problem of the rules of evidence (taken up in the next chapter).

Magistrates

Among the most important figures during the colonial period were the magistrates, or justices of the peace. From the sixteenth through the eighteenth centuries they were powerful officials. In the seventeenth century Coke gave them fulsome praise: the justices, he wrote, provided "such a form of subordinate government for the tranquillity and quiet of the realm as no part of the Christian world hath the like." Numerous treatises described the metes and bounds of their authority. One of the first was William Lambard's *Eirenarcha; or, Of the Office of Justices of Peace* (1581). He suggested that the commissions under which they acted "doth leave little (or nothing) to the discretion of the Justices of the Peace, but bindeth them faste with the chaines of the Lawes, customes, ordinances, and Statutes."[3] An important limit was that a single justice could not order anyone executed. Still, as Michael Dalton put it, there was scope for a discretionary justice because "all considerable circumstances" could not be "foreseen at the time of the making of the statutes."[4]

In the seventeenth and eighteenth centuries their powers of summary conviction, as Norma Landau observed, were "impressive." Summary jurisdiction meant that magistrates could hear and determine cases sitting alone, often in their own homes. They could fine the "idle, lewd, and disorderly." The "catalogue" of their summary jurisdiction "seems endless and indicative of powers . . . sufficiently arbitrary to insure dominance of a neighbourhood." Landau also noted that "almost all the powers allotted to the single justice directly affected only the least substantial inhabitants of his vicinity." One of their most important powers was the authority to require people to enter into a recognizance to keep the peace or be of good behavior.[5]

Magisterial discretion, however, did have its critics. Among the more amusing was Henry Fielding, who was himself a justice in the English countryside. He pilloried a variety of justices throughout his ribald writings. Justice Frolic, in *Joseph Andrews*, for example, enjoyed a "little stripping and whipping."[6] More significant were the more formal expressions of concern. One fear was that voiced by a commentator on the office in the 1750s: "the power of a justice of the peace is in restraint of the common law, and in abundance of instances is a tacit repeal of that famous clause in the great charter, that a man should be tried by his equals."

Blackstone, about the same time, condemned summary convictions as "funda-
mentally opposed to the spirit of our constitution." But his real concern was with
the decline in the "quality of the sovereign's justices." "Gentlemen of rank and
character" were declining the office, and venal place seekers were moving in.[7]

Beginning in 1680, at the time when white Virginians turned to black slavery as
the number of white indentured servants declined, the burgesses began to extend
the jurisdiction of the single justices. A magistrate could order thirty lashes "upon
due proofe made thereof by the oath of the party" that a slave had presumed "to
lift up his hand in opposition against any christian." No defense was allowed. By
1705 the word "slave" was dropped as the jurisdiction was extended to cover any
offending "negro, mulatto, or Indian, bond or free."[8]

During the remainder of the colonial period statutory authority was given to
single justices when slaves were charged with stealing hogs or killing deer, attending unlawful meetings, or being off a plantation with a dog (this was to protect
sheep). The most detailed statutes involved hog stealing. By "one evidence," the law
of 1699 read, "or by his owne confession" a slave would receive thirty-nine lashes
for the first offense on order of a single justice. A second offense was outside the
jurisdiction of just one magistrate: it went to the full county court. In 1748, in one
of the only instances during the colonial period, the jurisdiction of the single
justice was removed. He now conducted a preliminary hearing only in hog-stealing cases.[9]

After the Revolution the Virginia legislature added a jurisdiction that was copied widely throughout the South. As of 1792 a magistrate could order up to thirty-
nine lashes for slaves involved in "riots, routs, unlawful assemblies, trespasses and
seditious speeches." By 1819 he could order up to thirty lashes for blacks, bond or
free, who furnished passes to slaves to be off plantations and order thirty-nine
lashes for slaves who used "abusive and provoking language" to a white person.[10]

It is obvious that the single justice of the peace in Virginia was not used to
rooting out wickedness and foulness of spirit, as in early New England. He was an
instrument in maintaining a system of racial domination in general and slavery in
particular. This was aided by using a summary jurisdiction in relatively minor
cases so that the labor needs of the master were only briefly interrupted. This
pattern and the specific jurisdiction were repeated often, even though there were
some variations.[11]

Probably the sharpest contrast to the jurisdictional history of Virginia's single
magistrate came in South Carolina. In that colony the single justice of the peace
did not occupy the exalted position of the justices of Virginia. Governor James
Glen complained, by the mid-eighteenth century, that the position of justice of the
peace was an office of "no Profit and some Trouble," and few would accept the job
"unless they are much courted."[12]

The responsibilities of the magistrates in South Carolina were defined in William Simpson's work, *The Practical Justice of the Peace and Parish-Officer, of His
Majesty's Province of South Carolina* (1761). They were as follows: (1) preventative,

"by taking surety for the keeping of it [the peace], or good behaviour," (2) "pacify-
ing such as are actually breaking it," and (3) conducting preliminary examinations
of those persons who appeared guilty of offenses upon a complaint or an information. Under the third category Simpson noted that justices possessed "no power to
hear or determine any breach of the peace whatever" and had to turn offenders
over to the court of general sessions for trial, unless he had been given authority to
"meddle with" the matter by statute.[13]

He had been so authorized when slaves were involved as early as 1690. Single
justices could order a slave to be "severely whipped" the first time he or she "shall
offer any violence, by striking and the like, to any white person." The number of
lashes was discretionary. For a second offense the justice could direct, in addition
to a severe whipping, that the slave have "his or her nose slit, and face burnt in
some place." A third offense was a capital crime and could not be tried by a single
justice.[14]

By 1712, because "great mischiefs daily happen by petty larcenies," single justices
were given authority to order a whipping up to forty lashes in such cases. A grim
addition was added in 1712 for fugitives. A fugitive slave, gone twenty days or more,
was to be whipped severely by his or her master. If the master failed to do so and
someone complained to a justice, the magistrate would whip the runaway and
assess the master for the costs. The fifth offense was a capital one and outside the
jurisdiction of a single magistrate. But up to that point the punishments became
more and more vicious. On the fourth flight a male fugitive was castrated; a female
was severely whipped, was branded with an R on her left cheek, and had her left ear
cut off. This lasted until the 1720s, when the correction of runaways was left to the
owners. Magistrates, however, still could order up to forty lashes for slaves who
assisted a runaway. They also had the authority to prescribe the same punishment
for slaves guilty of the "stealing of fowles, robbing of hen-roosts, or any other lesser
crimes." At the same time, the lawmakers changed the regulation on striking
whites to require two magistrates to hear such cases. In the English system this was
called the "Double Justice."[15]

Following the Stono Rebellion the position of the single justice declined in
South Carolina. Even in noncapital cases he could no longer sit alone. He had to
summon two freeholders and could order corporal punishment only with their
assent.[16] Slaveowners' property interests outweighed the power of South Carolina
magistrates. In that colony the office apparently had already slipped into hands
other than those of "Gentlemen of rank and character."

Whether they were gentlemen of property and standing or men of a lower social
class, how they exercised their discretion is significant. Unfortunately, we do not
possess anything like the full records for Kent County, England, on which Landau
was able to rely. Still, we can form an impression. One justice who behaved like
Fielding's Justice Frolic was Landon Carter of Virginia. A case he dealt with in 1774
in Richmond County is revealing. On Saturday, August 6, he recorded the following
incident in his diary: "Yesterday Gri. Garland by Letter made a complaint against

Rob. Carter's Weaver who he had catched at his house; he had constantly lost his fowls and was at last told of this man's going there to his woman and though he could not prove it, did suspect that William and his wench must be concerned about it, and he only desired the man might be corrected for it. As a magistrate I ordered him as Constable to give him twenty-five lashes and send him home." Carter had ordered the whipping on a complaint based on a suspicion, even though the complainant admitted he could not prove that William had stolen anything.[17]

That was not the end of the episode. The diary entry continued:

> This morning by accident I asked after this man and was told that he was sick. I ordered him to come to me; he came out and there in a most violent passion swore he would not be served so by me or by anybody for he daresay I was glad to have people murdered. I ordered him to be tied. He rushed in, bolted his door, and as the people were breaking in to him he broke out of the window and run off. I sent after him and rode about; when I came in he was at my door; and there before John Selfe told me I was not his master and his master would not have let him be served so, nay, that I would not dare to have done it, on which I gave him a stroke with my switch and he roared like a bull, and went on with his tongue as impudent as possible so much as J. Selfe told him he ought to be made to hold his tongue. I then had him carried to a tree, and at last he humbled himself; but I fancy it was only the fear of another whipping, but he only got three cuts and was forgiven for this once.[18]

Here was magisterial discretion in a colonial slave-based society. The symbols of power and mercy were both displayed in this case,[19] and, above all, the fact that to have the power to be a "conservator of the peace" in colonial Virginia meant that slaves had to be humbled at all times regardless of any objective evidence of guilt.

By the nineteenth century magistrates, at least outside Virginia, behaved more circumspectly, especially as they were subject to appeals from their judgments. Arthur Howington discovered some very useful records of local magistrates in Maury County, Tennessee. Some of them went out of their way to provide elaborate hearings. In December 1860, for instance, Justice W. R. Mack brought thirteen witnesses to testify in the case before him. It is hardly imaginable that colonial justices like Carter would have taken so much trouble in minor criminal offenses of slaves.[20]

A splendid, if isolated, example of an appeal below the highest state court occurred in Warren County, Kentucky, in 1858. The case, B. C. Gordon et al. v. P. Hines, Judge of the Police Court, was heard in the county circuit court. Hines had ordered a number of slaves arrested and brought before him for trial on a charge that they had violated a town ordinance by "disorderly conduct by blowing hornes and beating tin pans." He found them guilty and sentenced each to ten lashes that could be commuted if the owners paid $3 for each slave owned by him and one-thirteenth part of the court costs. The circuit judge, Asher W. Graham, overturned this judgment. He noted that a slave guilty of a misdemeanor could be punished by

stripes, and that a justice of the peace had jurisdiction to try and inflict punishment on persons guilty of breach of the peace. He also ruled that police courts had
exclusive jurisdiction of all breaches of the bylaws or ordinances of the city and
concurrent jurisdiction with justices and the circuit court of all misdemeanors
subject to punishment up to thirty-nine lashes. In the case before him the charge
was a violation of a municipal ordinance against disorderly conduct, not a violation of state law. But the problem was that the town charter allowed lashes for
slaves only for the offense of "gaming," even though it gave power to suppress
disorderly conduct. The slaves, therefore, could not be ordered to be whipped.[21]

Beyond these petty offenses the magistrates also had roles to play in the felony
trials of slaves. Sometimes they conducted preliminary examinations, and sometimes they participated in the trials themselves. The latter was especially true
during the colonial period. Virginia enacted one of the first laws in 1692. It was
adopted to assure the "speedy prosecution of negroes and other slaves for capital
offences" so that other slaves would be "detered by the condign punishment"
inflicted and so that they would "vigorously proceed in their labours." The sheriff
was to have a slave "well laden with irons" upon jailing him on a capital charge,
and then he was to notify the governor. The governor in turn issued commissions
of oyer and terminer "to such persons of the county as he shall think fitt." They in
turn would arraign, indict, take evidence, and render a verdict and pass judgment
"as the law of England provides." Despite the apparently cumbersome process, the
intent was to ensure speedy trials, the punishment of the guilty, and the docility of
those workers in bondage. The special commission of oyer and terminer was ideal
for those purposes.[22] Its value was that it could be issued to any person and to any
number who were authorized to hear cases. It was not necessary to wait until a
scheduled sitting of a regular court. Without the use of such a device, slaves would
be tried as free men and women, and that involved a truly laborious process.[23]

The planter justices of Virginia, however, were not satisfied because this scheme
gave the royal governor the power to issue commissions to those he thought "fitt."
They wanted them to be a pro forma grant of jurisdiction to the sitting justices of
the peace of the county.[24] By 1765 this resulted. From that time forward the law
provided that four or more justices of the peace (with at least one being "of the
quorum," which meant that he was to be learned in the law) would execute the
office of justices of oyer and terminer in the trials of slaves for their lives. In 1772
the burgesses added that no death sentence could be passed "unless four of the
court . . . being a majority, shall concur in their opinion of his or her guilt." This
produced a chilling blast from Landon Carter in his diary on May 6, 1772: "The
Court discharged" the slave Peter "though every presumption was as strong as
could be. But indeed by the New law, a negro now cannot be hanged, for there
must be 4 Judges to condemn him, and such a court I am persuaded will never be
got." The reason for the change was "Public frugality" because of the concern that
there were "too many Slaves to be paid for." The owners of slaves who were
executed were compensated from the public treasury. Carter was disgusted with

such parsimony: "Frugality go on with your destruction; and prosper thou the country whom thou intendest to serve if thou canst. My word for it, this law will not stand long."[25] He was wrong. It remained the basic framework for the capital trials of slaves until the end of slavery in 1865.

A variation in felony slave trials was developed in South Carolina. In 1690 the proprietary government stipulated that slaves would be tried in capital cases by two magistrates sitting with a specified number of slaveowners. The code of 1740 then provided that in capital cases two magistrates sitting with between three and five freeholders would hear the case; in noncapital cases it was one justice and two freeholders. In capital trials a quorum could consist of either two justices and one freeholder or one justice and two freeholders. The norm in capital cases, nonetheless, was the Double Justice system modified to include some slaveholders. By a law of 1839 the justices were required to sit with three freeholders.[26] These magistrate-freeholder courts, which continued to be used until the death of slavery, were special ad hoc tribunals. Once the freeholders joined the magistrates, they possessed the same power and duty as the magistrate who summoned them. There was no separation between the application of legal rules and fact-finding. Moreover, like the single justice, these courts would assemble at any designated spot. For instance, in Fairfield District during the 1840s a trial of a number of slaves for a breach of the peace was held at Colonel A. W. Younge's plantation, and a case of insolence was tried at the home of the complainant, Turner Turket.[27] Delaware used a similar system until 1789, and Georgia used it when it adopted South Carolina's slave code late in the colonial period; Georgia maintained the system until 1811.[28]

North Carolina's jurisdictional history differed. Under its 1741 code, trials in capital cases were before at least three county justices of the peace, who would sit with four slaveholders.[29] This system lasted until 1793, when it was changed to provide for trial in the regular county court unless that court was not scheduled to meet within fifteen days from the time the slave was committed. In that event, three county justices would hold the trial with a regular jury. The jurisdiction of the justices of the peace in capital trials, finally, was removed in 1816. There remained one possibility for their involvement in trying slaves, however: in cases of conspiracy, insurrection, or rebellion special courts of oyer and terminer would be called to hear the charges.[30]

The Role of Juries

By the mid-eighteenth century commentators were pointing out that the discretionary power of magistrates undermined the guarantee of a trial by peers. This concern had not always been that clear. Dalton did not mention the tension in his treatise. During the seventeenth century, however, regard for the jury trial rose dramatically.[31] By the end of the century there appeared an edition of Dalton's treatise that began with an expression of concern about the growth of the "absolute discretional, and extra-curial power" of the magistrates. The complaint was even more precise: it was that "in very many cases, in matters both of liberty and property, the fundamental course of accusation by Indictment found and Conviction after Issue joynd by Verdict of Twelve Jurors, and of Judgment given in open Court on mature deliberation, concurrency of Opinion, and publick and solemn Determination thereof, are in a great measure abrogated."[32]

By the end of the eighteenth century the jury trial was extolled as the very "palladium of liberty."[33] Seen as a powerful weapon against an oppressive state, it was an institution in which the law-finding and fact-finding functions were not wholly separated.[34] Nineteenth-century judges brought the juries under some measure of control through instructions and even, on occasion, directed verdicts. They instilled into the jurisprudence the notion that juries were to take the law from the court and then find the truth or the falsity of the facts alleged. But this resulted from a continuing historical struggle between judges and juries through the first half of the nineteenth century.[35] At the time when some states extended the right to a trial by jury to slaves, it was held in perhaps the highest esteem it has ever achieved. Some legalists outside the common law world expressed doubt about the institution and saw it more as an institutional expression of community values and prejudices.[36]

From the latter perspective there was really little to chose between judgments by magistrates or by jurors. There remained important differences between the justice administered by magistrates and that determined by juries. Among the qualities that distinguished the jury trial from the judgment of magistrates singled out in the 1677 edition of Dalton, for instance, was that the judgment was in open court, which meant that it was more solemn. Moreover, it came after a more "mature deliberation," and it required the agreement of several different persons.[37]

What was the role of the jury in the trials of slaves? The abolitionists Goodell and Stroud were critical of the fact that jury trials were only used in limited contexts. Goodell noted that a "a trial by jury is granted in *capital* cases" in some states but that was a fraud. "The proper idea of trial by jury includes a trial by the '*peers*' or EQUALS of the accused. *There is no such jury trial for the slave!* Trial by jury of slaves would soon upset the 'legal relation' of slave owner!" Stroud was a bit more careful in his analysis, but having admitted that jury trials did exist in some states, he spent most of his effort condemning the forms of trial in the three states where they were not used—South Carolina, Virginia, and Louisiana. On the other side, T. R. R. Cobb's treatment of the use of juries is more curious, but it points out how highly regarded trial by jury was, as well as the fact that people held somewhat imprecise notions about "juries." He made only one comment: "a fair trial by jury, in all graver cases, is granted by the statutes of every State." Cobb, who usually cited a statute or a case precisely, simply listed the states as support. If he believed this, he must have taken the view that the freeholders who sat with magistrates, as in South Carolina or in Louisiana, were to be viewed as jurors, and that five of them were sufficient. What confuses the matter for twentieth-century observers is that we approach the problem with fairly set ideas about what trial by jury must mean. But the records of the magistrate-freeholder courts indicate that South Carolinians, for instance, regarded the freeholders as jurors. They were often called "jurors," and there is an occasional reference to the "jury." In Anderson District those who tried the slave John for arson in 1855 were called "the jury."[38] On the other hand, there are references to the judgment of the magistrate-freeholders as the judgment of "the court."[39] Part of the difficulty is that freeholders and magistrates had precisely the same power and authority to find law and fact, and to set the punishment. Are we then dealing with trials by jury? South Carolinians apparently thought so. Yet O'Neall roundly condemned it as "the worst system which could be devised." It was a fact, he believed, that "the passions and prejudices of the neighborhood, arising from a recent offence, enter into the trial and often lead to the condemnation of the innocent."[40] But even if we concede that the freeholders who sat with the magistrates in South Carolina and Louisiana might be called a jury, what can be said about Cobb's inclusion of the state of Virginia, where trials were held before "Gentlemen Justices" alone?

The actual laws and experiences with jury trials in Southern jurisdictions are more complicated than might appear. An opening question is to determine when juries began to be used. According to Stroud, "African slavery . . . originated in the foulest iniquity," and "in but few, if in any, of the colonies, was trial by jury allowed to the slave."[41] In fact, such trials did take place in Maryland.

Maryland's use of juries in slave trials was part of one of the most intricate jurisdictional schemes in the Southern colonies. Hurd noted that in Maryland, by a law of 1751, "a trial by jury and justices of assize, as in cases of other persons, appears to be contemplated." What that law really provided was that in capital cases, the slave would be tried either by the county court of magistrates or by one or more of the assize justices at the next assizes, whichever court sat first. Unlike the county magistrate, an assize justice moved about the country on circuit under a special commission. The law also stated that the slave could be convicted by his confession or by "the verdict of a jury." But there is evidence that slaves had been tried by juries in Maryland well before 1751. As early as 1701, in *His Majesty v. Smiths Negro Man*, a jury found the slave Tom guilty of hog stealing. A year later John and Lieutenant were acquitted by a jury on a charge of "thefts." In 1737 Ben was indicted by a grand jury and tried by a petit jury before the court of magistrates of Prince Georges County, Maryland. And a year after that several slaves were tried by a jury on a charge that they were involved in a conspiracy to murder a slaveowner.[42]

There were anomalies. Whereas Tom, John, and Lieutenant received jury trials, Fortuno, charged with killing and removing a hog, did not. Moreover, special commissions of oyer and terminer were used on occasion—normally only in extraordinary situations, such as in the trial of alleged slave insurrectionists in Prince Georges County in 1739. But the year before Anne Arundel County employed them in ordinary felony trials of slaves for burglary, robbery, and murder.[43]

It is also clear that assize justices heard cases before 1751. In 1743 the justices of assize of the western shore sitting on circuit heard a case against Jack for breaking into a stable and stealing a horse.[44] After 1751 the assize judges continued to hear cases, special commissions of oyer and terminer were issued, trials by jury were held, and even on rare occasions a trial might be conducted in the provincial court. The provincial court consisted of the governor and one or more of his councillors functioning as associate judge.

If the Maryland system is set aside as unique, however, the first real break toward the use of juries came in Delaware in 1789, when it was decided that slaves would be tried in capital cases by juries in the regular county general sessions court. The next alteration was in North Carolina in 1793. There were oddities. From 1793 to 1816 trials in North Carolina were to take place in the county court, unless they were not scheduled to be held within fifteen days of the jailing of the slave. In that event three justices would hear the case with a regular twelve-man jury. After 1816 North Carolina abandoned the use of magistrates as triers, and felony trials were held only in the regular county court. Georgia dropped the use of magistrates in 1811, when it gave jurisdiction over slave felonies to county inferior courts. This was later changed to the superior courts. Mississippi, from 1822 to 1833, provided for trials by magistrates sitting under oyer and terminer commissions, but they would hear the case with a regular twelve-man jury. A particularly odd experiment occurred in Alabama from 1836 to 1852. Felony trials were to be held either before the county judge sitting with two magistrates or before three magistrates sitting with a regular jury. After 1852 this approach was dropped in favor of regular jury trials before the county court. Elsewhere in the South jury trials in felony cases became the norm, but in some places they were limited to capital offenses.[45]

Of the states that allowed juries to hear slave cases, only North Carolina required that all the jurors must be slaveholders.[46] This applied in Tennessee, which based its code on that of North Carolina, until 1831. It then shifted. If a jury of slaveowners was impracticable, it became lawful to use "householders" to round out the panel of prospective jurors. Five years later Tennessee made all persons competent to hear cases of free whites competent to hear slave cases. Some jurisdictions adopted a mix. Alabama, in 1836, stipulated that one-half of the twenty-four-person panel would have to be slaveholders, but it did not expect that the twelve chosen to sit on the jury would fit a mathematical profile. In 1852, however, it specified that two-thirds of the actual jurors must be slaveowners.[47]

North Carolina provided that slaveowners alone would try slaves, and Alabama and Mississippi used a technique that assured that some, if not all who heard the case, would be. In Louisiana and South Carolina the freeholders who sat with the magistrates were required to be slaveowners. Five states thus made it certain that slaveowners would dominate the trials of slaves for felonies.

Although not all jurisdictions expressly provided that the jurors who tried slaves must be disinterested, some chose to do so. One of the first was North Carolina. As of 1793 it decreed that jurors "shall not be connected with the owner of such slave, or the prosecutor, either by affinity or consanguinity." A narrower requirement appeared in the law of Florida of 1828: "No person having an interest in a slave shall sit upon the trial of such slave." In some jurisdictions no express provision was made. Presumably, the matter was to be handled by means of juror challenges. But as Michael Hindus suggests, freeholders who tried slaves in South Carolina may not always have been as disinterested as they ought to have been. In five cases he found that the owner of the slave tried and one member of the jury had the same last name; therefore, in rural counties with close family ties they were possibly related.[48]

If we accept the notion that the freeholders who sat on trials in Louisiana and South Carolina should be seen as "jurors," then jurors actually could find the facts in all, and even sentence defendants in nearly half, the slave states of the South. What, then, was the actual difference between trials by magistrates alone, as in Virginia, or by jurors? Were the procedural form and the substance closer than we allow? Surely there was a substantive difference between the conduct of the Virginia justices and the magistrate-freeholders of South Carolina and Louisiana, on one side, and that of those who acted within a system that on the surface tried to provide for trials by disinterested jurors before impartial judges, on the other. Although the distance between them is less than assumed, there was a distance. There was a more "rational" rule in the trials of slaves outside South Carolina, Louisiana, and Virginia than within those systems. Other jurisdictions exercised some discretion, of course, but it was not as freewheeling as can be found in the trial records of Virginia and South Carolina, for instance. Outside of those states it would be difficult to find a verdict such as that in the case against Green in South Carolina's Spartanburg District in 1849. "The court have decided," the judgment read, "that the charge is more of trespass than theft, but think it is a liberty that a Negro ought not to take and have decided that he receive eighteen lashes on the bare back." Or consider two examples from Virginia. In 1767 in Fauquier County, Prince was found not guilty of rape, but the magistrates added that "he ought to receive corporal punishment for the said crime" and ordered thirty-nine lashes. Occasionally, the justices rendered judgments that were not directly related to the charge against the slave. In 1782 in Sussex County, the slave Charles was found not guilty of breaking into a storehouse. The court admitted that the evidence, though strong, was insufficient to convict him. Nonetheless, he received thirty-nine lashes because he "has greatly misbehaved in the County in Gaming and Corrupting the Negroes in the Neighborhood."[49] Verdicts like these would be unimaginable outside the magistrates' court of Virginia or the judicial systems used in South Carolina and Louisiana. There was something to be said, after all, for the notion that a verdict given by a jury in "open court on mature deliberation" and following some reasonably certain rules would restrict discretion, even if it did not eliminate it.

Grand Juries

Goodell followed William Jay's assertion that "in no one State . . . is it thought worth while to trouble a *grand jury* with presenting a slave." Yet Stroud acknowledged that Kentucky, North Carolina, and Tennessee used the grand jury in slave trials. Cobb, on the other side, did not even mention the grand jury, but at one time or another every Southern jurisdiction used grand juries except for Virginia, South Carolina, and Louisiana.[50]

One of the more intriguing examples is Mississippi, precisely because its constitution provided that the grand jury indictment was unnecessary in slave trials. In Wilkinson County the slave Burt went on trial in 1862 for assault and battery with intent to kill. The first document in the file papers was the grand jury indictment. And in Adams County on November 4, 1857, the circuit judge quashed an indictment against the slave Peter for an assault on a white with intent to kill. The next day the grand jury brought in a new indictment against Peter.[51] The abolitionists were simply wrong, but whether the use of grand juries actually mattered is another question.

Grand juries have been extolled as a vital protection against oppression, and they have been damned as supine engines of prosecutorial vindictiveness. Daniel Flanigan argued that they might be very harsh, but the evidence is just not clear. Ultimately, the depth of slaves' powerlessness, based on the juridical notion of persons as things, might mean that no trial form really had much significance. The basic structure might matter little, unless, of course, it was linked in the minds of those who held the strings of power with the concept of right or a rule of law that bound discretion. Granting slaves procedural rights would then mean granting them rights to as fair a trial as the system could provide. Fundamental fairness could have been an ethical norm that infected the forms of trial, in other words. Another point concerns the property interests of slaveowners. To the extent that those interests were involved, the use of grand juries might have worked to the advantage of slaves if "gentlemen of the best figure," as Blackstone described those entitled to sit on grand juries,[52] rather than nonslaveholding whites dominated them. Before any conclusion can be reached, we need much more information on the composition of the grand juries in Southern communities.

Process upon Trial

At the same time that he criticized the requirement that four magistrates would be needed to condemn a slave, Landon Carter decried the technicalities increasingly introduced into slave trials. Carter lodged his complaint in 1772, but if he had lived until 1792 he would have been truly aghast. In that year Virginia became the first Southern state to provide that in capital cases slaves would be entitled to legal counsel and the fee would be paid by the owner.[53]

With the more frequent use of lawyers came the development of questions of procedure in the trials of slaves in ways that would have shocked Carter. Criminal trials, in the common law world, were essentially local affairs regardless of the problem of prejudice. Lawmakers slowly provided the statutory foundation for authorizing the change of venue in criminal trials, but it had not spread far, at least in the trials of slaves, by the time of the Civil War, and the practice was very thin. The first effort was a North Carolina law of 1816.[54]

Even with the possibility of a change of venue, there was no guarantee that it would be granted. That remained essentially within the discretion of a trial court, and I have found next to no cases in which the highest appeals courts ordered a new trial because of the abuse of that discretion. One of those appeals cases, however, is worth some attention. In *Fanny, (a slave), v. State* (Missouri, 1839), Fanny was indicted in Lincoln County Circuit Court for the murder of a white man. Her master successfully petitioned the court for a change of venue for a trial in Warren County. She was convicted and sentenced to death. The court ruled that the grant of the change of venue was a reversible error. The theory was that the master could not make the application for the slave. In a criminal trial the law viewed a slave as a "free agent," the judges reasoned. Therefore her "assent" to the application for a change of venue could not be "implied." She had "to petition in person as required by law."[55] The implications of this reasoning are significant: in some jurisdictions courts held that masters possessed some duties and rights in the trials of their slaves, but that was not the case in Missouri.

Provincialism was a powerful element in the trials of slaves throughout most of the South most of the time. There were, nonetheless, ways the dangers might be tempered. One of the strongest possibilities was the challenge of prospective jurors, but in the case of slaves the use of the challenge came late. Challenges for cause could be for several reasons, but the most relevant concerned a suspicion of bias and the qualifications of the juror: was he a "lawful" juror—for instance, was he a slaveowner? These could be "without stint," according to Blackstone. But the other form of challenge was of equal importance in criminal cases where, in his view, the law was *in favorem vitae*. The right of peremptory challenge showed the law to be "full of that tenderness and humanity to prisoners" of which English law was well known. So that this form did not become absurd the common law set a limit on it: there could be challenges up to thirty-five, one short of three full juries. This deeply rooted right to have some role in the construction of the jury that would try one for one's life was not initially extended to slaves at all. Stampp noted that despite the right to challenge, slaves often faced prejudiced juries. And Flanigan observed that peremptory challenges might be quickly exhausted, and it was often very difficult to obtain a jury in a rural community that did not include some members who had formed a view of guilt or innocence.[56] These points are surely correct as far as they go, but they are wholly irrelevant before the second decade of the nineteenth century.

Until the 1810s such questions did not apply, as slaves did not have the right to challenge. Without any explanation, for example, the court of quarter sessions of

Sussex County, Delaware, ruled in 1797 in *State v. Negro George* that the law that provided for the indictment and jury trial of slaves in capital cases did not include the right to peremptory challenges. Even by the teens the rules were changed slowly. Georgia adopted a law in 1811 requiring that twenty-four jurors be summoned from a list of twenty-six to thirty-six. Out of those called for the trial of a slave, the "owner or manager" was allowed to challenge seven. The court, acting for the state, could challenge five, and the remaining twelve would hear the case. One of the earliest states to grant slaves the right to be tried by a jury did not at first provide for the right to challenge jurors. It was not until 1816 that the challenge appeared in North Carolina, and then it was limited to capital cases. The law also stated that the slave was to be "entitled to the right of challenge for cause only, which challenge shall be made by and with the advise and assistance of his owner, or in his absence, of his counsel."[57] Two years later this restrictive law was dropped in favor of a rule that the slave in capital cases "shall, by himself, his master or counsel, have the same right to challenge jurors, that a freeman is now entitled to by law."[58]

South Carolina provided in 1839 that a freeholder could be challenged for cause. Virginia, on the other hand, did not adopt a statute permitting slaves to challenge a magistrate. Nonetheless, in one case a magistrate's qualifications to sit were considered. It was not on a challenge, however, but on a motion in arrest of judgment after the trial. The motion was made on the ground that one of the justices was not "legally a justice in the County of Lunenburg."[59] In other states the right to challenge was expressly dealt with in statutes from the 1820s onward.[60]

The experiences under these late statutory rules was not deep. It was not common for slaves, their masters, or counsel to challenge prospective jurors, and virtually all examples come from the last decade before the Civil War. In 1857 in Harrison County, Texas, the slave Alfred was found guilty of manslaughter following a murder indictment a year before. The special panel called for his trial was exhausted, and the court had to summon an additional twenty men before the trial jury could be filled. In Pulaski County, Arkansas, the slave Toll was indicted in June 1853. His case was continued because of the absence of witnesses, and when the case came up for trial in December, only two men of the original panel were selected. The rest had either failed to appear or were discharged for cause or by peremptory challenge. The counsel for Toll moved to have a whole new panel, but the court overruled this and counsel excepted. Two days later the state filed a motion for reconsideration of the defense counsel's motion for a new panel, and the court agreed. A new panel was to be called, but before that happened the trial was moved to Saline County because "the minds of the inhabitants of this County are so prejudiced against the said defendant that a fair and impartial trial of the issue in this case cannot be had." Three years later a panel of jurors was exhausted in the murder trial of Bob in Chatham County, Georgia. Twenty-four new prospective jurors were summoned, and the jury selected found Bob guilty but recommended him to mercy. The court sentenced him to hang.[61]

By the 1850s, the evidence suggests, the number of cases involving challenges to prospective jurors was on the rise. In Adams County, Mississippi (which included the city of Natchez), three cases in the mid-1850s involved challenges.[62] Yet the fact remains that the number of slave trials in which the record clearly established that there were challenges involving jurors is very small. It was a right that was not used often, and one likely reason is that slaveowners had to live with their neighbors and would be reluctant to challenge them, even the nonslaveholders among them who might end up on a jury. As Susan Dabney Smedes put it when commenting on a case involving a slave on the family plantation, "she was tried for her life, and would have been hung if her master had made any attempt to save her. He thought she ought to suffer the penalty of the law and made no move in her defence, and this conduct influenced the jury to bring in a verdict of manslaughter in self-defence, and she was acquitted."[63]

One pretrial motion that would not necessarily challenge one's neighbors was the motion to quash an indictment. An example of this legal process is provided by Mississippi. Lawyers for slaves often began defenses with motions to quash indictments. In Wilkinson County in June 1853, the counsel for John moved the court to quash because the indictment for burglary failed to charge that the house the defendant allegedly broke into was a dwelling house. He also argued that the indictment did not show with sufficient certainty who owned the house and the nature of the goods allegedly stolen. The court sustained the motion to quash this indictment, and subsequently a new one was entered, but it was not for burglary but for grand larceny.[64]

Once a case went to trial the most critical rule of law concerned the admissibility of evidence, but that is a sufficiently complex issue that it will be dealt with separately. Still, the role of lawyers and procedural rules were of importance in other ways, as in requested instructions to jurors and motions in arrest of judgment, for new trials, or for appeals.

What is evident from the lower court records, at least from the 1820s forward, is that lawyers did attempt to apply basic procedural rules to the trials of slaves. To that extent, slaves increasingly were granted legal rights, and they and their owners had the expectation of procedural regularity when their cases, at least capital cases, came to trial. One piece of evidence of this is the request for instructions to jurors as to the legal rules applicable to the facts. Such requests could be used to try to influence legal change, as in the case of the slave Celia in Missouri in the 1850s. Her counsel tried to defend her in her trial for murder on the ground that her master had brought on her violent response because of his sexual exploitation of Celia. Had the court accepted the counsel's requested instructions, it would have threatened the very basis of racial slavery in the South. Most requested instructions were not that bold, but they are still interesting. To illustrate, in Scip's trial for attempted rape in Lowndes County, Mississippi, counsel requested a number of instructions. One of them focused on the problem of Scip's intentions. It was this: "If the jury believe from the testimony that the intention of accused was only to have carnal intercourse with Mrs. Gibson & not to ravish her by force they must acquit of the charge in the indictment." Given the common assumptions about the attitudes of Southern whites toward interracial sexual relations, this was not a timid request.[65]

Occasionally the focus of requested instructions was on the constituent elements of the offense. Burt, for instance, was indicted in Wilkinson County, Mississippi, in 1859 for an "assault with intent to kill" his overseer. He had struck back "in resistance to legal chastisement which was then and there about to be inflicted" by the overseer. Among the instructions requested was this: "If the Jury belive [sic] from the evidence that the prisoner did *not intend* to kill Henderson but only made the assault to escape from prison they cannot find the prisoner guilty of an assault *with intent* to kill as charged in the indictment."[66] Burt was acquitted.

Another procedural move made by counsel for slaves was the motion in arrest of judgment. Unlike some of the other procedural rules, the motion in arrest was well established in the common law by the mid-eighteenth century.[67] Despite the firm lineage, the number of motions in arrest of judgment among the lower court records for the thousands of cases studied is miniscule. In all, I found only eighteen, and twelve of those occurred after 1840. Eight of the eighteen, moreover, came from two states, Alabama and Mississippi. The remainder were scattered among Maryland, Florida, Tennessee, and North Carolina.[68]

A particularly striking case occurred in Adams County, Mississippi, in 1843. Bill was indicted for an assault and battery on a white person with intent to murder. The jury returned a verdict of guilty of assault and battery with intent to commit manslaughter. The motion in arrest was because Bill was not guilty of "any offence known to the law of the land," because the court had no jurisdiction over assaults and batteries committed by slaves, nor did it possess the authority to inflict any "legal sentence" on Bill, and, finally, because the verdict amounted to "an acquittal."[69] Bill was ordered discharged.

Still another move was the motion for a new trial. New trials were not frequent in the common law and were granted only for misdemeanors. The practice in felonies was to stay an execution so that an application could be made for a pardon, not for a new trial. Generally, the authority to grant new trials was the creature of statute law. One example was the 1822 Mississippi law that authorized the trial judge to grant new trials in capital cases. Motions for new trials in the South also were not frequent, with the largest number among the counties studied once again coming from Mississippi.[70]

Despite the relative infrequency and late appearance of motions such as those to change the venue, arrest the judgment, or request a new trial, the fact that they appeared at all in the capital trials of slaves is significant. Jurists, Tushnet suggested, "may have wished to relax various technicalities in slave cases, but they ran the risk that elimination of concern for technicality in slave cases would reflect back onto cases involving whites, which formed part of the permissible range of analogy." As logical as this might seem, it is ahistorical. Southern jurists were not relaxing technicalities that had existed for some time in the trials of slaves so much as lawyers and legislators were successfully introducing them in the first place. The problem with the formulation is that it does not take into account the actual history of the introduction of procedural rules into slave trials. During the colonial period they hardly existed, and it was only very late that some made their appearance, with an increase in their use during the last decade before the Civil War. It is certainly true that some appellate judges expressed dismay, if not disgust, over the "technicalities" in the criminal law. One example of that was the remark in a Tennessee rape case, *Isham, (a slave), v. State* (1853), that "the day has now passed for rescuing the guilty upon mere technicalities."[71] This, however, had no reference to the trials of slaves alone. Rather, the lower court trial records show that the growth of legal professionalism and the increasing development of procedural rules in criminal trials became a part of the trials of slaves. It was lawyers applying the law as they knew it, but in doing so they brought slaves under the so-called rule of law and accorded them, despite the ambiguities, a cluster of rights that protected them as persons just as it protected the property interests of their owners from being injured without just cause.

One last legal rule that could be raised at the trial level was the claim for the benefit of clergy in an otherwise capital case. It was an antiquated common law rule that had been used to soften the bloodthirsty quality of the criminal law. It originated in medieval England as a way to keep the literate clergy within the jurisdiction of the ecclesiastical courts and out of the secular courts. And it rested on the notion that the lay public was not literate and if one could read he must be a man of the cloth. If a person successfully prayed the clergy, the trial was transferred to the ecclesiastical courts, where there could be no death penalty. By the seventeenth century the privilege of clergy had been extended to lay persons, and it was no longer necessary to be literate by virtue of a statute of 1707. It was granted to first offenders found guilty of those crimes considered clergyable. Some crimes were excluded. The two clergyable crimes under English law that were of most importance in the history of the criminal trials of slaves were manslaughter and larceny.[72] Slaves who received benefit of clergy were to be burned in the hand and then given thirty-nine lashes.[73]

Although this English legal rule has been studied by George Dalzell, its actual use in slave cases remains as a dark cave. If the lower court records are a fair measure, this much can be said: practice did not always follow the law, and as a practical matter the privilege was used in only two jurisdictions to a large degree, Virginia and North Carolina. But in the absence of fuller records from other colonies, this must be taken as a tentative conclusion. In Virginia, the benefit of clergy was abolished in 1796,[74] yet there are instances in Southampton, Fauquier, and Orange Counties where the privilege was expressly claimed and granted from that time down to 1815.[75] South Carolina kept the benefit all the way through the Civil War,[76] although there are no cases of its use in the magistrate-freeholder trials of Fairfield, Anderson, or Spartanburg Districts.

Although used in slave cases earlier in Virginia, the benefit of clergy was expressly secured by a statute in 1732,[77] only to be abolished in 1796. When North Carolina first used the privilege is not clear, but that state abolished it in 1854.[78] All the examples of benefit of clergy in Virginia fall between 1741 and 1815.[79] One notable thing about the cases is that they reinforce the notion that justice was parochial and we need to be very sensitive to local variations. In North Carolina, for instance, nearly all the cases in New Hanover County involved convictions for grand larceny, whereas nearly all the cases in Northampton County were for manslaughter.[80] Local practices and conditions defined the actual experience with legal rules.

Appeals

Although these various procedural rights were important, and, except for the benefit of clergy, were more widely used at the trial level as we approach the Civil War, the right of broadest importance was the right to appeal from the trial court to a higher court. One needs to keep in mind the scope of the appeal allowed: for instance, under the Louisiana black code "no proceedings shall be annulled or impeded by any error of form." The other point is to note the courts to which a slave had the right to appeal at all. Maryland, Virginia, and South Carolina did not provide the right to appeal to the state's highest court. Louisiana had no criminal appeals until 1847 because its constitution limited the right to appeal to civil cases involving matters over $300.[81] There were no appeals in Maryland's court through-out the history of slavery, and in Virginia there was one case, *Elvira, (a slave)*, that finally made it to the highest appellate court, but that was not until 1865. Elvira had been found guilty of attempting to poison the family of her master. Because the judgment was not unanimous, her owner appealed to the Petersburg Circuit Court for a *habeas corpus* for her discharge. The writ issued, but the court ruled that unanimity was not required. Elvira's owner sought a writ of error from the court of appeals, which was allowed. Judge Richard Moncure decided the case on the merits, in favor of Elvira. "It is unnecessary," he wrote, "to express any opinion on the question arising in this case as to the jurisdiction, as well of this court as the court below; this court being equally divided in opinion on that question, and being therefore unable to decide the case on that ground."[82] In South Carolina, after 1839, slaves were allowed to appeal to a single judge of the highest court,[83] but they possessed no right to a hearing by the full court. Georgia did not have a supreme court until the early 1850s. Generally, there was a right of appeal to the highest court in a county from judgments of magistrates unless all trials were clearly limited to special courts, as in South Carolina and Virginia. Appeals could be taken to the new state supreme court in Georgia after 1850, when that state fell into line behind most of the other Southern jurisdictions.

In South Carolina there were about a half-dozen appeals in the Anderson and Spartanburg Districts, all in the 1850s and 1860s. In every case the judge ruled in favor of the slave's petition. Two of the cases—one involving burglary and the other arson—arose on appeals for writs of prohibition. One was for the prohibition against the execution of the sentence and the other for a cessation of all further proceedings in the case. The second case concerned the trial of the slave Thornton, who allegedly burned a stillhouse, in Anderson District. Thornton had been tried once and acquitted of the charge, but he was rearrested and tried again. He was found guilty and sentenced to be banished from the state. Judge Robert Munro upheld the prohibition on the ground of the prior acquittal, a traditional common law bar to a prosecution.[84]

Three years earlier in Spartanburg District Judge Withers issued the prohibition against the punishment of Hamp on a burglary charge. The slave had been sentenced to over one thousand lashes, one of the most barbarous sanctions, short of execution, I have ever come across. There were several grounds of appeal, but it really came down to the prejudice of the presiding magistrate in the trial. He was known to harbor hostility both to the slave and to the slave's master. The sentence was halted by the prohibition issued by Withers, who also ordered a new trial. On the second trial Hamp was found guilty of receiving stolen goods. He was sentenced to twenty-nine lashes and banishment from the state.[85] The remaining applications were all for new trials, and a number of them turned on precise legal definitions. In Anderson District in 1863, for instance, Judge Munro ordered a new trial in a burglary case because the indictment did not note that the place broken into was a "mansion house" or a "dwelling house," which was an element in the common law definition of a burglary.[86]

Outside of these unique cases slaves generally possessed the right of appeal to the state supreme court by the nineteenth century. One of the more important issues was the scope of the review allowed, and, for the most part, it was quite wide. The focus of the review might be on the critical elements of the offense charged, and occasionally this required the judges to go to the heart of the master-slave relationship, such as with "provocation." Aside from such central issues, review often focused on procedural questions. It can be said that there has emerged strong, if not universal, agreement that jurists who heard appeals at the highest level displayed a remarkable degree of sensitivity to procedural regularity.[87]

A final mode of "appeal" was the normal mode in the common law during the eighteenth century, the application for a pardon.[88] The use of this technique can be seen in the colonial records of Maryland. One function of a pardon was mercy. Whatever might touch the feelings of a trial court, or those who knew the defendant, might be presented to request a pardon. In colonial Maryland, however, it also had a wider function. The request for a pardon filled a place later taken over in large part by the appellate process. It could also be used to mitigate the severity of the bloodthirsty common law of crimes, which provided capital punishment for over two hundred offenses in the eighteenth century.

Two elements in appeals for pardons that show up often were the youth of the offender and/or the fact that he or she possessed a "good character." For example, the council that reviewed capital sentences in colonial Maryland and made recommendations for pardons, or to affirm executions, suggested that Isaac, found guilty of burglary and robbery in Anne Arundel County in 1738, should be pardoned because he "had bore a good Character and was [a] real Object of Compassion." In contrast, the slave York was ordered executed for the crime of horse stealing in 1747 in Anne Arundel because the report reviewed by the council showed that he "bears a very ill Character."[89] Slaves who were insolent, defiant, lazy, or drunken, for instance, were not likely to be the objects of pleas for pardons.

The pardon also functioned as an appeal, as it did in the case of the slave Ben in Talbot County in 1769. Ben had been tried by the justices and a jury and sentenced to death for an assault with "Intent to Ravish Eve Shanahan." The justices, however, informed Governor Horatio Sharpe that the evidence "had such uncertainty in it, that it was neither clear the said Ben was the Felon, (the attempt having been made in the Night, and in an House without Light, where Objects could not well be discovered,) nor (if he was the Person) that his Intention was to Ravish." They, therefore, urged a pardon. The jurors likewise wrote to the governor. They also urged mercy, but their reasons were different. They recommended it because "the Law in that Case is extremely severe, and being satisfied that the attempt made upon the Woman brings him within the Description of that Act, yet Notwithstanding, as the Fellow before bore a good Character, the Attempt but small, and the Evidence not so clear as we could wish, we hope your Excellency will grant Pardon to the said Ben." The pardon was issued on the advice of the council.[90]

Despite all of the extraordinary as well as procedural ways in which unbridled discretion was reined in, the fact remained that slave justice could not be a truly rational system in a formal sense, even though that was the trend. Southern parochialism and the nature of the jury trial, not to mention the powers of magistrates, assured that. But an even more critical legal factor concerned the problem of evidence and testimony.

10

Slaves and the Rules of Evidence in Criminal Trials

The negro, as a general rule, is mendacious.

T. R. R. COBB, *Law of Negro Slavery* (1858)

In 1853 Goodell searingly observed that the slave becomes " '*a person*' whenever he is to be *punished*! . . . He is under the *control* of law, though *unprotected by* law, and can know law only as an enemy, and not as a friend." Goodell's argument that slaves were outside the protection of the law rested on two legal rules, one evidentiary and one substantive. The substantive rule was the simple assertion, as articulated by O'Neall in *State v. Maner,* that the slave was outside the protection of the common law. The evidentiary rule was another matter. Slaves could not testify against whites. As Chief Justice Drewry Ottley of St. Vincent noted, the result of exclusion was that "the difficulty of legally establishing facts is so great, that White men are in a manner put beyond the reach of the law."[1] This was changed in the West Indies during the 1820s as the British colonies inched toward abolition. The whites would receive the testimony of slaves who could show that they were Christians and understood the significance of an oath. Even then, there remained a vital exclusion: the testimony would be excluded if a white were on trial for his life.[2] No shift in policy occurred in the American South. The wholesale exclusion remained in force until the end of slavery.

Basic Rules

A major change, however, did occur in the rules of evidence as they applied to free blacks and Indians. From the Revolution down to the 1820s the evidence of slaves began to be admitted against such people of color. Prior to that, slaves could not testify in capital trials, although there is evidence that their testimony was received, albeit reluctantly, in noncapital cases. For instance, as of 1717 in Maryland the evidence of slaves was received in actions against any black or Indian as long as the case did not involve depriving them "of Life or Member." At the same time slaves' testimony against "any *Christian,* White Person" was excluded.[3]

North Carolina, one of the first jurisdictions to expand the rule on the admissibility of slave evidence to include capital cases, adopted such a law in 1777. A
typical statute was that of Mississippi (1822): "any negro or mulatto, bond or free,
shall be a good witness in pleas of the state, for or against negroes or mulattoes,
bond or free, or in civil pleas where free negroes or mulattoes shall alone be
parties, and in no other cases whatever."[4] The deterioration in the legal position of
free blacks was a product of the Revolutionary generation. But in practice there
were not all that many cases where the testimony of slaves figured prominently in
indictments against free blacks.

Race, as well as status, had become the basis for exclusion, and the exclusion of
the testimony of slaves against any white understandably was scored by critics of
the laws of slavery such as Stroud and Goodell.[5] But what happened when the slave
was not the victim of violence but was the person who committed the criminal
offense? In many cases the answer was that the person never reached the courts.
Occasionally, slaves were victims of mob violence. For example, in 1843 near
Copiah, Mississippi, a group of whites took off from the plantation and summarily
hanged two slaves who had allegedly raped a white woman. According to the
newspaper account, the slaves were "hung according to a statute of Judge Lynch,
'*in such cases made and provided.*'" Moreover, although many petty offenses, such
as thefts of chickens and fights among the slaves, were handled on the plantations
themselves, capital cases normally went to the public courts.[6]

Once they got there, what rules of evidence applied? There is a fine debate about
the history of evidentiary rules for the exclusion of certain kinds of testimony, such
as hearsay testimony or the evidence of prior convictions. James Bradley Thayer
contended that the rules emerged during the eighteenth century in order to control the discretion of juries. John Langbein suggested that it was to control lawyers.[7] But neither jury discretion nor unethical lawyers mattered that much to
slaves during the eighteenth century. Of much more consequence were the rules
that concerned the competency of someone to testify at all and the credibility
accorded their testimony if they were ruled competent.

Two rules used in seventeenth-century English criminal trials were of significance in the trials of slaves. Both derived from Christian doctrine. The first was the
two-witness rule found in Deuteronomy 17:6. The second rule was that witnesses
had to take an oath before they would be admitted to testify. The theory behind the
oath in the seventeenth century was that it was a way to bring forth immediate
divine vengeance upon false swearing.[8] This was a time when the belief in divine,
as well as devilish, intervention in the affairs of human beings was very deep.[9] By
the nineteenth century, when such doctrines were less secure, the oath had become
a way to remind the oath taker of a future punishment for false swearing. As Simon
Greenleaf, a master of the law of evidence, put it in 1842, "one of the main
provisions of the law, for the purity and truth of oral evidence, is, that it be
delivered under the *sanction of an oath*. Men in general are sensible of the motives
and restraints of religion, and acknowledge their accountability to that Being,

from whom no secrets are hid." The oath, then, was used to lay "hold on the conscience of the witness."[10]

Not everyone, however, was allowed to take an oath. The opinion of Coke was that only a person who believed in a Christian God could take a valid oath, and therefore the only competent witness was a Christian. Holdsworth maintained that this view was breaking down because of "commercial considerations." The work of Sir Matthew Hale at the end of the seventeenth century reflected transformation. He thought that an oath other than that required of Christians was acceptable "in cases of necessity, as in forein [*sic*] contracts between merchant and merchant." Hale also was disturbed by the notion that a murder might not be punishable if it was committed "in presence only of a Turk or a Jew, that owns not the Christian religion." Hale would allow non-Christians to testify under an oath that derived from their own religion. He did this grudgingly, however, and ended with the observation "that the credit of such a testimony must be left to the jury." Notwithstanding, there had to be an oath of some sort.[11]

Whereas the demands of market capitalism opened courts to some, social status closed them to others. Holdsworth noted that the person who had been reduced to villenage had "lost his law." Cobb made much of this. Only free men, he wrote, were "*othesworth*" (worthy of taking an oath), and wherever villenage or slavery existed in the past the testimony of those in the menial or degraded social position was excluded altogether. Cobb, in fact, came very close to saying that *law* was a system only for the free. One theory behind the exclusion, according to him, was reflected in the assertion of the early Jewish historian, Josephus, that the testimony of servants was not admitted "on account of the ignobility of their soul." Masters, moreover, were ever reluctant to give up their property interests lightly, especially to have them subject to the testimony of the ignominious. This presented a serious problem for the legal order. As the Maryland lawmakers observed in 1717, "it too often happens that Negro Slaves, &c. commit many Heinous and Capital Crimes, which are endeavoured to be smothered, and concealed, or else such Negroes, &c. are conveyed to some other Province, and Sold by their Owners, who for the sake of the Interest they have in their Lives and Services, suffer them to escape Justice." The answer was not to admit the testimony of slaves. It was to provide compensation to the owners of slaves who were executed.[12] If the social position of slaves, as well as the property interests of their masters, generally barred slaves from the public courts as witnesses *altogether*, we have missed something.

The first Virginia statute that dealt with evidence in slave trials is conclusive. It was a law of 1692 "for the more speedy prosecution of slaves committing Capitall Crimes." The rules of evidence concerned testimony in capital cases. There is no indication of what rules applied in noncapital trials before the county justices. In capital cases the only testimony of a slave ever mentioned was the confession of the accused. The other evidence consisted of the "oaths of two witnesses or of one with pregnant circumstances."[13] According to Hale's 1678 treatise, the evidence *for* the prisoner in English courts was often not given under oath, and the examination of the prisoner prior to trial also was "not upon Oath."[14] The 1692 Virginia law went further. It excluded all testimony not under oath, except for the confession of the defendant. By the time the English colonies established slavery in the seventeenth century, the exclusion was not expressly social as it had been in the case of villenage. The exclusion now was religious. As Sir William Hawkins observed in the 1720s in his *Treatise of the Pleas of the Crown*, it was a good reason to exclude a witness because he was "an Infidel; That is, as I take it, that he believes neither the Old nor New Testament to be the Word of God; on one of which our Laws require the Oath should be administered."[15] The evidentiary rule in the 1692 law first referred to the "oaths of two witnesses," and second it mentioned "or of one with pregnant circumstances." In either case a person had to take an oath, and the overwhelming majority of slaves at that time were non-Christians. They could take no oath in an English court. And seventeenth-century slaveowners notoriously obstructed efforts to proselytize among them for fear that conversion would lead to emancipation.[16]

As early as 1680, Godwyn complained about this. Savage black slaves could not testify in Christian white English courts in cases where slaves were on trial for their lives, except to confess. Wholely consistent with this conclusion was an evidentiary rule buried deep within an elaborate 1705 statute establishing and regulating the proceedings in the general court. It read "that popish recusants convict, negroes, mulattoes and Indian servants, and others, not being christians, shall be deemed and taken to be persons incapable in law, to be witnesses in any cases whatsoever."[17]

Whites never viewed slaves as paragons of truthfulness. In 1777, for example, Landon Carter wrote: "Do not bring your negroe to contradict me! A negroe and a passionate woman are equal as to truth or falsehood; for neither thinks of what they say." And Cobb, in the next century, argued that "the negro, as a general rule, is mendacious, is a fact too well established to require the production of proof, either from history, travels or craniology."[18]

The result of such beliefs and the corresponding legal rules was that down to 1723 slaves could not testify (except to confess) in any capital case in a Virginia court. They were largely outside the legal order except as objects of the law of property. But in that year the evidentiary rule was changed, and the reason shows that it could arise directly from a concern to maintain domination as much as to ensure justice. The preamble made clear the reason for changing the evidentiary rule: it was to remove the difficulties of punishing secret plots and conspiracies "known only to such, as by the laws now established, are not accounted legal evidence."[19] Some years later Governor William Gooch explained that one of the problems that faced white Virginians in many slave cases before 1723 was that "there could be no legal proof, so as to convict them." The change in the evidentiary rule was occasioned by white fears of slave insurrections, but it was not limited to rebels. It applied to all capital cases. In any event, the burgesses dropped the two-witness requirement but added that the trial court could accept "such testimony of Negros, Mulattos, or Indians, bond or free, with pregnant circumstances, as to them shall seem convincing." Even in England the two-witness rule was transformed during the eighteenth century. By the end it was retained only in cases of perjury and treason.[20] The requirement that the evidence of blacks be supported by pregnant circumstances, however, was the functional equivalent of the two-witness rule.

Once the testimony of slaves was admitted, the problem of perjury arose. Coke defined the crime of perjury at common law in such a way that it could not apply to the testimony of the overwhelming majority of slaves in colonial Virginia. "Perjury," he wrote, "is a crime committed, when a lawfull oath is ministred by any that hath authority, to any person, in any judiciall proceedings, who sweareth absolutely, and falsely in a matter materiall to the issue." This definition would not do; nor would the normal punishment for perjury, which was a fine and/or imprisonment. The law of 1723 therefore provided a charge from the court that included the penalty that was designed to ensure that slaves as non-Christians would be under "the greater obligation to declare the truth." The charge was this: "You are brought hither as a witness; and, by the direction of the law, I am to tell you, before you give your evidence, that you must tell the truth, the whole truth, and nothing but the truth; and that if it be found hereafter, that you tell a lie, and give false testimony in this matter, you must, for so doing, have both your ears nailed to the pillory, and cut off, and receive thirty-nine lashes on your bare back, well laid on, at the common whipping-post." Six years after the adoption of this law, Toney and Jone, slaves in Richmond County, learned its deadly seriousness. So did the slave Mary in Lancaster County in 1752. However, by that time this law was not always strictly followed. In Lancaster County in 1754 Alce, who was found guilty of having given false evidence against two fellow slaves, received only six lashes. And in the same county in 1756 Will received thirty-nine lashes for "letting a Lye in his Evidence Relating to Sambo," who was on trial for hog stealing.[21] Despite the vagaries of enforcement, the 1723 law remained the basis for the admission of evidence in capital trials of slaves in Virginia until the end of slavery in 1865.

Before the rules in other colonies and states are taken up, a word is needed about the phrase "pregnant circumstances." The legal treatises that guided Virginians, such as Dalton's, or Hales's, or Hawkins's, did not use the term. J. H. Baker, in his study of the criminal courts and procedure from 1550 to 1800, noted that "strong and pregnant presumption" was all that was necessary, according to some, to show that Crown evidence was sufficiently "meet" or "fit" to proceed to trial. He did not say that it was sufficient or necessary to convict.[22] Hale had referred to strong presumptive evidence, but he warned against it. He cited as an example the case of a man who was found riding a horse that had been stolen. This created a strong presumption that the man stole the horse, and indeed he was executed. Later the real thief confessed.[23]

Blackstone discussed what he called "*circumstantial* evidence or the doctrine of *presumptions.*" His categorization included "violent," "probable," and "light, or rash" presumptions. The first was "many times equal to full proof; for there those circumstances appear, which *necessarily* attend the fact." It is unlikely that the Virginians had that in mind. A violent presumption could be full proof, and it would be unnecessary to admit the testimony of a savage black slave at all. The next category comes closer. A probable presumption arose from a set of circumstances that "*usually*" attend a fact and should be given "due weight." This kind of circumstantial evidence could be used to lend credibility to the testimony of a slave precisely because the last category, "light, or rash," was not entitled to any consideration whatsoever.[24]

To return to the rules in the colonies, the code in Delaware is not clear. The law simply authorized the court to "acquit or condemn according to their Evidence" and to condemn "upon due Proof to them made." In Maryland an evidentiary history similar to that in Virginia developed. Inferentially, at least, the testimony of slaves was inadmissible in capital slave trials. The first mention of separate capital trials came in a law of 1729, nearly contemporary with the critical Virginia law. It referred only to a slave "convict, by confession, or verdict of a jury."[25] There is no reason to believe that slaves testified in such trials in Maryland any more than in Virginia. Aside from the evidence from the 1717 law, and from the fact that the basic common law system prevailed, there is additional corroboration in the colonial perjury law of 1699. The Maryland law punished perjury by fines or a year in jail; persons who could not pay the fine were to have their ears nailed but not cut off, and to be forever precluded from being sworn as a witness. There was no other perjury statute, and this one did not embrace non-Christian slaves who could not swear an oath. The Delaware law provided that those guilty of perjury would be punished according to the law of Great Britain.[26] The language in the first direct law in Maryland on slave testimony in capital cases lends more support as far as Maryland is concerned. The law of 1751 referred to a conviction of a slave "upon his, her or their voluntary confession, or the verdict of a jury, upon the testimony of one or more legal or credible witness or witnesses, or even the testimony or the evidence of other slaves, corroborated with such pregnant circumstances as shall convince and satisfy" those hearing the case. The punishment for perjury by a slave followed Virginia. To the south, the colony of North Carolina adopted the Virginia law in 1741.[27]

The evidentiary history in South Carolina differed. Its law of 1690 mentioned only that a magistrate was to conduct a *preliminary examination* where he would have "all persons to come before him that can give evidence." It is not certain that this meant only those persons who could give evidence in an English court. The trial that followed was to be based on the testimony of the "evidences." In English West Indian colonies, according to Elsa Goveia, "at the discretion of the courts, the evidence of slaves was admitted for or against other slaves" during the eighteenth century. But Cobb stated this was similar to the rule in the French colonies, where judges could use such testimony only to "illustrate other testimony."[28] The evidence for South Carolina is inconclusive. The next law, that of 1712, charged the court trying a slave with "diligently weighing and examining all evidences, proofs and testimonies." "Violent presumption and circumstances" could be considered in cases of murder. In actions for petty larceny, slaves could be found guilty by "confession, proof, or probable circumstances."[29] Finally, in a separate part of the statute this statement appeared:

> That the confession of any slave accused, or the testimony of any other slave, that the justices and freeholders shall have reason to believe to speak truth, shall be held for good and convincing evidence in all petty larcenies or trespasses, not exceeding forty shillings; but no negro or other slave shall suffer loss of life or limb, but such as shall be convicted, either by their own free and voluntary confession, or by the oath of christian evidence, or, at least, by the plain and positive evidence of two negroes or slaves, so circumstantiated as that there shall not be sufficient reason to doubt the truth thereof, and examination being always made, if the negroes or slaves that give evidence, do not bear any malice to the other slave accused; excepting in the case of murder, in which case, the evidence of one slave, attended with such circumstances as that the justices and freeholders shall have no just reason to suspect the truth thereof, of which they are hereby made judges, or upon violent presumption of the accused person's guilt.

This was a complex effort to construct different layers of evidentiary rules depending on the seriousness of the offense. In minor crimes the rule resembled the Virginia law of 1723 on major slave crimes. The two-witness rule, possibly reenforced by something like the "pregnant circumstances" rule, applied to slave testimony in major crimes, except for murder, where once again the rule resembled the Virginia law of 1723. South Carolina abandoned this confusing language in 1735. By then the evidentiary rule was basically the same as elsewhere: "the confession of any slave accused, or the testimony of any other slave or slaves, attended with circumstances of truth and credit, shall be deemed good and convincing evidence on the trial of any slave or slaves for any of the crimes aforesaid, or any other crimes, capital or criminal; of the strength of which evidence, the said justices and freeholders who try the same, are hereby made sufficient and competent judges." By 1740 the rule took its final form in South Carolina. Now the evidence "of any slave, without oath, shall be allowed and admitted in all causes whatsoever, for or against another slave accused of any crime or offence whatsoever; the weight of which evidence being seriously considered, and compared with all other circumstances, attending the case, shall be left to the conscience of the justices and freeholders." Georgia adopted this law in 1770.[30] There was no oath, no two-witness rule, and no *requirement* that the testimony of slaves be corroborated by pregnant circumstances. The only voice raised in protest against the South Carolina law of 1740 was that of Judge O'Neall in 1848, by which time many slaves were Christians. O'Neall suggested the propriety of taking slave testimony under oath:

"Negroes (slaves or free) will feel the sanctions of an oath, with as much force as any of the ignorant classes of white people, in a Christian country."[31] The legislature did not agree.

Virginia and South Carolina displayed a legal atavism found nowhere else. Both retained the evidentiary rules framed between 1720 and 1740.[32] In 1808 Maryland provided that the testimony of slaves was admissible either for or against a slave defendant in all criminal prosecutions. There was no reference to pregnant circumstances. Georgia modified its rule slightly in 1816: "on the trial of a slave, or free person of color, any witness shall be sworn, who believes in God, and a future state of rewards and punishments."[33]

Without a doubt, however, the most interesting transformation occurred in *State v. Ben, (a slave)*, where the issue of slave testimony, and especially the pregnant circumstances standard, came before the North Carolina Supreme Court. Here different views, missing from the black letter of a statute, were articulated by judges. Flanigan, one of the few scholars to analyze this decision, condemned the reasoning of the majority opinion of Chief Justice Taylor that overthrew the pregnant circumstances rule and led to the execution of Ben for burglary. It was based on a "superficial equalitarian rhetoric" blind to the realities of slavery and to the fact that the pregnant circumstances rule was actually both a "relic" and an "important statutory protection" for slaves.[34] There were some important assumptions in this analysis. One was that the rule should have been retained. But why? The assumption that this was an important protection for slaves may have rested on the notion that Southern whites were correct after all: slaves could not be trusted to tell the truth because they were not free agents, and therefore no slave should ever be condemned on the testimony of slaves alone without some corroboration. This was the view of the abolitionist critics Stroud and Goodell. They had argued that the testimony of slaves against slaves was especially suspect because Southern law allowed the emancipation of slaves for "meritorious services" and that one of those was *"giving information of crimes committed by a slave."*[35] This was fanciful, except in the case of insurrections, where it did hold true.[36] But it also rested on a pejorative view of the slaves themselves, of their sense of community and solidarity. Susan Rhodes, a former slave, recalled, for example, that "People in my day didn't know book learning but dey studied how to protect each other, and save 'em from such misery as they could."[37] I do not mean to suggest that Flanigan had in mind a negative view of the sense of community among the slaves, only that it lay beneath the surface of the abolitionist argument. Another possible unwritten assumption, which I do not share, could be that because of the cruelty of human bondage, almost all slave offenses should be viewed as "political." They were protests against degradation, and therefore rather ordinary rules of law used to convict rather ordinary felons should not apply. Whether the point is that slaves could not be trusted to tell the truth or that slave offenses were political, the result seems to be the same. Slave testimony should not have been tested by the ordinary rules. In any event, Taylor's opinion did not proceed on such assumptions. He argued that from 1793 forward, basic common law rules of evidence applied in the trials of slaves. The law of that year granted trial by jury to slaves, and Taylor argued that it drew "after it, as an incident, the common-law principles of evidence and all the consequences of common-law proceedings."[38]

There was one exception that Taylor admitted, and it is ironic. A law of 1802 retained the evidentiary rule from 1741 in trials of slaves for insurrection or conspiracy to rebel. This was a narrow exception in his view and was "passed soon after some disturbances had arisen among the slaves in the lower part of the State, and the clause was probably re-enacted for the purpose of tempering that excess which public excitement had produced in the trials for these offenses."[39] The irony, of course, is that the rule originally had been tied to a law designed to uncover slave insurrections, but it was retained in order to protect slaves against white hysteria about such insurrections.

Judge Hall vigorously dissented. "That the policy of the law of 1741," he wrote, "was founded on a sense of the degraded state in which those unhappy beings existed, no doubt, will be ceded. Being slaves, they had no will of their own, and a humane policy forbade that the life of a human being (one of themselves) should be taken away upon testimony coming from them, unless some circumstance appeared in aid of that testimony."[40] The testimony of social subordinates simply was not to be believed. They lacked free will. The majority of the court, however, disagreed with Hall's analysis based on social status.

Outside of the older colonial slave societies, the pregnant circumstances requirement appeared for a time in Kentucky, Tennessee, Mississippi, and Alabama. It was not used in other states, and these four dropped the rule between the 1830s and the 1850s.[41] Elsewhere the evidence of slaves was sufficient to convict or acquit, and in Georgia and Louisiana it could be testimony taken under oath.[42]

Whether sworn or not, and it usually was not, by the nineteenth century the evidence of slaves could be sufficient to convict or acquit other slaves. The problem of perjury was universally dealt with by corporal punishment. Most states, however, had substituted a whipping for the mutilation adopted in Virginia, but it could be severe. In some states the number of lashes was thirty-nine, and in Alabama the number could reach one hundred and the perjurer would then be branded with a *P*.[43]

Practice

Although the rules of evidence regarding the admissibility of the testimony of slaves in the trials of slaves had changed considerably by the nineteenth century, the question remains, how did the system work in practice? Was it common for slaves to be convicted or acquitted solely on the basis of the testimony of other slaves? Betty Wood, in her study of a handful of slave trials in Georgia, suggested that it was not. She found only one trial where the verdict was "(at least in theory) entirely dependent upon evidence supplied by other slaves." The defendant was convicted and hanged, and his head was put up on a pole.[44] This case does not show that a slave had been convicted solely on the testimony of other slaves, for they had attempted to establish his innocence. Although slaves often tried to help one another with their testimony, it was not always so.

In 1746 in Lancaster County, Virginia, the slave Guy was convicted on the testimony of three slaves, two of whom belonged to Guy's owner, Landon Carter, of stealing breeches valued at one shilling. Guy received thirty-five lashes. In 1750 in the same county, Sarah at first pled not guilty when placed on trial, but later she changed her testimony and admitted to having "rec^d Sundry" goods. She then implicated seven slaves in all, and only one of them was discharged. Sarah apparently testified in order to minimize her own punishment.[45] In capital burglary trials some slaves turned state's evidence in order to save their lives.

In 1741 Ben and Dedan were indicted for breaking and entering the public warehouse and stealing a hogshead of tobacco. The evidence against Ben was given by Jacob, George, and Dedan, all slaves. Dedan was "released from his tryal" because he had become "a material evidence for our Sovereign lord the King." Although found guilty, Ben was not executed because he was granted the benefit of clergy.[46] Slaves were no more heroic or ignominious than anyone else, and to overlook this obvious fact is to slip into romanticism.

Similar impressions emerge from the nineteenth-century records. In Fairfield District, South Carolina, four slaves and a free black were tried for "violating the peace" in 1849. The testimony came from two slaves, Tom and William. Tom testified that George and Levy "were Quarreling at the time he Saw George have a knife in his hand and open and heard him say to Levy that if he did not Stand away from him he would Cut or Stick him[. H]e saw Levy go to the fence and Get a piece of a Fence Rail[. H]e was persuaded to and did lay the Rail down." William testified that Elijah Bond, the free black, "commenced the Quarrel with George."[47] It was when conflicts erupted within the slave or black community that one could expect cases to rest solely on the testimony of slaves.

One special category of crime was the conspiracy to commit an insurrection. This was precisely the crime that had led Southern whites to admit slave testimony in the first place. Clearly, such testimony was critical in convicting the slave defendants.[48] It was crucial in the insurrection panic that hit the iron fields of Tennessee in 1856, for instance. But in insurrection conspiracy cases slave testimony was obtained in clear violation of normal common law rules. On some occasions it came as the result of confessions or accusations that followed torture.[49] Torture was commonplace in civil law systems, such as in Spanish Louisiana. In 1771, for example, a Louisiana slave was ordered to "be tortured to make him confess who were his accomplices."[50] The use of torture was not a feature of the common law, however. Southern whites nonetheless were not squeamish about using the whip despite the common law tradition, and this was especially true in cases of insurrection.

The major insurrection trials are well known. But the use of force to obtain evidence or confessions was also used on lesser occasions. In Spartanburg District, South Carolina, slaves were "tried" at Otts Bridge on September 24, 1860. A number of whites conducted this ad hoc trial. They even kept written testimony that was turned over to the lawful authorities. The result, after slaves such as John and Glenn testified about some mysterious white man, was that seven slaves were blindfolded and whipped between thirty and eighty-five lashes apiece. On September 28 there was a formal indictment against Jerry, Anderson, Ellis, Andy, and Steve for a conspiracy to raise an insurrection in the neighborhood. The trial before the magistrate-freeholders began on October 2, 1860. The primary witness was the same John who had been tried and found guilty at Otts Bridge. He testified that he had not told the whole truth there because he was afraid; his current evidence came after he was "whipped in jail and made to tell it." According to John, he had been at a cave where there were some runaways. "Anderson was talking about being set free—people wer [*sic*] coming from the North to set them free—said he expected the black people would have to fight and he would fight if he was obliged to[.] Ellis said about the same." There was virtually nothing mentioned about the other slaves, and on the testimony of John the magistrate-freeholders reached this verdict: "the boys Anderson and Ellis they think are guilty to some extent. . . . they think that they may have had some thought and made some preparation of an insurrectionary tendency." The magistrate-freeholders ordered them to receive fifty lashes each.[51]

Despite such occasional reliance on the "evidence" of slaves, the overwhelming majority of criminal trials of slaves in the South did not turn on the statements of slaves alone.[52] Some proceedings—such as those concerning rapes or assaults on whites, or attempts to kill whites—necessarily relied on white witnesses. The few crimes that did involve only the testimony of slaves were slave insurrection conspiracies, crimes arising out of some disruption within the slave community itself, or, finally, the handful of criminal cases where slaves turned state's evidence in order to minimize or escape punishment.

The Confession

The "confession," however, had always been admitted into evidence. Greenleaf noted that confessions of guilt were to be received with considerable caution. Among the reasons was the fact that a prisoner might be "oppressed by the calamity of his situation" and influenced by motives of "hope or fear." Nevertheless, if the threshold problem of admissibility was crossed, "*deliberate confessions of guilt*" were to be viewed as "the most effectual proofs in the law." This rested on the view that "they are deliberate and voluntary, and on the presumption, that a rational being will not make admissions prejudicial to his interest and safety, unless when urged by the promptings of truth and conscience."[53]

A suggestive view of lower-class defendants is that they often behaved with submissiveness and deference when brought into court before their social "betters."[54] One test of this view when applied to slaves would be the commonness of confessions. By this test slaves must have been a disappointment. They rarely confessed. In eleven Virginia counties examined for the eighteenth century, for instance, I found only fifteen confessions. The relative number of confessions did not rise in the next century, either.[55] One of the early Virginia cases, moreover, is not really a confession at all. In 1729/30 Harry lost his ears in Richmond County for stabbing another slave. The only evidentiary entry was that he was adjudged guilty "not Denying What is laid to his charge."[56] This is an example of a slave whose refusal to plead was taken as a confession of guilt.

One of the more interesting actions involved a murder. It is interesting because it was so rare—one of the only cases that arose before the admission of slave testimony in 1723. In Lancaster County in 1722 Wapping was tried for the murder of Guy, another slave, whom Wapping said he had assaulted with "Axes Clubs &c."[57] If slaves could not testify against each other before the 1720s, and if almost none "confessed" like Wapping, how much criminal conduct by slaves was not punished in public courts as a practical matter before that time? Scholars have often claimed that slave crimes increased by the mid-eighteenth century,[58] but they have failed to see that one reason for the statistical increase was the earlier exclusion of slave testimony. This skews the picture and may well present a false impression of the magnitude of the increase.

Evidence in the Quarters

We know, of course, that owners often punished offenses on the plantation, but what happened if the offender or the offense never came to the attention of the whites? Was there some mode of social control among the slaves in their conduct toward one another? Were they in the process of creating a body of norms in terms of respect for possessions or the regulation of sexual relationships that if violated resulted in some sanction by the slaves themselves? Scholars have recognized the degree to which slaves created first a pidgin and then a creolized language within the quarters, and the fact that they firmly grasped, even when they modified, the various elements of African culture. This included such things as rhythmic patterns, religious practices, and folk tales.[59] But if they retained all of this in syncretic forms, why should we assume that they failed to retain any of the various African notions of legal right and wrong and legal means of social control? Unfortunately, the degree to which slaves might have held onto African ways to define acceptable behavior within the quarters, and to sanction deviations, is beyond recall. Nonetheless, one very suggestive piece of evidence is recounted by Thomas Webber in his work on the significance of the "spirit world" among the slaves. It concerned the manner of uncovering thieves within the quarters:

> The third way of detecting thieves was taught by the fathers and mothers of the slaves. They said no matter how untrue a man might have been during his

life, when he came to die he had to tell the truth and had to own everything he had ever done, and whatever dealing those alive had with anything pertaining to the dead, must be true, or they would immediately die and go to hell to burn in fire and brimstone. So in consequence of this, the graveyard dust was the truest of the three ways in detecting thieves. The dust would be taken from the grave of a person who had died last and put into a bottle with water. Then two of the men of the examining committee would use the same words as in the case of the Bible and the sieve, "John stole that chicken," "John did not steal that chicken," and after this had gone on for about five minutes, then one of the other two who attended to the Bible and the sieve would say, "John, you are accused of stealing that chicken that was taken from Sam's chicken coop at such a time." "In the name of the Father and the Son and the Holy Ghost, if you have taken Sam's chicken don't drink this water, for if you do you will die and go to hell and be burned in fire and brimstone but if you have not you may take it and it will not hurt you." So if John had taken the chicken he would own it rather than take the water.[60]

Such a "trial" with its rules of evidence shows it is a reasonable speculation that slaves maintained a quasi-legal order among themselves despite their exclusion for most purposes from the courts of whites. Surely the legal notions of Africans did not suddenly disappear any more than their view of appropriate family relationships, the significance of magic, or the ring shout.

Voluntariness

There was, then, enormous complexity and ambivalence in the ways that slave conduct was controlled and sanctioned if it disregarded accepted norms, and public law was only one level of control. Offenses might be dealt with outside the public courts by whites on the plantations or by the blacks themselves unobserved by whites, not to mention the discipline that existed in the Southern churches.[61] But the immediate question is that of slave evidence in the courts of whites. And with the evidence in the public courts serious problems were presented above all by the confession. They focus around the question of "voluntariness."[62] In some cases, there is no doubt whatever that the confession was not the result of a voluntary act by the accused. For instance, in 1818 in Richmond, Virginia, the Common Council verified a charge that an "engine of torture," which turned out to be a finger screw, had been used by public authorities to extort confessions from black defendants regardless of the crime. Or consider the matter-of-fact entry in the case of the trial of Ben for burglary in Southampton County, Virginia, in 1821. After his arrest he "was . . . taken out and with small cords Suspended by the thumbs for about one minute, but the prisoner made no confession[. H]e was then tied by the toes and drawn up but not entirely off the ground," but he still did not confess. After he spent the night in the custody of a young man he did confess, although the record does not show why. He was sentenced to hang with a recommendation that he be banished from the state. His counsel made no complaint.[63]

There was an even deeper question about voluntariness than that posed by the use of violence. If slaves were without wills of their own, how could their confessions ever be voluntary and therefore admissible? This issue came up in the context of both judicial and extrajudicial confessions. Cobb, for one, argued that extrajudicial confessions when made to masters should not be admissible as evidence. According to him, the slave "is bound, and habituated to obey every command and wish" of the master. The slave

> has no will to refuse obedience, even when it involves his life. The master is his protector, his counsel, his confidant. . . . Every consideration which induces the law to protect from disclosures confidential communications made to legal advisers, applies with increased force to communications made by a slave to his master. Moreover, experience shows, that the slave is always ready to mould his answers so as to please the master, and that no confidence can be placed in the truth of his statements.[64]

Southern jurists usually did not go that far. Although nearly all of the appellate cases came during the 1850s, the first notable one—*State v. Charity, (a slave)*—was decided in North Carolina in 1830. This action turned on the admissibility of a master's evidence. Ruffin focused on the question of whether masters could testify for or against their slave, but in the course of his analysis he mentioned that confessions "being to the master, may or may not be of that voluntary character which the law, not less in wisdom than humanity, requires." Nevertheless, this case did not require an examination of that problem, which presented "not a little difficulty." Hall remarked that the slave might object to her master giving her confession to him as evidence because "he is authorized to defend her; and because she is his slave, and by various means, against which slavery could make but little resistance, he might exact from her any confessions he pleased." He added, however, that "upon this part of the case I give no opinion." Chief Justice Henderson believed that the confessions of slaves to masters should always be excluded as evidence. "The master," he noted, "has an almost absolute control over both the body and mind of his slave. The master's will is the slave's will. All his acts, all his sayings, are made with a view to propitiate his master. His confessions are made, not from a love of truth, not from a sense of duty, not to speak a falsehood, but to please his master."[65]

Courts that faced the issue later did not go as far as Henderson urged in 1830 or Cobb suggested in his late 1850s' treatise. Still, judges often were suspicious of confessions made by slaves to those with direct authority over them. Edwin and Nelson, for instance, were tried for murder in Louisiana in 1848. The court overturned the guilty verdict against Nelson and affirmed that against Edwin. Judge George Rogers King held that Edwin had repeatedly and voluntarily confessed; the only constraint on him was that necessary "for his safe custody." Nelson's case was different. He confessed to the overseer, who was the owner's son, while he "was in the stocks" and after the son declared that "it would be better for him to tell what he had done." The court was not disturbed by the fact that Nelson was in the stocks. This did not "authorize the conclusion that threats or violence were used to extort confessions." He was in the stocks "only for safekeeping." The problem concerned the remark made by the overseer. The confession to him came "strictly within the rules which should have excluded it from evidence. It was made to his young master . . . to whose authority he habitually submitted, to whom he would naturally look for protection . . . the admonition coming from such a source was well calculated to inspire the slave with the hope of protection from the consequences of his act if fully confessed," and it should have been excluded.[66]

An Alabama court reached a similar conclusion in an 1854 arson case, *Wyatt, (a slave), v. State*. Chief Justice William P. Chilton did not contend that all confessions made to masters by slaves should be excluded, but he did believe that the court should consider "with caution, whether the confessions of guilt made by a slave in interviews had with his master, or one having dominion over him, were not elicited or controlled by the relation, and predicated upon the fear of punishment or injury, or upon the hope of some benefit to be gained by making them." The court ruled that the confession to the master in this case was not voluntary and should have been thrown out. A final example, from Florida in 1853, also involved arson. In *Simon, (a slave), v. State*, Simon was examined by the mayor of Pensacola, who told Simon that if he had burned the house "he would be put upon his trial and would be certainly hung; that if he had any accomplices he would, by testifying against them, become State's evidence, and they would be put upon their trial and not him." The mayor noted that there was a loud crowd outside that said the prisoner should hang. Simon asked for his master, to whom he would tell the whole truth. He confessed. According to his master, Simon "was under a great state of excitement . . . was laboring under great terror, and . . . he never saw any one more terrified." Judge Semmes, for the majority, ruled this and subsequent confessions inadmissible. "Independent of these confessions," Semmes wrote, the fact that the accused was a slave who had confessed to his master was "entitled to the most grave consideration. The ease with which this class of our population can be intimidated, and the almost absolute control which the owner . . . [has] over the will of the slave, should induce the Courts at all times to receive their confessions with the utmost caution and distrust."[67]

A major exception to this line of cases occurred in Mississippi in 1857 in *Sam, (a slave), v. State*. Sam's owner had captured his slave, "chained his legs together, and brought him home in the stage-coach." He asked him why he burned the gin-house, and Sam allegedly replied because he "wished to be hung." Judge Alexander Handy, for the court, upheld the conviction based in part on the confession. His reasoning was that "the relation which the slave bears to the master, is certainly one of dependence and obedience, but it is not necessarily one of constraint and duress." Patriarchalism had a severe price, not the least of which was this charac-

terization of the master-slave relationship. "It is not to be presumed," Handy
continued, "that the master exercises an undue influence over his slave to induce
him to make confessions tending to convict him of a capital offence, because
besides the feelings of justice and humanity, which would forbid such efforts, it
would be against the interest of the master that the slave should make confessions
which would forfeit his life; for he would thereby sustain a loss to the amount of
one-half of the value of the slave." It thus would be extremely dangerous to exclude
the confessions of slaves to masters:

> Such confessions are not incompetent upon any sound legal principle; and to
> establish the rule that they are incompetent, would be highly impolitic and
> dangerous; because, from the nature of the connection between master and
> slave, if confessions fully made to him should not be admissible, they would
> not be likely to be made to any others; and thus, however true the confessions,
> and however strongly corroborated by circumstances, all violations of law
> committed by slaves, the proof of which depended on that sort of evidence,
> would go unpunished in the courts of justice. And the consequence of this
> would be, that a disposition would be created to punish slaves, otherwise than
> according to the rules and restraints of the law, which should operate, both in
> its protection and in its punishments, upon them, as well as upon white
> men.[68]

Obviously, a different legal problem was presented when slaves "confessed" to
the murder of those with direct authority over them. Now the significance of
subordination or deference to those to whom confessions were given became
murky. All of the appellate cases in which the problem was considered came after
1850. That the issue arose at all and when it did reflected a heightened concern on
the part of Southern jurists with fairness in slave trials.

One of the first cases in which this problem was considered was *Alfred and
Anthony, (slaves), v. State*, a Tennessee action decided in 1853. The court upheld the
convictions of the slaves for the murder of their master despite objections to the
admissibility of certain evidence. Under the law of Tennessee, a magistrate before
whom defendants were brought was to "record the examination of the party" and
transmit the written record to the trial court. It appears that each slave made a
confession to someone other than the committing magistrate. These confessions,
the court noted, "were attended by such circumstances as to render them incompetent." The court had held them to be so, yet it permitted them to go to the jury.
But the real question for the appellate court concerned the confessions taken by
the magistrate. These were held "competent." The court argued that if a defendant
"be cautioned by the magistrate that whatever he may say may be used against
him, and that he is not bound to criminate himself, but that it is his privilege to
submit to an examination or not, at his option, there certainly can be no good
reason why any statements or confessions he may make under such circumstances
should not be good evidence against him." Slaves possessed a right against self-

incrimination and were to be warned by a committing magistrate of this right.[69] At least they possessed the right in the abstract.

Three years later the Georgia court confronted this issue in *Rafe, (a slave), v. State* (1856). Rafe confessed to the sheriff of Liberty County, who was bringing him back from Savannah. On the way the sheriff met others, and an interrogation followed. During the course of it the sheriff told Rafe that the people of the county believed he had killed his master. The sheriff then said that "if he did do it he had better acknowledge it, but if he did not do it not to acknowledge it; that if he lied, it would be adding sin to sin: that the people of Liberty were so satisfied he did it they would hang him anyhow." After that Rafe confessed, but, as the sheriff put it, the "prisoner has confessed and denied several times since to me and others." The court ruled the confessions admissible because they were "not elicited by promises or threats; and although they may have been induced by the remarks and interrogation of the Sheriff, the record shows that they were voluntarily made." The court, through Judge McDonald, hastened to add that it disapproved "of the manner in which they were obtained—spiritual exhortations had better be left to the clergy."[70]

In the same year the Mississippi high court also ruled on an important confessions case. In *Dick, Aleck, and Henry, (slaves), v. State* the defendants had confessed to white persons who did not have authority over the slaves as either magistrate or master. The slaves were found guilty of murdering their master, whom they allegedly had choked to death. Counsel for the slaves made a bold effort to invalidate their confessions. They had come late in the evening after some whites had been with the slaves all day, and not until about eighteen to twenty whites surrounded the bondsmen after they had been arrested, chained, and told to confess did they do so. "The man who is born a slave, raised a slave, and knows, and feels his destiny and lot is to die a slave," counsel argued, "always under a superior, controlling his actions and his will, cannot be supposed to act or speak voluntarily and of his free will while surrounded by fifteen or twenty of those to whom he knows he is subservient, and by the law bound to obey." He continued: "such a being, in his physical, moral, and intellectual faculties, is, and must ever be, more or less subservient to the will and wishes of the freeman having the control over him; and when in chains, and informed that it would be better for him to confess, is under duress. Place man physically and morally, in perpetual slavery, and how can the intellectual man be free? Perpetual slavery and free will are incompatible with each other." Cobb agreed, but then so did Rousseau. Precisely because of their social status the confessions of slaves should always be suspect, and to the point of total exclusion.[71]

The Mississippi court, however, did not rise to this challenge, anymore than it would a year later in Sam's case. It focused on the fact that the confessions were not made before an officer during a judicial examination: that "no warning of any kind whatever, was given to the prisoners of their rights—and that they were not bound to make any confession, by which they would criminate themselves."[72] But this was a right that existed only in the context of an official examination. As long as no effort was made by private parties to induce the slaves to confess by "threats or promises," the confessions would be held to be "perfectly voluntary." Subordination, even to all whites, did not preclude "voluntariness" in Southern courts. The court, of course, did not discuss the notion that from the point of view of slaves, all whites were persons in "authority." This was a question of considerable significance. Goodell, for instance, cited a number of Southern statutes showing that slaves were believed to be in subjection to all white persons. And the South Carolina Supreme Court ruled in *Ex parte Boylston* (1847) that it was a criminal offense, triable in a magistrate-freeholders' court, for a slave to be insolent to a white.[73] Would not such a view of the relationship between slaves and all whites necessarily raise a serious question about the voluntariness of any confession given by a slave to any white? And would that not, in turn, bring us back to the notion that because of the "ignominy of the soul" that flowed out of social degradation, the testimony of slaves, including their confessions, should be excluded?

Tushnet has suggested that courts began to recognize that coerciveness was essential in the master-slave relationship and that this was "ultimately subversive of the general rule of arbitrariness." The rule could be preserved only if it were preserved for third parties, "particularly representatives of the state," who were independent of the master class. This proved impossible, in Tushnet's view, because of the "threat to public order and self-conception" that a special slave law created. I agree up to a point. But this position overlooks the significance of race. It was impossible to completely preserve voluntariness not solely because of the threat to public order, and that was genuine, but also because whites in general were not always conceptually separated from the "master-class." Slaves were considered to be subordinate to all whites, and, therefore, voluntariness could not have been preserved even for third parties. This would not necessarily mean that all confessions had to be excluded from evidence, even though that was one strong answer. Another might have been to admit all confessions and leave it to the court or jury to give them what weight they deserved in the circumstances. This was the approach of Scottish law, as Tushnet noted, and was applauded by Chief Justice Lumpkin, an opponent of legal technicality, in *Stephen, (a slave), v. State* (1852).[74] This would have amounted to treating slave confessions in a fashion similar to slave testimony generally in the West Indies during the eighteenth century. It was ultimately a matter of policy, and Southern whites had always shown themselves to be quite supple about such matters.

Legal traditions, religious values, the imperatives of social subordination, racism, and even property interests could determine whether a person would be admitted as a witness in a criminal case, and they could determine the way evidence was weighed if it was received. But this was contingent. Down to the 1720s slaves usually were excluded from Southern courts, except in noncapital cases, with the possible exception of South Carolina. Fear of the violent resistance of the slaves compelled the admission of their testimony, even though with conditions and restraints. As in the West Indies the testimony would be accepted, but the weight of it was for the triers of fact, and it had to be corroborated, at least in capital cases. For slaves, law was more often the rules of the plantation or even their own norms and sanctions. As Judge David Wardlaw of South Carolina observed in a leading slave insolence case, the law as to slaves was but "a compact between his rulers" with which the slaves had nothing to do.[75] On occasion this meant, especially before the 1720s, that some slave "crimes" were not punishable in the public courts of the South. It was a price Southern whites paid for refusing to allow the testimony of pagan blacks. Slaves thus existed in a sort of limbo, the abode of souls barred from heaven because of not having received Christian baptism. They were at times also barred from Southern courts and existed only in the shadows of the legal order. It was the fear of violent resistance coming from those shadows that finally overcame the legal traditions derived from England.

As the Civil War approached there was evidence that the testimony of slaves would be regarded more seriously, either by being taken under oath or by being allowed without corroboration by pregnant circumstances. This was another dimension of the fact that slaves were increasingly drawn into the normal criminal justice system. The end result of this line of legal development could have cut deeply into the claims and prerogatives of masters, a result with very serious consequences. But in the face of such developments and threats Southern whites erected their ideological defenses of their social order,[76] which brought to the fore the problem of social subordination. This, in turn, raised serious questions about slave confessions, questions that had never been openly asked or considered before.

Forced to confront a relationship that ultimately rested on the whip, some argued by the nineteenth century that confessions of slaves to masters were suspect and ought to be wholly excluded. The logic of this position could not have been kept within bounds, as Southern whites argued that black slaves were to show deference to all whites. There was no principled way to limit the analysis as long as the slave system was inextricably tied in Southern white discourse with the problem of race. The result could have been a swing back to the medieval view that had excluded the evidence of villeins. This, however, was in tension with modern legal developments whereby slaves were granted more and more procedural rights in Southern courts, including such legal securities as the right to a jury trial, the right to counsel, and the right to an appeal.[77]

There clearly were contradictory tendencies at work in Southern criminal law as it applied to slaves, and there was no inevitable resolution of the tensions. The resolution came as a result of the blood bath that began in 1861, but before that it was far from certain. One thing, however, was. Rules of evidence, rules fashioned to control juries and lawyers, were also constructed to ensure the property interests of slaveowners and the domination of whites over blacks. Some of the rules of evidence might have been evenhanded for those who possessed property, or at least who were entitled to acquire it, but generally those examined here would never be that for persons of color, especially for those who were held as property. There had even been times when slaves were not only unprotected at law, as Goodell noted, but also not even admitted to the mysteries of the criminal side of the legal order, unless the case was minor or they confessed. As Cobb had observed, law was for the "*othesworth*," and that meant it was for the free.

11

Masters and the Criminal Offenses of Their Slaves

Procuring counsel for his slave . . . is in return for the profits
of the bondsman's labor and toil.

Jim, (a slave), v. State (Georgia, 1854)

Goodell claimed that there were rare cases "where the interests of the 'owner,' the wants of society, or the exigencies of the Government require an anomalous departure from the principle of slave chattlehood, by the temporary and partial recognition of their humanity. Such exceptions and modifications are never made for the benefit of the slave."[1] Did Southern law treat slaves as autonomous moral beings separate from their masters? To suggest so overlooks the importance of the property claims of masters, of the master-slave relationship, and of the relationship masters had with the rest of society.

Douglas Hay suggested that one function of criminal law was the affirmation of authority and power.[2] There is evidence that Southern whites were sometimes mindful of this. During late 1859 the Reverend Charles Colcock Jones of coastal Georgia turned his slave Lucy over to the local magistrates for trial. Lucy had concealed the death of her child, and Jones believed that she might have killed it. By December her trial was over, and she was sentenced to eight days in the county jail plus ninety lashes at intervals of two and three days. "It is my impression," Jones later wrote, "that if owners would more frequently refer criminal acts of their servants to the decisions of the courts, they would aid in establishing correct public sentiment among themselves in relation to different kinds of crimes committed by the Negroes, give better support to their own authority, and restrain the vices of the Negroes themselves." This was not necessarily the norm. About five years earlier, and just a few miles to the north on St. Helena Island in South Carolina, Thomas B. Chaplin had noted in his diary that "Helen's last child died today, regularly murdered. The mother deserves a good whipping, & I think she will get it yet." There is no indication that she did, and there is none that he turned her over to the public authorities. The next to the last entry in his diary reads: "Helen had a girl, Flora, Oct. 1860."[3]

There was a time, however, when some planters were more conscious of the possible use of the criminal law in the fashion of Reverend Jones. As early as 1693 in Charles City County, Virginia, a prominent early tobacco planter, Colonel Edward Hills, brought a complaint before the county court against two white servants and one slave who had killed and eaten a hog on his plantation. All three belonged to Hills. Instead of whipping them on the plantation, Hills turned to the public forum.[4]

Throughout the colonial period, in Virginia at least, some slaveowners turned to the courts to affirm their power and authority. Two men, for example, accounted for five separate cases. They were Benjamin Harrison and Landon Carter, two of the wealthiest of all the eighteenth-century Virginia planters. But equally significant was the fact that they were also magistrates.[5] They used the law to control their slaves and validate their power precisely because they also controlled the law. The justices dominated what A. G. Roeber has called the "rituals of court day."[6]

Landon Carter provides an illustration of the practice. On February 4, 1771, two of his slaves were charged with hog stealing before the county court. One was found guilty and received thirty-nine lashes, whereas the second, Simon, was acquitted. The next year, on August 3, 1772, the court heard a complaint against Simon again. This time the complainant was Carter. The court found Simon guilty of a "misdemeanor," rather than of hog stealing. Carter was listed as a member of the court on August 3, and there is no indication that he excused himself. Even if he did, his presence must have been felt. On August 4, the day after Simon's trial, Carter recorded in his diary: "Still very cool wind all day at Northwest. Simon whipped for killing a hog." He did not mention that the whipping followed a formal trial at which he was present or that he brought the complaint. Power and mercy were blended in the judgment when the court found Simon guilty of a misdemeanor. A second conviction for hog stealing would have cost the slave his ears. That the danger was real was shown on November 2, 1772, when Carter "surrendered up his Negro Fellow Charles for hog stealing." Charles was the other slave tried in 1771. He was found guilty again, and the record concluded that "this is the second offense whereupon it is ordered that he be punished according to law."[7]

Twenty-five years earlier Carter also had resorted to the Richmond court. The charge was burglary of his mansion house and the theft of such items as "Four Torinton Rugs" and "two Dozen of Hose." Manuel was found guilty on October 6, 1747, and sentenced to hang.[8] On April 26, 1770, Carter confided to his diary what this case was truly about. Manuel had been one of Carter's most exasperating slaves. "However," Carter noted, "I kept my temper and resolved to sell Mr. Manuel. He was once a valuable fellow, the best plowman and mower I ever saw. But like the breed of him he took to drinking and whoring till at last he was obliged to steal and robbed my store of near half the shirts and shifts for my people besides other things. For this I prosecuted him and got him pardoned with a halter round his neck at the gallows."[9] There is no doubt that men like Landon Carter and

Benjamin Harrison wielded enormous power at the local level and could manipulate the criminal law for the reformation of their own slaves, not to mention the validation of their power.

Powerful planters like Carter, or later an influential slaveowner and clergyman like Reverend Jones, might turn to public law to prosecute their own slaves, but there is no reason to believe that the middling or poorer slaveowners would do so. And, as Richard Beeman's study of the Southside Virginia county of Lunenburg shows, the justices themselves did not always occupy the exalted status they did in the long-established and wealthy Tidewater. By the nineteenth century, moreover, society was becoming increasingly democratized, and the economic power of the big planters of the tobacco-based society of colonial Virginia was disrupted. By then justices did not always come from the gentry, and wealthy planters would not turn to lesser persons to judge their slaves. An example of this transformation came later in Lunenburg County. In 1862 the court heard a charge against Emanuel for breaking into a home with intent to rape. He was found guilty and sentenced to death. His counsel moved in arrest of judgment on the ground that one of the justices was not "legally a justice in the County of Lunenburg." The challenged jurist said that he had been living in Richmond "superintending" a home for wages, but most of his family lived in Lunenburg and he frequently came to the county. When he did, he stayed in the local hotel. That was enough, and he qualified. The contrast between this man, J. Stokes, walking over from the hotel to hear a case against a slave, and Landon Carter riding to the courthouse from his beautiful Georgian home, Sabine Hall, could hardly be sharper. Power was no longer firmly in the hands of an established and wealthy gentry. A power that had rested on the domination of tobacco cultivation and large numbers of slaves had been diffused with the spread of wheat and the democratization of society, and with it had died the tendency of the powerful to turn to the public courts that they controlled to validate their authority or to reform their slaves. Another factor in the transformation was the growth of the legal profession. Judicial discretion could be circumscribed by the presence of lawyers, and their emergence corresponded with the decrease in the power of the justices. The rise of legal professionalism shifted power within the legal system.[10]

Masters, under these various pressures, turned away from the use of the law to reinforce their authority over their slaves by prosecuting them for crimes unless they were capital offenses such as murder, rape, or arson. But masters were involved in other ways. They could be held legally liable for the criminal conduct of their slaves, such as in requirements that they pay the legal costs for the successful prosecution of their slaves or make some restitution for the injuries caused by them. The theoretical assumption was that a liability derived from the power exercised by masters over slaves. Another way they could be involved was by providing protection or defense for their indicted slaves.

One form of slaveowner liability developed at the end of the eighteenth century. States imposed a responsibility on owners to provide legal counsel for an accused slave, a duty that would have made no sense before the number of lawyers had increased. Not all states did so, however. In a major slave case in a state that did not impose this liability, Georgia, Judge Starnes explored one possible ground for a duty owed by the master. Although it was obiter dictum, it captures the point: "it is my opinion," he observed in *Jim, (a slave), v. State* (1854), "that this duty of procuring counsel for his slave . . . is in return for the profits of the bondsman's labor and toil, is as binding on the master, as the obligation to procure for that slave, medical attendance in his sickness, or food and clothing at all times."[11] But this was not a binding opinion, and there was no statute in Georgia, which proved fatal in this case.

Three years after Jim's trial the Georgia Supreme Court ruled directly on the question. The case, *Lingo v. Miller & Hill* (1857), involved an arson indictment against the slave of John R. T. Lingo in Marion Superior Court. The slave was acquitted. Lingo had refused to employ counsel or to pay the attorneys appointed by the court. In this action for fees the lower court charged the jury that even though Lingo had refused to hire counsel, "there was a legal obligation resting upon the master so to do, arising out of the relation of master and servant." The jury found for the attorneys, but this judgment was overturned on appeal.[12]

Judge Henry L. Benning observed that there was no positive law in Georgia requiring masters to provide counsel. If there was such a duty it would have to arise from some general principle, but Benning could find none. "Nor," he added, "does it seem, that there is any great need, that such an obligation as this, should be imposed on the master. *Every* master has an interest to prevent his slave from being punished, an interest that increases with the increase of the punishment to which the slave is exposed. *Nearly* every master, together with nearly every member of his family, has also an affection for his slave." Self-interest and humanity, in Benning's analysis, led to the denial of any duty to employ counsel. A master would do so voluntarily if he believed the slave to be innocent, but if he refused, "the case is one in which the master ought not to be required to employ them. It may be pretty safely assumed that every such case will be a case in which the master, a juror biased, by both interest and affection, to acquit, has convicted."[13]

Although Georgia did not require masters to furnish counsel, other Southern states—beginning in the 1790s—did. In 1792 Virginia provided that in capital cases slaves would be entitled to counsel whose fee was to be paid by the owner. The next year North Carolina determined that counsel would be assigned if the owner was unknown or resided outside of the state. Owners living in the state were not burdened with the duty. In 1822 Mississippi stated that the court trying slaves could assign counsel to defend "according to the circumstances of the case." It was not mandatory, and fees were not mentioned. The next year the state required owners to pay fees, and the court was obliged to appoint counsel if the owner did not do so. Kentucky, in 1834, made it the duty of owners to provide lawyers and set the fees. As of 1836 Alabama required counsel for slaves; Tennessee introduced the right to counsel in 1836 and South Carolina in 1839. Tennessee stipulated that fees could be recovered against a master by action of debt. A final example is Florida, which required the assignment of lawyers as early as 1828.[14]

Sometimes the assessment of fees against the owners of slaves who declined to employ counsel took bizarre forms. In Sussex County, Virginia, David Mason refused to employ a lawyer in a case against his slaves in the 1790s. The court assigned counsel for the slaves, and Mason was ordered to pay the lawyer his fee for defending them. The quixotic element is that the charge was "plotting the murder of said David Mason." Mason, who had been allegedly poisoned, petitioned the legislature for compensation for the execution of his slaves, which he received. In 1824, in Lunenburg County, Robert Hayes was faced with the same peculiarities of Virginia law. He had to pay counsel to defend two of his slaves charged with putting broken bottle glass, among other things, in his food and with threatening his family. Hayes did not have the satisfaction of Mason. His two slaves were acquitted.[15]

Missouri took a different approach in *Manning v. Cordell* (1840). The court argued that the assignment of counsel at the trial did not rest on the master-slave relationship, as Starnes had tried to establish in Georgia. Because it did not, the counsel in this case could not collect his fees in a civil action against the owner. "The counsel acts in such case," the court reasoned, "as an officer of the court, and for the furtherance of justice, and not upon any contract with the master, nor can any be implied."[16] The contractual analysis was not followed elsewhere, but it did exonerate Missouri masters from this form of duty or legal liability.

In some states masters were legally obligated to provide counsel for slaves on trial for their lives, and in some they were not. Where they were, the imposition of liability rested on the idea that the master owed a duty to the slave in exchange for his or her labor and the power he exercised over the slave. Conceptually tension existed. While masters in some jurisdictions were obligated to pay fees to defend their slaves, they were also liable to pay the costs of prosecuting them. Moreover, the payment of compensation to masters whose slaves were executed stood in contrast to these liabilities. It rested in part on a claim on society by slaveowners for some protection of their property interests.

Most Southern states adopted some provision for compensation in the case of executions. An initial purpose behind these laws was to assure that masters would not attempt to protect their property interests by shielding their slaves from public justice. Another was to shift the costs of public justice to the public at large and balance the owner's interests and public security.

The first compensation law adopted was that of Virginia in 1705. The justices who condemned a slave would put a value on him, and from this the assembly would make a "suitable allowance" to the master. There was never a statutory or case law definition of that phrase, but at least it meant that the owners would not always receive the full market value. In 1786 the state changed the law and did provide full value (in 1801 this was extended to cover slaves whose sentence was commuted to banishment).[17] North Carolina used the "suitable allowance" language from 1741 to 1796.[18]

Full value was allowed in some colonies and states for extended periods of time, but this did not always mean full market value for a prime field hand or domestic, for instance. The "market value" of the slave was diminished by his or her conviction. Virginia required this by law in the last few years of slavery.[19] In 1855 the court in Lunenburg County that found Phillis guilty of arson and sentenced her to transportation out of the United States added that she should be valued by each member of the court "as in his opinion the said slave would bring if sold publicly under a knowledge of the circumstances of her guilt." Maryland allowed full value from 1751 until the end of slavery. South Carolina, on the other hand, permitted it only for a brief period and then began to experiment with compensation. Full value was paid to owners from 1712 to 1714 because the loss otherwise "would prove too heavy for the owners" to bear and so that "the owners of negroes and slaves may not be discouraged to detect and discover the offenses of their negroes and slaves, and that the loss may be borne by the public, whose safety, by such punishments, is hereby provided for."[20] Few slaveowners in South Carolina held large numbers of slaves at that time, and this would explain the first concern. This generous approach proved too costly. In 1714 the law was changed because the treasury had been "exhausted by the extraordinary sums that have been allowed for criminal slaves." A ceiling of 50 pounds was placed on the valuation. Three years later, still complaining of an exhausted treasury, the assembly changed the law. Full value would be allowed except in cases of slaves convicted of murder. Moreover, instead of the money being appropriated by the assembly it would come from an assessment levied on all slaveowners of the parish where the slave was executed. In 1722 the law was revised once again to provide a ceiling of 80 pounds, which would come from an assessment on the land as well as slaves. Now non-slaveholders had to help subsidize the loss of executed slaves. In its landmark code of 1740 South Carolinians took still another approach. Of the assessment, not to exceed 200 pounds current money, the owner of the slave would receive up to one-half and the remaining one-half would go to the person injured by the criminal conduct of the slave. Victim compensation was not followed in other jurisdictions, but allowing masters only a portion of the appraised value was. In 1751 the law was again adjusted. This time the exemption in the case of murderers was deleted, and the value was set at 40 pounds proclamation money. Finally, in 1843 South Carolina set the maximum figure at $200.[21] No other state experimented as much with compensation, but some adopted significant laws.

The laws of North Carolina of 1796 and Alabama of 1836 are of special interest. Both predicated compensation on a finding that the masters bore no responsibility for the criminal conduct. The Alabama law provided that the jury would value a slave and a master would receive up to one-half of that sum. The jury was to say what amount he or she should have. "And the prosecuting officer shall inquire as to all facts which would go to show the portion of blame attached to the master, that the jury may rightly assess the amount he shall have."[22] There is nothing to suggest that the matter of "blame" referred solely to whether or not the master was a principal or an accessory to the crime. Other states excluded all compensation under those circumstances.[23] This followed the maxim that no one should profit from his or her own wrong.

According to North Carolina's law of 1796, the jury that valued the slave should also "enquire whether the owner of the said slave did or did not feed, clothe and treat him or her with the humanity consistent with his or her situation." If it was proved that the owner did not, he or she would receive nothing.[24] This law was grounded on a slightly different notion than that in the laws that assessed costs against masters. In the latter masters bore a measure of liability because of a failure to control their potentially dangerous "property," whereas here it was that masters actively created the conditions that led to crime. North Carolina used both conceptions. It had provided for the assessment of costs against masters three years earlier. Alabama and Louisiana were the only states that refused compensation during the nineteenth century for a particular crime, insurrection, the ultimate failure of a master.[25]

The most widely adopted limitation in the compensation laws was on the amount. In South Carolina, Mississippi, Alabama, and Texas, it was, at one time or another, up to one-half of the appraised value. In North Carolina and Louisiana, for a time, it was up to two-thirds. It was also two-thirds in Delaware.[26] The reasoning behind such limits is not clear. One possibility was the need to encourage slaveowners to allow their slaves to be tried at all balanced against the need to use a cost-effective approach. Another might have been that masters deserved some compensation because it was unfair to make them bear the whole economic burden: on the other side, the public should not do so either. Finally, it is probable that masters were not granted full compensation on the assumption that they bore some responsibility because of the failure to fulfill a duty to society to control their "property."

Nonetheless, according to a pioneering study of the compensation law in colonial North Carolina, the planters "suffer little or nothing."[27] One foundation for this judgment was the source of the money paid to slaveowners. Normally it was from the public fisc so that the whole community, nonslaveholders included, bore the burden. But there were variations. From 1717 to 1722 in South Carolina only slaveowners contributed to the fund. In Alabama and North Carolina the tax to create the fund was on the blacks of those states, slave and free. Finally, Maryland provided that the county would pay for the slave out of its regular tax assessment, but if the slave was sentenced to prison rather than execution, the county could be reimbursed by the sale of the slave once his or her term was completed. In Louisiana, another state where slaves could be sentenced to prison, owners would receive compensation from the state to which they transferred the title to the slave. An example of this occurred in St. Landry Parish in 1839, when Pierre Ozere conveyed his slave Azelie to the state because she had been sentenced to "perpetual imprisonment on a charge of attempting to poison."[28]

Masters, of course, were directly involved in criminal trials when they testified for their slaves. Some jurisdictions made statutory provision for such testimony. As early as 1705 Virginia determined that a master "may appear at the tryall and make what just defence he can for such slave, so that such defence do only relate to matters of fact, and not to any formality in the indictment or other proceedings of the court." In the absence of a statute, the normal common law rule of evidence applied: parties interested in the result of a lawsuit were not competent to testify in favor of their interest, nor could they be compelled to testify against it. An early confrontation with the rule came in the Delaware case of State v. Negro George (1797). The court, without explanation, held that the master should not be excluded as a witness in capital cases on account of interest.[29]

In State v. Charity, (a slave), the North Carolina Supreme Court considered the matter in the late 1820s. The master of Charity was called to prove her confession to an act of infanticide, but he objected to testifying against her. The lower court ordered him to do so. She was convicted, but on appeal a new trial was ordered by a divided court. Judge Ruffin argued that the master could not testify for his slave, and therefore he could not be forced to testify against her. The case had to be decided on "general principles" as there was no relevant statute. Were the interests of the master involved? Clearly, they were. "The whole property in the slave is in jeopardy, and the master is liable for the costs in case of a conviction." "His interests are essentially at stake," Ruffin contended, "as much as the life of the slave is." The only testimony that would be received was voluntary testimony against the slave. Judge Hall agreed that the master was precluded from giving evidence for his slave because of interest. The "master is not a party in form to the proceeding. But he is substantially so." "The conviction of the slave," Hall continued, "is a judgment against him to the amount of her value. In addition to this, he is made liable . . . for costs."[30]

Chief Justice Henderson wrote an opinion he characterized as a concurrence "so feeble that it almost amounts to a dissent." He was not happy with the effect of the common law rule. When money only was involved, "to exclude a witness on the score of interest, however small, is applying a scale of morality to our nature sufficiently humiliating." But it was worse when the life of a "fellow-being" was at stake. To decline to hear a witness in such a case on the ground of "interest" would be to view man as filled with "more depravity" than he would admit. For him, masters could be good witnesses for their slaves, but that also meant that they could be compelled to testify against them. The problem in Charity's case, however, was that the evidence to be given concerned a confession. Could her master be compelled to testify as to a confession? Ruffin and Hall declined to decide the case on that question. Henderson concurred because of it. He would exclude the evidence of the confession because of the master-slave relationship. He was very suspicious of confessions made by slaves to masters. But, additionally, he would exclude the compelled testimony from the master for the following reasons: "The master from his situation, from the duties which the legislature have imposed on him, is the guardian and defender of his slave. It is a moral duty of the highest grade to see that no injustice is done him. The relation subsisting between them imposes upon him a load of obligations, and he should not be permitted, even if willing, to disregard them."[31] It was such reasoning, incidentally, that had led some judges to hold that free blacks could not own slaves—they could not wholly fulfill the duty of protection.

The Tennessee Supreme Court took a different route from that of the North Carolina majority. In *Elijah, (a slave), v. State* (1839), Judge Reese admitted the obvious: a master of slaves had a pecuniary interest in his property. But the master-slave relationship, he reasoned, had been altered when the state intervened to try the slave for crime. "The law," Reese argued, "upon high grounds of public policy, pretermits, for a moment, that relation, takes the slave out of the hands of his master, forgets his claim and rights of property, treats the slave as a rational and intelligent human being, responsible to moral, social, and municipal duties and obligations, and gives him the benefit of all the forms of trial which jealousy of power and love of liberty have induced the freeman to throw around himself for his own protection." Viewed in this light, the next step was easy. Public policy and common humanity outweighed the common law rule of evidence in the criminal trials of slaves.[32] Still, the property interest reattached if the slave was executed.

When courts in Alabama and Mississippi later ruled on the same problem, they followed the judgment in Tennessee and not in *Charity*. In Mississippi, in *Isham, (a slave), v. State* (1841), Chief Justice William L. Sharkey observed that "the servant has such an interest in the testimony of his master as will outweigh mere pecuniary considerations; nor can he be deprived of that testimony from the accidental circumstance that in a civil point of view he is regarded by the law as property." Finally, in *State v. Jim, (a slave)* (1856), the North Carolina Supreme Court, in an opinion by Judge Pearson, ruled that in a felony trial a master was a competent witness for his slave. He contended that there was no precedent in North Carolina directly in point, and he had seen no other decisions on the issue. Pearson suggested that the grounds taken in *Charity* were too dispersed to provide a satisfactory answer. He confronted the problem as follows:

> The idea, when a prisoner calls a witness to prove his innocence, who, it may be, is the only person on earth to whom a fact is known that will save his life, that he must be repulsed by the cold announcement, "he is your master—he has an interest in saving your life, and at all events he is liable for the costs of this prosecution, and, therefore, has a pecuniary interest which makes him incompetent, so he cannot be heard in your behalf," shocks all the best feelings of our nature, and extorts the exclamation, "This ought not to be a rule of evidence!"

He castigated the "almighty dollar" when placed in the scale with human life. Pearson concluded that the testimony "of the master cannot be excluded without manifest inconsistency. The slave is put on trial as a *human being*, entitled to have his guilt or innocence passed on by a jury. Is it not inconsistent, in the progress of the trial, to treat him as property, like a chattel—a horse, in the value of which the owner has a pecuniary interest which makes him incompetent as a witness?"[33]

On whatever theory—either that the relationship between master and slave was suspended or that the right of a slave to a master's testimony when the slave's life was at stake outweighed the reason to exclude the master's testimony—masters were entitled to give evidence for their slaves in all slave state jurisdictions. The old common law evidentiary rule had broken down in the face of the humanity of the slave.

Besides the ways in which masters were involved in slave trials as protectors of their slaves, there were those in which they were accounted liable for their criminal actions. The states began to impose liability for costs in the late eighteenth century.[34] But not always, as the judgment of the Texas Supreme Court in *Grinder, (a slave), v. State* (1847) demonstrates. The owner of a slave executed for murder in Fannin County was required to show cause why judgment should not be entered against him for the costs of prosecution. Lipscomb held that there was no legal foundation for the assessment. According to him, the state "in the prosecution of the slave belonging to the appellant, sought no pecuniary compensation; all that was asked was satisfaction for her violated laws; and this not at the hands of the owner of the slave, but from the person of the offender." Public justice was completely "satisfied in the person of the slave" by his execution. Without an appearance or defense on the part of the master, he concluded, there was "nothing in law to authorize a judgment against him."[35]

Two appellate cases—one in North Carolina, the other in Missouri—suggest some of the issues involved in the assessment of costs. In North Carolina, *State v. Carter Jones* (1828) was a state action against Jones, of Northampton County, for costs in the prosecution of his slave Charles, executed for the crime of rape. Counsel for Jones argued before the county superior court that he was not liable because Charles had become the property of the state when he was "taken out of the owner's possession by the operation of the criminal law to satisfy public justice." This was consistent with the ruling of the Tennessee court on the matter of testimony, but it was not accepted in North Carolina, either by the superior court or later by the state supreme court.[36]

The final case, *Reed v. Circuit Court of Howard County* (1839), involved an analysis of a fairly typical statute. The Missouri law provided that "if a slave be convicted of any offense in a case, where, if the convict was a free person, he would be liable to pay costs, such slave shall be sold to satisfy such costs, unless the owner or master appear and pay the same within sixty days after they become due." The issue was liability. Reed owned the slave but had hired him out for a year. During that year the slave was convicted of arson and sentenced to be removed from the state for twenty years. Reed wanted to shift the costs to the hirer. When the Howard County court refused to do so, he sought a mandamus to order it to do so.

The supreme court refused on the ground that the words "master" and "owner" in the law were virtually synonymous, and Reed, not the hirer, was liable.[37]

There was an even more direct liability when owners were required to enter peace recognizances, or stand as sureties of the peace for their slaves, or to make some form of restitution for the damage done by the criminal conduct of their slaves. Because the peace could be sworn before a single justice of the peace, the number of such cases is undoubtedly much higher than appears in the reports of courts of record. But, even there, there are occasional references. One of the first appeared in the minutes of the higher court for North Carolina in 1684. "Whereas Mr. John Burnby," the report reads, "hath given in upon Oath that he goes in Danger of his Life for feare of one Andrew a Negroe belonging to Mr. John Culpeper It is Ordered that Mr. Jno. Culpeper take Care of him and bring him to the next Court and also give in good bond for his good behaviour to the next Court."[38] In Prince Georges County, Maryland, in 1738 John Beall alleged that a number of slaves owned by others, along with some of his own, had attempted to poison him. After their acquittal, Beall swore the peace against the slaves of the other owners, who were required by the court to enter into recognizances by providing security for the good behavior of their slaves toward Beall.[39]

In the 1770s Richard Posey's slave Sam surfaced in the records of Granville County, North Carolina. John Howard Jr. feared that Sam would kill him; he also charged that Sam had stolen a "negro wench" of his. He "therefore pray'd Security of Peace against him."[40] As a final example, in Mercer County, Kentucky, Absalom W. Scales swore the peace in 1852 against John, the slave of Thomas Elliot. Scales alleged that he feared the slave otherwise would harm him or his property.[41] The very monotonousness or commonness of such entries in the records indicates the resistance of slaves. It also testifies to the fact that liabilities were placed on masters. Such liabilities rested on the notion that masters owed a duty to the rest of society to control their slaves.

A final mode of liability was the most direct of all: it was the requirement that masters make some form of restitution for the criminal offenses of their slaves. Most often this was limited to property crimes and was an adaptation of the English rules on the restitution of stolen property. The English law, however, provided for restoring the actual property taken,[42] whereas the adaptations in the South went further. One example would be the Virginia laws on hog stealing in the colonial period, although these were later dropped. By 1705 the owners of slaves convicted of the offense had to pay the owners of the hogs a stipulated amount of tobacco. There are not many cases where this applied, but there are some. For instance, in 1741 the owner of Rippon, in Charles City County, was ordered to pay two hundred pounds of tobacco to the owner of the stolen hogs, as well as the expenses of the witnesses who appeared to testify against his slave.[43]

The most extensive examples come from Missouri and Louisiana. In 1835 the Missouri legislature approved an adaptation of continental civil law. It provided that "every person who shall be injured by the commission of any offense against his person . . . committed by a slave, shall have an action against the master or owner of such slave for the time, to recover any damages by him sustained by the commission of such offense, not exceeding in amount the value of the slave." This statute was at issue in a series of cases heard by the Missouri Supreme Court beginning with *Jennings v. Kavanaugh* (1837). In this action the slave of the plaintiff had been killed by the defendant's slave in a fight. The court ruled against recovery. The basis for the judgment was that the slave, as property, had to come under the terms of the statute that pertained to crimes against property. The killing of a slave as a nonperson was not among the offenses listed in the damages statutes.[44]

The next case, *Ewing v. Thompson* (1850), also involved the killing of one slave by another. This was a common law complaint, however. The complainant charged that the slave of the defendant was known to the defendant to be of a "dangerous and murderous disposition." The principle of law on which he hoped to recover, according to Judge Napton, was that the "responsibility of the owner of the slave for the willful wrongs of that slave is at least as extensive as his responsibility for the injurious acts of his dog or his ox." The court did not accept the theory. Under the laws of Missouri the power of a master was limited, and "his responsibility is proportioned accordingly." It did not include a responsibility for the wanton aggressions of his slave except where expressly covered by statute. Napton reasoned: "we understand the slave to be a responsible moral agent, amenable, like his master, both to the laws of God and man for his own transgressions—that the law which regulates our dominion over the brute creation is not the one which governs the relation of master and slave—that our municipal laws have not given to the master that absolute dominion over his slave which would enable him absolutely to prevent the commission of crime." The master then "could not be held responsible for such remote consequences as the murder of another slave, should such a consequence be traced to a laxity of discipline not tolerated by our laws."[45] Despite the statutory extension of liability on masters for some criminal offenses of their slaves, none of the appellate cases actually sustained claims, and *Ewing* rejected a common law foundation.

An obligation based on continental civil law was a different matter. Article 180 of the Louisiana code provided that "the master shall be answerable for all the damages occasioned by an offence or quasi-offence committed by his slave, independent of the punishment inflicted on the slave." Article 181 incorporated the *actio noxalis*. The master could "discharge himself from such responsibility" by turning his slave over to the person injured. The injured party would then sell the slave at public auction and return to the original owner any balance after the deduction of damages and costs.[46] The language of the code and the principle was not limited to civil wrongs; it embraced criminal conduct as well. The theory of liability was the mirror image of the reasoning in Missouri. The theory was that a master possessed absolute power by law, and absolute power created an absolute obligation to control.

One case may show how wide that liability was. In *Collingsworth v. Covington*

(1847), the state supreme court dealt with a case where the overseer of the slaves was wounded by one of them. He sued his employer for damages. The judgment in the lower court favored the owner, but the supreme court overruled it. The evidence, Judge King observed, was that the plaintiff was a "good manager, attentive to the health, discipline, and good government, of the slaves under his charge, and exercised no unnecessary severity." It was also in evidence that the owner, Covington, maintained a "loose discipline" on his plantation and had made his slaves "unmanageable" by "over indulgence." It is hard to see why this was mentioned unless King felt some discomfort, because it did not matter in the least to the legal ruling. There simply was no exception in the code for such a case. The master's liability was complete.[47] Despite such theories, of course, masters never could control their slaves completely whatever claims they might have to absolute power or whatever obligations were imposed on them by law.

12

Obedience and the Outsider

Servants be obedient to them that are your masters.

Ephesians 6:5

Southern slaves maintained, as best they could, ties of kinship and culture.[1] But from the perspective of the free, the slave was an outsider without recognizable culture. Patterson defined slavery as the "*permanent, violent domination of natally alienated and generally dishonored persons*." Finley stressed "kinlessness" as one of the three components of slavery—the other two were the totality of power of the master over the slave and the status of the slave as property. His description of the first was this: the "totality of the slaveowner's rights was facilitated by the fact that the slave was always a deracinated outsider—an outsider first in the sense that he originated from outside the society into which he was introduced as a slave, second in the sense that he was denied the most elementary of social bonds, kinship." David Brion Davis noted the "modernity" of the slave that "lay in his marginality and vulnerability, in his incomplete and ambiguous bonding to a social group." He was a "replaceable and interchangeable outsider." Exemplifying scholars' view of slaves as ultimate victims, Oakes observed that "slavery in the American South shared the basic characteristics of slavery everywhere. Perpetual outsiders, non-citizens stripped of virtually all legal rights, southern slaves were totally subject to the authority of masters, who could be kind or cruel or, perhaps most terrifying, kind and cruel by turns, arbitrarily and without warning." As complete and perpetual outsiders who transferred nothing but bondage to their children, slaves had no rights of any kind. Having no rights they had no duties, as W. W. Buckland observed was the case in Roman law. Without duties, obligations, or rights, all that remained was raw power. This was the view captured wonderfully by Garrison Frazier, the black minister, when he defined slavery in 1864 for General Sherman and Secretary Stanton as submission to "irresistible power." Submission to such power would carry no intrinsic duty or obligation, as Hobbes understood: "slaves, have no obligation at all; but may break their bonds, as the prison; and kill, or carry away captive their master, justly."[2]

Southern whites hardly saw it that way. They constructed a different social world in which they could live with a system that Hegel described as an "outrage" because it rested on the falsehood that someone could be an extension of someone else's will. Slaveowners could not live for long in a Hobbesian world in which authority rested on power alone, and those who labored in the field did so only to "avoid the cruelty of their task-masters."[3] The world they created was one in which patriarchs bore a paternal duty to guide, govern, and protect all the members of their "family," including the slaves. Masters had a jurisdiction to govern and subordinates had a corresponding duty to obey. But it was far from a perfect world, as they had to face the insubordination or breach of duty of their subordinates, or "my people," as William Byrd II called them.[4] Theirs was a hierarchical order in which everyone had his "station" and his "duties,"[5] and that included the slaves.

There were different sources for the notion that slaves possessed a duty of obedience, even allegiance. One of those was a conservative social tradition in England that infected all social relationships. The sweep of that tradition was expressed well by Matthew Bacon in his *Abridgement* of English law, which began to appear in the 1730s: "The relationship between a master and a servant from the superiority and power which it creates on the one hand, and duty, subjection, and as it were, allegiance, on the other, is in many instances applicable to other relationships."[6] Slavery was one of those relationships in the plantation societies. English colonials could and on occasion did see slavery in terms of traditional master-servant relationships, and those contained a duty of submission or obedience, even "allegiance." The fact that English master-servant relations were based on voluntary contracts (at least they were voluntary agreements in theory) and slavery was not voluntary could be conveniently ignored. Slaves could be seen as analogous to servants, who possessed a duty of obedience. In the colonial plantation societies it was all part of a patriarchal social order. "Patriarchal masters," as Philip Morgan observed, "stressed order, authority, unswerving obedience, and were quick to resort to violence when their authority was questioned." By the nineteenth century patriarchalism coexisted with and was giving way to paternalism: "paternal masters . . . expected gratitude, even love from their slaves; they were keenly interested in their slave' religious welfare; their outlook was far more sentimental."[7]

This was another phase in the history of authority. The conception of property was changing with the emergence of liberal capitalism, and because authority rested on property the conception of authority was changing as well. Still, while the latter changed the claim of an obedience due remained, although by the nineteenth century it was not framed in the harshest terms. "If the state of Slavery is to exist at all," Harper wrote, "the master must have, and ought to have, such power of punishment as will compel them to perform the duties of their station. And is not this for their advantage as well as his? No human being can be contented, who does not perform the duties of his station."[8] But increasingly the argument was framed in religious terms. The Reverend Thornton Stringfellow of Virginia was an influential example. In his *Bible Argument; or, Slavery in the Light of Divine Revelation* he relied on St. Paul's letter to the Ephesians. In that letter,

Stringfellow noted, "The relative duties of each state are pointed out; those between the servant and master in these words: 'Servants be obedient to them who
are your masters, according to the flesh, with fear and trembling, in singleness of
your heart as unto Christ.' "[9] Charles Colcock Jones of Georgia, in *The Religious
Instruction of the Negroes in the United States*, agreed with Stringfellow's emphasis:

> the servant recognizes a superintending Providence, who disposes of men
> and things according to his pleasure; that his Gospel comes not with reckless
> efforts to wrench apart society and break governments into pieces, but to
> define clearly the relations and duties of men, and to lay down and render
> authoritative, those general principles of moral conduct which will result in
> the happiness of the whole, and in the peaceable removal of every kind of evil
> and injustice. To God, therefore, he commits the ordering of his lot, and in
> his station renders to all their dues, obedience to whom obedience, and
> honor to whom honor.[10]

In legal discourse conservative social and religious notions were expressed in
several categories, and none more so than age-old ideas of treason. J. G. Bellamy
found two different views of treason in the medieval law of England, the Germanic
and the Roman. "The Germanic element," he wrote, "was founded on the idea of
betrayal or breach of trust (*treubruch*) by a man against his lord, while the Roman
stemmed from the notion of *maiestas*, insult to those with public authority."[11]
Medieval English legal conceptions of treason remained vibrant into the eighteenth century (and to some extent in an altered condition into the nineteenth
century), and they were transferred to the English settlements in the form of high
treason and petit treason. Both treasons appeared in the way the free used the law
when slaves murderously rejected the notion that they owed a duty of submission
or allegiance by a resort to revolt or homicide of those who claimed a lawful
authority to command their labor—masters, overseers, and hirers.

High treason in seventeenth-century English law assumed different forms, but
the central idea was expressed by Dalton as a "grievous offence, done or attempted
against the estate regall." Hobbes, in *A Dialogue between a Philosopher and a
Student of the Common Laws of England*, had his lawyer (who represented Sir
Edward Coke) sound befuddled when asked what treason was at common law. The
lawyer replied that, because no lawyer had tried to say what amounted to high
treason, no one should expect him to do it "on such a sudden." The philosopher
(Hobbes) cut to the heart of the matter, of course: "you know that *salus populi* is
suprema lex, that is to say, the safety of the people is the highest law; and that the
safety of the people of a kingdom consisted in the safety of the King, and of the
strength necessary to defend his people, both against foreign enemies and rebellious subjects."[12] Ultimately the crime of treason was a threat to the stability of
society as a whole, and the concept was retained easily after the Revolution by
substituting the people for the king.[13] The punishment for anyone guilty of high
treason was ghastly. Men would be "drawn to the Place of Execution, and be there

hanged by the Neck, and cut down alive, and . . . his Entrails . . . taken out and burnt before his Face, and his Head cut off, and his Body divided into four Quarters, and his Head and Quarters disposed of at the King's Pleasure." Women would be drawn to the place of execution and burned to death.[14] Petit treason was also considered a horrible offense, but not as awful as high treason. Dalton defined the former this way: "Pety treason is when wilfull murder is committed (in the estate Oeconomicall) upon any subject, by one that is in subiection, and oweth faith, duty, and obedience, to the party murdred." Blackstone referred to it as a breach of the "lower allegiance, of private and domestic faith." The punishment for a man was to be drawn to the place of execution and hanged. The drawing added an element of spectacle and humiliation, if not prolonged terror. If the convicted killer was a woman, she would be sentenced to the same form of death as if guilty of high treason.[15]

Conceptually there were problems with applying these legal notions to slaves, especially in the case of high treason. If the slave was an outsider, one who did not owe "allegiance" to the society as a whole or the state, it would be hard to find such a person guilty of a breach of an allegiance due. And to treat him as though he was guilty of high treason in the event of rebellion would be to treat him as if he were a citizen of the state in some fashion or other. Allegiance is an illusive concept. It was rare for slaveowners to deal with the idea in depth, but one of the most expansive discussions before the Civil War occurred in South Carolina in 1834. It stemmed from a test oath imposed by the nullifiers on all officeholders in the state. Nullifiers contended that South Carolinians owed allegiance only to the state of South Carolina and nothing other than obedience to the federal government. The oath was challenged before the state court of appeals, where it was struck down. O'Neall led off the judgment in *M'Cready v. B. F. Hunt* with a discussion of allegiance, which he equated with obedience and held was due by South Carolinians to both the state and federal governments. Specifically, he maintained that although the word *allegiance* came from feudalism it did not retain its feudal meaning, and by the nineteenth century it meant "the duty which the citizen, or subject, owes to the sovereign." Johnson agreed with O'Neall, but Harper did not. He argued that allegiance was "that obedience which, in matters of government, is due in prefer-ence to all other obedience," and that higher duty was to the people of South Carolina, not the federal government.[16] The slave—when seen as property—did not fit into either view of the relationship between persons or between the individ-ual and society. High treason was linked to allegiance, and to apply it to slaves would imply that they were subjects or members of society with rights as well as duties, and not really outsiders. Southern judges never resolved the tensions al-though they tried to apply the law of treason to slaves. There was less difficulty with the notion of petit treason—although it could raise the question of the existence of legally enforceable duties of masters to protect slaves. The classic formulation in English law, and this carried over in the plantation societies, was that of Coke in *Calvin's Case* (protection equaled allegiance).

Of course, other legal categories might apply when slaves revolted or killed their masters. The two most significant were insurrection and murder. But insurrection presented the same problem as high treason. One of the first relevant references to the word *insurrection* in English law is in Coke's *Third Institute* (1644). "An insurrection against the Statute of Labourers," he wrote, "for the inhancing of salaries and wages, was a levying of war against the King." Class struggles and insurrection were linked in English legal thought—insurrection did not stand without a context. Insurrection by workers to raise wages was considered waging war against the king, and because that was high treason, insurrection was a form of high treason. The connection was made explicit in Hawkins's work in the early eighteenth century. He used the word insurrection only in his section on high treason: "those also who make an Insurrection in order to redress a publick Grievance, whether it be a real or pretended one, and of their own Authority attempt with Force to redress it, are said to levy War against the King . . . which manifestly tends to a downright Rebellion."[17]

Colonial Developments

There is no question that slaves resisted bondage despite the pre–Civil War claims of Southern whites that blacks were "natural slaves" and despite the thoughtful, although controversial, claim by Stanley Elkins that Southern slavery was so dehumanizing that it led to infantilization of slaves. One of the first incidents occurred in Virginia in 1644, for which two tantalizing entries appear in the council records. The first reads simply "*Septr* 3. 1644 Concerning the rioutous & rebellious conduct of Mrs *Wormleys* negroes." The second entry is this: "*Sep^t* 10. 1644 psons apprehended for rebellion (phaps Mrs *Wormleys* Servants *Sept* 3d.)."[18] Virginians were lumping different legal concepts (riot and rebellion) in a hodgepodge. But this may be making much too much out of a simple one-line entry in the journal. The first act on slave uprisings, the 1680 law "for preventing Negroes Insurrections," is clearer. This law alluded to the "frequent meeting of considerable numbers of negroe slaves under pretence of feasts and burialls"; it concluded that these were "judged of dangerous consequence." The law did not prohibit such meetings. Rather, it made it unlawful for slaves to carry clubs, staffs, guns, swords, or other weapons, and it stipulated that they should not leave their master's property without a certificate from the master, mistress, or overseer, and then only "upon particular and necessary occasions."[19] Presumably, they could still gather to put shards of vases and other pieces of property on the burial mounds of those they mourned.

Thirty years later two slaves were executed for high treason. Their case led Governor Alexander Spotswood to urge the adoption of a stronger law:

I Would Willingly Whisper to You The Strength of Your Country and The State of Your Militia; Which on The foot it Now Stands is so Imaginary A

Defence, That we Cannot too Cautiously Conceal it from our Neighbours and our Slaves, nor too Earnestly Pray That Neither The Lust of Dominion, nor The Desire of freedom May Stir those people to any Attempts The Latter Sort (I mean our Negro's) by Their Dayly Encrease Seem to be The Most Dangerous; And the Tryals of Last *Aprill* Court may shew that we are not to Depend on Either their Stupidity, or that Babel of Languages among 'em; freedom Wears a Cap which Can Without a Tongue, Call Togather all Those who Long to Shake of the fetters of Slavery and as Such an Insurrection would surely be attended with Most Dreadfull Consequences so I Think we Cannot be too Early in providing Against it, both by putting our Selves in a better posture of Defence and by Making a Law to prevent The Consultations of Those Negros.[20]

It was over a decade later, however, before the burgesses acted on Spotswood's suggestion. The 1723 law made it a nonclergyable offense for five or more slaves to consult, advise, or conspire to rebel or make insurrection, or to plot or conspire to murder someone.[21] The law was adopted when it was because of two insurrection conspiracies. The first was uncovered in late 1722. Lieutenant Governor Hugh Drysdale informed the Board of Trade that one consequence would be "stirring up the next Assembly to make more severe laws for the keeping of their slaves in greater subjection." During the spring of 1723, when the second conspiracy was uncovered, Drysdale urged the burgesses to correct the "Lameness" of the laws insofar as insurrections were concerned.[22]

A quarter of a century later the Virginia burgesses modified the law soon after a number of serious slave uprisings or alleged conspiracies in the English colonial world, such as Antigua in 1736; Stono, South Carolina, and Prince Georges County, Maryland, in 1739; and New York City in 1741. In the 1748 law they noted the need for "effectual provision" in order to detect and punish the "secret plots, and dangerous combinations" of the slaves. Therefore, they reenacted the law of 1723, but without the requirement that five slaves be involved.[23]

In 1751 the Maryland assembly provided that it would be a felony without benefit of clergy to "consult, advise, conspire or attempt to raise any insurrection within this province." This law included "attempts," which had not been mentioned in the Virginia law. According to Francis Sayre, a number of writers "viewed the law of criminal conspiracy as an outgrowth of the larger law of criminal attempts." Joel Prentiss Bishop wrote that criminal conspiracy "is not called in the books 'attempt,' but it is such in nature and effect."[24] Sayre noted that the link was not altogether appropriate. The Maryland law, in any case, treated them separately. The whole concept of criminal attempts will be considered fully in Chapter 14, where the law of rape is taken up.

The statutory experiments at controlling servile insurrections were more extensive in South Carolina than elsewhere. Death or any other punishment thought "fit" was stipulated as of 1690 for any slave who made an insurrection or raised a "rebellion against their master's authority," made "any preparations of arms," or held any "conspiracies for raising mutinies and rebellion." If the comment of the Reverend Johann Martin Bolzius is correct, the punishment South Carolinians might consider "fit" could be sickening. He wrote that "the agitators of rebellion are punished in a very harsh and nearly inhuman way (which is generally not the way of the English), for example, slowly roasted at the fire."[25]

This law was more advanced than those of other colonies in that it recognized a number of different legal categories. It dealt with conspiracies or what might be an attempt (the preparations provision), a murder, resistance to the authority of a master, and insurrection. Although the law distinguished legal categories, it also allowed discretionary punishments.

Twenty-two years later the South Carolina legislators revised the law. They separated murder from insurrection. They dropped the notion of rebellion against the master, so that punishment now followed "if any negroes or other slaves shall make mutiny or insurrection, or rise in rebellion against the authority and government of this Province, or shall make preparation . . . in order to carry on such mutiny or insurrection, or shall hold any counsel or conspiracy for raising such mutiny, insurrection or rebellion." The motivation behind this law was captured in the preamble:

> WHEREAS, the plantations and estates of this Province cannot be well and sufficiently managed and brought into use, without the labor and service of negroes and other slaves; and forasmuch as the said negroes and other slaves brought unto the people of this Province for that purpose, are of barbarous, wild, savage natures, and such as renders them wholly unqualified to be governed by the laws, customs, and practices of this Province; but that it is absolutely necessary, that such other constitutions, laws and orders, should in this Province be made and enacted, for the good regulating and ordering of them, as may restrain the disorders, rapines and inhumanity, to which they are naturally prone and inclined; and may also tend to the safety and security of the people of this Province and their estates; to which purpose . . .

Slaves may have been outside society, but they were persons capable of committing serious criminal acts that flowed out of barbarism and inhumanity, not out of a yearning for freedom (which was Spotswood's view).[26]

One striking feature of the law was a section that applied a concept that had appeared in earlier laws on crimes other than insurrection. The governor and council were given the authority to order "that only one or more of the said criminals should suffer death as exemplary, and the rest returned to their owners." The owners of the slaves allowed to live had to bear the loss of the executed slaves proportionately.[27]

A classic philosophy of punishment was Kant's retributive theory. A person who committed an offense deserved to be punished and must be punished. If a state was collapsing, the last act it should perform would be the execution of those sentenced to death.[28] It is an extreme version of the theory. South Carolinians adopted no such idea of punishment. Nor did they endorse an extreme deterrence theory, according to which the execution of anyone, regardless of guilt, could be justified as an example if it would in fact deter others from committing the offense. They required that a slave selected to die deserved it. Still, as H. L. A. Hart has argued, the purpose of punishment need not be singular. There can be a blend of answers to the question, why do we punish? South Carolinians, in 1722, blended retributive and deterrent theories. One must deserve to be executed and might be in order to provide an example to other slaves. Executions could be "freakishly imposed," and individual slaves, however "just" their execution might have been according to a purely retributive theory, might be saved to labor among the rice fields of their owner.[29]

In 1735 South Carolina's legislature revised the law again, and in doing so it showed how deeply engrained racism was. The crime now was to make, raise, or confederate or conspire to raise an insurrection not against masters, but against the authority and government of the province, "or to rise against the white people." Four years later came the major slave insurrection in the Southern continental colonies at Stono. The year following the offense became to "raise or attempt to raise an insurrection in this Province." The judges were allowed to mitigate the sentence if they thought mercy was due, but this could not apply to any slave who had been convicted of killing a white. There was an all-important proviso: "that one or more of the said slaves who shall be convicted of the crimes or offences aforesaid, where several are concerned, shall be executed for example, to deter others from offending in the like kind."[30] North Carolina mandated death, after 1741, "if any number of negroes or other slaves, *that is to say*, three or more, shall at any time hereafter consult, advise or conspire to rebel, or make insurrection."[31]

Did such legal orders matter in times of feared uprisings? One of the first significant accounts of the way whites responded to an alleged slave uprising concerns the events in 1709–10 in Virginia that provoked Spotswood's remarks to the council. The council noted, on March 21, 1709, that "there hath been lately happily discovered a dangerous Conspiracy formed and carryed on by great numbers of Negros, and other Slaves for makeing their Escape by force from the Service of their Masters and for the destroying and calling off such of her Maj[tys] Subjects as should oppose their design." The council was anxious to bring to "condign and speedy punishment" those involved in "this pernitious design according to the nature and Quality of their respective faults." It ordered the justices to take in writing the examination of the slaves and to sentence to such correction as they thought fit those slaves who "have been ignorantly drawn into the said Conspiracy or have been only so far concerned therein as barely to consent or to conceal the same." Those found to be "Principal Contrivers" were to be held until further order from the council.[32]

In the interests of a speedy prosecution, two justices of Surry County were ordered to bring a number of named slaves before the general court. These were to give evidence in the trial of the slaves who had been arrested. According to the rules of evidence, the slaves should not have been allowed to testify at all because they could take no oath in an English court. The trial of the principals occurred sometime between April 18, 1710, when this order was issued, and April 27, 1710, when the council recorded the sentences it imposed. It noted that two slaves, Salvadore (an Indian) and Scipio (a black), had been found guilty of *high treason.* Their execution therefore would be an "exemplary punishment" so as to have a "due effect for deterring other Slaves from entering into such dangerous Conspiracys." Salvadore was to be executed in Surry County, and his head and quarters were to be publicly displayed—his head in Williamsburg, one quarter in James City, one quarter in New Kent County, and the other two quarters in Surry County. Scipio faced the same fate but in different counties.[33]

What can we make of this gory spectacle? First of all, the indictment and the crime did not correspond to the statute law of Virginia. Virginia did not even make the offense of conspiracy to raise an insurrection a capital offense by statute until 1723, and yet the references throughout (until we arrive at the conviction—which was for high treason) are to the offense of conspiracy. The insurrection was a flight for freedom and a declared willingness to fight. But was the insurrection against the authority of their masters or against the society and government of Virginia? Because the slaves were executed for high treason, it must have been seen as the latter. Slavery was not viewed solely in terms of the property rights of individual owners.

Although there were numerous conspiracies, or scares, during the 1720s and 1730s,[34] there is little firm evidence about the use of the legal process until the 1740s. The major uprising at Stono was suppressed by the militia and did not end in the courts. One of the major conspiracy scares of the colonial period, that of 1741 in New York, is another matter.[35] Though outside the scope of this study, it is worth mentioning as another precedent for the later responses of Southern whites to fears of slave uprisings.[36] If one accepts the concept of conspiracy as a legitimate legal category, there was little exceptionable about the New York trials. At the same time they show how dangerous the notion could be, as blacks, in hopes of saving themselves, accused each other. It was a tragically misplaced aspiration in view of the deep-seated fears of the white community. Only blood or burned flesh would do.

At almost the same time that the slaves of New York City were being "impeached" and "impeaching" one another to save themselves from execution, another slave went on trial in Charleston. This conforms to the findings of scholars that there was an increased level of slave resistance about the mid-eighteenth century throughout the English slave-based settlements.[37] In New York the hysteria ran from about April to July/August 1741. The events in Charleston, in July and August, involved a fire and an alleged plot to burn the city.

In Charleston someone allegedly set fire to a bundle of straw on the roof of a house in Unity-Alley. It was discovered and put out. Catherine was "taken up on strong Suspicion; in the Afternoon she was tried according to Law, and denied the

Fact for which she was apprehended." However, "a strong Evidence appearing against her, she was convicted, brought in guilty and condemn'd." Jenny, an "old Negro Woman," had provided the evidence. She was in the house when it was set on fire, and "no Body had been with her but *Kate* [Catherine] for some time before the People cried-out Fire." Catherine was convicted on this evidence but refused to confess or implicate any accomplice until she saw the preparations being made for her execution and was promised a pardon if she would name the person or persons involved.[38] This was a technique used in New York in 1741 and earlier in Antigua in 1736.[39] She then accused the slave Boatswain. He, in turn, tried to follow the same tactic. "On his Tryal after much Prevarication and accusing many Negroes, who upon a strict Examination were found to be innocent, he confessed that none but he and *Kate* were concerned." Here there is a striking difference from the events in New York, where the hysteria was such that practically no one was found innocent. Charleston's authorities in 1741 behaved with the same restraint as did the South Carolina officials eight years later at the time of another serious conspiracy scare. Boatswain, but not Kate, was "burnt to Death." The *Gazette* concluded that "there was no Plot in the Case, but the Effect of his own sottish wicked Heart, especially since he looked upon every white Man he should meet as his declared Enemy."[40]

White colonials used but were not confined by the English notions of high treason, rebellion, insurrection, and conspiracy. They showed little concern with conceptual fidelity (something that did appear among strict common law pleaders in civil cases): they simply reacted with ruthless violence to punish those who were a danger to them. What is certain is that they were determined to ensure that owners retained the labor of their slaves and that the social order resting on that labor would not be shaken.

Post-Revolutionary Developments

Fears of insurrections rose during the American Revolution. This was especially true in the wake of Lord Dunmore's proclamation of freedom for those slaves who fled to British lines. But from a legal standpoint there was no change until after the upheaval. Virginia reenacted its 1748 law in 1792 (and again in 1819), and this law was the inspiration for later statutes in Kentucky, Tennessee, Mississippi, and Florida.[41] In 1802 North Carolina provided the death penalty for any slave "found in a state of rebellion or insurrection." It also covered those who agreed to join "any conspiracy or insurrection," persuaded others to join one, or aided or assisted such actions, as by furnishing arms. This law was an outgrowth of the Gabriel conspiracy in Virginia and events in Virginia and North Carolina around the years 1800 to 1802.[42]

There were, of course, other statutes adopted in the nineteenth century, but usually they were not linked to a particular insurrection or insurrection scare. Some are worth mentioning. The law of Texas, for instance, was one of the only measures to define the crime, "insurrection of slaves." Any "assemblage of three or more with arms, with intent to obtain their liberty by force" was an insurrection. In Alabama the offense was complete if one were involved in a conspiracy to rebel or in a rebellion "against the white inhabitants of this state, or the laws and government thereof." In Louisiana death was mandated for a slave "who shall encourage or excite any insurrection or revolt in this state." The key terms were not defined, but another section provided that slaves could be punished at discretion if they should "revolt or rebel against any white overseer, appointed by his owner to superintend the conduct of his slaves, when being punished by him, or another, under his orders."[43]

One of the most elaborate laws was that of Missouri (1845). Execution awaited slaves who were guilty of "actually raising a rebellion or insurrection," who did "rebel or make insurrection," who entered into "any agreement to rebel or make insurrection," or who plotted "the death of any person" or the commission of arson "in furtherance of such conspiracy, and shall by any overt act attempt to accomplish such purpose." It also called for the punishment of slaves involved in "consulting, plotting, conspiring or attempting to raise any rebellion or insurrection . . . although no overt act be done."[44]

All the laws, except those of South Carolina and Georgia, mentioned conspiracy. Georgia, in 1816, listed "insurrection, or any attempt to execute it."[45] Most states, on the other hand, did not mention attempts. Only Texas defined the crime of insurrection in terms of intention, and it was to obtain individual freedom, not to subvert society. Most laws simply referred to rebellion or insurrection and left it at that.

Some Nineteenth-Century "Insurrection" Cases

The nineteenth century opened with a major conspiracy trial in Richmond. According to one man who witnessed the prosecution of Gabriel Prosser and his coconspirators, the slaves received fairly openhanded treatment: "the Judges conduct themselves with a degree of humanity highly honorable. The least doubt, the smallest suspicion, or contradiction on the part of the witnesses (who are kept in separate compartments) will often acquit Negroes who are really criminal." Gerald Mullin agreed that "this is a fairly accurate picture of the proceedings." It seems more likely, in Douglas Egerton's view, for those tried after the first wave of executions, when Jefferson and James Monroe made it clear that some blood was needed but not too much. Later, in 1831, the trials of Nat Turner and his followers were held in regular oyer and terminer courts in Southampton County.[46]

The story in South Carolina is a contrast. The most famous conspiracy there was of Denmark Vesey in Charleston in 1822, the leadership of which was centered in the city's black churches. This was a conspiracy, not an actual uprising like Turner's.[47] The court admitted that it departed "in many essential features, from the principles of the common law, and some of the settled rules of evidence." But it attempted to conform with those rules wherever possible. Moreover, it allowed slaves to have counsel, which was not secured in South Carolina slave trials until 1839. The most questionable evidentiary decision was patterned after earlier insurrection trials. It was that "witnesses should be confronted with the accused, and with each other, in every case, except where testimony was given under a solemn pledge that the names of the witnesses should not be divulged, as they declared in some instances, that they apprehended being murdered by the blacks, if it was known that they had volunteered their evidence."[48]

Following the convictions the presiding magistrate, Lionel Kennedy, passed sentence. The charge, he noted, was "attempting to raise an Insurrection." He summarized Vesey's intentions this way: "Your professed design was to trample on all laws, human and divine; to riot in blood, outrage, rapine . . . and conflagration, and to introduce anarchy and confusion in their most horrid forms." Moreover, he said, "in addition to *treason* [emphasis added] you have committed the grossest impiety, in attempting to pervert the sacred words of God into a sanction for crimes of the blackest hue." From Kennedy's point of view the slaves involved had been treated with greater decency and lenity than was true of most. "Every one is more or less subject to controul; and the most exalted, as well as the humblest individual, must bow with deference to the laws of that community, in which he is placed by Providence. Your situation, therefore, was neither extraordinary nor unnatural." He further lectured those he was about to sentence to death for their ingratitude and treason: "Servitude has existed under various forms, from the deluge to the present time, and in no age or country has the condition of slaves been milder or more humane than your own. . . . You are exempt from many of the miseries, to which *the poor* are subject throughout the world. In many countries the life of the slave is at the disposal of his master; here you have always been under the protection of the law."[49] Kennedy neglected to mention that before 1821 the most severe punishment for killing a slave in South Carolina was a fine.

Kennedy at least confronted the defendants as persons in a hierarchical social order, not just as "things." The same cannot be said about a ruling pronounced during the summer of 1829, when a conspiracy scare rocked Georgetown District. A number of slaves were executed, and one was to be transported from the state. It is the latter, Quico, whose case is of legal significance.[50] His owner brought a motion for a writ of prohibition against the magistrates and freeholders who tried him. The opinion in the case, *Kinloch v. Harvey* (1830), was by Judge Bay. Counsel argued that the rules of evidentiary law were not followed and the proceedings of the court were irregular. He also contested the transportation as unwarranted by South Carolina law. If the first point were conceded, Bay argued, it would mean that slaves were entitled "to the rights of citizens, secured by *magna charta*, or the common law of the land." But "they have no rights, other than those which their masters or owners may give them. They are the property of their masters or owners, and are considered in this State, in law, as goods and chattels, and not as persons entitled to the benefits of freemen." In countries where slavery existed, he continued, the leading principle by which they are governed, is a sense of coercive necessity, which, leaving no choice of action, supersedes all questions of absolute right. Every endeavor, therefore, to extend positive rights to this class of people, is an attempt to reconcile inherent contradictions. The great security and happiness of the slave, is the humanity and kindness of his master, and the interest he has in the preservation of his health and bodily labor; which, in return, requires of his master protection, kindness, and every necessary support for his sustenance and comfort.

He concluded, without realizing that he left little foundation for his position when applied to slaves, that "the offence of insurrection is . . . high treason against the State, as well as against the happiness and tranquility of the families in the State." How someone who was solely property, outside the protection of the laws, could be guilty of high treason is puzzling. But Bay was not concerned with fidelity to legal notions. He upheld the sentence of transportation from the state, even though admitting that it was not the ordinary punishment, because it was the only mitigation that would secure the community against stirring up "murder, bloodshed, and plunder." The judge, who was likely either cold-blooded or very nervous about slave insurrections, was little bothered by procedural irregularities either. He argued that when "the dreadful nature and consequences of the insurrection of slaves in South Carolina, are taken into consideration," it would be dangerous for higher court judges to interfere in the "exercise of these summary jurisdictions; and they ought not to be eagle-eyed in viewing their proceedings, and in finding out and supporting every formal error or neglect, where the real merits have been duly and fairly attended to, and determined according to justice."[51]

A set of South Carolina "insurrection" cases gives us a glimpse of how the "summary jurisdictions" mentioned by Judge Bay actually functioned. In 1852, for instance, the slave Mattison went on trial in Anderson District. The charge was an "insurrection with attempt to kill" his owner. Judge Joseph N. Whitner was more measured than Bay had been. He ordered a new trial because the offense could not have been committed. Insurrection, he noted, "is distinguishable from mere resistance to the authority of the master by a single slave." At the new trial the court settled for a conviction for assault with an intent to kill. The sentence was an immediate 125 lashes and 100 more each sale day for the next three months (one day a month), and then Mattison was to be returned to his owner.[52]

Ten years later, during the Civil War, three slaves were tried in Anderson District for "attempting to raise an Insurrection at Cross Roads church on the 30th of March last and other unbecoming language." It appeared that Aleck made a remark about a white person who had told a "damned lie" regarding a couple of alleged deserters. It was enough to bring the charges. In the end Aleck alone of the three slaves was convicted. He received fifty lashes for the offense of "improper language." Or consider the conviction of Jerry, Andy, and Sam in Spartanburg District two years earlier on a charge of attempted insurrection. There was no evidence to convict, but the court believed that the slaves were "guilty to some extent" and concluded that "they may have had some thought and made some preparation of an insurrectionary tendency." They were whipped.[53]

All in all, few trials were recorded in South Carolina and elsewhere; the outcome of some of them is rather surprising. To illustrate, in Maury County, Tennessee, in 1842, Edmund and Lewis were indicted for "conspiring to Rebel or make an insurrection." Despite the charge, both slaves were admitted to bail and released. In Savannah a few months after the Vesey conspiracy, Robin and Shadrack were tried for an attempted insurrection and for an attempted poisoning of their master. They were acquitted on both charges. The judgment in the case of Rayl in Fauquier County, Virginia (1819), for a conspiracy to "Rebel & make insurrection" and for stabbing his owner with an intent to kill was also lenient. Rayl was acquitted of the first charge and found guilty of the second, for which he was sentenced to thirty-nine lashes and to be burned on the hand.[54]

More in line with our assumptions, no doubt, was the case of Dick, who was charged in Southampton County, Virginia (1802), with "Rebelling[,] conspiring and plotting to murder his said master." The testimony was that the owner had gone into the cornfield to charge Dick with a theft. Dick did not answer and the owner hit him with a stick. As he turned to go, Dick grabbed him and a fight ensued. The owner yelled for help, but when a slave approached, Dick told him "to stand off for that he meant to finish him." Another frightened slave ran away, and so on. Dick was hanged.[55]

A final example demonstrates that fidelity to legal rules and notions was not characteristic of the justice slaves faced when whites feared they were in "rebellion or insurrection." In September 1861 William J. Minor had hurried back to Natchez from New Orleans when he received word that "there was trouble among the negroes." After the examination of those "arrested," he concluded that they "had it in view to murder their master & violate their mistresses." It was the classic Southern white view of black insurrectionaries. But this group also had liberty on their minds. Their action was to depend on the "whipping" the Southerners got in the war; the slaves "would be made free," and then they would rise. It was an odd, after-the-fact revolution. What is of moment insofar as *law* is concerned is a diary entry made a couple of days later. Minor mentioned an "Examination Comtee." Ten male slaves, he wrote, "were hung yesterday by order of the committee. From what I learned, I think the testimony was Sufficient to justify the action of the Comtee."[56] The slaves died in expiation of the fears of an ad hoc committee of safety. It is clear enough that slaveowners did not often treat slaves as guilty of high treason, thereby avoiding for the most part any problems about *allegiance* due to society.

The Homicides of "Masters"

The "estate Oeconomicall," where there was no greater offense than the killing of a superior by a subordinate, raised different questions of obligation. Such an act was a breach of a lesser allegiance. In the English plantations, however, the fit was not neat. Colonials had a legal category based on a social relationship involving trust and duty, but they sometimes were candid enough not to try to describe the master-slave relationship that way. William Byrd II lamented that a slaveowner must be "either a fool or a fury" in dealing with slaves, and that slaves must be "rid with a tort rein."[57] More candid yet was the preamble to the only colonial statute that dealt directly with the offense of petit treason. Maryland's legislators of 1729 believed that two conditions made it necessary to modify the common law. One was that slaves "have no sense of shame, or apprehension of future rewards or punishments." The other was that the common law was not severe enough "to deter a people from committing the greatest cruelties who only consider the rigour and severity of punishment." The law met the alleged cruelty of slaves with the cruelty of whites, who provided that the right hand should be cut off, the killer hanged, and the body quartered regardless of gender.[58] Slavery was grounded not in trust and duty, but in force. In the view of colonial lawmakers, slaves were savages who could only be controlled by terror.

The English law of petit treason was not altered in other colonies, but that did not mean it was always followed in practice. One of the earliest executions occurred in 1687 in North Carolina, where a "Negroe boy named Exeter" was hanged for the "Murther" of his master.[59] This could have been a case of petit treason, but the punishment imposed was for murder only. North Carolinians were either indifferent to or ignorant of the English law. In Newbern in 1770 five slaves were tried for the murder of their master. "Two wenches" were "executed, and one burnt at a stake, one made his escape, and is not yet taken, the other, who made the confession, is saved." Only the case of the woman who was burned at the stake conformed to the law of England.[60] North Carolinians did not strictly adhere to the common law when slaves were found guilty of murder. The same was true for South Carolinians. In 1733 the *South Carolina Gazette* recorded that a slave of Thomas Fleming of Charlestown was "hang'd" for killing his overseer with an ax.[61]

Virginia also deviated from common law norms. In 1736 a slave woman who murdered her mistress with a broadax in Nansemond County was "since burnt."[62] This followed the law of England. Another case six years earlier in Richmond County did not. James, a slave of Christopher Petty, was jailed for the murder of Petty's daughter. He died in prison before he could be tried. Nevertheless, the court ordered the following: the sheriff was to "take the body of the Said Negro James and cutt it into four Quarters and hang and [a] Quarter up at Potoskey Ferry, and [a] Quarter at Captain Newtons Mill, and [a] Quarter at Mortico Mill and the other Quarter in William Griffins old Field and Stick his Head on a pole at the Court house."[63] James's "punishment" was not that for petit treason or for any statutory offense by the laws of Virginia. It was all that was left of the possible punishment for high treason once he had died. The justices acted out of repulsion at a heinous offense and with the purpose of terrorizing the county's slave population.

Even though Maryland had modified English law by statute, it did not always adhere to the provisions of the colonial law. In 1761, for instance, a slave who killed his mistress, her child, and a slave woman in St. Mary's County was hanged in chains. This was a horrible punishment that amounted to slow starvation, but it was not the punishment specified by the 1729 law. In June 1745, on the other hand, a slave who had murdered his overseer was executed according to the law. Seven slaves who murdered their master in 1742, however, were simply ordered hanged. In 1770 in Prince Georges County Jack Wood, Davy, and Jack Crane—all slaves— were sentenced to have their right hands cut off and then to hang, but the provincial court remitted the severing of the hands. In Charles County Anthony and Jenny were hanged in chains for poisoning the "late Master." Most of these sentences did not follow English law, and about half of them did not even abide by the law of Maryland.[64]

The legacy, by the end of the eighteenth century, was of a ghastly use of law to assure the tractability of the slaves and a relative indifference to traditional common law concepts. There was no systematic discussion of the social theory that was the basis for treating killers of "superiors" as guilty of a breach of duty. It was taken for granted. Not until it no longer was assumed did people articulate the theory as far as slaves were concerned. At the same time, slaves who killed masters in the colonial world were treated more savagely than if they had been convicted of simple murder. The notion, and sometimes the term *petit treason*, remained, but practice was too confused for the law to be sustained very long.

In 1777 the committee of revisers of the law of Virginia agreed that "Treason and Murder (and no other Crime) to be punished with Death, by Hanging and Forfeiture." In the case of "Petty-treason, parricide, Saticide," the revisers added, the "Body to be delivered over to Surgeons to be anatomized."[65] Conceptually, petit treason remained and was given substance with the proposal for dissection, which echoed the notion that the body was at the king's disposal. Elsewhere the offense was being eliminated or undermined. In 1787 Delaware stipulated that anyone convicted of petit treason would no longer suffer an exemplary death but would be sentenced as in any other capital case. Previous punishments were considered "too severe and contrary to the mild spirit of the constitution and laws of this state."[66]

Petit treason began to disappear during the 1780s. In many states it slipped from view, whereas in others it was expressly rejected. Maryland abolished the crime in 1810. Arkansas, in 1848, was one of the last to act, but by then it was a case of cleaning up the statute books. Petit treason collapsed as a concept with the growing humanitarian sensibilities of the late eighteenth century, when the Beccarian idea of certainty rather than brutality in punishment spread.[67] This does not mean that grisly punishments and horrifying theatricals ended. In King George County, Virginia, in 1795, for instance, Nelson, who was found guilty of the murder of his master, was hanged, and his body was "hung in Gibbets at the s^d lower Fork of the road."[68] One other case makes the point clearly. In Edgefield District, South Carolina, in early 1820 Ephraim and Sam murdered their master. "Sam was burnt and

Ephraim hung, and his head severed from his body and publicly exposed." The writer who described the executions was most concerned with the death of Sam. As he wrote:

> The burning of malefactors is a punishment only resorted to, when absolute necessity demands a signal example. It must be a horrid and appalling sight to see a human being consigned to the flames—Let even fancy picture the scene —the pile—the stake—the victim—and the mind sickens, and sinks under the oppression of its own feelings—what then must be the dread reality!—From some of the spectators we learn, that it was a scene which transfixed in breathless horror almost every one who witnessed it—As the flames approached him, the piercing shrieks of the unfortunate victim struck upon the heart with a fearful, painful vibration—but when the devouring element spread upon his body, all was hushed—yet the cry of agony still thrilled in the ear, and the involuntary and sympathetic shudder ran through the crowd. We hope that this awful dispensation of justice may be attended with salutary effects as to forever preclude the necessity of its repetition.[69]

Feelings stirred the writer of this ghoulish description, but there was no condemnation of the sentence. People could still accept awful punishments of slaves who murdered those with authority over them. Southerners, however, missed an opportunity to retain a legal notion and adapt it to the master-slave relationship in order to create a truly autonomous law of slavery.[70] Grim punishments, of course, continued in the nineteenth century, but they were discretionary, which meant that there was no clear legal norm.

The law of petit treason was gone, but the social foundation of the old common law offense remained an important part of Southern legal discourse during the nineteenth century. It was thought proper in legal analysis to take into account the idea that one in "subiection" did "oweth faith, duty, and obedience." Subjection or subordination, of course, is one thing, but a duty owed goes beyond that: it is a moral category.[71] It was the servant, not the slave, who stood at the center of the discussion in English law.[72] Would it make any sense to retain the idea of obedience due and apply the idea in cases involving masters and slaves after the emergence of the idea of free labor among other workers? Ruffin, in State v. Mann, considered the question and found little reason to do so. It came down to this: "What moral considerations shall be addressed to such a being to convince him what it is impossible but that the most stupid must feel and know can never be true—that he is thus to labor upon a principle of natural duty, or for the sake of his own personal happiness, such services can only be expected from one who has no will of his own; who surrenders his will in implicit obedience to that of another. Such obedience is the consequence only of uncontrolled authority over the body."[73] This was obedience extracted by force, but did it create a duty "owed"?

At about the same time Mann was decided, the North Carolina court (in State v. Tom, (a slave), 1830) construed a law of 1802 under which the slave Tom was indicted for involvement in a conspiracy to rebel and a conspiracy to murder his master. The question was whether the second count was good. The court held that it was: "The crime of conspiracy among slaves against the lives of those to whom they owe immediate domestic allegiance is . . . more to be apprehended than that of general insurrection."[74] Slaves now owed not just obedience, but allegiance to their masters. The author of the opinion was Ruffin. He did not attempt to provide a foundation for the claim of such a *duty*. If this opinion was to be reconciled with *Mann*, it must have been that the duty arose from force and not "moral considerations." But obedience or allegiance that was claimed over one without a will and solely because of "uncontrolled authority over the body" must be an ethical curiosity.

An alternative was to ignore the logic of *Mann* and find another foundation, such as the reciprocal duties of protection and allegiance grounded in traditional legal thought or perhaps a duty of obedience in the word of God. Religious arguments for slavery occasionally found their way into judicial opinions, especially in those written by Lumpkin of the Georgia Supreme Court.[75] Sometimes other judges used a contractarian analysis such as had been the basis of the traditional master-servant law in England. There was a direct legal precedent for this approach in the argument in *Chamberlaine v. Harvey*, an English king's bench case of 1697, although Southern judges did not rely on it even when they were familiar with English case law. The argument was that slavery could exist by virtue of a quasi-contract whereby the master provided food and clothing in exchange for "power." Reduced to this level (and overlooking such elements of slavery as the heritability of lifetime bondage), slavery was little more than a variation of the unfree labor of a contract of indenture. Southerners moved toward such a notion late in the history of slavery when they adopted voluntary enslavement laws in the 1850s. Some employed something like it when they discussed the obligations of owners to "protect" their slaves as well. For instance, the notion of an implied contract surfaced in the opinion by Starnes, Lumpkin's colleague, in *Jim, (a slave), v. State* (1854). This was an idea that is similar to Genovese's suggestion that the master-slave relationship rested on "reciprocal duties."[76] It was the duty of masters to protect their slaves. Slaves, in turn, owed a faithful discharge of their duties and the grant of their labor. These duties could carry legal consequences.

The notion of a duty owed defined a social relationship, and that brought into play the problem of "provocation." One of the earliest cases that dealt with this was *State v. Will, (a slave)* (North Carolina, 1834). In Will's case, a dispute between two slaves over a hoe led ultimately to the death of their overseer. Will claimed the hoe. He took it and went to pack cotton with a screw. The other slave, the foreman, informed the overseer, Richard Baxter, of the dispute, and Baxter took his gun and went after Will. When he got to the screw he ordered the slave down, and the "prisoner took off his hat in an humble manner and came down." The two exchanged words, and Will then "made off" and the overseer shot him in the back. Will tried to flee but was caught by Baxter and some other slaves. Will had a knife and in the struggle cut Baxter on the arm. That wound proved fatal. Will was found guilty of murder and sentenced to die.[77]

The one case that seemed to be in point was *Mann*, which had ruled that a hirer of a slave could not be held criminally liable for an assault and battery on that slave. Would it make sense to excuse a slave who killed such a person, or to allow the violence to stand as a "legal provocation"? Gaston believed that it did make sense. "Unconditional submission is the *general* duty of the slave," he wrote, "unlimited power is, in general, the *legal* right of the master." But there were exceptions. A master could not slay, and Gaston concluded that the slave had the right to defend himself "against the unlawful attempt of his master to deprive him of life." He added that although there might be other exceptions, the matter was "so full of difficulties, where reason and humanity plead with almost irresistible force on one side, and a necessary policy, rigorous indeed, but inseparable from slavery, urges on the other, I fear to err should I undertake to define them."[78]

The question before the court in Will's case required refinement. Did the facts show the malice necessary to establish a case of murder? For all I know, this was the first time anyone ever discussed the question of malice in a trial of a slave for killing one with authority over him. Counsel for Will understood that he was in a touchy area. He admitted that the court "must pass through Scylla and Charybdis," but, nevertheless, "they may be assured that the peril of shipwreck is not avoided by shunning with distant steerage the whirlpool of Northern fanaticism. That of the South is equally fatal. It may not be so visibly seen, but it is as deep, as wide and as dangerous."[79]

Counsel on the other side saw shoals with different contours. If a slave could "wreak his vengeance without incurring the punishment of death" in a case such as Will's, what would follow? The terrible answer was clear. "It will increase the importance of the slave, and beget a spirit of insubordination, the most dangerous to the peace and safety of the community." "Begin the humane work of advancing them in the scale of moral beings," he continued, "and it may be discovered, when too late, that such policy must result in the destruction of the rest of society, or of the slave population. They would become discontented; one privilege or indulgence would beget desires for another, until nothing short of absolute emancipation would satisfy. It must then be had, or an alternative the most shocking to humanity would then be resorted to."[80]

Judge Gaston tried to steer a measured course. He did not hold that Will had committed a justifiable homicide, as his conduct put him in the wrong. "In attempting to evade punishment," he was guilty of a "breach of duty." Nonetheless, it was a "breach" that amounted to neither "*resistance* nor *rebellion*, and it certainly afforded no justification nor excuse for the barbarous act which followed." If Will had died, Baxter, according to Gaston, might have been indicted for murder. But did that possibility reduce Will's offense to manslaughter? This was a fresh question: "if the passions of the slave be excited into unlawful violence by the inhumanity of his master or temporary owner, or one clothed with the master's authority," Gaston wrote, "is it a *conclusion of law* that such passions must spring from diabolical malice?" "Unless I see my way clear as a sunbeam," he answered, "I cannot believe that this is the law of a civilized people and of a Christian land." Because there was no statute that covered the case before the court, it had to be analyzed according to the common law, "which declares passion, not transcending all reasonable limits, to be distinct from malice." "The prisoner is a human being," Gaston continued, "degraded indeed by slavery, but yet having 'organs, dimensions, senses, affections, passions' like our own." Neither express nor implied malice could be found in Will's case; he was thus guilty of manslaughter but not of murder.[81]

No other appellate case had this result, although one judge in essence agreed. Turley for the majority of the Tennessee court in *Jacob, (a slave), v. State* (1842) held that

> the right of obedience and submission, in all lawful things on the part of the slave, is perfect in the master; and the power to inflict any punishment, not affecting life or limb, which he may consider necessary for the purpose of keeping him in such submission, and enforcing such obedience to his commands, is secured to him by law, and if, in the exercise of it, with or without cause, the slave resist and slay him, it is murder, and not manslaughter; because the law can not recognize the violence of the master as a legitimate cause of provocation.

This was not altogether forthright as Turley referred to punishment "not affecting life or limb," "all lawful things," and "with or without cause." It is not clear what these phrases would cover. Judge Green, in any event, added in his concurrence that it was possible that "the killing of a master by his slave would be manslaughter. What circumstances of torture, short of endangering life or limb, would so reduce a homicide, it is not easy to indicate. . . . The rights and duties of the parties must form the *criteria* by which an enlightened court and jury should act." Green's analysis, however, differed from Gaston's on the question, how much must the slave endure within his station? Gaston had held that the attempt to take the life of the slave was an "attempt to commit a grievous crime" that might be resisted. He had said nothing about "torture" short of threats to life or limb.[82]

Georgia's judges reached a conclusion close to Turley's in *Jim, (a slave), v. State* (1854). Jim, a "stout man," knocked his overseer down with an ax and kept hitting him even though the "youth weighing about 100 lbs" fled from him. The reason was that the overseer, who died, had raised a maul and attempted to hit Jim. On the appeal of Jim's conviction, Judge Starnes emphasized the master-slave relationship. "Implicit obedience" was due from the slave to the master and his agent, the overseer. To maintain the system at all, masters and overseers must possess the right "to give moderate correction." But they possessed no other right. The constitution and laws of Georgia required punishment if a master or overseer willfully killed or maimed a slave. "Up to the point of endangering the life of the slave," he continued, it must necessarily leave to the master, and not to the slave, the right of judging, as to the nature and degree of that chastisement, subject to his responsibilities to the Penal Law. If the master exceed the bounds of reason and moderation . . . the slave must submit . . . and trust to the law for his vindication. He cannot . . . undertake to redress his wrong, unless the attack upon him be with an instrument, or in the use of means calculated to produce death. In such event, he being in the peace of God and of the State, and not able, otherwise, to avoid or escape the assault, if he kill his assailant, he is justified; and in such event only. The law so making that allowance for his fear of death, which it refuses to make to his passion.

The law of Georgia refused any "indulgence to the passion of the slave." To do so would be to make the slave the judge of the reasonableness of "that patriarchal discipline which the master is permitted to exercise," and this would "place him continually in a state of insubordination, and . . . encourage servile insurrection and bloodshed." "Our law," Starnes argued from a conservative utilitarian viewpoint, "thus wisely lessens the privileges of the comparatively few, for the greatest good of the whole."[83] The legal result was that the killing of a master or overseer by a slave in Georgia, unlike North Carolina, might be justifiable homicide or murder. It could never be manslaughter.

The significance of ameliorative statutes was one possible reason for the different analyses. North Carolina had no criminal laws against cruel or inhumane punishments by masters, whereas Georgia did. Starnes could point to the *law* in his state as a security for slaves, but unless a North Carolina judge could find some doctrine, such as "legal provocation," there was nothing there. Starnes could say that slaves could not react to unlawful violence precisely because the state could protect them, whereas Gaston could not. It is ironic, however, that there was greater recognition of the autonomy of the slave as a human being in the absence of legislation protecting the slave than where such laws existed. The more absolute the power of the master in theory, the more recognition of the slave's humanity.

Mississippi's judges tried something different in 1859. The problem of the limits of obedience surfaced in *Wesley, (a slave), v. State*, a case where the principle legal issue involved an evidentiary rule. Wesley had been tied with a strap and put in the smokehouse of his owner by the overseer, William G. Ford. Ford later went to the smokehouse with his wife to get some meat. After opening the door, he was hit on the head with an instrument large enough to "knock a bull down with." Ford died the next day, and Wesley was condemned for murder. He was described as "an obedient and submissive slave," whereas Ford "was proven to be cruel and violent in his treatment of slaves." The evidence as to Ford's character was excluded, and this was assigned as error.[84]

Chief Justice Smith for the court began with the fact that the only direct testimony, from Ford's wife, showed that Wesley "was in no present danger . . . and that there was not reasonable ground to apprehend that the deceased meditated taking the life of the accused, or designed to do him some great bodily harm, and there was imminent danger." Smith did not say that a different case would exist if the facts had shown such danger, but he implied it.

The admission of the evidence as to Ford's character, he noted, should be governed by the general rule, which was to exclude it unless it was part of the *res gestae*.[85] The proper question was "whether the general management of slaves, on a plantation, by the deceased, as characterized by violence and cruelty, and whether specific acts of severity and cruelty committed by him, while acting in the capacity of an overseer, may be proved as circumstances going to justify a homicide, by a slave, committed upon him while acting as such overseer." To allow such evidence the court would have to hold the following proposition, which Smith believed "utterly untenable":

> a slave charged with the murder of his master or overseer, may excuse or justify the deed upon the ground that, being about to be chastised by his master or overseer, or being apprehensive that he would be punished for some real or imputed delinquency; from the known violent and cruel charac- ter of the deceased in the management of slaves, and from the fact he had been guilty of particular acts of great cruelty upon other slaves under his charge, he had good reason to apprehend, and in fact did believe, that some great bodily harm would be inflicted upon, or that his life would be taken.

If the court held this, Smith reasoned, slaves "will be incited to insubordination and murder, and the life of the master exposed to destruction, either through the fears or by the malice of his slaves." Justifiable homicide could exist if the danger was "actual, present, and urgent" or if there were "reasonable grounds" to fear that great bodily harm was imminent, and the jury would determine the reasonable- ness of the slave's conduct.[86]

There could be no legal provocation in Mississippi, anymore than in Georgia, to reduce a killing to manslaughter. Both states had ameliorative laws, but in this class of cases the notion of "subjection" or of obedience owed eliminated a defense of provocation. In these states the starkness of power was masked by the law that allegedly protected slaves from the cruelty of their owners, whereas in a state like North Carolina cruelty was restrained by the notion that the common law took into account the frailties of humanity, even when in bondage.

Such legal questions were of little significance for the majority of slaves, for they were issues dealt with at the appellate level only in the twilight of American slavery. For most, their cases did not pass beyond the county and a prompt execution. In fact, only one of the trials from the sample counties ended in an acquittal. That was the case of Elliott or Ellick tried in Caroline County, Virginia, in 1818 for the murder of his master with a "sythe blade."[87] If his case is removed, the conviction rate in such actions was 100 percent, that is, at least one person was convicted although a codefendant might be acquitted. No other crime, not even insurrection, came close to this conviction record.[88] Insurrection cases often rested on fear, not fact. A dead master was a fact.

What the record shows, in over sixty cases from the selected counties, is a richness of texture in the relationships between slaves and masters that ended in homicide. No simple characterization can capture the scope of that violence. It ranges all the way from the poisoning of a master by a single slave, to assault in self-defense in cases such as Will's in North Carolina, to the death of John Hamlin in Lunenburg County in Virginia's Southside. In the last case, Commonwealth v. Davy et al. (1827), sixteen of Hamlin's slaves were tried for his murder. It contains among the largest number of indictments for this offense. Hamlin was buried alive, and then his corpse was burned. He was a particularly brutal master who, when informed that there was a conspiracy against his life, had said that he "would give them one thousand lashes for he was afraid of none of them, and if they chose to do it, let them do it." They did. Nine of the sixteen were sentenced to hang, two were acquitted, and the others were never formally tried. Mercy was recommended for two of the persons sentenced to death because of their youthful ages (fifteen and seventeen).[89]

Perhaps two killings in Adams County, Mississippi, in 1857 can stand as surrogate for the others. This will allow some development of texture without the undue details of trial upon trial. In the first case, a coroner's jury originally ruled that Duncan Skinner, overseer of the Sharp plantation, had died accidentally as the result of a fall from a horse. His body had been found in the woods, and his neck was broken. But Skinner's brother was unsatisfied and got a number of his neighbors together to "help him in an investigation." On the morning the inquiry began, all the slaves on the Sharp plantation were called together and placed "upon a line before the company assembled." The cook was taken aside and told that "something badly had happened upon the place,—that it could not happen without her knowing it,—and that she had better tell all about it." She opened up, and the probe began in earnest. Three slaves were implicated: Reuben, Henderson, and Anderson. At the time Anderson was a runaway and was being hidden by slaves at a nearby plantation. In the course of the interrogation of the slaves it was revealed where he was, and he was captured. The slaves were "put under the lash," and confessions followed. Reuben, for example, said that Skinner was killed because he "*harryragged him so.*"[90]

The full story, however, related by Alexander Farrar, a large neighboring slave-owner,[91] was far more intricate than the simple reaction of slaves to rough treatment. According to Farrar, the real instigator of the crime was a white man named McAllin. His account, corroborated by some of the slaves, was that McAllin wanted to marry the widow Sharp but Skinner opposed the match. McAllin allegedly had had a long-standing affair with Darcas, a slave on the plantation. He supposedly told her and the others that if Skinner were gotten rid of, he could marry the widow and the lot of the slaves would be much improved. Moreover, he informed Darcas that he could do much more for her as the husband of her owner than in his present comparatively low position.

One evening, Farrar continued, McAllin was standing at a window looking out at the slave quarters and listening to a disturbance there. When he asked some of the slaves what was going on, they told him that Skinner was whipping slaves and that it was a common occurrence. McAllin responded that the slaves lacked any courage at all if they put up with such treatment. It was after that that the three slaves who would stand trial went into Skinner's room and bludgeoned him. Then they took him to the woods, and while he showed some signs of life they broke his neck and staged the theatrical to make it appear that he had died in a fall from his horse.

Shortly after Skinner's death three slaves of William Fowles—John, Tom, and Reuben—allegedly killed Fowles's overseer. A few days after the investigation at the Sharp plantation "a number of us," according to the Farrar account, met at Fowles's. The slaves who were in jail for the overseer's killing were brought back to the plantation "in order to give them an opportunity of providing corroborating testimony. They produced the watch, hat, shoes &c . . . & made a clear confession of every thing. From their statements we were satisfied that they knew the Sharp negroes had murderd their overseer, and as the 'white folks' didnt find it out, they were induced to make a similar experiment." The Adams County vigilantes had done their work well. Even though they had resorted to the lash to obtain confessions, they had uncovered what they doubtless feared all along: there was a serious danger of murder from the seething anger of slaves subjected to whipping, and there was a wide network among the slaves in Adams County.

The trials began in November 1857. Each set of three slaves was tried together, and two counsel were appointed to represent each set. On November 8, 1857, the special venire for the trial of Reuben, Henderson, and Anderson was exhausted so that it became necessary to draw the rest of the jury from the regular list. On the same day they were found guilty. On the twelfth of the month they were valued and sentenced to hang on December 11.

The second trial did not proceed in quite the same fashion. On November 10, 1857, John, Tom, and Reuben were tried and found guilty and valued on the twelfth along with the Sharp slaves. But one day later a new trial was ordered for Reuben; John and Tom were sentenced to hang one week after the Sharp slaves. The motion for a new trial was based on the admission of "illegal evidence affecting the position of Reuben in this case" and the fact that the jury had "disregarded the instructions of the court in his behalf." The new trial for Reuben began in May 1858. When the special and regular venires were exhausted, the court had to turn to bystanders to fill out the jury. The defendant was found not guilty on May 9, 1858. That was by no means the end of the case, however. On May 11 a true bill was brought against Reuben for being an "accessary [sic] to murder after the fact." On the thirteenth the case against Reuben was continued by consent. It did not come up again for a year. On May 6, 1859, a motion to quash the indictment was sustained, and Reuben was remanded to jail to await any further action by the grand jury. At this point the district attorney entered a nolle prosequi against the consent of the defendant. The case was over.[92]

This complex set of cases from Adams County with all of the legal maneuvering would, of course, have been unlikely much earlier. During the colonial period the suspected slave or slaves seldom faced anything more than a quick hearing and a grisly execution. Some things had changed, at least in form.

Outlawry

It may seem curious to end this chapter with a brief discussion of the slave as insider who was capable of being placed outside the law, but he was—through the process of outlawry. When he wrote about insurrections, Cobb noted that "mere insubordination does not (amount to insurrection), else every fugitive slave would be in a state of insurrection"; "and yet," he observed, "to a certain extent, every runaway is rebelling against the authority of the master."[93] One way to deal with such resistance was through outlawry, which meant treating breaches of obedience as so subversive as to place a person completely outside the law. It was the ultimate alienation.

All the laws providing for formal proclamations of outlawry date from the colonial period. In 1705 the Virginia burgesses adopted the first formal law on outlawry. It was aimed at runaways who were out killing hogs and committing other injuries. Two justices were authorized to issue a proclamation against such runaways requiring them to surrender and to direct the sheriff to raise a force to go after them. The proclamation was to be published on a Sunday at the door of all the churches in the county. If a runaway slave did not then surrender, he was outlawed and could be killed by anyone. If the slave was captured alive, the same law authorized the owner to apply to the county court for an order to dismember the slave as a punishment "or any other way, not touching his life, as they in their discretion shall think fit, for the reclaiming any such incorrigible slave, and terrifying others from the like practices."[94] There are two instances in the sample where an owner applied for such authority, and in both it was the same man, Robert "King" Carter. Carter obtained an order in March 1707/8 to cut off the toes of Bambarra Harry and Dinah and a similar order in September 1722 for another slave.[95]

There is ample evidence that slaves were outlawed, as well as maimed, under these Virginia laws, and that some were killed. For instance, in Lancaster County Mingo, a slave of Robert Carter, was killed after being outlawed in 1730. In Fauquier County James "being outlawed was killed" in 1766.[96] A good grasp of the use of outlawry can be obtained from the diary of Landon Carter. During the 1760s and 1770s he acted against four of his slaves—Simon, Bart, Guy, and Robin. On April 24, 1766, he recorded that "Simon, one of the Outlaws, came home. He run away the 12th of March and by being out and doing mischief was outlawed in all the Churches 2 several Sundays." The next day Bart returned. According to Carter, he was the "most incorrigeable villain I believe alive, and has deserved hanging; which I will get done if his mate in roguery can be tempted to turn evidence against him." Simon did not. Over the next few days the evidence mounted that Simon and Bart had been harbored by other slaves in various places in the quarters, even in Carter's kitchen vault. By 1770 Carter wasted no time with references to villainy. On March 17, 1770, he recorded: "Guy actually run away. Outlawries are sent out against him for tomorrow's publication." On the twenty-second he noted that "Guy came home yesterday and had his correction for run away in sight of the people."[97] Carter, in other words, employed outlawry in the case of a simple runaway. One reason to use it in such cases was to call to the slaveowner's aid an organized force to help with the recapture. Another was to protect the community against the depredations of notorious runaways. Still another was economic, as a formal proclamation of outlawry provided the foundation for a claim of compensation from the public treasury.[98]

By 1792 Virginia dropped the whole process of proclamations of outlawry and adopted a law that a number of the newer Southern states followed after the turn of the century. This law provided that two justices of the peace were to direct the sheriff (who in turn could gather a sufficient force) to recapture runaway slaves and bring them in for "further trial." All of the process remained, in sum, except outlawry itself. This was true even when it remained on the lawbooks, as in North Carolina. A case in 1829 in Northampton County shows that it was a dead letter. Three slaves were indicted for murder. Two of them were bailed, and one of them was outlying. An outlying slave thought to have been guilty of murder was surely a candidate for a proclamation of outlawry. Instead, the court ruled that if he was caught, he too would be bailed.[99] This form of using law to assure that slaves in "insurrection" were treated as true outsiders was confined to the colonial world.

"Every planter knew," wrote Jordan, "that the fundamental purpose of the slave laws was prevention and deterrence of slave insurrection."[100] But insurrection was not a rock-solid concept, so that Jordan's point needs refinement even while it has considerable force. Some Southerners counted revolt against a master's authority or running away as insurrection, along with using violent means to obtain one's freedom, wreaking vengeance on the one person to whom a "domestic allegiance" was due or subverting the social order.

Scholars have tried to find some categorical coherence, or precision of definition, in the wealth of small details and large that made up slave resistance. John Blassingame defined "revolt" as "any concerted action by a group of slaves with the settled purpose of and the actual destruction of the lives and property of local whites." Early slave revolts, in Genovese's view, occurred in precapitalist societies that saw society as "a hierarchically ordered community or household." They were reactions against exploitation or efforts to secure individual freedom, not efforts to destroy the social order. By the 1790s and the uprising in Saint-Domingue, capitalism had emerged and rebellion had become revolutionary.[101] Like scholars, slaveowners also tried to control and to order slave resistance, but for them it was a matter of life and death. Law was one instrument at hand to reduce the danger. But they put on old clothes that appear ill-fitting when applied to a slave society that rested on violence and race. They used common law notions like high treason and petit treason, and even after they discarded the latter they kept the fundamental idea that underlay both forms of treason—protection equaled allegiance, or at the very least an obedience that was due to society as a whole or to identifiable individuals in society.

There was some truth in the formula that protection equaled allegiance because masters were seen, at least in the more thoughtful proslavery writings of the nineteenth century, as providing protection in exchange for a faithful exercise of labor—never mind that the protection was in the form of food, clothing, and shelter, which represented a part of the labor of the slaves themselves or was a protection against the cupidity and violence of other free persons or even protection against the law. There was also some truth in the formula in that slaves were given some protection, even against excessive force by masters, by the state through legal intervention in the master-slave relationship or through security against the violence of third parties. To that degree the notion of the slave as an outsider overstates the degradation of Southern blacks precisely because they possessed obligations. It was a conservative social order in which everyone had a station and duties—at least that was the more sophisticated proslavery view. In some slave societies the slave as outsider has to be qualified by the fact that slavery was an institution that eventually led to full enfranchisement of a slave's children, if not the slave himself or herself. This was not the case in the South, where the slave as outsider was defined differently. There the nature of the degraded social position resulted from race and from the intellectual and legal traditions used to order and control the violent reactions of slaves to their bondage: they were traditions that placed the master-slave relationship within boundaries that included the idea that each party possessed obligations and rights. To the extent slaves possessed obligations with legal consequences, the absoluteness of the property claims of their masters was reduced. Moreover, an obedience due, however ill-fitting the garments, placed limits around the slave as alienated outsider in the intellectual world of the free, and that was what counted for an understanding of the workings of the law.

Slaves were neither wholly outsiders nor the absolute property of their masters, but they did occupy the lowest possible social position, one subject to the authority of other people in ways no others were. That was reflected in the way the legal concept of provocation was used. The history of authority of a free society did not correspond to the history of authority in a slave society. The law that affirmed authority had to be adapted in some particulars to the special social relationships of a slave society based on race.

13

Slaves' Violence against Third Parties

Legal rules were to be adapted to the "actual conditions of
human beings in our society."
State v. Jarrott, (a slave) (North Carolina, 1840)

Slaves had a duty of obedience not only to their owners, but also to all whites (at
least under some circumstances). The right of whites, including nonslaveowners,
to use force against slaves and the limits on that right have been considered. The
reverse side of that relationship became a legal issue when slaves resisted. Slave
resistance to third parties ranged from "insolence" to assaults, to homicides. Each
crime presented different legal problems. What was illegal "insolence," or was
there such an offense? Assaults increasingly became a tough legal problem as states
adopted laws on "assaults with intent to kill": the problem then became one of
"intention." Finally, in homicides the question that arose was whether or not it was
possible for a slave to be guilty of the crime of manslaughter when the victim was
white—and that turned on the issue of "provocation," which brought to the fore
the social relationship of slaves to all whites.

The problem, to a large degree, was one of drawing lines, and that lent itself to
legislation. Generally, policy choices on punishments overshadowed discussions of
legal concepts like "provocation" when the resistance of the slaves was violent
because the choice was to make all violent assaults on whites by slaves capital
offenses.

One of the earliest statutory decisions was in the 1740 South Carolina law: it was
a capital offense in the case of any slave "who shall be guilty of homicide of any
sort, upon any white person." Exceptions were allowed for accidents or homicides
in defense of one's owner. In Mississippi, the "manslaughter of any free person" by
a slave became a capital offense. In 1852 Alabama made the voluntary manslaughter of a white person by a slave a capital offense. It also made it capital for a slave to
commit involuntary manslaughter on a white in the commission of "any unlawful
act." In 1859 Texas law provided that an assault and battery by a white on a slave
that did not inflict great injury would not be a "sufficient provocation" to mitigate
the offense from murder to manslaughter.[1]

Provocation in Cases Involving the Deaths of Whites

Some judges considered the problem in the absence of statutes, but not until the 1840s and 1850s. For instance, Georgia's Judge Lumpkin asserted in *John, (a slave), v. State* (1854) that manslaughter "cannot exist under our law, as between a slave and a free white person, where the former is the slayer." Any such killing "is murder, or justifiable homicide." Lumpkin, speaking for himself, obscured the point: "it is supposed, that where a slave is under an absolute and inexorable necessity, to take the life of a white man to save his own, who has no right to punish him or control him in any manner whatever, that such killing will be excusable. And it may be so. For myself, I have formed no very definite opinion upon this subject." The law in Georgia would never take into account the passions of a slave so as to reduce the killing of a white from murder to manslaughter. This followed from a "stern necessity."[2]

A major exception to this line of statutes and adjudications were two North Carolina cases decided in the 1840s. It made sense to raise the issue in North Carolina because it was a state that retained the benefit of clergy (down to 1854), and one of the leading clergyable offenses was manslaughter, which rested on provocation. In the first case, *State v. Jarrott, (a slave)* (1840), Jarrott and Thomas Chatham had argued at a late night card game; the slave had been very "insolent" to the white. A fight broke out, and Jarrott hit Chatham with a long, curled hickory stick and killed him.[3] Jarrott was tried and convicted of murder.

Judge William Gaston, for the court, ordered a new trial. Courts, he contended, should keep in view the distinction between a malicious homicide and one committed "in a transport of passion" excited by a "grievous provocation," even though the slayer was a slave and the victim a free white. Once this crucial concession was made, the problem was to determine what might be a legal provocation. "Sufficient provocation" would differ between whites and slaves. The difference "in the application of the same principle arises from the *vast* difference which exists, under our institutions, between the social condition of the white man and of the slave." Common law principles applied, but they had to be adapted to the "actual conditions of human beings in our society." It did not matter that the white had debased himself by a "familiar association with a slave," because the "distinction of castes yet remains, and with it remain all the passions, infirmities, and habits which grow out of this distinction." Without a doubt most Southern lawmakers and judges would have agreed. There was a notable exception. In 1859 Texas provided that if on the trial of a slave for killing or injuring a white it was proved that the white, unless under eighteen, was in the habit of associating with slaves or free blacks, "and by his general conduct placed himself upon an equality with these classes of persons," then the rules used when a slave killed or injured a slave or free black would be used.[4]

In any event, a new trial was ordered for Jarrott because of misleading instructions on the right of a third party to correct an insolent slave. Insolence, Gaston reasoned, did not justify an *excessive* battery. But this brought back the whole question of provocation. "That is a legal provocation of which it can be pronounced," he wrote, "having due regard to the relative condition of the white man and the slave, and the obligation of the latter to conform his instinct and his passions to his condition of inferiority, that it would provoke well disposed slaves into a violent passion. And the application of the principles must be left, until a more precise rule can be formed, to the intelligence and conscience of the triers."[5] Force could be met by force, but whether it would reduce homicide to manslaughter if the killer was a slave and the victim a white would be left to the judgment of local jurors in North Carolina.

Nine years later the issue of provocation came up again, in *State v. Caesar, (a slave)* (1840). Caesar and another slave, Dick, were in a field when two drunk whites appeared. The whites claimed to be patrollers and cuffed the slaves slightly. When Dick refused to get a whip, he was hit more severely over the head. At that point Caesar grabbed a fence rail and struck back. One of the whites later died from the blows, and Caesar was convicted of murder.[6]

Judge Pearson, in ordering a new trial, noted that the legislature had not dealt with the question of whether the same rules regarding manslaughter applied when slaves killed whites as in other cases. The law was left to be declared by the courts "as it may be deduced from the primary principles of the doctrine of homicide." The same rules did not apply. The slave, accustomed to "constant humiliation," would not react to slight blows the same way a white would. Brutalize a person enough and you create the slavish personality. Once done, if a slave killed it must "be ascribed to a 'wicked heart, regardless of social duty.' " Still, there could be occasions when the killing of a white by a slave was manslaughter. If a white without authority to whip slaves did so he might be indicted in North Carolina. If such a white "wantonly inflicts" on a slave severe or repeated blows "under unusual circumstances" and the slave strikes "*at that instant,*" it could be manslaughter.[7]

There was a complication in this case, however, because the killer was not the one who had been severely hit. By the common law it was sufficient to see a friend viciously assaulted to create an excited passion that would reduce a homicide. Pearson held that this applied to a slave. Slaves were not obliged to give up the "feelings and impulses of human nature" under all circumstances. But property interests of owners were also involved. Considerable "caution is required to protect slave property from wanton outrages, while, at the same time, due subordination is preserved."[8]

Judge Nash agreed with Pearson and wanted it understood that a basic reason was that he did not wish to be caught in the "mazes of judicial discretion"; rather, he felt that he must adhere to the common law because it "gives him a safe and fixed rule to govern himself by." Ruffin heartily disagreed with both judges. He was not constrained by the common law because of the "dissimilarity in the condition of slaves from anything known at the common law" and because the rules that governed the relationship between whites and slaves "must vary from those applied by the common law between persons so essentially differing in their relations, education, rights, principles of action, habits, and motives of resentment." The case should be decided on principle and precedent.[9]

Judge Ruffin concluded that an ordinary assault and battery was not a legal provocation so as to reduce a homicide to a manslaughter, and that was what was involved in *Caesar*. What was at stake, he believed, was nothing less than the proper relationship between slaves and whites in North Carolina. This involved a discipline necessary to extract "productive labor" from the slaves and "enforcing a subordination to the white race, which alone is compatible with the contentment of the slaves with their destiny, the acknowledged superiority of the whites, and the public quiet and security." Whites felt the superiority and slaves a "deep and abiding sense of legal and personal inferiority." The appropriate rule was that if a slave killed when he was assaulted by a white in a way not likely to kill or permanently injure, the slave's action sprang "from a bad heart—one intent upon the assertion of an equality, social and personal, with the white." Was it allowable for a slave to make a judgment about the extremity of the violence? Slaves should not, Ruffin held, "assume to themselves the judgment as to the right or propriety of resistance." If allowed, it could lead to a denial of "their general subordination to the whites," end in slaves "denouncing the injustice of slavery itself, and, upon that pretext, [they] band together to throw off their common bondage entirely."[10]

The next year, in *Nelson, (a slave), v. State* (1850), the Tennessee Supreme Court agreed with the North Carolina majority. If the punishment inflicted on an insolent slave was "excessive," the killing of a white might be manslaughter. The homicide in this case had occurred at a cornhusking, where the son-in-law of the owner of the slaves was put in charge of putting away the husks. He hit one of the slaves and Nelson responded "insolently." Sellars, the victim, then hit Nelson with a hickory stick "as large as a chair-post." Later they confronted one another again. Nelson, who would have confirmed Ruffin's fears, said that "if you will give me a white man's chance, I will whip you like damnation." Sellars hit him several times and knocked him to his knees. Nelson stabbed Sellars. On those facts the state supreme court ordered a new trial for Nelson.[11]

Only in North Carolina and Tennessee was it ever expressly ruled that the homicide of a white by a slave could be reduced from murder to manslaughter. It is unlikely that the North Carolina–Tennessee majority line of reasoning would have made much of a dent if the lower court records are a fair measure of jurors' attitudes. Among the thousands of cases I examined there was not one of a slave convicted of the manslaughter of a white person. Every trial ended in a murder conviction or a not guilty verdict. Despite the agonizing of judges like Gaston in North Carolina or Nathan Green, the author of the Tennessee decision, the record strongly supports the view that Southerners did not believe there could be a legal provocation to reduce the homicide of a white person to manslaughter, regardless of the nature of the violence or the law.

"Assaults with Intent"

The offense of assault with intent to kill is absent from the colonial records. There were laws on maiming whites or on striking them, but none that dealt with assault with intent to kill: still, the concept was not completely unknown. Blackstone mentioned an "assault with an intent to murder." This was subject to a heavy fine, imprisonment, and the pillory.[12]

English colonials, despite the English rule, did not indict slaves for the offense. A few samples from the Chesapeake region make that clear, and in a sense they are surprising, even for seasoned readers of these trials. In 1721 in Essex County, Virginia, two slaves received thirty lashes because they had "much abused & beaten" Cornelius Lelor. In the same county in 1739 James sustained thirty-nine lashes for the "felonious stabing [*sic*]" of William Compton "with a large knife under his left shoulder." In 1772 in Princess Anne County the slave Jimmy was whipped thirty-nine times after he was found guilty of beating and wounding John Lovet, a white man.[13] Not one of these cases, in other words, was treated as assault with intent to kill, not even where slaves stabbed whites. There was no statutory foundation, and criminal attempts law was about as "inchoate" as assault itself, which Blackstone described as "inchoate violence."[14] Legal categories were crucial. There surely is no reason to believe that colonials were more sanguine about interracial violence than were nineteenth-century Southerners.

The *statutory* offense of assault with intent to kill or murder, when committed by a slave on a free white person, emerged in the second decade of the nineteenth century. One of the first laws was that of Georgia in 1816. It listed, among the capital offenses, "assaulting a free white person with intent to murder, or with any weapon likely to produce death." The statute in Mississippi was one of the more interesting and the one in Virginia one of the more oblique. Mississippi in 1822 made it a capital offense for a slave to assault a white with intent to kill. In 1829 the legislators added that if implied malice only was shown, the sentence would be up to three hundred lashes, unless the assault was on a master.[15] The difference between express and implied malice was important. According to Blackstone, "express malice is when one, with a sedate deliberate mind and formed design, doth kill another: which formed design is evidenced by external circumstances discovering that inward intention; as laying in wait, antecedent menaces, former grudges, and concerted schemes to do him some bodily harm." "Also," he continued, "if even upon a sudden provocation one beats another in a cruel and unusual manner, so that he dies, though he did not intend his death, yet he is guilty of murder of express malice; that is, by an express evil design." Malice was not necessarily directly related to a specific "intention." It could be "any evil design in general; the dictate of a wicked, depraved, and malignant heart."[16] Malice was a deep wickedness. This was significant in Mississippi.

Finally, there was the 1819 law of Virginia concerning malicious and unlawful shooting, stabbing, maiming, and disfiguring. This statute provided prison terms for whites. For slaves it merely said that those guilty would be considered "felons" and "suffer as in case of felony." Practice under the law of Virginia is not especially helpful. In Charles City County, for example, James was found guilty in 1852 of assault with intent to kill a white. He was ordered to be transported outside the United States, which was the alternative to execution. In 1844 Amos received thirty-nine lashes although charged with assault and battery with intent to kill. The reason was that the court could not agree on Amos's "intention." The record suggests that the justices either were uncertain whether the offense of assault on a white with intent to kill was a capital offense or they did not care all that much, preferring to decide each case according to the particular facts and community values. In 1798 Bob was executed in Richmond County for an assault with intent to kill, whereas in 1831 Dan was transported for the same offense. Some cases from Petersburg reveal quite different sentences for the same crime. In 1819 Benjamin White, a slave, was burned in the hand and given thirty-nine lashes. He had stabbed a white with intent to kill.[17] As a comparison, in six cases from the city of Richmond from 1838 to 1857, slaves found guilty of stabbing other slaves or free blacks with intent to kill received sentences ranging from twenty to thirty-nine lashes.[18] A particularly bizarre contrast occurred in Fauquier County, where in 1819 a slave stabbed another slave with intent to kill. His punishment was to be burned on the hand and receive twenty-five lashes. In the same year another slave stabbed a white laborer with intent to kill and was sentenced to be burned on the hand and receive twenty lashes.[19] It is likely that the facts of each case and the social position of the white victim account for the dissimilarities.

There was no doubt at all in Mississippi that assault with intent to kill a white was a capital offense if express malice could be established. In that state a number of trials turned on efforts by defense counsel to argue the legal issue of "express malice." One example occurred in Lowndes County in 1849–50. Charles, a runaway, was accused of assault with intent to kill Richardson W. Watson with an ax. One jury charge requested by defense counsel, and granted by the court, was that "if from the evidence the jury shall entertain a reasonable doubt as to what was the intention of Charles in cutting Watson whether to kill him or so to disable him without having any intention to kill him with malice express, they cannot find him guilty of an assault and battery with intent to kill with express malice but are bound to acquit him of this offence." Counsel also asked the court to instruct the jury that he was not guilty of the offense charged if he cut Watson in order to get away from him and not to kill him. The verdict was, "We the Jury find Charles the prisoner guilty Implied Malace [sic]." Although he got a severe whipping, Charles escaped the hangman's rope because of the express malice provision of the Mississippi law.[20]

The express malice issue was finally considered by the state supreme court in *Anthony, (a slave), v. State* (1850). James Tinnin, the white victim, went to one of the "Negro houses" and asked Adaline if anyone was there. She hesitated but finally said that Anthony, a runaway, was inside. Tinnin ordered him to come out. As he did so he hit Tinnin in the head, a blow that laid him up for five weeks. Anthony was sentenced to death, but the sentence was overturned on appeal because of errors in the trial judge's instructions to the jury. He had refused to say that express malice required a deliberate intention formed sometime prior to the commission of the act, that it was not express malice if the violence grew out of the circumstances of the moment rather than a fixed intention to kill Tinnin, and, finally, that the jury could not find express malice if the indictment did not charge it. The state supreme court relied on the failure to give the last charge. But instead of remanding the case, the court substituted the punishment for an assault with intent to kill, but on implied malice only. Anthony was to receive up to one hundred lashes a day for three successive days.[21]

The express malice provision of the Mississippi law presented a way for slaves to escape execution for assaulting whites. In Alabama, the law was more inclusive. *Nancy, (a slave), v. State* (1844), is an illustration. Nancy had been found guilty of assault with intent to kill Mary Beasley, a white woman. The primary issue, according to Judge Henry Goldthwaite, was "whether an assault by a slave on a white person, with intent to kill, under circumstances which would not make the killing murder, if the assault had been fatal, is a capital crime." The statutes of Alabama, he concluded, left only one possibility—such an assault was a capital offense.[22]

Georgia offers a useful contrast. In Baldwin County, in 1818, Alick pled guilty to a charge of striking Pleasant Hightower with the intent to kill him. Under the 1816 Georgia law that should have been a capital crime. Despite the charge and the plea, however, the court entered a judgment of guilty of striking a white and sentenced him to a total of 150 lashes, 50 at a time. In Hancock County, in 1849, Israel was tried on a charge of "assault with attempt" to murder George Reynolds with a "wood axe." Defense counsel asked the court to instruct the jurors that the assault had to be with an instrument likely to produce death. The state asked for a charge that it was implied malice to attack with a club and that if Reynolds had died it would have been murder. Israel was found guilty and sentenced to 500 lashes spread over ten days. The court added, with no sense of the absurd, that the punishment was "to be executed with humanity." After that Israel was to be branded with an *M* on his cheek.[23]

As a matter of policy, the statutory offense was a capital crime. Like manslaughter, it was treated in the nineteenth century like the actual murder of a white person. Moreover, experience with the offense was not extensive, and in many states it began to appear only late in the history of slavery. In some states not a single case turned up in the sample county records. This was true in Texas, North Carolina, Maryland, Louisiana, and Delaware. My claim is not that there were no such cases in those states, only that they were rare. Where trials occurred, they were late. With the major exception of a 1798 case in Virginia, they surfaced in some states by the teens and in most others much later than that.

Assaults

Still another form of criminal violence was the striking, wounding, or maiming of a person without any claim that the intent was to kill. South Carolina dealt with this in 1740, when it required the death penalty for any slave who "shall grievously wound, maim or bruise any white person" unless on command of, or in defense of, the person or property of the owner or individual in charge of the slave. If a slave presumed to strike a white person at all, he or she would be punished at the court's discretion for the first and second offenses and executed for the third. Aside from Virginia, it was the Deep South that followed the lead of South Carolina. Normally the laws were capital statutes. Provocation was not relevant: there was no excuse, justification, or mitigation. Nonetheless, very few cases were tried. In Putnam County, Georgia, Ben was hanged in 1813 for striking, wounding, and bruising a white man. He had cracked his skull with an iron mattock.[24]

In South Carolina an important supreme court adjudication did not come until 1848, when the slave Nicholas was sentenced to death for the "grievous wounding" of a white man. One ground of appeal was that the injuries were superficial and therefore not "grievous wounds." The court, over a hundred years after the law was adopted, had to provide some definition of "grievous wounding, maiming or bruising." Judge David Wardlaw admitted that the jurists had "attained no distinct conclusion as to the meaning of the words." All believed, however, that the violence must be "with evil intent, and be severe." Intention was central in Anglo-American criminal jurisprudence. It was the notion of *mens rea*, the so-called guilty mind. Without the requisite intention there would be no crime, although there certainly might be a civil wrong. A large problem, of course, was the evidence that might establish "intention." Some inferred it from social position and expected conduct—a deferential slave might not be presumed to have behaved with a wicked purpose, whereas a saucy one might. Regarding the other matter, that of "severity," the South Carolina judges had some difficulty. The "degree of severity," Wardlaw wrote, "is not sufficiently expressed by saying that it must inflict pain, distress and suffering." Moreover, it was "hard by many words to attain the precision which is desirable. Some of us think that this grievous wounding, maiming or bruising must be such as ensues from an attempt to commit murder or other felony, and is likely to endanger life."[25] Those who adopted this view leaned toward equating this offense with a criminal attempt to commit murder—in other words, an assault with intent to kill.

Insolence

Insolence was a nonviolent mode of resistance that directly challenged white domination. Frederick Douglass described how slaves might be guilty of this crime: "in the tone of an answer, in answering at all; in not answering; in the expression of countenance; in the motion of the head; in the gait, manner and bearing of the slave."[26] Deference, critical in a slave-based society, would be undermined if insolence was not treated as a criminal act, but as a crime dealt with in courts or before magistrates insolence normally involved language, not simply a gait or bearing. Moreover, oddly enough, it was not until 1819 that any Southern state criminalized language by statute. In that year Virginia amended its law on persons of color lifting a hand against whites, adding the phrase "[or] use abusive and provoking language to." On the oath of the offended party a justice of the peace could order up to thirty lashes for the offense. Mississippi and Florida followed this statute in the 1820s. In the 1830s North Carolina provided that "it shall not be lawful for any slave to be insolent to a free white person." Tennessee adopted the Virginia law in the 1850s but did not limit the number of lashes, and Missouri's law was essentially the same. More traditionally, Texas stipulated that a free white could punish a slave by a "moderate whipping" if the slave used "insulting language or gestures towards a white person."[27]

Prior to 1819 it was rare that an insolent slave was ever brought before a court on a criminal charge, and the records of single magistrates simply do not exist in sufficient number to give much information. The case dealt with by Landon Carter, however, suggests that impudent slaves might well have been whipped by some magistrates. One formal exception occurred in Lancaster County, Virginia, in 1745. Tom was sentenced to twenty-five lashes after he was found guilty of using "threatening language." Undoubtedly, the more common way to deal with an insolent slave was to whip him immediately on the roadside, in the ordinary (tavern), or on one's plantation, or else demand that a master do so. One early significant case suggests this. *White v. Chambers* (South Carolina, 1796) was not a criminal action, but a civil suit brought by the slave's owner for a battery committed on his slave. The defendant claimed that the slave was insolent, that the beating was only in proportion to the nature of the "insolent language," and that it was essential to the preservation of the system that slaves were to be subordinate to all whites. The owner countered that this would put the slaves at the mercy of "every violent or vindictive" man in the state. In the court's view, the "best rule" would be that if a "slave behaved . . . with rudeness or incivility to a free white man, to complain to the master." Republicanism involved a sense of community and responsibility to one's neighbors. However, if a slaveowner proved to be lacking in a sense of community, the white victim of the insolent slave could appeal to a magistrate whose duty it was to "see that reparation was made, according to the nature and circumstances of the case."[28]

By 1847 South Carolina judges were less satisfied that "community" was enough. In *Ex parte Boylston* the court upheld the view that it was proper to try a slave for insolent language and behavior even though it was nearly impossible to define the concept of "insolence." In fact, it claimed, slaves had been tried for insolence frequently since 1796. In dissent, John O'Neall argued that the legislature had never declared insolence a crime, and in his thirty-three years of legal experience in the state this was the first case he had seen. O'Neall even found something slightly charming in an impudent slave: "some of the most faithful and devoted slaves have been remarkable for their liberty of speech . . . and who has ever dreamed that an open-mouthed, saucy negro, is the deep intriguer calculated to raise . . . an insurrection?" There was danger, moreover, in trying slaves for this so-called offense. Give the authority to magistrates and freeholders to try slaves for insolence "and the result will be that passion, prejudice and ignorance will crowd abuses on this inferior jurisdiction to an extent not to be tolerated by slave owners."[29] Nonetheless, legal intrusion was increasingly seen as a replacement for community in a republican society.

Although O'Neall had a point, most people, even South Carolinians, were not about to suffer the saucy slave gladly as a series of cases from Fairfield illustrates. One year after the *Boylston* decision Turner Turket complained that while he was working on the public road Anthony had insulted him, and it had not been possible to "get satisfaction for the said gross insult" from the owner. Anthony received one hundred lashes. John was no more fortunate. Francis McKleduff, the superintendent at Asaph Hill's Gin House, complained that John had been abusive. The slave had been told a number of times not to go through McKleduff's yard, but he continued to do so. When stopped, he replied that "he would be god damd if he did not go where he pleased." McKleduff hit John, and John "laid hold of him and said that he should not hirt [*sic*] him." The other whites who testified tried to exonerate the slave. John Stevenson, for instance, said that McKleduff was half drunk at the time and was "somewhat fractious when drinking." Asaph Hill stated that his employee was drinking and that the slave John was always "humble." It was not enough. John also got a hundred lashes.[30]

Considerably worse, however, was the case of the slave Sole or Solomon. He was tried in 1851 for insolence to a patrol. One of the patrollers was David Coleman, who testified that Sole used "some very improper or unbecoming language such as asserting his Equality with any man and that he would die before he would submit to being whipt to death." Another patroller stated that Sole had said that "all men was made of flesh and Blood." This was more than the magistrate-freeholders could stand, and they sentenced him to two hundred lashes.[31]

Generally, the behavior that brought Anthony, John, and Sole before the full magistrate-freeholders' courts in Fairfield would have been handled by single magistrates elsewhere. One example is the case of Charles in Davidson County, Tennessee, in 1841. Charles was brought before the circuit court on a charge of "throwing Rocks at Robert Bradfate & giving him ill language." The court, however, remanded the case to a magistrate who had exclusive jurisdiction over such actions.[32]

A substantive and important case, *State v. Bill, (a slave)*, reached the North Carolina Supreme Court in 1852. The court upheld the refusal of the county court to award a jury trial as the case was properly handled by a single magistrate. Judge Nash, writing for the court, faced a definitional problem similar to that of the *Boylston* court, but he began his analysis with a jurisdictional point. The law that gave magistrates the authority to inflict punishment in noncapital cases gave magistrates the power to "make and declare the law."[33] This was analogous to the old common law power of judges to punish offenses *contra bonos mores*, a power Virginia's judges declined to use in cases of cruelty by masters to their slaves.[34] The insolence of slaves was different, but it also raised problems. "It was utterly impossible," Nash wrote, "to specify and enumerate all the actions of a slave" that might "violate the domestic order of the State, and which, if tolerated, would and must inevitably lead to higher and worse offenses. . . . Standing in the relative position which the white man and the slave occupy, there are and must be a great variety of the acts of the latter which cannot and ought not to be suffered, and which could be highly calculated to exasperate." If the law provided no remedy, individuals would take what they thought to be "justice into their own hands."[35] The property interests of slaveowners required that they allow others, on occasion, to bring their slaves to public justice for impudence, or else they would indeed see their interests subject to the violence and caprice of all whites, especially with the erosion of deference and the rise of the great unwashed with the spread of democracy in the nineteenth century.

But the legal problem remained—what would constitute "insolence"? "What acts in a slave towards a white person," Nash wrote, "will amount to insolence it is manifestly impossible to define; it may consist in a look, the pointing of a finger, a refusal or neglect to step out of the way when a white person is seen to approach." All such conduct would "destroy that subordination upon which our social system rests." Such conduct had to be punished, and the best way was to leave the matter to the "sound discretion" of local magistrates. There would be no clear legal boundary, nor need there be. The ultimate objective, of course, was deference, subordination, and the security of the social order based on the enslavement of persons of color, even if this had to be secured by some slight whittling away of the prerogatives of masters.[36]

Slaves as Victims of Slaves

Violence among slaves was dealt with under different legal rules and doctrines by white judges, jurors, and lawmakers. Sarah Fitzpatrick, an Alabama slave born in 1847, remembered that "Niggers didn't kill one 'nudder much in dem days. . . . Back dere 'Niggers' jes' had fights 'mong de'selves, ef day got too bad white fo'ks whup'em." Sarah was ninety when she was interviewed, and her memory, as well as her expectations of what her interviewer wished to hear, may have affected her responses.[37] Nevertheless, she expressed a strong perception shared by scholars— violence among slaves rarely ever became the concern of the law as it did not threaten the system.

Viewed from this perspective, the majority of slave crimes were directed outside the slave community, and thus most criminal conduct of slaves can be analyzed in terms of either a functional or a conflict theory of crime, to use the terms of Terry

Chapman. The first theory is that "criminal law is the embodiment of moral consensus in society." Criminal acts are acts that "offend strong collective sentiments." One function of punishment is to make a statement that some acts are not acceptable and they should not be done or repeated. The conflict theory derives from the work of Marx. It holds that criminal law is "not oriented to the idea of justice but is a means of dominance."[38] "Crime" becomes social protest, and the "criminals" are "primitive rebels."[39] Such notions provide a powerful model for the analysis of some slave crimes, but does it apply to violence within the slave community itself? If a slave poisoned another slave, or stabbed him, or attacked a spouse who had taken a lover, for instance, does it make much sense to talk about social protest or rebellion? Does the conflict theory of crime help us? And does the functional theory? If most violence among slaves was ignored by whites, does the functional theory suggest that the moral consensus of white society was not offended by such violence? If there was such a moral consensus, it amounted to saying that violence among the lowest orders in society did not challenge the authority or the interests of those with power, and therefore they rarely used law to punish that violence.

It is not true, however, that violence among slaves was always ignored by the law, especially if a slave died at the hands of another. Why would masters turn to the criminal law in such cases? If the victim who died and the killer were owned by the same master, what purpose would be served by prosecuting at all? One reason is that owners would be compensated for slaves who were executed, and at the same time they would be rid of a disruptive slave. If the slaves were owned by different persons, why bring a criminal prosecution of a slave when a civil action against the owner of the defendant for damages might work? An answer is that owners could not be held civilly liable for the criminal conduct of their slaves. But this answer is incomplete because slaveowners were held liable in Louisiana and Missouri. Another point is that we should not forget that some masters, such as the Reverend C. C. Jones, turned to the criminal law because they believed that the conduct of their slaves was morally wrong, as well as criminal by law, and should be punished.[40]

Whatever the reason, slaves were indicted for the murder of fellow slaves but, as Sarah Fitzpatrick correctly recalled, not often. Moreover, the great majority of verdicts were not for murder, but for manslaughter. Aside from the files for the whole state of Virginia,[41] the records from the Southern counties consulted show that there were thirteen murder convictions, two convictions for second-degree murder, and forty-two convictions for manslaughter. This is not surprising precisely because legal provocation among the equally degraded presented no conceptual barrier.

The evidence in most of these cases is not extant, but where it exists it suggests a classic form of manslaughter, that is, someone was killed in a fight. Nothing, however, could capture the full texture of this side of slavery but an exhaustive study of the causes of violence among slaves, a subject beyond the scope of this book.

Two illustrations from Kentucky show the commonness of these cases and the variety of responses among whites. In the 1850s a number of whites from Grant County petitioned Governor C. S. Morehead to mitigate the punishment of John, who had been convicted of the manslaughter of George. George and Charles had been in a fight "after night." A "considerable number of slaves" were present. While George and Charles fought, John hit George in the head with a stone. The injury did not appear to be serious, and George continued his normal work after the fight. One slave put a wad of tobacco chew in the wound. Over a week later George became sick, developed a fever, and a few days later he died. John was convicted of manslaughter and sentenced to receive 175 lashes. The white petitioners asked Morehead to reduce the number of lashes because they thought it was "excessive and inhuman." The governor declined because there was no statement from the judge who had sentenced John, no affidavit of the facts, and therefore insufficient grounds to act.[42]

In the other case the governor granted a full pardon after the intervention of some powerful Kentuckians, such as Garrett Davis, who became a leading unionist in the state during the Civil War.[43] After leaving their work at a brick kiln, Daniel and George had something to drink and wound up fighting. The argument started when Daniel said that "he was the best man that was ever on that walk." George declared that he was not, shook his fist in his face, and the ruckus began. When it ended George had been mortally cut. Daniel was convicted of murder, but a number of Bourbon County citizens urged the governor to pardon him. They firmly believed that he was only guilty of manslaughter. One petition emphasized that there was no malice, and that Daniel had always been a "vary [sic] peaceable & well behaved slave" and "has been singularly submissive, humble & proper." Davis added that if Daniel "had been a white man this jury would not have convicted him of a higher offence than manslaughter."[44] Justice and mercy remained in the hands of whites; if slaves were properly deferential, they might expect some mercy.

A special form of homicide among slaves was infanticide. Some slave mothers killed their children because they did not want them to be slaves,[45] others probably because of the psychological stress of postpartum depression. Some slave women faced criminal trials. In Fauquier County, Virginia, the slave Sall was tried for murder. She allegedly beat to death the male child "which she was delivered of alive in the peace of God and the said Commonwealth." The court adjudged Sall innocent, and she was freed. Jenny was tried in the Richmond Hustings Court for infanticide and acquitted, as was Nancy in Petersburg in 1821 on the same charge. Matilda, tried in Chambers County, Alabama, in 1847, was also acquitted. Harriet was another slave who escaped "justice." Owned by Nelson Warren in Lowndes County, Mississippi, she was indicted in September 1848. At the time she allegedly beat her baby to death with a stick, the child was "in the peace of God & our said State." Harriet was fortunate because she was never tried. From 1848 to 1852 five separate processes were issued for her arrest, but each time she was listed as "not found."[46] Her owner had probably removed her from the county. I found no cases of infanticide that were brought before the courts in the colonial period.

Cases in which slaves got into fights, sometimes vicious fights, are more frequent in the records. In the Petersburg, Virginia, Hustings Court in 1804 the slave Dick was tried for a felony in that he did "Bite of the Ear" of Jacob, another slave, with intent to disfigure him. The court was not unanimous that Dick intended to disfigure Jacob. It therefore found him guilty of a misdemeanor and sentenced him to twenty lashes. Finally, in the same court in 1828 Tom was sentenced to be burned on the hand and lashed twenty-five times for biting off the ear and lip of another slave.[47]

Routinely, fights among slaves were dealt with not as assaults with intent to kill, but as simple assault and battery cases that ended in whippings. One illustration of the normal treatment of violence among slaves is the record in Anderson District, South Carolina. From 1819 to 1865 about thirty simple assault and battery cases—out of over four hundred total actions—were tried in the local magistrate-freeholders' court.[48] The overwhelming majority of these cases ended in a guilty verdict for one or more defendants; their sentences ranged from five to thirty-nine lashes.[49] The norm was in the twenties, and in one case the slave was sentenced to sixty lashes.[50]

Social equality, or equal degradation, put violence on one level, while subordination led to an elevation in the seriousness of violence. The intention behind an act was inferred from social relationships. As the North Carolina judges observed in 1840, legal rules had to be adapted to the "actual conditions of human beings in our society."[51] Increasingly, lawmakers made fatal violence by slaves against any white person a capital offense regardless of the circumstances, and they added "insolence" to the list of slave crimes. Doubtless most agreed with Judge Ruffin that such legal rules were necessary to assure the subordination of slaves "to the white race, which alone is compatible with the contentment of the slaves with their destiny."[52]

14

Slaves, Sexual Violence, and the Law

The presumption that a white woman yielded . . . to the

embraces of a negro, without force . . . would not be great.

Pleasant, (a slave), v. State (Arkansas, 1855)

Black male sexuality has been a subject of fascination, ribaldry, and considerable fear among whites. Scientific thought and deep-seated sexual insecurity led whites to write "sexual retaliation" into law, to use Jordan's phrase. Lazarus, one of Eldridge Cleaver's characters in *Soul on Ice*, understood. He also understood the relationship between miscegenation and rebellion: "the white man forebade me to have the white woman on pain of death. Literally, if I touched a white woman it would cost me my life. Men die for freedom, but black men die for white women, who are the symbol of freedom." Fear of white retaliation ran deep.[1] A very different chord was struck in the classic work of W. J. Cash, *The Mind of the South*. Cash discussed the "rape complex," which critics of the South believed to be a "fraud, a hypocritical pretext behind which the South has always cynically and knowingly hidden mere sadism and economic interest." The "ultimate secret of the Southern rape complex" rested in the perceptions of Southern white women, who were identified with the "very notion of the South itself." This came, Cash believed, "from the natural tendency of the great basic pattern of pride in superiority of race to center upon her as the perpetuator of that superiority." More recently, Suzanne Lebsock suggested another view. She concluded that the "mythology of rape" developed after the Civil War as a way to reestablish the hegemony of white men. "In the myth of rape, the suppression of blacks and the suppression of women came together with new and sickening clarity." None of this, of course, wholly captures the range of sexual relationships between black and white people in the American South. Considerable evidence of miscegenation is explored in the work of scholars like James Hugo Johnston and Joel Williamson.[2]

Cases in which people crossed a color line can be multiplied from all over the South throughout the history of slavery, even though it did not occur as often as in Brazil or the Caribbean.[3] Whatever the frequency it did occur, and occasionally it became a legal matter. For example, in 1849 in New Hanover County, North Carolina, a jury was asked to support a request for divorce because the husband, "by habits of adultery with his slave Lucy: by degrading his wife . . . by beating her, by insulting her and by abandoning her bed, for that of the slave Lucy," had given ample cause for the action. In 1859 in Lowndes County, Alabama, William K. Mangum was fined $100 after he pled guilty to a charge of "fornication & adultery with a slave, Ann."[4] Consensual sex occurred across racial lines, and the images of sexually aggressive black males and whites with profound sexual insecurities are only part of the story. Still, it is a very important part, and it is reflected in the history of the law of rape. Scholars have often commented on sexual retaliation. Bertram Wyatt-Brown, for instance, argued that "it goes without saying that the penalty for a slave who dared lust after white women's flesh was castration, first by the law of the slave code, later by community justice alone."[5]

It is often noted that the number of actual rapes or attempted rapes brought before the courts was small. There is disagreement about the significance. Some use it to suggest that there was little sexual violence. Jack Williams noted that in antebellum South Carolina rape cases amounted to only one-half of 1 percent of all arraignments. Wyatt-Brown, on the other hand, responded that "the figure means little." "Shame, guilt, and family pride" kept victims from reporting sexual assaults, just as they often do today. Caution is in order. Not all of the indictments were legitimate, a fact that Wyatt-Brown also noted: a white woman caught in an "improper" relationship with a slave might claim a rape in order to preserve what little remained of her honor. Johnston found that nearly half of the sixty rape cases studied for the period from 1789 to 1833 in Virginia rested on evidence so weak that whites testified for the slave and alleged that the sexual relationship was consensual.[6] If those tried were often enough innocent, despite the verdicts, and if the number tried is no reflection of the actual number of sexual assaults, which is higher, we are caught in statistical cobwebs. This is one area of law where impressions are as valuable as statistics that decline to give up their secrets.

Rape: Definitional Problems

The basic definition of rape was the "carnal knowledge of a woman forcibly and against her will." Because it had to be "against her will," there would be no rape if she consented. But a child could not "consent." Lumpkin of the Georgia Supreme Court played on this theme when he wrote that the victim "like all other children . . . lacked the instinctive intelligence to comprehend the nature and consequences of this atrocious act—to reason upon duty—to distinguish, morally and legally, between right and wrong—to have the consciousness of guilt and innocence clearly manifested." Because of such ideas there could be no common law offense of rape of a child under ten years old. By a statute of the reign of Elizabeth, a sexual assault on such a young female was made a capital offense without benefit of clergy. And, of course, there would be no rule about consent: with or without it the crime was complete.[7]

There was one limit in the common law of importance in appellate rape cases in the South. This was that a woman who was raped "ought presently to levy huy & cry, or to complaine thereof presently to some credible persons as it seemeth." If shame or fear deterred her from immediately filing a charge against her attacker, she would endanger a prosecution.[8] In *State v. Peter, (a slave)* (North Carolina, 1860), the victim had waited two weeks before reporting that Peter had raped her and bloodied her clothes. The rule about silence, Chief Justice Pearson held, was not a rule of law but concerned an inference of fact to impeach the credibility of the witness. The basis of the rule was "that a forcible violation of her person so outrages the female instinct, that a woman, not only will make an outcry for aid at the time, but will instantly, and involuntarily . . . seek some one to whom she can make known the injury and give vent to her feelings." The absence of the "involuntary outburst" tended to show consent. It was not an absolute rule of evidence, however, and the weight to which the presumption was entitled would be left to the jury.[9] The law of rape in the South was clearly affected by sexist, as well as racist, presumptions. Women lived in a psychological world that bore little relationship to the images of men, but those images conditioned the rules of law.

The "carnal knowledge of a woman forcibly and against her will," whatever the limitations, was a *capital* offense by the common law and the statutes of England by the end of the seventeenth century. As Wyatt-Brown noted, castration was provided by the "law of the slave code." However, this was only the case in three jurisdictions. In Virginia castration was allowed for a variety of offenses until 1769, when it was limited to slaves convicted of rape or attempted rape on a white woman. This lasted until 1823.[10] North Carolina permitted castration from 1758 to 1764: according to Jordan, this was only to save the colony the expense of paying for slaves who were executed. The third jurisdiction was Missouri. By its law of 1845 a black rapist, free or bond, would be castrated.[11] Although some jurisdictions were removing capital punishment in rape cases for white defendants, all of them retained it for slaves during the nineteenth century with the exception of Missouri.[12] Most states made express provision for slaves and in some cases for all blacks.[13]

Race, age, and status were all elements in the law of rape in the South. Every state that adopted statutes to deal expressly with rapes committed by slaves (and in some cases free persons of color) added that the victim was to be a white female. On occasion this entered into appellate adjudications. In *Grandison, (a slave), v. State* (1841), the Tennessee court ruled that the fact that the victim was a white woman "must be charged in the indictment and proved on the trial." And in *Pleasant, (a slave), v. State* (1852), the Arkansas court held that the jury could not find the alleged victim to be a white woman solely on its own inspection because the accused slave might be able to show that she had a black grandmother, for instance.[14] On the other side, no white could ever rape a slave woman. But what about the sexual violence of blacks, free or slave, against slave women, or of male slave sexual assaults on free women of color? I have seen no case that concerned the sexual assault of slave women by free blacks. There is limited evidence concerning the other possibilities.

Slaves, on *very* rare occasions, were indicted for the rape of slave women. There were two such cases in Westmoreland County, Virginia, one in May 1778 and the other in July 1783. The most intriguing is the first, a charge brought against Kitt, a slave of Robert Carter. He was indicted "for having forcibly and against her will had Carnal Knowledge of the Body of Sarah a Negro Woman Slave the property of the said Carter." Kitt was found guilty and sentenced to hang. Five years later another slave named Kitt was accused of raping Fan, a slave of John Yeatman. No one appeared to testify so he was discharged.[15] The justices of Westmoreland County obviously considered it possible to indict, try, and condemn a slave for the rape of another slave. But they were unique.

So were a local judge, E. G. Henry, and a jury in Madison County, Mississippi, in 1859. Tried for the rape of a slave under ten years of age, the slave George was convicted and sentenced to death. The critical point was not the victim's age, but her status. John D. Freeman argued that rape could not exist between "African slaves" in Mississippi. He contended that "our laws recognize no marital rights as between slaves; their sexual intercourse is left to be regulated by their owners. The regulations of law, as to the white race, on the subject of sexual intercourse, do not and cannot, for obvious reasons, apply to slaves; their intercourse is promiscuous, and the violation of a female slave by a male slave would be a mere assault and battery."[16] Violence between slaves in general was subject to indictment, and Freeman admitted that sexual violence would be also. The problem was that it could not be a *rape*, a view consistent with the notion that by their very nature "African" slaves copulated freely. The early English had believed that black women copulated with chimpanzees or what were thought to be orangutans.[17] Blacks were randy and that was that.

In a brief, but important opinion Judge Harris adopted the view that neither by the statutes of Mississippi nor the common law could a slave be indicted for the rape of another slave. The common law, despite an earlier case to the contrary, *State v. Jones* (1820), did not apply to slaves. As to the notion that slaves were covered by the general rape law, Harris maintained that they were never included in statutes unless mentioned expressly. By a law of 1860 "the actual or attempted commission of a rape by a negro or mulatto on a female negro or mulatto, under twelve years of age, is punishable with death or whipping, as the jury may decide."[18] Within less than a year of the decision, in other words, the state legislature extended the protection of the law to young black females, free or slave.

Generally, black women, whether bond or free, were not protected by the law in the same way as white women were. Virginia made some exceptions. In 1797 in Surry County the slave Peter was executed for the rape of a free mulatto woman. Then in 1829 in Mecklenburg County Lewis was hanged for the rape of a free black woman. He had broken into her home and announced that "he came for *cunt* and *cunt* he would have, that he had been told there was aplenty of it there and he would have his satisfaction before he left the house or kill" her and the other person in the home. Allegedly the woman had entertained a number of white and black men, but the majority of the whites who testified spoke of her good reputation. Philip J. Schwarz, who discussed this case, also mentioned four other cases in Virginia between 1790 and 1833. Virginia, however, was unique. The distinction made by most states was expressed in the Tennessee case, *Grandison, (a slave), v. State* (1841). Judge Nathan Green ordered a new trial because the indictment did not note that the victim was a *white* woman. "Such an act committed upon a black woman would not be punished with death," he stated. The white race of the victim "gives to the offense its enormity."[19]

English law had drawn a line based on age, and this also entered into the law in some Southern jurisdictions. None drew a line based on the age of the defendant, which English law did (it was set at fourteen on the theory that below that age males were physically incapable of sexual relations). The age of the victim was another matter. In their zeal to draw a firm racial line and protect white womanhood, Southern legislators were not always careful draftsmen. A number of states simply made it a capital crime for any slave (or in some cases a free person of color as well) to rape "any" white female. In Kentucky the offense was the rape of "a white woman of any age."[20] But this obscured the traditional element of consent or no consent. If the definition of "rape" held, theoretically—albeit absurdly—slaves could allege that the female had consented to the sexual intercourse regardless of her age. This would wipe out any sensitivity to the problems identified by Lumpkin in Georgia.

A small number of states adopted age-specific statutes. One of the first was Virginia, which in 1792 provided the death penalty for any slave "to unlawfully and carnally know and abuse any woman child" under ten. Mississippi legislators, in 1822, made the sexual assault on a female under twelve a rape. In 1857 they apparently realized the evidentiary problem. Now it was a capital offense for a slave to rape or attempt to rape "any white woman" or to have "carnal connexion with any white female child" under fourteen.[21] Presumably, consent or no consent was irrelevant in indictments under the second category, whereas it could be crucial under the first.

Missouri, which used the traditional age distinction in cases of rape by whites, did not extend the distinction to sexual assaults committed by blacks. The only other state that adopted an age-specific statute was Tennessee. In 1829, in its general rape statute, it provided ten to twenty years, as was the case in Virginia, for "any person" who should "unlawfully and carnally know and abuse" any female under ten. It was not until 1852 that the state applied an age-specific provision to slaves or free blacks. Its law was like Mississippi's statute of 1822. Six years later, like Mississippi, the law was changed. Now it was raping a "free white female" or attempting or having intercourse with a free white female under twelve.[22]

These were the laws of rape applied to slaves in the South. Nonetheless, they do not begin to touch upon the offenses for which most slaves were indicted, which was not rape as such, but an assault with intent to commit a rape or an attempt to commit a rape.

Attempts

Central to all discussions of the common law of criminal statutes are its theoretical underpinnings. Sir William Hawkins observed that "the bare Intention to commit a Felony is so very criminal, That at the Common Law it was punishable as Felony, where it missed its effect through some Accident, no way lessening the Guilt of the Offender." The theory was that what was punished was the evil intention as much as any social harm. But, Hawkins continued, "it seems agreed at this Day, That Felony shall not be imputed to a bare Intention to commit it, yet it is certain that the Party may be severely fined for such an Intention."[23] A criminal attempt had become a misdemeanor.

Blackstone believed that the severity of the social harm was the standard to determine punishment. "A design to transgress," he stated, "is not so flagrant an enormity, as the actual completion of that design. For evil, the nearer we approach it, is the more disagreeable and shocking; so that it requires more obstinacy in wickedness to perpetrate an unlawful action, than barely to entertain the thought of it." The prevention of a social harm was connected with a moral theory to sustain a particular system of punishment. Blackstone thought that to view the matter this way would be "an encouragement to repentance and remorse, even till the last stage of any crime, that it never is too late to retract."[24]

The first important analysis in an American law treatise was that of Joel Prentiss Bishop in the mid-nineteenth century. According to him, "Whenever a man, intending to commit a particular crime, does an act toward it, but is interrupted or some accident intervenes so that he fails to accomplish what he meant, he is still punishable. This is called a criminal attempt." Action and intention had to be present. But proportionality was also appropriate.[25]

After the Civil War Holmes raised the discourse on attempts to a high level of abstraction. The reason we punish at all, he argued, was "to prevent some harm which is foreseen as likely to follow that act under the circumstances in which it is done." Or, as he put it earlier in his discussion of attempts, "If an act done of which the natural and probable effect under the circumstances is the accomplishment of a substantive crime, the criminal law, while it may properly enough moderate the severity of punishment if the act has not that effect in the particular case, can hardly abstain altogether from punishing it, on any theory. . . . Acts should be judged by their tendency under known circumstances, not by the actual intent which accompanies them." Holmes, however, had to admit that there were some "punishable attempts" where "actual intent is clearly necessary." Some acts (such as lighting a match near a haystack) normally would not amount to a crime unless they were "followed by other acts on the part of the wrong-doer." If no such acts followed, the law could not assume that they would. "They would not have followed it unless the actor had chosen, and the only way generally available to show that he would have chosen to do them is by showing that he intended to do them when he did what he did." But it was not the intention that was being punished, that was evidentiary. Yet there had to be some point in the chain of actions beyond which the law would not be used to punish conduct that on its face might be innocuous. Here Holmes provided a sharp insight. Where do societies draw the line? "The principle," he observed, "is believed to be similar to that on which all other lines are drawn by law. Public policy . . . legislative considerations, are at the bottom of the matter." The leading example he used to justify his point about policy was the law of Alabama on assaults by slaves with intent to rape white women.[26]

More recently the problem of criminal attempts was taken up in a new way by H. L. A. Hart, a legal positivist. The law, he argued, "does not punish bare intention, [it] does punish as an attempt the doing of something quite harmless in itself, if it is done with the further intention of committing a crime and if the relationship between the act done and the crime is sufficiently 'proximate' or close." Hart, however, was much more concerned with the argument that criminal attempts should be punished less than the actual completion of the crime. For him a retributive theory of punishment is on slippery ground because what is being punished is the "wicked intention." But there is "no difference in wickedness, though there may be in skill, between the successful and the unsuccessful attempt." The distinction Blackstone had attempted to make about an "obstinacy in wickedness" and a lesser degree of evil is lost in Hart's approach. Hart assumed that the offender failed because of clumsiness rather than that he desisted because he simply was not of a deep-dyed evil mind and would persist regardless of the consequences.[27]

A reformatory and deterrent, rather than retributive, theory of punishment is in no less difficulty. An offender who failed in the attempt might need as much punishment to reform as if he had succeeded. Hart tried to minimize the notion that the law is a proper means to promote morality. The real reason for the different levels of punishment was not different degrees of wickedness or the desire to encourage people to abandon their criminal designs. The real reason was based on the amount of social harm plus something captured in the sermon of Bishop Butler on resentment. There is a close connection between "blame and resentment," and people more deeply "resent" the greater harm. But for Hart the law should not rest on a theory of resentment.[28] Hart, unfortunately, did not provide a principled basis for deciding which offenses ought to be punished and those for which proportionality might be appropriate.

When Southerners began to incorporate the law of criminal attempts into the law of sexual violence by slaves against white females they anticipated the position of Holmes and Hart, and they abandoned the thought that had dominated common law ideas about criminal attempts as that law developed in the eighteenth century. Proportionality was no part of the Southern legislative policy. The first attempt statute was that of Delaware, adopted some time before 1741. The punishment for an attempt to rape "any White Woman or Maid" was to stand four hours in the pillory with both ears nailed to it and then to have the ears cut off close to the head. In 1794 the penalty was changed—the defendant to receive thirty-nine lashes, stand one hour in the pillory with the ears nailed, and have the soft part of the ears cut off. By 1852 it was to be whipped with sixty lashes, stand one hour in the pillory, and then to be transported out of Delaware.[29] Delaware's noncapital approach was unique.

The first capital attempt statute was Maryland's of 1751. It made it a felony without benefit of clergy to "attempt . . . rape on a white woman."[30] Marylanders' concern had risen dramatically by the mid-eighteenth century. In 1735 county officers in Prince Georges County, for instance, were enjoined to deal with "all manner of felonies Witchcrafts Enchantments Sorceries Arts Magick Trespasses Engrossing Regrateings Forestallings and Extortions whatsoever." There was no mention of slaves and none of rape. The charge of 1769 began that they were to be responsible for "all manner of Felonies Petty Treasons, Murders, Rapes upon White Women . . . and all other capital offences, done or perpetrated by any Negroe or other Slave."[31] The concern was sufficiently deep that criminal attempts were dealt with the same as the completed offense when committed by slaves.

In 1769 Virginia prohibited castration for any offense except the rape or attempted rape of a white woman. But it was not mandatory because the law provided that castration "may" be imposed. In 1782 a slave was castrated for attempted rape, and the slave Bob was castrated in 1783 in Southampton County although he was convicted not of attempted rape but of "carnal knowledge of Elizabeth Vick . . . without her consent." On the other side, the slave Ben was executed in Essex County in 1786 for attempted rape.[32] The provision for castration was eliminated in 1823. Maryland changed its law in 1845, when it determined that in attempt-to-rape cases slaves would be treated the same as free persons. In the Carolinas no "attempt" statutes were adopted. In 1816 Georgia made any attempt by a black, bond or free, to rape a white woman a capital offense.[33]

Other states adopted "attempt" language much later. The Independent Republic of Texas did so in 1837, when the offense was made capital if committed by a slave. Missouri acted in the same decade, but it provided for castration, not death. The slave Lee, for example, was castrated in Saline County in 1854 for attempting to commit rape.[34]

Attempts were part of the civil law tradition, so it is no surprise that Louisiana incorporated the concept. Yet there were few cases. In the view of Derek Kerr, the Spanish rarely ever convicted anyone of rape (much less "attempted rape") because they assumed that the woman had invited the sexual connection. Nonetheless, attempts were part of the normative system in Louisiana.[35]

Most states punished attempted rape by slaves the same as actual rape. About half of the states did not have attempt statutes until the last decade of the antebellum years. The use of the concept of criminal attempt in slave rape cases was, generally, a late development. Yet this picture is incomplete. We need to pick up the laws on assault with intent to rape. Most of these laws also came late. In the 1852 Delaware law, legislators dropped attempt in favor of assault with intent to rape.

The first absolutely clear law on assault with intent to rape by slaves was the one adopted by North Carolina in 1823. The statute read: "That any person of colour, convicted by due course of law, of an assault with intent to commit a rape upon the body of a white female, shall suffer death without benefit of clergy." South Carolina followed twenty years later. Its law made it a capital offense for any slave or free person of color to commit "assault and battery" on a white woman. This was an odd law because it did not mention "with an intent to rape," but the actual use of the statute suggests that was the intention. Finally, in a law of 1840 Florida made it a capital crime for a slave to assault a white woman with intent to rape.[36] The three states that did not have attempt laws adopted ones on assault with intent to rape.

These laws might be seen as conceptually interchangeable. A complication arises, however, because of laws passed in Missouri, Texas, and Tennessee. All three states had attempt laws, but all three also adopted statutes on assault with intent to rape.[37] Tennessee's law was similar to that of South Carolina in that it did not deal with a simple assault, which under the common law did not necessarily involve violence. Tennessee's law of 1833 provided the death penalty for "assault with violence and force with intent to commit such rape."[38] Six states had adopted assault with intent laws, and three of these also had attempt laws. What relationship existed between these two legal categories?

Firm categorizations did not exist. For instance, in the Georgia case of *Stephen, (a slave), v. State* (1852) the indictment charged a rape and an attempt to commit a rape. Stephen was found guilty on the second count. But the Georgia Supreme Court began its analysis with a reference to his indictment on a charge of assault with intent to commit a rape. Conceptually the two categories were interchangeable to the Georgia judges. Or consider some of the evidence from the trials of slaves in Anderson District, South Carolina. The statute of that state merely mentioned assault and battery on a white woman. In 1856 Lewis was tried for assault with intent to rape on a complaint from Rachel Francis Ann Holeman. He had allegedly thrown her on the ground, pulled her clothes over her face, and threatened to kill her if she did not "yield to him." Moreover, he had "otherwise maltreated and abused her, and . . . used every means in his power to Ravish her." In 1843, on the other hand, Wallis had been tried in the same district for "attempting to commit Rape on Sally White." Finally, in 1864 a slave of R. B. Hutchinson was tried for an "assault on a white woman." This was closer to the statute, but it did not allege "assault and battery." The evidence was that the slave had stopped Milly Holy and was talking to her when he "laid his hand upon her shoulder & said mistress canot [*sic*] you give me a little." She screamed and he fled.[39] That was the assault. Was it with intent to rape? Does this set of cases show any conceptual clarity?

There was more clarity in an opinion by North Carolina's Ruffin in *State v. Martin, (a slave)* (1832). The indictment under the statute of 1823 read that the slave Martin "did feloniously attempt to ravish and carnally know." It did not charge a felonious assault with intent to ravish. Was the word "intent" necessary in the indictment, or would "attempt" do? He held that it would not. First of all, "attempt" was not the word used in the statute, and it would be enough, he reasoned, to reject the indictment because it did not follow the wording of the statute. This was a common statutory analysis in criminal cases. But, Ruffin continued, the words were "not even synonymous. *Intent* referred to an act denotes a state of mind with which the act is done. *Attempt* is expressive rather of a moving towards doing the thing than of the purpose itself. An *attempt* is an overt act itself. An assault is an 'attempt to strike,' and is very different from a mere intent to strike. The statute makes a particular intent, evinced by a particular act, the crime."[40]

Were attempt and assault with intent statutes viewed as the same? The answer is sometimes. It depended on the particular case, or the judge, or the level of legal knowledge, or lack of it, of those who tried slaves. Occasionally jurists acted as if attempt and assault with intent were the same, and occasionally they did not; three states treated them as separate in statutes. Why all the confusion? The probable reason is that the concept of criminal attempt was itself not well developed. Conceptual rigor is not always found in law, especially when it is a legal concept being developed or transformed, and we should not expect otherwise.[41] Perhaps the only thing that should be added to S. F. C. Milsom's idea that manipulation of ideas was consciously done by lawyers who wanted to win cases is that sometimes it was done because of a lack of understanding of the implications or complexities within a given legal notion, even by those trained in the law and who used it on a day-to-day basis. It would be illogical to expect much else.[42]

Problems of Evidence and the Elements of the Crime

Although the concern here is with the *law*, it is important to remember that some slaves never received a trial when suspected of sexually attacking a white woman. In Saline County, Missouri, in 1839 James was on trial for attempted rape. He was in jail with a slave who had been convicted of murder the same day and a third slave who was to be tried for assault with intent to kill. James's jury had broken for dinner when a mob took all three slaves out and hanged them. And, at the outset of the Civil War, a slave charged with rape and attempted rape was taken out of a jail in Georgia and burned to death. The man who purchased him tried to avoid full payment on his note, but the state supreme court ruled in 1866, in *Middlebrook v. Nelson*, that he was obligated, even though it was a "hard case" for him. The court did not mention how hard it was for the slave.[43]

Such grim events did happen, but my immediate concern is how slaves were dealt with when they received complete trials. Among the problematic areas were questions about the admissibility of testimony about the character of the prosecutrix, the nature of the evidence used, and the elements of the offense. One of the first cases recorded involved the woman's character. In Henrico County, Virginia, in 1681, Katherine Watkins, the wife of a local Quaker, charged that a slave, Jack Long, had raped her. There was evidence that she had been treated roughly, but there was also a question about her conduct and character. The justices admitted some damaging testimony into evidence. Whether they were so inclined because she was a Quaker rather than an Anglican we shall never know. In any event, it appeared that there had been an interracial party where there was a lot of drinking. A white witness testified that Watkins had lifted the shirt of one black man and announced, "Dirke thou wilt have a good long thing." She allegedly had thrown another on the bed, kissed him, and "putt her hand into his Codpiece." Finally, it was reported that she had gone into a side room with Jack.[44] Unfortunately, there is no recorded disposition of the case, but clearly the character of the woman was considered legitimate evidence in the trial of a slave for rape.

The admission of such evidence persisted. In a case of assault with intent to rape in Brunswick County, North Carolina, in the 1820s the "general moral character" of Mary Rittenhouse was "seriously impeached." Another illustration is the Georgia trial of Wesley in 1847 for the attempted rape of Nancy Fleetwood. Fleetwood alleged that the defendant "broke open the door of the Dwelling house"; she fled to the woods, but he caught her and tried to throw her down and rape her. When examined, she stated that she had not arranged for any visitors to come to her house and that she "never kept company with Brown Peltersons boy." It is obvious that she had a dubious reputation among local whites. There was also evidence that Wesley had been whipped and that she had said "she would be sorry if the negro was hung for she had not as much against the negro as she had against Major Carpenter." Wesley was pronounced not guilty.[45]

A final example received one of the fullest discussions of this problem. *Pleasant, (a slave), v. State* (1855) was an assault with intent to rape case brought on the complaint of Sophia Fulmer in Union County, Arkansas. She said that Pleasant, whom she knew, had ridden into her yard and asked for liquor; he took a drink, "then caught her by the bosom and asked for tobacco." She pulled loose, gave him the tobacco, and hoped he would leave. But he "caught her by the arm, drew her towards him, threw her several times violently on the floor, then threw her on the bed, pulled her clothes over her head, and smothered her with them; then got upon her—she drew up her legs, and offered such resistance as to prevent him from penetrating her body—that he seemed to satisfy himself—then got off of her." At the trial, however, witnesses were asked a series of questions concerning the character of Fulmer and her husband. The husband allegedly offered to drop any charges if the owner of Pleasant paid him a sum of money. All the critical questions were ruled out of order by the trial judge and became the basis of the appeal. Sample questions included: "Did she, or not, tell you she liked to hug up a man in her arms, and tangle legs with him of a cold night?" "Do you, or not, know that Sophia Fulmer has had criminal connection with some other person than her husband, repeatedly during the year 1849, 1850 and 1851?" "Do you, or not, know that she is a base and lewd woman, and was such in 1849, 1850 and 1851?" Some witnesses were also asked about her general reputation for chastity. The supreme court ruled that the last question, under basic evidentiary rules, was proper, but

that the specific questions were not. Had there been evidence of criminal connection with the defendant, that would be admissible.[46] This harkened back to the
view that the sexual connection of a person with his concubine was not rape,
although the sexual assault on a strumpet could be.

The reason for the admission of testimony about general reputation for chastity
was "not for the purpose of furnishing a justification or excuse for the offence, but
for the purpose of raising the presumption that she yielded her assent." Such a
view would not stand up under modern rules of evidence, but it was commonplace at that time. The court, however, could not forbear to add: "But surely, it may
not be unsafe, or unjust to the prisoner, to say, that, in this State, where sexual
intercourse between white women and negroes, is generally regarded with the
utmost abhorrence, the presumption that a white woman yielded herself to the
embrace of a negro, without force, arising from a want of chastity in her, would
not be great, unless she had sunk to the lowest degree of prostitution."[47] Having
applied the normal evidentiary rule to the trials of slaves, the court then raised a
higher barrier for slaves to cross. Although evidence of the general character of a
white woman might be introduced, it would have an effect only if she were known
to be promiscuous precisely because the countervailing racist presumption was so
firm. This was an accommodation between sexism and racism within the legal
presumptions used by Southern white males.

Another element that cut across this analysis was class. Lower-class white
women, especially those thought to consort with slaves, were highly suspect. It was
rare that a charge of rape or attempted rape was brought by a woman of social
position. In the sexual assault cases tried in South Carolina's Anderson and Spartanburg Districts, for instance, almost every complainant was an illiterate.[48]

In some cases the testimony of lower-class women simply was not sufficient to
convict or at best led to fairly moderate sentences. For instance, Jane Elizabeth Bile
in Anderson District complained that Frank did "insult her by offering or Solicit-
ing her to let him Gratify his brutal propensity" and threatening that if she did not
do so he would waylay her another time and accomplish his "designs." Another
person testified that he heard the prisoner say this, and that he would "kill her and
have the accommodation any how." However, still another witness stated that at
the time of the alleged offense, Frank was at the Good Hope Camp Meeting. The
magistrate-freeholders' court did not consider Frank a potential necrophiliac, and
it disbelieved Bile's testimony. Or consider the case of Wallis, who allegedly
grabbed Sally White, an illiterate white woman. He was "stark naked," used "vulgar" words, and said he intended to "affect his purposes." He was found guilty but
was sentenced to only thirty-nine lashes, about the same as for a petty larceny.
Tom, in Spartanburg District, was charged not with attempted rape, or assault
with intent to rape, but with "rude and insolent behavior." Tom was found guilty
of having been insolent on a number of occasions, but it was always for the same
basic conduct. He stopped, or "accosted," the complainant, Mary Manus, another
illiterate, on one occasion "with his private parts entirely exposed and expressed a

desire to have Intercourse with her Saying he would give her a dollar." Tom was convicted but hardly castrated: his sentence was twenty-five lashes.[49] Would this have been the punishment if the complainant had been a woman of considerable influence in the district?

Legal practice was not based *solely* on race. This is demonstrated by a North Carolina case decided in 1859. *State v. Elick, (a slave)*, involved a conviction for assault with intent to ravish Susannah Pickett, whose character was "proved to be very good for truth and chastity." One person testified that Elick had told him that "Susannah Pickett is a very pretty girl" and that he "intended to ask for some." When informed that she would probably resent it, he replied that he would "knock her in the head, and then he would do as he pleased." The important point concerned evidence of intent, which the court concluded showed that "he had predetermined to force her to his will." One reason was this: "the inference of intent on the part of the prisoner . . . is to be drawn from the character of the young woman whom he assaulted, and from the respective social conditions of the parties."[50] Class relationships could be significant: it is doubtful that poor white women like Nancy Fleetwood in Georgia or Sophia Fulmer in Arkansas could pass the test of character or social condition. The degree of protection given women was not only based on a racial line, but on a class line as well.

Nevertheless, when brought to trial male slaves were the ones who faced execution. Whether they died depended on the nature of the evidence and what a jury would believe. A logical intuition is that evidentiary rules were lax in such trials.[51] Because it is impossible to recover the evidence admitted into the vast majority of slave trials, any conclusion must be impressionistic. For Michael Hindus the supporting evidence came from Spartanburg District, South Carolina: "one slave was convicted of rape despite the fact that the court described the alleged victim as an imbecile incapable of reasoning. Her testimony would not have been admitted had the defendant been white. Another slave was convicted of the same crime even though the alleged victim did not know her age, the meaning of a sworn oath, or what the Bible taught would become of anyone who spoke falsely." A third defendant was prosecuted for rape even though testimony revealed that "he never touched the prosecutrix or her dress."[52] There is certainly evidence that occasionally slaves were convicted on testimony that contemporaries considered less than credible. For instance, in 1752 Harry was found guilty in Baltimore County, Maryland, of ravishing a widow. However, he was pardoned on the recommendation of the justices who oversaw his trial because "the Evidence was not sufficient to convict him."[53]

We must take care that our intuitions do not lead us astray. The three cases cited by Hindus, for instance, were not all indictments for rape. Only one was, and the results of the trials are not what one might assume. It would be a reasonable guess that all were convicted and executed. But in the case of the young woman who did not know her age, the slave was found guilty of "an assault and misdemeanor." The indictment was for an assault and attempt to rape. The sentence was fifty lashes.

The testimony of the prosecutrix was that he had asked her to have intercourse with him, she said no, and he "caught hold of her around the waist and tried to pull up her clothes." She told him to stop, and he did. He then went down the road, stopped two hundred yards away, unbuttoned his pants, and "showed his person to her." The rape indictment was brought against Harry in October 1851, but he was convicted not of rape, but of a "high misdemeanor." His sentence was five hundred lashes spread over five weeks, followed by banishment from the state. There is no disposition recorded in the final case. The actual charge against Redman was not for rape; rather, it was for "asking Miss Elizabeth Cargil indecent questions and pursuing her on the road . . . and ordering her to stop from the maner [sic] he approached and pursued the intent was to commit rape though he did not get hold of her." Cargil said that he made known "his wishes," and that she "threatened him with his master and he backed out." She added that she thought she would say nothing because he was young, and threatening him with his "master would be sufficient to break him." People sometimes relied on the power and authority of the master before they turned to the law, even in such a delicate area as sexual connections between white women and slaves. In this case, however, it was not enough. On another day Cargil was riding along when she heard something. Looking around she saw Redman, who "seemed to be trying to steal up on me but when I turned he spoke to me." He allegedly told her to stop; she said that she "mended my gait and he his" and he nearly got hold of her, but he did not. Cargil concluded: "I am Sattis fyed [sic] his intention was to commit rape though he did not get hold of me."[54] There is no disposition recorded in this case.

Whites, of course, did not always scrupulously follow common law rules of evidence. The admission of the testimony of the young woman who did not know her age and so on was definitely outside the normal rules of evidence.[55] With the limited evidence available, however, we can miss the subtlety and complexity in these trials and come to the simplistic and erroneous conclusion that all blacks were automatically found guilty and executed or castrated.

One case suggests how diverse the responses of whites might be and the nature of the evidence used to convict slaves. This was the trial and conviction of Charles for the rape of Eglantine Williams in Northampton County, North Carolina, in 1824. It began with a complaint by Williams in August 1824 that she had been raped by Charles, the slave of Carter Jones. In September the justices of the peace concluded their preliminary examination and ordered Charles bound over for trial. Despite the seriousness of the charge, Charles was brought before the superior court in April 1825, when he was granted bail. In October 1825 and again in May 1826 the case was continued by consent of the attorney general. Charles's owner had requested the continuances because the case "has been a Subject of much conversation amongst the people of this county for some time," and some "individuals of influence in the county, have busied themselves very much in exciting prejudices, unfavorable to Defendants case." Because of the widespread prejudice there could be no "fair & impartial trial." He concluded that he believed Charles was innocent.[56]

Charles was tried in May 1827, found guilty, and sentenced to hang.[57] All of the testimony, however, did not support the view that Charles had raped Eglantine Williams. According to Williams, the wife of an overseer, Charles had "hold of her & caught her by her legs & threw her down and wrapped her clothes around her head, & said if she . . . did not hush hallowing that he would kill her—that she hallowed as loud as she could, & after she had become completely exhausted he committed the rape." She further stated that she was "well acquainted with Charles and knew him as soon as she saw him altho' he was disguised by having his face besmeared with yellow clay. That he had on an old coat which she had never seen before, and an old hat which belonged to a negroe boy named Britton." She then went to the home of local whites where she reported the rape: although she said she knew who it was, she did not name Charles at that time. Two slaves testified that they saw Charles after the alleged rape and that he was wearing white pantaloons and a shirt. Some whites vouched for Charles. Sally Davis was one of them. One of the first persons Eglantine Williams met after the attack, Davis said that Williams had come to her house "stript of all of her clothes but her shift. That she had her frock either in her hands or under her arms, and she was very dirty, and her hair much dishevelled and full of straw & leaves." When asked what happened, she "replied that some person had been beating her and tried to ravish her too, but that she did [not?] know whether they had done it or not." When asked if she knew who it was, she responded "that she should always believe who it was tho' she might be mistaken." Britton Snipes, another white, added that Williams said that "she thought it was Charles who had committed the act, but would not say what it was that had been done her."[58] These witnesses, in other words, raised doubt about her identification of Charles and even about what had happened.

This was the evidence, and the jurors believed Williams. There is not much here to suggest that they had no valid reason to do so. Charles was hanged on June 3, 1827.[59] Nevertheless, elements of doubt concerning his trial linger. Was the jury caught up in the prejudice that had led Carter Jones to ask for the continuances? Who were the influential people who were stirring up the community and for what reason? Were they effective, and did they have sufficient power to predetermine the outcome? But if that were so, why did some whites testify on behalf of Charles?

A final example gives more flavor to the evidence used to convict slaves. This was a trial for rape, in Orange County, Virginia, during August 1818, that ended in an execution. Unlike Charles's case, this one was not prolonged; in fact, it lasted only a day. Moreover, no whites testified for Jack. The prosecutrix, Elizabeth Wright, was cross-examined by counsel, however. Although described as a "spinster," Wright admitted on cross-examination that she had a child "and is now in a state of pregnancy and has never been married." These admissions did not discredit her testimony before the justices. She claimed that Jack forced open the door of the house, despite her resistance and those of her mother and niece. He forced her out, holding her arm in one of his hands and "an ax in the other." He then raped her. Again on cross-examination, Wright testified that she had in fact opened the door a bit to see who was there, and that the "prisoner said he was determined to have criminal intercourse with one of the family, or words to that amount." Jack, as well as Wright, must have been unusually legally literate to say the least of this testimony. Two slaves unsuccessfully tried to provide Jack with an alibi.[60] Although we can never know whether Jack actually raped Elizabeth Wright, there remains something unsettling about her testimony.

Occasionally evidentiary questions went beyond the question of credibility and touched on the essential elements of the offense charged. Among the elements required at common law were penetration and emission. In Delaware, in *State v. Negro George* (1800), the attorney general asked the victim: "Did you perceive or were you sensible by any marks that he spent or emitted while with you?" She answered that she did. In charging the jury in this case, Chief Justice James Booth began: "on an indictment for this offense it is necessary the facts of penetration and emission be proved. The witnesses for the State . . . have proved these facts."[61] A real difficulty could arise when the victim was mentally dim. A good example of this occurred in Cumberland County, Virginia, in 1819. The victim claimed that the slave got on her and acted "violently." She said he did not force his way inside her, although "he done as he pleased Rogered her and got off: after satisfying himself." The prosecutor, in obvious exasperation, then asked, "In plain english, did he fuck you?" Her answer was that he did, but she later admitted that she did not understand when asked about the meaning of entering her body. Finally, she claimed that there was penetration and emission, and that she was a virgin.[62]

Another problem concerned the issue of intention. How could it be determined, and by whom? In *State v. Elick, (a slave)* (1859) the North Carolina Supreme Court inferred intention from the relative social positions of the slave and the victim. Earlier, Judge Nathan Green of Tennessee had also considered the question of intention when he defined attempt and assault with intent to rape as separable in *Henry, (a slave), v. State* (1842). The evidence was that the slave had caught the victim "by the back of the neck and choked her down several times; that she cried out, and he left her." What crime was this? According to Green, "No attempt was made to ravish her; no embrace, or word, or action indicating a wish to have carnal knowledge of her." This was not a criminal attempt to rape. But was it an assault with intent to rape? Possibly it was. "From this evidence," Green continued, "if any motive of anger or ill-will could have been shown to exist, we should be clearly of opinion that the assault and choking were referrible to that, rather than to the intent to ravish. But there is no evidence of such motive, and the jury were, perhaps, warranted in arriving at the conclusion that the assault was commenced with an intention to ravish, but which intention was immediately abandoned . . . hence, we would feel scarcely authorized to give a new trial upon this evidence."[63]

The intention, in other words, might be inferred from the act, unless other evidence demonstrated a different intention, and the inference would be left in the hands of a local jury. Provincialism meant that local whites would determine intention, and there were practically no guidelines to limit their discretion.

This area of the law of rape was ill defined. Community norms would be ritualistically affirmed when jurors found the necessary intention to rape from the mere fact of putting one's hands on a white woman. But this does not help grasp another dimension of the law in regard to sexual offenses by slaves, and that is the actual criminal "attempt" as seen by Green and Ruffin. It is clear that they viewed an intention as a state of mind and an attempt as some act. What conduct by slaves did white jurors and courts view as an "attempt" to commit a rape on a white female?

Henry suggests that in Tennessee courts there would have to be evidence of a sexual intent,[64] but even that might not be enough in some jurisdictions unless there was physical violence as well. For instance, in one of the South Carolina cases described by Hindus the slave clearly indicated a sexual purpose when he grabbed the woman, tried to pull up her clothes, asked her to have intercourse with him, and later unbuttoned his pants and exposed himself.[65] Could this legally have been viewed as a criminal attempt to commit a rape? There was some action and an intention, but was the action sufficient to constitute the crime? The magistrate-freeholders' court in South Carolina did not treat it as a criminal attempt to rape or an assault with intent to rape. A possible reason is that the slave desisted and walked away when the woman told him to stop, and this did not show the necessary intention to have a sexual relationship by force and against her will. We are at a borderline. Under the common law if a person stopped short of committing the offense of rape, it could still be punished as an attempt, even if with a lesser punishment. This was the view taken by the North Carolina Supreme Court in *Elick* in 1859. The court ruled that if the slave began his assault with the intent to ravish but "changed his purpose upon being resisted, and concluded not to do so," it was still assault with an intent to rape. The Arkansas Supreme Court, however, in *Pleasant* held the opposite. "Where force is used," it reasoned, "but the assailant desists, upon resistance being made by the woman, and not because of an interruption, it could not be said that his intention was to commit rape."[66] In Harry's case discussed earlier there was no attempt because he did nothing to indicate that his assault was intended to be sexual, but it could be an assault with intent to rape nonetheless. There was, after all, violence in the assault, and the intention might have been sexual. Still, there was no attempted rape. In contrast to that case, consider the behavior of the slave toward Milly Holy. He had put his hand on her shoulder "very lightly" and asked her to give "me a little." She screamed and he fled. His sentence was five hundred lashes and banishment from the district. This was an "assault on a white woman."[67]

One element that needed to be present in criminal attempt was force, because without it there would be no evidence of intention to commit a rape. This issue came up in two appellate cases: *Wyatt, (a slave), v. State* (Tennessee, 1852) and *Charles, (a slave), v. State* (Arkansas, 1850). *Wyatt,* which focused directly on the common law definition, held that the element of force was absolutely essential in a rape indictment: "fraud and strategem . . . cannot be substituted for force, as an element of this offence."[68] And, by inference, some element of force would be required in a criminal attempt. The same conclusion was reached in Arkansas. Charles had been found guilty of an assault with intent to rape a fourteen-year-old girl. He had partly undressed and entered a bedroom where she was asleep with four other girls. He made an effort to turn her over, but she woke up, saw the man, and yelled for help. When he tried to flee, she grabbed his pants, but he took her hand, pulled free, and left. The Arkansas Supreme Court, following a ruling in a Virginia case involving a free black,[69] held that this did not establish an intention to commit a rape. "It is certain that the accused in this case used no force, nor is it probable, from all the surrounding circumstances," the court reasoned, "that the idea of force entered into his original design. . . . We do not think that the testimony evinced that settled purpose to use force, and to act in disregard of the will of the prosecutrix, which the law contemplates as essential to constitute the crime." This possible escape route from severe punishment for lusting after white women bothered the supreme court judges, who added this remark: "Whether there should not be an amendment of the statute so as to punish, as a distinct offence, and more severely than it can be, under existing laws, the carnal knowledge of a white woman by a slave, or the attempt of it, by fraud, and without force, or the attempt without consummation in consequence of her resistance, is, in our opinion, worthy of the serious consideration of the legislature."[70] The legislature did not act on this suggestion.

The historical experience with the trials of slaves for sexual offenses is complex. Whether there was a "rape myth" or "rape complex" in the sense described by Cash, for instance, must remain elusive. There is little doubt that some Southern whites did view white women as the embodiment of the South. There is no question, moreover, that Southern whites were profoundly racist. George Sawyer, a Louisiana slaveholder, probably spoke for the majority of whites when he wrote in 1858 that "lust and beastly cruelty" are what "glow in the negro's bosom."[71] But whether that meant that white males' "sexual retaliation" found vent through law is another question. The number of cases is small, and among them assaults with intent to rape and attempt actions loom large. It was not until about the 1820s, however, that Southern states uniformly adopted statutes to cover criminal attempts. When they did they anticipated the reasoning of Hart. It was not wickedness or intention alone that was to be punished; punishment was to prevent a deeply feared social harm.

The trials themselves will forever be opaque. The evidence that was recorded has a dull sameness about it. The slave allegedly grabbed the woman, pulled her clothes above her head, and either tried to rape her or did so. Despite the opaqueness, however, some things can be learned from these cases. To begin with, it is misleading to suggest that slaves charged with such offenses were immediately castrated, burned to death, or hanged. The social position and reputation of the alleged victim could turn in favor of the slave. And we should never forget that slaves were valuable property, and the property interests of the owners, not to mention the social power they might wield in the local community, could be an element as well.

Social relationships, racism, and perceptions of women all played a role, as did the legal rules and presumptions that derived from the common law and the fact that those rules and presumptions were being transformed. The law that dealt with sexual offenses was a mockery for black women. Its fullest protection was reserved for white women of some social standing whose reputations were what Southern white men believed they ought to be. If a woman fell below these standards, her charges of sexual abuse by slaves might be disbelieved or the defendant might receive a fairly modest punishment.[72]

From the standpoint of legal ideas alone, one of the most important was the concept of criminal attempt. This notion of criminal jurisprudence was employed in more than rape cases, but in the pre–Civil War South that was its most significant use. The way Southerners punished criminal attempts to rape by slaves was a significant harbinger of the idea that a society would determine how severely it would punish an offense on the basis of the perceived social harm. Punishment was a matter of policy, Holmes said. And the perceived harm was seen as very significant. As Chief Justice Lumpkin put it in *Stephen, (a slave), v. State*: "I would not put common seduction upon the same footing, and confound it with rape. In the present case, however, the consequences are pretty much the same to the unhappy victim, her family and friends, and to society at large. Over her and them, the defendant's unhallowed lust, has thrown a dark cloud, which will hang over them forever. The entrance of sin into this lower world, has brought no sorrow like this."[73]

15

Property Crimes and the Law

The morality of free society could have no application
to slave society.

FREDERICK DOUGLASS, *My Bondage and My Freedom* (1855)

E. P. Thompson's notion that criminal acts are often efforts to establish a "moral economy" by oppressed lower-class people has informed some efforts to find meaning in slave crimes against property. Alex Lichtenstein, for instance, saw them as attempts to "redefine and extend the bounds of paternalism" and as "incipient class-conflict over the forms the slave economy would take and the claims to its profits." Slaves, he believed, "used theft to reject, not accommodate to, their condition of slavery."[1] The views of slaves and the recollections of ex-slaves are filled with discussions of thefts. They were often justified as a "taking" rather than stealing. As Frederick Law Olmsted put it, "the agrarian notion has become a fixed point of the negro system of ethics; that the result of labour belongs of right to the labourer, and on this ground, even the religious feel justified in using 'massa's' property for their own temporal benefit." Others felt unease about stealing. One ex-slave commented: "See old Marse and Missus give us such little rations led her slaves to stealin'. . . . We knowed hit was de wrong thing to do but hunger will make you do a lot of things." There is little doubt that some felt personal degradation because of it, as the case of Frederick Douglass shows. But he ultimately rationalized thefts because the "morality of free society could have no application to slave society."[2]

Thefts of food from masters were not the only offenses against property committed by slaves, and petty stealing—as opposed to a crime like burglary—did not usually become a legal problem. Masters simply punished the slaves on the plantations for stealing chickens, which is why property crimes played a relatively small role in *legal* experience. This level of the struggle between masters and slaves was largely outside the public law. Law was involved only in that authority to punish was permitted to masters. As James Henry Hammond noted, "we try, decide, and execute the sentences, in thousands of cases, which in other countries would go into the courts."[3]

This was not the case with arson. William Faulkner caught the profound unease aroused in Southern whites by fire. The image of the burning house in *Light in*

August is memorable, as is the fear Flem Snopes generated when he arrived in town with a reputation for a barn burning in *The Hamlet.* Arson was an easily concealed crime,[4] and it was often thought to be an act of resistance. As early as 1820 a Northern insurance company declined to provide fire insurance in Virginia because of a supposed tendency of a "species of population" to use fire as revenge.[5]

Historians, however, have not always seen arson through the same lens. Stampp claimed that "next to theft, arson was the most common slave 'crime.'" Fire "was a favorite means for aggrieved slaves to even the score with their master." Genovese took a more circumspect approach. Arson was of a "restricted character." If a slave "burned down the Big House, which few ever did, or the carriage house, or some other building of little direct economic significance, the slaves might easily sympathize with and protect them." It was different if they burned the "corncrib, smokehouse, or the gin-house." The reason was that "destruction of food stores meant their own deprivation. Destruction of the cotton meant severe losses to their master, but this furious vengeance also threatened the sale of one or more members of the slave community, or worse, bankruptcy and the breakup of the community altogether."[6] At the heart of these different views is the question of whether slave crimes should be seen as acts of accommodation or resistance. For Southern whites that probably was a question unasked: for them the problem was simply the "criminal" conduct of those in bondage, not the motives or meaning underlying that conduct. The theft of chickens was surely an annoyance, but that form of "crime" was something they could live with. Crimes like larcenies, burglaries, or arson, however, were a different matter. Larcenies of chickens from neighbors could also be grievous, as they might involve the relationships among the free, not just those among masters and slaves.

Larceny

Most slave crimes against property fell in the category of larceny. "Simple larciny," according to Blackstone, "is the felonious taking, and carrying away, of the personal goods of another." A compound larceny included an element of aggravation as in a "taking from one's house or person." One form was robbery. As Pearson put it in *State v. John, (a slave)* (North Carolina, 1857), "Robbery is committed by force; larceny by stealth." Larceny from the person was not simply a crime against property. "Open and violent larciny from the *person*, . . . is the felonious and forcible taking," Blackstone noted, "from the person of another, of goods or money to any value, by putting him in fear." The compound larceny of stealing from a house shaded off into burglary, but it could be different. Under the common law a burglary involved breaking into a house at night.[7]

There was a further breakdown between petit or petty larceny and grand larceny. Policy determined the distinction and the punishment. During the late eighteenth century Sir Matthew Hale argued that public order might require the death penalty for some thefts if they became too widespread and thereby threat-

ened social stability. Grand larceny was a capital, but clergyable offense and occurred whenever the goods stolen were over twelve pence in value. Petit larceny,
the theft of property valued under twelve pence, was punished by imprisonment
or whipping at the discretion of the magistrate.[8] By the eighteenth century hanging a person for the theft of goods over twelve pence in value troubled many
people, and juries would sometimes save a person by the "pious perjury" of
valuing goods below that sum no matter what the true value.[9] In the slave societies
of the South the law might be bent in different ways as public order, and thus
policy, could be satisfied by the justice of the plantation in some cases but not in
others.

Hog stealing was one of the most frequent thefts in the South and one of the first
dealt with specifically in a statute. Throughout the region hogs were relatively
plentiful and formed a major part of people's diets. If a hog was valued over twelve
pence, the hog stealer would be guilty of a capital offense under English law. By an
act of 1699 Virginia's burgesses provided that a slave would receive thirty-nine
lashes "well laid on" for the first offense. For a second he was to stand in the pillory
for two hours with both ears nailed to it, and then the ears would be cut off. By a
law of 1705 a third offense was made capital without benefit of clergy, which is what
it would have been under the common law for a second theft of a hog valued over
twelve pence if clergy had been granted for the first crime.[10]

The treatment of sheep-stealing slaves contrasted with the practice and the
statutory development for the theft of hogs. Virginians did not directly follow the
English law. In England, where sheep cost more than hogs, sheep stealing was a
capital offense without benefit of clergy. It remained nonclergyable in colonial
Virginia in theory but not always in practice. In 1763 Cupid was burned on the
hand in Westmoreland County after his conviction for sheep stealing. But two
years earlier Sam was hanged in Princess Anne County for the same crime.[11]

By the nineteenth century the distinction between grand and petit larceny was
collapsing, and statutory limits had been set on punishments. Any functional
difference between the two larcenies was eliminated in 1822 in Mississippi, for
instance. The categories remained but there was no point. Grand larceny was the
theft of goods valued above $20, and petit larceny the theft of goods below that
figure. The punishment, however, was identical—thirty-nine lashes.[12]

By its law of 1856 North Carolina abolished the distinction. This statute was
construed by the state supreme court a year later in *State v. Harriet, (a slave).* Nash
noted that there had been a distinction at common law, but "morally speaking,
there is no difference; each is equally forbidden by the great Lawgiver." North
Carolina's lesser lawgivers agreed. They abolished the distinction and provided
that the offense, unless otherwise specified, would be punished as a petit larceny in
all cases. They diminished grand larceny, "a change which the spirit of the times
demanded."[13] A major exception to this trend was a Louisiana law of 1856: "any
slave who shall be guilty of larceny, shall be punished at the discretion of the
court." Discretion was retained, but the distinction was not. One illustration of the

use of this discretion is an 1831 case from St. Landry Parish. George, who had taken cash, clothes, a pocket knife, and so on from different people, was convicted of larceny. The judgment of the court was that his owner was to pay unspecified damages, the value of the property taken from one of the victims, and court costs. George himself was whipped thirty-nine times with a cow skin and had "an Iron Collar of five pounds weight with three prongs put upon & round the neck." He had to wear the collar for one year.[14]

Statutes sometimes retained the distinction but removed the unbridled discretion. In Alabama's 1852 law a magistrate was authorized to sentence a slave up to thirty-nine lashes for a petit larceny. If he felt that the offense warranted more, he could consult two "respectable freeholders" and with their assent order up to one hundred lashes. Maryland was unique in that it provided prison terms for slaves convicted of grand and petit larceny.[15]

Throughout the South sentencing practices for slaves found guilty of larceny collapsed distinctions. The procedure in New Hanover County, North Carolina, for the period 1821–56 illustrates the point. There were eleven cases involving charges of grand larceny and none of petit larceny. Benefit of clergy is mentioned in several of these cases, and the sentences with guilty verdicts ranged from twenty-five lashes to thirty-nine lashes on two separate occasions.[16]

Probably the most extreme example of the older common law approach to larceny was in South Carolina, which adopted no significant statute on slave thefts, kept the common law language, and allowed the magistrate-freeholders discretion in sentencing.[17] In Anderson District sentences for simple larceny ranged from the ten lashes given Linda in 1832 for stealing to one hundred lashes given Marshele and Pleasant in 1865 for hog stealing. In 1852 Wash and Jim were involved in the theft of bacon. Wash was the principal, and Jim was found guilty of being an "accessory before and after the fact." Jim was sentenced to fifty-five lashes "moderately well" laid on, whereas Wash was not tried at all. The telling reason was that Wash's owner allowed him to be flogged by the owner of the bacon and then flogged him himself, but Jim's owner refused to allow Jim to be whipped.[18]

Although the distinctions in the common law offense of simple larceny were collapsing, the same was not true of compound larceny. Robbery and "larceny from the house," however, do not appear often. Robbery is mentioned most often in the records of the old slave societies along the Atlantic coast. Generally, when a trial for robbery ended in a guilty verdict, the slave was hanged.[19] A rare exception occurred in Chatham County, Georgia, in 1813. Elijah was found guilty of robbery but the jury recommended mercy, and he was sentenced to receive thirty-nine lashes on two separate occasions.[20]

At the opposite extreme was the treatment of Nathan, the slave of Gabriel South (South Carolina, 1851). His case involved two trials on separate charges based on the same event. Elizabeth Mitchell claimed that Nathan had assaulted her. He was choking her and released her only when she promised to give him what money she had, which was one dollar. He then left. On these facts Nathan was first tried on a charge of assault and battery with intent to rape. He was found guilty of assault and battery and was sentenced to receive fifty lashes on two separate occasions. After this was carried out he was indicted on a charge of robbery on the same facts, found guilty, and sentenced to hang. O'Neall issued a writ of prohibition because the first conviction was a bar to the second trial and because "if there was no intent to commit a rape, the delivery of the money was without such a putting in fear, as the law requires to make the offence of robbery." When the case was appealed to the state supreme court, O'Neall's ruling was overturned. The majority of the court held that whatever Nathan's intent, his acts that followed the assault and battery "(when explained and characterized by his previous violence,) show such a taking by putting in fear, as constitutes a case of robbery." The justices also held that the first trial was no bar. O'Neall in dissent contended that the first trial showed that there was no assault and battery with intent to rape, and therefore the facts could not be used to prove force or fear so as to constitute the offense of robbery. "Indeed there is no larceny: it is the delivery of a dollar without compulsion." The rest of the court was satisfied that "justice" would be done with the execution of Nathan for robbery. "If the prisoner was a white man," O'Neall asked, "and not a negro, could such a course receive the countenance of any one?"[21]

The other compound larceny, "larceny from the house," rarely appears. Spencer was sentenced to seventy-five lashes in Chambers County, Alabama, in 1853 for this offense.[22] Cases of breaking into stores, storehouses, and meat houses, on the other hand, are numerous indeed, especially in urban communities.[23] Oddly enough, it does not clearly appear in the records for some states at all, or some cities, such as Natchez.

Burglary

A commonsense view of burglary is breaking into some building and stealing things, but this is misleading. Coke defined a burglar as "he that by night breaketh and entereth into a mansion-house, with intent to commit a felony."[24] Obviously, there is a property element here, but that is not all. The intention had to be to commit a "felony," and that included more than theft.

According to Hawkins, moreover, the "currant Opinion" in early eighteenth-century England was that the place broken into had to be a dwelling, but outbuildings, such as barns, were considered part of the dwelling unless far removed. There could be no burglary, in his opinion, in a shop or workhouse alone. In the *Historia Placitorum Coronae*, Hale noted why: burglary involved the "habitation of man, to which the laws of this kingdom hath a special protection." Blackstone pointed out that the reason burglary was so serious was that it created a "midnight terror." The "malignity of the offence" was based on the fact that it occurred "at the dead of night; when all the creation, except beasts of prey, are at rest; when sleep has disarmed the owner, and rendered his castle defenceless." Burglary was not simply a crime against property, it was one of only two "crimes against the habitation." The other was arson.[25]

A shift in emphasis toward the more modern perception appeared in Adam Smith's *Lectures on Jurisprudence*. He treated burglary in his discussion of thefts. According to him, "theft appears naturally not to merit a very high punishment. . . . But there is one case wherein thefts of the smallest value are punished with death both by the Scots and English law, that is, where a house is broken open in the commission of it. The security of the individuals requires here a severer and more exact punishment than in other cases. Burglary therefore is always capitally punished."[26] The crime was essentially one involving theft. This was not a correct summary of English law, and Smith did note that the reason it was a capital offense was to protect people, not property rights. But for Smith—for whom property rights were so important, and who discussed burglary among "thefts"—and for those influenced by his thought, it was easy to end seeing burglary as a property crime.

During the colonial period some lawmakers tinkered with the elements of common law burglary. Georgians and Carolinians left them intact, but Marylanders did not. The section of their 1729 law on burglary removed the benefit of clergy for the felonious breaking and entering of shops, storehouses, or warehouses, even though they were not used as dwellings or even contiguous, if the goods stolen were worth at least five shillings. Whereas other jurisdictions treated such crimes as larcenies, Maryland squeezed them under the rubric, "burglary." It shifted the emphasis toward the property element in the offense. A similar law was adopted in Virginia in 1748, except that the Maryland law applied to slaves alone, whereas the Virginia law did not.[27]

In 1719 Delawareans provided the death penalty for anyone convicted of burglary, which was defined as follows: "a breaking and entering into the dwelling-house of another in the night time, with an intent to kill some reasonable creature, or to commit some other felony within the same house." Later they stipulated that anyone who entered the dwelling of another, by night or day, with intent to commit a felony would be guilty of burglary. The same law made it a capital offense, without benefit of clergy, to break or enter "any dwelling-house, out-house or other house whatsoever" in the daytime with an intent to "kill some reasonable creature, or to commit some other felony."[28]

Post-Revolutionary experimentation was erratic. In 1806 Georgia required the death penalty for any slave who broke open a dwelling "or other building whatsoever." Most of the experimentation did not concern the definition of the crime, but the punishment. But there were some changes in the nineteenth-century South. In Louisiana and Texas the emphasis shifted toward viewing burglary as a property offense. By 1856 Louisiana made it a capital offense for a slave to commit a traditional common law burglary, or to break into a "store, or house of any kind, or who shall attempt to do so," whose purpose was to "steal or commit any other crime." Missouri was a state that modified burglary law in a general criminal code and created different degrees of the offense.[29] A number of states eliminated the death penalty for burglary and substituted either a prison term or severe whippings. Severity was being moderated in the wake of the campaigns against cruelty and the movement in favor of institutionalization for deviancy.[30] This did not always work to the advantage of slaves, of course.

The most intriguing modification came in Alabama and Mississippi in the 1850s. In 1852 Alabama changed the definition of dwelling: no building would be considered a dwelling "unless some white person is in such house at the time the act is done or offence committed." Statutory burglary was defined by race. It could not be such a "burglary" to break into a free black's home, or into a slave cabin with the intent to commit a felony, unless, of course, a white person was there, a none too likely—although not impossible—condition. Five years later Mississippi provided the death penalty for slaves "guilty of burglary, some white person being at the time in the house broken."[31] The Alabama law was noted in one of the only appellate cases that involved the elements of the crime. In *Ex parte Vincent, (a slave)* (1855), Judge Goldthwaite wrote that the meaning of the "dwelling" was narrowed because it was believed that the old law punishing all burglaries by slaves was too severe. This did not help Vincent, however: he broke into a white man's store at night when the owner and his brother were sleeping in the back room.[32]

These were the principal statutory alterations in burglary law. The tendency, outside of the old colonial states, was to reduce the punishment and to experiment with altering the various elements of the offense. Everywhere the crime increasingly was a crime against property, but the crime as one against the habitation was not wholly lost. Indictments were still brought against slaves for burglaries that did not involve theft. For instance, in 1824 in Culpeper County, Virginia, Dick was tried for burglary and felony. The burglary was breaking into the dwelling of John Wale with the intent to "ravish Lucy Wale spinster." He was found guilty and hanged a month after his trial.[33] There were also burglary cases involving attempted rape in, among other places, Anderson District, South Carolina, in 1830; Jessamine County, Kentucky, in 1843; and Lunenburg County, Virginia, in 1862. In Lunenburg County, moreover, the slave John was tried for burglary in 1860 for breaking into a dwelling and stabbing a slave with intent to kill.[34]

Burglary Cases

Because burglary was not as difficult to prove as arson, we might expect to see a high conviction rate, but that was not so. Although burglary was a capital offense, colonial Virginians actually convicted and executed far less than one-half of those slaves indicted. Hindus found a 60 percent conviction rate for all crimes against property, including burglary, in the nineteenth century in Anderson and Spartanburg Districts, South Carolina. The punishments could be brutal, yet the slaves convicted of burglary in those districts were not always sentenced to death.[35] By the 1770s, according to Philip Schwarz, Virginians began to focus much more attention on burglary. His figures for the counties he examined show a notable increase in the number of cases, and the conviction rate rounded off to 65 percent. Of those convicted of felonies, however, 42 percent were granted benefit of clergy. In addition, a little over 9 percent were convicted of misdemeanors rather than the felonies with which they were charged. From the 1780s on, moreover, Virginians hanged fewer slaves for property crimes: they viewed "major stealing by slaves as less reprehensible and dangerous as time passed."[36]

Intuitively we would guess that the greatest variations or deviations from the strict legal conception of burglary occurred in the lower—rather than the appellate—courts. This is a sound instinct; even so, it does not capture how skewed things could sometimes be, as one illustration shows. Will's road to the gallows in Charles City County was convoluted. He was tried in November 1761 for breaking and entering the stable of John Christian and stealing a horse. If the stable was adjacent to the dwelling, this would be a common law burglary. He was acquitted of the charge, but without any new indictment he was found guilty by the same court at the same trial of the theft of a gun belonging to John Johnson. His sentence was that of a slave granted benefit of clergy. In July 1762 Will was tried again. Three of the men who sat on the earlier trial were involved in this one. The charge was burglary: Will was indicted for breaking into the dwelling of Agness Parish and stealing property valued at twenty shillings. His owner testified against him, but he was found not guilty. Yet again he was confronted with a new information for the same offense but in a different dwelling. Will pled guilty to stealing but denied breaking into the dwelling. He was found guilty of housebreaking and hanged. The problem, of course, was that he had already had his clergy, a fact the court noted.[37]

By the nineteenth century technical legal arguments appeared even at the trial court level, where slaves were defended by legal counsel. An example was the argument made in the case of John in Wilkinson County, Mississippi, in 1853. John was indicted for burglary and larceny. One of the points made by his counsel in a motion to quash the indictment was that it did "not alledge, or show that the House into which the defendant is said to have burglorously entered was a dwelling." The court sustained the motion, quashed the indictment, and remanded John for further proceedings. Two days later he was indicted on a charge of grand larceny, and two days after that he was acquitted. In 1844 in Screven County, Georgia, Guy escaped the gallows after a conviction for burglary, robbery, and assault. The "evidence did not authorize a conviction for Burglary inasmuch as it established that there was no breaking of the house but the door was opened to him."[38]

A variation on the theme occurred in South Carolina, where the magistrate-freeholders did not always show much regard for technical definitions, and where the right of appeal from their judgments was very limited. One case did reach the state supreme court. In *State v. Ridgell* (1831) the court granted a prohibition against the execution of the slave because the storehouse he broke into was about one hundred yards from any dwelling, was separated from the nearest dwelling by a public road, and was not used "as a place for sleeping by any person at the time when it was broken open." Nonetheless, the magistrate-freeholders had found the slave guilty of burglary and sentenced him to death. This, the court held, was inappropriate.[39] A rather rare exception in the records of these courts is that of the trial of Philip for burglary and larceny in Anderson District in 1854. The magistrate-freeholders found him guilty of larceny only and sentenced him to thirty-six lashes. They noted that they could not find him guilty of burglary "from the fact that the law Requires to constitute Burglary the breaking and entry must be done in the night time & of which there was no evidence & we could not presume it was done in the night."[40]

The actual practice varied a great deal from jurisdiction to jurisdiction and over time, with more and more formalism as time passed. In some jurisdictions the old common law definition of burglary remained firm, and in others it did not, either in practice or because of statutory modifications. One thing that the lower-court records do make clear is that we need to be careful with legal categorizations and not overly rely on statistical evidence, or we will sketch an erroneous picture of the actual historical experience. At the same time, there is no doubt that the spread of capitalism led to an increased emphasis on the offense of burglary as a crime against property.

The Use of Fire

Early seventeenth-century treatise writers sometimes discussed "burnings" rather than "arson."[41] By the time Hawkins wrote a century later, the crime of arson was viewed as "maliciously and voluntarily burning the House of another by Night or by Day." He added that it "seems Agreed" that "not only a Mansion-House, and the Principal Parts thereof" but also "any other House, and the Out-buildings, as Barns, and Stables, adjoining thereto; and also Barns full of Corn, whether they be adjoining to any House or not, are so far secured by Law, that the malicious burning of them is Arson." Neither a "bare intention" nor an "actual attempt" would amount to the felony unless a part of a house were in fact burned. Blackstone defined arson as "the malicious and wilful burning the house or out-house of another man." Arson was especially pernicious, he believed, because "it is an offence against that right of habitation, which is acquired by the law of nature as well as by the laws of society."[42]

By the time of the settlements the punishment for arson was hanging. Colonials began to modify the law in the 1720s. As of 1729 a slave in Maryland would have his right hand severed, and then his body (after he was hung) would be quartered and distributed about the countryside. The punishment was not applied to the whole range of possible "burnings." In 1751 it became a capital offense without benefit of clergy for any slave to burn "any house or houses" or to attempt "to burn any dwelling-house, or out-houses contiguous thereto, or used with, any dwelling-house, or any other house wherein there shall be any person, or persons, or any goods, merchandise, tobacco, Indian corn or other grain or fodder."[43] This law blurred the distinction Hawkins had made between an actual burning and an attempt. It also blended Blackstone's crime against the habitation with purely economic crimes against property. The specific crops covered, of course, were adjusted to correspond to those of Maryland.

The Maryland law dealt with slaves only. The law of Virginia did not. In 1730 "all and every person" could be executed who burned "any tobacco-house, warehouse, or storehouse, or any house or place, where wheat, Indian corn, or other grain, shall then be kept, or any other houses whatsoever." The property element was uppermost in the minds of the burgesses rather than the protection of the habitation. Virginia adopted this law because "divers wicked and evil disposed persons, intending the ruin and impoverishing his majesty's good subjects" had resorted to burnings.[44]

South Carolina's first statute on fires was that of 1690. Among the crimes listed was the "burning of houses." This was repeated in 1712. By 1740 it was added that any person of color who burned "any stack of rice, corn or other grain, of the product, growth or manufacture of this Province" or who burned "any tar kiln, barrels of tar, turpentine or rosin, or any other the [sic] goods or commodities of the growth, produce or manufacture of this Province," would be executed without benefit of clergy.[45] These statutes concerned economic crimes. The common law against the burning of dwellings was supplemented by these laws, which did not use the word *arson*.

Stampp's claim that arson "was the most common slave 'crime'" after theft has force if we view the use of fire as protest or resistance against slavery, or even as simply an act of revenge by an individual slave. We intuitively would expect to find a fair number of cases, especially if we also accept Hindus's argument that despite the difficulties of conviction without witnesses to this "anonymous" crime, whites brought slaves to trial because of fear and the seriousness of the offense. What is surprising is the paucity of trials for arson or burnings of any kind in some jurisdictions. In the sample of Virginia counties for the colonial period, for instance, I found only one true case of burning. After his trial in Caroline County in 1743, Phill was hanged for burning a tobacco house, a corn house, and a "dary." Earlier, in 1729, the owner of a slave in Princess Anne County was ordered to guarantee his good behavior or else transport him out of the colony on the complaint of two men that the slave had "threatened to burn the house of ye said John & other injuries" and had behaved in an "impudent & churlish manner."[46]

The number of cases in Maryland is much higher. In 1751 Jenny and Grace, two slaves of Joseph Galloway, were executed for burning his tobacco house. The *Gazette* mentioned the acquittal of a black tried for barn burning "on a strong Suspicion."[47] In 1762 Abram was sentenced to death, but pardoned, for attempting to burn a kitchen. The next year, in Talbot County, Tim was found not guilty of setting fire to a thatched house containing Indian corn. Also in 1763 Adam was sentenced to death for "advising consulting and attempting" to burn his master's storehouse. This, however, was not simply an arson case, as he was also found guilty of "advising and Consulting to Murder his Master." Finally, in 1766 Beck was executed for burning her master's tobacco house.[48]

One of the most dramatic cases of arson in the colonial South was tried in Charleston in 1741. Originally Kate was indicted for setting a fire with an intent to burn the whole city to the ground. But as she faced execution, she implicated Boatswain, who, the evidence showed, had an abiding hatred of whites. He was certainly out to do more than simply burn a stack of grain or even the Big House of a plantation. Boatswain was a victim of the *lex talionis* of early English law. He was burned to death even though neither the statutes of South Carolina nor the law of England expressly required this sentence for arson.[49]

The rules of law, as well as the actual experience with the trials of slaves for arson, changed after the Revolution. One of the most common changes was the expansion of the places covered in laws on burnings. In 1789 Virginia made it a felony without benefit of clergy to engage in common law arson and the willful burning of a courthouse, a county jail or public prison, or an office of a clerk of a court. In 1798 the slave Claiborne was executed in Petersburg for setting fire to the county jail. His case, however, is complex. In 1797 and 1798 he had been held in the jail on two separate occasions under indictments for burglary. In 1819 Virginia mandated death for anyone guilty of arson, as well as death for slaves who were accessories. It was death for anyone who was guilty of burning any house in a town and death for slaves convicted of burning barns, stables, and so on. It was also a capital offense if a slave burned wheat, barley, oats, and so forth.[50]

By 1860 South Carolina's law had also been revised, but not without complaint. When he drafted a code for the state James L. Petigru included two sections under arson. Both were capital crimes. One was traditional arson, and the other, which had been added by statute in 1860, was the "wilful and malicious burning of any state-house, court house, or church." Petigru was unhappy with the addition. In a lengthy footnote he argued that the new law was "defective in the disregard of natural distinctions." Common law arson, the "burning of a dwelling-house in the nighttime," was a crime of "great enormity, being perpetrated against the defence-less in the hours of sleep." He did not mention that arson, according to Hawkins, could be committed in the daytime as well. And he did not comment on the fact that arson included burning a barn or stable containing grain or corn. Nonethe-less, arson, as he saw it, was marked by the aggravation that it endangered life.[51]

Legislators were less careful. In Alabama, for instance, death was provided for slaves guilty of "arson," which occurred if a slave burned "any dwelling house, or out house appurtenant thereto, store house, office, banking house, ware house, or other edifice, public or private, corn crib, gin house, cotton house, stable, barn, cotton in the heap to the value of one hundred dollars, or in bale to any value, or any ship or steam boat." The notion of a burning as a crime against the habitation was obliterated. Texans tried to be precise, influenced as they were by the civil law tradition and the notion in Napoleonic code making—define, define. They used the word "arson," which was defined as the burning of any house, which in turn was defined as "any building, edifice, or structure, enclosed with walls and covered." Tennessee provided death for "arson," which it left undefined. Juries were given discretion to sentence short of life or limb in the following cases: if a slave set fire to or attempted "to burn any barn, stable, crib, out-house, gin-house, manufacturing establishment, bridge, steamboat, or lighter; or any valuable building, or any building containing valuable property therein; or any stack of grain, fodder, straw or hay; or any water craft." Tennessee treated arson in the traditional Blackstonian sense as different from other burnings. Missouri's law was the most complex and modern. Like burglary, it established precise degrees. There were four degrees, with different punishments attached.[52]

Burnings Trials

The pattern of trials and convictions under these various schemes is tangled. In the sample counties examined for Missouri, Texas, Arkansas, and Delaware there were no cases of arson or burnings. Trials occurred, but convictions were difficult to obtain in Mississippi, Alabama, Kentucky, Florida, Tennessee, and Louisiana. One conviction was won in St. Landry Parish, Louisiana, where Patrick Woods sold his slave Mary to the state in 1838 for half her value after she was found guilty of attempting to burn a house. She was sentenced to life in prison.[53] In all, there was only one clear conviction in this set of states, and it did not result in the death penalty. In the other states the trials either ended in acquittal or the disposition is unknown.

Experience in the remaining states and within given jurisdictions diverged. There were differences, for instance, between the trials in the rural and urban communities of Virginia. In Petersburg, from 1784 to 1840, thirteen indictments were brought against slaves for arson or other burnings, but only two slaves were convicted.[54] In 1793 Dennis and Isaac were indicted for setting fire to a lumber house. Dennis was acquitted, but Isaac was found guilty of an attempt to burn. He was lashed thirty-nine times and jailed until his master either entered into a bond to guarantee his good behavior for life or transported him out of Virginia. The second conviction was that of Claiborne in 1798.[55] The remaining twelve cases all ended in not guilty verdicts. Temporally, there were two cases in the 1790s, three between 1800 and 1810, one in the teens, four in the 1820s, and two in the 1830s. The only convictions came in the 1790s. The objects burned were a lumber house, the jail, a coach maker's shop, a dwelling, a store (this was also a robbery case), a house near an old shed, the home of the person to whom the slave was hired out, a smokehouse, a house used as a tobacco factory, and a tobacco factory. In the remaining cases the charge was simply arson, without specifying what was burned.

Of the six cases in Richmond, three were in 1858. The 1858 case against Frank and George charged them with burning a tobacco factory valued at $15,000 and with breaking and entering the tobacco factory. They were found guilty only on the second count and received thirty-nine lashes. The same year Victoria was discharged on an indictment for stealing and attempted arson of a building. The only exception to this pattern was in the third case from 1858—that of Lewis, who was hanged for burning a dwelling in the city. This was common law arson.[56] The indictments in both Petersburg and Richmond were for more than simple arson— they were for stealing, or robbery, or breaking and entering, as well as for the use of fire.[57] These were instances of arson used to cover another offense rather than an outburst at enslavement or resistance to the system of oppression per se.

Outside Virginia's major urban centers the story is different. In Caroline County, for instance, Andrew and Malina were hanged in 1861, Andrew for burn- ing the master's dwelling and Malina for setting fire to his barn, stable, corn house, and tobacco house. These slaves were clearly out to destroy everything their owner possessed, except presumably themselves. In Sussex County Lewis and Caesar were discharged on an indictment in 1801 for burning a house when no evidence was produced against them. The same did not happen in Fed's case in Charles City County in 1833. Although he was not convicted of arson, the court remained deeply suspicious, so much so that it "doth recommend to the owner of the said Fed or the person who has charge or management of him to sell him forthwith."[58] Among the things to note about these cases is the high proportion that included two defendants and the fact that none contained charges other than for straight burning or arson. The same conclusions can be drawn from the records of Lunen- burg, Orange, and King George Counties.[59]

Burnings in the cities of Virginia differed from those in the countryside. Because the overwhelming majority of these cases ended in not guilty judgments, it is feckless to conclude that slaves burned this or that with a particular motive in mind. What the records show is the perceptions whites had of slaves and the ways they would employ the law to deal with the perceived use of fire. Arson was always difficult to establish, but the willingness of whites to acquit slaves of this horrifying offense is remarkable. After the turn of the century the overwhelming majority of convicted slaves were never executed, and in fact most were found not guilty.

Perhaps one of the more intriguing legal issues concerned intention. An exam- ple of the problem is Mary's case in 1819 in Prince William County, Virginia. She was transported because she was not really moved by malice and was not "fully sensible" of the enormity of her crime. Because malice was an essential ingredient of arson, it is a wonder that she was convicted at all. The issue of malice also came up in one of the only arson cases to reach the appellate level, aside from those that also involved other issues such as confession. In *Jesse, (a slave), v. State* (Mis- sissippi, 1854) the court reversed the conviction and sent the case back because the charge against the slave had not included the claim that the offense was done with malice, and the 1822 state statute "does not dispense with the averment of mal- ice."[60] There were more arson or burning cases in Maryland, the Carolinas, and Georgia than outside the eastern seaboard slave communities.[61]

The story in Georgia is different again. In 1819 Rodney was hanged for burning his master's ginhouse with cotton inside. In 1821 Susan was acquitted of burning her master's home in Savannah, whereas three years later Molly was hanged on a similar charge. The oddest case was that of Adeline, who was found guilty of arson for burning a dwelling in 1849. Under the state code this was a capital offense, but her sentence was fifty lashes for three consecutive days, and then she was to be branded with an *H* on her right cheek and a *B* on her left, doubtless for "house burner."[62] The Georgia experience comes closer to what we would intuitively expect—a high conviction rate and arson associated with the property of masters, especially their dwellings.

There were a larger number of indictments and a very high number of acquittals in North Carolina. The most striking thing about the record there is that a disproportionate number of the cases came from one county, New Hanover. The experience of masters and slaves in any given locale was different from that of slaves in another, even within the same state or region. Too often we lose sight of the fact that localism is as important as regionalism in the study of the law of slavery. The experience of masters and slaves with crime—as with much else—differed, for instance, between Texas and South Carolina and Virginia, but it also differed between Lowndes and Wilkinson Counties in Mississippi. In any event, the one North Carolina lower court that pronounced a guilty verdict was that of New Hanover in 1843. Sandy and John were indicted for arson, and Sandy alone was convicted.[63]

The final state, South Carolina, produced some interesting findings. Hindus identified twenty-six cases of arson in Spartanburg and Anderson Districts between 1818 and 1860. This amounted to 2.5 percent of all crimes and made arson the tenth most frequent offense. The number is higher than elsewhere in the South.[64] Only one of the cases in Anderson District led to an execution. Jane was hanged in 1863 after she confessed to burning a dwelling. Five cases ended in acquittal. Finally, there was the case of John in 1855. He was charged with the burning of a carriage house, workshop, and adjacent dwelling. The magistrate-freeholders recorded that "while many *strongly suspicious circumstances*, arise in our minds against the Prisoner, yet, the nature of the *Evidence*, does not authorise us, to found a verdict of Guilty."[65]

The pattern in Spartanburg is not the same. Of the seven cases there, all involved only one defendant, and three ended in acquittal. In 1855 Adam was sold out of state for burning a carriage workshop, and in 1860 Alfred was hanged for burning a dwelling. Miles was executed in 1864, but he was found guilty of the murder of his master as well as arson. Finally, on April 28, 1865, George was acquitted of robbery and arson.[66]

One thing that is clear from this record is that, except for the punishments provided, the statutory changes made within these categories of property crimes were less because of an effort to accommodate the common law rules to a slave society than they were to accommodate the growth of capitalism. A clear exception is the Alabama and Mississippi burglary statutes, which required that a white person be present before a home could be a "dwelling" at law. Many of the statutory changes would have occurred even in the absence of slavery. During the eighteenth century some of the statutes do show a particular concern with the criminality of slaves, but some also reveal a concern with the criminality of lower-class people in general, "divers wicked" people. Lower-class people, regardless of status, would be punished severely if they tried to control the distribution of goods by stealing, for instance.

But what does the actual experience with the enforcement of these laws against thefts, burglary, and burnings show regarding the treatment of slaves? Was there any serious effort to obtain "justice"? Were the crimes charged examples of an attempt to claim the profits of slavery? Were they acts of accommodation or resistance to slavery? Were they efforts to establish a "moral economy," or is it as fruitful to see them in terms of the notion that criminal law is a marginal element in a legal order? One thing we should not lose sight of is the fact that many of these offenses were handled by the "complementary system of plantation justice" rather than in a public forum. But insofar as the public law was concerned, the answers to the above questions depend on whether the questions are addressed from the viewpoint of the slaves, or of the masters, or of whites generally. From the latter two perspectives, the most probable response would be that slaves who were charged with violating the norms of any civilized society, especially one based on a regard for property rights, were treated justly. From the viewpoint of the slaves, of course, the answers would be different. As Douglass had finally resolved, the "morality of free society could have no application to slave society."

16

Police Regulations

An Act for the Better Ordering of Slaves
South Carolina, *Statutes at Large* (1690)

A central objective of the slave codes was the control of labor to work the plantations, farms, mines, factories, and railroads of the South. The codes supplemented (and limited) the controls of slaveowners. To that end lawmakers adopted patrol laws and laws that restricted or denied to slaves all of the rights Blackstone considered the basic rights of people secured by English law—the "right of personal security, the right of personal liberty; and the right of private property." The first of these was discussed in Chapter 8. Blackstone defined the right of personal liberty as "removing one's person to whatsoever place one's own inclination may direct; without imprisonment or restraint, unless by due course of law." This right was denied to slaves, for, as Cobb noted, "the right of personal liberty in the slave is utterly inconsistent with the idea of slavery, and whenever the slave acquires this right, his condition is *ipso facto* changed."[1] This right was restrained by pass laws, laws requiring the presence of whites on plantations or at gatherings of slaves, laws on slaves who were allowed to go at large as though they were free or hiring themselves out, laws on unlawful assemblies, and laws on slave runaways.

The last of the "absolute" rights of man was the ownership of property.[2] Abolitionists and proslavery writers agreed that slaves had no right to property. Stroud observed that "whatever property they may acquire belongs, in point of law, to their masters." He had a crucial qualification. This "harsh doctrine" could be affirmed only for "*negro* slavery." In the ancient world slaves "were permitted to acquire and enjoy property of considerable value, as their own." The same was true in the Spanish and Portuguese colonies. It was even true, to some extent, in the British West Indies—at least as a practical matter. Cobb agreed as to the *law* in the South, but he disagreed as to the *practice*: "though our law allows of no *peculium* to the slave, yet, as a matter of fact, such *peculium* is permitted, *ex gratia*, by the master." The right to possess or own property was covered by laws on trading with slaves and laws directly concerning the ownership of property. All of these features of the slave codes are obvious enough, and all have been cited by scholars. A fine summary is that of Stampp.[3] However, even this summary conceals tensions, inconsistencies, and variations within the codes. A crucial fact was that the restraints and denials of rights grew or changed over time. Above all, the law often *required* owners to *use* their property in certain prescribed ways: they could not do whatever they wished with their slaves. To that extent they had no absolute right of property—the law intruded on their prerogatives. References by Southerners to "absolute" property, then, ought to be read with skepticism.

Restraints on Personal Liberty

Cobb claimed that slaves enjoyed a "*quasi* personal liberty." The "long hours of the night, the Sabbath day, and the various holidays" were among the times when this "right" was enjoyed. At these times "it cannot be expected that the watchful eye of the master can follow them." This led to the creation of the "policemen or patrol." But, in Cobb's view, "to restrain the slave altogether from leaving his master's premises, during the time that he is not employed in his master's business, would be unnecessarily harsh towards that dependent class." Therefore, masters could grant their slaves permission to be off the plantations for various purposes. The legal evidence was a pass of some sort.[4]

The first statute requiring slaves to possess passes was a Virginia law (1680). A single magistrate could order twenty lashes inflicted on a slave who was off "his masters ground without a certificate from his master, mistris or overseer." Although there were no sanctions on owners, the pass laws were an early indication that masters had duties to control slaves in the interest of society at large. The pass requirement appeared in "an act for preventing Negroes Insurrections." There was a similar link in the South Carolina pass law of 1740. Anyone could apprehend slaves off their plantation without a "letter from their master, or a ticket" or without a white person with them. The slaves could be whipped. The Louisiana law of 1806 stated that the pass law was needed "in order to keep slaves in good order and due submission."[5] In time all slave jurisdictions adopted a pass law of one sort or another.[6] The pass laws had multiple purposes. One was to confine the labor of the slaves to the plantations and to keep them in "due submission." At the same time, the pass laws allowed slaves a condition of "*quasi* personal liberty."

Another form of restraint on an owner's discretion were laws that required masters to keep whites on plantations when there were over a certain number of slaves resident. These laws were confined to the Deep South. The first was that of South Carolina (1740), which authorized fines against masters who failed to keep a white on "plantations settled with slaves." No precise number of slaves was mentioned, but the reason for the law was to prevent such plantations from becoming "harbours for runaways and fugitive slaves." Florida's patrol law of 1846 was similar. It required the owner of "any settled plantation" who did not keep a white on the land had to pay a fine for every "working slave." Most of the laws specified the number of slaves involved, and after 1800 South Carolina's did so as well (the number was "ten workers"). The white had to be capable of performing patrol duty. These laws may have been self-enforcing, for actions against slaveowners were rare. There were a few in Adams and Lowndes Counties, Mississippi, and Lowndes County, Alabama. The Alabama cases were all during the Civil War. In 1863 Francis A. Turner pleaded guilty to a charge of failing to keep an overseer on his land and was fined $100. In contrast, the Mississippi cases date from 1851 to 1860. During that decade there were three actions in the two counties.[7]

A serious problem was created by owners who allowed slaves to hire themselves out as though they were free. An example of a self-hire is Harriet Tubman, one of the most courageous of slaves. When interviewed in 1863, she said that "She once 'hired her time,' and employed it in rudest farming labors, ploughing, carting, driving the oxen, ec., to so good advantage that she was able in one year to buy a pair of steers worth forty dollars."[8] Such a relaxed relationship undermined the subordination of slaves to masters. Owners *had* to exercise some control, claim some rights, impose some discipline.

Statutory consideration of the issue came late. A notable exception was South Carolina, which considered it as early as 1712. Masters would be fined unless they kept the "whole of what the slave shall earn" and maintained the slave's "care and direction," or unless they expressly gave such authority to someone to whom the slave was hired. The difficulty was that some masters permitted "their said slaves to do what and go whither they will, and work where they please" on condition that they brought the master an agreed-upon sum. This encouraged theft and subsidized "drunkenness and other evil courses" among the slaves.[9]

North Carolina used a different sanction after 1777. Slaves allowed to hire themselves out would be apprehended by a magistrate or a freeholder (but not a free white or person of color who was not a freeholder) and kept up to twenty days at hard labor. After 1794 owners would be fined and the slave hired out for one year with the benefit of his or her labor to go to the poor. After 1831 masters were subject to a fine of up to $100 if they allowed a slave "to go at large as a free man, exercising his or her own discretion in the employment of his or her time" or to "keep house to him or herself as a free person."[10]

By a law of 1782 Virginia provided that slaves permitted to go at large as free or to hire themselves out would be seized and sold. A similar approach was used in 1822 in South Carolina, which held it "unlawful to hire to male slaves their own time" subject to seizure and forfeiture. Nothing, inexplicably, was said about female slaves.[11] A number of states fined owners, and some provided that the slave would be seized and sold if the fine was not paid.[12]

The overwhelming majority of cases that arose under these laws date from the years after 1840.[13] The exceptions come from Virginia and North Carolina. For instance, a number of cases brought in 1809 in Fauquier County, Virginia, involved slaves who had been allowed to go at large, and in 1798 in Petersburg's Hustings Court a slave was ordered sold for moving about the community as a free man and operating a tavern.[14]

Pass laws, laws requiring overseers in certain instances, and laws prohibiting slaves to hire themselves out or to go at large all placed responsibilities on masters to keep their slaves under control. They were statutory intrusions into a master's authority that arose from his or her claim of property rights and governance.

Runaways

One of the most frequent threats to the notion of the person as a thing, of course, was the slave runaway. As Peter Wood noted, "no single act of self-assertion was more significant among slaves or more disconcerting among whites than that of running away." Runaways were violating an alleged duty or obligation owed to their masters. They were also potential insurrectionaries, and by the time the Northern states began to abolish slavery they were a potential source of volatile sectional conflict.[15]

Chief Justice Roger Taney, in his concurring opinion in *Prigg v. Pennsylvania* (U.S. Supreme Court, 1842), suggested that every state in the Union had a constitutional duty to follow the course of the South.[16] A constant throughout the history of Southern slavery was that lawmakers deferred to the right of masters to punish runaways however they thought fit. For most runaways the *law* was the whim of their masters. The range of punishments meted out by masters varied with their personalities and imagination. In 1740 William Byrd II gave three of his slaves "a vomit for going off the plantation and staying all night, which did more good than whipping." Bennett Barrow, in nineteenth-century Louisiana, varied his responses from humiliating the slave in front of the other slaves to whippings.[17]

Newspapers from the eighteenth century onward were filled with advertisements for runaways.[18] Some contained more than simple descriptions of the slave, offers of rewards, or threats of prosecution against those who harbored the slave. In 1745, for instance, James MacKelvey of St. John's Parish, South Carolina, wrote that "Toney is an obstreperous sawcey Fellow, and if he should be kill'd in taking, I am wiling to allow any Man that will bring me his Head Ten Pounds." One of the most resolute runaways was General. His master, Landon Carter, advertised for him in December 1784. General was "remarkable as a runaway [*sic*] having lost both his legs, cut off near the knees." Carter's self-proclaimed paternalism stopped short of mercy in General's case. He offered five dollars above what the law allowed "provided the taker up do chastise him before he brings him home; and his ingratitude, and want of pretence to leave me, forces me to enjoin severity in the chastisement."[19]

Two scholars, Peter Wood and Schwarz, have suggested that runaways committed theft: they stole themselves. Wood wrote that "in a society where slaves were defined as property and where blacks were becoming artful in appropriating things they were denied, these were the people who, in a real sense, elected to 'steal themselves.' " Wood's image is striking but misleading if it is taken as a statement of the way Southern whites considered runaways as a *legal* problem. Wood did not say that Southern lawmakers saw it that way, he merely said in a "real sense."

Schwarz carried the image to the next step. Running away was a "prevalent and powerful form of slave resistance. It was, according to the law, also another form of theft."[20]

Sometimes runaways were linked with the law of theft, but not quite that way. The law applied to persons who aided or enticed slaves to run, rather than to the actual act of running itself. According to the Mississippi law of 1857, "any person who shall counsel, advise, aid, assist or procure . . . any slave to runaway, with a view to the emancipation of such slave, shall, if such slave shall actually escape from his master, whether he be retaken or not, be guilty of slave stealing." Or consider the case of John Johnson, an inmate of the Missouri State Penitentiary. He was an "African negro" who in 1861 had been sentenced to serve five years for "Grand Larceny ('assisting Slaves to Escape')."[21] However, no statute ever defined running away itself as an act of theft so that if it were to be considered that way, it would have to come under the common law of thefts. The conceptual problem was the intention of the act. The relevant technical phrases are *animo furandi* and *lucri causa.*[22] The first meant that the act was done with the intention of stealing and the second that it was done for profit. Runaways acted not to "steal" themselves. Rather, they acted on an intention to transform their position from property to persons—or perhaps with a lesser motive such as to escape a whipping, to get some rest, or to reunite with a spouse. It would be a stretch to describe such acts as theft at common law. It was defiance but not theft. Slaves were punished for disobedience, not stealing themselves.

During the eighteenth century whites turned to an expanded use of patrols to control slaves and to capture runaways. The Virginia law of 1691 was a precursor of the more formal patrol laws of the later years. It was an act for "suppressing outlying Slaves." Two justices of the peace were authorized to order the sheriff to apprehend them, and the sheriff was authorized to raise what force he thought necessary to do the job. Apprehension was one thing, but punishment *at law* was another. It was not until 1705 that Virginians considered this, and when they did their commitment to maintain their control of a dependent labor force tore large holes in the mask of paternalism. Edmund Morgan was correct when he said that they were prepared to maim slaves in order to get them to work on the plantations of the colony.[23]

Two other colonial assemblies believed that it was justified in providing for the maiming of runaways under some circumstances. In Maryland, under the law of 1751, runaways could be ordered to be whipped, cropped, or branded in the cheek with the letter *R* "or otherwise, not extending to life, or to render such slave unfit for labour." This would be done on application to the justices of the county court by the master or the party injured by the slave.[24]

The South Carolina law of 1712 was unique. It imposed a duty on masters to punish, and in lieu of that it provided for a progressive range of savage punishments. This law also stipulated that anyone could stop a slave and ask to examine his or her lawful ticket to be off a plantation; for the "security" of people who tried to apprehend runaways or examine passes, it was lawful "for any white person to beat, maim or assault," or to kill if necessary. By the law of 1722 the grim list of specific maimings was gone, as was the lawful duty of a master to inflict them. What replaced it was a provision for the death penalty for any slave who ran away "with intent to go off from this Province, in order to deprive his master or mistress of his service." By 1740 any white could "moderately correct" a slave off his plantation who refused to be questioned.[25]

The preambles to the South Carolina laws suggest that South Carolinians held somewhat different views of their peculiar institution at different periods, and this led to different treatment for runaways. The preamble to the brutal 1712 law, for instance, read as follows:

> Whereas, the plantations and estates of this Province cannot be well and sufficiently brought into use, without the labor and service of negroes and other slaves; and forasmuch as the said negroes and other slaves brought unto the people of this Province for that purpose, are of barbarous, wild, savage natures, and such as renders them wholly unqualified to be governed by the laws, customs, and practices of this province; but that it is absolutely necessary, that such other constitutions, laws and orders, should . . . be made . . . for the good regulating and ordering of them, as may restrain the disorders, rapines and inhumanity, to which they are naturally prone and inclined.[26]

In the preamble to their 1740 statute South Carolina lawmakers expressed a slightly more humane perception:

> Whereas, in his Majesty's plantations in America, slavery has been introduced and allowed, and the people commonly called negroes, Indians, mulattoes and mustizoes, have been deemed absolute slaves, and the subjects of property in the hands of particular persons, the extent of whose power over such slaves ought to be settled and limited by positive laws, so that the slave may be kept in due subjection and obedience, and the owners and other persons having the care and government of slaves may be restrained from exercising too great rigour and cruelty over them. . . . We pray your most sacred majesty that it may be enacted . . .[27]

Except for the Maryland code of 1751, then, the maiming of runaway slaves by law had ended. This is not to say that slaves were not maimed, savagely whipped, and branded for running away after midcentury. Rather, deference to masters instead of resort to law became the norm. Maiming and branding continued in the eighteenth century and less so in the nineteenth, as the descriptions of runaways in newspaper advertisements show.[28] Law, however, played a different role.

What remained were statutes that provided legal support for the recovery of runaways. Most of these laws allowed little or no punishment at the hands of authorities for the slaves recaptured. "Few slaves," Stanley Campbell wrote, "actually ran away—not because they were satisfied with their plight, but because they feared the severity of the laws designed to curtail their flight and of their punishments."[29] Insofar as law is concerned, this would hold true before the middle of the eighteenth century, but it is doubtful after that.

Lawmakers offered some aid in the recovery of runaways early on, and by the nineteenth century a common statute provided that a person who apprehended a slave would deliver him to a justice of the peace. The slave would be jailed. If the owner was known, he could go and claim the slave, or the slave might be sent to him after he paid a reward to the individual who made the capture and the relevant fees. If the owner was unknown, the slave would be advertised in the local newspapers. If no one claimed him or her after a specified period of time, the slave would be sold. Some statutes provided that slaves could be hired out until they were claimed. In the nineteenth-century laws there was rarely any reference to a punishment other than the jailing of the runaway.[30]

These laws were reasonably useful to slaveowners. One example would be a series of cases involving runaway slaves in the magistrate-freeholders' trial records for Anderson District, South Carolina. There are records for thirteen cases between 1819 and 1848.[31] Some of them contain the oath of the man who caught the slave, a description of the slave, and the name of the owner. If the time the slave was committed to jail is recorded, it was relatively short—about a month. Only a few records contain anything about the claimant, and none suggest any punishment inflicted by the jailer.[32]

One barrier to the effective operation of these laws was presented by those who sheltered runaways. All slave jurisdictions provided punishment for harboring slaves: slaves were whipped, and free persons received fines and/or were imprisoned. Sometimes the number of lashes would be specified.[33] Only the law of Texas defined the offense of "harboring." It was the "act of maintaining and concealing a runaway slave; the person so harboring having knowledge of the fact the slave is a runaway." Judge Benning of the Georgia Supreme Court, in *Cook v. State* (1858), wrote that the offense of harboring a slave "was, in grade, one of no great enormity."[34] Harboring presented no great danger to the social order, but it was nettling.

Those most likely to actually conceal a runaway slave would be other slaves. Such conduct rarely led to formal trials. There is a set of such cases from Anderson District. Whether this set was typical of the rest of the South is impossible to tell, but it is instructive. The cases reveal, however dimly, one side of life in slave communities. For one thing, the majority of the cases in Anderson District involved more than one defendant. In one case in 1854, for instance, there were nine defendants. Four were found not guilty, and one who was convicted had her whipping remitted because of "extreme age." One slave woman who pleaded guilty stated that Bob came to her and said Alfred, a fugitive from Alabama, was "near and [he] wished to make arrangements for Alfred to be concealed." He had been staying at Bob's, but as the "hunters being in pursuit" he had to move. The sentences for those who aided Alfred ranged from twenty to forty lashes.[35] One might contrast this record with those from the general sessions court in Fairfield District, where whites were tried. The extant records cover the years 1825–29, 1840–63, and 1863–68. Only one case was presented to the grand jury involving the harboring of a slave (it was in April 1829), and the grand jury returned a no bill.[36]

Related to harboring slaves were offenses such as enticing them to run away and helping them to escape. But these were not simple crimes, and the offense of "slave stealing" added a further complication. By the last few years before the Civil War these violations were often lumped together. One crime that Southerners transformed by statute was "inveigling" or "enticing" slaves to leave their masters. The conduct that could lead to such a charge was wide-ranging. In some cases slaves were enticed to flee with promises of freedom. In 1853, for instance, Morgan Granet was found guilty in Adams County, Mississippi, of counseling a slave to run away and go to a free state. This was very different from the conduct of John S. Sullivan, in Catahoula Parish, Louisiana, who in 1849 enticed the slaves of St. John R. Liddell to work for him transporting lumber after midnight without Liddell's knowledge.[37] The motives behind efforts to persuade slaves to leave masters ranged from the benevolent to the venal.

By the mid-eighteenth century inveiglement of a servant to leave a master was not considered a crime at common law. It did give rise to a special action on the case. Inveigling was "an ungentlemanlike, so it is also an illegal act" in that it induced a breach of contract.[38] But it was not a crime. Earlier Southern lawmakers, however, had begun to view inveiglement as a public offense as well. According to a South Carolina law of 1712, for instance, "evil and ill-disposed persons" attempted to steal slaves by the "specious pretence of promising them freedom in another county." Something more was involved than ungentlemanly behavior. The law provided that anyone guilty of tempting or persuading a slave to leave his master's service with an intent to take him out of the province, regardless of the ultimate motive, would forfeit 25 pounds to the master. If the person was unable to pay the sum, he would become a servant to the slaveowner for up to five years. In 1722 this was dropped and a whipping was substituted, but civil liability remained. However, if the slave was taken out of the province, the act became not inveigling but slave stealing, and that was punished with death.[39]

The actual line between inveigling and slave stealing was blurred in the colonial period. In Virginia, by a law of 1753, the punishment was death for anyone to "steal" a slave "out of, or from the possession of the owner or overseer of such slave." One year later South Carolina adopted a sweeping statute: "all and every person and persons, who shall inveigle, steal and carry away any negro or other slave or slaves, or shall hire, aid or counsel any person or persons to inveigle, steal or carry away . . . so as the owner or employer of such slave or slaves shall be deprived of the use and benefit of such slave or slaves, or that shall aid any such slave in running away or departing from his master's or employer's service was guilty of a felony without benefit of clergy."[40]

In colonial Maryland and North Carolina, on the other hand, the offense was treated in a mixed fashion. By its law of 1741 North Carolina provided a fine plus a forfeiture to the master to be recovered by an action of debt for anyone who did "tempt or perswade" or "give Encouragement to relieve, assist, harbour, or entertain, for any Space of Time whatsoever." If the intention was to help the slave get out of the province, the amount of money owed to the master was higher; if the slave was conveyed away, the defendant would be "condemned as guilty of Felony." By its law of 1751 Maryland stipulated that anyone who "shall entice and persuade" a slave to run away when the slave actually did so would be liable to the master for the full value of the slave. If unable to pay, the defendant would be imprisoned for one year.[41]

By the nineteenth century most states with inveigling or enticement statutes had transformed the offense from a civil to a criminal act. By its law of 1816 Georgia provided one year in prison and then sale as a slave for life for any free person of color guilty of "inveigling or enticing away" any slave with the intention of helping the slave to leave the service of an owner. In 1824 the provision for sale into slavery was deleted.[42] By midcentury the offense was treated as highly criminal in a number of states. In Mississippi and Kentucky, anyone who persuaded or enticed a slave to flee could receive a sentence ranging from two to twenty years in prison.[43] And if there were gaps in the laws, the courts stepped in, as occurred in Alabama in *Crosby v. Hawthorn* (1854). Crosby was brought into court for trying to persuade two slaves to leave Hawthorn's premises. The court held that "one who procures a slave to run away . . . by such means as beget and strengthen the slave's determination to do so . . . is guilty of aiding" a slave to run away. Otherwise, the door would be wide open for the "disaffecting of the slave population . . . by the vile and fanatical, with impunity, and would greatly depreciate the value, if not endanger the permanency of the institution itself."[44]

The peculiar problems of a slave society, one in which a large number of whites owned no slaves at all, and one that faced an increasingly hostile section of the same nation in which slavery did not exist, led to a major transformation in an old common law legal notion, inveigling. What was once only "ungentlemanly" was now highly criminal. Slaveowners were concerned with the relationships among poorer Southern whites and slaves, as well as with the attraction of the free states. Property interests of masters had to be secured, and the social relationship between the lower classes in the South had to be kept under firm control.

The perception that this required a harsh approach is evident from the fact that all over the South people, often whites, were indicted for assisting slaves to escape or for enticing them to do so. Nearly all of these cases, as one might expect, date from the last three decades before the Civil War when the issue of runaways became especially significant. One notable case in Maryland was one of the latest. It is striking because of the sentence. In January 1861 George Thomas was found guilty in Anne Arundel County of assisting a slave woman to run away. He was sentenced to be sold "out of state as a slave for the term of 15 years."[45]

The runaway slave was clearly a person who displayed self will and was thus a danger to the social order. And the whites who dealt with them were as well. A different form of self-assertion involved conduct that whites often came to regard as "unlawful assemblies," gatherings of slaves to worship God, to learn to read and write, or just to have a "frolic." The last gathering, if permitted by masters, was rarely viewed as a threat at all. It might be broken up by a patrol, especially if things got out of hand (too much drink and too much fighting, for example) or if the temper of whites was frayed by fears of an uprising. A principal means to control this was the patrol, and one of its duties was to break up unlawful assemblies of slaves.

Unlawful Assembly

Unlawful assembly was an offense usually related in the treatises to riots.[46] Like all legal categories, unlawful assembly was malleable. What was constant was that at least more than one person had to be involved. It had to be an assembly, and the purpose had to be unlawful.

Southern whites found a number of assemblages of slaves sufficiently threatening as to be unlawful—particular targets were get-togethers to learn to read and write and religious meetings. Another type of law made the gathering of slaves unlawful no matter what the purpose. An example is the Florida patrol law of 1846: "All assemblies and congregations of slaves, free negroes and mulattoes, consisting of four or more, met together in a confined or secret place, is hereby declared to be an unlawful meeting."[47] Seen from the standpoint of Hawkins, such laws become intelligible. He wrote:

> An unlawful assembly, according to the common opinion, is a disturbance of the peace by persons barely assembling together with an intention to do a thing which, if it were executed, would make them rioters, but neither actually executing it nor making a motion towards the execution of it. But this seems to be much too narrow a definition. For any meeting whatsoever, of great numbers of people, with such circumstances of terror as cannot but endanger the public peace and raise fears and jealousies among the king's subjects, seems properly to be called an unlawful assembly.[48]

Whereas other commentators tended to tie unlawful assembly to riots, this approach cut it loose to wander at will. In societies based on slavery, any assembly of slaves might arouse fear. But it was not always written into the law of unlawful assembly.

Some of the statutory considerations of unlawful assembly were narrower. The law of Mississippi provided that any assembly of slaves or free persons of color above five "at any place of public resort, or at any meeting-house or houses in the night, or at any school for teaching them reading or writing, either in the day time or night, under whatsoever pretext shall be deemed an unlawful assembly." Often a precise exception was carved out for biracial religious activities. The same Mississippi law, for instance, allowed masters to give written permission to slaves "for the purpose of religious worship, provided such worship be conducted by a regularly ordained or licensed white minister, or attended by at least two discreet and respectable white persons, appointed for that purpose by some regular church or religious society."[49]

South Carolina's catchall statutes of 1800 and 1803 led to one of the only appellate cases involving such laws. The law of 1800 forbade assemblies of slaves without whites or even with whites in a "confined or secret place of meeting." Patrols were authorized to break into such places and disperse the assembly. The same law prohibited meetings of slaves for "religious or mental instructions" at night. The law of 1803 modified this by prohibiting breaking into places where "members of any religious society are assembled, before 9 o'clock at night, provided a majority are white people." If the majority were blacks, no matter what the time of day the meeting could be broken up and lashes administered. In *Bell ads. Graham* (1818) the South Carolina judges overturned a verdict in favor of a member of the militia who had brought a malicious prosecution action against a Methodist class leader. The patrol had broken up a religious meeting at the Shady Grove Methodist Church and whipped a slave. The evidence did not show that there were more blacks than whites at the meeting. According to O'Neall, writing thirty years later, this case rested on the notion that a patrol did not have the right to break up a religious meeting in the daytime when whites were present, even if a majority of the congregation was black. O'Neall, a deeply religious man, was even more emphatic: the laws of 1800 and 1803 were "treated now, as dead letters. . . . They ought to be repealed. They operate as a reproach upon us in the mouths of our enemies, in that we do not afford our slaves that free worship of God, which he demands for all his people. They, if ever resorted to, are not for doing good, but to gratify hatred, malice, cruelty or tyranny."[50]

Reading and Writing

Although unlawful assembly laws were enforced, statutes that prohibited teaching slaves to read and write often were not. In a sardonic jab at his state's attitude toward teaching, Francis Lieber, a professor at the University of South Carolina, wrote: "there are now schools for Cretins and Idiots in France, Germany etc. S.C. prohibits reading to negros."[51] Indeed it did, as early as 1740. What is surprising perhaps is that a number of Southern states never did legislate against slave literacy, a point admitted by Stroud. In fact, about half of the slave states did not prohibit teaching slaves to read and write, whereas states like South Carolina, Louisiana, and Georgia did.[52] Virginia's law of 1849 deemed any gathering of blacks for the purpose of instruction an unlawful assembly: the blacks were to be whipped and any whites involved fined and jailed.[53]

The North Carolina act of 1830 explained why such laws were adopted: it was because the "teaching of slaves to read and write, has a tendency to excite dissatisfaction in their minds, and to produce insurrection and rebellion to the manifest injury of the citizens of this State."[54] Occasionally, however, countervailing values surfaced in arguments against such laws or for their repeal. A strong effort was made in Civil War Georgia to modify the law,[55] and in 1848 O'Neall articulated an argument against such laws:

> This Act [1834] grew out of a feverish state of excitement produced by the *impudent* meddling of persons out of the slave States with their peculiar institutions. That has, however, subsided, and I trust we are now prepared to act the part of wise, humane and fearless masters, and that this law, and all of kindred character, will be repealed. When we reflect, *as Christians, how can we justify it, that a slave is not permitted to read the Bible?* It is in vain to say there is danger in it. The best slaves in the State, are those who can and do read the Scriptures. Again, who is it that teach your slaves to read? It generally is done by the children of the owners. Who would tolerate an indictment against his son or daughter for teaching a favorite slave to read? *Such laws look to me as rather cowardly.* It seems as if we were afraid of our slaves. Such a feeling is unworthy of a Carolina master.[56]

The fact that the overwhelming majority of slaves remained illiterate was just as likely the result of the indifference of whites toward teaching slaves to read and write combined with the exhaustion or resignation of the slaves as of the laws against teaching. This is one of those cases where the law was more symbolic than significant. The law was much more important in controlling slaves' movements than their minds.

The Right of Property

There are various ways to view the question of whether slaves owned property in the South. One of those has been to compare the legal situation there with that under Roman law. In Louisiana slaves were allowed the *peculium*. It appears, for example, as article 174 of the civil code of 1838: "all that a slave possesses belongs to his master; he possesses nothing of his own except his *peculium*, that is to say, the sum of money or moveable estate which his master chooses he should possess."[57]

Some conclude that the *peculium* was the personal property allowed to a slave by a master. We need to be more precise. W. W. Buckland, the early authority on Roman slave law, defined a *peculium* as follows: it "was a fund which masters allowed slaves to hold and, within limits, to deal with as owners. It was distinct from the master's ordinary property—the *patrimonium*, and though in law the property of the master, it is constantly spoken of as, *de facto*, the property of the slave." Such property could be very valuable; it could even include other slaves. Even though the concept of the *peculium* existed in Louisiana law, no one ever argued there that a slave could own a slave. One of the limits under Roman law on the rights a slave could have over the *peculium* concerned alienation. The power of disposition was restrained under Roman law. "The mere possession of a *peculium*," Buckland wrote, "did not in itself increase the slave's power of alienation: the *voluntas* [willingness or consent] of the *dominus* was still necessary." The consent, however, could be generous; it could give the slave the full power of disposition, "which did away with the need of special authorisation in each case."[58] Watson noted another restraint: "Technically, the peculium belonged to the slave's master, since a slave could own nothing. Nor indeed could the slave have lesser legal rights, such as possession. The legalist Papinian was the source of this notion: 'Those who are in another's power can hold property forming part of a *peculium*; but they cannot possess it, because possession is not only a matter of physical fact but also of law.' "[59] This is an important distinction. Slaves, even under Roman law, could have no *legal possession* of property. They could use property and even dispose of it, but only with the consent of their master. To the extent to which Southern slaveholders allowed slaves to accumulate and use property as a practical matter there seems little difference. But occasionally legislators placed restraints on the right of slaves to use or dispose of property, even with the consent of the master.

The earliest restraint was also the most obvious. A Virginia law of January 1639/40 stipulated that "all persons except negroes to be provided with arms and ammunition or be fined at the pleasure of the Governor and Council."[60] Virtually all colonies, and later states, had statutes that prohibited slaves from possessing weapons. Virtually all of them provided that the weapons could be seized and condemned, and often they provided that the slave could be whipped or the master fined. But the prohibition was rarely absolute. Owners might allow selected slaves to carry weapons to protect crops. Florida, beginning in 1828, permitted slaves to have firearms but only with a special license from the master, and then it was only good for one week and could only be used to kill game, birds, beasts of prey, "or for any other necessary and lawful purpose." If this law was violated, the slave would receive the usual thirty-nine lashes. Tennessee's code was another variation: "no slave shall have or carry a gun in any plantation where a crop is not tended; nor shall more than one slave carry or have a gun where a crop is not tended, nor after the crop is housed." Such laws rested on the requirement to accommodate the needs of masters while protecting society at large from the danger of violence at the hands of armed slaves. The problem, however, appears in the court records rarely. During 1856–57 two masters were fined for slaves bearing arms in Union County, Arkansas, but that is about the extent of it.[61]

Legislators sometimes put restraints on the possession of other forms of property by slaves. One of the earliest such limitations was in a Virginia law of 1692. The statute generally addressed capital crimes committed by slaves, but in it this appeared: "all horses, cattle and hoggs marked of any negro or other slaves marke, or by any slave kept" and not "converted by the owner of such slave to the use and marke of the said owner" would be forfeited to the use of the parish poor.[62] One notable thing about this law is that it seemed to acknowledge that property, in some fashion or other, could "belong" to a slave. What might be said of other "possessions" not mentioned, things like clothes, vegetables, fish, chickens, tools, wagons, or even money? Another crucial point is that the law *required* masters to exercise their authority over their slaves in certain ways.

In its 1740 code South Carolina provided for the forfeiture of any boat, perriaguer (pirogue) or canoe, or horses, mares, neat cattle, sheep, or hogs held for the use or benefit of the slave. This condition was included because "several owners of slaves" had allowed them these benefits, but this gave them the "opportunity of receiving and concealing stolen goods" and "to plot and confederate together, and form conspiracies dangerous to the peace and safety of the whole Province." The law, however, rested on the assumption that a slave could possess or own something with the consent of the master. By 1848 O'Neall summarized the law in South Carolina: "A slave may, by the consent of his master, acquire and hold *personal* property. All, thus acquired, is regarded in law as that of the master."[63]

Because most of these laws provided for seizure and forfeiture before a single justice of the peace, it is not possible to determine legal practice throughout the region. One exception is worth noting. In Maury County, Tennessee, a number of masters were fined in the circuit court. In 1845 five different men pleaded guilty and were fined on charges such as "suffering a slave to own a horse" or "suffering a slave to own property."[64] There were also cases in that county in 1846, 1848, 1849, and 1852.[65] In a seven-year period there were ten separate actions.

Perceptions of property "held," "possessed," "belonging to," or even "owned" by slaves were not as clear as we might suppose. This was obvious during the Civil War. In June 1863, for instance, Colonel Higginson testified before the American Freedmen's Inquiry Commission in Beaufort, South Carolina, that when slaves left plantations to follow Union troops, "they have an intense desire to take their property away with them. It is almost provoking to see the way in which they cling to their blankets, feather beds, chickens, pigs, and such like. But this is to be expected—these things represent the net result of all their labors up to this time." A much more legalistic view of slave property was taken by General Sherman, who, as commander of the Fifth Division of the Army of the Tennessee, wrote to a Captain Waterhouse in October 1862. Waterhouse had sent a party of soldiers to the home of a fugitive's owner to take clothes and other articles "belonging to a fugitive negress." Sherman upbraided him. "The Clothing & effects of a negro are the property of the master and mistress & whilst we admit the right of a negro to run away we must not sanction theft robbery or violence." He ordered the property returned to the master and concluded that "we must not encourage the negroes in their propensity to steal and be impudent." Presumably the "negress" would not have been guilty of stealing if she had run away naked.[66]

Philip Morgan, who studied the claims made by freedmen before the Southern Claims Commission after the war, has shown that the matter was complex. He found, for instance, that ex-slaves from Liberty County, Georgia, listed among their property losses such things as hogs, fowl, rice, corn, horses, cows, wagons, beehives, and a variety of foodstuffs. Slaves themselves often testified that the property was theirs and not their masters. Prince Wilson claimed that he was the "only one who has any legal right to the property." Henry Stephens said that he "never heard of a master's claiming property that belonged to his slaves." Joseph Bacon, on the other hand, did admit that "legally the property was his [master's] but a master who would take property from his slaves would have a hard time," and, he added, his had "never interfered with me and my property at all." This situation, however, may have been unique. As Morgan noted, the task system used in the low country of South Carolina and Georgia allowed slaves greater freedom to accumulate material effects than would have been possible under the gang system.[67]

Trading with Slaves

Notions about possessions could be less than clear, but then so could notions about law, as a revealing sexist story recorded by Mary Chesnut shows:

> John Chesnut is a pretty softhearted slave-owner. He had two negroes ar-
> rested for selling whiskey to his people on his plantation and buying stolen
> corn from them. The culprits in jail sent for him. He found them (this snowy
> weather) lying in the cold on a bare floor. And he thought that punishment
> enough, they having had weeks of it. But they were not satisfied to be allowed
> to evade justice and slip away. They begged him (and got it) for five dollars to
> buy shoes to run away in. I said, "Why, that is flat compounding a felony!"
> And Johnny put his hands in the armholes of his waistcoat and stalked
> majestically before me. "Woman, what do you know about law?"[68]

Normally, the law on trading with slaves was clear enough, but there were some ambiguities that John Chestnut would have appreciated. Implicitly they rested on the notion that slaves might have some lawful possession of property, even if it was not full ownership. They also rested on a class-based concern that lower-class whites should not be allowed to develop too close an association with slaves. Virginia's law of 1705 was the first to deal with the issue. It made it a criminal offense for anyone to buy, sell, or receive from any slave "any coin or commodity" without the consent of the master.[69] The assumption here was that the slave was trading in goods stolen from the master.

In 1737 the grand jury sitting in Charleston complained of the "practice of Negroes buying and selling Wares in the Streets of *Charlestown*, whereby stolen Goods may be concealed and afterwards vended undiscovered." Three years later slaves were prohibited from buying or selling or bartering in Charleston any goods whatsoever except fruit, fish, and garden stuff and then only with a license.[70] Throughout the colonial period, however, grand juries complained that the laws were not being enforced: slaves had obviously carved out an area of marginal economic activity in the city that could not be stopped. One grand jury, for instance, protested in 1770 about "a general SUPINENESS and INACTIVITY" on the part of magistrates in enforcing the "NEGRO ACTS" inasmuch as slaves were "being suffered to cook, bake, sell fruits, dry goods, and other ways traffic, barter, ec. in the public markets and streets of Charles-town." By the end of the century lawmakers stipulated heavy fines for those who traded with slaves without tickets, and by 1817 the penalty stood at a fine of up to $1,000 and up to one year in jail.[71]

Georgia focused its enforcement efforts on the slaves themselves. By 1824 they would receive thirty-nine lashes for selling any amount of cotton, tobacco, wheat, rye, oats, corn, rice, or poultry without a ticket. Most jurisdictions fined those dealing with slaves without the master's permission. Mississippi added that in all cases the burden of proof that the consent had been given, either in person or in writing, was on the defendant. Sometimes the goods being vended would be seized and sold at public auction. This was the case under an 1806 Louisiana law that prohibited, with one major exception, slaves from being involved in the exchange of any goods whatever. The exception was that persons who lived outside New Orleans could allow their slaves to sell or exchange the goods of the master.[72]

These laws were designed to prevent thefts by slaves. They also worked to assure that they remained economically marginal. Implicitly as well, they acknowledged that slaves might possess property and might dispose of it, at least by sale, trade, or barter. The lower court records are full of cases involving violations of these laws. Here is a point where lower-class whites were crossing the class and racial lines of Southern society in ways those above them found dangerous. From 1853 to 1860 four cases of unlawful trading or buying from slaves were brought against whites in Harrison County, Texas, and in West Feliciana Parish, Louisiana, a white was fined and jailed in 1856 for the unlawful purchase of corn from a slave. Possibly one of the most bizarre was a case brought against a slave woman in Jessamine County, Kentucky, in 1844. She was charged with selling liquor "for a proffit" without a license to keep a tavern. One can only wonder what would have happened had she applied for the license.[73]

The sale of liquor to slaves was a special variation on the theme of trading or dealing with slaves. What is odd at first blush is the fact that the laws, and the cases that involved this relationship, were quite late. Some slaveowners, such as Landon Carter, railed against their drunken slaves again and again,[74] but they did not turn to the law. By the nineteenth century, however, Southern whites showed a special concern for the unlawful sale of liquor to slaves. A bottle supplied by the owner over the Christmas holidays was one thing, but a besotted slave mingling with debased whites was something altogether different.

In 1819 Virginia required precisely the same penalty (four times the value of the commodity to be paid to the owner, plus a fine) for giving slaves liquor without the owners' consent as it did for unlawful trading in general. South Carolina adopted a vicious alternative: by a law of 1831 any black, free or slave, was forbidden from keeping a still or working at vending liquor on a possible sentence of up to fifty lashes. And most states imposed a fine on those who sold liquor to slaves without the owner's consent.[75] Virtually all of the cases came after 1820, and, with a few exceptions, they were indictments of whites for selling liquor to slaves.[76]

The exceptions were rare. They occurred in Virginia and Kentucky. The Virginia case, however, was not really focused on the sale of liquor. In 1798, in the Petersburg Hustings Court, a slave was sold because his owner had allowed him to go at large and deal as a free man. It was noted that he kept a "tipling House," but that was not the real charge. The Kentucky actions related to the vending of liquor, including a couple of cases in Warren County in the 1850s. In 1857 a slave was indicted for operating a "tipling house."[77]

Even though slaves obviously had to have money to buy liquor, the real apprehension was not that this might suggest that they possessed property. Nor is it altogether clear that it was a concern with drunkenness among slaves as such, despite the fact that passage of these laws may have been spurred in part by the temperance movement of the nineteenth century. Some Southern judges and lawmakers were temperance men, despite the movement's lack of success in the region. O'Neall, for instance, during a larceny case in 1815 involving a white, noted: "Drunkeness [*sic*] the cause of crime!!!" Over thirty years later he wrote to Lumpkin that "the temperance course is healthier with us than it has been for years." A few months earlier Theobald Mathew had informed Lumpkin that he took enormous pleasure in the "personal acquaintance of so zealous and distinguished a Fellow labourer in the cause of temperance."[78] Such views may have played some role in the adoption of the laws against supplying slaves with liquor, but a stronger concern—especially in view of the relative weakness of the temperance movement in the South—was with the relationship that might exist or develop between debased white people and black slaves. It was but one more effort to provide for the "better ordering" of the slaves of the South. Slaves must be kept tractable, propertyless, sober workers, and they should never be allowed to develop too close a relationship with rowdy, drunken, propertyless whites.

17

Wrongs of Slaves and the Civil
Liability of Masters

As if the injury was effected by the natural elements of air, or fire.

Cawthorn v. Deas (Alabama, 1835)

Despite the efforts of slaveowners to control slaves, there were many occasions when they could not do so. A significant legal question, then, became when, and on what principles, masters were held liable in civil actions for the intentional or unintentional injuries inflicted on others by their slaves. A first glance at the case law can easily leave one confused. Judge Harry I. Thornton, for example, concluded for the Alabama Supreme Court in *Cawthorn v. Deas* (1835) that for many victims of slave wrongs "it is, as if the injury was effected by the natural elements of air, or fire." There would be no compensation. Six years later the Louisiana Supreme Court, in *Gaillardet v. Demaries* (1841), argued that a master's liability was "one of the burthens of this species of property; it is absolute and exists whether the slave is supposed to be acting under their authority or not."[1] What lay beneath the apparent muddle, of course, was choice of policy.

Guido Calabresi has shown that the whole question of allocating the burdens of accidents is a matter of choice, and "what we choose, whether intentionally or by default, will reflect the economic and moral goals of our society." Interpretation of the emergence of torts as a distinct legal category has been raised to a high level by the work of Horwitz and G. Edward White, among others. Horwitz argued that in the United States tort law underwent a revolutionary transformation during the first few decades of the nineteenth century. The most important development was the destruction of the notion of strict liability, which had stood in the way of the development of the idea of carelessness as a central element in negligence actions. It was also necessary to break the concept of negligence away from its contractual foundations. This development was pronounced in Pennsylvania, Massachusetts, and New York, and was associated with the rise of industrialization—in fact, it preceded it and was one of the conditions that aided its rise. The end result was that "after 1840 the principle that one could not be held liable for socially useful activity exercised with due care became a commonplace of American law."[2]

White admitted that "changes associated with industrial enterprise did provide many more cases involving strangers, a phenomenon that played a part in the emergence of torts as an independent branch of law." But this was not the only fact in the emergence of torts. The increase in cases associated with industrialization came at a time "when legal scholars were prepared to question and discard old bases of legal classification. The emergence of torts as a distinct branch of law owed as much to changes in jurisprudential thought as to the spread of industrialization."[3]

White, moreover, placed the emergence of torts as a distinct category somewhat later than Horwitz. "The crucial inquiry in tort actions prior to the 1870s," in White's view, "was not whether a defendant was 'in fault' or had otherwise violated some comprehensive standard of tort liability, but whether something about the circumstances of the plaintiff's injury compelled the defendant to pay the plaintiff damages." Before the mid-nineteenth century "individual 'tort' actions . . . tended to be decided with reference to their own features and to current perceptions of equity and justice."[4]

Despite the value of these works, and it is considerable, there is a weakness. They paid little attention to the South. The fact that the wealthiest class in the region owned land and slaves rather than factories and railroads, at least until the last few years before the war when they began to diversify, created unique legal questions. But Southern law, in Tushnet's view, was not static. "Slave law," he claimed, "recognized regulation by law rather than sentiment more readily the closer the circumstances came to involve purely commercial dealings. In a sense slave law asserted jurisdiction only over market transactions, leaving other relationships to be regulated by sentiment."[5] But market analysis is of little use in the area of slave torts, as most of the injuries inflicted by slaves fell outside market relationships (such as the death of one slave at the hands of another or the spread of a fire from an owner's field). It is hardly much of an insight to point out that many conflicts that a legal system must attempt to resolve fall outside of market relationships. This is not to suggest that Tushnet's analysis is without force, only that it is of limited use.

Interpreting the efforts of Southern judges to define a master's liability involves an understanding of moral and economic choices. A choice by "default" was often made by jurists who answered the question "Should a master pay?" by a reference to common law categories and standards of liability. Although these categories and standards were framed to meet the needs of a totally different socioeconomic system, they were what Southern judges had learned as students of the law, and many continued to function within that familiar intellectual world.[6] Occasionally a judge would cut through the technical rules to suggest that the real basis of the judgment was a sense of fairness grounded in the idea that someone should not pay for the wrongs of someone else unless that person was under their control.

This, of course, raised the critical question about the nature of a master's power and responsibility over his or her slaves. Was a slaveowner's power absolute, and, if so, was liability absolute? If power was limited, what theory of limitation could be used to mark the boundaries of responsibility for the misconduct of slaves?

Common Law Patterns of Dealing with Accidents

There have been two main streams of thought in the common law world about the nature of civil liability for wrongs. One, the most congenial to nineteenth-century individualist thinking, emphasized the notion that without fault there could be no liability. Holmes was one of the first to develop this idea of a full-blown theory of torts. "At the bottom of liability," he wrote, "there is a notion of blameworthiness but yet that the deft's [defendant's] blameworthiness is not material." What this meant was that Holmes defined "fault" or "blameworthiness" in external terms, that is, in terms of "a certain average of conduct." The moral state of the defendant was irrelevant. Not all American legal thinkers agreed, but by the end of the century most did believe that fault was essential to liability. The other stream has broadened and deepened considerably in the twentieth century. It is one side stream running into a larger current that Roscoe Pound described as the "social-ization of law." It is the notion of liability without fault or of absolute liability.[7]

Southern judges did not have the advantage of the conceptualism of a Holmes or a Pound. The latters' views were developed after a revolution had already occurred in the way people thought about noncontractual wrongs, after "negli-gence" had emerged as a separate tort, and after torts had begun to appear as a coherent legal category alongside contracts and crimes. In short, Southern judges' earlier responses were channeled by the common law, the civil law, or statutes as they existed before the emergence of a fully developed concept of torts.

At the end of the eighteenth century there was no substantive category of law called torts. Rather, there was a cluster of individual wrongs for which the law provided a precise remedy through a particular writ, and each writ had its own standard of liability and rules of pleading. The two forms of action relevant to an understanding of a master's liability for the acts of slaves were trespass and trespass on the case, or case. The most important question is not which writ applied to which set of facts but rather the nature of the liability associated with the writs. Some have argued that trespass rested on a notion of strict liability whereas case required proof of negligence or wrongful intent.[8] This neat formulation, however, has been undercut. Horwitz noted, for example, that liability in fire cases had been strict because of the duty not to allow fire to spread. But the action was in case. What *is* clear is that at the beginning of the nineteenth century there was no separate tort created solely by negligence: there was no legally imposed respon-sibility of care owed by all persons to all other persons independent of special relations. "The dominant understanding of negligence at the beginning of the

nineteenth century," Horwitz has written, "meant neglect or failure fully to perform a preexisting duty, whether imposed by contract, statute, or common law
status."[9]

Until this was broken down and the notion of carelessness as a distinct ground
of liability emerged, Southern judges continued to work within the older common
law writ system. That meant that they faced the problem of finding an appropriate
analogy in that system to the position of slaves in Southern society. Among the
possible analogies used were cattle, domestic animals with vicious habits, and
servants. If cattle strayed onto the land of another and trod down herbage, the
owner of the cattle would be answerable in trespass. This was because the owner
had a duty to keep the cattle fenced in, and if they strayed (as dumb beasts are apt
to do) the plaintiff had an action. If slaves then were analogized to cattle, a strict
liability could be imposed on the master under the common law. Of course, one
problem with this was that it might immunize slaves from punishment because the
analogy denied moral agency.

The other property analogy had the same problem. The liability of the owner of
a domestic animal with bad habits was not strict, and therefore this analogy
differed from that of cattle. The assumption was that domestic animals, as a
category, were not dangerous. The rule, then, was that the owner, of a dog for
example, must have knowledge of the bad character of the particular animal. The
basic common law rule in master-servant relationships was that masters were
liable for the negligence of servants in their employ. Knowledge of the conduct that
led to an injury was not essential. Liability was grounded on a contract theory:
there was an implied contract between the master and strangers that the servant
would perform with skill. A master, however, would not be liable for the intentional wrongs of the servant unless they were done with the authority of the
master, either express or implied.[10] None of these analogies was truly apposite to
the condition of the slave in American society. But they were all that was available.

The Analogies to Cattle and Vicious Animals

Only one case contained any discussion of the analogy to cattle—*Campbell v.
Staiert* (North Carolina, 1818). Taylor rejected it out of hand. A master was not
bound to keep his slaves confined like cattle, and that was that. Taylor's opinion
was less than half a page; it would be pointless to attempt to decide whether Taylor
was more concerned with treating slaves as persons or with removing what would
otherwise have been an unfair burden on masters. Perhaps it was a little of both.[11]

The second analogy crept into cases more often. In both *Wright v. Weatherly*
(Tennessee, 1835) and *Ewing v. Thompson* (Missouri, 1850), it was rejected and on
precisely the same grounds. In *Wright* it was because the slave was not an animal
but rather "an intelligent moral agent" liable for his own wrongs, and in *Ewing*
because slaves were "responsible moral agents" answerable for their own miscon-

duct. Alabama came as close as any state to use of the vicious animal analogy, but, in *Brandon v. Planter's & Merchant's Bank* (1828), it did so without any direct reference to the common law rules.[12]

The Master-Servant Analogy

What remained was the master-servant analogy. This was preferable to dealing with slaves as though they were cattle or dogs. However, the problems with this analogy emerged in an early tort case in South Carolina, *Snee v. Trice* (1802). The facts in *Snee* were that the slaves of Trice, the defendant, had built a fire in a field that was being cleared prior to planting, probably for cooking, "as is usual among Negroes." It was made in the morning when there was no wind, but by midday a breeze blew up "which is very common at that season of the year," and the fire spread while the slaves were elsewhere in the field. It burned down Snee's corn house and destroyed three hundred bushels of corn inside. Snee then sued Trice in a special action on the case for the value of the corn "upon the ground that this loss was occasioned by the negligence or misconduct of defendent's negroes."[13]

In his charge to the jury Judge Bay observed: "If the doctrine, laid down by Mr. *Blackstone* in the extent in which he has placed it was to prevail in this country, to make masters liable for the negligences of their slaves, it would place all the slave-owners in the state at the mercy of their numerous slaves, who might commit what trespasses, or be guilty of what neglects and omissions they thought proper, to the ruin of their masters." Blackstone had written that masters were liable for the negligence of their servants; that was the extent of his view.[14] The problem, of course, was that slaves and servants were *not* truly analogous. Servants in England normally were skilled craftsman who had contracted with a master to perform a limited set of duties. Slaves in South Carolina, on the other hand, were the property of their master for life—they were always under the power or jurisdiction of the owner, or the agent of the owner, or a hirer.

Bay did not allow the master an absolute immunity, even though he sought to carve out an area of immunity from legal responsibility for the wrongs of slaves. There were instances, he wrote, where an owner was liable, "as in all cases where negroes are permitted to perform any public duty, or to carry on a handicraft trade or calling, or to perform or superintend any other kind of business where public confidence is to be reposed." In other words, to the extent that the status of a slave was nearly identical to that of a servant, the liability of the slave's master was exactly the same as under the common law. Under no circumstances, however, would a master be liable "where any unauthorized act is done by a slave in his private capacity, without the knowledge or approbation of his master."[15] Bay thus treated the position of the slave as though it was nearly the same as the servant under English law. What he ignored was the fact that the slave might always be presumed to be under the authority of the owner.

Twenty-three years later, in *Wingis v. Smith* (1825), Nott held that the rule in *Snee* was that masters were "not liable for the negligence of" servants. "Tradesmen, ferrymen, carriers and others acting in such like capacities are exceptions to the rule." He concluded that "the interest of the master affords a higher security against misconduct or negligence of his servants than any liability which the law could impose." This "allocation to sentiment," however, had gone too far. *O'Connell v. Strong* (1838) overruled *Wingis*: "the proposition may be laid down that in all cases a master would be held liable for the negligence or misfeasance of a slave whilst in the lawful and authorized employment of the master . . . in other words, the distinction between slaves and other servants, so far as it regards the liability of the master for non-feasance and negligence, does not obtain in South Carolina."[16]

This was about as far as the analogical reasoning of the common law would carry Southern judges. Within common law categories, they could impose a wide liability by analogizing slaves to animals or a narrower liability by attempting to squeeze the slave into the status of an English servant. The latter choice, however, tended to leave some victims of slave wrongs without any compensation.[17]

Standing alone, this choice would leave slaves without any burden. This would be intolerable, and the *Snee* court had an answer. "Other salutary checks have been found by experience," wrote Bay, "more efficacious than that of recovering damages from masters." Although he did not say what they were, there could be a hint in the earlier slave insolence case, *White v. Chambers* (1796). In *White* the court, which included Bay, suggested that "the best rule would be, in all cases where a slave behaved amiss, or with rudeness or incivility to a free white man, to complain to the master . . . of such offending slave, who, if he was actuated by curtesy [*sic*] and civility to his neighbor, would on such application, give him the necessary satisfaction for every insult or piece of improper conduct which a slave had offered." It is entirely possible that the "salutary" control Bay had in mind would be a private remedy. For judges who believed in a republican society controlled by a responsible aristocracy, such a proposal made perfect sense. A decent master would surely provide some remedy on the request of an injured neighbor. To believe otherwise might even involve questioning some of the basic assumptions about one's society. Snee ought to have simply asked Trice to assume the burden of the accident without resorting to the courts. Tushnet's idea about allocation to the sentiment of the master class is, of course, fully supported by the approach of the *Snee* court, as well as the *Wingis* court.[18]

The law, then, would not impose a liability on a master beyond that defined by the analogous rules of English master-servant law. Further than this, there could be remedies for the victims of slave wrongs, but they would not always be imposed by law. Instead, they would flow from the sense of decency and responsibility of slaveowners. If a given master's standards of conduct fell below those of society at large, the only recourse a victim would have would be a criminal action, if the facts sustained it. Otherwise, victims were left where the Alabama court found them. This choice undoubtedly was reinforced by the view that it would be unjust to make someone liable in a court action when no fault could be imputed to that person.

Negligence and Fault

The notion of fault, however, was itself undergoing a significant transformation in the early nineteenth century with the emergence of a new idea of negligence. This was the idea of due care, a legally imposed responsibility of care owed by all persons to all persons independent of special relations.[19] To what extent did this transformation apply to defining a master's liability for the misconduct of slaves?

A logical starting point is *Snee v. Trice*, the first case, according to Horwitz, that contained some "creative impulses." It was, he believed, the "first unambiguous recognition in American law of a legally imposed standard of care not arising out of contract."[20] To fully understand this side of the case, it is necessary to know what negligence meant in the common law in proceedings involving fire. Most scholars, including Horwitz, thought that it had meant nothing more than "neglect" or "failure" to keep the fire from spreading. There was no standard of due care as that is understood today: if the fire spread, it was because of a failure to contain it. Liability in such cases would be strict. The only clear ground of exemption was in the event of "inevitable accident." An early eighteenth-century English statute exempted a master from any liability for fire-spreading damage caused by the "negligence" of a servant. The servant would have to pay a fine to be distributed among those injured or else be committed to the workhouse. This was the status of English law when *Snee* was decided.[21]

Did the *Snee* court develop new standards? Did it impose or recognize a standard of prudent conduct arising out of a general duty to all? To answer this it is necessary to return to the court's description of the event on Trice's plantation: "the morning was still, and the fire had burnt down, but towards the middle of the day, the wind arose, and blew up the sleeping embers which communicated the fire to the buildings; this, therefore, had more the appearance of accident than negligence." Then came the following two sentences; "but be that as it may, the master, Mr. Trice, knew nothing of it; he was away from home and did not even hear of it until his return. To make him therefore chargeable, would be very rigorous and unjust."[22] A reasonable interpretation would be that unless the fire spread because of inevitable accident, the master would be liable, but if and only if he had knowledge of the conduct. Did this change the English common law rule? Yes it did, but not with a new standard of "due care."[23] The English rule did not require a master to have specific knowledge of a servant's conduct, because the servant was presumably acting on the master's authority. What *Snee* ruled was that the court would not rest liability on the presumption that slaves were always under the authority of the master. Furthermore, because the master-slave relation was involved, the court did not break away from basing liability on an implied contract between masters and strangers that the slave would perform with skill.

It is not, finally, to the decision in *Snee* that we ought to look for evidence of a modern standard of negligence. It is, rather, to the decision in *O'Connell v. Strong* over thirty years later. The facts in *O'Connell* were similar to those in *Snee*, except that the servant involved was a white man employed on a farm and not a slave. The worker was using fire in clearing new ground. "Having done so by the consent of the defendant," Judge Butler wrote,

> if it had been shown that he used it with a reckless indifference to the plaintiff's rights and property, as by setting fire to the log heaps at an improper time, or that the fire escaped from his not having taken proper precautions to prevent its spreading, there is no reason why the defendant should not have been held answerable for the consequences. But if the fire escaped by inevitable accident, or in any way which common prudence could not have prevented or remedied, the liability could not have attached.[24]

We now find quite modern standards such as "reckless indifference," failure to take "proper precautions," and "common prudence."

Negligence was also addressed in a North Carolina proceeding, *Garrett v. Freeman* (1857), but probably the clearest commitment to a modern standard of due care or negligence came in a dissent in a Louisiana case on the very eve of the Civil War. *Maille v. Blas* (1860) involved an action to recover the value of a slave who was killed in a fight with the slave of the defendant. Judges Buchanan and Albert Voorhies ruled that the master was indeed liable: the code provision was absolute. Chief Justice Merrick dissented. He attempted, by reference to railroad negligence trials, to introduce into the case the concept of contributory negligence: "It is then apparent, that a party's right to recovery for the loss of his slave depends in many cases upon the question whether the slave, for which he claims recompense has or has not acted lawfully and prudently, or whether he has not brought the injury upon himself by his negligence, his malice or felonious intent."[25]

These were the sole cases concerning slave misconduct in which modern notions about negligence made an appearance. It is hardly an impressive record. The only South Carolina proceeding in which the standard of liability was adopted actually involved a white servant rather than a slave. There was one case in North Carolina and one dissent in Louisiana. But that is all.[26] One possible reason for this meager record is that the need simply was not there. Slaveowners were hardly weighted down by what Horwitz described as the "crushing burden of damage judgment that a system of strict liability entailed." The same was not true for those in the North—for example, those who were building milldams that flooded riparian owners' land. If Horwitz is correct, Northern courts set out to construct rules that would exempt entrepreneurs from civil liability "for socially useful activity exercised with due care," and by about 1840 they had succeeded.[27] Perhaps it was commonplace, as Horwitz claimed, and that may account for its occasional appearance in slave misconduct cases, but it was hardly a major consideration in the law of slavery.

Yet the notion of fault need not be viewed solely in the context of modern standards of due care owed to all by all regardless of relationship. It was also seen in terms of one's responsibility for the misconduct of others, modern standards of negligence apart. The idea was that it was simply not fair to impose liability on one person for the wrongs of another.

Liability and Class Relationships: Masters and Slaves

Fairness required that masters should not pay for the wrongs of slaves not under their control. But inevitably this principle raised the vital question of the nature of a master's power and responsibility. Was a slaveowner's power absolute? If so, was liability absolute? If power was limited, what theory of limitation marked the boundaries of responsibility for the misconduct of slaves? Answers depended, to some extent at least, on whether the judge worked within a system defined by statutes, civil law traditions, or common law traditions.

Formal rationality has long been regarded as an attractive feature of the civil law.[28] Rules about the liability of slaveowners are a good example. Under the civil law, liability was complete and absolute; it flowed out of "ownership," as the Louisiana Supreme Court observed in *Gaillardet v. Demaries*, and was one of its "burthens." There is some dispute about the theoretical ground for this liability, but, in the view of Buckland, it may have been representational: because a slave could not be civilly liable, the master must represent or stand in the position of *defensor*.[29] Such a notion certainly has the neatness of rationality. Still another possible foundation for liability might be found in a provision of *Las Siete Partidas*: Slaves were not allowed to testify under oath, but they "should . . . be tortured . . . because slaves are, as it were, desperate men, on account of the condition of servitude in which they are, and every person should suspect that they will easily lie and conceal the truth when some force is not employed against them."[30] Duplicity and rebelliousness were the natural results of the desperation of slavery. If slaves were viewed this way, it *could* reasonably follow that those who owned slaves had an affirmative duty to control them in the common interest. Wrongs committed by slaves resulted from the failure of the owner to control, and this failure or neglect became the foundation of civil liability. A principled ground for complete liability could be that slaves were always presumptively under the master's control. Culpability rested on the failure of the master to control the slave.

Whatever the theoretical foundation might be, article 180 of the code of 1838 provided that "the master shall be answerable for all the damages occasioned by an offence or quasi-offence committed by his slave, independent of the punishment of the slave."[31] A "quasi-offence" under Louisiana law corresponded to what we think of as a tort under the common law. A master, therefore, was civilly liable under the code for all criminal or civil wrongs of a slave. As under the Roman law of slavery, however, a master was allowed to limit the impact of this responsibility through the *actio-noxalis*. Article 181 of the code described this process:

> The master however may discharge himself from such responsibility by abandoning his slave to the person injured; in which case such person shall sell

such slave at public auction in the usual form, to obtain payment of the damages and costs; and the balance, if any, shall be returned to the master of the slave, who shall be completely discharged, although the price of the slave should not be sufficient to pay the whole amount of the damages and costs; provided that the master shall make the abandonment within three days after the judgment awarding such damages shall have been rendered; provided also that it shall not be proved that the crime or offence was committed by his order; for in case of such proof the master shall be answerable for all damages resulting therefrom, whatever be the amount, without being admitted to the benefit of the abandonment.[32]

Although the liability was absolute, the consequences of that liability could be limited. The *actio-noxalis* retained the principle of complete responsibility at the same time that it allowed a distribution of the damages.

A case that shows the extent of liability was *Gaillardet*, where the plaintiff sued the hirer of a slave. The slave, while in the employ of the defendant, drove a dray against the gig of the plaintiff, "breaking it to pieces and injuring his servant." The damage was alleged to have resulted from the "negligent and unskillful conduct of a slave." The defendant contended that the owner of the slave was liable for the damages under the code, but that he, as a mere hirer, was not. The court, however, ruled that the plaintiff had an action against both the owner and the employer of the slave. The master's liability, said the court, flowed out of the ownership and existed whether the slave was supposed to be acting under his authority or not. The liability of the hirer was narrower. The hirer would not be liable for the willful wrongs of the slave, only for damage resulting from the neglect or unskillfulness of a slave in the course of employment.[33] In other words, the common law rules of master and servant liability applied in Louisiana to the hirer of the slave, but not to the master, whose responsibility was absolute.

The dilemma presented by the code to a judge who shared the view that a person should not be liable for someone else's wrongs cropped up in another Louisiana case, *Boulard v. Calhoun* (1858). The plaintiff, Antoinette Boulard, sought vindictive damages against the defendant, Meredith Calhoun. Calhoun's slaves removed the plaintiff's property from her home, put it and her on a flatboat, and set it adrift on the Red River. They then burned her house to the ground. They were under the direction of Calhoun's overseers (he had four plantations), among others, who had decided to run Boulard out because she was supposedly a notorious illegal trader with slaves. The facts developed at the trial showed that Calhoun had not only not supported the action, he had positively tried to dissuade the white leaders. Nevertheless, Judge Buchanan was compelled by the code to find the defendant guilty, but it bothered him. To extend the accountability for vindictive damages "to other cases than those in which the owner of the slave was an active participant in the tort or crime committed by the latter, would constantly expose the master to ruin by the acts of a vicious slave, without any fault of his own; and would thereby operate as the greatest of discouragements, to the holding of that species of property; a consequence which we conceive to be at variance with the policy of the law of Louisiana."[34]

Under the common law the problem of defining the precise boundaries of a master's power proved more difficult. This is perhaps nowhere better evident than in the work of Judge Ruffin in North Carolina. In *State v. Mann* (1829) he argued for the total subordination of the slave. If a master's power was absolute, then absolute liability for wrongs committed by the slave logically followed. Twenty years after the *Mann* decision, however, in *Parham v. Blackwelder* (1848), Ruffin refused to carry the logic to this conclusion. The case did not deal with negligence, but with a more traditional trespass—cutting timber on someone else's land. Despite *Mann*, Ruffin refused to make the master liable. His reasoning was as follows: "we believe the law does not hold one person answerable for the wrongs of another person. It would be most dangerous and unreasonable if it did, as it is impossible for society to subsist without some persons being in the service of others, and it would put employers entirely in the power of those who have, often, no good-will to them, to ruin them." Besides, he noted, the slave would be criminally liable for his trespasses.[35] Ruffin, in other words, had hardly strayed an inch from the reasoning of the South Carolina Constitutional Court in *Snee*.

One dramatic effort to go beyond the approach of the South Carolina court was made in Tennessee in 1835. *Wright v. Weatherly* involved the death of one slave at the hands of another. To avoid the dilemma of a false analogy to the servant in English law, the court unsuccessfully suggested that the legislature adopt the *actio noxalis* of the civil law.[36]

The response in two other states, Arkansas and Missouri, was somewhat different. Both made masters civilly liable for a specified series of trespasses, and many of these were indictable offenses as well. In Arkansas, a number of trespasses, previously only torts, became indictable offenses (such as killing, maiming, or administering poison to domestic animals). An Arkansas statute also provided that in "all trespasses, and offences less than felony" committed by a slave, the master could "compound with the injured person and punish his own slave, without the intervention of any legal trial or proceeding; but if he refuse to compound, the slave may be tried and punished, and the damage recovered by suit against the master."[37]

In *McConnell v. Hardeman* (1854) this statute was given a narrow interpretation: the law was restricted to trespasses that were indictable offenses or acts expressly listed in the statutes. Liability was broad but not unqualified. Here the court ruled that the tortious act of "taking the plaintiff's horse" was not listed in the statute, and therefore the master was not liable. But it invited the legislature to consider "whether the true interests of slave-holders would not be promoted by making them liable for all trespasses committed by their slaves, thus removing many causes of jealousy and ill-feeling against the owners of that species of property, and at the same time protect them by limiting their liability, as at the civil law, to the value of the offending slaves."[38]

Missouri moved a little closer to the civil law than did Arkansas. It provided that masters would be civilly liable for injuries that resulted from certain stipulated offenses, but that the damages could not exceed the value of the slave. The Missouri Supreme Court, in interpreting the statute, was far less sympathetic to the victims of slave offenses than either the Arkansas or Tennessee courts. Judge Napton, for example, argued that "the power of the master being limited, his responsibility is proportioned accordingly. It does not extend to the willful and wanton aggressions of the slave except where the statute has expressly provided."[39]

Arguments favoring a wider statutory liability then existed under a common law master-servant analysis claimed that it flowed from the nature of the master-slave relationship. This was true, for instance, in Louisiana and Tennessee. Such analysis focused on the view that slaves were not merely docile extensions of a master's will but independent, responsible "moral agents."

The same premise existed for those who attempted to *limit* the liability of a master. Bay in *Snee* had described slaves as a "headstrong, stubborn race of people" who could ruin their owners if the latter were made absolutely liable. Only one court, as far as I am aware, clearly adopted the theoretical position that a master's liability was limited because his power was limited. That was the Missouri court in *Ewing v. Thompson* (1850).[40]

It is difficult to explain why a given judge took one side or the other in this debate. Bay, Ruffin, and Buchanan all fell back on the notion that if owners were always to bear the costs of accidents, it could lead to their ruin. Such a position would place power in the hands of slaves. Buchanan, who worked in a civil law code state, could only use this notion to reject vindictive damages, not to remove all liability for certain accidents. But the general idea remains the same. What is impossible to tell, of course, is whether or not these judges were really that timid. Did they truly believe that making masters responsible for the cost of accidents would lead to their ruin? Perhaps Ruffin, who in *Mann* noted that nothing but absolute power could keep slaves in submission, was indeed uncertain about the stability of his society. Bay, with the recent bloody slave insurrection on Santo Domingo before his eyes, may have been equally sensitive to the dangers from a servile population, as he later showed in *Kinloch v. Harvey* (1830). Whatever the answer might be, one thing is reasonably clear: these judges tended to fashion rules of law and make policy choices based on the master-slave relationship. Was this relationship also the focus for those who attempted to justify a wider liability for slaveowners?

Cost Distribution and Nonslaveholders

It is plausible to argue that Southern judges, especially in view of the confused state of tort law development in mid-nineteenth-century America, were moved by a concern that injured plaintiffs be compensated under some circumstances. Still, class relationships and perceptions often played an important role in the way Southerners grappled with the problem of civil liability for slave wrongs. The importance of class relationships in the shaping of legal rules cannot be ignored, but we simply must not fall into a reductionist trap. Calabresi properly states that "fairness" played a role, and it was not always defined by class relationships.

Surely there were deep-seated ambiguities in the minds of nonslaveholders. Some undoubtedly agreed with Hinton Helper's hostility to slavery, whereas others hoped eventually to own a slave or two at least. Some, like Andrew Johnson of Tennessee, the future president, absolutely despised the large slaveholders, and many supported slavery because without it they feared they would have to compete with black labor and be degraded in the process. In the final analysis Genovese is correct: "How loyal, then, were the nonslaveholders? Loyal enough to guarantee order at home through several tumultuous decades, loyal enough to allow the South to wage an improbable war in a hopeless cause for four heroic years. But by no means loyal enough to guarantee the future of the slaveholders' power without additional measures."[41] One of these "measures" may well have been an effort to impose a wider responsibility on masters for the misconduct of their slaves. Because we still know little, despite some superb recent studies,[42] about the nonslaveholders (farmers, urban workers, "poor white trash," etc.), their *precise* role in shaping the law remains uncertain. There is enough evidence, however, to show that the influence was there.

There is little documentation that judges like Ruffin, Bay, or Nott fashioned a theory of liability with an eye to nonslaveholders. Chief Justice George C. Watkins in Arkansas and Judge Nathan Green in Tennessee, on the other hand, certainly did. Watkins, in *McConnell v. Hardeman*, urged the legislature to widen a master's liability, "thus removing many causes of jealousy and ill-feeling against the owners of that species of property." And Green, who was no ardent proslavery judge, faced a full-scale assault on the institution of slavery from counsel representing the plaintiff in *Wright v. Weatherly*. "The people of this country," counsel contended, "deprecate slavery as an evil—to be rid of which would be a great public blessing." He further argued that "it is not the policy of the law to encourage slavery." (Such an argument, it need hardly be said, would have been unthinkable before a court in South Carolina or Georgia.) Of equal interest was Green's response to the request for a rule imposing a wide liability. After urging the legislature to impose it, he observed that "such a provision would be fair and equal among the slaveholders themselves; and, in relation to a large majority of the people of the state, who do not own slaves, it is imperiously required."[43]

The nature of slavery and the class structure among whites in Tennessee provoked a different analysis of the problem than that pursued in the Carolinas. The *Wright* case was decided one year after a debate between proslavery and antislavery forces in the state. Antislavery sentiment clearly existed in Tennessee, even though it did not prevail.[44] In Arkansas, hostility to slaveholders was also evident. At the time of the movement to acquire statehood, for example, a correspondent wrote to the *Little Rock Times*:

> Of the whole white population, for one who has twenty slaves, we will find you twenty who have no slaves. The one, then, will be the sufferer by the abolition of slavery in the Territory, and to enable him to loll in ease and affluence and to save his own delicate hands from the rude contact of the vulgar plow, the twenty who earn their honest living by the sweat of the brow are called upon with the voice of authority assumed by wealth to receive the yoke. They must consent to a tenfold increase of tax for the support of a state government, because my lord is threatened with danger of desertion from his cotton field if we remain as we are.[45]

This, of course, was an unsuccessful plea against statehood, but the point lies in the writer's unconcealed hostility toward slaveholders.

Such sentiments were relatively strong in states like Arkansas, Missouri, and Tennessee—states not dominated by a slave population.[46] Arkansas and Missouri modified the rules on a master's liability by statute, but despite Judge Green's plea, this did not happen in Tennessee. Perhaps, and this must be speculative, the reason is that though all three states were common law jurisdictions, Tennessee was the oldest and most traditional. The newer states of the West often showed a greater willingness to depart from the common law. States like Alabama and Mississippi, of course, were also newer states that showed a willingness to move by statute to significantly modify common law rules, as in the Married Women's Property Laws;[47] but in regard to civil liability of slaveholders for the misconduct of slaves, they differed sharply from the other western slave states, because they had very large slave populations. In those states the master-slave relationship was of greater significance than the relationship between nonslaveholding whites and slaveholders. It was easier for an Alabama judge to accept the fact that in many cases the victim of a slave wrong had to be content with the notion that the injury was as if "effected by the natural elements" than it was for a judge in Arkansas or Tennessee. The behavior of North Carolina is also striking. Why, since it had produced Hinton Helper and harbored opposition to slavery in the up-country as well as in some communities around Albemarle Sound, did an analysis like that of Green or Watkins fail to break the surface? Here the purely human element must be brought in. Tushnet and A. E. Keir Nash appropriately placed a great deal of weight on the differences in the abilities and views of various judges and courts. Ruffin simply did not view slavery the same way Green did. It is not altogether correct, however, to leave the impression that the class structure in North Carolina produced no one who inclined to the Green or Watkins approach. Pearson's charge to the jury in *Parham* in the 1830s suggests otherwise. He, at least, was prepared to create a much wider liability than Ruffin; and it is just as likely that he was reflecting the class pressures that existed in North Carolina as he was expressing some personal preference.[48] It also may be significant that Bay, for example, sat on the court of his state in the first years of the nineteenth century, whereas Watkins and Green were judges during the emergence of Jacksonian Democracy and the rise of a strong abolitionist movement in the North. The early South Carolina court's decision may have reflected a society largely unbattered by politically important class divisions. As democracy spread, slaveowners became increasingly concerned about the loyalty of nonslaveholders—especially because the Northern abolitionist movement was then launching its full-scale attack on slavery, and more and more moderate Northern political leaders were embracing the notion of containment.[49]

Nonslaveholding white Southerners, no less than the slaves themselves, were able by their demands to force slaveowners and their allies to make some adjustments within their legal order. But the range of choices was not infinite. Legal traditions and styles of reasoning, as well as class needs, affected the policy choices made by Southern jurists. A theory of responsibility, like a theory of liability from which it springs, is determined by complex social relations, conditioned by legal traditions.

IV

Manumission

18

Emancipation: Conceptions, Restraints, and Practice

The State has nothing to fear from emancipation,
regulated as . . . law directs it to be.
JOHN BELTON O'NEALL, *Negro Law of South Carolina* (1848)

Manumission is not a simple concept. Buckland long ago noted that it was like a conveyance, but it was not a conveyance. It was not the transfer to the slave of what the master "possessed," dominion—it was the release from dominion. Two scholars have used the anthropological idea of the *gift* to explain manumission. But the gift itself is not a simple concept. Gift exchanges in premarket societies involved a redistribution of goods at the same time that they created a variety of obligations, even though it appeared that the gifts were given freely. Manumission, Patterson argued, was the gift of social life "ideologically interpreted as a repayment for faithful service." It was, David Brion Davis agreed, the "negation of an already negated social life" and required "continuing gratitude and obligations to the master and his successors."[1]

In English common law, however, a "gift" was gratuituous. There is force to the Patterson-Davis view if we look at the practice among some Southern slaveowners and not at the law, or if we focus on the Roman law of slavery and those slave systems built on civil law foundations, like Louisiana's. One obligation in these was *obsequium.* In Louisiana if a freedman was "ungrateful" to a master who had freed him out of goodwill, "the master may, on that account, reduce him again to slavery, by complaining against him, and proving . . . [it] in court." The idea of ongoing obligations in the South did not exist outside a civil law state. As Coke remarked of the common law, "if a villein be manumised, albeit he become ungratefull to the lord in the highest degree, yet the manumission remaines good: and herein the common law differeth from the civill law."[2]

Finally, it bears emphasis that in the South manumission often did not create a *civis*, which occurred in Roman law. One illustration is the conclusion reached by Lumpkin in *Bryan v. Walton* (1853):

. . . the act of manumission confers no other right but that of freedom from the dominion of the master, and the limited liberty of locomotion . . . it does not and cannot confer *citizenship*, nor any of the powers, civil or political, incident to *citizenship* . . . the social and civil degradation, resulting from the taint of blood, adheres to the descendants of Ham in this country, like the poisoned tunic of Nessus . . . nothing but an Act of the Assembly can purify, by the salt of its grace, the bitter fountain—the *"darkling sea."*[3]

Some Southern states, fearful of the growth of a free black population, rarely, if ever, purified anyone with the "salt of its grace." At one time or another five of them (Alabama, Kentucky, North Carolina, Tennessee, and Virginia) even required freed people to leave the state within a short period or face reenslavement.[4] The cases of Patty Green and Betty in Charles City County, Virginia, illustrate that the danger could be real. They were found guilty of remaining in Virginia over a year after their "right to freedom accrued," and in June 1834 Judge Abel Parker Upshur ordered them sold back into slavery. Freed blacks in the rest of the South might not face reenslavement if they remained in the state, but they were not granted the full range of citizenship rights either.[5]

One thing often emphasized about manumission was that it was the renunciation of a property right. One Southern judge, however, bypassed a property law analysis. Manumission, he argued, was a question of "State policy, and should not be put upon these principles of *meum et tuum*, which regulate individual rights."[6] Most judges, nonetheless, did discuss it in terms of property law. But, as Hurd noted in the late 1850s, that left a problem: other "chattels, when derelict by the owner, are still chattels, and belong to whoever may then first take possession of them." The act of manumission was more than a renunciation of a property claim. Sir Thomas Littleton put it this way: "manumission is properly, when the lord makes a deed to his villeine to enfranchise him by this word (manumittere), which is the same as to put him out of the hands and power of another." Manumission was "essentially a release not merely from the owner's control, but from all possibility of being owned."[7]

Because of that, manumission fell within the bounds of public policy even when it was seen in terms of private rights. The state had to give legal consequences to an emancipation, and emancipators had to comply with the rules or their effort to release one from dominion would fail. To illustrate, South Carolina had a statutory provision that if a person was emancipated otherwise than according to the law of 1800, it would be lawful for any person to seize the slave as his or her property. In *Linam v. Johnson* (1831) an action was brought for Bill Brock, an alleged slave. Brock had purchased himself by having a white man use Brock's money for the sale. The new "owner" allowed Brock to act as free, and Brock obtained a guardian, as all free blacks were required to do. The new owner demanded Brock from the guardian, and after the guardian refused to give him up the new owner sued. Judge Johnson held that the action could not be brought because the putative owner was not the owner in light of the illegal emancipation. Brock was a "slave without an owner, and cast upon society as a derelict, which, according to the law of nature, any one might appropriate to his own use."[8]

Manumission as a "Legacy" or "Trust"

Special conceptual problems were presented when slaveowners tried to emancipate slaves by last wills and testaments that did not exist when the slaves were granted immediate freedom by deed during the lifetime of the owner. Was manumission by last will a "legacy," or was it better to regard it as a "trust"—in particular, a "charitable trust"? What legal or equitable issues arose when a testamentary emancipation was placed in one or another of these categories?

Judge Ara Spence of Maryland was one who saw a testamentary emancipation as a legacy. "The manumission, or bequest of freedom to a slave by last will and testament," he wrote in *State v. Dorsey* (1848), "confers on such slave the identical rights, interests and benefits, which would pass, if the testator had bequeathed the same slave to another person. . . . The conclusion . . . that a bequest of freedom to a slave is a legacy, is . . . clear." Ten years earlier Judge Ephraim M. Ewing in Kentucky was of the same mind. When "emancipated by will," slaves "occupy the double character of property and legatees or *quasi* legatees . . . freedom is a legacy" (*Nancy v. Snell*, 1838). Judge William Daniel in Virginia, in *Wood v. Humphreys* (1855), disagreed. "Bequests of freedom," he observed, "do in some respects differ from bequests of property: For no man can enjoy or acquire a right of property in himself." Daniel perceived the oddity of seeing a manumission, the discontinuation of a property right, as a grant of a property right. Nevertheless, even he referred to a manumission in a will as a "bequest."[9] Despite the oddity Southern judges often spoke of manumissions by will as legacies. They were struggling to find an appropriate place within known legal categories.

Did a slave have the capacity to accept the gift? The issue is illustrated in South Carolina judgments. In 1830, in *Lenoir v. Sylvester*, O'Neall wrote:

. . . a legacy cannot be given to a slave; for he can have no right, whatever, which does not, the instant it is transferred to him, pass to his master. Every thing which belongs to him, belongs to his master. In other words, he is in law himself chattels personal; and it would be absurd to say, that property can own property. The will directing them to be set free is not, therefore, to be regarded as bequeathing a legacy to persons who can take it; but as merely directory to his executors to do an act, on a particular event, which is then to confer freedom on the slaves, and make them capable of acquiring the rights of property.[10]

Twelve years later the judges in South Carolina considered another aspect of the problem in *Bowers v. Newman*. "Freedom," Earle wrote, "when bestowed upon a slave by will, is usually spoken of as a legacy, which requires the assent of the executor as other bequests. . . . Should the executor withhold his assent to the legacy of freedom to the slave, could the heir at law retain him in slavery?" If an executor withheld his assent the "enjoyment of the legacy in possession" might be delayed, but it would still vest at the death of the testator. The "title" to freedom would become "absolute and perfect" when the assent of the executor to the legacy of freedom would be presumed because of a lapse of time. It was a nice legal finesse, but it left a person a slave in the meantime. In a separate opinion Chancellor Harper held that a "slave could both take freedom and property, by the same instrument, a will."[11]

In North Carolina, Ruffin, in *White v. Green* (1840), ruled that "Slaves have not capacity to take by will, and a legacy to them is, like the direction for their emancipation, void." Judge Alexander M. Clayton of Mississippi, in *Wade v. American Colonization Society* (1846), adopted a different position. The "right to freedom is inchoate, and becomes complete when the subjects of it are removed. The bequest to the slaves is not void for want of capacity in the legatees to take."[12] Obviously, judges had difficulty squeezing postmortem manumissions into the boundaries of the notion of a legacy.

The idea of a testamentary emancipation as a form of trust or charity presented its own difficulties. What would count as a charity? How could trusts to emancipate be enforced, and which were valid in the first place? An important equitable concept to bear in mind was *cy pres*, which meant that the court would fashion a decree to carry out the intentions of the testator "as near as possible."

A momentous development in English law came with the adoption of the Elizabethan statute on charitable uses, which specified those gifts that would be considered gifts for charitable uses. The list included such things as gifts to relieve aged and poor people. Jurisdiction over charities was within the court of chancery, whose flexible remedial powers were used to enforce charitable bequests, even when there were problems with the will. By the time the law was considered in American slave cases, the normal mode of proceeding was by information filed by the attorney general in chancery to enforce the charity.[13]

The first crucial judgment on manumission as a charity was the Virginia decision in *Charles et al. v. Hunnicutt* (1804). Gloister Hunnicutt, a Sussex County Quaker, devised six slaves to the monthly meeting to be freed. Hunnicutt's son refused to free the slaves, but a deed of manumission was recorded by those appointed by the monthly meeting. The freedom of the slaves was affirmed by the court of appeals. Chancellor Roane observed that it was appropriate to "take official notice of the principles of that society, holding slavery in abhorrence." And he described the emancipation as an "emphatical species of charity." President Lyons began his opinion with the observation that "devises in favour of charities, and particularly those in favour of liberty, ought to be liberally expounded."[14]

Another early leading decision, going the other way, was *Haywood v. Craven's Ex'rs.* (North Carolina, 1816). It involved a bequest of three slaves and their offspring to three men in trust to emancipate them according to the law. The court held the trust void. The judges reasoned as follows: "With respect to the cases decided upon 43 Eliz., it is believed that not one can be found in which a court of equity has executed a charitable purpose unless the will so described it that the law will acknowledge it to be such. The disposition must be to such purposes as are enumerated in the statute, or to others bearing an analogy to them, and such as a court of chancery in the ordinary exercise of its power has been in the habit of enforcing."[15] There were no reasons given why a trust to free slaves could not be viewed as a charity by analogy.

By the time the court decided *Cameron v. Commissioners* in 1841 there were signs of a change in position. In this case slaves had been given in a will in trust to be transported to Africa, and some property was to be sold to defray the costs of transportation and settlement. Raleigh's city commissioners wanted the proceeds from the sale of the property to go to the hospital fund, not to the former slaves in Liberia. The argument was that the slaves, at the testator's death, were still slaves and so incapable of taking the property, and that "a trust for them or for their emancipation was illegal and void." The opinion was written by Gaston, who was the counsel for the blacks in *Haywood*. He observed: "It is true that as slaves at the death of the testator they were incapable of taking a beneficial interest under the will, and that this bequest cannot be upheld except on the ground of a devise or gift to a charitable purpose. . . . No definition is given in the statute of charitable purposes, but we see no cause to doubt that liberation from slavery, when not forbidden by law or inconsistent with public policy, is a purpose of this kind." Public policy, Gaston concluded, prohibited only the "manumission of slaves to reside amongst us." It never prohibited out-of-state emancipation as in some other states, such as Mississippi or South Carolina, and, therefore, the trust fund for that charitable purpose was not inconsistent with public policy.[16]

Thirteen years later, in *Hurdle v. Outlaw* (1854), Battle left the way open to apply the law of charities. "Whether the emancipation of slaves, directed in a will or assumed upon a secret trust," he wrote, "is such a public charity as will be enforced by a proceeding in the name of the Attorney General of the state, or whether it is a right which the slaves themselves can enforce, by a suit, are interesting questions which the present pleadings do not make it our duty to decide."[17] Other North Carolina judges, however, were not always receptive to the idea that trusts to free slaves could be viewed as charities.

In 1844, for instance, Ruffin mentioned *Cameron* in his opinion in *Thompson v. Newlin*. But it was not to endorse Gaston's views. He cited the case only to make the point that, since the law passed in 1830, it was lawful for a slaveholder to bequeath slaves for the purpose of their removal from the state, subsequent emancipation, and being "kept away."[18] In *Lemmond v. Peoples* (1848) Ruffin wrote that "every country has the right to protect itself from a population dangerous to its morality and peace; and hence the policy of the law of this State prevents the emancipation of slaves with a view to their continuing here . . . and when the purpose is that the emancipated slaves shall remain here, they cannot be carried away, because it is contrary to the trust, and the doctrine of *cy pres* does not exist with us." The next year, however, Ruffin affirmed the trust involved in the earlier *Thompson* case to remove slaves and free them. The critical point was that a trustee could be compelled to execute the trusts he accepted. The way was "either at the instance of the Attorney-General, by regarding such dispositions in the light of charities, or at the suit of the negroes themselves, upon the capacity imparted to them by their incipient right to freedom."[19]

The problem of valid trusts to manumit and the doctrine of *cy pres* was also noted in *Ross v. Vertner* (Mississippi, 1840). Isaac Ross's heirs filed their bills to set aside the bequests directing well over one hundred slaves to be sent to Liberia to be freed. Their counsel argued that the American Colonization Society could not take the property in slaves, and a slave could not be the beneficiary of a trust. "Are we then to be told," he argued, "that notwithstanding the void devises and inability of any person to execute the will, and the attempted fraud upon the laws and policy of the state, yet that the court will sustain the devises as charities, and execute the will according to the odious doctrine of cy-pres?" Judge James Trotter bypassed the question. The right to dispose of property by will was simply a "creature of the civil state," and if manumission by last will was against public policy, that was that. J. B. Trasher, the counsel, made it clear that there was a great deal at stake. His argument is striking:

> Slaves constitute a portion of the vested wealth and taxable property of the state. Without them her lands are worthless. Would it not therefore be contrary to the policy of the state, to part with this vested wealth, this source of revenue, with that which alone renders her soil valuable.
>
> Again, would it not be productive of mischief, and would it not be spreading a dangerous influence among the slave population of the country, for the slaves of whole plantations to acquire their freedom, take leave of the country and make their departure, proclaiming liberty for themselves and their posterity? Would this not render the other slaves of the country dissatisfied, refractory, and rebellious? Would it not lead to insubordination and insurrection? And if so, would it not be contrary to the policy of the law? So certain as the heavens afford indications of the coming storm, so certain will scenes of blood be the concomitants of such testamentary dispositions in this state.

The court was not impressed. It invoked the idea that a slave, the "subject of absolute dominion," could be freed precisely because of the power of the owner "to dispose of his own property as he pleases." At the same time, it did not adopt the notion that manumission by will came under the law of charities. Power, not piety, was the issue. That and the fact that out-of-state manumission did not violate the "policy" of Mississippi.[20] Two years later Mississippi prohibited manumission by last wills.

Whereas Mississippi's judges were reluctant to discuss the doctrine of *cy pres*, their counterparts in Georgia zealously took it on. The attack began with *Hunter*, *guardian v. Bass, Ex'r.* and *Adams, guardian v. Bass, Ex'r.*, both in 1855. These were companion cases involving the will of Robert Bledsoe whereby his slaves were to be removed and freed in Indiana or Illinois. After Bledsoe made his will Indiana passed a law prohibiting the introduction of blacks, and after his death Illinois did the same.[21] As Judge Benning put it in the first case, *cy pres* did not apply because the court could not say with "any degree of confidence, that he wished them to be free in Ohio or Massachusetts, Canada or Congo, Liberia or wherever else his executor or some Court might say." He concluded with the observation that he did not wish to see the "monstrous doctrine of *Cy pres*" given much latitude.[22]

Cy pres did not help the slaves in the second case because, according to Judge Lumpkin, Bledsoe failed to use language in his will that indicated a general intention to manumit his slaves. The intention was to move them to Indiana or Illinois where they would be free, but there was nothing to indicate a general intention to set them free. Lumpkin could not resist the chance to make his views about blacks well known:

> I do not regret the failure of this bequest. Look at the stringency of the laws of Indiana and Illinois and other Northwestern States against persons of color, and reflect upon their thriftlessness, when not controlled by superior intelligence and forethought, and what friend of the African or of humanity, would desire to see these children of the sun, who luxuriate in a tropical climate and perish with cold in higher latitudes, brought in close contact and competition with the hardy and industrious population which teem in the territory northwest of the Ohio, and who loathe negroes as they would so many lepers?[23]

Within a short time Lumpkin no longer wrote about the hardy people of the free states. Moreover, in *American Colonization Society v. Gartrell* (1857) he referred to "the odious doctrine of *cy pres*."[24]

Questions remained, however, even if the intention of a testator was clear so that *cy pres* was of no concern. One was how to enforce valid trusts set up in wills. Another was to determine which trusts were valid and which were not. The problem of trusts became fairly common in appellate cases from the 1830s forward, as a growing body of trust law converged with growing sectional tensions over slavery. In the tussle between policy and fidelity to the rules of trust law, judges and lawmakers often went in different directions. One of the first significant cases was *Frazier v. Frazier* (South Carolina, 1835), which overruled the earlier influential case of *Bynum v. Bostick* (1812) in which it had been held that a trust to free a slave violated the law and therefore could not be enforced. But if there was such a thing as a valid trust benefiting a slave, how could the slave require the enforcement of the trust in his or her behalf? "On a bill filed by the heirs to partition the slaves," O'Neall wrote, "the court would, if on looking into the will they should find that the executors could execute it by sending the slaves out of the State and there set them free, order them to so discharge the trust reposed in them by the testator."[25] Six years later the South Carolina legislature adopted a proscriptive statute stipulating that any postmortem provision for a trust whereby a slave was to be removed from the state and freed would be void and the slave would remain an asset in the hands of the administrator. This punitive law provoked O'Neall to chastise the legislators and urge repeal:

> The state has nothing to fear from emancipation, regulated as that law [the law of 1800] directs it to be. Many a master knows that he has a slave or slaves, for whom he feels it to be his duty to provide. . . . In a slave country, the good should be especially rewarded. Who are to judge of this, but the master? Give him the power of emancipation, under well regulated guards, and he can dispense the only reward, which either he, or his slave appreciates . . . with well regulated and mercifully applied slave laws, we have nothing to fear for negro slavery. Fanatics of our own, or foreign countries, will be in the condition of the viper biting the file. . . . As against our enemies, I would say to her, *be just, and fear not.* Her sons faltered not on a foreign shore; at home, they will die in the last trench, rather than her rights should be invaded or despoiled.

O'Neall could not know how prophetic he was, but his appeal to the legislators was unpersuasive.[26]

The next year, in *Thompson v. Newlin* (1849), Ruffin confronted the issue of the trust to operate postmortem. Once an executor accepted the trust, he claimed, he could be "compelled to perform it in those methods which the law prescribes for the benefit alike of the subjects of the trust and the public security." Lumpkin adopted a different line in *Sanders v. Ward* (1858). For him there was no problem. Executors were not faithless. "However faithless we may be to the living, we are rarely so to the dead." But there was another resolution, and it was the same as in *Frazier:* "If the heirs move in the matter, this will give the Courts jurisdiction, and they will compel by their decree an execution of the trust." *Slaves* possessed no remedy in Georgia, but they would benefit from the faithfulness that decent and honorable whites displayed among themselves.[27]

Which trusts were valid and which were not? Most of those held valid by the courts involved out-of-state manumissions. Most of those, but not all, pronounced invalid involved in-state manumissions or so-called quasi-emancipations. (These will be considered in the next chapter.) An exception involved bequests to those, other than slaves, incapable of taking the bequest. The most notable illustrations were trusts that failed because the trustees were Quakers or bequests were to the American Colonization Society.

Still another problem loomed above all the conceptual difficulties associated with postmortem manumission. The right to make a will "is one thing," counsel pointed out in *Ross*, and "the power to manumit a slave, by will, is another." The general right was "a power to continue property . . . whilst the other is a power to discontinue property, by a provision, that there shall be no owner."[28] This was in conflict with the right of inheritance. In *Vance v. Crawford* (1848) Lumpkin upheld a bequest of slaves to the American Colonization Society to be taken to Liberia and freed. Despite this, he ended his opinion as follows:

> great indulgence is extended to the declared wishes of testators, touching what they would have done with their property after their death. If it be true, however, that *families* are the original of all societies, and contain the foundation and primitive elements of all other social institutions, and as such deservedly claim the front rank in the protection of Courts, *wills*, which are calculated practically, to disregard and set at naught this divine ordinance, worth more than all that man in his wisdom has ever devised, cannot claim to be regarded with peculiar tenderness and favoritism by Courts of Justice.[29]

After a decade of bitter controversy among the members of the Georgia court, the state legislature, in 1859, adopted a law prohibiting all postmortem manumissions whether "within or without the State."[30]

One way to resolve the conflict between the right to "discontinue property" and the "right of inheritance," then, was to prohibit the postmortem manumission of slaves. The earliest effort to do that was in a Maryland law of 1752. This law was not absolute according to the Maryland Court of Appeals in 1821. It allowed freedom to be given by a last will if the will was not made during the last illness of the testator. The statute was repealed in 1796, and owners could then free slaves by last will if the slaves were under forty-five and able to "work and gain a sufficient maintenance and livelihood."[31] Implicitly, Virginia and North Carolina had prohibited manumission by will when they required that slaves could be freed only for "meritorious services," and those were to be judged by some public authority. Virginia imposed this restriction in 1723 and North Carolina did so in 1741. It was not until 1782 in Virginia and 1830 in North Carolina that owners were expressly authorized to free by last will.[32] In 1800 South Carolina's legislators adopted a restrictive law because owners freed slaves of "a bad or depraved character, or, [who from] age or infirmity, [were] incapable of gaining their livelihood by honest means." To control such duplicitous conduct only manumission by deed was allowed. In 1820 South Carolina limited manumissions to those granted by the legislature. Nonetheless, it still was necessary to deal with the problem of postmortem manumission as late as 1841. After that any bequest, deed of trust, or conveyance that took affect after the death of the owner whereby a slave was to be removed from South Carolina to be emancipated was illegal. The next year Mississippi followed and prohibited manumission by last will.[33]

The same point had been reached in Alabama four years earlier in a judgment in *Trotter v. Blocker* (1838). "That the owner of property is free to relinquish his right to it, at pleasure," Chief Justice Collier wrote, "will not be denied; and the manner of the relinquishment, in the absence of legal restraints, must be left to his discretion. But the imposition of restraints, upon the exercise of this natural right (the more especially as it respects slaves), is not only allowable, but the dictate of a wise policy." This was because "suitable guards" had to be placed around slavery in order to protect the interests of the "citizens at large." The constitution of Alabama said that the legislature had the "power to pass laws to permit the owners of slaves to emancipate them." Whatever form of emancipation the legislature chose, Collier reasoned, would be exclusive. The Alabama law of 1834 provided that masters would have to apply to a county probate judge and follow other rules before they could manumit a slave. There was no authorization to manumit by last will. *Trotter* was overruled in 1854 in *Prater's Adm'r. v. Darby.* "It would appear somewhat improbable that the people," Chilton wrote, "the true source of power in a republican government, should yield up to one of the departments of the State a natural, common-law right, thus making themselves ever afterwards dependent upon the Legislature to reinvest them with it." *Prater,* however, did not long command the allegiance of Alabama's judges. It was overruled in 1859 in *Evans v. Kittrell.*[34]

In some Southern states, in other words, public policy, especially after 1840, overroad the right of an owner of property to "discontinue" the claim to that property when the property was a slave. Public policy had cut deeply into possessive individualism. At the center of possessive individualism was human will, and in the late eighteenth and early nineteenth centuries this was given considerable respect in the construction of last wills and testaments. But as sectional tensions rose, Southern whites showed an increased concern over a free black population among them. One result was the subordination of the will of slaveowners to larger social needs. The expression of "will" by slaves, of course, was something else. The problem of will in slaves also had arisen in manumission cases in the South: it came up when the courts were asked to consider, first, whether contracts between masters and slaves for self-purchase were valid, and, second, whether slaves could ever "elect" freedom under a last will and testament.

Contracts for Manumission

Slaves had an enforceable legal right to purchase their own freedom through contractual arrangements with their owners in civil law jurisprudence. In Spanish law it was known as *coartacion,* gradual self-purchase. Rebecca Scott, however, has shown that the institution was of marginal significance in Cuba, and that the price of slaves put self-purchase well beyond "almost all slaves."[35] Was self-purchase, even if marginal, recognized in the South?

Because slaves lacked "will," they could not generally enter into contracts. Yet some people did enter into agreements with slaves whereby the latter did purchase their freedom. For example, James R. Starkey, a slave of Matthias Manly, a judge of the North Carolina Supreme Court, worked as a barber and accumulated some money. By 1851 Starkey paid the judge for his freedom and was emancipated.[36] Was this a contractual relationship? It was conduct that changed the relationship between the master and the slave, but normally it would not create an enforceable legal obligation. Yet there were exceptions even to this commonsense conclusion.

Some judges, in other words, held that there could be a contractual basis for freedom even when one of the parties to the contract was a slave.

During the 1790s in South Carolina a slave woman purchased and freed a slave, Sally. The manumission was contested on the ground that whatever a slave possessed belonged to her master, and therefore the slave woman could not emancipate another slave. Nonetheless, the judges, in *Guardian of Sally, a Negro, v. Beaty* (1792), supported the contract between the owner of Sally and the slave woman. As Chief Justice John Rutledge put it in the jury charge:

> if the master got the labour of his wench, or what he agreed to receive for her monthly wages, (which was the same thing,) he could not be injured; on the contrary, he was fully satisfied, and all that she earned over ought to be at her disposal; and if the wench chose to appropriate the savings of her extra labour to the purchase of this girl, in order afterwards to set her free, would a jury of the country say no? He trusted not. They were too humane and upright, he hoped, to do such manifest violence to so singular and extraordinary an act of benevolence.[37]

The jury returned its verdict in favor of Sally's freedom. A more predictable decision was reached in *Stevenson v. Singleton* (Virginia, 1829). In the words of Judge William Cabell, "it is not competent to a court of chancery to enforce a contract between master and slave, even although the contract should be fully complied with on the part of the slave."[38]

An important line of cases regarding contracts for freedom were heard in Tennessee. The first was *Ford v. Ford* (1846). There were numerous issues involved, but my immediate concern is Judge Green's remarks about a possible contractual foundation for freedom:

> A slave is not in the condition of a horse or an ox. . . . He has mental capacities, and an immortal principle in his nature, that constitute him equal to his owner but for the accidental position in which fortune has placed him. The owner has acquired conventional rights to him, but the laws under which he is held as a slave have not and cannot extinguish his high-born nature nor deprive him of many rights which are inherent in man. Thus while he is a slave, he can make a contract for his freedom, which our laws recognize, and he can take a bequest of his freedom, and by the same will he can take personal or real estate.[39]

Green's conclusion can be misleading, as subsequent cases show.

In 1835 Moses Lewis purchased his freedom. After he was freed Lewis obtained a note executed against G. F. Simonton. Simonton seized Lewis and imprisoned him. Threatening him with criminal prosecution, he forced Lewis to turn over the note. Lewis petitioned chancery to obtain the value of the note, plus interest. One ground of Simonton's defense was that Lewis could not bring the bill in equity because he was still a slave.[40]

Judge Robert McKinney, in *Lewis v. Simonton* (1847), disagreed. In Tennessee, he claimed, "the owner may part with his right of property in the slave . . . and thereby vest him with an imperfect right to freedom. This may be done by deed, or will, or *even by parol contract with the slave* [emphasis added]: and if in either of these modes the master has parted with his right, nothing remains to be done to entitle the slave to his freedom but the assent of government." McKinney held that a contract between a master and a slave could be a legitimate basis for emancipation. But the inducement to manumit was not the crux. It could as well have been religious scruples, anger at potential heirs, or caprice or money from the slave. The focus was not on the agreement with Lewis or on any "consideration." Rather, it was on the voluntary abrogation of property rights, so that this was not a case of an enforced contract.[41]

During the 1859 court term two more manumission cases involving possible contracts were decided in Tennessee. In *Isaac v. Sliger*, Isaac sued for his freedom on an alleged promise from his former master that he would be freed at the death of the master's wife if "he conducted himself properly." The owner died in 1834 and his wife in 1855. No provision had been made for Isaac's freedom. After the wife's death some of her children decided to sell Isaac, and he responded with a bill in chancery for freedom based on the alleged promise. Judge McKinney ruled that the owner had shown different intentions and had done nothing to secure freedom. The most that could be said was that there was "a mere voluntary declaration or promise, which imposed no obligation on the master, nor did it confer any right on the slave . . . in contemplation of law, it must be regarded a *nudum pactum*." He added a tantalizing remark: "we need not stop to discuss the validity of a contract entered into directly between master and slave for the freedom of the latter. It is settled by our courts, that such a contract—upon a consideration moving either from the slave, or from a stranger on behalf of the slave—is valid and obligatory."[42] The problem here was that there was no "consideration." Obviously, faithful service in a slave would not be seen as consideration because "faithful service" was what slaveowners demanded as their right. A contractual analysis meant that in Tennessee courts manumission would not be a gift of social life "interpreted as a repayment for faithful service."

The other 1859 case was *Isaac v. Farnsworth*. Isaac's owner died in 1829, and in his will he gave his widow the authority to hire out or sell his two slaves. She sold one of them and later proposed to Isaac that if he could get anyone to pay her $300 she would free him. Isaac made a contract with Michael George for the $300 in exchange for eight years of service, an arrangement that might even be seen as indentured servitude rather than slavery for a term of years. In any case, the widow executed an absolute bill of sale to George, with an understanding that he would free Isaac at the end of eight years. A little over a year before the end of the term of service the widow (by then about eighty years old), at the suggestion of Henry Farnsworth, sold Isaac to a man named McCampbell. She made an absolute bill of sale to take effect at the end of the eight years. George refused to acknowledge this title and insisted on his own, coupled with the trust to emancipate. The widow filed a bill to reform the sale to George to make it a contract for eight years' service only. George gave up his title along with Isaac to McCampbell on the latter paying him the balance for Isaac's term of service. Isaac entered his bill to enforce "his contract for emancipation."[43]

Judge Caruthers, who had himself agreed to sell one of his slaves for the purpose of manumission if the slave wished to be free,[44] was disgusted. "It would be as useless as disagreeable," he wrote, "to comment upon the picture of depravity and the perversion of truth among near relations and speculators." Moreover, it was "revolting to see to what an extent some men will go against the rights of the weak, in eager pursuit of gain." But did Isaac have an enforceable claim to freedom? The argument against him was that the widow possessed only a life estate and could not destroy the remainder over to her children by giving him freedom. Normally this would be true, Caruthers noted, but here the will gave her a power to sell, and that transformed the estate into an absolute one. Her arrangement with George was a consent to an emancipation "for a satisfactory consideration."[45]

Caruthers noted that George could not surrender the trust "to the prejudice of Isaac's rights" when Isaac was not a party to the compromise. Isaac, he continued, "was allowed by his mistress to become a party to this contract and arrangement for his benefit, and is entitled to the advantages of it, subject alone to the legal condition, that the judicial authorities acting for the State shall sanction it."[46] The latter had been done. In what sense was Isaac a party to the contract? The most likely was that Caruthers viewed Isaac as the beneficiary of the trust in his favor by the consent of his owner. If this was so, it meant that he held that slaves might possess equitable rights enforceable against their owner if their owner had made a contract with another person for the benefit of the slave. Even this would be saying a great deal.

The court clarified matters in *McCloud and Karnes v. Chiles* (1860), on the eve of the Civil War. The right of freedom, Judge McKinney wrote, "is not imparted by force of a formal contract in the legal sense, for the slave, as such, is incapable of making a contract for his freedom or of paying a valuable consideration, as he can have nothing to give. The right must therefore be regarded . . . as the pure gift of the owner, based upon some moral, and not on a legal, consideration." A moral obligation was an unenforceable, imperfect obligation.[47]

Tennessee judges were more sensitive to freedom than those in many other states,[48] and the same has been said for those in Kentucky. The first significant case in Kentucky was *Beall v. Joseph* (1806). Woods, the owner of Joe, sold some land to Edwards in 1799 and agreed that Edwards would also have Joe for four years; after that Joe was to be free. Edwards, however, sold Joe to Beall. The county court found in favor of Joe, but its decision was overruled. There were only two ways to emancipate in Kentucky: either by a deed in writing or by a testamentary disposition. Neither was involved here. "It is therefore clear," the court concluded, "that no declaration nor promise made to a slave in this state, or for his benefit, by the owner or any other person, can be enforced by a court, either of law or equity." A bare promise created no enforceable right.[49]

Three years later *Thompson v. Wilmot* (1809) went to the state supreme court. Ruth Wilmot had exchanged a slave named Will in Maryland for a slave named Harry, the property of Thomas Thompson, who was leaving for Kentucky. The consideration for the agreement was that Thompson would emancipate Will after seven years. Will "was persuaded by Thompson, to leave her and go with him to Kentucky, by the prospect of freedom." It was also provided that if Will, after one year, did not like Kentucky, he would be allowed to return to Maryland. Will stayed the full time, but Thompson did not free him. Suit was brought on Will's behalf, but it was held in 1805 that a written contract by which Thompson promised to emancipate did not amount to an emancipation and did not authorize a common law suit on Will's behalf.[50]

Ruth Wilmot filed a bill in chancery for a specific execution of the contract in Will's favor. In his answer Thompson referred to "the contract really made with Will in the presence of the complainant." The court found in favor of Will. The answer, according to Chief Justice Bibb, did "not afford a colorable pretext for withholding a performance of his engagement . . . under circumstances interesting to humanity and most obligatory upon a man of good conscience and unpolluted faith." The court concluded that "the contract in itself was not forbidden by any political institution, but is in unison with the dictates of natural right." A promise to emancipate was sufficient to sustain a contract if the parties were both free, even though the beneficiary was a slave.[51]

When several years later the Kentucky court faced a direct contract between a master and a slave for self-purchase, it took a more predictable turn. In *Willis (of color) v. Bruce and Warfield* (1848) Judge James Simpson ruled that "a promise to, or an executory agreement with a slave by his owner, that he shall be emancipated, is not obligatory, and cannot be enforced either at law or in equity." Moreover, any suit for freedom based on a claim that a master had promised freedom would fail as "contrary to the policy of the law, and inconsistent with the relation of master and slave." Fundamental rules of contract in the common law, as well as policy, meant that there was no room for the concept of *coartacion*. Simpson admitted that emancipation could result from self-purchase, but it would be because of the act of the master, not because there was an enforceable contract.[52]

But what about civil law Louisiana? Article 174 of the civil code stated that "the slave is incapable of making any kind of contract, except those which relate to his own emancipation." Schafer surveyed the proceedings arising on this article that reached the Louisiana Supreme Court. In all, she found sixteen cases that involved self-purchase contractual claims to freedom. Sometimes the claim was upheld, often it was not. The reason some slaves lost was because they failed to prove that they had paid the full purchase price for their freedom. To illustrate, Victoire brought suit for her freedom in 1815. She won in the lower court but lost in the supreme court because the only evidence she was able to produce was oral, and the rule was that oral evidence was inadmissible in actions involving the disposition of immovables.[53] Altogether the number of cases is not large, and I found none of self-purchase in the parish records. If this impression is sound, the experience of Louisiana slaves was similar to that of Cuban slaves. For most, self-purchase was out of the question.

The "Election" Cases

Contract law implicated questions of human will, but there was another area where it arose: when slaves were allowed to choose between freedom and continued enslavement. Most instances in which the view of the slave was considered occurred in testamentary dispositions. Doubtless, a logical intuition would be like that of the Alabama Supreme Court in *Carroll v. Brumby* (1848). The testator "did intend to give them [the slaves] the option of freedom or servitude." But, Judge Edward Dargan wrote, "they have not the legal capacity or power to choose—the law forbids this."[54]

As logical as this is, it was not universal. A particularly instructive line of cases in Virginia began with *Elder v. Elder* (1833). The testator, who died in 1826, provided in his will that certain named slaves would go to Gabriel Dissoway in trust to be sent to Liberia. The remaining slaves willing to go should also go to Dissoway, and those who preferred to stay in Virginia would go to the brother of the testator within a year of the testator's death. In the lower court the chancellor ruled that all the slaves except Mingo, who refused to accept freedom, would be allowed to go to Liberia. Two infants would also go upon the "election of their mother for them." The judges avoided the problem of choice in slaves.[55]

The next two cases were *Forward's Adm'r. v. Thamer* (1853) and *Osborne v. Taylor* (1855). In *Forward* the will of Arthur Savage began as follows: "I emancipate and set free all my negroes at the following dates . . . provided they shall remove and leave the state of Virginia within six months after they shall go free; but if they do not remove and leave the state aforesaid within the six months, then and in that case to becomes slaves to my estate forever." Green B. Samuels, for the court, held the condition void. Judge Daniel dissented, but without opinion. The slave Thamer was entitled to her freedom at the beginning of 1844. The condition of the will was not a condition on which freedom attached, but one that occurred after freedom attached. That was something slaveowners could not do. They could either keep slaves as slaves or they could free them. When persons were bequeathed as slaves, the testator could "annex no valid condition subsequent, which would be repugnant to the state of slavery." The reverse was also true. The *Forward* court was spared the problem of "election" because the gifts of freedom preceded the "condition."[56]

By the terms of the will in *Osborne*, slaves were either to be manumitted or to have the option of remaining in Virginia and choosing masters. If they selected the latter alternative, they were to serve until the death of the person chosen and then "they shall have the option of freedom or slavery, by making a second choice." Counsel argued that the slaves were to remain slaves until they elected freedom. Samuels felt that this misconstrued the will. In a "substantive clause" the will "distinctly manumits them; and afterwards, in another clause, gives them the election to remain in the state of Virginia, in a condition intermediate between slavery and freedom." This was against policy and void. He concluded that "the bequest of freedom is in no wise impaired by the impracticable and repugnant alternative offered to the choice of the slaves." The will had read in relevant part: "it is my further will and direction that the slaves embraced in this item be emancipated . . . but should a part or the whole of the negroes prefer remaining in the state, they can do so by choosing masters to serve during the life of the person or persons chosen." By voiding this "condition subsequent" the court again avoided any discussion about the capacity of slaves to exercise human will and choose between freedom and slavery.[57]

The year after Virginia adopted its self-enslavement statute the court decided the seminal case of *Baily v. Poindexter* (1858). This time the court was sharply divided. The law, counsel for the heirs of Poindexter argued, "regards a negro slave, so far as his civil *status* is concerned, as purely and absolutely mere property, to be bought and sold and pass and descend as a tract of land, a horse or an ox. From this it necessarily follows, that the condition of the negro in slavery is that of absolute civil incapacity, or rather that of an absolute negation of civil existence." The act of election, he said, "involves the exercise of civil rights and civil capacity; and an emancipation made dependent upon the exercise of civil rights or legal capacity by the slave, is necessarily void." Some civil cases acknowledged the humanity of the slave, but that was no problem. The true inquiry, he believed, was not "what is the moral and intellectual character or capacity of the negro race, or for what qualities or habits slaves are generally acquired or esteemed, but *what is the relation they sustain to the law of the land*?"[58] Legal positivism doomed slaves to civil negation. Moreover, the case relied on to show that slaves were viewed as moral beings did not deal with their status; it concerned moral and intellectual qualities as elements that helped define the value of the slave as property. A well-behaved, moral slave was worth more than a lazy or wicked one.[59]

Counsel on the other side conceded most of these arguments but attempted to validate the will on the ground that the slaves did not make themselves free by any choice of theirs. The crucial element was not their exercise of will, but the "will of their master, who has a right by the law to emancipate them." The majority of the court held that a master could not give his slaves a capacity to choose, it would be a legal "impossibility." Judge Daniel developed the main point as follows:

> when we assent to the general proposition, as I think we must do, that our slaves have no civil or social rights; that they have no legal capacity to make, discharge or assent to contracts, that though a master enter into the form of an agreement with his slave to manumit him, and the slave proceed fully to

perform all required of him in the agreement, he is without remedy in case the master refuse to comply with his part of the agreement; and that a slave cannot take any thing under a decree or will except his freedom; we are led necessarily to the conclusion that nothing short of the exhibition of a positive enactment, or of legal decisions having equal force, can demonstrate the capacity of a slave to exercise an election in respect to his manumission.

Slaves could *take* freedom under a will in Virginia, but they could not *choose* freedom under that will.[60]

Judge Moncure dissented, along with Samuels. "A master," he believed, "may emancipate his slaves *against* their consent. Why may he not make such consent the condition of emancipation?" The fallacy of the counterargument "consists in supposing that to make such an election would be to exercise a civil right or capacity." He did not say what he thought it would be. He tied the problem of election under a will to a voluntary enslavement under the Virginia statute. "Slaves emancipated absolutely," he pointed out, "still have an election between freedom and slavery. They may become slaves again under the provisions of the Code."[61] What he did not note, of course, was that if they made the choice to voluntarily return to slavery, they would do so at a time when they were free.

The *Bailey* decision was followed a few months later by *Williamson v. Coalter* (1858). This involved a will that provided that slaves would be freed and transported to Liberia "or any other free state or country in which they may elect to live, the adults selecting for themselves, and the parents for the infant children." Furthermore, if any of the slaves preferred to remain in Virginia, they were to be allowed to "select among my relations their respective owners." Allen, the president of the court, invalidated the bequests because slaves possessed no civil capacity to make an election. He distinguished the case before him from *Forward* and *Osborne* on the ground that here "there was no intention to emancipate without consulting the slave. The alternative of freedom or slavery was presented to the slave. Until acceptance, he remained a slave. If he declined he continued a slave, his *status* never having been changed."[62] By the late 1850s the majority of Virginia's judges had rejected the notion that a slave could *ever* select between freedom and slavery, a position A. E. Keir Nash characterized as "Continental Absolutism of a peculiarly twisted sort,"[63] whereas the state's legislators had affirmed the right of a free black to make that choice.

North Carolina's judges, on the other hand, believed that it was possible for slaves to elect freedom. Two decisions by Ruffin illustrate their reasoning. In *Cox v. Williams* (1845) Mary Bissell gave her slaves to the American Colonization Society to be sent with their consent to Africa. The next of kin contended that the provision for emancipation was against state law. Ruffin held that it was not. It grew out of the "natural right of an owner to free his slaves: and was restrained to the extent that the freedmen would have to leave the state." The society could take the bequest, but it depended on "whether the negroes, who are adults, are willing to go to Africa or not." "We are not sure," Ruffin wrote, "that it would be proper to send them abroad against their will, even if there were no such restriction in the charter of the society—since, if a slave has capacity to accept emancipation, it would seem that he must have the power also of refusing it, when the offer of his owner is upon the condition of his leaving the country, and when he is not compelled by law." If an adult chose not to go, he or she would be sold and the proceeds would go to benefit those who did. The children posed a problem. Ruffin's solution was that those "under, say the age of fourteen" would have the choice made by their parents. The age was selected as a measure of an "age of discretion." He also considered the issue of those who lacked parents, and he confronted a question others finessed or saw as no problem: what if the parents chose slavery? In either case, Ruffin ruled that "liberty must be reserved," the children to "make their election, when they shall arrive at the age of fourteen." No one could choose slavery for another, they could only choose freedom.[64]

Ruffin had another opportunity to explain his views in *Redding v. Findley* (1858). "It is not true in point of fact or law," he argued, "that slaves have not a mental or a moral capacity to make the election to be free, and, if needful to that end, to go abroad for that purpose. From the nature of slavery, they are denied a legal capacity to make contracts or acquire property while remaining in the state." But, Ruffin stated, "they are responsible human beings, having intelligence to know right from wrong, and perceptions of pleasure and pain, and of the difference between bondage and freedom, and thus, by nature, they are competent to give or withhold their assent to things that concern their state."[65]

Civil negation rested heavily on legal positivism, and Ruffin countered with natural law. "No one ever thought that it required a municipal law to confer the right of manumission on the owner, or the capacity of accepting freedom by the slave. They pre-exist, and are founded in nature, just as other capacities for dealings between man and man."[66] Ruffin analyzed slavery in terms of human relationships—it was a problem of domination and submission. Those judges who viewed manumission as a legacy or a bequest had some difficulty with the question of election. A property analysis and legal positivism tended to civil negation more than the harsh judgments of Ruffin in a case like *Mann* or the opinions of Lumpkin, opinions that affirmed the racial basis of American slavery and emphasized the power and domination of slaveowners, even more than they did "property" rights.

Freedom and the Claims of Creditors

At the outset of his discussion of manumission Stroud wrote: "Having degraded a rational and immortal being into a *chattel*,—a thing of bargain and sale,—it has been discovered that certain incidents result from this degradation which it concerns the welfare of the community vigorously to enact and preserve. One of these is, that the master's benevolence to his unhappy bondman is not to be exercised, by emancipation, *without the consent of his creditor.*" Stroud was correct, and one could add that the claims of widows on the estates of husbands could also defeat or delay freedom granted to slaves. This danger arose when a widow renounced her husband's will and claimed her dower rights, or thirds.[67]

The cases of creditors defeating claims to freedom, however, were much more significant. Nearly every proceeding in which judges dealt with creditors' claims included a reference to an equitable maxim: one must do justice before one does benevolence. The duty to fulfill one's obligations took precedence over piety or charity. Nearly all Southern states that allowed manumission saved the rights of creditors. The first statute was Virginia's law of 1782.[68]

Ten years later David Bradley recorded a deed of manumission for a number of slaves in his possession. He later married Eliza, the widow of John Harrison. Six years after that the distributees of Harrison brought an action against Bradley and his wife for an account of their administration of Harrison's estate. Bradley functioned as an administrator along with his wife. The distributees won in chancery, and they later brought an action of debt against Bradley and his wife. On this action they obtained an execution against the slaves freed in 1792; those people had been enjoying their freedom for nearly twelve years. St. George Tucker's opinion, in *Woodley v. Abby* (Virginia, 1805), was favorable to the former slaves. Tucker admitted that slaves were liable to be used to satisfy debts. But that was only the case while they were under the executor's control. Once he assented to the legacy of a slave, as to the son of the testator, the slave was no longer liable, he had become the property of the son. By analogy, St. George Tucker concluded, "an emancipated slave ought not to be put in a worse situation than the voluntary donee, or legatee, of a slave, who has obtained possession by the act and consent of the donor, or by the assent of the executor."[69]

Judge Paul Carrington also favored the slaves. He relied on the fact that there was a gap in the law of 1782 that was not filled until 1792. The saving clause in the 1782 law, he argued, "extended to vested rights in the property itself; and not to a case like this, where no specific right in the slaves had been acquired." In 1792 this was added to the statute: "all slaves so emancipated, shall be liable to be taken by execution, to satisfy any debt contracted by the person emancipating them before such emancipation is made."[70] But *Woodley* originally arose before passage of the 1792 law, and there was no saving clause involving creditors of testators who had no contractual claim to the particular slaves.

Judges Roane and William Fleming wrote separate opinions unfavorable to freedom; President Lyons agreed with them, so that the emancipated slaves were placed at risk. The law of 1782, Fleming believed, preserved the rights of creditors in general. "Any other construction would operate injustice to those who had trusted the owner upon the faith of that property." Roane relied on the law against fraudulent conveyances. It was "founded on principles of justice and fair dealing." Surely this was included in the words of the 1782 law, which had to be interpreted to "respect justice and vested rights." Nonetheless, the evidence did not show that it was necessary to levy the execution on the particular slaves who had been freed in order to fulfill Bradley's obligations. If Bradley had other property, including slaves or even other emancipated slaves, "such property and such slaves should be applied in exoneration and aid of the appellees [Abby and the other former slaves] by such rule and proportions as are equitable and just." The lower chancery court was directed to obtain the necessary information and to modify its original decree "to equalize the servitude of the appellees as much as possible, if such a proceeding is found to be indispensable."[71] This decree left considerable room for flexible equitable remedies. So far as the slaves were concerned, for instance, they might have been hired out for a time or sold.

Creditors' rights also were at issue in 1829 in *Dunn v. Amey et al.* Judge Cabell noted that the mere intention of the testator to free gave a "right to freedom" that "ought to be enforced in a court of equity." The right to freedom, however, was subordinate to the duty to pay debts. But before freedom was defeated, there should be an account of "the assets, both real and personal . . . (for we are of opinion, that the will subjected the real estate to the payment of his debts)."[72] If an emancipator was careful enough to mention that his real property was to be liable, along with his personal property, he could protect the freedom of his former slaves.

An opinion written four years later went further. Judge Carr wrote in *Nicholas v. Burruss* (1833) that the estate of the decedent was "fully sufficient, without the slaves, for the payment of all the testator's debts; and that, at the time of the trial, there were, forming a part of his estate, 4000 acres of land in the western country, and 600 acres in *Virginia*." He made no reference to language in the will expressly charging the land with liability for debts. Carr placed land and personal property together as a common fund for the payment of debts and suggested that creditors look to that fund before they looked to slaves who were to be set free.[73] Clearly some of Virginia's judges tried to find some way to secure freedom when that was the obvious intention of the testator. The crucial differences among them concerned how to balance claims to freedom and the fair claims of creditors.

Judges in Maryland approached the same problem from a number of different angles. In *Negro George et al. v. Corse's Adm'r* (1827) the testator freed his slaves and added that if his personal estate, excluding the slaves, was insufficient to pay his debts, his real estate should be sold. Judge Thomas Beale Dorsey supported the judgment against the slaves on the ground that the "sufficiency of real assets" was an issue that could not be tried between the administrator and the slaves "without 'prejudice' to creditors," because the creditors were not parties. Judge Stevenson Archer reached the same conclusion but for different reasons. He believed that it made no sense to say that creditors were prejudiced if by the manumission of slaves they were compelled to resort to the realty. The problem was that there were "no parties to the record competent to make the admission" that the realty was a sufficient fund because the executor dealt only with personal estate. Finally, Judge Richard Tilghman Earle sided with Dorsey, but he was even more forceful about the rights of creditors: "It was not in his [the testator's] power to confine them [the creditors] to a particular fund for the satisfaction of their debts, to whose demands the whole of his estate was equally liable." Unlike the conclusion in *Dunn*, Earle contended that a testator could not alter the rule.[74]

Eight years after this decision it was cited as authority in *Fenwick v. Chapman* (U.S. Supreme Court, 1835), a case that rested on Maryland law but arrived at the Supreme Court on appeal from the District of Columbia Circuit Court. In a unanimous opinion the Court declined to be bound by the reasoning in *Negro George* and construed Maryland law on its own. It ruled that in Maryland a testator, by "express words or manifest intention," could exempt his personalty from liability for debts and charge his realty. "The will is the executor's law."[75]

The Maryland judges responded to the reasoning in *Fenwick* in *Cornish v. Willson* (1848). They refused to follow the Supreme Court's reading of Maryland law. A charge on realty was not within the jurisdiction of a court of law. It was solely a question for equity, and in the case of manumitted slaves and an insufficiency of personalty a court of equity would intervene, suspend the legal proceedings, and order the sale of realty charged with the payment of debts. The slaves could then obtain their freedom in proper proceedings.[76] Testators could not change the legal rule, and a court of law, where creditors were not represented, lacked jurisdiction in such cases.

Well before this decision, Maryland's judges had made essentially the same point and had shown more sensitivity to manumission than appeared in *Negro George*. The proper remedy when there was a conflict between the claims of creditors and those entitled to freedom, the court ruled in *Allein v. Sharp* (1835), was by a bill in equity so that all parties' claims could be dealt with. Nonetheless, the court made it clear that the burden of proof, when manumission was involved, was on the creditor. It held, moreover, that the law of 1796 "charges the whole of the manumitter's property with the payment of his debts, in favor of his manumitted slaves, because the act of manumission is to be effectual, if not done in prejudice of creditors; which plainly and necessarily implies that the residue of his property is first to be appropriated to the payment of his debts, before the manumitted slaves can be made liable therefor." In *Thomas v. Wood* (1848) the judgment in *Allein* was cited to prove that persons manumitted were "not assets for the payment of debts." The manumission, even though in prejudice of creditors, was "valid." It was a startling conclusion, and the judges did not explain what risk, if any, manumitted persons ran if the rest of an estate was not sufficient to pay outstanding debts. They held only that if creditors could prove an insufficiency of property, "the proper relief would be accorded to them."[77]

Virginia's judges had treated slaves as though they were assets in the hands of executors, and the same was true in Tennessee. In *Harry v. Green* (1848), Judge Nathan Green held that the slaves were "legatees of their own freedom, and this is a specific legacy." If there was a "deficiency of assets first liable for the payment of debts," the freedmen had to "contribute, as specific legatees of personal property are bound in such case to contribute." The slaves would be allowed to pay the debt, but if they should "fail to raise the money" they would be hired out until the debts were paid.[78]

Finally, Kentucky jurists developed still another theory to balance the various claims. Beginning in 1830 with *Ferguson v. Sarah*, they embraced a lien theory. Chief Justice Robertson ruled that after manumission the person freed "is free as against the emancipator, and the world" except for *bona fide* creditors or persons with a better right to the slave than the emancipator. As for the creditor, his "right does not nullify the act of emancipation, nor otherwise affect it, further than as a lien for the ultimate security of the debt." Eight years later, in *Nancy v. Snell* (1838), the court admitted that slaves, as property, were "a fund for the payment of debts." However, as "freedom is a legacy, above all price, humanity, justice and the spirit of our laws, inculcate the propriety of placing them in the most favored class of legatees." Slaves would be protected against unnecessary sales whenever there was a sufficiency of other funds.[79]

Nancy was not as clear as it might have been because the court referred to a "legacy," and legacy referred to personal property. In Kentucky slaves passed as real estate. This was important in the judgment in *Caleb v. Fields* (1840). There the court noted that because slaves passed as land, they did not go to executors as assets but passed immediately to the devisee without the assent of an executor. Consequently, "in like manner a slave emancipated by will, is not assets in the hands of the executor, but . . . the title to freedom passes to the beneficiary immediately." The conclusion was that the "lien" in favor of creditors could not be enforced against the executor. Rather, there had to be some proceeding in which the person freed "would be entitled to defend his rights," and he should not be disfranchised "unless the debt of the pursuing creditor can not be otherwise made."[80]

The rule in Kentucky was made clearer in another case during the same term. In *Snead v. David* what the creditor possessed was "no right to his person [the freed person] or services, but only to his value." By the act of emancipation dominion was given to the former slave. It was not subject to the lien of the creditor. The value of the former slave was.[81] This meant that emancipated persons would be liable to contribute to the liquidation of debts up to their former market value. They would retain their freedom by paying that amount. Kentucky's judges leaned further toward affirming freedom in the face of creditors' claims than did any others.

Manumission in Practice: Virginia as a Case Study

The restraints or reservation of rights of creditors were only one danger to vesting freedom. The states had to assent to the attempted manumission, and Southern colonies and later states provided the ways a manumission could be done lawfully. There were numerous variations—such as rules involving age, ability to work, emancipation by deed or will, and so on. Still, a case study of the rules of one jurisdiction and the practice under those rules provide a point of reference for further inquiry. Since the comparative study of Tannenbaum appeared in 1946, there has been considerable agreement that a close relationship between racism and restraints on manumission existed. Scholars disagree about whether the British slave societies in the Caribbean and on the Continent were more closed than the non-British slave societies in the Caribbean and Latin America, as Tannenbaum claimed. Those who have tried to show that he overstated the hostility to manumission in the American South have focused on Virginia in the late eighteenth century. The legal history of manumission in Virginia, therefore, assumes an unusual importance.

As early as 1667 Virginia's burgesses closed off one possible road to freedom, Christianization of slaves. The preamble to the statute noted that "some doubts have arisen whether children that are slaves by birth, and by the charity and piety of their owners made pertakers of the blessed sacrament of baptisme, should by vertue of their baptisme be made ffree." The law was that baptism did not free a slave. After 1691 any slave freed had to be transported out of Virginia within six months. If the heirs or executor failed to carry out that requirement, they would be fined and the churchwardens would use the money to pay for the slave's transportation, with anything left going to the use of the parish poor. From 1723 to 1782, finally, no slave could be freed in Virginia "except for some meritorious service," and that would be judged by the councillors and the governor. If anyone freed a slave in any other manner, the slave would be treated as a derelict, taken up by the churchwardens, and sold at the next county court.[82] The "meritorious service" limit was a version of the Patterson-Davis idea of a manumission as a gift exchange for "faithful service." Manumission in the colonial South, in other words, was not seen in contractual terms. A contractual analysis did not emerge until the nineteenth century with the development of a coherent and significant body of contract law resting on the doctrine of "consideration." Before that, manumission was viewed in terms of a property rather than contract analysis: it was the right of an owner to discontinue property. But policy in the colonial world constrained the right of the owner to the extent that there had to be a demonstrated meritorious service. Practice, however, tended to fuse "meritorious" and "faithful"; thus manumission could be regarded in fact as a gift of social life by an owner for faithful service, if sanctioned by the state.

Manumission, in any case, was rare in the colonial world. The first request to grant a manumission came ten years after the passage of the law. It was an application from the executors of the will of Philip Ludwell. He freed only Jonathan Pearse in his will because of his "faithful Services." But the executors added that it was also because of his "having delivered to them one other Slave pursuant to a Clause in the said will . . . impowering them to exchange any of his Slaves in the Consideration of the Premises."[83] The next request was by Anne Alexander to free Robin in 1735. She was the widow and residuary legatee of John Smith, who had

had a great affection for Robin and had said that on his, Smith's, death, Robin should be freed "for his fidelity and Diligent Service." This was also granted. Meritorious service thus could be defined by an emancipator, and it was not infrequently defined as faithfulness. Despite these acts, few slaves were ever emancipated in colonial Virginia. Of the 215 sample wills from York County, only 2 instructed that their slaves be manumitted. And because there was no mention of these slaves in the records of the council, it is doubtful that they ever received their freedom.[84]

By the 1770s and 1780s, however, the pressures to manumit, and to authorize private manumissions, were building. Quakers, for instance, were turning against slavery. A January 1778 entry in the order book for Southampton County, which was inhabited by a large number of Quakers, reads: "It being represented to this court that several persons in this county have and are about to manumit their slaves therefore it is ordered that the churchwardens of the parishes of St. Luke and Nottoway make inquiry concerning the premises and deal with such slaves as the law directs." Virginia altered the law in 1782 in response to a number of petitions, largely coming from religious sources, asking that those "disposed to emancipate their slaves may be empowered so to do."[85] By virtue of that law, owners were authorized to free slaves by last will "or by any other instrument in writing." The slaves had to be of sound mind and body and between twenty-one and forty-five if male and between eighteen and forty-five if female. Slaves above or below those ages being freed had to be supported by the emancipators. By 1806 persons freed had to leave Virginia within twelve months, or they forfeited their right to freedom and would be seized and sold by the overseers of the poor. Thirty years later Virginia allowed persons freed after 1806 to apply to the local court for permission to remain in the county where they were freed. Finally, in its 1850 constitution this appeared: "Slaves hereafter emancipated shall forfeit their freedom by remaining in the commonwealth more than twelve months after they became actually free, and shall be reduced to slavery under such regulation as may be prescribed by law."[86] Virginians were experimenting with the rules on private manumission.

As early as 1913 John H. Russell wrote that "the removal in 1782 of restraints upon manumission was like the sudden destruction of a dam before the increasing impetus of a swollen stream. The free negro population . . . more than doubled in the space of two years. Instances of manumission, often of large numbers of slaves, became frequent." Russell concluded that "this period from 1782 to 1806 was the time when manumission was most popular in Virginia." Then, "In 1806," Jordan observed, "Virginia restricted the right of masters to manumit their slaves. On its face not a remarkable measure, in fact it was the key step in the key state and more than any event marked the reversal of the tide which had set in strongly at the Revolution. It was the step onto the slippery slope which led to Appomattox and beyond." This is a strong claim. But one of the strongest statements about the revolutionary generation of Southern slaveholders was that of Gary Nash, who noted that, even in the absence of a plan of compensated emancipation, "thousands of slaveholders were disentangling themselves from the business of coerced labor." He also believed that there was evidence "pointing to a widespread desire among Virginians (who represented about half of the nation's slaveowners) to be quit of slavery" along with a "simultaneous desire to be quit of blacks."[87]

There is evidence, of course, of opposition to slavery in general and of a number of large-scale manumissions. In 1785, for instance, Methodist leaders Francis Asbury and Thomas Coke brought a petition to Virginia legislators asking for a general emancipation law. Then there were the large private manumissions, such as those of John Pleasants, Robert Carter, and George Washington. Carter tried to free over five hundred slaves. And in his 1799 will Washington provided for the freedom of his slaves on the death of his wife. However, there is reason to be cautious about the idea that there was a rush to emancipate, or that big planters acted out of conscience to disassociate themselves from slavery. Thomas Jefferson is a case in point, as Finkelman has argued. Jefferson owned well over a hundred slaves, but he freed only eight, and of those he freed only two during the late eighteenth century. Moreover, proslavery petitions submitted to the assembly in 1784 and 1785 show that many Virginians were not happy with the liberalization of the manumission law. Some of those petitions developed a strong biblical defense of slavery, and all were deeply racist. One petition, calling for the rejection of any scheme of emancipation and repeal of the law of 1782, paraded a list of terrors associated with manumission, including "the Rapes, Murders, and Outrages, which a vast Multitude of unprincipled, unpropertied, revengeful, and remorseless Banditti are capable of perpetrating."[88]

Despite such horrifying rhetoric, the fact remains that slaves were freed. Was this widespread? Richard S. Dunn downplayed the rush to emancipate. "Most big Chesapeake slaveholders displayed little enthusiasm for manumission," he noted. John Tayloe, for instance, a rather decent low-keyed paternalist, had only one free black among the 225 slaves on his estate at Mount Airy. Nonetheless, "something was accomplished," Dunn admitted. His primary evidence came from Westmoreland County, where Robert Carter of Nomini Hall tried to free 509 slaves over a twenty-year period. According to his biographer, it is not clear whether Carter's relatives and neighbors were successful in blocking some of his efforts. Nevertheless, as Dunn noted, in 1810 Westmoreland had 621 free blacks, which gave it one of the "highest county totals in Virginia."[89] This county, then, ought to provide us with solid evidence of the early practice under the manumission law, but I have added data from some other counties for comparison.

I will begin with the wills probated in Westmoreland County between 1782 and 1806 and then take up manumission by deed during the lifetime of the owner. The first will freeing a slave following passage of the 1782 law was probated in November 1786, four years after the law allowed masters to manumit by last wills. Daniel Bailey freed only one slave, "old Black Daniel." More than ten years elapsed before another slave was freed by will in the county, and then it was a man, Samuel Sanford, who resided in Baltimore.[90]

In 1798 an important and complex will freeing a number of slaves was probated. Joseph Pierce, the testator, stated: "I have set Tom, Harry, Winny, Hannah & James at liberty and my desire is that they shall continue so." In the case of five others he noted that "I cant think of leaving them slaves for life—therefore they are to be set at liberty at the expiration of five years." Pierce set fifteen additional slaves free at various times in the future. He added a provision that if any of the females among the fifteen had children while they were still in "Servitude," the children would serve to the age of thirty-one and "so on until they all become free."[91] This brought into play the rule against perpetuities in cases of manumission (considered in the next chapter). In any case, between 1782 and 1806 only three men manumitted slaves by will, and only six slaves received immediate freedom.

What of those freed by deeds rather than wills? Nineteen people recorded deeds of emancipation between 1782 and the spring of 1807, and several of them had close ties to Robert Carter.[92] Only twenty-two slaves were freed by seventeen of the nineteen people during this quarter of a century.[93] Two men—John Brinnon and Robert Carter—freed a larger number, but the precise count is unclear as the record shows "sundry slaves." Ultimately, of course, Carter tried to free 509.[94]

Carter was a gradualist. According to Benjamin Dawson, the steward of Carter's estate, he feared that immediate emancipation would create serious problems for the slaves and "chaos for the community." He began his gradualist effort in 1792. Prior to that year only three slaves were freed by deed by two men, both of whom acted in April 1786. The deed of manumission recorded by John Rowand makes it clear that his motive was not opposition to slavery. Rowand had bought Frank Toulson as a slave for 100 pounds. Toulson, in turn, had purchased himself from Rowand.[95]

The record of manumission by deed is not particularly strong, except for that of Brinnon and Carter. No such deeds were recorded for four years after the adoption of the law, and none after April 1786 until February 1792, nearly six years later. But it was presumably between 1782 and the upheaval of 1785 (when proslavery petitions and the request for a general emancipation law reached the assembly) that the emancipationist sentiment was strongest. In any event, there was then a bulge during the period 1792–95, when Carter recorded several deeds involving "sundry slaves" and Brinnon freed a large number in 1792.[96] From 1797 to 1800 there were six separate manumissions of one slave each; thereafter, one emancipator recorded a deed a year, and in no case did the manumission involve more than two slaves until June 1804,[97] when Benjamin Dawson freed a number as a trustee of Robert Carter's estate. The record hardly supports the view that there was a flood of manumissions that betokened a strong commitment to disentangle Virginia's planters from forced labor.[98]

Evidence from other counties supports this conclusion. Moreover, as Schwarz and Peter Albert have shown, a number of early emancipators were free blacks liberating members of their family or immediate community. In some counties, such as York, Charlotte, Isle of Wight, Amherst, Powhatan, and Amelia a fairly large percentage of the emancipators were free blacks. Whereas no free blacks were among the emancipators in Westmoreland, they amounted to 39 percent of the number in Isle of Wight County. There were twelve black emancipators from 1782 to 1806.[99] Although Albert's study affirms the belief that there was no great rush to free slaves among the revolutionary generation of Virginia slaveowners, it also suggests that the story of manumission could vary from county to county.

This is confirmed by the evidence from Charles City County. Of approximately 3,100 slaves in that county, a little over 50 were liberated by deeds or wills recorded or probated between 1789 and 1805. In 1793 Benjamin Dancy freed 11 slaves by deed "from a sense of its being my duty." He retained the "service" of the males under twenty-one and the females under eighteen until they reached those ages.[100] What is more revealing, perhaps, were the manumissions by deed recorded by Charles Binns, Samuel Hargrave, and John Crew. Binns freed one slave from "principles of humanity" and the "dictates of my own conscience." Hargrave liberated slaves on three occasions and Crew on two. Hargrave emancipated five slaves in January 1791, four in January 1795, and six in January 1796. All three deeds began the same way: "fully persuaded that freedom is the natural right of all mankind, and being desirous of doing to others as I would be done" he did manumit. These were not cases of freeing a single, favored, or "faithful" old slave: the gift of freedom had nothing to do with faithfulness. The crucial point, however, is that these men were not the norm among Virginians, they were Quakers.[101] A little over eighteen people were freed in eight different wills recorded during this period.[102]

There were no emancipators among the large slaveholders in Charles City County. Benjamin Harrison, the owner of the beautiful Berkeley estate on the James River, divided up his slaves among his wife and children. He was not unmindful of the feelings of the slaves, however. In a codicil he directed that the slaves be put in "four as equal parts as possible without parting men and their wives."[103]

Records from counties outside Westmoreland show that there were numerous motives for freeing slaves, but that it was rarely because of opposition to the institution.[104] The notable exceptions were the Quaker emancipators and the free blacks. Moreover, none of the emancipators in the sample counties outside Westmoreland were large slaveowners. An emancipator like Robert Carter was not common. On this point, Dunn was surely correct. Many of the small-scale owners who freed slaves, finally, do not appear to have done so because of hostility to human bondage. In many cases they freed a faithful old slave and kept others in bondage. Freeing a slave in late eighteenth-century Virginia, in other words, often did not indicate opposition to slavery. Outside of the large-scale manumission attempted by Carter in Westmoreland, slightly more than one hundred slaves were freed in a slave population of several thousand.[105] This unimpressive record suggests that the law of 1782 did not open any floodgates holding back the hopes of

Virginia planters to disengage themselves from slavery. It was, of course, a concession to those opposed to slavery, particularly those with religious scruples who had
worked so diligently to obtain the right to manumit in the first place. At the same
time, the law was also congenial to the notion that one ought to be able to do what
one wished with one's own property, and that accommodated the "intention" of
the individual property owner in a liberal capitalist world.

Little regard had been paid to the intention or desire of individual owners to
free their slaves in the colonial period. Individual intention was subordinate to
"policy," and policy was very restrictive. Toward the end of the eighteenth century
some developments converged to allow room within the law for a "humanitarian
sensibility." For some people, to be sure, this led to a rejection of the whole
institution of human bondage, and for them it seemed reasonable to wonder when
and how slavery would be ended, not whether it would be. But they were a distinct
minority of Virginia's slaveowners, and their individual intentions faced an increasingly hostile policy that opposed the growth of a free black population. As a
result, Virginia required free blacks to leave the state after 1806, even though later
they could request permission to remain, and occasionally the legislature did grant
such requests.[106] Even then they did not possess the full range of citizenship rights.
A better test of the attitude of Virginians as the Civil War approached involved the
adoption of the voluntary enslavement law and the rigorous antifreedom reading
of the intentions of a testator such as occurred in *Bailey v. Poindexter* and *Williamson v. Coalter.*

By the 1840s and 1850s a devastating breakdown in comity among the states had
become frighteningly evident. Northern states were obstructing the recovery of
legitimate fugitive slaves, despite the injunction in the Constitution that they be
delivered up, and some of these states were closing their borders to slaveowners in
transit with their slaves. Slaveowners risked losing their human property if they
dared to enter some of the free states.[107] Southerners, for their part, increasingly
intruded on the right that owners of slaves possessed to discontinue their slaves as
property. Mississippi and South Carolina during the early 1840s had prohibited
manumission by will regardless of whether it was to take affect within or outside
the state. By the late 1850s a number of slave states prohibited manumission within
their borders. For example, in 1859 Arkansas adopted the following statute: "any
deed, last will, or other act emancipating any slave or slaves, shall, so far as the
emancipation is concerned, be deemed a nullity." By 1860 even Maryland, which
had not been especially hostile to individual manumissions, prohibited grants of
freedom by either deed or will.[108] An especially cogent illustration of the reaction
of some Southerners was the judgment in the case of *Mitchell v. Wells* (Mississippi,
1859). The appellee had been freed under Ohio law in the late 1840s and sought the
bequest in her father's will in Mississippi. William L. Harris, for the majority of the
court, posed the problem this way:

If Mississippi, by her public policy, has declared herself opposed to negro freedom, or to the emancipation of her slave population, and in favor of the continuance and perpetuation of slavery, then respect for that policy, as well as the great interests it was designed to promote, forbid that she should allow other States, opposed to her institutions, to interfere with that policy, and confer upon that inferior race, *within her limits*, rights and capacities, which, by our laws, they never enjoyed here, and in their nature wholly inconsistent with slavery.[109]

Harris's answer to the conditional "if" was a resounding yes: the policy of Mississippi completely denied the freedom of people of color.

The intentions of individual slaveowners, whether those intentions grew out of opposition to slavery, gratitude for the faithful service of an individual slave, or even malice toward potential heirs, were giving way to the interest in securing the social order in a Federal Union in which one section came to oppose the social order in the other. But piety never completely lost out in all Southern jurisdictions. Kentucky's rule on the liability of emancipated persons for the debts of testators is an example, but the extreme hostility of Georgia's judges to postmortem manumissions and the doctrine of *cy pres* stand as illustrations of a strong countertrend in Southern jurisprudence.

In any event few Southern slaveowners chose to free slaves and thereby disinherit or reduce the inheritance of their families, even during the late eighteenth century when the time seemed more propitious than any other. The right to discontinue property as property, to remove a person from "all possibility of being owned," had not been the easiest notion to grasp for those trained in the common law, and it had always been subject to constraints. First, there were the claims of those entitled to inherit and the claims of one's creditors. But, above all, there were the claims of the society as a whole, claims reflected in the numerous restrictions placed on those who tried to grant freedom to enslaved people of color. For Southern whites, well before the collapse of comity in the last few years before the Civil War, there had been more than a grain of truth in O'Neall's conclusion that policy throughout the region meant that "the State has nothing to fear from emancipation, regulated as . . . law directs it to be."[110]

19

Quasi and *In futuro* Emancipations

There is no middle ground . . . between freedom and slavery.

Sidney v. White (Alabama, 1848)

In *Cannibals All* Fitzhugh observed that "great as the difficulty is to determine what is Liberty, to ascertain and agree on what constitutes Slavery is still greater."[1] Southern manumission meant liberty even when the act of granting freedom was framed in terms of Anglo-American property law: liberty was a "legacy" beyond all price. But manumission also introduced questions about the meaning of slavery. There was no doubt, of course, that slavery was involuntary, as well as unfree— at least until the voluntary enslavement laws of the 1850s. In addition to involuntariness, were there particular disabilities and incapacities that Southern judges and lawmakers considered essential to any definition of slavery? To a large extent that turned on the question of "control" and "compulsion." Apart from "police regulations," how much control a master had or *must* exercise for a slave to be a slave in Southern thought was an issue primarily in the nineteenth century, when a free labor ideology had also emerged as a clear contrast.[2] This was an issue especially in a number of cases involving testamentary dispositions of slaves. Sometimes it was because the attempt to emancipate occurred in states in which it was difficult, if not unlawful, to free a slave in-state. This raised the so-called quasi-emancipation problem. And sometimes the question came up because an owner chose not to grant immediate freedom, but freedom *in futuro*. Manumission *in futuro* began in the late eighteenth century, and one of the wrenching questions related to the status of the female slave, which in turn involved the status of children she had before she became free. Another concern was less personal—was manumission *in futuro* a "perpetuity," a continuation of property claims in opposition to the claims of a commercial market and free alienation?

Quasi-Emancipation

An early illustration of the first issue occurred in *The Trustees of the Quaker Society of Contentnea v. William Dickenson* (North Carolina, 1827). This case involved both the capacity of Quakers to take property in slaves and the concept of "quasi-emancipation." The Quaker society, Judge Taylor noted, had been incorporated and had the capacity to acquire property. However, it did not have the right to acquire property for the benefit of persons other than those in the society. The true beneficiaries in the case before him were the slaves who were held only nominally as slaves. Taylor admitted that an "individual may purchase a slave from gratitude or affection, and afford him such indulgences as to preclude all notion of profit." But an incorporated society was different. "When the law invests individuals or societies with a political character and personality entirely distinct from their natural capacity, it may also restrain them in the acquisition or uses of property." What the Quakers did was in fraud of the law. "Mischief" would result if the trust was upheld: "Numerous collections of slaves, having nothing but the name, and working for their own benefit, in the view and under the continual observation of others who are compelled to labor for their owners, would naturally excite in the latter discontent with their condition, encourage idleness and disobedience, and lead possibly in the course of human events to the most calamitous of all contests, a *bellum servile.*"[3]

Hall wrote a penetrating dissent. To him the Quakers had the right to acquire property and were not averse to holding title to slaves. It was enough that a person, or an incorporated society, possessed a legal title and a potential right to claim the use of the property.[4] Taylor relied on policy, whereas Hall depended on legal abstractions and on the rights derived from possessive individualism. The first was an example of proslavery republicanism and the second of nineteenth-century liberalism in a slave society.

The Quakers, policy, and qualified emancipation were also involved in *Thompson v. Newlin* (1844). Sarah Freeman appointed John Newlin, a Quaker, as her executor. Her intention was that after her death her slaves would receive her personal estate and be freed, or they would be "held by some person in a state of qualified slavery." Ruffin noted in the *Thompson* decision that "slaves can only be held as property, and deeds and wills, having for their object their emancipation, or a qualified state of slavery, are against public policy."[5]

Precisely what was a qualified state of slavery in North Carolina? In *Huckaby v. Jones* (1822) there was a bequest of slaves to whites "to be their lawful property, for them to keep or dispose of as they shall judge most for the glory of God and the good of the slaves." In *Stevens v. Ely* (1830) there was a trust "to permit the negroes to live together on his land and to be industriously employed and continue to exercise a controlling power over their moral condition and furnish them with the necessaries and comforts of life." In *Sorry v. Bright* (1835) an absolute bequest of slaves was followed by a "request" that the donee would "admit said negroes to have the result of their own labor, but ever to be under his care and protection."[6] All of these were held to be unlawful trusts in favor of slaves that would leave them in a state of qualified slavery.

In *Lemmond v. Peoples* (1848) Judge Ruffin confronted another situation in which the "real purpose" was unlawful. The intestate had conveyed a mulatto woman and her daughter to the defendants. He also sold them a tract of land in Mecklenburg County. The conveyances were absolute on their face, and the defendants insisted that a legal property was transferred to them. Ruffin would have none of it. He did admit that the "property" belonged to the defendants, "that is, apparently and literally speaking." Ruffin conceded that emancipation was not necessarily intended by the conveyances. "But still that would not come up to the claim of the property, absolute and unconditional, in the sense in which the defendants wish it to be understood, and as it must be understood in order to exclude the right of the plaintiffs." What was involved, he concluded, was one of the plainest cases of quasi-emancipation "in violation and fraud of the law" that could be imagined. The true purpose of the conveyances was "to provide for the protection, comfort, and happiness of the woman and her children."[7] Some control and the exaction of "moderate labor" were minimal elements in the status of slavery in North Carolina.

An absolute property right was not necessarily absolute, however, precisely because the owners of property *had to exploit* that property as well as control it. They could not do with it what they wished. This was also clear in an opinion by Pearson in *Lea v. Brown* (1857): "it may seem hard that one is not allowed to dispose of his own property as he pleases; but private right must yield to public good." The language in the bequest in *Lea* could not have been clearer. It provided land and money for a family of slaves "so that they may not be made to work like other negroes." This was a "mistaken charity which the law forbids. The result, if his intentions are to be carried out, will be to establish in our midst a set of privileged negroes, causing the others to be dissatisfied and restless, and affording a harbor for the lazy and evil disposed."[8] It was not enough in North Carolina that a person was owned as property by someone else. The "benefit" of the property had to belong to someone other than the slave, and it had to be "used." Moreover, the slaves must labor, at least as long as they were fit, and their work must be controlled by and for the interest of someone else. Finally, the slave could not possess "privileges" enjoyed by the free.

A series of cases in South Carolina provides a contrast to the North Carolina set. One of the first involving quasi-emancipation reached the highest court in the state in 1833. In *Cline v. Caldwell* an action was brought for the wrongful conversion of a slave. Cato Gallman, a free black, sold John to Elizabeth Cline, a free mulatto. John was her husband. The question was whether he had ever been at large and manumitted, and whether he had been seized as derelict property by the defendant because he had been manumitted in violation of state law. According to O'Neall on circuit (and the high court agreed), the law of 1820 did not declare a deed absolute on its face but really intended as a "covert emancipation," to be void. The bill of sale of John conveyed the right of property to Cline. Until he was actually emancipated, the right of property was in Cline, John's wife.[9]

To emancipate required parting with the "possession" of slaves and allowing them to go at large and act as free persons. Without these acts the slave remained under the "control" of the owner. O'Neall, who clearly disagreed with the North Carolina judges, wrote that "in the case before us, there may have been an inchoate intention to set John free"; indeed, he may have been really free even though technically the slave of his wife. But unless he was "*to be at large without an owner,* he could not be legally captured." He was not abandoned property. John was "under the control of an owner . . . generally, he lived with his owner, and there was as much actual possession of him as ever does exist between master and slave."[10] In South Carolina slavery existed as long as there was a bare possession by an owner and something called control. Given the facts in *Cline,* possession and control were stretched to the point of disingenuousness.

Judge O'Neall elaborated his position in *Carmille v. Carmille's Adm'r.* (1842). A white woman tried to overturn the provisions of her father's will that favored her mulatto half-brothers and half-sisters who were lawfully slaves. The father had deeded the slaves for a nominal consideration on condition that they be allowed to work for themselves and pay one dollar to their alleged owners. O'Neall denied that the woman should win, although she sought to void her father's deed on the ground of fraud. She claimed under him and could have no "superior equities" to her father. O'Neall contended, moreover, that the slaves had not been actually manumitted. "They were still, to all intents and purposes, slaves. . . . The hire which they pay, however inconsiderable, is a constant recognition of servitude." The same might have been said of the rents and duties owed in a feudal society or even in a modern industrial one. O'Neall was more candid yet. There was nothing in the statutes of South Carolina that prevented quasi-emancipation. And he did not believe it necessary for the judiciary to fill the void by general reasoning regarding the necessary elements of slavery. How much control, beyond mere possession, would be needed to define the master-slave relationship was a matter for *meum et tuum*; it was a question for the individual "owner," not a question of policy.[11]

Lumpkin in Georgia sharply disagreed with this,[12] as did two South Carolina chancellors, George Dargan and F. H. Wardlaw. The latter expressed the basis for their disagreement in *Broughton v. Telfer* (1851). William Remley, in an 1831 trust deed, sought to give to six slaves, who were his children, the "benefit of their labor, and to suffer them to enjoy, as far as practicable, all the privileges of free persons." Chancellor Dargan felt hemmed in by the earlier decisions, especially *Carmille,* and he took the occasion to express his displeasure. The precedents upheld frauds on the law and validated "flimsy and barefaced evasion" of the prohibition against manumission. Chancellor Wardlaw held that the conveyance of the slaves with the trusts passed the title to the grantee "practically discharged from the trusts, whether these be legal or illegal." If the trusts were legal because they fell outside the 1841 law against manumission, the beneficiaries, being slaves, could not enforce their performance in court. They were trusts "of imperfect obligation, depending upon the benevolence of the trustee." If they were illegal, of course, they were simply void. By 1856, as sectional conflict heated, the chancellors took a stronger stand against trusts that were quasi-emancipations. George Broad of St. Johns Berkley Parish executed a will that provided that his executors took the slaves and were required to allow them "to apply and appropriate their time and labor to their own proper use and behoof." The will was invalidated as a clear trust in violation of the law against manumission.[13]

Manumissions In futuro

In futuro manumissions also raised serious problems for Southern judges, especially when the person to be freed was a female slave. Was she in a state of "absolute slavery," "qualified slavery," or even "indentured servitude"? The answer was vital for her children and takes us further into the thinking of Southern judges about the necessary elements in any definition of slavery.

One of the first to confront the problem, which originated in the late eighteenth century, was Chancellor George Wythe of Virginia in 1798, when he construed the wills of John Pleasants and Jonathan Pleasants, one of the sons who took some of the slaves under his father's will and then drafted a similar one of his own. In 1771 John Pleasants provided that if the "laws of the land" permitted, all his slaves "now born or hereafter to be born, whilst their mothers are in the service of me or my heirs," would be set free at the age of thirty. Wythe concluded that the bequest took effect in 1782, when the legislature passed the law allowing manumission by will. In his decree he concluded that the slaves who were thirty at that time and those born since the statute were entitled to immediate freedom; those not yet thirty in 1782 would be freed when they reached that age. This decree was modified in the leading case of *Pleasants v. Pleasants* (1799).[14]

Chancellor Roane agreed with Wythe. The crucial problem concerned the status of those under thirty in 1782. The contingency in the Pleasants's wills had happened. All the slaves then thirty were immediately freed. As for those under thirty, "their right to freedom was complete, but they were postponed as to the time of enjoyment," and they could not be considered slaves until the "time of enjoyment." "They were in the case of persons bound to service for a term of years; who have a general right to freedom, but, there is an exception, out of it, by contract or otherwise."[15] Although he did not explain his remark about "contract," one possible analytic point was that Pleasants had included in his will the provision that the slaves were to be freed "if they chuse it when they arrive to the age of thirty years." Election introduced the element of will, which was the foundation of contract, and indentured servitude was the result of a contractual relation. However, this is a very circuitous argument if it is what he had in mind. It assumes that the right to freedom was "complete" as of 1782, but that it was postponed because of "contract or otherwise." If it was postponed because of contract, it could only be because the freed slaves had agreed to serve as indentured servants. This approach to the problem was similar to the ancient Greek institution of *paramone*.[16] But there is no evidence of such an agreement, and the language of the will had to be twisted to suggest that there could be: it was "shall be free if they chuse it *when they arrive to the age of thirty years* [emphasis added]."[17] Despite the weakness of Roane's argument, it is clear that he considered the females under thirty as free persons in a state of indentured servitude. But what about "or otherwise"? It is difficult to fathom what he had in mind, but there is one possibility. The other jurists based their judgments firmly on the intention of the testator, and one of the most basic rules of interpretation was that the intention of the testator should prevail, unless it was illegal or impossible.[18] It is possible that Roane was suggesting that one analytic peg was to give effect to the intention of the testator and that was to free his slaves, but to postpone the enjoyment of that freedom. This would be a non-contractual analysis.

What was the status of the children born to the females under thirty? Were they free immediately, or was their freedom also postponed to the age of thirty? Both Roane and Wythe argued that they were free immediately. "The condition of the mothers of such children," Roane observed, "is that of free persons, held to service, for a term of years, such children are not the children of slaves." If the intention of the testator was to place the children in the state of indentured servitude until the age of thirty, it was void because it was illegal: "The power of the testator . . . has yielded to the great principle of natural law, which is also a principle of our municipal law, that the children of a free mother are themselves also free."[19] How then could free mothers who were not thirty in 1782 have been kept in some form of bondage by "or otherwise"? The reasoning is puzzling.

In any event, it was not to be. Carrington and Edmund Pendleton formed a majority against Roane. Carrington based his analysis not on a mixture of property and contract concepts, but solely on the law of property and the interpretive rule that the intention of the testator should prevail. By the law of 1782 the right of the "owner of a slave . . . to emancipate" was restored. The right was based "upon the principle of having a right to dispose of his own property as he pleased." The children of mothers under thirty had to serve until the age of thirty. The probable reason that age was picked was "with a view to the labour of the slaves affording some compensation, for the trouble and expence of taking care of the aged or infirm, and rearing the children." Carrington did not say whether he considered the mothers as in a state of "qualified slavery" or as "indentured servants."[20]

"I am of opinion," President Pendleton wrote, "that the paupers are not legally emancipated under the wills of the testators and the several acts of Assembly; but if they are entitled to relief, at all, it is on the ground of a trust created by the will's, that their manumission should take place, upon a contingent event." The event, the passage of the law, happened. But what was the status of the children? The legislature had not expressed its view of the "middle state." The closest analogy was the mulatto born to a free white woman by a black, but that law was no longer in force after 1764. Still, the legislators, Pendleton believed, "have permitted a voluntary unlimited emancipation."[21] Emancipators had to support some, such as males under twenty-one and females under eighteen. Pendleton apparently endorsed the decree that placed the children in servitude until age thirty on the ground that he was attempting to accommodate the intention of the testator to the legislative condition. As for the children, he seemed to accept the notion that there could be some sort of "middle state." If this was so, Pendleton did not adopt the view that the children were absolute slaves for life anymore than their mothers. The problem of perpetuities in such cases will be considered later.

Scholarly examination of *Pleasants* has tied it to the later case of *Maria v. Surbaugh* (1824). For Robert Cover, *Maria* marked an abrupt shift in judging in Virginia courts away from the "natural rights" grounds relied on by Roane and a repudiation of an earlier profreedom form of judging. For A. E. Keir Nash, the factual situation was sufficiently different from *Pleasants* to make it "less clear" that *Maria* represented a major shift. Moreover, other cases about the same time "delimited *Maria*" in such a way as to suggest that it did not really signify the abandonment of an earlier, more decent tradition of judging.[22]

Maria is a crucial case: as Ruffin noted, it was "the leading and most authoritative one upon this point of American jurisprudence." The facts were that Mary brought an action for herself and her children, including Maria, for freedom under a will of 1790. Mary had been bequeathed to the son of the testator with the provision that she was to be free at age thirty-one. In 1804 the son sold her. She reached thirty-one in 1818, and by then she had four children. The lower court affirmed Mary's freedom but denied it to her children.[23] This decision was unanimously upheld by the court of appeals.

The most important opinion was that of Judge John Green. He began with a remark that supports the view of Cover, as well as Nash's characterization of the opinion as marked by "chilly neutralism" and "continental conservatism." "In deciding upon questions of liberty and slavery," Green opened, ". . . it is the duty of the Court, uninfluenced by considerations of humanity on the one hand, or of policy (except so far as the policy of the law appears to extend) on the other, to ascertain and pronounce what the law is; leaving it to the Legislature, as the only competent and fit authority, to deal as they may think expedient, with a subject involving so many and such important moral and political considerations."[24] But where did judicial restraint leave him?

Green rejected the claim that Mary was a slave until age thirty-one because the legacy to her did not vest until then and if she died before that time it would have lapsed without effect. The position he rejected might seem to be a reasonable one for a proslavery judge to accept, and it might seem odd that Green did not. Scholars have ignored this portion of Green's opinion in *Maria*, but the reasoning was crucial. It concerned the whole notion of manumission. "This conclusion would be just," he wrote, "if the preliminary proposition were true, and emancipation was in effect, a transfer of the property in a slave, to himself." But this was not acceptable: "no man can take or hold a property in himself. If he could, he might sell himself, and, by his own act, become a slave. Emancipation is an utter destruction of the right of property. If it be conditional or future, the condition being performed, or the time come, then, and not till then, the right of property is wholly gone."[25] Other judges did treat manumission as a "legacy." Green rejected this. Manumission, he claimed, was the "utter destruction of the right of property." Green's argument was that the basic reason a man could not hold property in himself was that if he could, he could sell himself into slavery. This was unthinkable to Green, whose view was similar to that of the antislavery views of Rousseau. Later Southerners disagreed as they adopted the voluntary enslavement laws.

According to Green, if manumission were a grant of property in a slave to himself, an unacceptable conclusion would follow. The "legacy having in fact vested in the mother the property in the children would also be vested in her. By the common law in relation to animals, the owner of the female is entitled . . . to the increase." "The consequence is," he wrote, "that if the testator gave the property in *Mary* to his son, until she attained the age of 31, and afterwards to herself, the son was entitled to her issue until she attained that age, and *she* then became entitled to them."[26] Mary, in effect, would be the remainderman entitled to the estate after the end of the estate for years. Green did not say why this was unacceptable except for his argument that a man could not own himself because if he could, he could sell himself into slavery. This was surely a *liberal* perception of property law, but it was one that condemned Mary's children to slavery. It affirmed slavery even while it affirmed individual freedom. It was also a bourgeois notion of property built on possessive individualist conceptions and natural law premises, despite the apparent legal positivist position with which he began. Yet the final point about Green's opinion is that his rejection of the notion that a man could sell himself into slavery should caution us against characterizing his position too quickly as a stark retreat from an earlier natural law way of judging in cases involving liberty and slavery.

Once he rejected the proffered suggestion, Green turned to the relevant Virginia law. Children followed the condition of the mother, but that did not answer the question of Mary's condition before she reached thirty-one. There were various possibilities, such as that the right to freedom was dependent on some condition, and until the contingency occurred she was a slave. Another was that she possessed a vested right to future freedom and was in the condition of "one free, but bound to service for a limited time."[27] In Virginia jurisprudence only *Pleasants* dealt with the issue, so Green turned to it.

One problem with Roane's opinion, from Green's standpoint, was that the former owner could not be required to provide support for any children because he did not free them, they were born free. "The consequence . . . would be, that the public, in consequence of the emancipation of the mother, with an obligation to future service, would inevitably be burthened with the support of the children, until they arrived to an age when they could be bound out as apprentices." This, Green believed, was "contrary to the policy of the law." There were weightier legal objections. A person in the position described by Roane would have all the privileges of a free black even though a slave. The result would be a "middle state between slavery and absolute freedom." This again raised the question, exactly what qualities were essential to define a person as a "slave"? It was not, in Green's view, some middle state. In any event, the person defined by Roane would be free but bound to service, and he would be allowed to sue and be sued, and own property. Because this had been the condition of indentured servants in colonial Virginia, it is not clear why Green found it wholly unpalatable. One strong possibility, of course, was race. Whereas indentured servitude for whites had given way to a free labor system, bondage for blacks remained completely correct in the minds of Southern whites. But the final point was that if the Roane-Wythe approach was correct, the law of 1782 authorizing manumission would be defeated. The reason concerned the intention of the testator. If he intended to free the children not at birth but at thirty, his intention ought to prevail, but if the children were freed at birth it "would be to emancipate by law, and not by will."[28]

Pleasants, however, affirmed the notion that the children were to be freed at age thirty and not that they were slaves for life, the latter being the position adopted in *Maria*. The crucial point was "intention." The grant of freedom to the children at the age of thirty "was avowedly founded wholly on the directions of the will to that effect." In other words, the children did not follow the condition of their mothers, they were themselves bequeathed by the testator as slaves until they became thirty. The vital difference was that the children were mentioned in the wills in *Pleasants* but not in *Maria*. To turn Green's point around, the children in *Pleasants* were dealt with according to the will, whereas the children in *Maria*, about whom no intention was expressed, had to be dealt with according to law. The law was that the children followed the condition of the mother. The conclusion Green derived from *Pleasants* was this: "that, a testator might emancipate upon a contingency, and that the children born of mothers who were to be free upon the happening of the contingency, and before the contingency happened, were born slaves, and were not entitled to the benefit of the contingency upon which the mother was to be entitled to her freedom, so as to be free upon the happening of the contingency; nor were to be considered as born free by relation." The contingency had to occur before the "mother was to be entitled to her freedom." Until then she was a slave, and so were her children.[29] The will of the testator prevailed, and, sadly, in *Maria* the testator had failed to mention the children. As Green concluded:

> The only other ground upon which the children of *Mary* could claim to be free, is, that it may be supposed that the intention of the testator was to emancipate them also, and that this may be fairly gathered from the will. I have no doubt, but that, if the idea had occurred to him, that she would probably have children before she attained her age of 31, he would have expressly provided that they also should be free, which could have been effected by the addition of these words, "and her increase." His not having done so, satisfies me entirely, that he never thought of, or intended to make any provision for the children. And if so, it was a subject in relation to which

he had no thought, or will, or intention, and is consequently to be disposed of according to the law of the land.[30]

The intention of the testator was critical. This is one of the primary reasons *Maria* should not be seen as a rapid retreat from *Pleasants*. Because, despite Roane's opinion, the actual decision of the earlier case was in the hands of the majority, Pendleton and Carrington, and they decided it according to the intention of the testator. Judge Green did provide guidance for those who drafted wills in the future. All Virginia emancipators had to do, if conscientious and desirous of freeing all their slaves, was to use some language that would show such an intention.

If the judges in *Maria* seem to have been grossly insensitive to claims of freedom, the next case may come as a surprise. Four years after *Maria* Green wrote the opinion for the court in *Isaac v. West's Ex'r.* (1828). In 1806 Abel West freed Jenny by deed. Isaac was Jenny's son. There was a problem because a clause in the deed required the slaves to serve West during his life. Such a clause, Green contended, "seems to indicate that he did not intend to reserve his original and general power over them, as a master entitled to dispose of them during his life, at his pleasure, by selling them to others, but only to impose on them the obligation to *serve him personally* as he should require." One of the essential elements of slavery was the power to dispose of slaves by sale, and the language used gave up that right. "The effect," Green wrote, was that "he renounced all his right and title as master, from that moment, reserving a right to claim their personal services to himself only, as a condition of the emancipation. If this condition was against Law, as inconsistent with the right granted, it would not frustrate the grant."[31] There could be no conditional manumission in Virginia. Once a person became free, he could not be bound by the act of the emancipator. There was no legal requirement of *obsequium* outside of Louisiana. Isaac was entitled to immediate freedom.[32] For good measure, Green added an observation that weakens Cover's reading of his earlier opinion: "if this construction is doubtful," Green ended, "some weight is due to the maxim, that every Deed is to be taken most strongly against the grantor, and to the spirit of the Laws of all civilized nations which favours liberty."[33]

Following *Maria* the judges began to "delimit" and move away from its harsh implications, at least until the last few years before the outbreak of the Civil War.[34] Language was once again at issue in a case decided ten years after *Isaac*. The claim in *Erskine v. Henry* (1838) was based on a will of 1803 that gave slaves to Rebecca Crouch and provided that at her death "all my negroes to be free and at full liberty." Crouch died in 1828 and left a will freeing all the slaves, except those who were "not of age." The latter were to be hired out until they became the appropriate age for freedom. Brockenbrough, for the court, ruled that the children were entitled to freedom. The "*right* of the *child* to freedom is identical and contemporaneous with that of the *mother.*" The children, by the grant to Mrs. Crouch, were to be her slaves for life, as were their mothers. The reasoning was not that the children followed the condition of the mothers, however. It was that they were part of the estate of the testator, and they were covered by the phrase "all my negroes" precisely because the testator had not freed individual slaves by name.[35]

Within a year President Henry St. George Tucker had had enough of prospective manumissions. According to Tucker, prospective manumissions such as in the case before him, *Crawford v. Moses*, were not authorized by the 1782 statute. Manumission was immediate, not prospective. "If the act be not executed, but executory," he claimed, "it is but a contract for freedom between the master and slave, which is void. If, on the other hand, the act be considered as executed, it must take effect immediately, and intermediate servitude is incompatible with it." For Tucker there should be no such thing as a vested right to freedom the enjoyment of which was postponed. Nevertheless, he accepted prospective manumissions because they had been "so long recognized" in Virginia.[36]

Two additional Virginia cases should add sufficient flavor. *Anderson's Ex'rs. v. Anderson* (1841) was based on the will of Jordan Anderson probated in 1805. He gave to one of his sons the raising of "my young negroes, namely *Anaca's* increase, and *Tom* and *Patt* and *Peter, Phillis's* children, and *her future increase.*" To another son he gave the labor and raising of some other of his "young negroes," including "future increase," until they reached twenty-one. All the slaves then twenty-one who were living with Anderson, or the sons, were to be free on the first of January after the death of Anderson and his wife. The woman Patt was freed in 1821 and became Patty Anderson. She had two children, Green and Henry, before her own freedom. She tried to establish their immediate freedom or, in the alternative, the right to freedom when they reached twenty-one. The executors of the estate of one of the original testator's sons claimed that they were absolute slaves, as they were born while their mother was a slave. The lower court, however, had ruled that they were free from birth. Surprisingly enough, Allen, for the majority of the court of appeals, affirmed the lower court decision: the will "intends a disposition of his whole estate," and there was no doubt that the intention of the testator was to "emancipate the whole of his slaves." The point followed *Erskine* closely. But the court held that the slaves were bound to service until they were twenty-one, even though the lower court had ruled that they were free from birth. The most likely reading of the lower court position was that it was based on the Roane view, whereas the court of appeals based its position on the majority view in *Pleasants* (the intention of the testator should prevail) as fleshed out by the hint of Green in *Maria* (use language such as "future increase") and the decision in *Erskine* (the significance of the phrase "all my negroes"). A footnote added by the editor of the report suggested that the reason for any confusion was that the lower court decision had been upheld generally, and by the time the court of appeals rendered its decision the boys were already twenty-one.[37]

President Tucker dissented. Patty Anderson had successfully sought an injunction in the court of chancery to prevent the executors from selling or removing her sons. Chancery had been used to protect the future interests of the boys. This was dangerous in Tucker's view, and the injunction should have been dissolved. He reasoned:

> Their case is a hard one; every case of slavery is a hard one: but there are considerations connected with it of a very delicate nature. The rights of the master must be controlled, the moral influence that subjects the slave to the master disregarded, and a spirit of hostility engendered while they continue to be slaves, calculated to diminish their value while slaves: the property of the master is to be invaded in a manner subversive of the institution of slavery, and likely to have an influence on those who are slaves for life; and the next step may be to interfere with the master in their case also, if the humanity of the court is appealed to.

The court of chancery should not be the "guardian of . . . infant slaves, and thereby . . . enfeeble the master's rights while they continue slaves."[38]

In 1849 Virginia's legislators tried to put the whole question of the status of children to rest. They stipulated that "the increase of any female so emancipated by deed or will hereafter made, born between the death of the testator or the record of the deed, and the time when her right to the enjoyment of her freedom arrives, shall also be free at that time, unless the deed or will otherwise provides."[39] Intention still mattered, but in the absence of an expression of intention children became free at precisely the same time as their mothers.

This was the situation after 1849, but that did not affect *Wood v. Humphreys* (1855), a case involving a provision in the will of Joseph Pierce of Westmoreland County. The fact that a proceeding concerning his will could arise fifty-seven years after it was probated shows how such prospective manumissions worked. One of the women to be freed was Nancy, and she had a daughter, Julianna, before she was entitled to freedom. Before Julianna reached thirty-one she had daughter, Frances Wood, who brought suit for freedom on reaching that age.[40]

The vital point was intention. The court, Moncure claimed correctly, had repeatedly found in favor of freedom "whenever any words have been found in the deed or will which could fairly be construed to express" an intention that children should be free as well as the mother. The testator here had included the words "and so on, until they shall all become free." That was enough. "These words," he wrote, "indicate that the testator intended to emancipate the mothers and all their descendants," and that took the case "out of the operation of the principle of *Maria v. Surbaugh*."[41]

In futuro *Manumissions and the* Partus *Principle*

Manumission was the discontinuation of a property right. Therefore many judges, logically enough, considered the status of the mother and of her "increase" in terms of property law. One rule of property law, as Brooke noted in *Maria*, only to reject its application, was *partus sequitur ventrem*. Outside Virginia *partus* was applied in Kentucky, beginning with *Ned v. Beal* (1811), in Delaware in *Jones v. Wootten* (1833), in North Carolina in *Mayho v. Sears* (1842), and in Alabama in *Sidney v. White* (1848). In all, it was a captious use of the maxim. In the Delaware case *partus* was treated as a rule about status, not the ownership of property. "The rule—*Partus sequitur ventrem* must prevail—if she was free then he was free—if she was then a slave, he also was a slave." This did not resolve *who* owned the slave children. Delaware was one of two states that held that "increase" should be viewed as profits owned absolutely by the temporary owner of the mother.[42]

The Kentucky case, *Ned v. Beal*, was even more perfunctory. Chief Justice Boyle said that the children "follow the condition of their mother at the time of their birth, according to the maxim *partus sequitur ventrem*." As in Delaware, there was no discussion of the legal rules to determine who owned the slaves. It was Beal, but we do not know his relationship to the testator, Isaac Cox, or the basis of his claim to the slaves. In *Mayho v. Sears* Judge Ruffin confronted a case of trespass to try a right to freedom based on a Virginia deed of manumission. His conclusion was that, under relevant Virginia law, the "issue, born of a female while in that state of slavery and with the prospect of emancipation before her, must be slaves, results conclusively from the maxim, *partus sequitur ventrem*." Ruffin apparently did not realize that the Virginia court had not used that maxim. Finally, the Alabama court in *Sidney v. White* used the "maxim of the civil law" to conclude that "the child born whilst the mother was a slave, is also a slave"; it backed its conclusion with references to *Maria* and *Crawford*, the Virginia decisions, *Ned v. Beal*, and the Louisiana case of *Catin v. D'Orgenoy's Heirs* (1820). The problem was that neither *Maria* nor *Crawford* relied on the maxim. It was used in *Ned* and *Catin*. But in the Louisiana civil code of 1838, adopted ten years before the Alabama decision, the rule in *Catin* was discarded.[43]

Additional Rules of Property

The maxim, *partus sequitur ventrem*, was not often used, and when it was the judges did not pursue a deeper property analysis. Decisions in North Carolina and Tennessee, on the other hand, rested squarely on the rules of succession to property. It is useful to begin with *Maria*. One of the arguments was that the legacy of freedom vested in Mary when she was thirty-one. Judge Green rejected it because a person could not hold property in himself. It was an approach, however, that became the basis for decisions in North Carolina and Tennessee.

Campbell v. Street (North Carolina, 1840) was based on a Virginia testamentary disposition. The testator freed one slave immediately and "all the rest" after the testator's youngest child reached the age of twenty-one. Gaston admitted that there was a difference in Southern states about "the question what becomes of the increase of slaves under a limitation whereby a temporary use or ownership is granted to one, and the future and absolute dominion given over to another." In North Carolina and Virginia, he noted, the increase went to the remainderman.

Employing this analysis, rejected as applicable by Green in *Maria,* would set up a claim to freedom for the increase on their mother reaching the fixed age for her freedom or at least that she was entitled to her children. In *Campbell,* however, this was not vital because the testator had made disposition of the increase. The person here "was in law his property, as an incident to and fruit of the property which he held in her mother, and he, by law, had a right to emancipate *her* with her mother."[44] I do not claim that Gaston intended to apply his reasoning about the claims of the remainderman in a *Maria* situation, but the reasoning was there for future use.

In another significant case, *Caffey v. Davis* (North Carolina, 1853), the testator freed a slave couple if they could comply with the state law on the termination of his wife's life estate in the couple. The two children of the couple were given to a grandson, but on condition that they would go with their parents if the slaves fulfilled the condition. If the couple failed, Battle reasoned, "their issue or increase would have gone with them into servitude to the remainderman, whether such issue or increase were mentioned in the will or not. . . . why then should not the issue go with them into freedom . . . ? Why any more necessity that the testator should mention issue or increase, to give liberty to such increase, than to doom it to slavery?" The conclusion was that "upon a condition in a will to emancipate a female slave, either immediately or at a future time, after a temporary enjoyment by another, the issue of such female slave, as an incident to and fruit of the mother, must, when nothing to the contrary appears in the will, follow the condition of the mother and be emancipated also." Now no words indicating an intention to free the increase, such as "all my negroes," were even needed. Battle, however, did not favor manumission. The "true principle of our law in relation to the emancipation of slaves," he wrote in *Myers v. Williams* (1860), "is that it *permits,* but does not *favor* it." It was more a question of the rights and intentions of property owners, than of slaves, that had conditioned his earlier approach. As for prospective manumissions, his view was that the policy of allowing them "is carried far enough already."[45]

The sharpest contrast to *Maria* was the 1834 decision in Tennessee in *Harris v. Clarissa.* There is disagreement about how to characterize the ruling in *Harris.* A. E. Keir Nash described it as "highly libertarian" and as "prejudiced" in favor of liberty as "*Maria* was against." Arthur Howington suggested that although it showed sensitivity to the humanity of slaves, it did not "indicate support for the principle of absolute, unrestricted, universal liberty."[46]

The judgment of Chief Justice John Catron was that Clarissa was entitled to "a present right to freedom at the testator's death, encumbered with a condition to serve fifteen years." As for the children, those

> born of Clarissa in the state of Tennessee came into existence impressed with the rights our laws confer. They were not slaves for life of William Harris. They could only be his slaves until the termination of twenty-five years from

the birth of their mother. Her state and condition fixed that of her increase, during the particular estate, and also after its termination. With us the remainder-man takes the increase of slaves born during the term . . . if the termer has no further title, and there be no one to take in remainder, slavery ceases of course. Such we take to be the condition of the three children born of Clarissa before she was twenty-five.

Catron used a partial property analysis to affirm freedom, but this requires some explanation. Manumission, counsel had argued in *Maria*, was essentially a legacy. If so, then the legatee at the end of a life estate, or term for years, would be a remainderman. Mary would be the remainderman and would be entitled to her own children, but as "increase" or property. They would not automatically be freed. But Catron reached the position that the children in *Harris* were free with the mother. The reason was that he did not begin with the proposition that manumission was a "legacy." Because Clarissa was not viewed as being given "title" to herself as a legatee, she could not be a remainderman after the termination of the limited estate. "The law," Catron concluded, "does not separate the title; they go to the remainder-man together, and, if there be no remainder-man to take the mother, the child goes with her."[47]

Although the ruling in *Harris* was in favor of freedom, it is difficult to see the decision as "libertarian." The result was in favor of freedom, but the analysis was based squarely on the law of property, and slaves were treated within that law. There was no effort to undermine the notion of slaves as disposable chattels; the question was precisely how the testator disposed of them. Perhaps the greatest irony in these cases is that those judges who analyzed the status of children born to women entitled to future freedom from the point of view of property law ended with affirming freedom. Those who viewed the problem from the standpoint of the complete destruction of property (as did Green in *Maria*), or in terms of what they perceived to be a rule involving the status of human beings (*partus sequitur ventrem*), tended to believe that the children were slaves for life. The first group saw them in the context of property law and found for freedom, the second group viewed them in the context of their humanity and found for slavery.

Statutes and Status

Some states tried to resolve the problem by statutes. One of the first efforts was that of Maryland in 1809, and the solution was that reached in *Maria*. A person granting a conditional emancipation was allowed to determine the status of offspring born to a woman to be freed *in futuro*, but if he did not the child would be a slave.[48] Later statutory approaches went the other way.

One of the first laws in the newer set was Louisiana's statute of 1838, which must be seen in the context of the decision of the state supreme court in 1820 in *Catin v. D'Orgenoy's Heirs*. Judge Mathews held the lower court judgment to be correct "in considering the mother to have been of that class of persons, known to the Roman law, by the appellation of statuliberi, and that children born from her, while in such a state, are not entitled to freedom." By 1838 Louisiana legislators adopted a rule change: "the child born of a woman after she has acquired the right of being free at a future time, follows the condition of its mother, and becomes free at the time fixed for her enfranchisement, even if the mother should die before that time." This became the basis for affirming the freedom of some slaves in 1856 in *Heirs of Henderson v. Rost & Montgomery.* By the "humane dispositions of our law" the children became free at the time fixed for the enfranchisement of their mothers. Regrettably, Louisiana law did not remain so "humane." The year after *Heirs of Henderson* was decided, the state prohibited manumission. A number of cases followed in which the liberation of persons granted future freedom before 1857, not to mention their children's, was defeated. The court ruled that all efforts to free slaves after 1857 were invalid. In *Julienne (f. w. c.) v. Touriac* (1858), for instance, the court admitted that there was a legitimate claim to freedom based on the condition in a sale in 1837 but determined that "the Act of March 6th, 1857 . . . is a bar to the action. . . . If it should hereafter become possible, the plaintiff will have a remedy."[49]

Other states that dealt with the problem by means of statutes were Delaware (1810), Kentucky (1852), and North Carolina (1854). The Delaware law of 1810 provided that "slaves freed in future were slaves until the time arrived" and that "any children born before that would also be slaves, males until age 25, females age 21."[50] The question debated passionately by the Delaware judges in *Jones v. Wootten* concerned whether this statute operated retrospectively. The majority held that it could not because to read it that way "*violates* vested rights or the rights of property." Judge Samuel M. Harrington, in dissent, argued that it did not violate justice to allow the law a retrospective operation. "It is true," he noted, "that slavery is tolerated by our laws; but it is going too far to say that this kind of property in slaves is precisely like every other species of property. The spirit of the age and the principles of liberty and personal rights as held in this country are equally opposed to a doctrine drawn from the ages and the countries of despotism, and founded proximately or remotely in oppression." The real basis of the law of 1810, in his view, was that if the children were free at birth, a possibility, the master of their mother might be obliged to maintain them until she became free. That seemed unjust, so to compensate him a compromise was adopted: slavery for a set number of years.[51]

The remaining statutes all came much later, from the Virginia law of 1849 (already noted) to the North Carolina law of 1854. The 1852 Kentucky law was as follows: "The issue of a slave emancipated by deed, born after the date of the deed, shall have the same right to his freedom that the mother has under said deed, and shall be treated accordingly. The issue of a slave willed to be free, born after the death of the testator, shall have the same right to freedom as the mother, and be treated accordingly, unless it shall manifestly appear by the provisions of the will that such issue is not intended to be emancipated." And the law of North Carolina of 1854 provided: "Whenever a female slave shall by will be directed to be emancipated, all her issue, born after the date of the will, shall be deemed to have been likewise intended by the testator to be emancipated; and the court shall so declare, unless a contrary intent appear by the will, or by some disposition of the slave so born, inconsistent with such presumed intent."[52] Obviously, the "authoritative" decision in *Maria* was too much for many Southerners. Whenever they considered the problem as a law-making problem they adopted statutes more favorable to the children than the ordinary rules of property law allowed. At the same time, they did accommodate the intention of slaveowners, but only in the sense that if an owner wished the children of a woman he freed to be slaves for life, he would have to say so.

In futuro *Manumissions and the Problem of Definition*

On occasion, judges who dealt with prospective manumissions of females faced the task of defining the elements of slavery. Roane had tried to resolve the problem by saying that the mothers were not slaves at all. Except for Wythe, all other Virginia judges rejected that view. Most of them said that the persons were slaves until the contingency or condition was fulfilled. Pendleton, in *Pleasants*, had referred to a "middle state," but he did not define what that was. In *Maria* Green rejected Roane's view because it would create a "middle state between slavery and absolute freedom." For him, the children in *Pleasants* actually were born as "absolute slaves."[53] Other Virginia judges and many judges outside Virginia merely said that the mother was a "slave" until the appropriate time, and that the children born to her before that time were slaves as well. They made no effort to define the elements that would constitute her slavery.

A Maryland decision in 1823 and an Alabama decision in 1848 give us good examples of some jurists who went further. The Maryland judgment in *Hamilton v. Cragg* was particularly full. The mother

> at the time of his birth, who, though to become free, on the death of . . . the legatee, was during her life-time, not in the capacity of a servant, but in the state and condition of a slave; she had no civil rights, and could have pursued no legal remedy against her mistress on any account; she could have made no will, and was incapable of taking either by purchase or descent; the product of her labor belonged to her mistress; she could neither plead nor be impleaded, and was subject to all the disabilities and incapacities incident to a state of slavery; she was a mere chattel, the property of her mistress, who could have sold or transferred her at pleasure. Her becoming free depended on the contingency of her surviving Sarah Turner.[54]

Alabama's Ormond, in *Sidney v. White*, claimed that the mother was a slave "for there is no middle ground known to our law, between freedom and slavery. Until the event happened . . . she continued a slave, subject to all the disabilities of that condition."[55]

Maryland's judges mentioned that among the incidents of slavery was the liability to be sold. That element of ownership is crucial. Exactly what did it mean? The Virginia court held in *Isaac* that the owner had given up his claim as a master and had converted the persons involved into servants. One of the elements that constituted slavery, from this perspective, was that the slave was subject to sale at the owner's pleasure. The same view was taken in *Hamilton.* But a power of sale did not have to be unqualified: entailed slaves, for instance, could not be sold at the pleasure of the tenant in tail, but no one would doubt that they were slaves or that the tenant was in some sense the "owner."

What the judges in *Isaac* and *Hamilton* did not explore was what power of sale was necessary. Could the owner sell the person for life even though the person was "entitled" to freedom on the happening of some contingency? Would purchasers purchase taking upon themselves the risk that the contingency would not happen and the person would never be freed? Another view would be that owners could only sell what interest they had a right to claim, and that interest was limited to a term for years because of the right the slave possessed to freedom on the happening of the contingency. All the judges ever said was that owners possessed a right to sell or that "all" the disabilities attached to the slave entitled to future freedom. Conceptually, the result would be that at the very least the temporary owner of the slave to be freed in the future possessed a right to sell that slave for the time that remained between the sale and the vesting of freedom. A right to sell and the danger of being sold, however qualified or limited, constituted one of the elements of slavery. It was a necessary, but not a sufficient condition, however, as the owners of the time of indentured servants had the right to sell that time as well.[56] What should also be clear is that judges who said that "all the disabilities" attached, but who knew that the slave was to be freed at a certain age, had to admit that lifetime servitude was not a necessary element in the definition of slavery. We normally think of slavery in the South as lifetime servitude, and normally it was, but not necessarily. The 1852 revised statutes of Delaware made that point explicit: "the term 'slave,' as used in this chapter, means a negro or mulatto slave, and is applied to a slave for a limited time, as well as to a slave for life, or indefinitely."[57] In all cases where judges held that the mothers were slaves subject to "all the disabilities" of slavery, the status of the children was the same. If born before the freedom of the mother attached, they were born slaves.

Not all Southern judges adopted the view that the mothers were in a state of unqualified slavery. Judge Harrington, in the Delaware case *Jones v. Wootten,* dissented. From his standpoint, the act of manumission, even though to operate prospectively, gave the mother "a vested right: the master has no longer an unlimited control over her services, and it would seem to follow, that he had no longer an unlimited control over the services of her offspring." However, unlike Roane, who argued that the person was free but bound to service, Harrington admitted that the person was a slave. But "the mother is not in the condition of absolute slavery, but only of limited slavery, owing services for a limited period." As for the child, it "follows the condition of the mother" and "being in the same condition it is that of limited slavery, measured by the term of its mothers servitude."[58]

Chief Justice Catron, in *Harris*, wrote: that "Clarissa rested under *most of the disabilities* [emphasis added] pertaining to a state of slavery is true; but that she took a vested and undoubted right to freedom by Thomas Bond's will is equally true." What "disabilities" she remained under he did not say, except that it is clear enough that the length of her servitude was limited. And so was that of her children. Her condition before freedom was not simply that of "slave" as many judges elsewhere held, it was a slave for years.[59]

Judge Reese, in *Hartsell v. George* (Tennessee, 1842), was even more expansive. He claimed that "it was an act of emancipation *in praesenti* to be enjoyed on the part of the slave in future . . . the services of her who had been a slave continued indeed to be due to the master until his death, but the character of slave ceased."[60] A serious problem with this approach was ignored by Reese. On what basis could a free person, a person emancipated "*in praesenti*," be bound at all? Roane had referred to "contract or otherwise," but it was a weak part of his analysis, and Reese presented none at all. The only possible basis would be fictional or a contract by implication. Slaves elected freedom with the understanding that they also accepted the condition of a continuing obligation to serve for a time. This view is not illogical, but there is no evidence judges generally accepted it.

Judges, in sum, were not very successful in identifying crucial legal elements in slavery when they dealt with *in futuro* manumissions. There was no universal agreement. Judges were no more productive in obtaining unity in their responses to the efforts of some owners (usually in the late eighteenth and early nineteenth centuries) to create an ongoing, although temporary bondage, within a slave community. Such owners, in effect, tried to create perpetuities at the same time that they granted freedom *in futuro*.

Prospective Manumission and the Rule against Perpetuities

This last effort brought into play the English rule against perpetuities. One critical point in the development of the rule came in 1681 in *The Duke of Norfolk's Case*. According to A. W. B. Simpson, Lord Nottingham, who ruled against perpetuities in the case, was not interested in promoting a free market economy, the usual view of the rule. "His objection to perpetuities," Simpson argued, "was grounded in natural law. Human laws should be appropriate to the nature of man, and man, unlike God, possesses only a limited ability to foresee what will happen in the future. Hence a landowner should not be allowed to settle the devolution of family lands too far into a future which he could not foresee. Hence perpetuities 'fight

against God, by effecting a stability which human providence can never attain to.' "
Nottingham did not set the precise limit in the rule against perpetuities, and the
religious foundation did not last. Blackstone wrote that the law "abhors" a perpetuity because "estates are made incapable of answering those ends, of social
commerce, and providing for the sudden contingencies of private life, for which
property was at first established." As Simpson noted, the rule was especially "valued as favouring a free market in land." One thing that should be kept in mind,
however, is a point made by W. Barton Leach. Although the rule did derive from a
general policy "against withdrawal of property from commerce," it should not be
seen as one of the rules against restraints on alienation, such as those involving
entails. Restraints on alienation operated after an interest in property vested,
whereas the rule against perpetuities held an interest void because it vested too
remotely; the interest "may be, and usually is, freely alienable at all times."[61]

Was the rule against perpetuities applied by Southern judges in cases involving
prospective manumissions? The first proceeding in which the issue arose was
Pleasants v. Pleasants. John Wickham, on one side, contended that the devise was
void because the contingency—the passing of an act allowing manumission—was
too remote. He treated this as a restraint on alienation. The will was a "devise of
the slaves in absolute property, with a condition, that the devisee shall not alien."
But the right of alienation, as Coke had written, was central to the right of property. Wickham did not actually apply the rule against perpetuities. His complaint
was a little different: "must it be, that the plaintiffs and their progeny to all
generations shall, in succession, be entitled to freedom at thirty? This would be to
allow the testator to create a new species of property, subject to rules unknown to
the law. But this is what no man can do." John Randolph, on the same side, used
the rule against perpetuities. Slaves, he pointed out, were to be conveyed as chattels, and "as such a limitation of a chattel would be too remote and therefore void,
it follows that this is so likewise."[62]

John Marshall, on the other side, claimed that the "great question . . . is, as to the
perpetuity." For him, the condition in the will did not "run forever, or to an
unreasonable time." The reason was that it related to several subjects. For mothers
born at the testator's death, the time would not be too remote. He conceded that
"the mothers born after the testators death may perhaps form a class of different
cases."[63] This timid concession was quite a concession. He did not spell out the
possible implications, but if the rule against perpetuities applied, and he did not
deny that it would to cases of bequests of prospective freedom, his concession
would have condemned to slavery a number of the slaves to be benefited by the
wills. The critical question, therefore, was "whether the rule against perpetuities
was applicable to a bequest of liberty."[64]

Roane held that the rule applied in cases other than those involving land. "If it
be contrary to the policy of that law," he wrote, "to render unalienable, for a long
space of time, real estates of inheritance, on reasons of public inconvenience and
injury to trade and commerce, these reasons apply, with much more force, as to

interests of short duration in lands and personal chattels: not only because the latter are better adapted to the purposes of trade than the former, but also, because of their transitory and perishable nature." The law abhorred perpetuities in chattels as well as in land, but did the rule apply to cases of *in futuro* manumission of slaves? The answer was that he did not have to answer because the limitation of the property interest had vested in the slaves at the age of thirty. They were entitled to freedom even though its enjoyment was postponed. The children, who could have been in real danger under Marshall's reasoning, were never slaves at all. Therefore, Roane noted, he was spared "the necessity of a very delicate and important enquiry: Namely, whether the doctrine of perpetuities is applicable to cases in which human liberty is challenged?"[65]

Despite this Roane proceeded to comment on the "delicate" matter. "Restraints," he observed, "rightly imposed on the alienation of inheritances, to prevent perpetuities are founded principally. . . . on considerations of public policy and convenience." But "it is also clear, that neither the particular species of property now in question, nor the case of a remainderman (if I may so express it) claiming his own liberty, were in contemplation of the judges, who established the doctrine on this subject; which therefore may not apply." Roane treated the rule against perpetuities as though it was among the rules against restraints on alienation, which, if Leach is correct, was a misreading of the rule. In any event, the real question was whether it would apply, and Roane had something to say. If it was necessary to decide the issue, which it was not, "it would be proper to weigh the policy of authorizing or encouraging emancipation," which was "dear to every friend of liberty and the human race," against those "secondary considerations of public policy and convenience; which appear to have supported and established the doctrine of the law, on the subject of perpetuities, as relative to ordinary kinds of property."[66] Roane, if forced to decide, would have avoided using the rule against perpetuities in cases of grants of freedom to operate in the future, even through generations.

Carrington believed that the devises should be upheld and that they were "not liable to the rule respecting chattel interest, limited on more remote contingencies, than the law allows." The reason was that the "subjects of the devises are different; inasmuch as in the doctrine of chattels, property only, is concerned; but liberty is devised in this case." Pendleton also chose not to implement the rule. It "would be too rigid," he wrote, "to apply that rule, with all its consequences, to the present case."[67] Here was one situation where jurists found it unpalatable or too harsh to utilize a basic common law rule. Two judges expressly denied its applicability, and the third, Roane, said he did not have to decide and then proceeded to show how he would.

The next time Virginia judges considered the perpetuity was fifty-five years later, in *Wood v. Humphreys.* Now there was less agreement. Moncure, for himself and George Lee and Samuels, began with *Pleasants.* But, he noted, because only two judges had said that the rule was inapplicable, they did not consider themselves bound by it as a precedent. The notion that *stare decisis* required unanimity is odd, to say the least. Despite this, Moncure traveled a path close to *Pleasants* and concluded that it should govern.[68]

He placed considerable weight on the "manifest difference between a gift of freedom and a gift of property." Manumission was a "renunciation of the relation of master and slave." Obviously, it did not make much sense to apply the rule against perpetuities. It would hardly be "applicable to a gift of freedom, because it is applicable to a gift of property. It is applicable to a gift of property, because it is against the policy of the law that property should be rendered perpetually inalienable. It may not be applicable to a gift of freedom, which is a renunciation of property."[69]

William Daniel, on the other side, rejected *Pleasants*. He disliked prospective manumissions and held that the right to emancipate was subject to "general principles of public policy regulating the transmission and acquisition of property." He did agree, however, that "bequests of freedom do in some respects differ from bequests of property: For no man can enjoy or acquire a right of property in himself." Nonetheless, the ordinary rules applied. A slaveowner had the right to emancipate his slave, but only his slave. "In what legal sense," he asked, "can a bequest of freedom by a testator to a slave to be born centuries hence, be called a bequest of freedom to *his* slave."[70] For Daniel the rule against perpetuities did apply.

It also applied for Allen, who believed that those descendants of slaves born after the death of the testator were free from birth, rather than when their ancestors became entitled. Aside from *Pleasants*, which was not binding, there were no Virginia cases that "affirmed the right of the master to attach a condition or quality to slaves so to be emancipated *in futuro*, which will follow their posterity through all succeeding generations." Regarding them as "property merely," the reverse would violate the rule against perpetuities. As persons there was also a problem. The law did not empower "the owner of slaves to create this new *status*, by which his slaves and their posterity through all time shall occupy this anomalous position of being slaves up to the prescribed age, and free persons thereafter."[71]

The rule against perpetuities was significant in a small number of cases outside Virginia. At issue in *Harris* (Tennessee, 1834) was the charge of the circuit judge that the mother was a slave until she was twenty-five, and her three children were likewise slaves until they reached twenty-five. Catron noted that "if this construction be the true one, we have in perpetuity slaves for a term of years." This was not acceptable, and Catron got around the difficulty by claiming that the status of the mother was of one entitled to freedom immediately, but a freedom burdened with a condition to serve some years. The condition of the children was that of the mother, and they became free when she reached twenty-five.[72]

One case, a sad one, in which the rule against perpetuities was held to apply was *Ludwig, (of color), v. Combs* (Kentucky, 1858). The proceeding involved a deed recorded in 1824. It provided freedom for Hannah when she reached thirty-one and for her children when they were twenty-five, "and their children and grand-children, &c., to the latest generation, are to be slaves until they shall respectively arrive to the full age of twenty-five years." The testator's intent was straightforward: as long as "one of the breed" was in being, he or she was to be a slave until age twenty-five. In 1831 the owner, Alexander Adams, made his will with essentially the same conditions. The grandson of Hannah brought the suit for his freedom. Combs purchased the grandson from a man named Beauchamp, who sold the grandson as a slave for life even though he had purchased Hannah's remaining time. The circuit court dismissed Ludwig's petition for freedom, and the state supreme court, in an uninspired opinion by Judge Alvin Duvall, affirmed the ruling. Duvall merely cited the rule against perpetuities and noted that "tested by this . . . rule" the provisions of the deed and will were void. According to Duvall, if Hannah had died a year after Ludwig's birth, his right to freedom could not have vested within the time limit specified in the rule against perpetuities. He would have been about twenty two, and his freedom was not provided for until he was twenty-five.[73]

In a final example, *Myers v. Williams* (North Carolina, 1860), the will was attacked on a number of grounds including the fact that it created a perpetuity. The will provided that the increase would be freed and sent to Liberia on reaching the age of twenty-five, if they chose. This allegedly created a perpetuity. Judge Battle, for the court, held that the scheme for emancipation was against policy and void. He did not directly apply the rule against perpetuities, despite the argument of counsel. Battle's point was that other cases involving quasi-emancipation made it clear that the policy of the state was against a position for "favored slaves," who would be "idle and worthless" and would generate discontent. It would also induce disobedience and make them "unfit for the social state which is essential to the well being, the happiness, and even the very existence of both master and slave."[74] It was a matter of policy to protect the whole social order, not a question of applying a rule designed to keep property in the stream of commerce.

As sectional tensions grew, policy loomed large and ordinary rules of property gave ground. When confronted with cases involving prospective manumissions, judges turned increasingly to policy, and it did not favor "qualified slavery" or freedom within the state, even if, or perhaps especially if, it involved a "perpetuity." Such conditions amounted to anomalies. But so did the laws that allowed voluntary enslavement. When adopted, they stood as a contradiction not only to some of the basic ideas of a possessive individualist society based on market relationships, but also to the notion that a slave should always be subject to "all the disabilities and incapacities" of the status. Perhaps in time the voluntary enslavement laws would have been modified to assure that result, but we shall never know. All we do know is that, with the marginal exception of the qualifications in the voluntary enslavement laws of the 1850s, the general judicial trend was toward the discouragement of any form of "qualified slavery." But even then there remained the major exception of the judges in South Carolina. Despite that exception (and the legislators in South Carolina did not agree with the judges), and despite the idea that one could sell oneself "rump and stump" into slavery voluntarily, one of the most consistent elements that ran through these cases is that slavery was *involuntary* bondage, subjection to the *control* of another and to some claim of *ownership* by that other. Even these general notions did not go unchallenged. The voluntary enslavement laws, some of the quasi-emancipation cases, and some of the efforts to manumit *in futuro* created profound conceptual stress in Southern slave jurisprudence.

Conclusion

Southerners failed to agree among themselves on a formal definition of slavery, the institution that defined their social order. They were not alone—conceptual ambiguity has been as universal as the institution. "The Roman law of slavery," Buckland observed, "was developed by a series of practical lawyers who were not great philosophers, and . . . it seems unwise to base it [a definition of slavery] on a highly abstract conception which they would hardly have understood and with which they certainly never worked." C. Duncan Rice followed this cautious approach in his general history of the rise and fall of black slavery in the modern world: he declined to "formally define the characteristics of slavery." Nonetheless, many scholars have defined slavery in terms of ownership or property. Finley, who represented it in terms of powerlessness, indicated that to that end the notion of "chattelhood" was central. Patterson, on the other hand, claimed that it was misleading to suggest that one of the "constituent" elements of slavery is the "notion of property," because there are property claims in numerous human relationships that do not amount to slavery. The anthropologist Claude Mellissoux agreed. He pointed out that the "weakness of the legalistic approach is that it considers alienability as a characteristic specific to slaves," when it is not. Moreover, "efficient slave management implies a greater or lesser recognition of the slave's capacities as *Homo sapiens*, and thus a constant shift towards notions of obedience and duty which renders the slave indistinguishable, in strictly legal terms, from other categories of dependents."[1]

This last point was echoed during the 1850s by the Reverend C. F. Sturgis, author of the "Melville Letters," who wrote from Alabama that

> black people expect, and, by a kind of conventional usage, almost demand, a number of little rights and privileges, which, although like the "common law," not referable to any positive enactments, are, like it, also of very binding influence. . . . One of the most effectual modes of inducing servants to perform their duties with cheerfulness, is to recognize all those little points; not, perhaps, as matters of right, but as concessions cheerfully made from the feeling of good will that exists between master and servant.[2]

Hegel, on the other hand, claimed that "a slave can have no duties; only a free man has them." It was a nice summary from a legal philosopher, but Southern judges and lawmakers did not agree. According to Buckland, however, the practical Roman lawyers did to a point: "over a wide range of law," he wrote, "the slave was not only rightless, he was also dutiless."[3] This is not to say that the slave *never* possessed duties, or that once duties were imposed and legally enforced the person was no longer a slave, a consequence that would flow from the Hegelian view. And certainly by the nineteenth century, Southern judges often began their analysis with the notion of the duties owed by slaves.

Still, we can concede that no formal legal definition of slavery would apply to all forms of the institution and yet claim that the notion of the person as a *thing*, an object of property rights, was central. Without such a claim, in some strong sense, there was no slavery. A striking testament is T. R. R. Cobb's reasoning at the outset of his study of the law of slavery:

> *Absolute or Pure Slavery* is the condition of that individual, over whose life, liberty, and property another has the unlimited control. The former is termed a slave; the latter is termed the master. Slavery, in its more usual and limited signification, is applied to all involuntary servitude, which is not inflicted as a punishment for crime. The former exists at this day in none of the civilized nations of the world; the latter has, at some time, been incorporated into the social system of every nation whose history has been deemed worthy of record. In the former condition the slave loses all *personality*, and is viewed merely as *property*; in the latter, while treated under the general class of *things*, he possesses various rights as a person, and is treated as such by the law.[4]

Undoubtedly, there is no universally applicable legal definition of slavery. The closest Buckland came, for instance, was to say that Roman lawyers described the slave as the only human being who could be "owned," but even "ownership" is a complex notion in modern legal thought and includes ideas about a cluster of legal claims to an object (which could include the control of the labor power of a free person). That does not mean that there were not certain legal elements *usually* if not *universally* present in slave societies. Slavery normally involved a large range of diverse restraints, powers, rights, and duties. The absence of one or more, however, does not necessarily mean that slavery did not exist. Normally, people think of slavery as lifetime bondage, but lifetime bondage was not essential, as the Delaware law made clear.[5] Furthermore, some elements can also be found in other forms of dependent labor or social relationships. This would include a claim of ownership of some kind and a claim of the right of alienation. Another element is heritability of the slave. But this can be found in other statuses. One thing that is often missing is that the children born of a slave were likewise property subject to alienation and inheritance. But even here we must remember English villenage and Russian serfdom. In addition, the claim to the whole produce of the labor of the slave had parallels in the liabilities of those in debt peonage. Nonetheless, slavery, even if seen as part of a continuum, was the institution of greatest dependence and rightlessness, even when one might argue that it shaded off into some other form of subordination.

At a minimum slavery as a legal institution normally, and in its Southern form always, included a number of elements: a claim of ownership in the slaves beyond a simple claim to control or use their labor (the slaves themselves were a thing at law, a *res*, and not just their labor power, even when there were limits on the property rights of an owner, such as that the owner could not destroy the thing); a claim of alienability (even when restrained in the interests of the creditors and heirs of the owner); heritability (including the heritability of the children of slaves and the status of slavery deriving from birth); a claim to the whole product of the slave's labor (although some usually went back to the slave in the form of food and shelter); and a general, if not universal, rightlessness. There were, or could be, limits around any of these elements of slavery, and if the elements were too weakened or were eliminated the institution of slavery could be absorbed into other forms of dependence—perhaps indentured servitude. It is important to remember, moreover, the disparity between a body of complex, sometimes inconsistent doctrines and day-to-day practice at the local level. Yet doctrine, despite rough edges and inconsistencies, still reveals the fears and aspirations of those who framed it.

What, then, was the relationship of law as doctrine to the institution of slavery? None of those who reject a purely legalistic definition have claimed that law is of no importance in validating or supporting slavery in some way or other. They simply maintain that it makes no sense to look to the law for an intelligible definition that sets it apart from all other "institutions." Thus, did it really matter that Southern judges, lawmakers, and proslavery apologists did not agree on the meaning of slavery or the meaning of freedom? What importance was there, if any, in the fact that E. N. Elliott argued just before the war that all slaveowners claimed was the control of their slaves' labor, no matter what the "fictions" of the law might be?[6] Were the differences among judges about whether manumission was a legacy, or whether quasi-emancipation was legally allowable, of any significance? More broadly, were the differences in legal notions among the several slaveholding states so serious as to amount to a deep crisis of incoherence that would have been resolved only with the transformation of the social order toward some other form of dependent labor or even "free labor"?

Slave systems had been transformed before: they did not all end abruptly or in the midst of violence. Finley, in discussing the decline of slavery in the ancient world, wrote that "neither exhortations nor the rare legal enactments to treat slaves decently, were antislavery measures in intention or effect." According to him, "slavery is not a moral category, comparable to good manners or honesty; it is an institution performing various functions, in particular that of providing an important part of the labour supply. So long as that labour is needed, slavery cannot decline *tout court*; it has to be replaced." There was a slow "quantitative decline in slaves" in the Roman Empire that was not analogous to what happened in the nineteenth century. "New world slavery existed within the larger context of a European society based on free wage labour and growing industrialization." Slavery in the ancient world did not end abruptly, as modern slavery did, and it was replaced not with "free labor," as in the nineteenth century, but with "other forms of dependent labor."[7] G. E. M. de Ste. Croix, a Marxist historian of ancient slavery, believes that Finley came close to a correct explanation of the decline of the institution, only to falter. It was not enough to refer to some unexplained "trend" toward decline and note the depression of the *status* of lower-class free citizens. This legalistic approach (treating *status* as a legal concept) misses the crucial element of "exploitation." The exploitation of slaves in the ancient world was no longer producing the surplus it had earlier, so that the propertied classes "*needed* to put more pressure on the free poor."[8] Whatever the cause(s) of the decline of ancient slavery, it was not because of some crisis of legal incoherence or because of legal developments as such.

The same can be said for the medieval world. Marc Bloch, the great French historian, noted that there was an incoherence between legal categories and the social order of medieval Europe. "The abstract concept in Roman law," he wrote, "which made the *colonus* (a free man by personal status) 'the slave of the estate on which he was born,' in short the dependent not of an individual but of a thing, became meaningless in an age too realistic not to reduce all social relationships to an exchange of obedience and protection between beings of flesh and blood."[9] It was not incoherence within the legal order as such, or within conceptions about freedom, slavery, and dependence, that explained the transformation from slavery to villenage. Social reality changed, and the older legal concepts had to be discarded. Practice departed from doctrine, and a tension developed between the two. Within the South there were deviations as well, but they were largely of the kind that would be mediated by the legal system easily enough. A major exception might have developed if a large number of owners kept too loose a rein over their slaves in the sense of the quasi-emancipation that disturbed some judges. The number, however, was relatively small, and other judges found nothing in the practice that frightened them over much. Yet above and beyond the deviations between doctrines and practice there were the inconsistencies within the doctrines themselves.

These inconsistencies raise a serious jurisprudential and historical question. Martin Krygier posed it as follows:

> Unless social and legal values, doctrines and beliefs are static, and few are ever completely static, tensions and inconsistencies between those embedded in legal doctrine at any time are bound to occur. This allows, indeed makes necessary, choice in particular legal applications. This should be borne in mind by those "critical" lawyers and others, who take incoherence in doctrine as evidence of deep crisis. For it remains an important question in social and legal theory, insufficiently considered: when does incoherence within a tradition, which always occurs, amount to crisis, which only occurs sometimes?[10]

Did the inevitable incoherence within the legal traditions of the several Southern slave states amount to a deep crisis that would have led to a transformation of the legal order to correspond to a transformed social order? Was the legal order contributing to an incoherent social order or at least evidence of it? The closest scholars have come to saying so is in discussions about the relationship between slavery and liberal capitalism in the modern world, that is, a world, as Finley noted, increasingly dominated by the concept of "free labor."

Slavery and Liberal Capitalism

A number of scholars have examined the relationship between slavery and the rise of capitalism.[11] There has been an important debate that began in the 1940s with the work of Eric Williams, *Capitalism and Slavery*. Williams saw the end of slavery as the result, in part, of the marginalization of the colonial, slave-based economies within the British imperial scheme. Recent scholarship, however, has emphasized that nineteenth-century slave societies were often at the height of their importance in world markets, and that it was not economic stagnation or insignificance that brought them down. Fogel's assertion in *Without Consent or Contract: The Rise and Fall of American Slavery* is a strong statement of a widely regarded view: slavery died as the result of " 'econocide,' a political execution of an immoral system at its peak of economic success, incited by men ablaze with moral fervor. Slavery deserved to die despite its profitability and efficiency because it served an immoral end." Fogel and Engerman, in *Time on the Cross: The Economics of American Negro Slavery*, earlier argued that slavery was compatible with capitalism, that slaveowners (even though paternalistic) were shrewd calculators of markets, and that slaves often internalized a Protestant work ethic that made them efficient, diligent workers.[12] Slavery and capitalist values thus could be seen as congenial. Thomas Haskell has suggested an alternative view of the relationship. The values that arose with market capitalism—values such as a humanitarian sensibility associated with a high regard for individualism or the notion of a duty to live up to one's promises—created preconditions that could undermine slavery. Another view is that the collapse of slavery was linked in a subtle way to the emergence of free labor. Free labor, at the center of the new industrial capitalism of the nineteenth century, demanded some form of discipline of the workers, but the workers resisted. Anglo-American antislavery leaders often validated the discipline of industrial workers by their condemnation of the institution of human bondage and its inefficiency, and by their contrast of the two forms of labor.[13] Seymour Drescher, in a series of works, has sided with Fogel and discounted an economic analysis of the end of slavery. He has contended, for instance, that Dutch capitalism, in its various stages, never produced an antislavery movement.[14] This is an important debate about the relationship between capitalism, as a set of class relationships and as a set of market-generated values, and the growth of antislavery, and so the end of slavery in the nineteenth century. But another dimension of the relationship has been relatively—although not completely—overlooked. That is the "subversion" of slavery from the inside by the incorporation of capitalist values into slavery jurisprudence. The question is whether the relationship between slavery and Western liberal capitalism of the nineteenth century, as reflected in legal rules and norms, had become or was in the process of becoming a dangerously incoherent relationship.

Possibly the closest anyone has come to the view that it was is Oakes in his *Slavery and Freedom: An Interpretation of the Old South.* He claimed that "modern slave societies had come into existence to serve capitalism; they could not survive without capitalism; they went to their graves at the behest of capitalism." The Old South arose in a world in which there was a blend of Lockeanism and classic republicanism, and central to that world was "liberal individualism." At the center of that ideology was the notion of "rights." Slavery was defined as the opposite of a freedom that was made up of rights. Even slaveowners spoke in the language of rights. Although the South was not a full-blown liberal capitalist society, it existed and functioned within such a world, and in that world rights were cast in legal forms. A liberal capitalist society was preeminently one resting on law, on predictable legal rules that made market calculations rational. The unhappy result for slaveowners was that "in the end the universalization of rights and the dynamic force of free labor overwhelmed and destroyed slavery."[15]

Hurd's formulation in the late 1850s in *The Law of Freedom and Bondage* was a perfect expression of the liberal capitalist world that Oakes had in mind: "every recognition of rights in the slave, independent of the will of the owner or master which is made by the state to which he is subject, diminishes in some degree the essence of that slavery by changing it into a relation between legal persons." Oakes gave expression to the same idea: "any action that forced the legal system to recognize the slave as in any way independent of the master represented an implicit threat to the principle of total subordination. Grounded in the presumption of universal rights, the American political system at once defined the slaves as rightless and yet risked undermining slavery every time it recognized the legal personality of the slave." The crucial link with the legal order was that "the intrinsic ambiguity of slave law—the total subordination of the slave to a master who himself owed allegiance to the state—transformed a simple problem into a profound dilemma. For it was all but impossible for a liberal political culture to place limits on the masters' power without implicitly granting rights to slaves. This made the jurisprudence of slavery intrinsically subversive." Patterson might have found this a bit pointless because no slaveholding society ever existed, in his view, that "did not recognize the slave as a person in law" who possessed duties and rights in some sense or other. The notion of a slave as someone without a legal personality is, at best, a fiction of "western societies" that has had more interest for legal philosophers than for "practicing lawyers."[16] But was there something unique in the world of liberal capitalism that provided more force to Oakes's claim? Possible answers, aside from Oakes's, can be found in Marxist analyses of American slavery.

Even though slaveowners had individual property rights in slaves, Tushnet argued, they also had a collective duty to preserve the system of which they were the beneficiaries. However, they could not rely on "state and legal intervention to control shortsighted and selfish masters, for they could not overcome the contradiction inherent in the embedding of a slave society in a bourgeois world that recognized the absolute property rights of uncontrolled individuals." Oakes focused on the rights of slaves in a liberal capitalist world and Tushnet on the notion that there were serious dangers in eroding the "absolute property rights" of individuals in a bourgeois world. Oakes was concerned with slaves' rights and Tushnet with masters' rights, but they agreed that any legal intrusion into the absolute rights of masters threatened to topple or transform the social order. Fox-Genovese and Genovese tried to find a way around the apparent dilemma. Tushnet, they argued, made a critical mistake because the problem he described was endemic to any bourgeois society, and judges could provide "fictions" that would reduce the more dangerous tendencies, or they could just live with them. Besides, absolute property was not really absolute, and Southern slaveowners did not claim absolute rights in "property in general, as the modern bourgeoisie was to do, but in property in man." Fede, incidentally, also saw no problem, but his resolution differed. There was no dilemma because slaves had no "rights," and to claim otherwise was "obfuscation." Slaves were always nothing other than property.[17]

These interpretations suffer from the assumption that slaveowners throughout the South possessed some kind of absolute property in their slaves and implicitly that such absolute claims were necessary to uphold a slavery system. Admittedly, there are some illustrations of the broad claim in the writing of Southern judges. For instance, Gaston noted in an unpublished piece that the master was "regarded as to all civil purposes the absolute owner of the slave."[18] This was hyperbole, at least if applied to every jurisdiction. In Louisiana, even though lawmakers imposed an absolute liability for the civil wrongs of slaves on the theory that absolute power and absolute liability went hand in hand, they also retained forced heirship, which limited the absolute right of disposition of owners, and they prohibited owners from selling children away from their mothers. Louisiana granted absolute power in some sense, but not absolute property rights: elsewhere in the common law world the *tendency* was the reverse, a move toward the restraint on power along with a consolidation of property claims, but this was only a tendency and there were notable exceptions.

The nineteenth century—which saw the emergence of a liberal property law favoring consolidation of claims to promote the market—moreover, was different from the seventeenth or the eighteenth centuries when slavery was implanted in the English continental colonies. The colonial South, as Jack Greene has argued, was quintessentially an acquisitive society and more like modern America than the puritan North,[19] but that did not mean that it was a liberal capitalist world. A society in which some kind of absolute property rights were claimed in things began to arise in the nineteenth century, and then it was not complete. Fox-Genovese and Genovese came close to the point only to concede more than they needed: slaveowners did not claim an "absolute" property right in man. Ruffin, in *State v. Mann* (which might have been the source of their view), did not say that slaveowners had an absolute *property* right in slaves. He said that the "power of the master must be absolute, to render the submission of the slave perfect."[20] This absolute claim was not a property claim as such as against the rest of the world, it was a claim of authority in order to secure "implicit obedience" in the slave, and even then Ruffin diluted the claim elsewhere in his opinion. Property claims and claims of governance were related, of course, but they were not identical, and this allowed judges to approach the legal or equitable issue before them from one of two angles: some judges analyzed problems from the perspective of property law, of *meum et tuum*, and some from the perspective of the master-slave relationship.

During the nineteenth century, in any case, judges did not talk in terms of an absolute property right in chattels in the sense in which absolute had been used earlier in English law. Earlier it had been held that no estates could exist in chattels because it would be "contrary to the nature of ownership that the owner for the time being should not be able to do what he liked with the chattel, including its destruction."[21] This view was long gone. Yet, in terms of succession law, the property claim in chattels had been close to absolute, aside from dower. However, the definition of the slave as realty (with the intricate succession rules that went with that definition) did not leave an absolute property right in owners. But to observe that absolute power or claims to absolute rights of property was not *necessary* to maintain slavery is not the same as saying that slavery was on firm ground in Southern law.

The ground was like loose shale. Liberal capitalism, which rests on the idea that labor is a commodity to be bought, sold, or withheld in a market, appeared in a significant form only by the nineteenth century. Southern slavery began in a world that fell short of that. Freedom of labor contended with many forms of subordinate, coerced labor in the seventeenth and eighteenth centuries. Indentured servitude was the closest form to slavery. But some scholars claim that coercion has been an element even within so-called free labor systems of the nineteenth century. David Eltis, for instance, argued that it is "more useful to regard slave and non-slave labour as part of a continuum than as polar opposites," and, moreover, that "if slavery is the most extreme form of domination, there is an element of the latter in all arrangements between employer and employee, in that they include specific performance and payment expectations backed by law."[22] There is force to this view, but we ought not to push the various forms of subordination, coercion, and rightlessness too close together. The coercion in the use of law to command the specific performance of a labor contract is profoundly different from the sale of a child away from its mother and father, or the father from the mother, even if we describe the first as "wage slavery" and concede a point to pre–Civil War proslavery writers.

For another reason it was not inevitable (even if likely) that the emergence of liberal capitalism in the nineteenth century would lead to the destruction of slavery, even though it created tensions within slavery jurisprudence. Liberal property law could sustain slavery because slaves, and not just their labor power, were seen as commodities. Southern slavery, on the other hand, existed in a Western market capitalist world, not just in the United States, and the dominant metropolises in that world had rejected slavery. That would be another nonlegal source of pressure.

We will never know the exact form the resolution might have taken because slaveowners resorted to war to preserve a social system under pressure within a Federal Union.[23] Because the constitutional constraints in the American Union made a frontal assault on slavery all but impossible, it was nearly impossible that slavery would end as it did in a unitary state like the British imperial system. It is worth noting that some of the English precedents—such as that in Zanzibar studied by Frederick Cooper and in Guyana, by Walter Rodney—suggest that one strong possibility was that some kind of dependent labor system would replace the slavery system however slavery might end.[24] In the United States, in any case, there was a constitutional crisis around such questions as the extension of slavery into the common territories, the rendition of fugitive slaves from free soil, and the problem of the interstate transit of slaves with sojourning owners. By 1860–61 the crisis erupted into secession and civil war and, in the end, the abolition of slavery throughout the Union. Could slavery have been transformed, or was it being transformed internally, to mediate the internal contradictions that were emerging in the jurisprudence of slavery? If the answer is yes, then the carnage of the war becomes even sadder.

There is much at stake. David Potter raised a crucial issue. The result of the Civil War, he wrote, was this: "Slavery was dead; secession was dead; and six hundred thousand men were dead." For every ten Southern whites held in the Union and for every six slaves freed, one soldier died. We are entitled to ask "whether the Southerners could have been held and the slaves could not have been freed at a smaller per-capita cost." Fogel suggested that Potter's ethical question about the end of slavery makes sense largely if one assumes that slavery was no longer economically viable. It makes far less sense otherwise.[25] However, it might have been economically strong and still rent to a dangerous degree by incoherence in the legal system growing, in part, out of the very economic success in world markets. The point is that economic success encouraged judges to adopt more and more of the doctrines of liberal capitalism, doctrines that in turn threatened chattel slavery in the long run.

It is necessary, therefore, to grasp just how and when slavery jurisprudence incorporated the norms and ideas of liberal capitalism, and how much the human personality of slaves was recognized and in what situations. What rights did slaves possess as slavery matured in the South? It is important to begin with the point that slavery in the region existed for nearly 150 years before the widespread emergence of free labor and liberal capitalism. The legal and equitable rules of England during the period from about 1620 to 1750 bore the traces of an older social order. Many of the rules were like the impenetrable chambers of the gothic castle Blackstone wrote about at mid-century. The rules of succession to property were more fully developed and significant in those years than the doctrines of contract law, the body of law decisive in liberal capitalist thought. Many doctrines of contract law were still buried in the rules of forms of action, such as assumpsit, and the law of agency (which has been so prominent in modern corporate law) was largely unknown in its modern form whereas the old feudal succession law that recognized entails remained good law, well developed and well known.[26] This was true despite the fact that Virginia, to take one example, was described even in the eighteenth century as a "trading country." It was also the country of the grand patriarchal estates of the Carters and the Harrisons.

There was little consolidation of property rights in the eighteenth-century legal world—in Virginia at least, which allowed contingent and vested remainders, even in slaves, or executory bequests, along with the entail and primogeniture. The uses of property were restrained in numerous ways in the interests of heirs, and of the power and authority of propertied families, even while there were accommodations to merchants. By the end of the century, of course, the entail and primogeniture as restraints on alienation had been abolished. There was a move toward the consolidation of property rights in order to promote a free market, as standards as the rule in Shelley's case and the rule against perpetuities, were used more and more, including in slave cases. There is no doubt that some nineteenth-century Southern judges welcomed the norms of liberal capitalism and looked with considerable hostility on earlier legal rules that allowed such things as executory bequests or used trusts and remainders to amount to entails tying up property. An example is Reese, in Tennessee, who in 1836 wrote a judgment favoring the application of the rule in Shelley's case, which enlarged an estate in slaves and made them alienable much earlier, on the ground that it was in "perfect harmony" with the "liberal and commercial spirit of the age."[27] But this gesture toward liberal capitalism did not rest on any recognition of the "rights" of slaves or their "human personality." And it is true, on the other side, that Southern legalists did not always favor liberal capitalist ideas, which emphasized rights, an abstract equality, and dessicated legal rules at the expense of a "multi-level system of subordination based on patriarchal principles."[28]

Entails, remainders, trusts, and executory devises were ways to withstand the pressures of the market and protect the power and the authority of families against an emerging liberal property law. Nonetheless, that emerging law was powerful. By the end of the eighteenth century some of the remnants of the older, patriarchal legal order had crumbled, and some of them were under real pressure from the liberal thought expressed by Warner in an 1847 Georgia slave case: "wealth does not form a permanent distinction . . . every individual of every family has his equal rights, and is equally invited by the genius of the institutions, to depend upon his *own merit* and *exertions.*" And many agreed with the political economists like McCord that exempting slaves from seizure for debts due or attaching them to the soil was unacceptable.[29]

The notion of the "contract" was central to the liberal capitalist world of the

nineteenth century, and it was here more than in successions law that the jurisprudence of slavery incorporated the norms of the market. The contract was the law of
the parties to the contract, and they were usually honored by Southern judges,
whether they were contracts of sale, bailment, or mortgage. It was not common for
judges to act as protectors of the necessitous free debtor in his dealings with his
creditors, regardless of the impact on the slaves who might be the subjects of the
contract. Edward Dargan, in *Judge v. Wilkins* (Alabama, 1851), provided an example. The case involved an excessive price paid for slaves and land. Inequality in a
bargain was not evidence of fraud, either at law or equity, he believed. The courts
"must act upon the ground that every person, who is not under some legal disability, may dispose of his property in such manner and upon such terms as he sees
fit; and whether his bargains are discreet or not, profitable or unprofitable, are
considerations not for courts of justice, but for the party himself."[30]

Older paternalist notions did persist in some areas. They remained in warranty
law in a few states, especially the Carolinas and Louisiana, and they continued to
some degree in remedial law when courts decreed specific performance rather
than awarding damages for breaches of contracts. Little of the newer approach—
damage awards that rested on the interchangeability of "commodities" (including
slaves, of course)—existed in the legal world of the seventeenth or eighteenth
centuries. There might have been glimmerings of the new in the old, as in *Waddill
v. Chamberlayn* in Virginia in the mid-eighteenth century in which losing counsel
argued against the notion of any implied warranty, but they were glimmerings at
best. For its part, specific performance was not a common remedial right of
slaveowners, and usually it rested on some demonstrable "uniqueness" of the slave
involved, as in "family slaves." It was not the case that specific performance came to
be a common remedy because all slaves "by their nature *merely*," as one Virginia
judge noted, were unique.[31] But such recognition of the individuality of slaves as
occurred in implied warranty and specific performance jurisprudence did not
amount to a recognition of the rights of slaves as against their masters. Generally,
moves toward the inclusion of liberal capitalist property and contract notions into
slavery jurisprudence rather favored a freer market in slave transfers at the expense
of the slaves and their families.

Personality, Rights, and Reform

Reforms in the laws of slavery, on the other hand, often served to block some of the
harsher effects of liberal capitalist ideas as they did recognize the humanity of the
slaves against abstract market values. Many of these grew out of the values associated with the spread of evangelical Christianity, others out of the emphasis on the
individual and the humanitarian sensibility that also went along with the growth
of capitalism in the later eighteenth century.

Patterson was correct when he noted that all slave systems recognized the slave
as a person at law, although he was not correct to imply that all "western societies"

accepted the fiction that the slave lacked a "legal personality."[32] But we must not confuse those instances in which legal norms accommodated the fact that slaves were human beings with those in which there was a direct acknowledgment of some kind of "legal personality." The humanness of slaves, in other words, conditioned legal rules in at least two different senses: (1) when those rules were adjusted to take human qualities into account, and (2) when the legal personality of slaves was the basis for the allocation of rights and duties. Oakes's thesis rests on the second sense.

Before I take that up, however, a few words are in order about how Southern judges and lawmakers wove humanness into slavery jurisprudence without creating rights in slaves. An example is in warranty law. It readily enough included the diseases of human beings as covered under the doctrine of implied warranties of soundness that arose from the full price paid; the same could have been said for cattle or horses. The implied warranties of moral or mental soundness were more problematic. South Carolina judges excluded the former. Moral qualities, they reasoned, depended on things they could form "but a very imperfect opinion of," such as the treatment a slave received that might condition his moral behavior and thus his value in the market. This had nothing to do with any rights in the slave. A different approach might be that of the Alabama judges, who chose to include mental soundness in their state's general warranty law because the word *person* included the whole man. This concerned the value of the slave and the duties of buyers and sellers of human beings; it did not involve any rights possessed by the slave.[33]

Numerous other examples could be cited. In Louisiana the otherwise normal recording law in the sale of realty (slaves were so defined in that state by statute) was ruled inapplicable because "being semorentes considered as men" slaves "cannot strictly speaking be held to be immoveables." Much earlier, in seventeenth-century Virginia the English Statute of Distributions of the chattel property of intestates was altered because of the "difficulty of procureing negroes in kind as alsoe the value and hazard of their lives." A final illustration might be some of the adjustments made in the early nineteenth century in the law of slave hires. In Tennessee, for instance, slave hirers, in the absence of an agreement in the contract, were made insurers of slaves who died or fled "by a contingency to which it is naturally subject." The "it," of course, was the slave. The flight of human beings from bondage was taken as an element in construing the duties and rights of the parties to hire contracts, but such contractual rights and duties created no rights in the slave. On the other hand, the imposition of implicit obligations through assumpsit rested on the duty of a hirer to protect the health of a hired slave, and, in some sense, this might be seen as a right in slaves as well as a right in masters to have their property cared for.[34]

There were even lesser but notable examples where the humanness of slaves altered legal practice when it did not actually alter the legal doctrine. In early nineteenth-century South Carolina, for instance, juries abused the trover action to turn it into something like the equitable action of specific performance.[35] This suggests, along with the other examples cited here, that the special character of the property claimed sometimes altered practice or doctrine because of the slaves' humanity even though there was no recognition of rights or personality in the sense modern scholars have in mind.

One of the most obvious cases in which the personality of slaves was recognized was in their prosecution for the alleged commission of crimes. Anglo-American criminal justice relied heavily on the notion of *mens rea*, the guilty mind, and Southern slavery jurisprudence did not deviate from that concept. Even an abolitionist like Goodell, who argued that slaves were essentially regarded as cattle, noted that in this area they were accorded a "personality," one they doubtless would have preferred to relinquish. The "only real exception" to the idea that slaves were "BRUTES," in Goodell's view, was this: "where the interests of the 'owner,' the wants of society, or the exigences of the Government require an anomalous departure from the principle of slave chattelhood, by the temporary and partial recognition of their humanity. Such exceptions and modifications are never made for the benefit of the slave. They enable the Government to *punish*, as a human being, the poor creature whom, in *no* other respect, it recognizes as such!"[36] There is no doubt that slaves were treated as human beings for the purpose of state-sanctioned punishment. But there were other ways in which a legal personality was woven into the law. By the nineteenth century, at least, when confronted with the violent punishment of slaves by masters, Southern judges often enough acknowledged that violence was necessary to control slaves. Slaveowners possessed a duty and a right to discipline slaves, and slaves had a duty of obedience.[37] The duty owed by slaves as human beings was one foundation of the right of punishment by masters. Still another way in which a legal personality was recognized was in some election cases in manumission law. This was not universal. Virginia judges denied any legal weight to the will of slaves in such cases, whereas their North Carolina counterparts gave legal force to the election of freedom by slaves given that chance by masters.[38]

Slaves also possessed some rights by law, but these virtually never derived openly from the common law. Efforts to find some measure of protection against the cruelty of masters in the common law power of judges to punish offenses *contra bonos mores* always failed.[39] What rights they possessed can be found in statutes and occasionally in equitable decrees.

Rights found in equity were tenuous. A good example of a right in the slave found in equity comes from South Carolina. It shows that the right in the slave was linked with a right in the potential owner of that slave. Chancellor DeSaussure adopted a rule that the children of slave women born during the lifetime of the testator followed the mother to the ultimate owner, even though the testator failed to mention the children in his will. "Sound policy," he wrote, "as well as humanity, requires that everything should be done to reconcile these unhappy beings to their lot, by keeping mothers and children together. By cherishing their domestic ties, you have an additional and powerful hold on their feelings and security for their good conduct."[40] The equitable rule adopted by DeSaussure, however, lasted only a short time. Nonetheless, the equitable recognition of humanity could carry with it something like a right, in this case the right of the mother to her child and the right of the child to stay with the mother, at least as long as the child was a "suckling child."

But it was in statutes that we find the clearest recognition of humanity and of rights in slaves, and it was in the nineteenth century that statutory law rose in importance compared to the common law. During the colonial period a few attenuated rights were built into statutes, such as in the prohibition against certain forms of cruel punishment in the South Carolina law of 1740.[41] Significant statutory amelioration of slavery and the creation of rights, however, began in the late eighteenth century and was most notable after about 1830.

One of the strongest expressions of the late antebellum reform impulse was the attempt to protect the slave family, or parts of it. An article published in *DeBow's Review* in 1855, for instance, entitled "Slave Marriages," cited an effort in North Carolina to "render legal the institution of marriage among slaves," to "preserve sacred the relations between the parents and their young children," and to allow slaves to learn to read. It then cited a piece from the *Port Gibson [Mississippi] Reveille* to the effect that the "main features of the movement" had already been put into practice by planters, but that it was entirely possible that the reforms would be written into law throughout the South. If that happened, the "enemies of the institution will be robbed of their most fruitful and plausible excuses for agitation and complaint." The Mississippi editor could not help but conclude, however, that there would be "objections to be answered in the adoption of such a modification."[42] Indeed there were, and the movement to reform the laws of slavery collapsed for the moment. Nonetheless, even some of those most committed to the plantocracy in the South remained troubled. "We are reproached that the marriage relation is neither recognized nor protected by law," wrote one such person, Robert Toombs of Georgia. "This reproach," he admitted, "is not wholly unjust, this is an evil not yet remedied by law, but marriage is not inconsistent with the institution of slavery as it exists among us, and the objection therefore lies rather to an incident than to the essence of the system."[43] Disrespect for the marriage relationship among slaveholders made many decent Southern slaveowners uneasy, if not guilt ridden, and they tried to respond to the complaints.

There were problems with the protection of slave marriages. Cobb, who felt uneasy about the matter and hoped to see some improvement, provided an example of one of the difficulties. "The unnecessary and wanton separation of persons standing in the relation of husband and wife," he wrote, "though it may rarely, if ever, occur in actual practice, is an event which, if possible, should be guarded against by law. And yet, on the other hand, to fasten upon the master of a female slave, a vicious, corrupting negro, sowing discord, and dissatisfaction among all his slaves; or else a thief, or a cut-throat, and to provide no relief against such a nuisance, would be to make the holding of slaves a curse to the master." Still, there was a limited remedy possible: "It would be well for the law, at least, to provide against such separations of families by the officers of the law, in cases of sales made by authority of the Courts, such as sheriffs' and administrators' sales. How much further," he cautioned, "the law giver may go, requires for its solution all the deliberation and wisdom of the Senator, guided and enlightened by Christian philanthropy." O'Neall in South Carolina made a similar suggestion about slaves in 1848.[44] The most that ever occurred was the adoption of statutes in a small number of slave states, usually during the 1850s, that placed limits on the sale of children away from their mothers, not spouses from one another.[45] Genovese put his finger on a reason for the relative failure when he noted that for slaveowners "reforms threatened the economic viability of the capital and labor markets. No other issue [slave marriages] so clearly exposed the hybrid nature of the regime; so clearly pitted economic interest against paternalism, and defined the limits beyond which the one could not reinforce the other."[46]

To protect the slave family, to use Oakes's formulation, would be to extend rights to slaves. The problem here, of course, was that this extension of rights was in opposition to the market. In fact, many proposed reforms, even those that arguably extended legal rights to slaves at the expense of the masters' power, were designed to affirm, validate, and uphold the system of human bondage, not to subvert it in favor of a world based on liberal capitalist values.

Statutory rights were extended, from the late eighteenth century on, in still other ways. Some of these extensions of rights impinged on the authority of masters, and some did not. One body of law that cut both ways concerned procedural protections of slaves when they were criminal defendants. Sometimes this involved the simple modification of procedural rules in the trials of slaves (such as the grant of rights of juror challenges and appeal), and sometimes it involved the imposition of duties on masters (the requirement in some states that they provide legal counsel). The imposition of duties on masters in criminal trials brings us to the heart of the master-slave relationship as conceived of by Southern lawmakers. By the nineteenth century there was an increasing equation within the proslavery argument between a duty of obedience on the part of the slave and a duty of protection on the part of the master. The protection-allegiance formula, dating in Anglo-American legal thought at least from Coke's judgment in *Calvin's Case* in the early seventeenth century,[47] was the foundation for numerous statutory duties imposed on masters. These included the responsibility to provide adequate food, clothing, and medical care,[48] as well as legal counsel. These rights of slaves and duties of masters also contained statutory limitations on the right of masters to punish slaves. There are numerous examples of states prescribing limits on what was deemed cruel punishment. This was, if anything, one of the strongest curbs that ameliorationists succeeded in imposing on the authority of masters. In exchange for labor and the incidents of ownership, masters had not only rights but duties, as well as limits on their rights. They could punish, but not in any fashion they wished, and they had to provide adequate food, shelter, medical care, and clothing. By the 1850s Georgia owners were even limited in the amount of labor they could demand from a slave, although it is hard to see how this could have been enforced. In fact, enforcement of any of the rights of slaves was always difficult, although it is erroneous to claim that they were never enforced. Masters, as well as third parties, were indicted for cruelty to slaves, and they were required to provide legal counsel. The rights of owners were limited, and the limits were increasing as the system matured in the nineteenth-century world of liberal capitalism. The humanitarian sensibility and the liberal individualism associated with liberal capitalism did create tensions within slavery jurisprudence, but not necessarily to the degree seen by Oakes, precisely because slaveowners never did possess an *absolute* property right or a total power at law, not even in the harsh colonial world of the seventeenth and eighteenth centuries. Nonetheless, the ameliorationist trend was pushing Southern slavery closer to other forms of dependent labor. At the same time, some of the tension could be mediated by policies and fictions incorporated into legal rules.

Reform efforts, however, could not always be canalized in safe banks, and the pace of reform pressures was accelerating. Encrusted systems could be formidable barriers against subversive reforms, but encasing crusts could also be brittle under pressure. Reform or ameliorationist impulses could be strong counterweights, along with traditional common law and equitable rules, against a clean victory for liberal capitalism and a legal victory for market relations, rational calculation, and so forth. But the mores of Western capitalism were also powerful. Amelioration, in short, might have improved the day-to-day lives of slaves, even creating rights without subverting the whole system; but, then, it might have subverted the system, as there is some force in what might be called the Hurd-Oakes view. The future was indeterminate, and factors other than law would have resolved or redirected the legal tensions and incoherencies. In the end, reform never rose to the level of widespread policy.

Southern Slavery and Legal Policies

Legal policies are not ineluctable, they are choices among possibilities, and those are limited by legal knowledge and heritage, among other socially defined values. Although I believe that it is vital to understand the legal heritage, I also agree with William Fisher III, who has pointed out that much of the "rhetoric of the law of slavery" flowed from sources other than continental or English legal traditions. This was especially true during the nineteenth century, when much of it came, to use Fisher's words, from "vocabularies, images, and arguments developed in Southern fiction, political economy, formal defenses of slavery, and the popular political debate."[49] That debate would incorporate and mediate religious values, as well as class relationships among Southern whites and the struggles that erupted within the Union among the free and slave states.

Such policies, in any event, were guides to judgment for those given the authority to evaluate socially defined rights and wrongs. But those choices were not all of similar importance. In the broadest sense, policy choices serve to preserve the existing social order from outside assault, and from pressures within that push at the outer edges of the distribution of power and authority that defines social relationships. An example would be those Southern states that prohibited the manumission of slaves.[50] Widespread manumission would have weakened a society based on the labor of predial slaves on large plantations. This would have been exacerbated in a Federal Union in which half of the states' legal orders were based on a free labor system. Not all policy choices were of such a magnitude. And some of those choices were not hostile to rights in slaves, although the prohibitions on the right of owners to emancipate slaves surely undercut a potential right in slaves to freedom.

One of the most important of all the policy choices was the choice to base slavery on the race of the workers: Southern slavery was truly an "Institution of African Service." During the seventeenth century, when a huge number of Southern laborers were white indentured servants, race was less vital than it would be toward the end of the next century and into the nineteenth, when whites were viewed in the context of a free labor system. The separation among the degraded became wider and wider, and the distinguishing mark of the chasm was race. The initial policy choice in the seventeenth century in Virginia, but not in Maryland, was to derive the status of a person from the status of his or her mother. This was likely based on the English law of bastardy and a concern for the property interest of the owners of slaves as much as on the idea that fornication between blacks and whites was so repulsive that it had to be penalized.[51] Whatever the initial basis of the policy choice, once it was in place many other choices followed. For example, as manumission became more commonplace toward the end of the eighteenth century, the rule that race raised the presumption of slavery whenever there was any doubt about the legal status of the person became the norm. Slavery in the South was racial, and to assure the continuation of that type of bondage it made sense to erect a high wall between the races. The tendency was for free whites to avoid any alliance with free nonwhites, and to push the latter more and more toward the status of slaves, or else to exclude them from the state altogether. The initial policy choice that persons derived their status from their mother led to the view, reached in the last decade before the war, that all blacks should be slaves, despite the absence of a legally universal definition of who would be seen as a "black."

The decision to create a biracial society in which one race was free and the other slave was promoted in different ways. One way was to prohibit any free blacks from entering the state, and another was to exclude anyone who was freed or to enslave anyone who was free who remained in the state after a certain date. Another way was for a state to prohibit manumission and encourage voluntary enslavement for the free blacks who remained. Voluntary enslavement, however, stood in basic antagonism to the liberal idea that it made no sense for anyone to sell himself into slavery precisely because he had no property right in the whole self. But these policy choices were not universal, even when the current was strong. Blacks owned slaves in some states but not in others, and not all states adopted laws excluding freed blacks (Virginia reversed its policy on this point).[52]

Moreover, some legal doctrines or rules were grounded in status rather than race and some in a combination of the two. Slave hire law derived from the property claims of the owners and not the color of those in bondage,[53] whereas in criminal law race was often crucial. It was of overwhelming importance in the law of rape, assault with intent to rape, and attempted rape. Chattelhood had next to nothing to do with the punishments meted out. What lawgivers did was to assign the same punishment, most often death, to any black—slave or free—found guilty of rape or attempted rape of a white woman. Policy meant, as Holmes later wrote, the drawing of lines, and as evidence of this fact he cited the Alabama law on the attempted rape of a white woman by a slave.[54] Moreover, jurists chose not to allow any room for consideration of the doctrine of "provocation" in homicide cases when the victim was white and the defendant was black, free or slave. But, of course, even this was not uniform, as some North Carolina judges were prepared to give some weight to the doctrine even while they kept in mind the relative social positions of blacks and whites.[55] It is worth noting that in reflecting on cases, they often wrote as though all blacks were slaves, not just presumptively so. Georgia judges, on the other hand, gave no weight to provocation because that would be to give legal force to judgment in a slave, a black slave. Southern slavery was racial slavery, and as time passed Southerners increasingly pushed to assure not only that it remained so, but also that the society they created would rest on freedom for the members of one race and slavery for another, however one might categorize racial elements in a given person. It had not always been the case, but by the eve of the Civil War the trend was all too clear. All "blacks" should be slaves. It was a matter of social judgment, and that judgment found expression in several legal policies chosen. Slavery had been "encrusted" in race, as Tannenbaum noted.[56]

People of color were slaves, but that was only the initial policy choice. Slaves were in bondage to provide labor, and it was to assure control over that labor that many legal policies were adopted. A persistent internal danger to the social order was the "obstinacy" of the slaves, and Southerners adopted a wide range of policies to reduce the danger: some were ruthless uses of criminal law, some were police regulations, and some were more gentle adaptations of noncriminal law rules. Often enough the policy chosen depended on the view held of slaves. During the colonial period, most lawgivers framed criminal statutes around the assumption that slaves were desperate, barbarous people and would work only under the lash and in the face of savage punishments. The echo of such views, perhaps, could be found in judgments by Georgia's judges that were based on the idea that blacks were so degraded in the scale of humanity that they had to be guided at every step and controlled at all times, even if control required those with authority over slaves, such as hirers, to keep them in chains.[57] An alternative was adopted by Brockenbrough in a case to determine whether it was legally possible to indict an owner in Virginia for cruelty: "with respect to the slaves," he argued, "whilst kindness and humane treatment are calculated to render them contented and happy, is there no danger that oppression and tyranny, against which there is no redress, may drive them to despair."[58]

Policies were far from uniform throughout the South, and they were not always based on simple economic concerns or interests. In *On Law in Economy and Society*, Weber observed that "economic interests are among the strongest factors influencing the creation of law. For, any authority guaranteeing a legal order depends, in some way, upon the consensual action of the constitutive social groups, and the formation of social groups depends, to a large extent, upon constellations of material interest." The relationship was subtle. Law, he continued,

> guarantees by no means only economic interests but rather the most diverse interests ranging from the most elementary one of protection of personal security to such purely ideal goods as personal honor or the honor of the divine powers. Above all, it guarantees . . . positions of authority as well as positions of social preeminence of any kind which may indeed be econom-ically conditioned or economically relevant in the most diverse ways, but which are neither economic in themselves nor sought for preponderantly economic ends.[59]

In the South authority, honor, and economic power were demarcated by many lines, none of which was more significant than race. The "Institution of African Service" placed severe limits on the possibilities of legal subversion precisely be-cause it rested on racial subordination. That is not the same as saying that race made any transformation away from slavery to some other form of dependent labor impossible in the American South. A different set of historical experiences, political configurations, and social-economic relationships made change possible, despite race, in such Caribbean societies as Jamaica, Barbados, Antigua, Guyana, Guadeloupe, and Martinique.[60] Race, like class relationships, memories of oppres-sion, religious values, or ethnic differences placed powerful obstacles in the way of change but did not, any more than the others, make it impossible. Such things limit options and define strategies for achieving social transformations.

Southerners showed signs of adjustment. They were responding to the external criticisms and the internal inconsistencies and doubts. The differences among judges were evidence of a social order under severe stress. It was precisely because they were adapting the laws of slavery, or considering modifications and ameliora-tion, that it is possible to see some movement toward changing chattel slavery into some other form of dependent labor. Although some Southerners tried to preserve a patriarchal social order in the face of the pressures of liberal capitalism by reforming the system, others warmly embraced the newer world of liberal capital-ism, a world of rights. The result, however, could be the same: a possible transformation toward something other than that which currently existed—chattel slavery within a healthy economic system at a high level of involvement in markets. How far the transformation would have gone is an open question.

As slavery in the American South was changing, not because of economic marginalization, but because of outside criticisms, internal incoherence, and uneasiness, there remained a possibility that significant change might have come without violence. Race was a powerful barrier, however, and some people fought against restraints on the authority of owners because they cut too deeply into their material interests and their paternal social order. In the end, however, a nonviolent transformation was turned aside by the conscious decision of the South. Southerners of all classes rallied to the resolution of the region's leaders to withdraw from a union in which their social order was considered of the deepest wickedness and their honor beneath contempt. As O'Neall, who did not favor secession and considered it a tragedy, put it as early as 1848, the sons of South Carolina "will die in the last trench, rather than her rights should be invaded or despoiled." Cobb, who did favor secession in the end, explained it to his daughter shortly before his death in the Battle of Fredericksburg: "These hypocritical, fanatical miserable lying Yankees will not leave us alone to worship God and seek our happiness as He has given us the right to do. They invade our country. They burn our homes, ruin our property, steal our slaves and imprison our men and women and cruelly treat our children. What can we do but war with them?"[61]

Notes

ABBREVIATIONS

Court Reporters

Alabama:
Minor	Henry Minor
Port.	Benjamin F. Porter
Stew. and P.	George N. Stewart and Benjamin F. Porter

Delaware:
Harr.	Samuel M. Harrington

England:
Ld. Raym.	Lord Robert Raymond
Lofft	Cappel Lofft

Georgia:
Dudley Ga.	G. M. Dudley

Kentucky:
Bibb	George M. Bibb
Dana	James G. Dana
Hardin	Martin D. Hardin
Littell	William Littell
A. K. Marsh.	Alexander K. Marshall
J. J. Marsh.	J. J. Marshall
Met. Ky.	James P. Metcalfe
B. Mon.	Ben Monroe
T. B. Mon.	Thomas B. Monroe

Louisiana:
Mart. La.	François X. Martin
Mart. N. S.	François X. Martin

Maryland:
Gill	Richard W. Gill
G. and J.	Richard W. Gill and John Johnson
H. and J.	Thomas Harris Jr. and Reverdy Johnson
Har. and McH.	Thomas Harris Jr. and John McHenry
Md. Ch.	Maryland Chancery Reports

Massachusetts:
Met.	Theron Metcalf

Mississippi:
Fr. Miss. Ch.	John D. Freeman
How.	Volney E. Howard
Smedes and M.	W. C. Smedes and T. A. Marshall
Walker	R. J. Walker

North Carolina:
Devereux	Thomas P. Devereux
Dev. Eq.	Thomas P. Devereux (Equity Reports)

Dev. and Bat.	Thomas P. Devereux and William H. Battle
Hawks	Francis L. Hawks
Iredell	James Iredell
Jones	Hamilton C. Jones
Jones Eq.	Hamilton C. Jones (Equity Reports)
Martin N. C.	François X. Martin

South Carolina:

Bay	Elihu H. Bay
Bailey	Henry Bailey
Brevard	Joseph Brevard
Cheves	Langdon Cheves Jr.
DeSaussure	Henry W. DeSaussure
Dudley	C. W. Dudley
Harp.	William Harper
Harp. Eq.	William Harper (Equity Reports)
Hill	W. R. Hill
Hill Eq.	W. R. Hill (Equity Reports)
McCord	D. J. McCord
McCord Eq.	D. J. McCord (Equity Reports)
McMul.	J. J. McMullan
McMul. Eq.	J. J. McMullan (Equity Reports)
Mill	John Mill
N. and McC.	Henry J. Nott and David J. McCord
Rice	William Rice
Rice Eq.	William Rice (Equity Reports)
Rich.	J. S. G. Richardson
Rich. Eq.	J. S. G. Richardson (Equity Reports)
Speers	R. H. Speers
Strob.	James A. Strobhart
Strob. Eq.	James A. Strobhart (Equity Reports)

Tennessee:

Coldwell	Thomas H. Coldwell
Haywood	John Haywood
Head	John W. Head
Humphreys	W. H. Humphreys
Sneed	John L. T. Sneed
Yerg.	George S. Yerger

Virginia:

Call	Daniel Call
Dana	James G. Dana
Grattan	Peachy R. Grattan
Hen. and M.	William W. Hening and William Munford
Leigh	Benjamin W. Leigh
Mun.	William Munford
Rand.	Peyton Randolph
Va. Ca.	William Brockenbrough and Hugh Holmes
Wash.	Bushrod Washington
Wythe	George Wythe

State Archives

AHC	Arkansas History Commission, Little Rock
GDAH	Georgia Department of Archives and History, Atlanta

KSA   Kentucky State Department for Archives and History, Frankfort
LSA   Louisiana Archives and Records Service, Baton Rouge
MDAH   Mississippi Department of Archives and History, Jackson
MHR   Maryland Hall of Records, Annapolis
MoSA   Missouri State Archives, Columbia
NCDAH   North Carolina Department of Archives and History, Raleigh
SCDAH   South Carolina Department of Archives and History, Columbia
TSLA   Tennessee State Library and Archives, Nashville
VSL   Virginia State Library, Richmond

INTRODUCTION

1. Quoted in Quarles, *Negro in the Civil War*, 322–23.

2. Quoted in Faust, *Ideology of Slavery*, 112.

3. Hutchinson, *Code of Mississippi*, 510; Ormond, Bagley, and Goldthwaite, *Code of Alabama*, 300.

4. Goodell, *American Slave Code*, 19–20.

5. On the property claim in free labor see Steinfeld, *Invention of Free Labor*; on the claim in indentured servitude see Abbot Emerson Smith, *Colonists in Bondage*.

6. Genovese, *Roll, Jordan, Roll*, 47.

7. Watson, *Roman Slave Law*, 53.

8. Quoted in Watson, "Thinking Property at Rome," 1355.

9. Coke, *First Part of the Institutes* (hereafter cited as *Coke on Littleton*); Blackstone, *Commentaries*; Hawkins, *Treatise of the Pleas of the Crown*; Powell, *Essay upon the Law of Contracts*.

10. Rose, *Slavery and Freedom*, 18–36.

10. Berlin, "Time, Space, and the Evolution of Afro-American Society," 44.

12. Fox-Genovese and Genovese, *Fruits of Merchant Capital*, 392.

13. Edmund S. Morgan, *American Slavery American Freedom*, 308; *Negro Population . . . 1790–1915*, 57.

14. *Negro Population . . . 1790–1915*, 57; Main, *Tobacco Colony*. Barbara Jeanne Fields (*Slavery and Freedom on the Middle Ground*, 6) pointed out that Maryland was "in effect, two Marylands by 1850: one founded upon slavery and the other upon free labor. Northern Maryland . . . was an overwhelmingly white and free labor society, the only region of the state in which industrial activity had grown to significant proportions. . . . Southern Maryland . . . was a backward agricultural region devoted primarily to tobacco, though wheat production made inroads during the 1850s, particularly in areas of large and concentrated landholdings."

15. Kulikoff, *Tobacco and Slaves*.

16. *Negro Population . . . 1790–1915*, 57; Essah, "Slavery and Freedom in the First State."

17. Coclanis, *Shadow of a Dream*.

18. *Negro Population . . . 1790–1915*, 57. According to Evarts B. Greene and Virginia Harrington (*American Population*, 156, 173), in 1677 there were 1,400 tithables "a third part whereof at least being Indians, Negroes and women" in the area that became North Carolina, whereas in 1732 there were 6,000 blacks in the same place. South Carolina, in 1703, had a slave population that looked like this: 1,500 black men, 100 Indian men, 900 black women, 150 Indian women, 600 black children, and 100 Indian children.

19. *Negro Population . . . 1790–1815*, 57; Betty Wood, *Slavery in Colonial Georgia*.

20. *Negro Population . . . 1790–1815*, 57; Coleman, *Slavery Times in Kentucky*; Mooney, *Slavery in Tennessee*.

21. James C. Cobb, *Most Southern Place on Earth*, 7–28.

22. *Negro Population . . . 1790–1915*, 57; John Hebron Moore, *Emergence of the Cotton Kingdom*; Sellers, *Slavery in Alabama*; Thornton, *Politics and Power in a Slave Society*.

23. Orville W. Taylor, *Negro Slavery in Arkansas*; Hurt, *Agriculture and Slavery in . . . Little Dixie*.

24. *Negro Population . . . 1790–1915*, 57.

25. Julia Floyd Smith, *Slavery in . . . Antebellum Florida*; *Negro Population . . . 1790–1915*, 57.

26. *Negro Population . . . 1790–1915*, 57; Campbell, *Empire for Slavery*.

27. Gwendolyn Midlo Hall, *Africans in Colonial Louisiana*, 9, 276.

28. *Negro Population . . . 1790–1915*, 57; Joe Gray Taylor, *Negro Slavery in Louisiana*; Tadman, *Speculators and Slaves*; Malone, *Sweet Chariot*.

29. Fields, *Slavery and Freedom on the Middle Ground*, 5.

30. Tocqueville, *Democracy in America*, 1:380.

31. Ronald L. Lewis, *Coal, Iron, and Slaves*.

32. Ransom and Sutch, *One Kind of Freedom*, 52–53.

33. Wright, *Old South, New South*, 19–20; Bateman and Weiss, *Deplorable Scarcity*; Wright, *Political Economy*; Ronald L. Lewis, *Coal, Iron, and Slaves*.

34. Trespass on the case was a special form of common law action that grew up in the common law courts. It was always shortened in the appellate record and in legal discussions to the one word—case. It was a different action from the more ancient action of "trespass." The word *case*, when the discussion is of the proper form of action, means trespass on the case. Special rules of pleading, as well as liability, were attached to each form of action—an example concerned the matter of possession. A person had to have actual or constructive possession of property to proceed under some actions but not necessarily under others. The real importance of trespass on the case, or case, however, was summed up by Maitland (*Forms of Action*, 67) this way: "Case becomes a sort of general residuary action; much, particularly, of the modern law of negligence developed within it." The context should alert the reader that case either refers to this special form of common law action or is rather a general reference to a case before the court.

35. Maitland, *Forms of Action*, 62.

36. Ibid., 4.

37. White, *Tort Law in America*, 8–12; Nelson, *Americanization of the Common Law*; Morton Horwitz, *Transformation of American Law, 1780–1860*.

38. A superb study of the place of "fictions" in Anglo-American law is Fuller, *Legal Fictions*. The fiction, he wrote, "represents the pathology of the law," and "we may liken the fiction to an awkward patch applied to a rent in the law's fabric of theory." The fiction was either "(1) a statement propounded with a complete or partial consciousness of its falsity, or (2) a false statement recognized as having utility" (pp. viii, 9).

39. Blackstone, *Commentaries*, 3:268.

40. Quoted in Hoffer, *Law's Conscience*, 10.

41. An excellent summary of equity appears in Katz, "Politics of Law," 259–60:

(1) *Equity remedies defects in the common law*. It takes notice of fraud, accident, mistake, and forgery. It administers relief according to the true intentions of the parties. It gives specific relief in actions for contract and tort, and it gives relief against the penalties assessed by other courts. It has unique powers of examining witnesses, and joining parties to a suit.

(2) *Equity supplies omissions in the jurisdiction of the common law*. It deals with uses and trusts, and, especially, with mortgages and equities of redemption. It disposes of the guardianship of minors and lunatics. It has competence in mercantile law, family settlement, female property, and divorce.

(3) *Courts of equity afford procedures not available at law:* the writ of subpoena, interrogatory process, discovery of evidence, written pleadings, judgment without jury trial, leeway for errors in pleading, specific performance, injunction, imprisonment for contempt, ability to act *in personam* rather than *ad rem* (that is, on the person rather than the thing), powers of account, and administration of estates.

42. Lieberman, *Province of Legislation Determined*, 182.

43. Ibid., 179–217. On codification in the United States see Cook, *American Codification Movement*, and Bloomfield, *American Lawyers*, chap. 3. One study of the movement in the South is Senese, "Legal Thought in South Carolina." For specific examples in the South see Petigru, *Portion of the Code of Statute Law of South Carolina;* Livingston, *System of Penal Law;* Grimké, *An Oration, on the Practicability . . . of Reducing . . . the Law;* and Wilson, *Codification.*

44. Plucknett, *Concise History of the Common Law*, 374.

45. Coke, *Third Part of the Institutes;* Hale, *Pleas of the Crown;* Hawkins, *Treatise of the Pleas of the Crown.*

46. Blackstone, *Commentaries*, 4:2.

47. Milsom, *Historical Foundations*, 355, 365.

48. Lipscomb to Lumpkin, March 5, 1853, Lumpkin Papers, University of Georgia, Athens; *Pridgin v. Strickland*, 8 Tex. 433–34 (1852).

49. Dargo, *Jefferson's Louisiana;* Haas, *Louisiana's Legal Heritage.*

50. A. E. Keir Nash, "Reason of Slavery," 10; Morton Horwitz, *Transformation of American Law, 1870–1960*, viii.

51. Watson, *Slave Law in the Americas*, 76; Fox-Genovese and Genovese, *Fruits of Merchant Capital*, 365.

52. Tannenbaum, *Slave and Citizen*, vii.

53. A. E. Keir Nash's "Reason of Slavery" (p. 25) holds that Southern judges did acknowledge moral personality. Finkelman, in "Slaves as Fellow Servants," "The Crime of Color," and "The Color of Law," takes the position that they rarely did. At one point Tushnet argued that so-called recognitions of humanity were a sham, but he changed his mind. Tushnet, "American Law of Slavery" (1975) and *American Law of Slavery* (1981). No one, however, has gone as far as Fede (*People Without Rights*, x) in repudiating the notion that Southern judges ever gave any real weight to humanity. In his view, "those instances of legal recognition of slaves as persons" were "rhetorical devices that legitimized the inhumanity of slave law."

54. A. Leon Higginbotham Jr., *In the Matter of Color*, 15, 39.

55. Higginbotham and Jacobs, "The 'Law Only as an Enemy,' " 975.

56. Fredrickson, *Arrogance of Race*, 3, 7.

57. Jordan, *White Over Black*, 4–11, 24.

58. Watson, *Slave Law in the Americas*, xiv, 64, 76, 130–33.

59. Tushnet, *American Law of Slavery*, 155; A. E. Keir Nash, "Reason of Slavery," 205; Fisher, "Ideology and Imagery in the Law of Slavery," 1057.

60. Elkins, *Slavery*, 49.

61. Macpherson, *Theory of Possessive Individualism*, 3.

62. Steinfeld, *Invention of Free Labor*, 80; Atiyah, *Freedom of Contract*, 30.

63. Fox-Genovese and Genovese, *Fruits of Merchant Capital*, 32; Oakes, *Slavery and Freedom*, 43.

64. Knight, "Slavery and Capitalism in the Spanish and Portuguese Empire," 62 n. 1; Fogel and Engerman, *Time on the Cross*, 71–73.

65. Appleby, *Capitalism and a New Social Order*, 9, 94.

66. Genovese, *Roll, Jordan, Roll* and *World the Slaveholders Made.*

67. Tushnet, *American Law of Slavery*, 72.

68. Ibid., 40.

69. Ibid., 42; Fox-Genovese and Genovese, *Fruits of Merchant Capital*, 369.

70. Quoted in Fredrickson, *Arrogance of Race*, 26.

71. Goodell, *American Slave Code*, 404.

72. Quoted in Tannenbaum, *Slave and Citizen*, 107–8.

CHAPTER 1

1. Godwyn, *Negro's & Indians Advocate*, 36. See also Vaughan, "Origins Debate," 311–54.

2. Jefferson, *Notes on the State of Virginia*, 133.

3. Aristotle's view of slavery was challenged by Francis Lieber in "Definition of Slavery," a one-page, undated scrap in Lieber on Slavery, Lieber Papers, Huntington Library, San Marino, Calif. Lieber was categorical: "the Aristotelian definition of a slave . . . is wrong."

4. Hanke, *Aristotle and the American Indians*, 47. See also Hanke, *Spanish Struggle for Justice*.

5. Jordan, *White Over Black*, 158–59.

6. Arthur O. Lovejoy, *Great Chain of Being*.

7. In addition to Jordan's study see Evans, "From the Land of Canaan to the Land of Guinea."

8. T. R. R. Cobb, *Law of Negro Slavery*, 46–47.

9. Hellie, *Slavery in Russia*.

10. Watson, *Slave Law in the Americas*, 76; Phillips, "Central Theme of Southern History," 31; Hoetink, "Slavery and Race," 267–68; Sio, "Commentary," 270, 272; Genovese, *Roll, Jordan, Roll*; Genovese, *World the Slaveholders Made*, 113 (Moreover, "To say that the race question has to be subsumed under the class question is not to make it a mere facade for class exploitation, nor to deny it a life of its own . . . racism restricted the options open . . . race gave shape to class hegemony, not vice versa" [p. 238]); Fredrickson, *Arrogance of Race*, 11.

11. Watson, *Slave Law in the Americas*, 767.

12. Tushnet, *American Law of Slavery*, 139–40; A. Leon Higginbotham Jr., *In the Matter of Color*, 39. See also Higginbotham and Kopytoff, "Racial Purity and Interracial Sex"; Higginbotham and Kopytoff, "Property First, Humanity Second"; and Higginbotham and Jacobs, "The 'Law Only as an Enemy.'"

13. A. E. Keir Nash, "Reason of Slavery," 205.

14. Edmund S. Morgan, *American Slavery American Freedom*, 99–100.

15. Duncan, "Servitude and Slavery"; McGowan, "Creation of a Slave Society."

16. Hening, *Statutes at Large*, 1:410. An earlier act of March 1654/5 expressly stated that Virginians "do engage that wee will not use them as slaves" but bring them up as Christians (p. 396).

17. Ibid. 455–56, 482.

18. Ibid., 2:283, 280–81, 346, 440.

19. Edmund S. Morgan, *American Slavery American Freedom*, 330.

20. Hening, *Statutes at Large*, 2:479–80.

21. Duncan, "Servitude and Slavery," 39, 41.

22. Parker, *North Carolina Higher-Court Records, 1697–1701*, 38.

23. Goodell, *American Slave Code*, 281.

24. *Hudgins v. Wrights*, 1 Hen. and M. 138–39 (Va., 1806). Judge Tucker drew a crucial legal presumption from this: "all American Indians are *prima facie* FREE."

25. O'Neall, *Negro Law of South Carolina*, 5.

26. *Seville v. Chretien*, 5 Mart. La. 275 (La., 1817). The court also turned aside a challenge based on natural law: "Slavery, notwithstanding all that may have been said and written

against it, as being unjust, arbitrary, and contrary to the laws of human nature, we find, in history, to have existed from the earliest ages of the world, down to the present day. . . . we are of opinion, that it may be laid down as a legal axiom, that in all governments in which the municipal regulations are not absolutely opposed to slavery, persons already reduced to that state may be held in it" (p. 285).

27. *Marguerite v. Choteau*, 3 Mo. 286 (1834), overruling *Marguerite v. Choteau*, 2 Mo. 71 (1828).

28. *Marguerite v. Choteau*, 3 Mo. 289–90 (1834).

29. *Somerset v. Stewart*, Lofft 1, 98 Eng. Rep. 499 (K. B., 1772). See Wiecek, "*Somerset*"; James Oldham, *Mansfield Manuscripts*, 2:1221–40; Shyllon, *Black Slaves in Britain*.

30. *Marguerite v. Choteau*, 3 Mo. 301 (1834).

31. T. R. R. Cobb, *Law of Negro Slavery*, 67.

32. *State v. Dillahunt*, 3 Harr. 551 (Del., 1840). On slavery in Delaware see Essah, "Slavery and Freedom in the First State."

33. T. R. R. Cobb, *Law of Negro Slavery*, 67 and n. 4.

34. *Code of Virginia, 1849*, 458; T. R. R. Cobb, *Law of Negro Slavery*, 22; O'Neall, *Negro Law of South Carolina*, 5.

35. Jordan, *White Over Black*, 168: Hening, *Statutes at Large*, 3:252.

36. Hening, *Statutes at Large*, 3:252.

37. McIlwaine, *Minutes of the Council*, 479.

38. Hening, *Statutes at Large*, 3:252.

39. Patterson, *Slavery and Social Death*, 142.

40. Case of Susannah Barnes, October 15, 1679, Charles City County Orders, 1650, 1672–73, 1677–80, 1685, 1687–95, VSL. See also the case of Ann Churchman, April 15, 1678, in the same order book.

41. Hening, *Statutes at Large*, 3:87 (the 1691 provision was part of a law entitled "An act for suppressing outlying Slaves"), 453 (the 1705 provision was part of the general law, "An act concerning Servants and Slaves"), 4:133, 8:34.

42. Case of Joseph Barham, July 13, 1744, Charles City County Orders, 1696, Order Book, 1737–51. See also Case of Elizabeth Sanders, October 8, 1736, Caroline County Order Book, 1732–40, and Case of Priscilla Palmer, May 13, 1723, Lancaster County Orders No. 7, 1721–29, VSL.

43. Hening, *Statutes at Large*, 12:184; Jordan, *White Over Black*, 168; Maxcy, *Laws of Maryland*, 1:116; Cushing, *Earliest Printed Laws of North Carolina*, 164.

44. Williamson, *New People*.

45. McLaurin, *Celia*, 91; Wright and Tinling, *Diary of William Byrd*; Faust, *Hammond and the Old South*; Woodward, *Mary Chesnut's Civil War*, 29. In another part of her entry that day, March 18, 1861, Chesnut wrote: "we live surrounded by prostitutes. An abandoned woman is sent out of any decent house elsewhere. Who thinks any worse of a negro or mulatto woman for being a thing we can't name? God forgive us, but ours is a *monstrous* system and wrong and iniquity."

46. Lord Proprietary v. Mallatto (*sic*) Jane, August 1740, Prince Georges County Court Record, August 1740–March 1741/2, MHR. See also Lord Proprietary v. Sarah Battling, November 1751, March, November 1752, and Case of Martin Maddin, November 1752, Talbot County Court Criminal Judgments, 1751–55, MHR.

47. For "promulatto bias" see Toplin, "Between Black and White." See also Sheldon, "Black-White Relations in Richmond," and Ingersoll, "Old New Orleans."

48. T. R. R. Cobb, *Historical Sketch of Slavery*, ccix–ccxx. This was the introductory essay to his study of slave law.

49. O'Neall, *Negro Law of South Carolina*, 5; T. R. R. Cobb, *Law of Negro Slavery*, 67.

50. *Historical Statistics of the United States*, 1:26, 29, 32, 34, 36.

51. *Gobu v. Gobu,* 1 N.C. 101 (1802); *Nichols v. Bell,* 1 Jones 34 (N.C., 1853).

52. *Hudgins v. Wrights,* 1 Hen. and M. 139–40 (Va., 1806).

53. *Gentry v. McMinnis,* 3 Dana 385 (Ky., 1835).

54. Tushnet, *American Law of Slavery,* 143.

55. *Daniel v. Guy,* 19 Ark. 130, 136 (1857).

56. Ibid., 131–36; Williamson, *New People,* 1–2. The one-drop rule had become almost universal by the 1920s.

57. *Daniel v. Guy,* 19 Ark. 134 (1857).

58. *Gary v. Stevenson,* 19 Ark. 583–84, 580, 586 (1858).

59. *Adelle v. Beauregard,* 1 Mart. (O. S.) 183–85 (La., 1810).

60. *State v. Scott,* 1 Bailey 270, 272–73 (S.C., 1829).

61. *State v. Davis* and *State v. Hanna,* 2 Bailey 559–60 (S.C., 1831); O'Neall, *Negro Law of South Carolina,* 6.

62. Hoetink, "Surinam and Curaçao."

63. Exclusion was common enough, but it became extreme in the 1850s and early 1860s when some argued for expulsion, not just exclusion of those born outside a state. Berlin, *Slaves Without Masters,* 360–64, 371–75. See also Michael P. Johnson and Roark, *Black Masters.*

64. *Revised Statutes of . . . North Carolina,* 1:590.

65. For nineteenth-century Southern whites this was one of the most embarrassing aspects of the law of slavery. It was a focus of some who sought to reform the law: see, e.g., "Slave Marriages," *DeBow's Review,* July 1855, 130.

66. In March 1848 there were indictments against Mary Clarke and Hardy Artis for "intermarrying with slave," and in September 1849 there were indictments against Jacob Boon, Eliza Powell, and Netty Sexton for the same offense. Northampton County Court, Appearance, State, and Trial Docket, 1840–49, NCDAH. Examples from New Hanover County would include the indictment against William Allen in Fall 1850 and one against William Martin in Spring 1851 for "cohabiting with a slave." New Hanover County, State Docket, Superior Court, 1836–51, NCDAH.

67. State v. Mariah Sweat, October 30, 1860, Northampton County, Minutes, Superior Court, 1845–68, NCDAH; Manuscript Census, 1860, Free Schedule, M 653, Reel 908. The judgment against Sweat was suspended on her paying costs. Two additional examples are Penny Wiggins, a thirty-five-year-old mulatto woman, and Mary Clarke, a thirty-year-old.

68. *State v. Edmund, (a slave),* 15 N.C. 280 (1833); *Session Laws of North Carolina, 1860,* 69; *Cline v. Caldwell,* Hill 424 (S.C., 1833).

69. Jackson, *Free Negro Labor,* 205–13; Michael P. Johnson and Roark, *Black Masters;* Mills, *Forgotten People.* See also Berlin, *Slaves Without Masters.*

70. Howell Cobb, *Compilation of the . . . Statutes . . . of Georgia,* 614; *Bryan v. Walton,* 20 Ga. 512 (1856).

71. *Davis v. Evans,* 18 Mo. 252 (1853).

72. *Tindall v. Hudson,* 2 Harr. 441–42 (Del., 1838).

73. *Ewell v. Tidwell,* 20 Ark. 144 (1859).

74. Elkins, *Slavery.*

75. Dew, *Review of the Debate,* 96. Dew concluded that free blacks were "the most worthless and indolent of the citizens of the United States. It is well known that throughout the whole extent of our Union, they are looked upon as the very *drones* and *pests* of society . . . idleness and improvidence are at the root of all their misfortunes" (p. 88).

76. Fitzhugh, *Sociology for the South,* 264. On Fitzhugh see Genovese, *World the Slaveholders Made,* Part 2, "The Logical Outcome of the Slaveholders' Philosophy."

77. Berlin, *Slaves Without Masters,* 372–80. On an effort to expel slaves in South Carolina

see Michael P. Johnson and Roark, *Black Masters*, chap. 7, and Wikramanayake, *A World in Shadow*.

78. *Session Laws of Alabama, 1859*, 63–64; *Session Laws of Florida, 1858*, 13–14; *Session Laws of Louisiana, 1859*, 214–15; *Session Laws of Maryland, 1860*, Law 322; *Session Laws of Tennessee, 1857*, 55–56; *Session Laws of Texas, 1857*, 75–77; *Session Laws of Virginia, 1855*, 37–38. Specific examples will be considered in the text. Wikramanayake (*A World in Shadow*, 183) found petitions for enslavement involving a half-dozen people in South Carolina. See also Berlin, *Slaves Without Masters*, 367; Russell, *Free Negro in Virginia*, 108; and Wilbert E. Moore, *American Negro Slavery*, 100.

79. Innes, *Work and Labor in Early America*, 3; Locke, *Essay concerning Civil Government*, quoted in Burtt, *English Philosophers*, 412; Waldron, *Right of Private Property*, 177.

80. Rousseau, *The Social Contract and Discourses*, 7; Kant, *Metaphysical Elements of Justice*, 98; Hegel, *Philosophy of Right*, 55, 241; Marx, *Capital*, 1:168; Genovese, "Slave States of North America," 259; Macpherson, *Theory of Possessive Individualism*, 54.

81. Blackstone, *Commentaries*, 1:411–41; Adam Smith, *Lectures on Jurisprudence*, 455.

82. Hellie, *Slavery in Russia*, 280, 384, 455, 580, 693–94, 704, 706.

83. Brown to Ferguson, July 18, 1818, St. Landry Parish, Conveyance Record, D-1, 236, St. Landry Parish Courthouse, Opelousas, La.

84. Fitzhugh, *Sociology for the South*, 267, 272.

85. Oakes, *Slavery and Freedom*, 68–69.

86. Blackstone (*Commentaries*, 1:125) reduced the basic rights to three—"the right of personal security, the right of personal liberty; and the right of private property." Oakes (*Slavery and Freedom*, 57) argues that by the eighteenth century "rights preceded all obligations, and they were inherent in the individual rather than conferred from on high. Liberalism was overtaking the ideal of an organically unified social hierarchy patterned on the model of the patriarchal family." "In the end," he believes, "the universalization of rights and the dynamic force of free labor overwhelmed and destroyed slavery. But southern slave society emerged within rather than apart from the liberal capitalist world, and that made a crucial difference. For the ambiguous relationship between slavery and liberal capitalism thereby became intrinsic to the Old South, not merely the basis of sectional animosity" (p. 79). There is also considerable evidence of a widespread patriarchalism among Southern judges, however. There was, in short, a fierce struggle going on between liberal capitalist thought and republicanism in a slave society, which meant patriarchalism. The whole concept of self-enslavement, which institutionalized the racial element in the proslavery argument, is a case in point. The concept was far from liberal capitalist thought.

87. Samuel, "Role of *Paramone* Clauses," 295.

88. *Session Laws of Louisiana, 1859*, 214–15; *Session Laws of Tennessee, 1857*, 55–56.

89. Berlin, *Slaves Without Masters*, 367; February 19, 1864, Leon County Circuit Court Minute Book, vol. 6, October 1855–May 1869, 341, Leon County Courthouse, Tallahassee, Fla. See Rivers, "Slavery in Microcosm."

90. There are documents covering sixteen people during the period 1857–60 in Auditor's Item 153, Box 10, VSL. Margarett Price was one of them. Ironically, Auditor's Item 153 generally is concerned with "condemned slaves." There are twelve more cases in the session laws down to 1861. One case, involving Willis and Andrew, was from 1854, before the general voluntary enslavement law was passed (*Session Laws of Virginia, 1854*, 131–32). The remaining ten came in 1861 (*Session Laws of Virginia, 1861*, 251–55). The petition of Araminta Francis, March 10, 1856, is in the Lunenburg County Minute Book, 1853–58, VSL.

91. *Session Laws of Georgia, 1861*, 121–22. Another case involves Jane Miller the following year. *Session Law of Georgia, 1862*, 96.

92. Petition of Lucy Andrews, a free person of color praying to be permitted to go into

slavery, no date, Legislative Petitions, SCDAH. Another petition in the collection is that of Elizabeth Jane Bug, December 1, 1859. She also had an eleven-month-old child. Additional examples, outside those in the text, are Bastrop County Deed Records, April 9, 1858, Bastrop County Courthouse, Bastrop, Tex.; act of 1859 allowing Emily Hooper to return to North Carolina from Liberia and go back into slavery, *Session Laws of North Carolina, 1859*, 370; *Session Laws of Alabama, 1859–60*, 599–600, 674–75, 662, authorizing voluntary enslavement for Ned Adkins, Tarleton Moss, William Patterson (aged twenty-five), Lucy Green, Cora, Lewis Wetherspoon, and Charles Short and eleven others, all related. The next year six slaves entitled to freedom were authorized to select a master "should it be the desire of the . . . named slaves to remain in slavery." *Session Laws of Alabama, 1861*, 259–60.

93. Godwyn, *Negro's & Indians Advocate*, 36.

CHAPTER 2

1. Stroud, *Sketch of the Laws*, 9.

2. John Taylor, *Elements of the Civil Law*; A. W. B. Simpson, "Rise and Fall of the Legal Treatise," 657.

3. Stroud, *Sketch of the Laws*, 9–10. According to Taylor, "Slaves were held *pro nullis: pro mortuis: pro quadrupedibus*. They had no head in the state, no name, title or register: they were not capable of being injured; nor could they take by purchase or descent: they had no heirs, and therefore could make no will: exclusive of what was called their *peculium*, whatever they acquired was their master's; they could not claim the indulgence of absence *republicae causa*: they were not entitled to the rights and considerations of matrimony, and, therefore, had no relief in case of adultery: nor were they proper objects of cognation or affinity, but of *quasi-cognation* only: they could be sold, transferred, or pawned as goods or personal estate; for goods they were, and as such they were esteemed: they might be tortured for evidence, punished at the discretion of their lord, or even put to death by his authority." John Taylor, *Elements of the Civil Law*, 459. See also Watson, *Roman Slave Law*; Buckland, *Roman Law of Slavery*; Nicholas, *Introduction to Roman Law*; and the collection of materials about ancient slavery by Wiedemann, *Greek and Roman Slavery*.

4. Stroud, *Sketch of the Laws*, 9.

5. Sio, "Interpretations of Slavery." See also Finley, *Ancient Slavery and Modern Ideology*.

6. An especially provocative examination of the role of generalizations among historians is "Generalizations in Ancient History," in Finley, *Use and Abuse of History*. It is not my contention that a "sound generalization" that will "hold true" is equivalent to "objectivity" in some strong sense. On this problem see Novick, *That Noble Dream*.

7. Patterson, *Slavery and Social Death*, 4. There is an increasingly sophisticated literature on various slave systems. In addition to Patterson's general study, one might begin with Parish, *Slavery*; Paul Lovejoy, *Transformations in Slavery*; Fredrickson, *White Supremacy*; Kolchin, *Unfree Labor*; Frederick Cooper, *Slavery on the East Coast of Africa*; and Watson, *Slave Law in the Americas*. Useful guides on the literature are Joseph C. Miller, *Slavery: A Worldwide Bibliography*, and John David Smith, *Black Slavery in the Americas*.

8. See *Bryan v. Walton*, 14 Ga. 199 (1853).

9. Quoted in Washburn, "Law and Authority in Colonial Virginia," 117. See also Handlin and Handlin, "Origins of the Southern Labor System," 205.

10. Watson, *Slave Law in the Americas*, 64.

11. Bush, "Free to Enslave," 457–58.

12. Ibid., 432–33.

13. Nicholson, "Legal Borrowing and the Origins of Slave Law," 40, 42.

14. This version is from Captain John Smith, *Generall Historie of Virginia*, reprinted in

Tyler, ed., *Narratives of Early Virginia*, 337. A variation is the report Rolfe wrote to Sir Edwin Sandys in January 1619/20 in which he referred to the fact that the Dutch brought "not any thing but 20. and odd Negroes." A convenient source for this letter is Rose, *Documentary History of Slavery*, 16.

15. Ballagh, *History of Slavery in Virginia*, 288–89; Handlin and Handlin, "Origins of the Southern Labor System," 203 n. 16, 204. See also Palmer, "Servant into Slave." The thesis was first seriously challenged in Ames, *Studies of the Virginia Eastern Shore*. A useful introduction to the debate is Noel, *Origins of American Slavery and Racism*. See also McColley, "Slavery in Virginia," 11–23. McColley argued that despite the absence of English statutes the English were well aware of slavery, and that the earliest blacks in Virginia were held as slaves, at least most of them. He does not, however, consider questions of law or "legal status."

16. Jordan, *White Over Black*, 73.

17. Billings, "Transfer of English Law to Virginia" and "Pleading, Procedure, and Practice"; Konig, " 'Dale's Laws,' " 354, 368 n. 21, 375.

18. Washburn, "Law and Authority in Colonial Virginia," 127, 129, 131. See, especially, Macpherson, *Political Theory of Possessive Individualism*.

19. Vaughan, "Blacks in Virginia," 472, 477.

20. Entry for September 27, 1627, in McIlwaine, *Minutes of the Council*, 72–73. In an earlier case the court swore in John Phillip and took his evidence on the last day of November 1624; he was "A negro Christened in *England* 12 yeers since" (p. 33). On March 31, 1641, the court entered the case of John Graweere. A "negro servant unto *William Evans*," he was permitted "by his said master to keep hogs and make the best benefit thereof to himself" provided he give Evans one-half of the increase. Graweere had a son by a "negro woman belonging to Lieut. *Robert Sheppard*" whom he wanted to make a Christian, and to that end he purchased his son's freedom from Sheppard. The court ordered the boy to be "free from the said *Evans* or his assigns" (p. 477). The only apparent claim Evans might have had to the child derived from his ownership of Graweere. This, in turn, would suggest that the status of a child derived not from the mother, but from the father.

21. Hening, *Statutes at Large*, 1:146. Two scholars have suggested possible alternative readings of this case. Finkelman (*Law of Freedom and Bondage*, 10) noted that one question was whether Davis was "whipped for fornication or homosexual activity." Edmund S. Morgan (*American Slavery American Freedom*, 333) asked whether Davis was punished because it could be a "case of sodomy rather than fornication." Despite the fact that sodomy is not easy to define, Morgan seems to have had in mind the same point as Finkelman. This view, however, is unlikely to be correct. Homosexuality was dealt with severely in early-seventeenth-century Virginia. In 1624/5, for instance, not only was Richard Williams (alias Richard Cornish, a seaman) executed in Virginia for buggery, but also an acquaintance who said he believed that Williams had been "put to death wrongfully" was ordered whipped from "the forte to the gallows and from thence be whipt back againe, and be sett uppon the Pillory and there to loose one of his eares, And that his service to S^r: *George Yardley* for seaven yeers Shalbegain from the psent day, According to the Condicion of the *dewtie* boyes he beinge one of them." McIlwaine, *Minutes of the Council*, 34, 42, 93.

22. McIlwaine, *Minutes of the Council*, 477, 483. A telling point was made by McColley ("Slavery in Virginia," 21): "the courts of early Virginia did indeed punish couples of different races for fornication. But the same courts far more often punished white servants for fornication and bastardy. Blacks were not punished for sexual relations among themselves, which is surely significant."

23. Blackstone, *Commentaries*, 4:65.

24. Hening, *Statutes at Large*, 1:240.

25. As late as 1648 there were only about 300 blacks in Virginia, and the number did not rise to about 2,000 until 1670. Greene and Harrington, *American Population*, 134–36, 143–

44. See also *Historical Statistics of the United States*, 2:1171–72, which suggests that headrights were granted for about 420 blacks as of 1662. An important study that emphasizes the small number of blacks in seventeenth-century Virginia is Craven, *White, Red, and Black.*

26. Littleton's position as a justice placed him among the elite of the county. Excellent studies of the prominence of these people are Sydnor, *American Revolutionaries in the Making*; Roeber, *Faithful Magistrates and Republican Lawyers*; and Isaac, *Transformation of Virginia.*

27. Ames, *County Court Records of Accomack-Northampton, Virginia*, 4, 324, 422–23. I am grateful to Christopher Tomlins for the Burdett reference. Inventory of the Estate of William Stafford, March 3, 1644, York County Order Book, VSL. For a similar later entry see the inventory of the estate of Lt. Col. Thomas Ludlove, recorded January 25, 1660, York County Order Book.

28. Breen and Innes, *"Myne Owne Ground,"* 5, 11–17.

29. Ibid.

30. Jordan, *White Over Black*, 3–44, 136–269; Breen and Innes, *"Myne Owne Ground,"* 19–36.

31. A. W. B. Simpson, "Rise and Fall of the Legal Treatise," 656. By the late eighteenth century and into the nineteenth Virginia judges cited Roman law more often. See Bryson, "Use of Roman Law in Virginia Courts."

32. *Waddill v. Chamberlayne* (1735), in Barton, *Virginia Colonial Decisions*, 2:45.

33. Davies, "Slavery and Protector Somerset," 534.

34. Finley, "Slavery," *International Encyclopedia*, 14:307.

35. Baker, "Property in Chattels," 217.

36. The evolution of various categories of English law can be examined in Holdsworth, *History of English Law*; Baker, *Introduction to English Legal History*; Milsom, *Historical Foundations*; and Harding, *Social History of English Law*. Also of interest are Levack, *Civil Lawyers in England*, and Veall, *Popular Movement for Law Reform.*

37. Stroud, *Sketch of the Laws*, 2. Hurd (*Law of Freedom and Bondage*, 1:211 n. 1) pointed out that "the phrase—partus sequitur ventrem is not, I believe, to be found in the *Corpus Juris*, and probably originated with the modern civilians."

38. Hening, *Statutes at Large*, 2:170.

39. Billings, "Cases of Fernando and Elizabeth Key," 473.

40. Swinburne, *Brief Treatise*, 43–44. An inventory of Col. Ralph Wormely's library in 1701 included "Swinborns Wills and Testaments," *William and Mary Quarterly*, 1st ser. (1893): 2:172.

41. Swinburne, *Brief Treatise*, 43–44. See also Holdsworth, *Some Makers of English Law*, 21.

42. Swinburne, *Brief Treatise*, 43–44.

43. Handlin and Handlin ("Origins of the Southern Labor System," 213) first suggested this link.

44. Botein, *Early American Law*, 13.

45. Billings, *Old Dominion in the Seventeenth Century*, 166, 168. For a full account see Billings, "Cases of Fernando and Elizabeth Key," 467–74.

46. Wiecek, "Statutory Law of Slavery," 262–63; Billings, "Cases of Fernando and Elizabeth Key," 473; Edmund S. Morgan, *American Slavery American Freedom*, 333. See, for instance, the case of Rebecca Corney from 1689 in Charles City County mentioned in Billings, *Old Dominion in the Seventeenth Century*, 163, or an earlier case from the same county: Ann Churchman was ordered by the county court to serve her master longer because she had "brought forth a bastard child begotten by a negro man." April 15, 1678, Charles City County, Court Orders, VSL; Vaughan, "Blacks in Virginia," 473. See also the inventory of the estate of William Stafford, March 3, 1644, York County Order Book, VSL.

His estate included two black men, two black women, and four children. This is not to suggest that sexual parity was the norm in Virginia or elsewhere in the English North American settlements. A study of the gradual emergence of stable family units in the Chesapeake is Kulikoff, *Tobacco and Slaves*. The question of the sexual composition of the earliest black groups brought to the region, however, remains a subject for further study. Botein, *Early American Law*, 13: Hening, *Statutes at Large*, 3:87.

47. Blackstone, *Commentaries*, 2:94.

48. Hurd, *Law of Freedom and Bondage*, 1:249.

49. Stroud, *Sketch of the Laws*, 1–2.

50. Maxcy, *Laws of Maryland*, 1:115–16; Whittington B. Johnson, "Origins and Nature of African Slavery"; Alpert, "Origin of Slavery."

51. Cushing, *Earliest Printed Laws of North Carolina*, 161–73.

52. Thomas Cooper and McCord, *Statutes at Large of South Carolina*, 7:352; Sirmans, "Legal Status of the Slave," 466. Sirmans referred to the definition in the law as "vague to the point of being cryptic."

53. Patterson, *Slavery and Social Death*, 142. Patterson described the Chinese pattern as one in which the "principle of *deterior condicio* operated: the child always took the status of the parent with the lower status." He indicated that the South Carolina law of 1717, rather than that of 1712, followed the Chinese pattern (p. 144), but the law of 1712 did so as well. Despite this omission, Patterson has been the only scholar to recognize the South Carolina law for precisely what it was.

54. Thomas Cooper and McCord, *Statutes at Large of South Carolina*, 7:397; Peter Wood, *Black Majority*.

55. Betty Wood, *Slavery in Colonial Georgia*.

56. Tannenbaum, *Slave and Citizen*; Scott, Lohinger, and Vance, *Las Siete Partidas*. A classic statement of the belief that Brazilian slavery was not as brutal as that of the American South is Freyre, *Masters and the Slaves*. Numerous studies have undermined this view of Latin American slavery. See, e.g., Degler, *Neither Black Nor White*; Stanley Stein, *Vassouras*; Stuart Schwartz, *Sugar Plantations*; Knight, *Slave Society in Cuba*; and the collection of documents by Conrad, *Children of God's Fire*.

57. Watson, *Roman Slave Law*, 95.

58. Ibid., 134–35.

59. Blackstone, *Commentaries* 2:94; A. W. B. Simpson, "Rise and Fall of the Legal Treatise," 655, 658. Blackstone, according to Simpson, was "essentially a civilian" whose "disappointed ambition was to become Professor of Civil Law at Oxford." Of somewhat greater importance is the fact that "the *Commentaries* do not arise from the common law. Though the scheme dates back to Hale, nothing remotely resembling them in execution had appeared in the English language before." In Simpson's view, Blackstone did precisely for the common law what had already been done with skill for the civil—to present it as a rational system built on firm foundations. But though he had considerable respect for the civil law, Blackstone was also a nationalist: "we must not carry our veneration," he wrote at the outset, "so far as to sacrifice our Alfred and Edward to the manes of Theodosius and Justinian. . . . [If] an Englishman must be ignorant of either the one or the other, he had better be a stranger to the Roman than the English institutions." A superb analysis of the intellectual transformations on which Blackstone built is Shapiro, "Law and Science."

60. Milsom, *Historical Foundations*, xi.

61. Hurd, *Law of Freedom and Bondage*, 2:4, 14, 146, 160–61, 192.

62. *Pridgin v. Strickland*, 8 Tex. 433–44 (1852).

63. Dargo, *Jefferson's Louisiana*. See also Haas, *Louisiana's Legal Heritage*. Especially relevant essays are those by Baade, "The Law of Slavery in Spanish Luisiana"; Yiannopoulos,

"The Early Sources of Louisiana Law"; and Billings, "Louisiana Legal History and Its Sources." And see Moreau and Carleton, *Laws of Las Siete Partidas . . . Still in Force.*

64. *Mayho v. Sears,* 3 Iredell 228 (N.C., 1842).

65. *Maria v. Surbaugh,* 2 Rand. 236–37 (Va., 1824). There is an extensive discussion of this landmark case in A. E. Keir Nash, "Reason of Slavery." It is also examined by Cover, *Justice Accused,* 74. These studies, however, were concerned with the conclusions of law, not with the sources of law.

66. *Maria v. Surbaugh,* 2 Rand. 245 (1824). The relative indifference to historical accuracy is hardly unique to Southern judges. See, e.g., Watson, *Sources of Law, Legal Change, and Ambiguity,* and Charles A. Miller, *Supreme Court and the Uses of History.* For a parallel case see the disturbing essay by Finley, "The Ancestral Constitution," in his *Use and Abuse of History.* After showing the way the Greeks abused and used the notion of an "ancestral constitution," he noted that professional historiography "threatens to render the past unusable" because it may "undermine a common interpretation of the past and therefore the social bonds that are fortified by a common identification with the past." See also Kammen, *A Machine That Would Go of Itself.*

67. *Maria v. Surbaugh,* 2 Rand. 246 (Va., 1824).

68. *Mayho v. Sears,* 3 Iredell 224, 228–29 (N.C., 1842).

69. T. R. R. Cobb, *Law of Negro Slavery,* 68–69.

70. *Guardian of Sally, a Negro, v. Beaty,* 1 Bay 260 (S.C., 1792).

71. Ibid., 261.

72. Ibid., 262–63. The irony is that although the court rejected the strictest interpretation of Roman law regarding the possession of property by a slave, it nevertheless, without reference, acted as though slaves in South Carolina possessed something akin to the *peculium.*

73. *Bynum v. Bostick,* 4 DeSaussure 266–68 (S.C., 1812). DeSaussure relied on Thomas Cooper's volume, the *Institutes of Justinian, with Notes by Thomas Cooper,* as well as the work of John Taylor. The former was published in Philadelphia in 1812, the same year DeSaussure rendered his decision in *Bynum.* Cooper's edition was based on the translation of the institutes by George Harris, which was first printed in London in 1761.

74. See, for instance, the argument from villenage by Chancellor F. H. Wardlaw while on circuit in *Willis v. Jollifee,* 11 Rich. Eq. 447 (S.C., 1860), or Chancellor Harper's argument from the status of alien enemies in *Fable v. Brown,* 2 Hill Eq. 378 (S.C., 1835).

75. A. E. Keir Nash, "A More Equitable Past?," 206–7.

76. *State v. Boon,* 1 N.C. 103, 107 (1801); Blackstone, *Commentaries,* 1:423.

77. Montesquieu, *Spirit of the Laws,* 325–50.

78. Herbert A. Johnson, *Imported Eighteenth-Century Law Treatises,* 52. Johnson's summary of the frequency of the use of civil law treatises, which was not often, provided this order: Domat, *The Civil Law; Digesti Justiniani Institutionum;* Wood, *New Institute of . . . Civil Law;* Noodt, *Opera Omnia Juridica;* and John Taylor, *Elements of the Civil Law.*

79. *State v. Reed,* 9 N.C. 255 (1823). The sketch of Henderson in the *Dictionary of American Biography (DAB)* (8:29) described him as an important law teacher, but as a judge who was respected more for his expression of sound judgment than for his knowledge of precedents. He was also a "religious free-thinker and seems to have made no profession of religion until at a very advanced age."

80. *State v. Reed,* 9 N.C. 256 (1823).

81. *State v. Jones,* Walker, 84–85 (Miss., 1821).

82. *Bryan v. Walton,* 14 Ga. 199–200 (1853).

83. Ibid., 200.

84. *George, (a slave), v. State,* 37 Miss. 316 (1859). According to the sketch in the *DAB* (8:27), Harris received his legal training in Georgia before moving to Mississippi. When the

state seceded in 1860, he was appointed as one of the commissioners to go to Georgia to urge cooperation.

85. *George, (a slave), v. State,* 37 Miss. 320 (1859). He did not identify the New York case.

86. Ibid.

87. Cf. Judge Hall's remarks in *Trustees of the Quaker Society of Contentnea v. William Dickenson,* 12 N.C. 126 (1827), where he referred to "our unfortunate connection with slavery" and added that "if we take a step into the moral world and contemplate the unbiased principles of our nature, we will discover for the exercise of our discretion a wide range between humanity and cruelty, and we might not find fault with those who mingled with their religion the dictates of the one and carefully abstained from the exercise of the other."

88. *Bynum v. Bostick,* 4 DeSaussure 267 (S.C., 1812).

89. *Coke on Littleton,* Book 2, sec. 107; Blackstone, *Commentaries,* 1:423. The classic historical study remains Vinogradoff, *Villainage in England: Essays in English Medieval History.*

90. *State v. Boon,* 1 N.C. 107 (1801).

91. *Coke on Littleton,* Book 2, sec. 190.

92. *Neal v. Farmer,* 9 Ga. 555 (1851).

93. *Bryan v. Walton,* 14 Ga. 185 (1853).

94. *Spicer Adm'r. Ex'r. of Stone v. Pope & al* (1736), in Barton, *Virginia Colonial Decisions,* 2:232 (1736).

95. *Fields v. State,* 1 Yerg. 143–44 (Tenn., 1829).

96. *Willis v. Jolliffe,* 11 Rich. Eq. 463–65 (S.C., 1860).

97. An excellent analysis of Hargrave's argument is Wiecek, "*Somerset,*" 103. Hargrave attempted to show that villenage, the only form of slavery that had ever existed in England, had been long dead.

98. *Willis v. Jolliffe,* 11 Rich. Eq. 465 (S.C., 1860).

99. Chancellor Harper, "Slavery in the Light of Social Ethics," in Elliott, *Cotton Is King.*

100. *Fable v. Brown,* 2 Hill Eq. 390, 392 (S.C., 1835).

101. An excellent critical introduction to the thought of Locke and Hobbes on slavery is David Brion Davis, *Problem of Slavery in Western Culture.* He points out some of the contradictions in Locke, for example. Locke wrote that "Slavery is so vile and miserable an Estate of man, and so directly opposite to the generous Temper and Courage of our Nation: that 'tis hardly to be conceived, that an *Englishman,* much less a *Gentleman,* shoud plead for 't." Yet it was Locke who drafted the Fundamental Constitutions of Carolina, which provided that "every freeman of Carolina, shall have absolute power and authority over his negro slaves." Ibid., 118.

102. See, however, *Heirn, Ex'r., &c., v. Bridault and Wife,* 37 Miss. 209 (1859).

103. Genovese, "*Slavery Ordained of God.*"

104. Ibid., 9.

105. T. R. R. Cobb, *Law of Negro Slavery.*

106. Genovese, "*Slavery Ordained of God,*" 12, 14.

107. T. R. R. Cobb, *Law of Negro Slavery,* 69.

108. This conclusion is drawn from comparing the language of some deeply religious judges, like William Gaston of North Carolina, in cases such as *State v. Will, (a slave),* 1 Dev. and Bat. 121 (N.C., 1834), with the views of men like Thornton Stringfellow, "The Bible Argument: or, Slavery in the Light of Divine Revelation," in Elliott, *Cotton Is King.* Most often, however, religious references were to Christian "benevolence," as in *Bynum v. Bostick,* 4 DeSaussure 267 (S.C., 1812).

109. *Commonwealth v. Richard Turner,* 5 Rand. 684 (Va., 1827); *Exodus* 21:5–6.

110. *Commonwealth v. Richard Turner,* 5 Rand. 684 (Va., 1827).

CHAPTER 3

1. Stroud, *Sketch of the Laws*, 11.

2. Finley, "Slavery," *International Encyclopedia*, 14:307.

3. Patterson, *Slavery and Social Death*, 21.

4. Oliver Wendell Holmes, *Common Law*; Honoré, "Ownership," in Guest, *Oxford Essays in Jurisprudence*, 80.

5. Almost any publication by an abolitionist would do. Albert Bledsoe answered one. It was Dr. William Channing's assertion that "this claim of property in a human being is altogether false, groundless. No such right of man in man can exist. A human being cannot be justly owned." Quoted in Bledsoe, *Essay on Liberty and Slavery*, 89.

6. Fitzhugh, *Cannibals All!*, 235.

7. Goodell, *American Slave Code*, 41.

8. Ibid.

9. Freidel, *Francis Lieber*.

10. Francis Lieber, handwritten piece entitled "Is There Any Insult to the South in Slavery Being Excluded from California," 1849, in Lieber on Slavery, Lieber Papers, Huntington Library, San Marino, Calif.

11. Elliott, *Cotton Is King*, vii.

12. Bledsoe, *Essay on Liberty and Slavery*, 89.

13. *Snead v. David*, 9 Dana 355 (Ky., 1840).

14. Blackstone, *Commentaries*, 2:4.

15. Baker, "Property in Chattels," 217; Blackstone, *Commentaries*, 2:385.

16. Randolph, in *Blackwell v. Wilkinson* (October 1768), quoted in Jefferson, *Reports of Cases . . . in the General Court of Virginia*, 73–74.

17. *Dunlap v. Crawford*, 2 McCord Eq. 171 (S.C., 1827).

18. Hening, *Statutes at Large*, 3:333; *Statutes at Large of Virginia, 1792–1806*, 1:128.

19. Sirmans, "Legal Status of the Slave," 464–65.

20. *Girard et al. v. City of New Orleans et al.*, 2 La. Ann. 901 (1847); English, *Digest of the Statutes of Arkansas*, 943–44; *Helton v. Caston*, 2 Bailey 95 (S.C., 1831); *Tennent v. Dendy*, 16 Dudley 83 (S.C., 1837); *McLeod v. Dell*, 9 Fla. 451 (1861).

21. Goodell, *American Slave Code*, 75–76. Even that would be open to abuse in view of the experience in Kentucky: ". . . Kentucky is one of the only two States in which statutes have declared slaves to be real estate, a tenure which, *if adhered to*, would attach the slave to the soil, and prevent separation of families. The *practice*, as sanctioned by custom and the courts, is in this case found to be less favorable to the slaves than the words of the statute, in their plain import. The people have been worse than their statutes, and the judges have conformed to the people." Ibid.

22. Ballagh, *History of Slavery in Virginia*, 63.

23. Sirmans, "Legal Status of the Slave," 465.

24. David Brion Davis, *Problem of Slavery in Western Culture*, 249–50 n. 38.

25. Graveson, *Status in the Common Law*, 2–7; Maine, *Ancient Law*, 170: "the movement of the progressive societies has hitherto been a movement *from Status to Contract*."

26. Tucker, *Blackstone's Commentaries*, 2:74, app. E.

27. O'Neall, *Negro Law of South Carolina*, 18.

28. Fox-Genovese and Genovese, "Slavery, Economic Development, and the Law," 26.

29. Richard Hall, *Acts Passed in the Island of Barbados*, 64–65.

30. Ibid.

31. Beckles, *White Servitude and Black Slavery*; Sirmans, "Legal Status of the Slave," 462; Thomas Cooper and McCord, *Statutes at Large of South Carolina*, 7:397.

32. Hening, *Statutes at Large*, 3:333.

33. Ibid.

34. Ibid.

35. The notion is captured in Holmes's opinion in *Pennsylvania Coal Co. v. Mahon*, 260 U.S. 412 (1922).

36. Oliver Wendell Holmes, *Common Law*, 351.

37. Ibid., 352.

38. Blackstone, *Commentaries*, 2:107, 113–15.

39. A good introduction to entails is A. W. B. Simpson, "Entails and Perpetuities."

40. Quoted in ibid., 143.

41. Hening, *Statutes at Large*, 4:225–26.

42. Ibid., 224.

43. Keim, "Primogeniture and Entail," 584. Nonetheless, Keim does examine some cases where slaves were entailed.

44. Will of James Burwell, September 15, 1718, York County Orders, Wills, etc., 1716–20, Will of Joseph Mountfort, June 19, 1738, York County Orders, Wills and Inventories, 1732–40, and Will of Philip Lightfoot, June 20, 1748, York County Orders, Wills and Inventories, 1745–59, VSL.

45. Hening, *Statutes at Large*, 8:457–60.

46. Ibid., 7:343–45. Lewis Burwell's various positions can be followed in McIlwaine, Hall, and Hillman, *Executive Journals*, 5:277, 345–46, 391. Philip Lightfoot's membership on the council can be followed throughout volume 5 of the executive journals. At one point he recorded an act docking an entail that vested the property in himself. He was sitting on the council that day. *Executive Journals*, 5:97.

47. *Burwell et ux. v. Johnson et ux.* (1762), in Joseph Henry Smith, *Appeals to the Privy Council*, 504–6.

48. See, e.g., Will of Richard Slater, November 17, 1718, and Will of John Tomer, January 20, 1718, York County Orders, Wills, 1716–20, and Will of John Butterworth, November 19, 1744, Orders, Wills and Inventories, 1740–46—all in VSL; *Taylor v. Graves* (1736), in Barton, *Virginia Colonial Decisions*, 2:56–59.

49. Hening, *Statutes at Large*, 5:43.

50. Jack Greene, *Diary of Landon Carter*, 1:98, 100.

51. Quoted in Hening, *Statutes at Large*, 5:432, n *.

52. Ibid.

53. *Blackwell v. Wilkinson* (October 1768), in Jefferson, *Reports of Cases . . . in the General Court of Virginia*, 73–74, 76, 82, 84.

54. Ibid., 84–85.

55. *Tucker v. Sweney* (1730), in Barton, *Virginia Colonial Decisions*, 1:39; Hening, *Statutes at Large*, 4:224.

56. *Goddin v. Morris* (1731), in Barton, *Virginia Colonial Decisions*, 1:82.

57. *Statutes at Large of Virginia, 1792–1806*, 1:128.

58. Jefferson, *Notes on the State of Virginia*, 131.

59. Littell and Swigert, *Digest of the Statute Law of Kentucky*, 2:157.

60. *Cox v. Ex'rs. of Robertson*, 1 Bibb 605 (Ky., 1809).

61. *Grimes v. Grimes' Devisees*, 2 Bibb 594 (Ky., 1812).

62. *Faris v. Banton*, 6 J. J. Marsh. 237 (Ky., 1831).

63. Ibid., 240, 244.

64. *Caleb v. Field and Others*, 9 Dana 346–48 (Ky., 1840).

65. *Snead v. David*, 9 Dana 350 (Ky., 1840).

66. Ibid., 355–58.

67. Stanton, *Revised Statutes of Kentucky*, 2:359.

68. English, *Digest of the Statutes of Arkansas*, 944.

69. *Gullett & Wife v. Lamberton*, 6 Ark. 117 (1845).

70. A brief overview of the general influence of *Las Siete Partidas* is Tannenbaum, *Slave and Citizen*, 48–52.

71. Moreau and Carleton, *Laws of Las Siete Partidas . . . Still in Force*; Baade, "Law of Slavery in Spanish Luisiana," 60.

72. Bullard and Curry, *New Digest of the Statute Laws of Louisiana*, 1:49.

73. *Girard et al. v. City of New Orleans et al.*, 2 La. Ann. 901 (1847).

74. Brissaud, *History of French Private Law*, 268–70.

75. Dargo, *Jefferson's Louisiana*.

76. Bullard and Curry, *New Digest of the Statute Laws of Louisiana*, 1:49; *Black's Law Dictionary*, 1346.

77. Upton and Jennings, *Civil Code of . . . Louisiana*, 521.

78. *Harper v. Destrehan*, 2 Mart. N. S. 390, 392 (1824).

79. *Monday v. Wilson et al.*, 4 La. 341 (1832).

80. *Girard et al. v. City of New Orleans et al.*, 2 La. Ann. 900–901 (1847).

81. May 1, 1851, West Feliciana Parish, Notarial Record, vol. K, 353–70, West Feliciana Parish Courthouse, St. Francisville, La.

82. Entry for January 6, 1852, ibid.

83. *Helton v. Caston*, 2 Bailey 97–98 (S.C., 1831).

84. *Tennent v. Dendy*, 16 Dudley 85 (S.C., 1837).

85. O'Neall, *Negro Law of South Carolina*, 10.

86. Chancellor Kent in Carter and Stone, *Reports of . . . the Convention of 1821*, 220. See the response of Peter R. Livingston: "If the title to land contributed to the elevation of the mind . . . there might be good reason for proportioning the right of suffrage to the acres of soil. But experience has shewn that property forms not the scale of worth, and that character does not spring from the ground" (p. 225).

87. *Hull v. Hull*, 3 Rich. Eq. 65 (S.C., 1850).

88. Ibid., 68, 70, 74.

89. Ibid., 91–92.

90. *McLeod v. Dell*, 9 Fla. 461–62 (1861).

CHAPTER 4

1. Goodell, *American Slave Code*, 73–74.

2. An excellent introduction is Waldron, *Private Property*, 241–51.

3. Ely, *Property and Contract*, 1:459.

4. Alexander, "The Dead Hand and the Law of Trusts," 1189 n. 1.

5. A. W. B. Simpson, *History of the Land Law*; Hale, *De succsssionibus apud Anglos* and *History of the Common Law*.

6. Blackstone, *Commentaries*, 2:208.

7. *Civil Code . . . of Louisiana*, 231–33; Katz, "Republicanism and the Law of Inheritance," 1–29.

8. Blackstone, *Commentaries*, 2:515–16.

9. Hening, *Statutes at Large*, 2:288.

10. *Statutes at Large of Virginia, 1792–1806*, 1:129.

11. O'Neall, *Negro Law of South Carolina*, 18; Howell Cobb, *Compilation of the . . . Statutes . . . of Georgia*, 636–37.

12. A. W. B. Simpson, *History of the Land Law*, 62.

13. Blackstone, *Commentaries*, 2:492. The law, Blackstone noted, had been altered by "imperceptible degrees."

14. *Civil Code . . . of Louisiana, 1825*, 231–33.

15. Waggoner, *Future Interests*; Blackstone, *Commentaries*, 2:163.

16. Blackstone, *Commentaries*, 2:164, 168–69.

17. Ibid., 173; Kent, *Commentaries on American Law*, 4:303. On perpetuities see A. W. B. Simpson, "Entails and Perpetuities," 143–63; Leach, "Perpetuities in a Nutshell"; and Waggoner, *Future Interests*, 165–69.

18. Blackstone, *Commentaries*, 2:242. For the rule in Shelley's case see Kent, *Commentaries on American Law*, 4:248–67.

19. A. W. B. Simpson, *History of the Land Law*, 223–35.

20. Blackstone, *Commentaries*, 2:174.

21. McGettigan, "Boone County Slaves"; Albert, "Protean Institution"; Schwarz, "Emancipators, Protectors, and Anomalies."

22. *Slaughter v. Whitelock* (1737), in Barton, *Virginia Colonial Decisions*, 2:251.

23. *Edmunds v. Hughes* (1730), in ibid., 35–39.

24. *Maulding et al. v. Scott et al.*, 13 Ark. 91 (1852).

25. *Ham v. Ham*, 21 N.C. 464–66 (1837); *Robinson v. McDonald*, 2 Ga. 116 (1847). For later uses of the rule in North Carolina see *Kiser v. Kiser*, 55 N.C. 24 (1854); *Williams v. Houston*, 4 Jones Eq. 277 (1858); *Thompson v. Mitchell*, 4 Jones Eq. 441 (1859); and *Hodges v. Little*, 52 N.C. 112 (1859).

26. *Polk v. Faris*, 9 Yerg. 233 (Tenn., 1836).

27. Will of John J. Wright, November 20, 1752, York County Orders, Wills and Inventories, 1745–59, and Will of William Rogers, December 17, 1739, York County Orders, Wills and Inventories, 1732–40, VSL.

28. Will of William Wise, November 7, 1718, York County Orders, Wills and Inventories, 1716–20, VSL; Will of Thomas McCullough, January 1844, Will of James Neil, October 8, 1849, and Will of John B. Pickell, January 21, 1851, Fairfield District: Office: Probate Judge, 1840–68, SCDAH.

29. *Robinson v. McDonald*, 2 Ga. 122–23 (1847).

30. *Jordan v. Roach*, 32 Miss. 484–85 (1856).

31. Ibid., 520–21.

32. Ibid., 617, 619–20.

33. Will of John Broadnax, August 17, 1719, York County Orders, Wills and Inventories, 1716–20; Will of Thomas Pattison, February 21, 1742/3, York County Orders, Wills and Inventories, 1740–45; Will of John Mundell, July 15, 1746 and Will of Philip Lightfoot, June 20, 1748, York County Orders, Wills and Inventories, 1745–59—all in VSL.

34. Lebsock, *Free Women of Petersburg*, 67.

35. Will of Rachel Griffin, June 1845, and Will of Jane Williamson, November 13, 1865, Fairfield District: Office: Probate Judge, 1840–68, SCDAH.

36. *Giles v. Mallicotte* (1738), in Barton, *Virginia Colonial Decisions*, 2:71–77.

37. See, e.g., Will of Robert Harris, November 19, 1716, and Will of William Davis, December 15, 1718, York County Orders, Wills and Inventories, 1716–20, VSL.

38. Will of William Trotter, December 17, 1733, York County Orders, Wills and Inventories, 1732–40, VSL.

39. Will of Robert Hamilton, 1842, Fairfield District: Office: Probate Judge, 1840–68, SCDAH; *Nelson v. Nelson*, 41 N.C. 417 (1849). See also *Carroll v. Hancock*, 48 N.C. 464 (1856).

40 *Nelson v. Nelson*, 41 N.C. 417 (1849).

41. See, e.g., Will of Drury Walker, March 1846, Fairfield District: Office: Probate Judge, 1840–68, SCDAH.

42. *Scott v. Dobson*, 1 Har. and McH. 160 (Md., 1852); *Smith v. Milman*, 2 Harr. 498 (Del., 1839).

43. *Holmes v. Mitchell*, 4 Md. Ch. 165–66 (Md., 1850).

44. *Holmes v. Mitchell*, 4 Md. 540–41, 452–53 (Md., 1853).

45. *Tims v. Potter*, 1 Martin N.C. 22 (178—); *Erwin v. Kilpatrick*, 10 N.C. 458 (1825); *Murphy v. Riggs*, 1 A. K. Marsh. 397–98 (Ky., 1819).

46. *Powell v. Cook*, 15 N.C. 499 (1834). Other cases involving the basic approach are *Mullinton's Ex'rs. v. Shipman*, 1 N.C. 243 (1800); *Jones v. Jones*, 1 N.C. 396 (1800); *Covington v. McEntire*, 37 N.C. 229 (1842); *Stultz v. Kiser*, 37 N.C. 398 (1843); and *Hurdle v. Reddick*, 39 N.C. 67 (1846). See also *Perry v. High*, 3 Head 349–50 (Tenn., 1859).

47. *Gayle v. Cunningham*, Harp. Eq. 124 (S.C., 1824); *Seibels v. Whatley*, 2 Hill Eq. 609 (S.C., 1837). First followed in *Tidyman v. Rose*, Rich. Eq. 294 (S.C., 1832).

48. *Gayle v. Cunningham*, Harp. Eq. 125, 128–30 (S.C., 1824).

49. *Coke on Littleton*, 124b; Blackstone, *Commentaries*, 2:129.

50. Cushing, *Laws of the Province of Maryland*, 154, 162–63; Shammas, Salmon, and Dublin, *Inheritance in America*, 35.

51. Hening, *Statutes at Large*, 2:303.

52. An example is the Will of John Brooks, November 17, 1729, York County Orders, Wills and Inventories, 1720–32, VSL.

53. Will of James Shields, July 17, 1727, York County Orders, Wills and Inventories, 1720–32, VSL.

54. Will of Isaac Arledge Sr., September 1847, and Will of William Watt, August 21, 1851, Fairfield District: Office: Probate Judge, 1840–68, SCDAH. See also Will of Bennoni Robertson, February 27, 1852, and Will of William Jones, September 25, 1854, ibid. In 1850 Robertson owned fifty-one slaves and Jones owned forty-seven. Manuscript Census, 1850 Slave Schedule, M 432, Reel 864.

55. Last Will and Testament of George Washington, in Fitzpatrick, *Writings of George Washington*, 37:275; Sobel, *World They Made Together*, 153, 287 n. 76: Flexner, *Washington*, 393.

56. Partition of Joseph B. Brinkley Estate, Orphans Court, Somerset County, 1836, and Partition of George A. Dashiell Estate, Orphans Court, Somerset County, January 1837, MHR.

57. *Herndon v. Herndon*, 27 Mo. 422 (1858); Cotton v. Cotton's Adm'r., January Term 1851, unreported, MoSA. See also Mary Cotton v. John J. Cotton's heirs, February 27, August 24, 1850, Boone County, Circuit Court, MoSA.

58. *Fitzhugh v. Foote*, 3 Call 16–7 (Va., 1801).

59. Cushing, *Laws of the Province of Maryland*, 154, 162–63; Gould, *Digest of the Statutes of Arkansas*, 944 n. A; *Hill's Adm'rs. v. Mitchell*, 5 Ark. 613 (1844). See also *Menifee's Adm'rs. v. Menifee*, 8 Ark. 49 (1847).

60. Will of Jacob Goodwin, January 19, 1718/9, York County Orders, Wills and Inventories, 1716–20, Will of John Mundell, July 15, 1746, Will of John Harris, February 20, 1748/9, and Will of Matthew Morland, February 17, 1755, York County Orders, Wills and Inventories, 1745–59; Will of William Gordon, December 21, 1730, York County Orders, Wills and Inventories, 1720–32—all in VSL.

61. Will of Robert Kilpatrick, 1842, Will of John Rabb, October 1844, Will of Nancy Yarbro, April 7, 1854, and Will of Hugh Gladney, December 4, 1854, Fairfield District: Office: Probate Judge, 1840–68, SCDAH. Gladney owned forty-three slaves in 1850. Manuscript Census, 1850 Slave Schedule, M 432, Reel 864.

62. *Southern Cultivator*, October 1853, 309.

63. Cited in *Corpus Juris*, 23:334–35.

64. Cushing, *Laws of the Province of Maryland*, 155; Hening, *Statutes at Large*, 4:224.

65. Prince, *Digest of the Laws of . . . Georgia*, 234, 233.

66. *Laws of the Territory of Louisiana*, 152–53.

67. *Revised Statutes of . . . North Carolina*, 265; Haywood and Cobbs, *Statute Laws of . . . Tennessee*, 1:244–45.

68. *Tucker v. Sweney* (1730), in Barton, *Virginia Colonial Decisions*, 1:39; *Goddin v. Morris* (1732), ibid., 82.

69. *Holderness v. Palmer*, 4 Jones Eq. 110 (N.C., 1858).

70. *Alexander v. Worthington*, 5 Md. 493–94 (1854).

71. *Logan v. Withers*, 3 J. J. Marsh. 389 (Ky., 1830); *Anderson v. Irvine*, 6 B. Mon. 233 (Ky., 1845).

72. Will of David Harrison, November 25, 1840, Fairfield District: Office: Probate Judge, 1840–68, SCDAH.

73. Will of David Johnson, January 15, 1855, Spartanburg District: Office: Probate Judge, Will Books A–D, 1810–58, SCDAH.

74. For Madison's will see McCoy, *Last of the Fathers*, 318. McCoy's judgment was this:

Surely his primary concern was for his wife. But it is also plausible to infer that Madison may have been more interested in the actual welfare of his slaves than he was either in clearing his conscience or in using them to make a political statement. Perhaps the will attests to Madison's humanity, in other words, as well as to his conservatism. Contrary to appearances, by providing for his slaves as he did, Madison may have given greater evidence of his concern and respect for them than he would have, had he merely released them into a hostile white world, or, for that matter, subjected them to involuntary deportation.

Ibid., 318–19. This is, I believe, a too generous reading of Madison's will. He certainly was most concerned with the welfare of Dolly, but there were ways, as other wills show, to have opened the door to freedom. He could have given the slaves themselves the election of freedom on condition of deportation.

75. Will of George Brewton, October 26, 1815, Spartanburg District: Office: Probate Judge, Will Books A–D, 1810–58, and Will of John A. Rosborough, April 24, 1840, Fairfield District: Office: Probate Judge, 1840–68, SCDAH.

76. Will of Charles Wise, November 17, 1740, York County Orders, Wills and Inventories, 1732–40, VSL; Will of Cassandra Farrow, 1859, Spartanburg District: Office: Probate Judge, Will Books A–D, 1810–58, SCDAH; Will of Edward Winning, January 28, 1861, vol. B, Saline County, Clerk of Circuit Court, Will Records, vol. A (1837–60), vol. B (1852–86) (two volumes in one), Saline County Courthouse, Marshall, Mo.

77. Will of John Rosborough, September 20, 1842, Will of Joseph Caldwell, October 1843, Will of William Mundles, December 1844, Will of Rachel Griffin, June 1845, Will of Nathan Cook, August 12, 1854, Will of M. A. M. Leggo, August 21, 1854, and Will of John Teacher, October 4, 1858, Fairfield District: Office: Probate Judge, 1840–68, SCDAH; Manuscript Census, 1850 Slave Schedule, M 432, Reel 864.

78. Jan Lewis, *Pursuit of Happiness*, 228; Will of Martha Golightly, November 17, 1860, Spartanburg District: Office: Probate Judge, Will Book E–F, 1858–87, SCDAH.

79. Will of Peyton Newlin, April 1837, vol. A (1837–60), and Will of Edward Winning, January 28, 1861, vol. B (1852–86), Saline County, Clerk of Circuit Court, Will Records, MoSA; Will of William Chapman, September 3, 1841, and Will of John Rosborough, November 19, 1860, Fairfield District: Office: Probate Judge, 1840–68, SCDAH.

CHAPTER 5

1. Stroud, *Sketch of the Laws*, 33.

2. Farnsworth, *Contracts*, 4: Atiyah, *Freedom of Contract*, 3.

3. Roover, "Concept of the Just Price," 418; Powell, *Essay upon the Law of Contracts*, 2:229.

4. A. W. B. Simpson, *History of the Common Law of Contract*.

5. Powell, *Essay upon the Law of Contracts* and *Treatise on the Law of Mortgages*; Sir William Jones, *Essay on the Law of Bailments.*

6. Joseph Story, *Commentaries on Equity*, chap. 18.

7. Morton Horwitz, *Transformation of American Law, 1780–1860*, 174.

8. Stowe, *Uncle Tom's Cabin*, 80.

9. Tadman, *Speculators and Slaves*; Stroud, *Sketch of the Laws*, 33; Thomas D. Russell, "South Carolina's Largest Slave Auctioneering Firm."

10. *Thomason v. Dill*, 30 Ala. 450 (1857). Occasionally, there is a jarring contrast among the appellate records to a case like *Thomason*. An example is *Turner v. Johnson*, 7 Dana 440 (Ky., 1838), in which the court included a ringing statement of concern for slaves. The court held that

> we are strongly inclined to the opinion, that a promise, founded upon a sufficient consideration, not to sell a slave at all, when prompted by the benevolent motive of preventing the husband from being separated from the wife, or the child from the parent, or of securing for the slave a good master, or the like, would be sustained. If the policy of trade and traffic would inculcate the propriety of treating such a promise as void, humanity and the eternal principles of justice would inculcate a different policy. It is true, slaves are property, and must under our present institutions, be treated as such. But they are human beings, with like passions, sympathies and affections with ourselves. And while we must treat them as property, we should not entirely overlook the obligations due to them as human beings.

Despite this gesture, however, the fact remains that the court upheld a contract not to sell a slave because it was "a promise, founded upon a sufficient consideration": the court, in other words, did not alter contract doctrine, it merely gave legal force to the benevolent intentions of the owner who included the promise not to sell in the contract.

11. Atiyah, *Freedom of Contract*, 178–79.

12. Domat, *Civil Law in Its Natural Order*, 1:238. Domat died in 1696.

13. *Waddill v. Chamberlayne* (1735), in Barton, *Virginia Colonial Decisions*, 2:45–50; A. W. B. Simpson, *History of the Common Law of Contract.*

14. *Waddill v. Chamberlayne* (1735), in Barton, *Virginia Colonial Decisions*, 2:46, 48–49.

15. Ibid., 49–50.

16. Atiyah, *Freedom of Contract.*

17. Paley, *Principles of Moral and Political Philosophy*, 104–5.

18. Atiyah, *Freedom of Contract*, 180.

19. Wooddeson, *Systematical View of the Laws of England*, 2:413–15; Powell, *Essay upon the Law of Contracts*, 1:iii, 92; Pothier, *Treatise on Obligation*, 1:15, 24.

20. *Timrod v. Shoolbred*, 1 Bay 324 (S.C., 1793). For other early uses of the doctrine of implied warranty see *Lester v. Graham*, 1 Mill 182 (S.C., 1817), and *Barnard v. Yates*, 1 N. and McC. 142 (S.C., 1818). See also McClain, "Implied Warranties in Sales," 213–20, and Fede, "Legal Protection for Slave Buyers."

21. *Timrod v. Shoolbred*, 1 Bay 325 (S.C., 1793).

22. *Rouple v. M'Carty*, 1 Bay 480 (S.C., 1795).

23. *Smith v. McCall*, 1 McCord 223 (S.C., 1821).

24. *Porcher ads. Caldwell*, 2 McMul. 332 (S.C., 1842).

25. *Watson v. Boatwright*, 1 Rich. 402–4 (S.C., 1845).

26. *Rodrigues ads. Habersham*, 1 Speers 316–27 (S.C., 1843). See also *Farr v. Gist*, 1 Rich. 69–70 (S.C., 1844).

27. *Evans v. Dendy*, 2 Speers 11 (S.C., 1843).

28. *Rupert v. Dunn*, 1 Rich. 101 (S.C., 1844).

29. On the emerging doubts in England see Atiyah, *Freedom of Contract*, 471–73, and

Rodrigues ads. Habersham, 1 Speers 316–17 (S.C., 1843). Yet the older doctrine held. See *Wood v. Ashe*, 3 Strob. 64 (S.C., 1848), and *Verdier v. Trowell*, 6 Rich. 166 (S.C., 1853).

30. *Galbraith v. Whyte*, 2 N.C. 371 (1797); William Wetmore Story, *Treatise on the Law of Contracts*, 333 n. 1; *Foggart v. Blackweller*, 26 N.C. 184 (1844); *Brown v. Gray*, 6 Jones N.C. 103 (1858).

31. *Smith v. M'Call*, 1 McCord 223 (S.C., 1821). See also *Owens v. Ford*, Harp. 25–26 (S.C., 1823).

32. *Caldwell v. Wallace*, 4 Stew. and P. 285 (Ala., 1833). See also *Wyatt v. Greer*, 4 Stew. and P. 322 (Ala., 1833).

33. *Sloan v. Williford*, 25 N.C. 215 (1843); *Simpson v. McKay*, 34 N.C. 104 (1851). See also *Eaves v. Twitty*, 35 N.C. 317 (1852).

34. *Belew v. Clark*, 4 Humphreys 506, 509 (Tenn., 1844); *Farnsworth v. Earnest*, 7 Humphreys 25 (Tenn., 1846); *Nations v. Jones*, 20 Tex. 302–3 (1857).

35. *Pyeatt v. Spencer*, 4 Ark. 570 (1842).

36. Schafer, *Slavery, the Civil Law, and the Supreme Court*, 127–48; *Black's Law Dictionary*, 1408; Schafer, *Slavery, the Civil Law, and the Supreme Court*, 132. Forty-seven of the 166 actions involved a form of tuberculosis.

37. Upton and Jennings, *Civil Code of . . . Louisiana*, 389; Schafer, *Slavery, the Civil Law, and the Supreme Court*, 135; Savitt, *Medicine and Slavery*, 248.

38. Schafer, *Slavery, the Civil Law, and the Supreme Court*, 128–30.

39. Petition of Recovery, Slave Suit, October 18, 1726, *Louisiana Historical Quarterly* 3: 420.

40. Schafer, *Slavery, the Civil Law, and the Supreme Court*, 132–48; *Berret v. Adams*, 10 La. Ann. 77 (1855); Benjamin Ballard to Bennett Barrow, March 28, 1824, West Feliciana Parish, Notarial Record, vol. AA (1824–28), 7, and Sydney Flower to William Flower Jr., December 22, 1849, West Feliciana Parish, Notarial Record, vol. K (1849–53), 4–5, West Feliciana Parish Courthouse, St. Francisville, La.; David Glenn to John Lyons, April 17, 1817, and Louaillier Freres to Jacques Charlot, January 26, 1818, St. Landry Parish, Conveyance Record, vol. D-1 (1817–18), St. Landry Parish Courthouse, Opelousas, La.

41. *Hyanis v. Bossier, curator*, September 9, 1841, Natchitoches Parish, District Court Record, vol. 6 (1840–48), Natchitoches Parish Courthouse, Natchitoches, La.; Schafer, *Slavery, the Civil Law, and the Supreme Court*, 132–48; *Riggin v. Kendig*, 12 La. Ann. 451–54 (1857). Bernard Kendig was notorious. See Tansey, "Kendig and the New Orleans Slave Trade."

42. *Roussel v. Phipps*, 10 La. Ann. 119 (1855).

43. *Berret v. Adams*, 10 La. Ann. 77 (1855); *Briant v. Marsh*, 19 La. Ann. 391 (1841); *McCay v. Chambliss*, 12 La. Ann. 412 (1857).

44. Schafer, " 'Guaranteed against the Vices and Maladies Prescribed by Law,' " 309, and *Slavery, the Civil Law, and the Supreme Court*, 132.

45. For the period July 1840–September 1848, for instance, I found only two cases involving recission claims in Natchitoches Parish: Houghtling v. Fisher, July 14, 1840, and Hyanis v. Bossier, curator, September 9, 1841, Natchitoches Parish, District Court Record, vol. 6 (1840–48), Natchitoches Parish Courthouse, Natchitoches, La.

46. Schafer, " 'Guaranteed against the Vices and Maladies Prescribed by Law,' " 311.

47. Case of Andrew Coussen by His Guardian John Coussen ex parte, January 1854, Davidson County Circuit Court Minutes, 1852–56, TSLA.

48. Kronman, "Specific Performance," 359; Tushnet, *American Law of Slavery*, 169.

49. Farnsworth, *Contracts*, 821.

50. *Young v. Burton*, McMul. Eq. 161 (S.C., 1841).

51. *M'Dowell ads. Murdock*, 1 N. and McC. 144 (S.C., 1818). Judge Gantt dissented without opinion.

52. *Martin v. Martin*, 12 Leigh 495–99 (Va., 1842).

53. *Brown v. Gilliland*, 3 DeSaussure 541 (S.C., 1813).

54. *Rees v. Parish*, 1 McCord Eq. 59 (S.C., 1825). On the hostility to equity in South Carolina see Cooper, "Chancery Law," 359. See also Fede, "Legal Protection for Slave Buyers," for a generally perceptive study of the South Carolina line of cases. Fede's conclusion that "the majority of Southern courts presumed that a slave owner or buyer had a right to specific performance" (*People Without Rights*, 203), I believe, however, overstates the case.

55. *Farley v. Farley*, 1 McCord Eq. 517 (S.C., 1826).

56. *Sarter v. Gordon*, 2 Hill Eq. 121 (S.C., 1835).

57. Ibid.

58. *Horry v. Glover*, 2 Hill Eq. 254 (S.C., 1837).

59. *Young v. Burton*, McMul. Eq. 255–56 (S.C., 1841).

60. Ibid., 257, 283.

61. Will of David Johnson, January 15, 1855, Spartanburg District: Office: Probate Judge, Will Books A–D, 1810–58, SCDAH.

62. *Young v. Burton*, McMul. Eq. 255 (S.C., 1841).

63. *Wilson and Trent v. Butler*, 3 Mun. 563–65 (Va., 1813).

64. *Allen v. Freeland*, 3 Rand. 170–73 (Va., 1825).

65. Tushnet, *American Law of Slavery*, 159–60; *Bowyer v. Creigh*, 3 Rand. 31 (Va., 1825).

66. *Allen v. Freeland*, 3 Rand. 176 (Va., 1825).

67. *Bowyer v. Creigh*, 3 Rand. 25 (Va., 1825).

68. Ibid., 25–26, 31.

69. Tushnet, *American Law of Slavery*, 161.

70. *Randolph v. Randolph*, 6 Rand. 197 (Va., 1828).

71. Ibid., 199.

72. Ibid., 202.

73. *Summers v. Bean*, 13 Grattan 404, 412 (Va., 1856); *Pearne v. Lisle*, cited in ibid., 411.

74. *Summers v. Bean*, 13 Grattan 412 (Va., 1856).

75. Tushnet, *American Law of Slavery*, 165; *McRea v. Walker*, 4 How. 456 (Miss., 1840); *Sevier v. Ross*, Fr. Miss. Ch. 531 (Miss., 1843).

76. *Baker v. Rowan*, 2 Stew. and P. 371–72 (Ala., 1832); *Hardeman v. Sims*, 3 Ala. 749–50 (1840).

77. Tushnet, *American Law of Slavery*, 169.

78. *Conway's Ex'rs. and Devises v. Alexander*, 7 Cranch 237 (1812); *Moss v. Green*, 10 Leigh 251 (Va., 1839). A. E. Keir Nash ("Reason of Slavery," 145) described Brooke as an extreme conservative among Virginia judges of the late 1820s.

79. Alan Harding, *Social History of English Law*, 106–7; Kent, *Commentaries on American Law*, 4:136–237; Holdsworth, *History of English Law*, 5:330–32, 7:663–64; Macauley, "Noncontractual Relations in Business," 55–67; Powell, *Treatise on the Law of Mortgages*, 1:13; Kent, *Commentaries on American Law*, 4:139. Friedman (*History of American Law*, 217), relying on Skilton's pathbreaking study of mortgage law, suggested that these clauses were often voided in Southern courts so that the trust deed became the "functional equivalent" of the mortgage with a power-of-sale clause. I have not found this to be the case in slave mortgage cases before the Civil War, however. Power-of-sale clauses were upheld, to give only two examples, in *Planters & Merchants Bank v. Willis*, 5 Ala. 770 (1843), and *Wootten v. Wheeler*, 22 Tex. 338 (1858). See Skilton, "Developments in Mortgage Law."

80. Adam Smith, *Lectures on Jurisprudence*, 471; Kent, *Commentaries on American Law*, 4:144 n. a; *Falls v. Torrance*, 11 N.C. 196 (1826); *Overton v. Bigelow*, 3 Yerg. 513 (Tenn., 1832).

81. Powell, *Treatise on the Law of Mortgages*, 1:25; Baker, "Property in Chattels," 217 (see also his discussion of chattel property in *Introduction to English Legal History*, 315–36); Eric Williams, *Capitalism and Slavery*; Solow and Engerman, *British Capitalism and Caribbean Slavery*.

82. *Jamieson v. Bruce*, 6 G. and J. 320 (Md., 1834); *Bryan v. Robert*, 1 Strob. Eq. 334 (S.C.,

1847); *Davis et al. v. Anderson*, 1 Ga. 176 (1846); *Bates v. Murphy*, reported with *M'Gowen v. Young*, 2 Stew. 162 (Ala., 1832). See also *Hannah, Adm'r. v. Carrington et al.*, 18 Ark. 185 (1856).

83. As late as the 1830s Chancellor Kent (*Commentaries on American Law*, 4:144 n, e) referred to the chattel mortgage as a more "benign contract than the conditional sale." By midcentury such sales were taking on new contours. A standard legal dictionary gave as a common example of such sales the so-called sale and return, "that is, the vendee is to return all that he does not sell. So goods may be sold on trial; the vendee is then to try them, and return them, if unsuitable, within a reasonable time." Bouvier, *Institutes of American Law*, 2:239. By the 1930s the *Corpus Juris* (44:1193) dealt with "so-called contracts for sale and return, or sales with agreements to repurchase" (the earlier forms of the conditional sale) as something other than a conditional sale. The latter was defined (following the Uniform Conditional Sales Act) as "a contract for the sale of personal property under which possession is delivered to the buyer, but title is retained in the seller until the performance of some condition, usually the payment of the purchase price." Finally, by the mid-twentieth century a standard treatise on sales noted that the "term 'conditional sale' has many different meanings. As used in current installment sales of chattels, it usually takes this form: a contract to sell when the buyer completes payment of all installments of the purchase price." Vold, *Handbook of the Law of Sales*, 281. Throughout the years before the Civil War, Southern courts continued to use the earlier definition of a sale with the right of repurchase.

84. Kent, *Commentaries on American Law*, 4:144. Representative cases include *Turnipseed v. Cunningham*, 16 Ala. 501 (1849); *Poindexter v. McCannon*, 1 Dev. Eq. 373 (N.C., 1830); *Secrest v. Turner*, 2 J. J. Marsh. 471 (Ky., 1829); and *Barnes v. Holcomb*, 12 Smedes and M. 306 (Miss., 1849).

85. Friedman, *History of American Law*, 217; *A. Pope & Son et al. v. Wilson, et al.*, 7 Ala. 690 (1845).

86. *Watkins v. Stockett's Adm'r.*, 6 H. and J. 435 (Md., 1820). Among the cases illustrating the admissibility of parole evidence are *Prince v. Bearden*, 1 A. K. Marsh. 169 (Ky., 1818); *Secrest v. Turner*, 2 J. J. Marsh. 471 (Ky., 1829); *Ross v. Norvell*, 1 Wash. 14 (Va., 1791); *Overton v. Bigelow*, 3 Yerg. 513 (Tenn., 1832); *Kent v. Allbritain*, 4 How. 317 (Miss., 1840); *Thompson v. Chumney*, 8 Tex. 389 (1852); and *Hudson v. Isbell*, 5 Stew. and P. 67 (Ala., 1833). Cases showing hostility to the rule are fewer, but the following should be examined: *Thompson v. Patton*, 5 Littell 74 (Ky., 1824); *Ransone v. Fraysers Ex'r.*, 10 Leigh 592 (Va., 1840); and *Montany v. Rock*, 10 Mo. 506 (1847).

87. *Boner v. Mahle*, 3 La. Ann. 600 (1848). Louisiana was a civil law state, and that meant that the system of mortgaging was different from that in common law jurisdictions. The term *mortgage* in Louisiana covered a variety of liens, including those created by the courts. It was not limited to agreements among private individuals.

88. *Turnipseed v. Cunningham*, 16 Ala. 501 (1849).

89. Of the twenty-four cases of slave mortgages recorded in Fairfield District, S.C., between 1854 and 1856, six were sales. In January 1855 six men mortgaged slaves to Mary A. Ellison. The terms of these "mortgages" made it clear that they were in fact purchases of slaves. The purchasers then gave Ellison a "mortgage" on the slaves she had just sold to secure the balance of the price. Fairfield District: Office: Clerk of Court: Deeds, 1854–56, SCDAH. See also McCuen, *Abstracts of Some Greenville County . . . Records.*

90. *Lewis v. Owen*, 36 N.C. 242 (1840); *McLaurin v. Wright*, 37 N.C. 69 (1841); *Colvard v. Waugh*, 3 Jones Eq. 335 (N.C., 1857); *Chapman v. Turner*, 1 Call 280 (Va., 1798). See also *English v. Lane*, 1 Port. 328 (Ala. 1835), where the court held that a "greatly inadequate price" does not by itself void a sale but a "gross inadequacy" might imply fraud. Two years before, the court, in *Hudson v. Isbell*, 5 Stew. and P. 67 (Ala., 1833), had said that a "very great inadequacy of the price" strongly suggested that the contract was a mortgage and not a conditional sale.

91. The areas discussed are illustrative of attitudes; this does not, of course, mean that others would not be. One problem, for example, was whether or not a mortgagor's "rights" were subject to execution sale by creditors other than the mortgagee. In *McGregory & Darling v. Hall*, 3 Stew. and P. 397 (Ala., 1833), the court ruled that they could be, even though the "ancient doctrine" was that a court of law could not touch an equitable estate. The reason was that this rule had been "giving way" in the case of real estate mortgages, and in the view of the court, no distinction between real property and personal property need be made. Tushnet (*American Law of Slavery*, 174), therefore, appears to be in error in observing that "southern courts accepted or rejected analogies to real property depending solely on whether the substantive rules could be supported independently by appeals to humanity." Cases upholding the liability to execution are *Wootten v. Wheeler*, 22 Tex. 338 (1858), and *McIsaacs v. Hobbs*, 8 Dana 268 (Ky., 1839). Examples of courts ruling the other way would be *King v. Bailey*, 8 Mo. 332 (1843), and *Thornhill v. Gilmer*, 4 Smedes and M. 152 (Miss., 1845). In *Prewett v. Dobbs*, Smedes and M. 432 (Miss., 1850), the court held that a right of redemption in a slave was not subject to a general execution in the satisfaction of debts but was liable to be distrained and sold in the satisfaction of rent due.

92. *Fleming v. Burgin*, 37 N.C. 430 (1843). On the other side see *Youngblood v. Keadle*, Strob. 121 (S.C., 1846); *Guerrant v. Anderson*, 4 Rand. 208 (Va., 1826); *Dearing v. Watkins*, 16 Ala. 20 (1849); and *Hughes v. Graves*, 1 Littell 317 (Ky., 1822).

93. *Johnson v. Bloodworth*, 12 La. Ann. 699 (1857).

94. *Gist v. Pressley*, 2 Hill Eq. 319 (S.C., 1835). In *Thompson v. Chumney*, 8 Tex. 389 (1852), the court noted that the contract "was in fact a loan of money, with the understanding that the services of the negro should be received in satisfaction of interest on the money loaned—a character of mortgage very common in this country."

95. *Maples v. Maples*, Rice Eq. 300 (S.C., 1839). A solitary case, in contrast, is *Robertson v. Campbell*, 8 Mo. 365 (1844), in which the court refused to apply the rules of real property mortgages to slaves. It declined to separate slaves from other chattels. In its view the difference in rules between land and chattel mortgages arose "partly from the inferior value and importance of personal property, and partly from a reluctance to impose any unnecessary restrictions upon its transfer."

96. *Fishburne v. Kunhardt*, 2 Speers 556 (S.C., 1844). On Frost see Perry's sketch in Brooks, *South Carolina Bench and Bar*, 1:129. Frost had someone else collect his legal fees for him while he was in practice. His sensibilities, however, did not prevent him from becoming president of the Blue Ridge Railroad Co.

97. *Ross v. Norvell*, 1 Wash. 14 (Va., 1791).

98. *Poindexter v. McCannon*, 1 Dev. Eq. 373 (N.C., 1830). Examples of cases involving possession by the mortgagee before debts were paid are *Byrd v. McDaniel*, 33 Ala. 18 (1858); *Kent v. Allbritain*, 4 How. 317 (Miss., 1840); *Kea v. Council*, 55 N.C. 286 (1856); and *Bailey v. Carter*, 2 N.C. 200 (1851).

99. *Roberts Admin. v. Cocke, Ex'r. of Thompson*, 1 Rand. 121 (Va., 1822).

100. *Perry v. Craig*, 3 Mo. 516 (1834); *Overton v. Bigelow*, 3 Yerg. 513 (Tenn., 1832); *Kenwick v. Macey's Ex'r.*, 1 Dana 226 (Ky., 1833); *Ewell v. Tidwell*, 20 Ark. 136 (1859). In *Sullivan v. Hadley*, 16 Ark. 129 (1855), the court gave a mortgagee three years to bring a bill to foreclose. This was the time to commence an action for the possession of slaves.

101. *Humphries v. Terrell*, 1 Ala. 650 (1840); *Falls v. Torrance*, 11 N.C. 196 (1826). The Georgia scheme is mentioned in the Alabama case.

102. *Bailey v. Carter*, 42 N.C., 200 (1851); *Robinson v. Lewis*, 45 N.C. 63 (1852); *Colvard v. Waugh*, 3 Jones Eq. 335 (N.C. 1857).

103. *Wilson v. Weston*, 4 Jones Eq. 350 (N.C., 1859); *Esham v. Lamar*, 10 B. Mon. 43 (Ky., 1849).

104. T. R. R. Cobb, *Law of Negro Slavery*, 317; McCash, *Cobb*.

105. *Webb and Foster v. Patterson*, 7 Humphreys 431 (Tenn., 1846); *Keas v. Yewell*, 2 Dana 248 (Ky., 1834).

106. *Boner v. Mahle*, 3 La. Ann. 600 (1848); *Hughes v. Graves*, 1 Littell 317 (Ky., 1822); *Evans v. Merriken*, 8 G. and J., 39 (Md., 1836).

107. *Ballard v. Jones and Ingram*, 7 Humphreys 439 (Tenn., 1846); *Harrison v. Lee*, 1 Littell 190 (Ky., 1822). See also *Overton v. Bigelow's Adm'r.*, 19 Yerg. 48 (Tenn., 1836); *May & May v. Eastin*, 2 Port. 414 (Ala., 1835).

108. *Bryan v. Robert*, 1 Strob. Eq. 334 (S.C., 1847). The modern common law does not compel specific performance of contracts in the future: it awards damages for breaches. Baker, *Introduction to English Legal History*, 263; Morton Horwitz, *Transformation of American Law, 1780–1860*, 174.

109. *Flowers v. Sproul et al.*, 2 A. K. Marsh. 54 (Ky., 1819).

110. *Lee v. Fellowes & Co.*, 10 B. Mon. 117 (Ky., 1849).

111. Morton Horwitz, *Transformation of American Law, 1780–1860*, 266.

112. Friedman noted that "security devices became almost indistinguishable. It was another example of the principle that nothing—neither the small specks of technicality nor large stains of legal logic and jargon—was allowed to interfere in the 19th century with what judges or the dominant public saw as the highroad to progress and wealth." *History of American Law*, 474.

CHAPTER 6

1. Fogel and Engerman, *Time on the Cross*, 56 (first quotation), 57; Shugg, *Origins of Class Struggle in Louisiana*, 87–88; Schlotterbeck, "Plantation and Farm," 190; Stampp, *Peculiar Institution*, 71.

2. See, e.g., Finch, *Law*, chap. 18.

3. Holdsworth, *History of English Law*, 7:452–54; Atiyah, *Freedom of Contract*, 177.

4. Sir William Jones, *Bailments*, 3–4, 9, 86; Blackstone, *Commentaries*, 2:396, 452.

5. Joseph Story, *Commentaries on the Law of Bailments*, 1; Dunne, *Justice Joseph Story*, 311–12; Sir William Jones, *Bailments*, 35–36. See also Pothier, *Traite du contrat e Louage*.

6. William Wetmore Story, *Treatise on the Law of Contracts*, 253, 275. The problem of the common carrier is explored in Wahl, "Bondsman's Burden."

7. *George v. Elliott*, 2 Hen. and M. 6 (Va., 1806).

8. *Harris v. Nicholas*, 5 Mun. 483–86 (Va., 1817).

9. Ibid., 487–89.

10. Savitt, "Slave Life Insurance," 583–600; *Harris v. Nicholas*, 5 Mun. 489 (Va., 1817).

11. *Hicks v. Parham Ex'r.*, 3 Haywood 225–27 (Tenn., 1817).

12. *Redding v. Hall*, 1 Bibb 537, 540 (Ky., 1809).

13. Ibid., 541.

14. *Outlaw and McClellan v. Cook*, Minor 258 (Ala., 1824).

15. *Helton v. Caston*, 2 Bailey 100 (S.C., 1831).

16. *Perkins v. Reed*, 8 Mo. 33 (1843); *Ewing v. Thompson*, 13 Mo. 132 (1850).

17. *State v. Mann*, 13 N.C. 168 (1829); *James v. Carper*, 4 Sneed 401 (Tenn., 1857).

18. *Harrison v. Murrell*, 5 T. B. Mon. 359–60 (Ky., 1827); *Young v. Bruces*, 5 Littell 281 (Ky., 1824).

19. *Harmon v. Fleming*, 25 Miss. 143 (1852); *Lennard v. Boynton*, 11 Ga. 111–12 (1852).

20. Quoted in Langum, "Role of Intellect and Fortuity," 4.

21. Ibid., 7. Langum himself cited the *Federal Union*, December 12, 1854, which carried the reaction in Milledgeville.

22. *Dudgean v. Teass*, 9 Mo. 867 (1846); *Towsend v. Hill*, 18 Tex. 425–27 (1857).

23. *Alston v. Balls*, 12 Ark. 664 (1852)

24. *Singleton v. Carroll*, 6 J. J. Marsh. 531 (Ky., 1830); *Alston v. Balls and Adams*, 12 Ark. 669–70 (1852); *Curry v. Gaulden*, 17 Ga. 75 (1855); *State v. Mann*, 13 N.C. 168 (1829); *Helton v. Caston*, 2 Bailey 99 (S.C., 1831).

25. *Jones v. Glass*, 35 N.C. 210–11 (1852).

26. *Craig's Adm'r. v. Lee*, 13 B. Mon. 98–99 (Ky., 1853).

27. A. W. B. Simpson, *History of the Common Law of Contract*, 222–25, 264–72.

28. *Latimer v. Alexander*, 14 Ga. 259 (1853); *Brooks v. Crook*, 20 Ga. 87 (1856).

29. Quoted in Langum, "Role of Intellect and Fortuity," 4.

30. *Hogan v. Carr & Anderson*, 6 Ala. 472 (1844).

31. *Sims & Jones v. Knox*, 18 Ala. 240 (1850).

32. *Alabama & Tennessee Rivers Railroad Co. v. Burke*, 27 Ala. 536–41 (1855).

33. *Wilkinson v. Moseley*, 30 Ala. 563–64, 574, 576 (1857). This case had been before the court earlier as *Wilkinson v. Moseley*, 18 Ala. 288 (1850), and *Wilkinson v. Moseley*, 24 Ala. 411 (1854).

34. Sir William Jones, *Bailments*, 121.

35. *Mullen v. Ensley*, 8 Humphreys 428–29 (Tenn., 1847); *The Mayor and Council of Columbus v. Howard*, 6 Ga. 214, 218–19 (1849).

36. Ibid., 220.

37. *Collins v. Hutchins*, 21 Ga. 273–74 (1857).

38. Sir William Jones, *Bailments*, 4, 7, 9, 21.

39. *Williams v. Holcombe*, 4 N.C. 28–30 (1814).

40. *Swigert v. Graham*, 7 B. Mon. 661, 663–64, 669 (Ky., 1847).

41. *Lunsford and Davie v. Baynham*, 19 Humphreys 268–69 (Tenn., 1849).

42. *Heathcock v. Pennington*, 33 N.C. 440 (1850).

43. Ibid.

44. *Jones v. Glass*, 35 N.C. 211 (1852).

45. *Couch v. Jones*, 49 N.C. 393 (1857).

46. Ibid., 395.

47. *Gorman v. Campbell*, 14 Ga. 143 (1853).

48. Finkelman, "Slaves as Fellow Servants"; Tushnet, *American Law of Slavery*; Kiely, "Hollow Words"; Wertheim, "Slavery and the Fellow Servant Rule"; *Black's Law Dictionary*, 743; *Farwell v. Boston & Worcester Railroad*, 4 Met. 49 (Mass., 1842).

49. *Black's Law Dictionary*, 1475; Wertheim, "Slavery and the Fellow Servant Rule," 1122 (quotation); *Corpus Juris Secundum*, 77:318.

50. Walker, *Introduction to American Law*, 243.

51. Konefsky, " 'As Best to Subserve Their Own Interests,' " 222–24.

52. Holdsworth, *History of English Law*, 8:252–53.

53. Reeve, *Law of Baron and Femme*, 358; Oliver Wendell Holmes, *Common Law*, 180. Holmes also wrote: "It is familiar that the status of a servant maintains many marks of the time when he was a slave. The liability of the master for his torts is one instance. The present [agency] is another. A slave's possession was his owner's possession on the practical ground of the owner's power over him, and from the fact that the slave had no standing before the law. The notion that his personality was merged in that of his family head survives the era of emancipation." Ibid., 179–80. An especially good analysis of the concept of agency in modern American law is that of Morton Horwitz, *Transformation of American Law, 1870–1960*, 39–51.

54. Blackstone, *Commentaries*, 1:423; Wilentz, *Chants Democratic*.

55. Wertheim, "Slavery and the Fellow Servant Rule," 1112–14; Sir William Jones, *Bailments*, 118–19.

56. *Corpus Juris Secundum*, 8:237; Blackstone, *Commentaries*, 2:454; *Coke on Littleton*, 89a, 89b.

57. Douglass, *Narrative of the Life of Frederick Douglass*, 87–88.

58. *Scudder v. Woodbridge*, 1 Ga. 195–98 (1846).

59. Ibid., 197–98.

60. Ibid., 198–99.

61. Ibid., 199–200.

62. Tushnet, *American Law of Slavery*, 186; Finkelman, "Slaves as Fellow Servants," 291; Wertheim, "Slavery and the Fellow Servant Rule," 1137–40.

63. *Ponton v. Wilmington & Weldon Railroad Co.*, 51 N.C. 246 (1858).

64. Ibid., 248–49.

65. Ibid., 249.

66. Finkelman, "Slaves as Fellow Servants," 303–4.

67. Tushnet, *American Law of Slavery*, 45–50.

68. Wertheim, "Slavery and the Fellow Servant Rule," 1134; *Ponton v. Wilmington & Weldon Railroad Co.*, 51 N.C. 249 (1858).

69. *Ponton v. Wilmington & Weldon Railroad Co.*, 51 N.C. 249 (1858), summarizes Ruffin's opinion in *Jones v. Glass*, 35 N.C. 211–12 (1852).

70. *Forsyth and Simpson v. Perry*, 5 Fla. 343 (1853).

71. Ibid., 344.

72. *Louisville and Nashville Railroad Co. v. Yandell*, 17 B. Mon. 595–96 (Ky., 1856).

73. *Howes v. Steamer Red Chief*, 15 La. Ann. 322–23 (1860).

74. *Murray v. South Carolina Railroad Co.*, 1 McMul. 403–6 (S.C., 1841).

75. *White v. Smith*, 12 Rich. 602 (S.C., 1860).

CHAPTER 7

1. Douglass, *Life and Times*, 67–68.

2. Goodell, *American Slave Code*, 195. Other expressions of the view that slaves were killed with impunity are Edmund S. Morgan, *American Slavery American Freedom*, 313; Leon Higginbotham, *In the Matter of Color*, 36; and Fede, "Legitimized Violent Slave Abuse." Stampp (*Peculiar Institution*, 218) suggested that "the great majority of whites who, by a reasonable interpretation of the law, were guilty of feloniously killing slaves escaped without any punishment at all. Of those who were indicted, most were either acquitted or never brought to trial." This was because blacks could not testify, because of racial solidarity that collapsed only under a "particularly shocking atrocity," and, finally, because white juries would not convict. He quoted a South Carolina jury foreman who said that he would never convict any white of "murdering a slave," and, Stampp added, "this was the feeling of most jurymen." The work of A. E. Keir Nash is a contrast to this view: see, e.g., "A More Equitable Past?," 215, 233, 235, 239.

3. Rosengarten, *Tombee*, 455–56. See also Haller Nutt to Alonzo Snyder, April 30, November 18, December 15, 1844, Snyder Papers, Louisiana State University Archives, Baton Rouge.

4. Goveia, *West Indian Slave Laws*, 33. The source for the assertion was Fortunatus Dwarris, a commissioner of legal enquiry in the West Indies. It was especially telling, she noted, that the Jamaica Assembly declined to accept a report in 1788 claiming that "negroes in this island are under the protection of the common law." Instead, the assemblymen accepted a statement that "negroes in this island are under the protection of lenient and salutary laws, suited to their situation and circumstances."

5. Hart, *Punishment and Responsibility*, 13–15.

6. Coke, *Third Part of the Institutes*, 47.

7. Ibid., 55.

8. Dalton, *Countrey Justice*, 224. In March 1654/5 Thomas Swann, who had been accused of killing his servant Elizabeth Buck in Surry County, successfully sued for his pardon after the jury returned a verdict of "homicide per misadventure." Hening, *Statutes at Large*, 1:406.

9. Dalton, *Countrey Justice*, 222, 225.

10. Ibid., 225.

11. Hawkins, *Treatise of the Pleas of the Crown*, 1:73, 76.

12. Hening, *Statutes at Large*, 2:270.

13. Ibid., 3:459.

14. Ibid., 4:132–33.

15. Ibid.

16. Don Higginbotham and Price, "Was It Murder for a White Man to Kill a Slave?," 596. Crow (*Black Experience in Revolutionary North Carolina*, 25) suggested that the bill was vetoed because Governor Josiah Martin was "piqued by his other conflict with the radical whigs."

17. Thomas Cooper and McCord, *Statutes at Large of South Carolina*, 7:346–47. On Stono see Peter H. Wood, *Black Majority*.

18. Thomas Cooper and McCord, *Statutes at Large of South Carolina*, 7:410–11.

19. Howell Cobb, *Compilation of the . . . Statutes . . . of Georgia*, 595–604.

20. Rutman and Rutman, *A Place in Time*, 134–38.

21. There is a good sketch of Clayton in the *William and Mary Quarterly*, 1st ser. (1901–3): 10–11:34.

22. These facts and all others relating to the case of Frances Wilson, unless otherwise noted, are in John Clayton to Board of Trade, December 20, 1716, CO 5/1318, Public Record Office, London, PRO 95–98.

23. A related accusation was that the governor "at the same time, knowingly to sufferr a favorite of his, to kill, destroy & maime as many Slaves of their own, & other people, as they please, without takeing notice thereof." Clayton dismissed this charge as confused at best: "wheither the Quarist means more favourits than one, or wheither the favourit, or favour-ites kill, destroy, & maime their own Slaves & the Slaves of other people, or other people that are not Slaves, not being plainly expressed; & it not being known to me, who is, or are meant by the favourite, or favourites, I cannot give a particular Answer thereto." Ibid.

24. Only two scholars mention the inquest jury finding. Parent correctly noted that Clayton found it "defective," but he did not say what the finding was. Arthur Scott said that the "coroners jury" found a verdict of "murder." The complete finding is in the text above. Parent, "Emergence of Paternalism," 99; Scott, *Criminal Law in Colonial Virginia*, 202.

25. A good survey of the jurisdiction of the general court in criminal cases is Chitwood, *Justice in Colonial Virginia*, 35, 44, 49, 52–53, 66–67.

26. It was the grand jury, not the coroners's jury, that claimed there was a murder. The grand jury indictment, as well as the inquest jury report, are included in the file with Clayton to Board of Trade. Parent ("Emergence of Paternalism," 115 n. 38), in an otherwise fine study, went a bit astray on the role of the grand jury. He suggested that John Custis, William Byrd II's brother-in-law, was on the grand jury that indicted Wilson, and that it was a divided body. The basis for this was a letter from Custis to Byrd in March 1717. Custis wrote: "it was my fate to bee upon a grand jury that petitioned the governor to sitt again in court." As he was a political opponent of Spotswood's this was uncomfortable for him, and he and other "male contents" opposed the petition. The mistake appears to be that Custis was referring to a petition from an October 1716 grand jury and not the true bill issued against Frances Wilson in the spring of 1713/14. The petition requested that Spotswood rejoin the councillors in the general court. After this petition he did so. The thing that likely

misled Parent was this sentence in the Custis letter: "I need not tell you the reason why he /absented?/the court; because I know you were then on the /be/nch and was one that opposd him; if you have forgot it was the tryall of Mrs. Wilson for the death of a Nigro wench." Byrd was on the bench of the general court, not the grand jury. The opposition was in the general court. The upshot is that the grand jury that indicted Frances Wilson may or may not have been unanimous. We will never know. John Custis to William Byrd II, March 30, 1717, Tinling, *Correspondence of the . . . Byrds,* 1:297. The remark of Spotswood is in Arthur Scott, *Criminal Law in Colonial Virginia,* 202.

27. Brown and Brown, *Virginia, 1705–1786,* 70; Dodson, *Alexander Spotswood,* 132 n. 62; Parent, "Emergence of Paternalism," 98–99, 216.

28. Rankin, *Criminal Trial Proceedings,* 89. It was not until 1734 that the law routinely allowed counsel in capital cases.

29. *Virginia Gazette,* November 23, 1729. Only two scholars have dealt with this case: Rankin (*Criminal Trial Proceedings,* 119) and Arthur Scott (*Criminal Law in Colonial Virginia,* 202).

30. The Byrn case is covered in Arthur Scott, *Criminal Law in Colonial Virginia,* 202; Rankin, *Criminal Trial Proceedings,* 112–13, 206–7; and Parent, "Emergence of Paternalism," 100. See also McIlwaine, Hall, and Hillman, *Executive Journals,* 4:206. Scott's account is a simple factual one, Rankin suggested that the governor acted on Byrn's behalf because he felt that the jury verdict was unjust, and Parent argued that the case "reveals the society's dedication to racial slavery at any cost." Parent also believed that the case rested more on a concern for the property rights of the owner than it did on the human rights of the slave. I am inclined to agree with his first point, whereas the second cannot, in my view, be sustained on the basis of the sparse record.

31. Hoffer and Scott, *Criminal Proceedings in Colonial Virginia,* 219 n. 142.

32. Ibid., 218–19.

33. Examination of Hannah Crump, January 8, 1747, discharged, March 11, 1747, Lancaster County Orders No. 9, 1743–52, VSL.

34. Examination of William Cox, March 29, 1752, Westmoreland County, Order Book, 1752–55, VSL.

35. Brown and Brown (*Virginia, 1705–1786*) are the only scholars who mention this case. They note that a slave was killed and no one was punished, but they do not discuss the facts of the case or attempt to analyze it. The details are contained in a series of documents (mostly depositions) in Prince William County Deed Book, 1761–64, 254–60, VSL.

36. Ibid., 257–58. See also Examination of John Collins, July 9, 1764, Orange County Order Book, 1763–69, and Examination of George Cannady, June 2, 1757, King George County Order Book, 1751–65, VSL. On the other side, see Examination of Matthew Welch, February 11, 1762, Westmoreland County Order Book, 1761–64, VSL. Welch was ordered to stand trial for the murder of Jack. It is likely that Cannady's social position was modest and that this was a factor in certifying his case for trial.

37. Pitman et al. v. Freeman, July 6, 1759, King George County Order Book, 1751–65, VSL. William Pitman sued Freeman again on September 4, 1761. On the same day Ezekiel Mathews sued Pitman in two separate actions. The Mathews case was settled by agreement in March 1762. Pitman was back in court the next year. He sued Benjamin Suttles and Moses Pitman (the relationship is not known) on July 7, 1763, and then Anthony McHellrich sued him. The case was heard by a jury on November 1, 1764, and Pitman assumed the obligation to pay the damages alleged. Then on May 2, 1765, a judgment on the petition was granted Abraham Outlam against Pitman.

38. A final piece regarding William Pitman appeared in the *Virginia Gazette* on February 2, 1786, when Isaac Pitman, the guardian of Mary, "Orphan of Wm Pittman dec'd," was ordered to settle the guardians account. Order Book, 1766–90, VSL.

39. *Virginia Gazette*, December 23, 1773.

40. Schwarz, *Twice Condemned*, 137–38.

41. Don Higginbotham and Price, "Was It Murder for a White Man to Kill a Slave?," 601.

42. *Maryland Archives*, 20:461.

43. *Maryland Gazette*, March 26, 1761, April 8, 1762.

44. *South Carolina Gazette and Country Journal*, October 31, 1769, January 23, November 1, 1770; *South Carolina Gazette*, February 1, 1768. George Roberts was an especially interesting case. He was fined in February 1768 for causing a white to be "whipt by negroes." *South Carolina Gazette*, February 1, 1768. In October 1769 he was found guilty of killing a slave in a sudden heat and passion but was granted a new trial. He was retried and again found guilty. *South Carolina Gazette and Country Journal*, October 31, 1769, January 23, 1770. An entry in the February 2, 1768, edition noted, without identifying the person, that among those sentenced, "A Person for killing a Negro in the Heat of Passion, was fined 350£."

45. *Maryland Gazette*, early 1760s, passim.

46. *South Carolina Gazette*, May 22–29, 1736; *South Carolina Gazette and Country Journal*, November 24, 1772. Other evidence of the brutish nature of colonial society can be found in Windley, *Runaway Slave Advertisements*. For "well" or "severely" whipped slaves see 1:15, 18, 34–35, 45, 51, 56, 60, 91, 96–97, 100–101, 121–22, 125–26, 137–38, 164, 179, 214, 218, 251, 309, 329, 339–40, 350. For the use of irons see 1:23, 264, 333–34, 2:88 ("an iron collar with a Bell fixed to it"), 90, 197, 199–200, 226, 234–35, 237, 246–47, 292. For branding see 1:7, 42, 57, 65–66, 121–22, 134, 196, 281, 311.

47. Wright and Tinling, *Secret Diary*, 133; Jack Greene, *Diary of Landon Carter*.

48. Wright and Tinling, *Secret Diary*, 494, 533.

49. Jack Greene, *Diary of Landon Carter*, 1:138, 366.

50. Kulikoff, *Tobacco and Slaves*. See also Kulikoff, "Origins of Afro-American Society in Tidewater Maryland and Virginia," and Tate, *The Negro in Eighteenth-Century Williamsburg*. The term "domesticated" is a variation of the felicitous title to a chapter in Rose, *Slavery and Freedom*, "The Domestication of Domestic Slavery."

51. Haskell, "Capitalism"; Beeman, *Evolution of the Southern Backcountry*, 190; Anesko, "So Discreet a Zeal"; Gallay, "The Origins of Slaveholders' Paternalism"; Gewehr, *Great Awakening in Virginia*, chap. 10; Drake, *Quakers and Slavery in America*; Mathews, *Religion in the Old South*; Albert, "Protean Institution," chap. 5. A convenient collection of documents is Bruns, *Am I Not a Man and a Brother*. The larger context is provided by David Brion Davis, *Problem of Slavery in the Age of Revolution*, *Problem of Slavery in Western Culture*, and *Slavery and Human Progress*. On the change in the Methodist position see Donald G. Mathews, *Slavery and Methodism*.

52. Aside from the works cited in n. 51 see Isaac (*Transformation of Virginia*, 309), who noted that "slavery could not go unchallenged in a world in which values were becoming focused on individuals and their quest for fulfillment."

53. Glenn, *Campaigns against Corporal Punishment*.

54. Masur, *Rites of Execution*.

55. Thorpe, *Federal and State Constitutions*, 2:801.

56. Wiecek, "Statutory Law of Slavery," 266.

57. Thorpe, *Federal and State Constitutions*, 1:112, 4:2154, 6:3564; Thornton, *Politics and Power in a Slave Society*.

58. *DAB*, 11–12:289–90. Lipscomb was originally from Abbeville District, S.C., and had studied law in the office of John C. Calhoun in South Carolina.

59. Hening, *Statutes at Large*, 12:681.

60. Haywood, *Manual of the Laws of North Carolina*, 2:141.

61. *Session Laws of Tennessee, 1801*, 187–88. Despite the title, the law of 1799 and laws other than those of 1801 are included.

62. Peirce, Taylor, and King, *Consolidation . . . of the Statutes of the State [Louisiana]*, 550; Howell Cobb, *Compilation of the . . . Statutes . . . of Georgia*, 604; O'Neall, *Negro Law of South Carolina*, 19; *Session Laws of North Carolina, 1817*, 18–19.

63. Ormond, Bagley, and Goldthwaite, *Code of Alabama*, 591.

64. *Ephesians* 6:5: "Servants, be obedient to them that are your masters according to the flesh, with fear and trembling, in singleness of your heart, as unto Christ."

65. Memorial from Christ Church for Alteration of the Act of 1821 for Killing a Slave, Legislative Petitions, 1829, SCDAH. See also Harper, "Memoir on Slavery," 97: "I am by no means sure that the cause of humanity has been served by the change in our jurisprudence, which has placed their murder on the same footing with that of a freeman."

66. Stampp, *Peculiar Institution*, 223.

67. Memorial from Christ Church, SCDAH.

68. *State v. Boon*, 1 N.C. 106–8 (1801).

69. Ibid., 110.

70. Ibid., 112.

71. Ibid., 113.

72. *State v. Reed*, 9 N.C., 255, 257 (1823).

73. Ibid., 255–57.

74. Ibid.

75. *State v. Jones*, Walker 84–86 (Miss., 1821).

76. *Fields v. State*, 1 Yerg. 160, 164–65 (Tenn., 1829).

77. *Chandler v. State*, 2 Tex. 309 (1847).

78. *State v. Fleming*, 2 Strob. 471 (S.C., 1848).

79. *State v. Weaver*, 3 N.C. 70–71 (1798).

80. *State v. Walker*, 4 N.C. 471 (1817).

81. *State v. Tackett*, 8 N.C. 104–6 (1820).

82. Ibid., 107.

83. *State v. Hoover*, 20 N.C. 393–94 (1839).

84. Ibid., 395.

85. Ibid., 396.

86. *Souther v. Commonwealth*, 7 Grattan 674 (Va., 1851).

87. Ibid., 680–81.

88. Ibid.

89. *State v. Raines*, 3 McCord 315 (S.C., 1826).

90. Ibid., 319–21.

91. *State v. Gaffney*, Rice 431 (S.C., 1839); *State v. Fleming*, 2 Strob. 464 (S.C., 1848).

92. *State v. Motley et al.*, 7 Rich. 327 (S.C., 1854).

93. A. E. Keir Nash, "A More Equitable Past?," 233.

94. Inquest into the death of Ador, September 1, 1827, quoted in Essah, "Slavery and Freedom in the First State," 60.

95. State v. Huff and Taylor, September 1–2, 1825, Granville County, Criminal Actions concerning Slaves and Free Persons of Color, 1820–57, NCDAH. Taylor was found guilty of manslaughter and granted benefit of clergy. He was burned on the hand. Huff, his overseer, was acquitted.

96. Examination of Robert Scott, October 9, 1817, and Examination of Pleasant Clarke, June 25, 1817, Lunenburg County Minute Book, 1817–19; Examination of Richard Straughan, June 26, 1815, Westmoreland County Order Book, 1814–18—all in VSL. Straughan's appearance at the March court in 1819 was required so that he would post a peace recognizance to maintain good behavior toward Thomas Barber. Also State v. Archibald Todd, October 7, 1816, Petersburg City Hustings Court Minute Book, 1800–1804; James H. Barrum, January–February 1834, Petersburg City Hustings Court Minute Book, 1834–35; State v. John Atkin-

son, January 1820, Westmoreland County Order Book, 1819–23—all in VSL. Additional cases from Westmoreland County were the Examination of Lee Griggs, March 18, 1784, and Examination of Thomas Sorrell, December 22, 1785 (the justices in this case were the same ones who had certified Mathew Welch for trial twenty years earlier), Order Book, 1776–86; Examination of William Thomas Davis, September 11, 1788, Order Book, 1787–90; Examination of Nathaniel Deane, March 26, 1782, Order Book, 1776–86—all in VSL. From Fauquier County there were the following examples: Examination of Isaac Johnson and Richard Risher, January 25, 1779, Minute Book, 1773–80; Examination of Elias Martin, January 7, 1802, Minute Book, 1801–3; Examination of Richard W. Chichester, March 28, 1815, Minute Book, 1815–16; and Examination of Fielding Sinclair, September 19, 1818, Minute Book, 1818–19—all in VSL. Other examples included the Examination of Temple Demoville, December 21, 1826, Charles City County Orders, 1823–29; Examination of John Morris, February 7, 1809, Charles City County, Order Book (Minutes), 1806–9; Examination of William Roberts, January 15, 1791, Petersburg City Hustings Court Minute Book, 1791–97; Examination of Billy Ash, January 27, 1802, Petersburg City Hustings Court Minute Book, 1800–1804; Examination of Joseph Lane, January 2, 1811, Southampton County Order Book, 1811–12; and Examination of Nathaniel Fells, August 28, 1818, Southampton County Order Book, 1816–19—all in VSL. Finally, there was the Examination of Thomas Hill, April 25, 1789, Sussex County Order Book, 1754–1807, VSL. Although one justice wanted Hill to stand trial, the other did not, so he was discharged. The persons certified for trial for the murder of their own slaves were Richard Straughan and John Atkinson from Westmoreland County, Pleasant Clarke from Lunenburg County, Richard W. Chichester from Fauquier County, and James Barrum from Petersburg. Possibly Archibald Todd ought to be added in that he was examined for the homicide of Ephraim, the property of William Colquhoun, but who was also identified as the servant of Todd. It is likely that Todd hired Ephraim, which gave him a temporary property in the slave.

97. State v. Drury Cheek, Fall 1835, Case 580, State v. William Craig, Fall 1852, Case 898, State v. Thomas and W. D. A. Dean, Fall 1859, Case 1085, State v. J. Goodman and J. Whitworth, Fall 1834, Case 559, State v. Hugh McClusky, Spring 1821, Case 343, State v. J. Templeton, Fall 1860, Case 1097, and State v. James Young, Fall 1850, Case 871, Index to Session Rolls, Laurens District, Clerk of Court, Court of General Sessions, 1801–1912, SCDAH. The cases from Marlborough District were State v. Robert D. Isgett, March 1866, Case 748, State v. W. B. Leggst, Fall 1860, Case 723, State v. L. L. McLaurin, Fall 1859, Case 679, and State v. Lewis A. J. Stubbs, October 1852, Case 485, Marlborough District, 1801–68: Office: Clerk of Court of General Sessions, Index. See also Petition of Dr. Reid, June 1828, Legislative Petitions, SCDAH.

98. Edwin Davis, *Plantation Life in the Florida Parishes of Louisiana*, 148; State v. Malichi Warren, September Term 1843, Lowndes County, Ala., Final Record, Circuit Court, 1840–43, Lowndes County Courthouse, Haynesville, Ala.; Commonwealth v. Theodore H. Davis, October 1850, Mercer County, Ky., Circuit Court Case Files, File C., 1850–51, KSA. A smattering of additional cases were State v. Wiley J. Ennis, May 15, 1846–September 1849 (this case was finally withdrawn from the docket), Chambers County Circuit Court Minutes, Chambers County Courthouse, Lafayette, Ala.; Texas v. Alexander Aiken, September 9, 1859, Civil Minutes, District Court, Harrison County Courthouse, Marshall, Tex. (despite the title of the record, this was a criminal case for the murder of a slave); State v. William Holcomb and William Andrews, June 25, 1821, and State v. William Fields, June 23, 1821, Maury County Circuit Court, vol. 1817–21, 510, 513, and vol. 1821–25, 18–19, 41–42, TSLA. Holcomb and Andrews were not tried. Fields, after a change of venue to Bedford County, was found guilty of manslaughter. His case was appealed to the state supreme court—see the discussion above regarding *Fields v. State*, 1 Yerg. 155 (Tenn., 1829). See also State v. Robert Stevens,

October 1806, Queen Anne County, Criminal Docket, 1807, MHR. I found no cases involving homicide indictments for the killing of slaves in the county records I examined for the states of Missouri, Arkansas, Louisiana, Georgia, and Florida.

99. State v. James Paul, 1843, Case 324, File 130–324 (1841–46), Lowndes County Department of Archives and History: Criminal File, Lowndes County Courthouse, Columbia, Miss.

CHAPTER 8

1. Douglass, *My Bondage and My Freedom*, 62.

2. Starobin, *Industrial Slavery*; Newton and Lewis, *The Other Slaves*; Ronald L. Lewis, *Coal, Iron, and Slaves*.

3. Finley, *Ancient Slavery and Modern Ideology*, 93. Fogel and Engerman (*Time on the Cross*, 147, 242) reduced the incidence of whipping. It was "an integral part of the system of punishment and rewards, but it was not the totality of the system," and the "failure to recognize the flexible and many-faceted character of the slave system, and the widely held assumption that systematic employment of force precluded the use of pecuniary incentives in any significant way, have led historians to exaggerate the cruelty of slavery." Slaveowners, in their view, tried to achieve a high level of productivity by instilling the Protestant work ethic into the slaves. The figures used by Fogel and Engerman to show that whipping was not as widespread as many have thought were, in turn, subjected to sharp criticism in Gutman, *Slavery and the Numbers Game*. Fogel (*Without Consent or Contract*, 394) reevaluated his position and put forward a number of judgments on "The Moral Problem of Slavery." Relevant here is that "slavery permitted one group of people to exercise unrestrained personal domination over another group of people. . . . The extreme degree of domination required by the system, and not percentages of masters who were cruel or benevolent in their operation of the system, was and is the essential crime. Cruelty was bound to be one of the consequences of unlimited domination because sooner or later it was necessary to sustain domination."

4. Flanigan, "Criminal Law of Slavery and Freedom," 147.

5. Genovese, "Treatment of Slaves in Different Countries," 203, and *Roll, Jordan, Roll*, 72–73.

6. Sartre, *Critique of Dialectical Reason*, 617.

7. Rose, *Slavery and Freedom*, 23. She also observed: "Judgments are fraught with hazards. Some matters may in time yield to statistical analysis: provision of clothing, food allowances, hours of work, even the extent of family disruption resulting from the interstate slave trade. Punishment and discipline probably never will" (pp. 30–31).

8. Fede, "Legitimized Violent Slave Abuse," 93, 101, 132.

9. Maxcy, *Laws of Maryland*, 1:115; Upton and Jennings, *Civil Code of . . . Louisiana*, 29–30; Scott and McCullough, *Maryland Code*, 1:454; Morehead and Brown, *Digest of the Statute Laws of Kentucky*, 2:1481–82; Thorpe, *Federal and State Constitutions*, 1:112 (Alabama), 6:3564 (Texas). T. R. R. Cobb (*Law of Negro Slavery*, 98) placed a good deal of weight on the Texas and Alabama constitutional provisions. He failed to note, however, that they required legislative implementation and that no statutes were passed.

10. Thomas Cooper and McCord, *Statutes at Large of South Carolina*, 7:410–11; Peirce, Taylor, and King, *Consolidation . . . of the Statutes of the State [Louisiana]*, 550.

11. Thomas Cooper and McCord, *Statutes at Large of South Carolina*, 7:410–11.

12. Grand Jury Presentment, Fall Term 1853, Fairfield District: Clerk of Court (General Sessions) Journal, 1825–29, 1840–63, 1863–68, SCDAH.

13. Hurd, *Law of Freedom and Bondage*, 2:100. Stampp (*Peculiar Institution*, 220) saw the qualification as a "nullifying clause." A closer reading of the law, I believe, is that it was an effort to balance, not to nullify.

14. Hurd, *Law of Freedom and Bondage*, 2:108; Howell Cobb, *Compilation of the . . . Statutes . . . of Georgia*, 635–36.

15. Upton and Jennings, *Civil Code of . . . Louisiana*, 27. McGowan ("Creation of a Slave Society," 284, 296) has argued that the allegedly humane *Real Cedula* of 1789 that the Spanish attempted to implement was a very reactionary code that denied "their [the slaves] living, human culture" and objectified "them as moral abstractions." It imposed Catholic forms and rituals on the slaves, for instance. McGowan does not dispute the fact that the code placed restraints on the power of masters and attempted to ensure that slaves would not be the victims of "immoderate" punishment. This, however, was a very narrow focus that obscured the reactionary nature of the code. Not until the early 1790s, under the Baron de Carondelet, was any effort made to intervene on the plantations in order to protect the slaves from brutality and violence. Carondelet believed that violence against slaves had stimulated an earlier revolt.

16. Peirce, Taylor, and King, *Consolidation . . . of the Statutes of the State [Louisiana]*, 550; Upton and Jennings, *Civil Code of . . . Louisiana*, 27.

17. Haywood, *Manual of the Laws of North Carolina*, 2:149. For an analysis of the earlier use of the law on compensation see Kay and Cary, " 'The Planters Suffer Little or Nothing.' " These authors concluded that the "planter rationally encompassed a willingness to kill or castrate slaves as well as a willingness to placate them. This was the situation in colonial North Carolina. There black slaves were terrorized; owners, especially the affluent, were subsidized; and the middle and lower class whites disproportionately financed the sorry spectacle" (p. 306).

18. Ormond, Bagley, and Goldthwaite, *Code of Alabama*, 390.

19. *State v. Maner*, 2 Hill 353 (S.C., 1834); *State v. Wilson*, Cheves 163 (S.C., 1840); *Turnipseed v. State*, 6 Ala. 664 (1844); *Eskridge v. State*, 25 Ala. 30 (1854); *Scott v. State*, 31 Miss. 473 (1856); *Markham v. Close*, 2 La. 581 (1831); *State v. Morris*, 4 La. Ann. 177 (1849); *State v. White and Ward*, 13 La. Ann. 573 (1858).

20. State v. John Wait, Fall 1847, Case 818, Index to Session Rolls, Laurens District, Clerk of Court, Court of General Sessions, 1800–1912, SCDAH.

21. *State v. Maner*, 2 Hill 355 (S.C., 1834).

22. *State v. Wilson*, Cheves 164 (S.C., 1840).

23. State v. Elihu Oglesby, December Term 1826, Liberty County, Superior Court Minutes, GDAH; Undated, untitled paper in folder 96, Gaston Papers, Southern Historical Collection, Chapel Hill. In this piece Gaston adopted a strikingly patriarchal and benevolent view of slavery in North Carolina and an elitist view of class relationships among whites: "It is difficult to imagine a state of slavery to exist more mitigated than that which prevails in North Carolina."

24. State v. William Samuel, September 19, 1850, Circuit Court Minutes, 1850–52, 89, Chambers County Courthouse, Lafayette, Ala.

25. *Turnipseed v. State*, 6 Ala. 664–67 (1844).

26. Ibid., 667. Nash ("A More Equitable Past?," 219) suggested that this case "genuinely required reversal" because the indictment was "defective." Fede ("Legitimized Violent Slave Abuse," 143–44) argued that the conviction could have been upheld but was not because the court had a "desired end." That was to apply a "sliding scale" of culpability based on the "class identity of the white defendant." One problem with the sliding scale notion is that it intimated that there might be some point along the scale where masters could properly be indicted for nonfatal abuse of their slaves. But that would have required a qualification of some kind in Fede's "fixed principle of slave law" which was that masters had "the unlimited

right to abuse their slaves to any extreme of brutality and wantonness as long as the slave survived." If I read Collier's opinion correctly, he was more concerned with finding some coherent line to define legal cruelty. Moreover, we should not overlook an insight of Roscoe Pound's *Criminal Justice in America.* A characteristic of criminal procedure in the nineteenth century was that there was a "hypertrophy of procedure" and an "extreme of record-worship" in which the reductio ad absurdum was the reversal of "written verdicts of 'guily' or of murder in the 'fist' degree" (p. 161).

27. Ormond, Bagley, and Goldthwaite, *Code of Alabama,* 592.

28. Texas v. J. C. Duval, October 12, 1857, Bastrop County, District Court Minutes, 328, Bastrop County Courthouse, Bastrop, Tex.; Texas v. Patton and Poag, July 1855, Civil Minutes, 36–37, District Court, Harrison County Courthouse, Marshall, Tex. See also Criminal Docket, July 1853, 106; Texas v. Morris Levy, March 6, 1856, Civil Minutes, 40–41, 396, Texas v. Maston Ussery, Spring Term 1857, Civil Minutes, 44–45, 400, and Texas v. William Smith, March 1860–June 1862, Civil Minutes, 394–97, Harrison County Courthouse, Marshall, Tex. There is a lot of information about slavery in Harrison County in Campbell, *An Empire for Slavery.* See also State v. Job Freeman, October 1862, and State v. John H. Hamilton, March 1863, Circuit Court Minute Book, vol. 6, 1855–69, 373, 391, Leon County Courthouse, Tallahassee, Fla.

29. *Markham v. Close,* 2 La. 587 (1831).

30. U. B. Phillips, *Revised Statutes of Louisiana,* 50.

31. *State v. Morris,* 4 La. Ann. 177–78 (1849).

32. State v. Elizabeth Rabassa, May 20, 1843, 5th Judicial District, St. Landry Parish, LSA.

33. State v. Felonise Israel Lapointe, District Court, Case 785, May 20, 1850, 5th Judicial District, LSA.

34. State v. William H. Rawley, May–December 1845, West Feliciana Parish, Minutes Record, 3d Judicial District, 1845–49, 32, 71–72, West Feliciana County Courthouse, St. Francisville, La.

35. *Scott v. State,* 31 Miss. 473 (1856).

36. An example is State v. James Stephens, June 1847–December 1848, Minute Book, Circuit Court, vol. 12 (1847–51), 10, 103, 193, Wilkinson County Courthouse, Woodville, Miss.

37. State v. Phillip Yancey, Case 793, and State v. Jesse Mitchell and Ebenezer P. Odeneal, Case 1139, Issue Docket, April 1855; State v. John Thompson, Case 2054, State v. Peter Nelson, Case 2129, and State v. William Motley, Case 2165, State Docket for April Term 1863; State v. J. D. Griffin, Case 1864, in File 1800–1999, 1859–60—all in Lowndes County Department of Archives and History, Lowndes County Courthouse, Columbia, Miss.

38. *Commonwealth v. Richard Booth,* 2 Va. Ca. 395–96 (1824).

39. *Commonwealth v. Richard Turner,* 5 Rand. 678 (1827).

40. Ibid., 685.

41. Ibid.

42. Ibid., 686–90.

43. Sartre, *Critique of Dialectical Reason,* 617. The most extensive commentary on *Turner* is in Fede, "Legitimized Violent Slave Abuse," 136. Fede believed that Brockenbrough's dissent was the key to unravel the case. Brockenbrough established the point that a slave's rights were "not to be defined by traditional common law notions," but by balancing the interests involved in the mistreatment of slaves. The criminal law was a tool, and it had to be used "very carefully and always with the best interests of the master class in mind."

44. Wiecek, *Sources of Antislavery Constitutionalism,* 143. Cover (*Justice Accused,* 77 n *) said that Ruffin's view showed that "the master-slave relationship is a creature of force and force alone and that the law must reflect the cruel origins of the relationship." Brady ("Slavery, Race, and the Criminal Law," 248–60) believed that the case has been taken too

far. Ruffin's "rhetoric was reckless," and the case decided only that a hirer or master would not be criminally liable for a nonfatal battery on a slave. See also Yanuck, "Ruffin and North Carolina Slave Law."

45. *State v. Mann*, 13 N.C. 168 (1829).

46. Ibid., 169; Stowe, *Key to Uncle Tom's Cabin*, 147–48.

47. *State v. Mann*, 13 N.C. 169–70 (1829).

48. Ibid., 170; "Address of Thomas Ruffin Delivered before the State Agricultural Society of North Carolina, October 18th, 1855," in Hamilton, *Papers of Thomas Ruffin*, 4:332–33.

49. Undated, unsigned paper in folder 96, Gaston Papers.

50. "Address of Thomas Ruffin," 4:330.

51. *State v. Mann*, 13 N.C. 170–71 (1829).

52. Ibid., 170.

53. *Worley v. State*, 11 Humphreys 174–76 (Tenn., 1850).

54. See, e.g., Sparks, "Religion in Amite County, Mississippi," 63–64.

55. T. R. R. Cobb, *Law of Negro Slavery*, 105.

56. Patterson, *Freedom*, 3; Skinner, "The Idea of Negative Liberty," 194.

57. Blackstone, *Commentaries*, 1:121, 125, 127; Edsall, *Anti-Poor Law Movement*.

58. Haywood, *Manual of the Laws of North Carolina*, 149; O'Neall, *Negro Law of South Carolina*, 17.

59. Thomas Cooper and McCord, *Statutes at Large of South Carolina*, 7:411; O'Neall, *Negro Law of South Carolina*, 20–21.

60. *State v. Bowen*, 2 Strob. 574–75 (S.C., 1849).

61. Ormond, Bagley, and Goldthwaite, *Code of Alabama*, 390; State v. Randall Cheek, Spring Term 1862–Fall Term 1864, Lowndes County Circuit Court, State Docket, 1861, Lowndes County Courthouse, Haynesville, Ala.; State v. Erasmus Murdoch, November 1853, Circuit Court Minutes, vol. 7, 222, State v. Samuel Callahan, March 1857, State v. Lettberry Sherrall, September 1858, State v. Benjamin Flea, September 1859, and State v. C. C. Caldwell, April 1863, Circuit Court Minutes, vol. 8, 43, 62, 105, 152, 259, Chambers County Courthouse, Lafayette, Ala.

62. State v. Peter Nelson, Case 2129, File 2000–2199, State v. Joseph W. Field, Case 1593, and State v. George Hairston, Case 1557, Lowndes County Department of Archives and History, Lowndes County Courthouse, Columbia, Miss.; Manuscript Census, 1850 Slave Schedule, M 432, Reel 386.

63. Howell Cobb, *Compilation of the . . . Statutes . . . of Georgia*, 635–36; Thomas Cooper and McCord, *Statutes at Large of South Carolina*, 7:413.

64. Albert, "Protean Institution," 190 (Asbury); Hurd, *Law of Freedom and Bondage*, 1:42.

65. Stroud, *Sketch of the Laws*, 67; Goodell, *American Slave Code*, 207.

66. Maxcy, *Laws of Maryland*, 1:68; Hening, *Statutes at Large*, 6:105; Haywood, *Manual of the Laws of North Carolina*, 129; Morehead and Brown, *Digest of the Statute Laws of Kentucky*, 2:1472; Ormond, Bagley, and Goldthwaite, *Code of Alabama*, 288; Hutchinson, *Code of Mississippi*, 513; Hardin, *Revised Statutes of . . . Missouri*, 2:1474; Gould, *Digest of the Statutes of Arkansas*, 1033.

67. Thomas Cooper and McCord, *Statutes at Large of South Carolina*, 7:99; Howell Cobb, *Compilation of the . . . Statutes . . . of Georgia*, 596; Bullard and Curry, *New Digest of the Statute Laws of Louisiana*, 54; *New Digest of the Laws of Louisiana*, 54; Thompson, *Manual and Digest of the Statute Law of . . . Florida*, 174; Ormond, Bagley, and Goldthwaite, *Code of Alabama*, 592.

68. Information v. James Nimmo, June 2, 1725, Princess Anne County Minute Book 3, 1717–28, and Case of Ziperus Degge, August 25, 1761, Westmoreland County Order Book, 1758–61, VSL; Grand Jury Presentment v. Josiah Coleman, March 1735, Anne Arundel

County Court Judgments, June 1734–June 1736, 409; Lord Proprietary v. William Wales and James Wrightson, March 1765, Talbot County Court Criminal Judgments, 1761–67, MHR.

69. *State v. Maner*, 2 Hill 454 (S.C., 1834).

70. See, e.g., *State v. James Jones*, 1 Del. 546 (1818).

71. *State v. Hale*, 9 N.C. 325–27 (1823).

72. Ibid., 327.

73. Ibid., 328.

74. Ibid.

75. *Commonwealth v. Lee and Bledsoe*, 3 Met. Ky. 230–31 (1860).

76. *Commonwealth v. Dolly Chapple*, 1 Va. Ca. 184–85 (1811); *Commonwealth v. Carver*, 5 Rand. 660 (Va. 1827).

77. *Revised Code of . . . Virginia, 1819*, 1:582.

78. *Commonwealth v. Carver*, 5 Rand. 665 (Va. 1827).

79. *Nix v. State*, 13 Tex. 575–76 (1855).

80. *State v. Wilson*, Cheves (Law, 1839–40), 163–64 (S.C., 1840); *State v. Boozer*, 5 Strob. 22, 25 (S.C., 1850); Woodward, *Mary Chesnut's Civil War*, 234. On Thomas Jefferson Withers, Mary Chesnut observed (June 4, 1861) that "the Judge abuses everybody—and he does it so well. Short, sharp, and incisive are his sentences, and he revels in condemning the world en bloc, as the French say" (p. 66).

81. *State v. Harlan*, 5 Rich. 471–72 (S.C., 1852).

82. Ibid., 472–73; *Witsell v. Earnest*, 1 N. and McC. 183 (S.C., 1818).

83. This includes unpublished lower court records from approximately fifty counties in all the Southern slave states.

84. The $150 fine was levied in the case of State v. Alfred E. Jones, January 20, 1853, Chatham County Superior Court Minutes, 1850–55, 273, GDAH. An example of a one cent fine is in State v. Bolton, September 2, 1857, Maury County Circuit Court Minutes, May 1855–January 1858, 543, TSLA. A typical sentence was a $10 fine imposed by Judge Wayne in State v. James Wilkins and William P. Bowen, Spring Term 1826, Liberty County Superior Court Minutes, 1824–42, GDAH. A few sample cases include State v. Fielding Brown, Fall Term 1838, Case 1061, Index to Session Rolls, Laurens District, Clerk of Court, Court of General Sessions, 1801–1912, SCDAH; State v. George Taylor, Joseph Wood, Cade Bodbold, October 22, 1856, Leon County Circuit Court Minute Book, October 1855–May 1869, Leon County Courthouse, Tallahassee, Fla.; State v. William Bass, August 18, 1857, Boone County Circuit Court, 1852–56 Index (despite the title, it is actually the minutes), MoSA; and State v. Samuel Craft, April 11, 1837–April 12, 1838, Chambers County Circuit Court Minutes, vol. 2, 1837–39, Chambers County Courthouse, Lafayette, Ala.

85. The period covered was Spring 1821–Fall 1848. The cases are scattered through the following volume: Chatham County, Superior Court, Criminal Docket March 1821–November 1848, Court of Common Pleas and Oyer & Terminer Book A, GDAH. Nearly one-half of the cases ended in acquittals, or nol pros were entered.

86. State v. Archibald Gilchrist, April 25, 1833, Maury County Circuit Court Minutes, 1831–34, 256–58, TSLA. Gilchrist was found not guilty in a case of assault with intent to commit murder (pp. 265, 478). The civil case, McGee v. Gilchrist, was in May 1831, 294.

87. State v. Douglass, May 14, 1845, Maury County Circuit Court Minutes, 1844–51, 377, TSLA. See also State v. Bolton, September 2, 1857, Maury County Circuit Court Minutes, May 1855–January 1858, 543, TSLA.

88. State v. Bolton, Maury County Circuit Court Minutes, May 1851–September 1852, 352, 425, 466; Circuit Court Minutes, 1855–58, 326, 441, 543, and 1858–66, 275, TSLA; State v. Alfred E. Jones, January 20, 1853, Chatham County Superior Court Minutes, 1850–55, 273, GDAH.

484   *Notes to Pages 203–13*

89. No disposition of any kind was recorded.

90. *White v. Chambers*, 2 Bay 71 (S.C., 1796); Morehead and Brown, *Digest of the Statute Laws of Kentucky*, 2:1481.

91. Bernard v. Alsop, March 5, 1802, August 2, 1804, King George County Order Book 6, 1799–1805, VSL.

92. Blackstone, *Commentaries*, 3:142.

93. *White v. Chambers*, 2 Bay 71–72 (S.C., 1796).

94. Ibid., 75.

95. Ibid.

96. *Goddard v. Wagner*, 1 McCord 100 (S.C., 1821); *Carsten v. Murray*, Harp. 115 (S.C. 1824).

97. *Grimké v. Houseman*, 1 McMul. 132 (S.C., 1841).

98. O'Neall, *Negro Law of South Carolina*, 43–44.

99. *Caldwell ads. Langford*, 1 McMul. 277–78 (S.C., 1841).

100. *Smith v. Weaver*, 1 N.C. 42 (1799); *State v. Weaver*, 3 N.C. 70 (1798).

101. *Richardson v. Dukes*, 4 McCord 93–94 (S.C., 1827).

102. *Wilson v. Fancher*, 1 Head 337, 339 (Tenn., 1858).

103. Ibid., 338; Christopher Morris, "An Event in Community Organization."

104. *Wilson v. Fancher*, 1 Head 339–40 (Tenn., 1858).

105. *Wheat v. Croom*, 7 Ala. 349 (1845).

106. *Sublet v. Walker*, 6 J. J. Marsh. 212–13 (Ky., 1831); *Townsend v. Jeffries' Adm'r.*, 24 Ala. 336 (1854); O'Neall, *Negro Law of South Carolina*, 18–19.

CHAPTER 9

1. Stroud, *Sketch of the Laws*, 88.

2. Atiyah and Summers, *Form and Substance in Anglo-American Law*, 38–39; Weber, *On Law in Economy and Society*, 63, 75, 213.

3. Milton, *English Magistracy*, 13; Lambard, *Eirenarcha*, 1st book, chap. 11, p. 64. See also Gleason, *Justices of the Peace in England*.

4. Dalton, *Countrey Justice*, 18.

5. Landau, *Justices of the Peace*, 23.

6. Quoted in Milton, *English Magistracy*, 11. See also Fielding, *Amelia*, 1:7.

7. The quotations are from Landau, *Justices of the Peace*, 343–44.

8. Edmund S. Morgan, *American Slavery American Freedom*; Kulikoff, *Tobacco and Slaves*; Hening, *Statutes at Large*, 2:481: "An act for preventing Negroes Insurrections," 3:459.

9. See, e.g., Hening, *Statutes at Large*, 4:425 (Killing deer, 1734), 3:179, 6:122.

10. *Statutes at Large of Virginia, 1792–1806*, 1:123; *Revised Code of . . . Virginia, 1819*, 1:423, 426.

11. Hardin, *Revised Statutes of . . . Missouri*, 2:1474; Gould, *Digest of the Statutes of Arkansas*, 1033; *Revised Code of . . . Mississippi, 1857*, 246–47; Morehead and Brown, *Digest of the Statute Laws of Kentucky*, 2:1472; Meigs and Cooper, *Code of Tennessee*, 508–9; Aikin, *Digest of the Laws of . . . Alabama*, 123.

12. Quoted in Sirmans, *Colonial South Carolina*, 234.

13. William Simpson, *Practical Justice of the Peace and Parish officer*, vi.

14. Thomas Cooper and McCord, *Statutes at Large of South Carolina*, 7:343.

15. Ibid., 355, 359–60, 380, 375, 377; Milton, *English Magistracy*, 11.

16. Thomas Cooper and McCord, *Statutes at Large of South Carolina*, 7:401.

17. Landau, *Justice of the Peace*, chap. on "Petty Sessions"; Flanigan, "Criminal Law of Slavery and Freedom," 89; Jack P. Greene, *Diary of Landon Carter*, 2:845.

18. Jack P. Greene, *Diary of Landon Carter*, 2:845.

19. For the symbols of power and mercy see E. P. Thompson, *Whigs and Hunters*, chap. on "The Rule of Law," and Isaac, "Communication and Control."

20. Howington, "Treatment of Slaves and Free Blacks in . . . Tennessee," 138, 140.

21. B. C. Gordon et al. v. P. Hines, Judge of the Police Court, November 3, 1858, Warren County Circuit Court Minutes, 1856–60, 174–76, KSA.

22. Hening, *Statutes at Large*, 3:102–3; Holdsworth, *History of English Law*, 1:274, 277.

23. For the basic process see Rankin, *Criminal Trial Proceedings*.

24. On the ongoing struggle between the governor and the planter justices see ibid.

25. Hening, *Statutes at Large*, 8:138; Jack P. Greene, *Diary of Landon Carter*, 2:676.

26. Thomas Cooper and McCord, *Statutes at Large of South Carolina*, 7:345, 400; O'Neall, *Negro Law of South Carolina*, 33.

27. State v. Tom et al., January 21, 1849, Case 13 (the trial at Colonel Younge's plantation; those found guilty received between 21 and 75 lashes); State v. Anthony, September 16, 1848, Case 10 (the trial at Turket's home; Anthony was found guilty of "misconduct" and received 100 lashes. Turket was insulted by Anthony while he, Turket, was working on the public road. He testified that he "cannot get satisfaction for the said gross insult" from Anthony's owner), Fairfield District Magistrate Freeholders' Trial Papers, SCDAH.

28. Cushing, *First Laws of . . . Delaware*, 3:943; Hurd, *Law of Freedom and Bondage*, 1:311; Howell Cobb, *Compilation of the . . . Statutes of . . . Georgia*, 607.

29 Cushing, *Earliest Printed Laws of North Carolina*, 171–72. In general, see the excellent piece, Watson, "North Carolina Slave Courts": "The justices and freeholders attempted to conduct dispassionate hearings," yet, in the end, "the courts left a legacy of injustice and discrimination" (pp. 27, 36).

30. Haywood, *Manual of the Laws of North Carolina*, 143; *Revised Statutes of . . . North Carolina*, 1:582–84.

31. Landau, *Justices of the Peace*, 343; Dalton, *Countrey Justice*; Pocock, *Ancient Constitution and the Feudal Law*, 44–45; Green, *Verdict according to Conscience*, 165. Green shows, moreover, that the Levelers pushed back the pedigree of the jury trial even further,

32. Dalton, *Countrey Justice* (1677 ed.), "to the reader."

33. Although the focus is on England, the best study of the jury and attitudes toward it, attitudes shared by Americans, is Green, *Verdict according to Conscience*.

34. On the power of juries generally and their power of nullification see ibid.

35. See, e.g., Morton Horwitz, *Transformation of American Law*, 28–29, 84–85, 228.

36. Weber, *On Law in Economy and Society*, 80, 213: "Because of the jury, some primitive irrationality of the technique of decision and, therefore, of the law itself, has thus continued to survive in English procedure even up to the present time."

37. Dalton, *Countrey Justice* (1677 ed.), "to the reader."

38. Goodell, *American Slave Code*, 314; Stroud, *Sketch of the Laws*, 88; T. R. R. Cobb, *Law of Negro Slavery*, 268–69; State v. John, June 18, 1855, Anderson District Magistrate Freeholders' Trial Papers, SCDAH. "The testimony on the part of the state was heard none being offered by the defence. Also the argument of council for and against the prisoner when the case was committed to the Jury." John was acquitted.

39. Almost any case would do, but, as one example, see State v. Negro Ann, June 10, 1861, Anderson District Magistrate Freeholders' Trial Papers, SCDAH. "The court after mature deliberation" acquitted her. Actually the verdict was "not guily [*sic*]."

40. O'Neall, *Negro Law of South Carolina*, 35.

41. Stroud, *Sketch of the Laws*, 88–89.

42. Hurd, *Law of Freedom and Bondage*, 1:254; Maxcy, *Laws of Maryland*, 1:236–37. Also His Majesty v. Smiths Negro Man, September Court 1701, and His Majesty v. John and Lieutenant, November 1702, Prince Georges County Court Record, 1699–1705, 129–129a,

201–201a; Lord Proprietary v. Ben, November Court 1737, and Lord Proprietary v. Forrester et al., March 1738, Prince Georges County Court Record, 1735–38, 600–601, 661–62—all in MHR.

43. His Majesty v. Fortuno, August Court 1802, Prince Georges County Court Record, 1699–1705, 171a, MHR; *Maryland Archives*, 28:188–90, 155.

44. *Maryland Archives*, 303.

45. Cushing, *First Laws of . . . Delaware*, 3:943; Haywood, *Manual of the Laws of North Carolina*, 143; *Revised Statutes of . . . North Carolina*, 582–83; Howell Cobb, *Compilation of the . . . Statutes of . . . Georgia*, 607, 634; Hutchinson, *Code of Mississippi, 1848*, 522; *Revised Code of . . . Mississippi, 1824*, 382; Aikin, *Digest of the Laws of . . . Alabama*, 124–25; Ormond, Bagley, and Goldthwaite, *Code of Alabama*, 595; Stanton, *Revised Statutes of Kentucky*, 2:377.

46. *Revised Statutes of . . . North Carolina*, 1:582: "entitled to a trial by a jury of good and lawful men, owners of slaves." Other statutes usually referred to a "jury trial," without any qualifications. Those jurisdictions that used "freeholders" expressly should probably be placed alongside North Carolina.

47. *Session Laws of Tennessee, 1825*, 21: the jury was to "consist of owners of slaves only," *1831*, 124, and *1835–1836*, 92; Aikin, *Digest of the Laws of . . . Alabama*, 125; Ormond, Bagley, and Goldthwaite, *Code of Alabama*, 596; State v. Henry, March 21, 1857, Chambers County Circuit Court Minutes, State Cases, vol. 9, 1856–70, 51–52, Chambers County Courthouse, Lafayette, Ala. A jury, "two thirds of whom were slave holders," found Henry guilty of assault with intent to kill a white. He was hanged.

48. Haywood, *Manual of the Laws of North Carolina*, 143; Thompson, *Manual and Digest of the Statute Law of . . . Florida*, 542; Hindus, *Prison and Plantation*, 155.

49. State v. Green, September 1849, Spartanburg District Magistrate Freeholders' Trial Papers, SCDAH; Trial of Prince, September 18, 1767, Fauquier County Minute Book, 1764–68, 311–12; Commonwealth v. Sam, June 25, 1831, Lunenburg County Minute Book, 1828–32; and Commonwealth v. Charles, April 29, 1782, Sussex County Order Book, 1754–1807—all in VSL.

50. Goodell, *American Slave Code*, 314; Younger, "Southern Grand Juries and Slavery"; Flanigan, "Criminal Procedure in Slave Trials" and "Criminal Law of Slavery and Freedom." See, e.g., Texas v. Washington, January 1849, Harrison County Civil Minutes District Court, vol. C (1848–50), 170, Harrison County Courthouse, Marshall, Tex.; State v. Tom, December 14–15, 1854, Union County (Ark.) Circuit Court Records, Books F–G, 1854, 1867, 50–52; State v. Mose, November 1859, Crittenden County Circuit Court Records, Books D–E (1853–69), 570–71, 580–81, AHC; State v. John, July 19, 1839, Saline County Circuit Court Record D, 1856–60, Marshall, Mo.; State v. Ben, October 1827–April 1828, Leon County, Superior Court for the Middle District of Florida, 1824–33, vol 1:41, 46, 61, 66, 76; State v. Henry, November 20, 1843, Leon County Superior Court Minute Book, 1843–47, 95, Leon County Courthouse, Tallahassee, Fla.; State v. Anthony, September 23, 1849, Chambers County Circuit Court Minutes, vol. 5 (1844–49), 519, 524, Chambers County Courthouse, Lafayette, Ala.

51. State v. Burt, December 8, 1862, File Papers, Wilkinson County Circuit Court Cases, 1859–60 [the papers for Burt's 1862 case are in this file], Wilkinson County Courthouse, Woodville, Miss.; State v. Peter, November Term 1857, Adams County Circuit Court Minutes, 1856–61, 175–77, 183–87, Adams County Courthouse, Natchez, Miss.

52. Leroy D. Clark, *Grand Jury*; Frankel and Naftalis, *Grand Jury*; Younger, *People's Panel*; Gwenda Morgan, *Hegemony of the Law*; Blackstone, *Commentaries*, 4:301.

53. Jack P. Greene, *Diary of Landon Carter*, 2:676; *Statutes at Large of Virginia, 1792–1806*, 1:126.

54. Baker, "Criminal Courts and Procedure"; Bloomfield, *American Lawyers in a Changing Society*; *Revised Statutes of . . . North Carolina*, 1:582.

55. *Fanny, (a slave), v. State,* 6 Mo. 141 (1839).

56. Blackstone, *Commentaries,* 3:362, 4:346; Flanigan, "Criminal Law of Slavery and Freedom," 112; Stampp, *Peculiar Institution,* 226–27.

57. *State v. Negro George,* 2 Del. 88, 95 (1797); Lamar, *Laws of . . . Georgia,* 799; Haywood, *Manual of the Laws of North Carolina,* 146; *Session Laws of North Carolina, 1816,* 10.

58. *Revised Statutes of . . . North Carolina,* 1:582–83.

59. O'Neall, *Negro Law of South Carolina,* 33; State v. Edmund, December 8, 1862, Lunenburg County Minute Book, 1859–66, VSL.

60. See, e.g., *Revised Code of . . . Mississippi, 1824,* 383; Aikin, *Digest of the Laws of . . . Alabama,* 125; and U. B. Phillips, *Revised Statutes of Louisiana,* 58.

61. Texas v. Alfred, September 1857, Harrison County, Civil Minutes, District Court, vol. F, 1856, 480, Harrison County Courthouse, Marshall, Tex.; State v. Toll, December 19–23, 1853, Pulaski County Records, Indictment Records Books B–C, 1848–63, AHC; State v. Bob, June 19, 1856, Chatham County Superior Court Minutes, 1855–59, GDAH.

62. State v. Cooper, November Term 1856, May Term 1857, and State v. Reuben, May 1858, Adams County Circuit Court Minutes, 1856–61, 67, 92, 119, 142, 269–70, Adams County Courthouse, Natchez, Miss. Reuben's case was part of a complex proceeding involving the trials of several slaves for the murder of an overseer. There is excellent coverage of it in Wayne, "An Old South Morality Play."

63. Smedes, *Memorials of a Southern Planter,* 9.

64. State v. John, June 18, 1853, Wilkinson County Circuit Court Minute Book, 13:1851–56, 173, 184, 188, Wilkinson County Courthouse, Woodville, Miss. He was acquitted of grand larceny.

65. McLaurin, *Celia,* 88–94; State v. Scip, File Papers, Box 2200–2498 (1860–63), Case 2211 Lowndes County Department of Archives and History, Lowndes County Courthouse, Columbia, Miss.; State v. Peter, November Term 1857, Adams County Circuit Court Minutes, 1856–61, 175, 183–85, 204, 260, 280, 291–93, Adams County Courthouse, Natchez, Miss.

66. State v. Burt, File Papers, Wilkinson County Circuit Court Cases, 1859–60, Wilkinson County Courthouse, Woodville, Miss.

67. Blackstone, *Commentaries,* 4:368.

68. I have no explanation for this odd pattern. The fact that the majority were after 1840, however, does suggest a growing concern with procedural formalism.

69. State v. Bill, 1843, Adams County Minute Book, 523, 577, Adams County Courthouse, Natchez, Miss.

70. *Corpus Juris,* 19:1117–19; *Revised Code of . . . Mississippi, 1824,* 383. See, e.g., State v. Mary, File Papers, Box 2000–2199, 1861, Case 2134, and State v. Charles, File Papers, Box 507–650, 1847–50, Case 527, Lowndes County Department of Archives and History, Lowndes County Courthouse, Columbia, Miss.

71. Tushnet, *American Law of Slavery,* 121–22; *Isham v. State,* 1 Sneed 115 (Tenn., 1853).

72. Dalzell, *Benefit of Clergy.*

73. See, e.g., State v. Primus, April 28, 1830, Northampton County Superior Court Minute Docket, 1818–34, 354–55, NCDAH.

74. Dalzell, *Benefit of Clergy,* 249. Speaking in favor of institutionalization of deviants through the construction of a prison and for the abolition of clergy, Major George Keith Taylor put the matter as follows: "This benefit of clergy is the application in open court of a hot iron for the space of about one second to the brawn of the criminal's thumb. The pain of the burn may perhaps continue for five minutes and the hand may be sore for three days or a week afterwards. There is no intermediate punishment between this and the halter. The one is as absurd as the other is shocking." Ibid.

75. See, e.g., State v. Dennis, August 11, 1815, Fauquier County Minute Book, 1815–16 (found guilty of the manslaughter of a slave, he was given thirty-nine lashes and was burned

on the hand); State v. Moses, April 6, 1808, Orange County Order Book (Minutes), 1806–11 (found "guilty of a clergiable offence," he was burned on the hand and given twenty-five lashes)—all in VSL.

76. Dalzell, *Benefit of Clergy*, 261.

77. Ibid., 99. It was not clear that clergy applied in the trials of slaves, however, until the mid-eighteenth century (p. 105). See also William K. Boyd, "Documents and Comments on Benefit of Clergy as Applied to Slaves," and Jeffrey K. Sawyer, "'Benefit of Clergy' in Maryland and Virginia."

78. Dalzell, *Benefit of Clergy*, 259–60.

79. An example was clergy granted in the Trial of Sambo, September 17, 1764, Orange County Order Book No. 7, 1763–69, VSL.

80. See, e.g., State v. Cesar, April 1837, New Hanover County Superior Court Minutes, 1835–42, and State v. Isham, April 29, 1830, Northampton County Superior Court Minute Docket, 1818–34, 356, NCDAH.

81. U. B. Phillips, *Revised Statutes of Louisiana*, 57; Schafer, "The Long Arm of the Law," 1250.

82. *Elvira, (a slave)*, 16 Grattan 570–71 (Va., 1865).

83. O'Neall, *Negro Law of South Carolina*, 34.

84. State v. Thornton, December 1860, Anderson District Magistrate Freeholders' Trial Papers, SCDAH. An earlier case, in December 1858, involved the same offence. State v. Thornton, George, Pete, and Phil.

85. State v. Hamp, February 1857, Spartanburg District Magistrate Freeholders' Trial Papers, SCDAH.

86. State v. Willis, November 1863, Anderson District Magistrate Freeholders' Trial Papers, SCDAH. See also State v. Mattison, April 1852, ibid.

87. Probably the strongest statements of this view are those of A. K. Keir Nash. See, e.g., his "Fairness and Formalism in the Trials of Blacks" and "The Texas Supreme Court and the Trial Rights of Blacks." There is even evidence of such solicitude in early cases. Allain and St. Martin, "Notes and Documents: A Slave Trial in Colonial Natchitoches."

88. Baker, "Criminal Courts and Procedure," 44.

89. *Maryland Archives*, 32:155, 399.

90. Ibid., 270–71.

CHAPTER 10

1. Goodell, *American Slave Code*, 309; *State v. Maner*, 2 Hill 453 (S.C., 1834); Goveia, *West Indian Slave Laws*, 33 (Ottley).

2. See, e.g., the law of Jamaica of 1826 entitled "An Act to Regulate the Admission of the Evidence of Slaves" in *British Parliamentary Papers: Slave Trade*, 73:39–40.

3. Cushing, *Laws of the Province of Maryland*, 199. This law was not repealed until 1847. *Session Laws*, chap. 27: "an act relating to the law of Evidence."

4. *Revised Statutes of . . . North Carolina*, 1:583; *Revised Code of . . . Mississippi, 1824*, 373.

5. Stroud (*Sketch of the Laws*, 44) noted that it was "the cause of the greatest evils of slavery." Goodell (*American Slave Code*, 303) observed that "a community or a Government that could tolerate such rejection of testimony—the testimony of the defenseless against those holding and daily exercising despotic power over them—must be resolutely bent on oppressing instead of protecting them."

6. *Mississippi Free Trader*, February 24, 1843; Hammond, "Letter to an English Abolitionist," 190. On the capital trials of slaves see, e.g., Hindus, *Prison and Plantation*, and Schwarz, *Twice Condemned*.

7. Thayer, *Preliminary Treatise on Evidence*, 180; Langbein, "Criminal Trial before the Lawyers," 306.

8. Barnes, *Book of the General Laws and Libertyes*, 54; Holdsworth, *History of English Law*, 9:189.

9. Even though the depth of religious belief might have been shallower in the colonial South before the Great Awakening than it was in New England, it was pervasive. One illustration comes from the daily entries William Byrd made in his diary. See Woodfin and Tinling, *Another Secret Diary*. Although there is no evidence that Southerners went so far in their condemnation of witchcraft as did New Englanders, they were concerned about it. On New England witchcraft one of the finest studies is Demos, *Entertaining Satan*. As as example from the South, consider the charge to the county officers in Prince Georges County, Md., in March 1735 to uncover "all manner of felonies Witchcrafts Enchantments Sorceries Arts Magick Trespassess." Prince Georges County Court Record, March 1735–March 1738, MHR. On the Great Awakening in the South see Gewehr, *Great Awakening in Virginia*, and Gallay, "Origins of Slaveholders' Paternalism."

10. Holdsworth, *History of English Law*, 9:189–90; Greenleaf, *A Treatise on the Law of Evidence*, 1:377; Deuteronomy 17:6—"At the mouth of two witnesses, or three witnesses, shall he that is worthy of death be put to death; but at the mouth of one witness he shall not be put to death."

11. Holdsworth, *History of English Law*, 9:190–92.

12. Ibid., 191–92; T. R. R. Cobb, *Law of Negro Slavery*, 227–29 ("the term 'law,' according to the common law, is defined to be a 'freeman's privilege of being sworn in Court as a juror or witness'"); Cushing, *Laws of the Province of Maryland*, 200. All jurisdictions, at one time or another, provided some compensation to the owners of slaves executed by law. See the pathbreaking article by Kay and Cary, "'The Planters Suffer Little or Nothing.'"

13. Hening, *Statutes at Large*, 3:298.

14. Hale, *Pleas of the Crown*, 262, 264. This was an outline of the larger study by Hale that was published posthumously in 1736.

15. Hening, *Statutes at Large*, 3:103; Hawkins, *Treatise of the Pleas of the Crown*, 2:434.

16. Hening, *Statutes at Large*, 3:103. See, e.g., Jordan, *White Over Black*, and Michael Anesko, "So Discreet a Zeal."

17. Godwyn, *Negro's & Indians Advocate*, 36; Hening, *Statutes at Large*, 3:298.

18. Jack P. Greene, *Diary of Landon Carter*, 2:1107 (in 1766 Carter had made the point more succinctly: "A negroe can't be honest" [1:301]); T. R. R. Cobb, *Law of Negro Slavery*, 233. There is an extensive scholarly literature. One might begin with Genovese, *Roll, Jordan, Roll*, and Fredrickson, *Black Image in the White Mind*.

19. Hening, *Statutes at Large*, 4:126.

20. Aptheker, *American Negro Slave Revolts*, 177–78 (Gooch); Hening, *Statutes at Large*, 4:127 (second quotation); Blackstone, *Commentaries*, 4:350–51.

21. Coke, *Third Part of the Institutes*, 164; Hening, *Statutes at Large*, 4:128; Hoffer and Scott, *Criminal Proceedings in Colonial Virginia*, 120; Trial of Davie, Robin, Daniel, and Moll, May 25, 1752, Trial of Dick and Tom, January 17, 1754, and Trial of Sambo, March 19, 1756/7, Lancaster County Order Book No. 10, 1752–56, VSL.

22. Dalton, *Countrey Justice*; Hale, *History of the Pleas of the Crown*; Hawkins, *Treatise of the Pleas of the Crown*; Baker, "Criminal Courts and Procedure," 19. Shapiro's *Beyond Reasonable Doubt and Probable Cause* is a superb study of the epistemological concern of the probabilities associated with human knowledge, and how philosophical notions in England were intertwined with and supported legal solutions to the problem of knowing something at the various stages of the criminal trial process.

23. Hale, *History of the Pleas of the Crown*, 2:288–89.

24. Blackstone, *Commentaries*, 3:371, 4:350.

25. Cushing, *Earliest Printed Laws of Delaware*, 65; Maxcy, *Laws of Maryland*, 1:191.

26. Cushing, *Laws of the Province of Maryland*, 2. This penalty followed the common law. See Blackstone, *Commentaries*, 4:137. Nailing the ears of free persons was an alternative only if they were unable to pay their fine. In this sense the perjury punishment for slaves in Virginia was similar to that of the common law, except that in Virginia the ears were cut off and there was a whipping instead of a fine, which, of course, slaves could not pay in any event.

27. Maxcy, *Laws of Maryland*, 1:237; Cushing, *Earliest Printed Laws of North Carolina*, 171–72. The exact language of the North Carolina law was that the court was "to take for Evidence, the Confession of the Offender, the Oath of one or more credible Witnesses, or such Testimony of Negroes, Mulattoes, of *Indians*, bond or free, with pregnant Circumstances, as to them shall seem convincing, without the Solemnity of a Jury." The penalty for perjury was the same as in Virginia, but this 1741 code did not require the justice to charge the slave the same way as in Virginia. In North Carolina the "first Person in Commission" who sat on the trial of the slave was to charge any black or Indian, "not being a Christian . . . to declare the truth."

28. Sirmans, "Legal Status of the Slave in South Carolina," 462–73; Thomas Cooper and McCord, *Statutes at Large of South Carolina*, 7:345 (first quotation); Goveia, *West Indian Slave Laws*, 34; T. R. R. Cobb, *Law of Negro Slavery*, 229: "By the Code Noir, the evidence of slaves was excluded in all cases in the French Colonies, whether for or against freemen or slaves. The Judges were allowed to hear their evidence, as suggestions to illustrate other testimony, but they were prohibited from drawing thence, '*aucune presomption, ni conjecture, ni adminicule de preuve*.' The same rule obtained in the British West Indies, and it is a little remarkable that the commissioners appointed to inquire into their condition, with a view to meliorating the *status* of the slave, hesitated to recommend a different rule, except in criminal cases."

29. Thomas Cooper and McCord, *Statutes at Large of South Carolina*, 7:355.

30. Ibid., 356–57, 389, 401. Georgia patterned its 1770 slave code after this 1740 statute of South Carolina. Betty Wood, *Slavery in Colonial Georgia*. See especially " 'The Better Ordering and Governing of Negroes,' " chap. 7.

31. O'Neall, *Negro Law of South Carolina*, 14. His general attitude toward the mode in which slaves were tried was summed up in his remark that it was the "worst system which could be devised" (p. 35). See also A. E. Keir Nash, "Negro Rights, Unionism, and Greatness on the South Carolina Court of Appeals."

32. See, for instance, the Virginia law of 1819 that codified the slave law of the state. *Revised Code of . . . Virginia, 1819*, 1:422, 431. Virginia's law could be misleading to the unwary. Two sections in the 1819 code were relevant: 5 and 44. Section 5, based on a law adopted in 1785, provided: "Any negro or mulatto, bond or free, shall be a good witness in pleas of the commonwealth for or against negroes or mulattoes, bond or free, or in civil pleas where free negroes or mulattoes shall alone be parties, and in no other cases whatever." Section 44 concerned "legal evidence" and provided that "the court may take for evidence the confession of the offender, the oath of one or more credible witnesses, or such testimony of negroes or mulattoes, bond or free, with pregnant circumstances, as to them shall seem convincing." The South Carolina rule is discussed in O'Neall, *Negro Law of South Carolina*, 14.

33. Maxcy, *Laws of Maryland*, 3:389; Lamar, *Laws of . . . Georgia*, 805.

34. *State v. Ben, (a slave)*, 8 N.C. 231 (1821); Flanigan, "Criminal law of Slavery and Freedom," 124–25. Flanigan considered this case "a classic of the law of slavery" because it "illustrated the Orwellian world the slave endured even when he approached equality with whites."

35. Goodell (*American Slave Code*, 315) merely followed Stroud's earlier statement (*Sketch of the Laws*, 93).

36. A very early example of this practice was the grant of freedom to Will in 1710. The burgesses took this action because he was "signally serviceable in discovering a conspiracy of diverse negros" in Surry County who were intent on "levying war in this colony." Will got his freedom for his "fidelity and for encouragement of such services." Hening, *Statutes at Large*, 3:537. One frustrating aspect of this case is that, according to the lieutenant governor, the "chief conspirators" were "tryed this General Court, found guilty, and will be executed." The records of the general court have not survived so that it is impossible to know what evidence was used to convict the two "chief conspirators." Given the existing rules of evidence, it is doubtful that Will's testimony would do. It is more likely that confessions were extorted from the slaves. Aptheker, *Negro Slave Revolts*, 170–71.

37. Quoted in Webber, *Deep Like the Rivers*, 63–64.

38. *State v. Ben, (a slave)*, 8 N.C. 233 (1821). One scholar who tends to view slave crime in a political sense is Schwarz. In a very useful article, for instance, he referred to a hog-stealing case as one where slaves "consciously challenged the system of slave control." Schwarz, "Gabriel's Challenge," 284. See also Schwarz, "Forging the Schackles," 125–46. For a critical review of this position see Finkelman, "Prosecutions in Defense of the Cornerstone," 397, 403.

39. *State v. Ben, (a slave)*, 8 N.C. 234 (1821). This provision on pregnant circumstances remained part of the law of North Carolina. See Moore and Biggs, *Revised Code of North Carolina, 1855*, 572.

40. *State v. Ben, (a slave)*, 8 N.C. 237 (1821).

41. The rule is in the Tennessee law of 1815 on the trial of slaves (*Session Laws of Tennessee, 1815*, 175), but by 1857 the state's code read simply that "the trial of a slave for a capital offence shall be conducted in the same manner as that of a free person." Meigs and Cooper, *Code of Tennessee*, 510. Mississippi, in its massive 1822 code, followed the Virginia pattern of 1819. Section 21 provided that blacks could testify, and section 58 considered "legal evidence" in terms of the testimony of blacks, slave or free, along with a pregnant circumstances requirement. *Revised Code of . . . Mississippi, 1824*, 373, 382. By 1857 the pregnant circumstances requirement had disappeared. *Revised Code of . . . Mississippi, 1857*, 249. The 1798 law of Kentucky that required the corroboration was patterned after the Virginia law. Morehead and Brown, *Digest of the Statute Laws of Kentucky*, 2:1475. By the 1850s slaves were to be tried "in the same mode and manner as free persons are tried." Stanton, *Revised Statutes of Kentucky*, 2:377. Alabama followed the pregnant circumstances rule as late as 1836. Aikin, *Digest of the Laws of . . . Alabama*, 123. By 1852 the state provided that, in general, the trials of slaves were to be "in the mode provided by law for the trial of white persons." Ormond, Bagley, and Goldthwaite, *Code of Alabama*, 595.

42. Howell Cobb, *Compilation of the . . . Statutes of . . . Georgia*, 610–11; U. B. Phillips, *Revised Statutes of Louisiana*, 58.

43. An example of the thirty-nine lashes approach is in Stanton, *Revised Statutes of Kentucky*, 377, and Ormond, Bagley, and Goldthwaite, *Code of Alabama*, 594. Mississippi continued to provide for the mutilation of slaves by cutting off ears. *Revised Code of . . . Mississippi, 1857*, 249.

44. Betty Wood, " 'Until He Shall Be Dead, Dead, Dead,' " 391–92; Edwards, "Slave Justice in Four Middle Georgia Counties"; Shingleton, "Trial and Punishment of Slaves in Baldwin County"; Hoffer and Scott, *Criminal Proceedings in Colonial Virginia*, 88–89. See also Lord Proprietary v. Kate, June Court, 1755, Talbot County Court Criminal Judgments, 1751–55, MHR.

45. Trial of Guy, March 25, 1746, and Trial of Sarah, September 6, 1750, Lancaster County Orders No. 9, 1743–52, VSL; Jack P. Greene, *Diary of Landon Carter*, 1:370–71, 415.

46. Trial of Ben and Dedan, September 11, 1741, Charles City County Order Book, 1737–51, VSL. See also Trial of Ned and Bob, January 26, 1762, Charles City County Court Orders,

1758–62, and Trial of Davie, Robin, Daniel, and Moll, May 25, 1752, Lancaster County Orders No. 10, 1752–56, VSL.

47. Trial of George et al., January 27, 1849, Fairfield District Magistrate Freeholders' Trial Papers, SCDAH. See also Trial of Martin and Dave, February 26, 1857, Spartanburg District Magistrates Freeholders Trial Papers, SCDAH. This case involved the accidental killing of a slave in a fight that erupted over a card game. Another example would be the case of Balaam, May 7, 1856, Anderson District Magistrate Freeholders' Trial Papers, SCDAH. Balaam was charged with breaking into the dwelling of Wade Dennis, a free black. The slave Brad testified that Balaam had claimed that he had "Dennis's papers." He told him that he later burned them. The slave Dover testified that Dennis had offered him $10 to find out who burned his fodder stack and robbed him. He said that Balaam "told him that he burn^d Wade Dennis' fodder." In this trial, however, a number of whites provided Balaam with an alibi, and he was acquitted. Slaves, of course, did not usually turn to the public courts. An example of a different approach occurred on the Dabney plantation in Mississippi where a number of slaves succeeded in having their owner sell a slave woman who had been a frequent thief in the quarters. Smedes, *Memorials of a Southern Planter*, 90. Genovese (*Roll, Jordan, Roll*, 606–7) noted that although we can never really know how often slaves stole from one another, it was a problem on some plantations.

48. Records of the trials in New York and Charleston appear in Horsmanden, *New York Conspiracy*, and Kennedy and Parker, *Official Report of the Trials of Sundry Negroes*.

49. Dew, "Black Ironworkers and the Slave Insurrection Panic of 1856," 329.

50. Porteous, "Official Investigation," 6–22.

51. In addition to the works cited in n. 48 above, see Peter H. Wood, *Black Majority*; Tragle, *Southampton Slave Revolt*; Oates, *Fires of Jubilee*; and Trial of Jerry et al., October 2–11, 1860, Spartanburg District Magistrates Freeholders' Trial Papers, SCDAH.

52. This is a firm impression based on reading the lower court records, as lean as they often are, for over fifty counties in all of the slave states.

53. Greenleaf, *Treatise on the Law of Evidence*, 1:250.

54. Hoffer and Scott (*Criminal Proceedings in Colonial Virginia*, xxxi), for instance, note that defendants in Richmond County were often quite submissive. They even declined to demand a jury trial when entitled to one. A similar observation in New York led Goebel and Naughton (*Law Enforcement in Colonial New York*, 78) to suggest that upper-class judges rarely confronted lower-class suspects in misdemeanor cases who demanded trials.

55. The eleven Virginia counties I examined were Caroline, Charles City, Essex, Fauquier, King George, Lancaster, Orange, Princess Anne, Richmond, Southampton, and Sussex. The periods covered ranged from ten to fifty years. Of the fifteen confession cases, only five involved capital sentences: four were burglaries and one was a murder. One of the slaves convicted of burglary received the benefit of clergy. The murder case is discussed in the text below. Trial of Wapping, May 30, 1722, Lancaster County Orders No. 7, 1721–29, VSL. All of the burglary cases were in Richmond County. Trial of Harry, July 1738 (he received the benefit of clergy), Trial of Dick, September 1749, Trial of Newman and Sam, September 1749, and Trial of Daniel, November 1753, in Hoffer and Scott, *Criminal Proceedings in Colonial Virginia*, xlix–l, 187, 240–42, 244–46. Newman and Sam "confessed that they were in some part guilty of the said felony and burglary but not of the Whole." They put themselves on the court for trial, were found guilty, and were sentenced to death (p. 242). Aside from the murder, the only other case of violence occurred when Harry stabbed another slave in 1730 (p. 123). This trial was also discussed in the text. All of the remaining cases were property crimes. One involved receiving stolen goods. Trial of Sarah, September 6, 1750, Lancaster County Orders No. 9, 1743–52, VSL. This case was discussed in the text above. The remaining eight cases all were charges of hog stealing: Trial of Will, August 12, 1748, and Trial of Jones, March 19, 1748/9, Caroline County Order Book, 1746–54; Trial of Citto, June 4, 1752,

King George County Order Book, 1751–65; Trial of Aaron, September 24, 1767, Orange County Order Book 7, 1763–69; Trial of Ned, November 7, 1771, Princess Anne County Minute Book 9, 1770–73; Trial of Rippon, January Court 1742, and Trial of Harry and Jack, December Court 1746, Charles City County Order Book, 1737–51; and, finally, Trial of Dick, October 4, 1758, Charles City County Court Orders, 1758–62—all in VSL.

For the nineteenth century, for example, I found no confessions in Elbert County, Ga., between 1837 and 1849 (the years for which full records are extant), and but one in Chatham County, Ga., which included Savannah, between 1813 and 1827, and between 1850 and 1859. On February 11, 1857, William pled guilty to voluntary manslaughter. Chatham County Superior Court Minutes, 1855–59, GDAH. A final example might be the confession of Ned in Jessamine County, Ky., in 1842. He was the only slave I found in the county's records for the years 1800–49 who confessed. He had admitted to his master that he sold some goods that had been taken in a burglary and had left some at his wife's home. Papers filed in Ned's case in Box 8, 1840–42, Circuit Court Clerk, Circuit Court Indictments, Jessamine County, KSA.

56. Trial of Harry, February 1729/30, in Hoffer and Scott, *Criminal Proceedings in Colonial Virginia*, 123.

57. Trial of Wapping, May 30, 1722, Lancaster County Orders No. 7, 1721–29, VSL.

58. See, e.g., Hoffer and Scott, *Criminal Proceedings in Colonial Virginia*, l–li.

59. Among the fine studies that might be consulted are Genovese, *Roll, Jordan, Roll*; Levine, *Black Culture and Black Consciousness*; Gutman, *Black Family in Slavery and Freedom*; Blassingame, *Slave Community*; Joyner, *Down by the Riverside*; Creel, *"A Peculiar People"*; Stuckey, *Slave Culture*. I learned of but did not see Michael Kay and Lorin Lee Cary's new volume, *Slavery in North Carolina, 1748–1775* (then in process), just before this book went to press.

60. Webber, *Deep Like the Rivers*, chap. 10, 120–21. This might be compared to some of the examples discussed in Hoebel, *Law of Primitive Man*.

61. On church discipline see Mathews, *Religion in the Old South*, 146–48. One interesting case arose in the Salem Baptist Church in Marlborough County, S.C., in the 1850s. A master charged his slaves with theft of hams from the smokehouse. The charge was before the church, not the local magistrate. The slaves unsuccessfully tried to defend themselves with the argument that because they had contributed to the preparation of the hams by their labor, they had merely taken what was theirs.

62. One of the fullest accounts of the voluntariness problem in confessions is Tushnet, *American Law of Slavery*, 127–37.

63. Sheldon, "Black-White Relations in Richmond," 32; Trial of Ben, 1821, Southampton County Court Order Book, 1819–22, 341, VSL.

64. T. R. R. Cobb, *Law of Negro Slavery*, 272.

65. *State v. Charity, (a slave)*, 2 Devereux 543 (N.C., 1830).

66. *State v. Nelson et al.*, 3 La. Ann. 497 (1848).

67. *Wyatt, (a slave), v. State*, 25 Ala., 9, 15 (1854); *Simon, (a slave), v. State*, 5 Fla. 285 (1853).

68. *Sam, (a slave), v. State*, 33 Miss., 347 (1857).

69. *Alfred and Anthony, (slaves), v. State*, 2 Swan 581 (Tenn., 1853). One case that emptied this right of any significance was *Seaborn and Jim, (slaves), v. State*, 20 Ala. 15 (1852). Chilton remarked that the fact that the confessions "were made to the examining magistrate, who did not previously caution them, as he undoubtedly ought to have done, as to the effect of such admissions, would not justify the court in excluding them. We find no case excluding confessions for want of such caution."

70. *Rafe, (a slave), v. State*, 20 Ga. 68 (1856). See also *Mose, (a slave), v. State*, 36 Ala. 211 (1860). Mose had admitted to two separate men that he had murdered a white man. One condition that preceded the confessions had been that he had been handed over to the

members of a "vigilance committee," some of whom suggested that they collect a fund to pay for him and execute him themselves. On this aspect of the case Chief Justice A. J. Walker commented: "His confession seems to have been prompted by a sense of religious duty, awakened by the apprehension of a speedy execution at the hands of lawless violence, and were not the result of the slightest hope of temporal benefit on account of the confession." The confessions were held admissible.

71. *Dick, Aleck, and Henry, (slaves), v. State*, 30 Miss. 593 (1856); Rousseau, *Social Contract and Discourses*, 5: "Aristotle was right: but he took the effect for the cause. Nothing can be more certain than that every man born in slavery is born for slavery. Slaves lose everything in their chains, even the desire of escaping from them: they love their servitude, as the comrades of Ulysses loved their brutish condition. If then there are slaves by nature, it is because there have been slaves against nature. Force made the first slaves, and their cowardice perpetuated the condition."

72. *Dick, Aleck, and Henry, (slaves), v. State*, 30 Miss. 593 (1856). Two cases where confessions were thrown out because they were obtained by violence inflicted by third parties who were not magistrates were *Jordan, (a slave), v. State*, 32 Miss. 382 (1856) and *Simon, (a slave), v. State*, 37 Miss. 288 (1859). Both involved the killing of slaves rather than whites.

73. Goodell, *American Slave Code*, 305; *Ex parte Boylston*, 2 Strob. 41 (S.C., 1847).

74. Tushnet, *American Law of Slavery*, 127; *Stephen, (a slave), v. State*, 11 Ga. 235 (1852).

75. *Ex parte Boylston*, 2 Strob. 41 (S.C., 1847).

76. Flanigan, "Criminal Law of Slavery and Freedom." There has been superb work on the proslavery argument as well as some excellent collections. Tise (*Proslavery: A History of the Defense of Slavery in America*) grounds many of the significant proslavery arguments in the conservative political philosophy of New England federalism and the conservative theology of New England congregationalism. An excellent collection of primary materials is Faust, *Ideology of Slavery*.

77. The relevant statutory extensions can be followed conveniently in Hurd, *Law of Freedom and Bondage*, 2:2–200.

CHAPTER 11

1. Goodell, *American Slave Code*, 289–90.

2. Hay, "Property, Authority, and Criminal Law."

3. Myers, *Children of Pride*, 1:528, 532–34, 544–46 (Jones); Rosengarten, *Tombee*, 622, 712 (Chaplin).

4. *William and Mary Quarterly*, 1st ser. 1 (1897–99): 6–7:211; October Court 1693, Charles City County Orders, 1650, 1672–73, 1677–80, 1685, 1687–95, VSL.

5. These cases include Trial of Will, September 3, 1760, and Trial of Ned and Bob, January 26, 1762, Charles City County Court Orders, 1758–62; Trial of Ben, September 1741, Charles City County Order Book, 1737–51—all in VSL. See the analysis of the justices in Chapter 9. See also the excellent discussion in Mays, *Edmund Pendleton*, chap. 4, "The Gentlemen Justices of Caroline."

6. Roeber, "Authority, Law, and Custom." See also Roeber's larger study, *Faithful Magistrates and Republican Lawyers*.

7. Trial of Charles and Simon, February 4, 1771, Trial of Simon, August 3, 1772, and Trial of Charles, November 2, 1772, Richmond County Order Book 17, 1769–73, 218, VSL; Jack P. Greene, *Diary of Landon Carter*, 2:709.

8. Hoffer and Scott, *Criminal Proceedings in Colonial Virginia*, 236–38.

9. Jack P. Greene, *Diary of Landon Carter*, 1:396.

10. Beeman, *Evolution of the Southern Backcountry*; Isaac, *Transformation of Virginia*;

Commonwealth v. Emanuel, December 8, 1862, Lunenburg County Minute Book, 1859–66, VSL; Schlotterbeck, "Plantation and Farm"; Hughes, "Slaves for Hire."

11. *Jim, (a slave), v. State*, 15 Ga. 540 (1854).

12. *Lingo v. Miller & Hill*, 23 Ga. 187 (1857).

13. Ibid., 190.

14. *Statutes at Large of Virginia, 1792–1806*, 1:126; Haywood, *Manual of the Laws of North Carolina*, 2:143–44; Aikin, *Digest of the Laws of . . . Alabama*, 124; *Revised Code of . . . Mississippi, 1824*, 385, 391; *Session Laws of Tennessee, 1835–1836*, 92; *Digest of the Laws of Kentucky, 1834*, 2:1286; O'Neall, *Negro Law of South Carolina*, 34; Thompson, *Manual and Digest of the Statute Law of . . . Florida*, 542.

15. Commonwealth v. Allen, Reuben, and Jeff, July 13, 1795, Sussex County Order Book, 1789–95; Commonwealth v. Allen and Reuben, 1795, Auditor's Item 153, Box 1; and Commonwealth v. Fanny, May 22, 1824, Lunenburg County Minute Book, 1822–24—all in VSL.

16. *Manning v. Cordell*, 6 Mo. 474 (1840).

17. Hening, *Statutes at Large*, 3:461, 12:345; *Statutes at Large of Virginia, 1792–1806*, 2:279–80. The history of the transportation of slaves in capital cases is covered in Schwarz, "Transportation of Slaves from Virginia."

18. Cushing, *Earliest Printed Laws of North Carolina*, 172; Haywood, *Manual of the Laws of North Carolina*, 149. For the way this operated see Kay and Cary, " 'The Planters Suffer Little or Nothing.' "

19. An example of how it worked is Commonwealth v. Phillis, June 11, 1855, Lunenburg County Minute Book, 1853–58, VSL. Each member of the court valued Phillis (she was transported outside the United States after a conviction for arson), "as in his opinion the said slave would bring if sold publicly under a knowledge of the circumstances of her guilt."

20. Commonwealth v. Phillis, June 11, 1855, Lunenburg County Minute Book, 1853–58, VSL; Maxcy, *Laws of Maryland*, 1:237; Thomas Cooper and McCord, *Statutes at Large of South Carolina*, 7:358.

21. VerSteeg, *Origins of a Southern Mosaic*, chap. 4; Thomas Cooper and McCord, *Statutes at Large of South Carolina*, 7:366 (quotation), 369, 383, 403, 424; O'Neall, *Negro Law of South Carolina*, 45.

22. Aikin, *Digest of the Laws of . . . Alabama*, 124.

23. See, e.g., Oldham and White, *Digest of the . . . Laws of . . . Texas*, 409.

24. Haywood, *Manual of the Laws of North Carolina*, 2:149.

25. Ibid., 143; Aikin, *Digest of the Laws of . . . Alabama*, 124; Bullard and Curry, *New Digest of the Statute Laws of Louisiana*, 64.

26. Thomas Cooper and McCord, *Statutes at Large of South Carolina*, 7:403; *Revised Code of . . . Mississippi, 1824*, 250; Ormond, Bagley, and Goldthwaite, *Code of Alabama*, 596; Oldham and White, *Digest of the . . . Laws of . . . Texas*, 409; Haywood, *Manual of the Laws of North Carolina*, 2:149; U. B. Phillips, *Revised Statutes of Louisiana*, 57; Cushing, *First Laws of . . . Delaware*, 1:103.

27. Kay and Cary, " 'The Planters Suffer Little or Nothing.' "

28. Thomas Cooper and McCord, *Statutes at Large of South Carolina*, 7:369, 383; Aikin, *Digest of the Laws of . . . Alabama*, 124; Haywood, *Manual of the Laws of North Carolina*, 2:149; *Session Laws of Maryland, 1845*, chap. 340, "An act respecting the punishment of slaves"; U. B. Phillips, *Revised Statutes of Louisiana*, 57; Pierre Ozere to the State of Louisiana, March 25, 1839, St. Landry Parish, Conveyance Record, 1836–41, I-1, J-1, 309, St. Landry Parish Courthouse, Opelousas, La.

29. Hening, *Statutes at Large*, 3:270–76 (1705), 6:107 (1748); Blackstone, *Commentaries*, 3:370; *State v. Negro George*, 2 Del. 95 (1797).

30. *State v. Charity, (a slave)*, 13 N.C. 352–55 (1828–30).

31. Ibid., 355–57.

32. *Elijah, (a slave), v. State,* 1 Humphreys 104 (Tenn., 1839).

33. *Isham, (a slave), v. State,* 6 How. 42 (Miss., 1841); *State v. Jim, (a slave),* 48 N.C. 352 (1856).

34. See, e.g., Haywood, *Manual of the Laws of North Carolina,* 2:149.

35. *Grinder, (a slave), v. State,* 2 Tex., 339 (1847).

36. *State v. Carter Jones,* 2 Devereux 48 (N.C., 1828).

37. *Reed v. Circuit Court of Howard County,* 6 Mo. 44 (1839).

38. Dalton, *Countrey Justice,* 140, 169 (on "suretie for the good Behaviour"); Parker, *North Carolina Higher-Court Records, 1670–1696,* 353. At the same term of court Culpeper was nonsuited in an action on the case against Burnby, and Burnby was nonsuited in a "pleas of defamation" against Culpeper and his wife (Parker, pp. 354, 356). Obviously there was ill feeling between the two.

39. Lord Proprietary v. Forrester et al., March 1738, Prince Georges County Court Record, 1751–54, 612, MHR.

40. Trial of Sam, May 1773, Granville County, Criminal Actions concerning Slaves and Free Persons of Color, 1764–1819. See also State v. Jack Lord, Samuel Cutter, Abel Mason, Mingo Lazarus, Cesar Mason, Bill Quince, slaves, November 3, 1831, New Hanover County Superior Court Minutes, 1830–35, NCDAH.

41. Commonwealth v. John, March 6, 1852, Mercer County Circuit Court Case Files, KSA.

42. Blackstone, *Commentaries,* 4:355–56. The common law also allowed individuals to recover their property by their own means wherever they found it, without a writ of restitution. This was essentially the right of recaption that became so explosive in the recovery of fugitive slaves in the North. Thomas D. Morris, *Free Men All.*

43. Hening, *Statutes at Large,* 3:277; Trial of Rippon, January 1741, Charles City County Order Book, 1737–51, 201, VSL. See also Trial of Jones et al., March 10, 1748/49, Caroline County Order Book, 1746–54, 130, VSL.

44. *Jennings v. Kavanaugh,* 5 Mo. 27–28 (1837).

45. *Ewing v. Thompson,* 13 Mo. 137–39 (1850).

46. Upton and Jennings, *Civil Code of . . . Louisiana,* 28.

47. *Collingsworth v. Covington,* 2 La. Ann. 407 (1847).

CHAPTER 12

1. See, e.g., Malone, *Sweet Chariot;* McDonald, *Economy and Material Culture of Slaves;* and Gutman, *Black Family in Slavery and Freedom.*

2. Patterson, *Slavery and Social Death,* 13; Finley, *Ancient Slavery and Modern Ideology,* 77, 75; David Brion Davis, *Slavery and Human Progress,* 15; Oakes, *Slavery and Freedom,* 31; Buckland, *Roman Law of Slavery,* 3; Quarles, *Negro in the Civil War,* 323 (Frazier); Hobbes, *Leviathan,* in Burtt, *English Philosophers,* 194.

3. Genovese, *Roll, Jordan, Roll,* 88 (Hegel); Hobbes, *Leviathan,* in Burtt, *English Philosophers,* 195.

4. Almost any daily entry in Byrd's diary would do. A typical jotting was this for March 22, 1740: "after dinner we talked and had tea and then played cards again till 9. I talked with my people and prayed." Woodfin and Tinling, *Another Secret Diary,* 46.

5. Bradley, "My Station and Its Duties," in *Ethical Studies,* 98–147.

6. Quoted in Steinfeld, *Invention of Free Labor,* 16.

7. Philip D. Morgan, "Three Planters and Their Slaves," 40.

8. Harper, "Memoir on Slavery," 97–98.

9. Quoted in Elliott, *Cotton Is King,* 481, 483.

10. Charles Colcock Jones, *Religious Instruction of the Negroes,* 211.

11. Bellamy, *Law of Treason in England*, 1.

12. Dalton, *Countrey Justice*, 213; Hobbes, *Dialogue between a Philosopher and a Student of the Common Laws*, 104.

13. Chapin, *American Law of Treason*; Kettner, *Development of American Citizenship*, 174–83, 194–202.

14. Hawkins, *Treatise of the Pleas of the Crown*, 2:443–44.

15. Dalton, *Countrey Justice*, 213; Blackstone, *Commentaries*, 4:75; Hawkins, *Treatise of the Pleas of the Crown*, 2:443–44.

16. *State ex rel. M'Cready v. B. F. Hunt*, 2 Hill 492–93, 521 (S.C., 1834).

17. Coke, *Third Part of the Institutes*, 9–10, 176; Hawkins, *Treatise of the Pleas of the Crown*, 1:37.

18. Elkins, *Slavery*; McIlwaine, *Minutes of the Council*, 502.

19. Hening, *Statutes at Large*, 2:481–82.

20. Quoted in Jordan, *White Over Black*, 111.

21. Hening, *Statutes at Large*, 4:126.

22. Quoted in Aptheker, *Negro Slave Revolts*, 176–77.

23. Gaspar, *Bondmen & Rebels*; Peter H. Wood, *Black Majority*; Horsmanden, *New York Conspiracy*; *Maryland Archives*, 28:188–90; Philip D. Morgan and Terry, "Slavery in Microcosm"; Hening, *Statutes at Large*, 6:104–5 (quotations).

24. Maxcy, *Laws of Maryland*, 1:236; Sayre, "Criminal Conspiracy," 399; Bishop, *New Commentaries on the Criminal Law*, 1:363.

25. Thomas Cooper and McCord, *Statutes at Large of South Carolina*, 7:346; Loewald, Starika, and Taylor, "Bolzius Answers a Questionnaire," 234.

26. Thomas Cooper and McCord, *Statutes at Large of South Carolina*, 7:356, 352.

27. Ibid., 346, 356.

28. Kant, *Metaphysical Elements of Justice*, 102: "Even if civil society were to dissolve itself by common agreement . . . the last murderer remaining in prison must first be executed, so that everyone will duly receive what his actions are worth and so that the blood guilt thereof will not be fixed on the people because they failed to insist on carrying out the punishment; for if they fail to do so, they may be regarded as accomplices in this public violation of legal justice."

29. Hart, *Punishment and Responsibility*, 76, passim; *Furman v. Georgia*, 408 U.S. 310 (1972) (Stewart concurring).

30. Thomas Cooper and McCord, *Statutes at Large of South Carolina*, 7:389 and 7:402–3 (quotations); Peter H. Wood, *Black Majority* (Stono). For Stono see also Wax, " 'The Great Risque We Run.' "

31. Cushing, *Earliest Printed Laws of North Carolina*, 171.

32. McElwaine, *Executive Journals*, 3:234–35.

33. Ibid., 236, 242–43.

34. See Aptheker, *Negro Slave Revolts*; Okihiro, *In Resistance*; Philip D. Morgan and Terry, "Slavery in Microcosm"; Watson, "Impulse Toward Independence"; and Crow, "Slave Rebelliousness and Social Conflict."

35. Horsmanden, *New York Conspiracy*; Thomas J. Davis, *A Rumor of Revolt*.

36. Edgerton, *Gabriel's Rebellion*; Kennedy and Parker, *Official Report of the Trials of Sundry Negroes*.

37. Aptheker, *Negro Slave Revolts*; Philip D. Morgan and Terry, "Slavery in Microcosm."

38. *South Carolina Gazette*, July 30–August 15, 1741.

39. Gaspar, *Bondmen & Rebels*.

40. *South Carolina Gazette*, July 30–August 15, 1741.

41. *Revised Statutes of Kentucky, 1852*, 2:375; Meigs and Cooper, *Code of Tennessee*, 509; *Revised Code of . . . Mississippi, 1824*, 380; Thompson, *Manual and Digest of the Statute Law of . . . Florida*, 537.

42. Haywood, *Manual of the Laws of North Carolina*, 2:153 (quotations); Edgerton, *Gabriel's Rebellion*.

43. Oldham and White, *Digest of the . . . Laws of . . . Texas*, 539; Ormond, Bagley, and Goldthwaite, *Code of Alabama*, 594, 596; U. B. Phillips, *Revised Statutes of Louisiana*, 50–51.

44. William C. Jones, *Revised Statutes of . . . Missouri*, 342.

45. Howell Cobb, *Compilation of the . . . Statutes of . . . Georgia*, 610.

46. Mullin, *Flight and Rebellion*, 201 n. 34; Schwarz, "Gabriel's Challenge"; Edgerton, *Gabriel's Rebellion*, 92–93; Tragle, *Southampton Slave Revolt*, 177–228. The warrant for Nat Turner's execution is in Auditor's Item 153, Box 6, VSL.

47. Cf. Wade, "The Vesey Plot."

48. Kennedy and Parker, *Official Report of the Trials of Sundry Negroes*, vii, vi.

49. Ibid., 177–78, 180–81.

50. Rogers, *History of Georgetown County*, 236–37.

51. *Kinloch v. Harvey*, Harp. 508, 517 (S.C., 1830).

52. State v. Mattison and Stephen, May 19, 1852, Anderson District Magistrate Freeholders' Trial Papers, SCDAH.

53. State v. Aleck, Bris, Martin, April 12, 1862, ibid.; State v. Jerry, Anderson, Ellis, Andy, Sam, October 11, 1860, Spartanburg District Magistrates Freeholders' Trial Papers, SCDAH. See also State v. Simon, Levi, Sally, May 3, 1864, Spartanburg District Magistrates Freeholders' Trial Papers, SCDAH.

54. State v. Edmund and Lewis, July 2, 1841, Maury County Circuit Court Minutes, May 1840–January 1844, TSLA; State v. Robin and Shadrack, September 13, 1822, Chatham County Inferior Court Trial Docket, 1813–27, GDAH; Commonwealth v. Rayl, October 25, 1819, Fauquier County Minute Book, 1819–20, VSL. Aside from these cases discussed in the text, see State v. Milly et al., November 1, 1831, State v. Elijah, November 1, 1831, and State v. Morris Chase et al., Slaves, New Hanover County Superior Court Minutes, 1830–35, NCDAH (these cases were connected to the hysteria that swept the region in the wake of the Turner uprising); Commonwealth v. Robin, Free Black, and Commonwealth v. Solomon, Slave, December 21, 1812, Westmoreland County Order Book, 1812; and Commonwealth v. Charles, Gabriel, and Jesse, November 4, 1801, Petersburg City Hustings Court Minute Book, 1800–1804—all in VSL. Of the latter three slaves, indicted for "consulting & devising or conspiring a rebellion or insurrection," only Jesse was found guilty and that was for "seditious discourse." He was sentenced to thirty-nine lashes.

55. Commonwealth v. Dick, July 30, 1802, Southampton County Order Book, 1802–3, VSL.

56. William J. Minor Plantation Diary, September 23, 25, 1861, Minor Papers, Louisiana State University Archives, Baton Rouge. See also Moses Liddell to Major St. John R. Liddell, July 21, 1841, Liddell Papers, ibid. Although admitting that a lot of it was rumor, Moses Liddell wrote: "since you left we have information that a number of negroes in the neighborhood of the Barrow settlement and Bayou Sarah here have been detected in a conspiracy and rebellion—a number about Eighty have been taken & are or have been in Jail." Tryphena Holder Fox Collection, letter dated December 16, 1860 ("We do not consider ourselves in any danger from the negroes *alone*—A free negro is to be hung at the Court-house . . . for attempting to incite insurrection"), MDAH. In addition to works cited earlier on insurrections, see Addington, "Slave Insurrections in Texas"; McKibben, "Negro Slave Insurrections in Mississippi"; and Jordan, *Tumult and Silence at Second Creek*.

57. The full text, in a letter of 1736 to the Earl of Egmont, was this: "Numbers make them insolent, & then foul means must do, what fair will not. We have however nothing like the inhumanity here that is practiced in the islands, & God forbid we ever shoud [*sic*]. But these base tempers require to be rid with a tort rein. Yet even this is terrible to a good naturd man, who must submit to be either a fool or a fury," Tinling, *Correspondence of the Byrds*, 2:488.

58. Maxcy, *Laws of Maryland*, 1:190.

59. Parker, *North Carolina Higher-Court Records, 1670–1696*, 378.

60. *Virginia Gazette*, September 6, 1770. The slaves went to their master's bedroom "and with an handkerchief attempted to strangle him, which they thought they had effected, but in a little time after they had left him, he recovered, and began to stir, on hearing which they went up again, and told him he must die, and that before they left the room; he begged very earnestly for his life, but one of them, his house wench, told him it was in vain, that as he had no mercy on them, he could expect none himself, and immediately threw him between two feather beds, and all got on him till he was stifled to death."

61. Sentence of Sanders, October 21, 1773, Granville County, N.C., Criminal Actions concerning Slaves and Free Persons of Color, 1764–1819, NCDAH; *South Carolina Gazette*, August 15–18, 1733. See also Loewald, Starika, and Taylor, "Bolzius Answers a Questionnaire," 234.

62. *Virginia Gazette*, February 4, 1736.

63. Hoffer and Scott, *Criminal Proceedings*, 133–34.

64. *Maryland Gazette*, April 30, May 14, 1761, June 14, 1745, January 30, 1751; June Court 1770, Prince Georges County Court Record, 1768–70, MHR; *Archives of Maryland*, 28:257, 31:69, 32:370.

65. Julian Boyd, Cullen, and Cantanzariti, *Papers of Thomas Jefferson*, 2:325, 494–95. A bill providing for dissection was presented in 1779 by a committee on revision of the laws of Virginia. It also provided that in cases of petit treason and murder, one-half of the lands and goods of the killer would go to the kin of the victim and the rest to the representatives of the defendant. This, of course, was not relevant in the case of slave killers. On the revision in general see Preyer, "Crime, the Criminal Law, and Reform in Post-Revolutionary Virginia."

66. Cushing, *First Laws of . . . Delaware*, 2:905–6.

67. Kilty, Harris, and Watkins, *Laws of Maryland*, 4:chap. 138, sec. 3; Gould, *Digest of the Statutes of Arkansas*, 328; Beccaria, *On Crimes and Punishments*; Foucault, *Discipline and Punish* (on the transformation in punishment from brutal torture of the body to efforts to control and modify the soul). See also Grand Jury Presentment, June 1801, Chatham County Superior Court Minutes, 1799–1808, GDAH.

68. Commonwealth v. Nelson, February 26, 1795, King George County Order Book 5B, 1792–1801, VSL.

69. The *Richmond Enquirer* (February 17, 1820) contains the account of the Edgefield case—the story was datelined Augusta, Ga.

70. Tushnet (*American Law of Slavery*) argues more forcefully than most that Southern lawmakers and judges tried to create an autonomous law of slavery.

71. Philosophies of ethics are legion. I claim no sophisticated grasp. Nonetheless, in the Anglo-American world it is reasonably clear that a strong current of philosophical thought views duty and obedience in moral terms. A good place to begin is Raphael, *British Moralists*. To take but one example, Richard Price, in *A Review of the Principal Questions and Difficulties in Morals* (1758), wrote: "*Obligation* to action and *rightness* of action, are plainly coincident and identical. . . . This may appear to anyone upon considering, whether he can point out any difference between what is *right, meet* or *fit* to be done, and what *ought* to be done" (2:161).

72. Steinfeld, *Invention of Free Labor*.

73. *State v. Mann*, 13 N.C. 169 (1829).

74. *State v. Tom, (a slave)*, 2 Devereux 569 (N.C., 1830).

75. On Lumpkin see Stephenson and Stephenson, " 'To Protect and Defend.' " The authors, however, do not emphasize the religious element in Lumpkin's opinions. A good example of that is *Moran v. Davis*, 18 Ga. 722–24 (1855). The case involved the liability when "negro" dogs ripped a slave savagely. Lumpkin spent half of his brief opinion quoting

biblical text to affirm the timelessness and divine origin of slavery. The American Bible Society even asked his "views as to the wholesome influence of that sacred Book, particularly in its bearings on civil and social life." J. C. Brigham to Joseph Henry Lumpkin, October 20, 1852, Lumpkin Papers, University of Georgia, Athens.

76. *Chamberline v. Harvey*, 3 Ld. Raym. 129 (1696/7); Wiecek, "*Somerset,*" 91; *Jim, (a slave), v. State*, 15 Ga. 540 (1854), involving the killing of an overseer; Genovese, *Roll, Jordan, Roll*, 91.

77. *State v. Will, (a slave)*, 18 N.C. 131 (1834).

78. Ibid. There is some confusion about the decision in this case. Stampp (*Peculiar Institution*, 220–21) implied that Will was freed; Genovese (*Roll, Jordan, Roll*, 36) suggested that Will had entered a plea of innocent by reason of self-defense and that the court "overturned Will's conviction and sustained the plea." The per curiam decision was this: "Judgment upon the special verdict, that the prisoner is *not* guilty of the *murder*, wherewith he stands charged, but is guilty of the *felonious slaying and killing Richard Baxter.*" *State v. Will, (a slave)*, 18 N.C. 179 (1834). Regardless, after the case was remanded Will's owner sold him out of the state, and he was later found guilty of killing a black in Mississippi and hanged. Genovese, *Roll, Jordan, Roll*, 36.

79. *State v. Will, (a slave)*, 18 N.C. 154 (1834).

80. Ibid., 170.

81. Ibid., 179.

82. *Jacob, (a slave), v. State*, 3 Humphreys 507, 509 (Tenn., 1842). There is an interesting set of letters involving Nathan Green in the *Advertiser and State Gazette* (Montgomery, Ala.), July–December 1858. Green had been giving lectures at a law school in Lebanon, Tenn., and William L. Yancey, a leading advocate of secession, charged that he was unfit because of his views on slavery. Green defended himself in the papers and the exchange began. He admitted having written a letter to the American Tract Society in which he had said that "I have not intended to defend the institution of slavery. I have long considered it an evil—an evil . . . morally, socially, and politically." Down to Calhoun's time all Southerners took that position, according to Green. He did not share Calhoun's view of slavery as a positive good. Slavery was an evil, but, he claimed, it was "a greater evil to the master than to the slave." Moreover, Green did not assert that "in the *relation of master and slave*, there is any thing wrong." He concluded by noting that he himself had owned slaves for fifty years. Green to *Advertiser and State Gazette*, July 14, 1858.

83. *Jim, (a slave), v. State*, 15 Ga. 543–44 (1854).

84. *Wesley, (a slave), v. State*, 37 Miss., 347 (1859).

85. *Res gestae* is an exception to the hearsay rule. It allows for the admission into evidence of acts and statements that were part of the thing done. *Black's Law Dictionary*, 1469.

86. *Wesley, (a slave), v. State*, 37 Miss., 1348 (1859).

87. Commonwealth v. Elliott or Ellick, February 9, 1818, Caroline County Minute Book, 1815–19, VSL.

88. Commonwealth v. Davy et al., March 19–21, 1827, Lunenburg County Minute Book, 1824–28, VSL; Schwarz, *Twice Condemned*, 245, 262. An excellent history of Lunenburg County is that of Beeman, *Evolution of the Southern Backcountry*.

89. Commonwealth v. Davy et al., March 19–21, 1827, Lunenburg County Minute Book, 1824–28, VSL.

90. Wayne, "An Old South Morality Play"; Jordan, *Tumult and Silence at Second Creek*. See State v. Reuben, Anderson, and Henderson and State v. Reuben (not the same man as in the first case), John, and Tom, Adams County Circuit Court Minutes, May 1856–May 1861, 175–76, 198–201, 211–12, 215–16, Adams County Courthouse, Natchez, Miss. Reuben from the second case appealed. This can be followed on these pages of the circuit court minutes: 217, 259, 269–71, 281, 285, 351, 375–77, 380.

91. Alexander Farrar to H. W. Drake, September 4 and 5, 1857, Farrar Papers, Louisiana State University Archives, Baton Rouge; Jordan, *Tumult and Silence at Second Creek.*

92. This account of the case is drawn from references to the appellate record in n. 90.

93. T. R. R. Cobb, *Law of Negro Slavery*, 275.

94. Hening, *Statutes at Large*, 3:460–61.

95. Petition of Robert Carter in the case of Bambara Harry and Dinah, March 19, 1707, Lancaster County Orders No. 5, 1702–13, and Petition of Robert Carter in the case of M. Jack, September 12, 1722, Lancaster County Orders No. 7, 1721–29, VSL.

96. April 2, 1730, Lancaster County Order Book, 1729–43. William Edwards and Thomas Crowdsor deposed that they killed Mingo, who was outlawed, July 8, 1766. Fauquier County Minute Book, 1764–68, VSL.

97. Jack P. Greene, *Diary of Landon Carter*, 1:79, 289–92, 370–71, 451; 2:648, 777–78.

98. Hening, *Statutes at Large*, 6:110–11.

99. *Statutes at Large of Virginia, 1792–1806*, 1:125; State v. Howell and Primus, November 4, 1829, Northampton County Minute Docket, Superior Court, 1818–34, 332–34, NCDAH.

100. Jordan, *White Over Black*, 111.

101. Blassingame, *Slave Community*, 215; Genovese, *From Rebellion to Revolution*, xiv, 1–2.

CHAPTER 13

1. Thomas Cooper and McCord, *Statutes at Large of South Carolina*, 7:402; *Revised Code of . . . Mississippi, 1824*, 381; Ormond, Bagley, and Goldthwaite, *Code of Alabama*, 594; Oldham and White, *Digest of the . . . Laws of . . . Texas*, 560.

2. *John, (a slave), v. State*, 16 Ga. 203 (1854).

3. *State v. Jarrott, (a slave)*, 23 N.C. 64–67 (1840).

4. Ibid., 68; Oldham and White, *Digest of the . . . Laws of . . . Texas*, 561.

5. *State v. Jarrott, (a slave)*, 23 N.C. 71 (1840).

6. *State v. Caesar, (a slave)*, 31 N.C. 270–73 (1849).

7. Ibid., 276–78.

8. Ibid., 280.

9. Ibid., 283, 287.

10. Ibid., 296.

11. *Nelson v. State*, 10 Humphreys 518 (1850).

12. Blackstone, *Commentaries*, 4:217. For laws on maiming whites or striking them see, e.g., Thomas Cooper and McCord, *Statutes at Large of South Carolina*, 7:405.

13. Trial of Bone and Frank, September 19, 1721, Essex County Order Book No. 5, 1716–23; Trial of James, November 17, 1739, Essex County Orders, 1738–40; Trial of Jimmy, July 3 and 9, 1772, Princess Anne County Minute Book 9, 1770–73; Trial of Sam, September 6, 1738, Princess Anne County Minute Book 5, 1737–44—all in VSL. See also Trial of Ben, November 1746, Charles City County Order Book, 1737–51, VSL, and Lord Proprietary v. Sam and Tobe, November 1737, Prince Georges County Court Record, 1735–38, 603, MHR.

14. Blackstone, *Commentaries*, 3:120.

15. Howell Cobb, *Compilation of the . . . Statutes of . . . Georgia*, 610; *Revised Code of . . . Mississippi, 1824*, 381; Hutchinson, *Code of Mississippi, 1848*, 532.

16. Blackstone, *Commentaries*, 4:199–200.

17. *Revised Code of . . . Virginia, 1819*, 1:582; Commonwealth v. James, November 18, 1852, Charles City County Court Minute Book, 1848–60, and Commonwealth v. Amos, December 19, 1844, Charles City County Circuit Court Order Book, 1831–52, VSL; Commonwealth v. Bob, December 1798 (Richmond County), Auditor's Item 153, Box 1; Commonwealth v. Dan, November 1831 (Page County) Auditor's Item 153, Box 6; Commonwealth v. Benjamin

White, Slave, February 13, 1819, Petersburg City Hustings Court Minute Book, 1816–19, VSL. See also Commonwealth v. Bob, February 17, 1831, Petersburg City Hustings Court Minute Book, 1829–31; Commonwealth v. Archie, September 17, 1840, Petersburg City Hustings Court Minute Book, 1838–40.

18. An example of twenty lashes is Commonwealth v. Billy Randall, slave, January 16, 1838, Richmond City Hustings Court Minute Book, 1837–40, and of thirty-nine, Commonwealth v. Morris, November 19, 1856, Richmond City Hustings Court Minute Book, 1856–57, VSL.

19. Commonwealth v. Nick, January 25, 1819, and Commonwealth v. Brister, May 24, 1819, Fauquier County Minute Book, 1818–19, VSL.

20. State v. Charles, September 1849–March 1850, Case 627, File 501–650 (1847–50), Lowndes County Department of Archives and History, Lowndes County Courthouse, Columbia, Miss.

21. *Anthony, (a slave), v. State*, 13 Smedes and M. 264–65 (Miss., 1850).

22. *Nancy, (a slave), v. State*, 6 Ala. 486 (1844).

23. State v. Alick, July 16, 1818, Baldwin County Ordinary Inferior Court Minutes, 1812–29, Trials of Slaves, and State v. Israel, April 1849, Hancock County Ordinary Inferior Court Minutes, Slave Trials, 1843–50, 8, GDAH.

24. Thomas Cooper and McCord, *Statutes at Large of South Carolina*, 7:405; Bullard and Curry, *New Digest of the Statute Laws of Louisiana*, 60: Howell Cobb, *Compilation of the . . . Statutes of . . . Georgia*, 599; State v. Ben, September 1813, Putnam County Inferior Court Records, 1813–43, Trials of Slaves, 1, GDAH.

25. *State v. Nicholas, (a slave)*, 2 Strob. 278, 280, 291 (S.C., 1848).

26. Quoted in Stampp, *Peculiar Institution*, 145.

27. *Revised Code of . . . Virginia, 1819*, 1:426; *Revised Code of . . . Mississippi, 1824*, 376; *Code of Tennessee, 1858*, 508–9; Hardin, *Revised Statutes of . . . Missouri*, 2:1474–75; Oldham and White, *Digest of the . . . Laws of . . . Texas*, 5443. The North Carolina law is discussed in *State v. Bill, (a slave)*, 13 Iredell 373 (N.C., 1852). The court admitted that it was not possible to define insolence precisely: "it may consist in a look, the pointing of a finger, a refusal or neglect to step out of the way when a white person is seen to approach. But each of such acts violates the rules of propriety, and if tolerated, would destroy that subordination, upon which our social system rests."

28. Jack P. Greene, *Diary of Landon Carter*, 2:845; Trial of Tom, August 9, 1745, Lancaster County Orders No. 9, 1743–52, VSL; *White v. Chambers*, 2 Bay 74–75 (S.C., 1796).

29. *Ex parte Boylston*, 2 Strob. 46–47 (S.C., 1847).

30. State v. Anthony, September 16, 1848, and State v. John, July 14, 1849, Fairfield District Magistrate Freeholders' Trial Papers, SCDAH.

31. State v. Solomon (Sole), February 5, 1851, ibid.

32. State v. Charles, May 1841, Davidson County Circuit Court Minutes, Civil and Criminal, 1839–41, vol. L–M, 352, TSLA.

33. *State v. Bill, (a slave)*, 35 N.C. 256 (1852).

34. See *Commonwealth v. Richard Turner*, 5 Rand. 678 (Va., 1827).

35. *State v. Bill, (a slave)*, 35 N.C., 256 (1852).

36. Ibid., 258.

37. Blassingame, *Slave Testimony*, 650 (quotation); Ferris, "Collection of Racial Lore," 261–62; Yetman, "Background of the Slave Narrative Collection."

38. Chapman, "Crime in Eighteenth-Century England," 139 (quotations); Hart, *Punishment and Responsibility*, 6.

39. Hay, "Property, Authority, and Criminal Law," 25; E. P. Thompson, *Whigs and Hunters*, 261; Hobsbaum, *Primitive Rebels*.

40. *Ewing v. Thompson*, 13 Mo. 132 (1850); Myers, *Children of Pride*, 1:528, 532–33, 541–47.

41. Auditor's Item 153, VSL.

42. Petition of Citizens of Grant County, no date, C. S. Morehead Papers, Folder 158, 1855–59, KSA

43. Garrett Davis led the fight against the Thirteenth Amendment in the U.S. Senate in 1864 and 1865.

44. Petition of Citizens of Bourbon County, June 5, 1858, and Garrett Davis to Judge W. C. Goodlow, June 4, 1858, C. S. Morehead Papers, Folders 116–17, KSA. The pardon was granted June 8, 1858.

45. Genovese (*Roll, Jordan, Roll*, 496, 767 n. 12) noted this as one motive for infanticide but suggested that it was a subject that required caution. One article, he argued, correctly I believe, went too far: Bauer and Bauer, "Day to Day Resistance to Slavery," 415–17.

46. Commonwealth v. Sall, December 12, 1793, Fauquier County Minute Book, 1793–95, 28, Commonwealth v. Jenny, July 6, 1824, Richmond City Hustings Court Minutes 8, 1821–24, 518, and Commonwealth v. Nancy, January 18, 1821, Petersburg City Hustings Court Minute Book, 1819–23, VSL; State v. Matilda, November 19, 1847, Chambers County Circuit Court Minutes, vol. 5, 1844–49, Chambers County Courthouse, Lafayette, Ala.; State v. Harriet, November 1848–January 1852, File 501–650, 1847–50, Lowndes County Department of Archives and History, Lowndes County Courthouse, Columbia, Miss.

47. Commonwealth v. Dick, October 1, 1804, Petersburg City Hustings Court Minute Book, 1800–1804, and Commonwealth v. Tom, January 28, 1828, Petersburg City Hustings Court Minute Book, 1827–32, VSL.

48. There is a checklist of cases, but it is not entirely reliable (case 291, for instance, is cited as a murder—he killed a dog), and not all the records are complete or intelligible.

49. For an example of five lashes see State v. Dianna and Sarah, June 8, 1826, and of thirty-nine, State v. Julius, September 3, 1850, Anderson District Magistrate Freeholders' Trial Papers, SCDAH.

50. State v. Jake, January 1, 1844, ibid.

51. *State v. Jarrott, (a slave)*, 23 N.C. 67 (1840).

52. *State v. Caesar, (a slave)*, 31 N.C. 296 (1849).

CHAPTER 14

1. Jordan, *White Over Black*, 157; Cleaver, *Soul on Ice*, 160. There has always been good reason for fearing white retaliation. A more recent, and particularly grisly, example is the killing of Claude Neal in Florida in the 1930s. The lynchers cut off some of his fingers, castrated him, cut off his penis and made him eat his genitals, and then hanged him. McGovern, *Anatomy of a Lynching.*

2. Cash, *Mind of the South*, 116–20; Lebsock, *Free Women of Petersburg*, 248; Johnston, *Race Relations in Virginia*; Williamson, *New People.*

3. Hoetink, *Caribbean Race Relations*; Freyre, *Masters and the Slaves.* But there was more hostility than is sometimes realized. See, e.g., Martinez-Alier, *Marriage, Class, and Colour in Nineteenth-Century Cuba.*

4. Hansley v. Hansley, April 24, 1849, New Hanover County Minute Docket, Superior Court, 1849–55, NCDAH; State v. William K. Mangum, Fall 1859, Lowndes County Circuit Court Final Record, 1858–60, 525, Lowndes County Courthouse, Lafayette, Ala.

5. Duncan, "Servitude and Slavery in Colonial South Carolina," 287; Hindus, *Prison and Plantation*, 152; Wyatt-Brown, *Southern Honor*, 50.

6. Cash, *Mind of the South*, 116–20; Jack Kenny Williams, *Vogues in Villainy*, 33–34; Wyatt-Brown, *Southern Honor*, 292, 316; Johnston, *Race Relations in Virginia*, 257.

7. Blackstone, *Commentaries*, 4:210 (definition of rape), 212; *Stephen, (a slave), v. State*, 11 Ga. 238 (1852).

8. Dalton, *Countrey Justice*, 256–57.

9. *State v. Peter, (a slave)*, 8 Jones N.C. 21–22 (1860).

10. Hening, *Statutes at Large*, 8:358. Jordan (*White Over Black*, 473) is in error. Jordan misread a law of 1805 that defined attempted rape as a felony and attached the same punishment as "heretofore." He assumed that the law of 1805 changed the punishment. It was not until 1823 that rape was made a capital offense, rather than the subject of castration, as in attempts cases. Schwarz, *Twice Condemned*, 206.

11. Jordan, *White Over Black*, 155; William C. Jones, *Revised Statutes of . . . Missouri*, 349.

12. The *Revised Statutes of Delaware, 1852*, did not impose the death penalty for assault on a white woman by a slave with an intent to rape. In the rest of the South, wherever an "assault with intent" statute was adopted, the death penalty was prescribed for slaves.

13. O'Neall, *Negro Law of South Carolina*, 29; Thompson, *Manual and Digest of the Statute Law of . . . Florida*, 537; Gould, *Digest of the Statutes of Arkansas*, 335; *Session Laws of North Carolina, 1823*, 42; *Session Laws of Tennessee, 1833*, 94; Stanton, *Revised Statutes of Kentucky*, 375; *Revised Code of . . . Mississippi, 1857*, 248; Kilty, Harris, and Watkins, *Laws of Maryland*, 4:chap. 138; *Revised Code of . . . Virginia, 1819*, 585 (this law expressly provided the death penalty for slaves and prison for the free, including free blacks); Jordan, *White Over Black*, 473. Jordan cites a judge in Georgia ordering a castration in 1824. The code, however, provided the death penalty, not castration, so that the sentence was not based on the statute. Bullard and Curry, *New Digest of the Statute Laws of Louisiana*, 67; Ormond, Bagley, and Goldthwaite, *Code of Alabama*, 594; Oldham and White, *Digest of the . . . Laws of . . . Texas*, 562–63; Lamar, *Laws of . . . Georgia*, 804.

14. *Grandison, (a slave), v. State*, 2 Humphreys 452 (Tenn., 1841); *Pleasant, (a slave), v. State*, 13 Ark. 376 (1852).

15. Commonwealth v. Kitt, May 29, 1778, and Commonwealth v. Kitt, July 29, 1783, Westmoreland County Order Book, 1776–86, VSL.

16. *George, (a slave), v. State*, 37 Miss. 319–20 (1859).

17. This whole subject is discussed in Jordan, *White Over Black*. Blacks recognized the "superior beauty" of whites, Jefferson believed. "Add to these" (some of the characteristics of the races), he wrote, "flowing hair, a more elegant symmetry of form, their own judgment in favor of the whites, declared by their preference of them, as uniformly as is the preference of the Oranootan for the black woman over those of his own species." Jefferson, *Notes on Virginia*, 133.

18. *State v. Jones*, Walker 83 (Miss., 1820); *George, (a slave), v. State*, 37 Miss. 320 (1859); Tushnet, *American Law of Slavery*, 72, 85 (quotation).

19. Case of Peter, 1797 (Surry County), Case 163, Auditor's Item 153, Box 1, VSL; Schwarz, *Twice Condemned*, 207; *Grandison, (a slave), v. State*, 2 Humphreys 452 (Tenn., 1841).

20. Cash, *Mind of the South*, 116–20; Lamar, *Laws of . . . Georgia*, 804 (a free person of color as well); *Session Laws of Tennessee, 1833*, 94 ("any" white female); Stanton, *Revised Statutes of Kentucky*, 2:375.

21. *Revised Code of . . . Virginia, 1819*, 585; *Revised Statutes of Mississippi, 1824*, 381; *Session Laws of Mississippi, 1859*, 102.

22. Hardin, *Revised Statutes of . . . Missouri*, 1:564–65; *Revised Code of . . . Virginia, 1819*, 585; *Revised Statutes of Mississippi, 1824*, 381; *Session Laws of Tennessee, 1851–52*, 251; Meigs and Cooper, *Code of Tennessee*, 509.

23. Hawkins, *Treatise of the Pleas of the Crown*, 1:65.

24. Blackstone, *Commentaries*, 4:15.

25. Bishop, *New Commentaries on the Criminal Law*, 264, 441.

26. Oliver Wendell Holmes, *Common Law*, 65–68.

27. Hart, *Punishment and Responsibility*, 128.

28. Ibid., 131.

29. Cushing, *Earliest Printed Laws of Delaware*, 67; *Revised Statutes of Delaware, 1852,* 257.

30. Maxcy, *Laws of Maryland,* 1:236.

31. Charge to County Officers, March 1735, Prince Georges County Court Record, 1735–38, and Charge to County Officers, March 1769, Prince Georges County Court Record, 1760–70, MHR.

32. Hening, *Statutes at Large,* 8:358; Commonwealth v. Ben, 1786 (Essex County), Case 36, Auditor's Item 153, and Commonwealth v. Bob, June 13, 1783, Southampton County Court Order Book, 1778–84, VSL; Schwarz, *Twice Condemned,* 150.

33. Schwarz, *Twice Condemned,* 206: *Session Laws of Maryland, 1845,* chap. 340, sec. 1; Lamar, *Laws of . . . Georgia,* 804.

34. *Session Laws of Texas, 1837,* 43; William C. Jones, *Revised Statutes of . . . Missouri,* 349; State v. Lee, November 9, 1854, Saline County Circuit Court Record, vol. C, 424, Saline County Courthouse, Marshall, Mo.

35. Kerr, "Petty Felony, Slave Defiance, and Frontier Villainy," 118, 363.

36. *Revised Statutes of Delaware, 1852,* 257; *Session Laws of North Carolina, 1823,* 42; O'Neall, *Negro Law of South Carolina,* 29; Thompson, *Manual and Digest of the Statute Law of . . . Florida,* 538.

37. *Session Laws of Tennessee, 1833,* 2; William C. Jones, *Revised Statutes of . . . Missouri,* 349; Oldham and White, *Digest of the . . . Laws of . . . Texas,* 562.

38. Blackstone, *Commentaries,* 33:120; *Session Laws of Tennessee, 1833,* 2.

39. *Stephen, (a slave), v. State,* 11 Ga. 230 (1852); State v. Lewis, August 14, 1856, State v. Wallis, October 6, 1843, and State v. Will Hutchinson, a slave, September 29, 1864, Anderson District Magistrate Freeholders' Trial Papers, SCDAH.

40. *State v. Martin, (a slave),* 14 N.C. 269–70 (1832).

41. Milsom, *Historical Foundations,* xi.

42. Langum, "Role of Intellect and Fortuity."

43. State v. James, July 19, 1839, Saline County Circuit Court Record, vol. D, 1856–60, 479, Saline County Courthouse, Marshall, Mo.; *Middlebrook v. Nelson,* 34 Ga. 506 (1866).

44. Billings, *Old Dominion,* 161–63.

45. *State v. Jim, (a slave),* 1 Devereux 508 (N.C., 1828); State v. Wesley, August–September 1847, Elbert County, Trial of Slaves, 1837–49, GDAH.

46. *Pleasant, (a slave), v. State,* 15 Ark. 646–47 (1855).

47. Ibid., 644.

48. There were eleven cases in those records spread over a thirty-four-year period. The earliest was State v. Sam, June 1, 1830, and the last, State v. Will Hutchinson, a slave, September 29, 1864. Anderson District Magistrate Freeholders' Trial Papers, SCDAH.

49. State v. Frank, November 8, 1851, and State v. Wallis, October 6, 1843, ibid.; State v. Tom, July 17, 1846, Spartanburg District Magistrate Freeholders' Trial Papers, SCDAH.

50. *State v. Elick, (a slave),* 52 N.C. 55 (1859).

51. Hindus, *Prison and Plantation,* 152.

52. Ibid.

53. *Maryland Archives,* 28:577.

54. State v. Daniel, January 15, 1859, State v. Harry, November 5, 1851, and State v. Redman, August 2, 1850, Spartanburg District Magistrate Freeholders' Trial Papers, SCDAH.

55. Hindus, *Prison and Plantation,* 152.

56. State v. Charles, August 9–September 22, 1824, Northampton County, Slave Records, 1785–1829; State v. Charles, 1825–26, Northampton County Minute Docket, Superior Court, 1818–34, 153, 166, 177, 202; Petition of Carter Jones in State v. Charles, Northampton County, Slave Records, 1785–1829—all in NCDAH.

57. State v. Charles, May 1827, Northampton County Minute Docket, Superior Court, 1818–34, 209, 211, 289–90, NCDAH.

58. File Papers, State v. Charles, Northampton County, Slave Records, 1785–1829, NCDAH.

59. State v. Charles, 1827, Northampton County Minute Docket, Superior Court, 1818–34, 211, NCDAH.

60. Commonwealth v. Jack, August 5, 1818, Orange County Order Book (Minutes), 1816–20, VSL.

61. *State v. Negro George*, 2 Del. 138–39 (1800). This is not the same case as that of 1797, although the titles are the same.

62. Schwarz, *Twice Condemned*, 206.

63. *Henry, (a slave), v. State*, 4 Humphreys 262–63 (Tenn., 1842).

64. Ibid., 262.

65. State v. Daniel, January 15, 1859, Spartanburg District Magistrate Freeholders' Trial Papers, SCDAH.

66. *State v. Elick, (a slave)*, 52 N.C. 55 (1859); *Pleasant, (a slave), v. State*, 13 Ark. 373 (1853).

67. State v. Harry, November 5, 1851, Spartanburg District Magistrate Freeholders' Trial Papers, SCDAH; Hindus, *Prison and Plantation*, 152; State v. Will Hutchinson, a slave, September 29, 1864, Anderson District Magistrate Freeholders' Trial Papers, SCDAH.

68. *Wyatt, (a slave), v. State*, 32 Tenn. 284 (1852).

69. *Commonwealth v. Fields, a free negro*, 4 Leigh 648 (Va., 1832).

70. *Charles, (a slave), v. State*, 11 Ark. 410 (1850); *Pleasant, (a slave), v. State*, 13 Ark. 373–74 (1852).

71. Sawyer, *Southern Institutes*, 222.

72. Bardaglio, "Rape and the Law," 761, 765, 771. I wholeheartedly agree with Bardaglio's conclusions that the procedures in the trials of slaves for rape were flawed because the slaves could not contradict the statements of whites (at least not directly), and that the property interests of owners as well as the lives of slaves were involved with efforts to achieve procedural fairness. I also agree with the idea that the law was thought to be a body of rules to be applied "equitably," and that this did affect the trials of slaves and free blacks. I do have a modest qualification to offer to his conclusion that though slaves received "substantial procedural protections," such protection was "offset" by the disparity in punishment of those convicted. There was no necessary *legal* connection between procedural securities and punishment.

73. *Stephen, (a slave), v. State*, 11 Ga. 239 (1852).

CHAPTER 15

1. E. P. Thompson, "Moral Economy of the English Crowd"; Lichtenstein, " 'That Disposition to Theft,' " 415, 433. See also Kay and Cary, " 'They Are Indeed the Constant Plague of Their Tyrants,' " 37–38, 52 ("Slaves in the colonies . . . wove criminal behaviour into the culture and value systems to deal with immediate problems, sustain the sense of morality and justice, and redistribute some of the power and wealth which surrounded them. . . . Almost all slaves derived from this criminality a heightened awareness of the destructive meanings of white treatment and definitions of slaves . . . whatever the heartrending, destructive paradoxes, slaves interwove in profound if often hidden ways murder, house-burning, running away, goldbricking, a sustaining religiosity, and expansive, powerful marital, familial, and communal ties."); Langbein, "Albion's Fatal Flaws," 97, 119.

2. Olmsted, the ex-slave, and Douglass are quoted in Ayers, *Vengeance and Justice*, 127–29.

3. Hammond, "Letter to an English Abolitionist," 190.

4. Genovese, *Roll, Jordan, Roll*, 613.

5. *Richmond Enquirer*, April 18, 1820.

6. Stampp, *Peculiar Institution*, 127; Genovese, *Roll, Jordan, Roll*, 613–15.

7. Blackstone, *Commentaries*, 4:230, 241, 240; *State v. John, (a slave)*, 5 Jones N.C. 170–71 (1857).

8. Berman, "Origins of Historical Jurisprudence," 1710 (Hale); Blackstone, *Commentaries*, 4:238–39. "And certainly the natural punishment for injuries to property seems to be the loss of the offender's own property: which ought to be universally the case, were all men's fortunes equal" (4:237).

9. Hening, *Statutes at Large*, 3:102, 179, 278.

10. Trial of Daniel, December 18, 1765, Orange County Order Book No. 7, 1763–69, VSL. Daniel was granted benefit of clergy after his conviction of steeling sheep valued at fifteen shillings.

11. Trial of Cupid, December 7, 1763, Westmoreland County Order Book, 1761–64, and Trial of Sam, October 3, 1761, Princess Anne County Minute Book, 1753–62, VSL.

12. Commonwealth v. Bob, September 6, 1831, and Commonwealth v. Granville, September 6, 1831, Charles City County Minute Book 2, 1830–37, VSL; *Revised Code of . . . Mississippi*, 1824, 381–82.

13. *State v. Harriet, (a slave)*, 4 Jones N.C. 265–66 (1857).

14. U. B. Phillips, *Revised Statutes of Louisiana*, 51; Parish Court Case: Parish of St. Landry v. George, August 1831, LSA.

15. Ormond, Bagley, and Goldthwaite, *Code of Alabama*, 595; Scott and McCullough, *Maryland Code*, 1:230, 434. The prison term applied to "any person." There was a second section providing that a slave convicted of petty larceny "may" be whipped up to forty lashes.

16. See, e.g., State v. Cesar, April 1837 (benefit of clergy granted in a grand larceny case, and the slave to be whipped thirty-nine times on two separate occasions), New Hanover Minute Docket, Superior Court, 1849–55, and State v. Alfred, Fall 1854 (thirty-nine lashes for grand larceny), New Hanover Superior Court, State Docket, 1854–67, NCDAH.

17. O'Neall, *Negro Law of South Carolina*, 33, 35: "The whippings inflicted by the sentence of Courts trying slaves and free negroes, are most enormous—utterly disproportioned to offences, and should be prevented by all means in our power." From Virginia, a clear example of where a court maintained the distinction is Commonwealth v. Paul, June 29, 1826, Lunenburg County Minute Book, 1824–28, VSL. Paul was found guilty of grand larceny (stealing $80 in silver and two tortoise shell combs). His sentence was severe: he was burned on the hand and also sentenced to fifty lashes. An example of where value was not noted is Commonwealth v. Bob, June 11, 1855, Lunenburg County Minute Book, 1853–58, VSL. Bob stole flour and bacon and was sentenced to twenty lashes.

18. State v. Linda, February 18, 1832, State v. Marshele and Pleasant, February 15, 1865, and State v. Jim, May 6, 1852, Anderson District Magistrate Freeholders' Trial Papers, SCDAH.

19. An example is Commonwealth v. Peter, November 27, 1799, Petersburg City Hustings Court Minute Book, 1797–1800, VSL.

20. State v. Elijah, June 18, 1813, Chatham County Inferior Court Trial Docket, 1813–27, 3, GDAH.

21. *State v. Nathan, (a slave)*, 5 Rich. 232–33 (S.C., 1851). See also *State v. Gabriel South*, 5 Rich. 489 (S.C., 1852). South was indicted for conveying Nathan away so that he could not be tried and punished. He was found guilty, and the verdict was upheld on appeal. Judge Frost observed that "a slave is the passive subject of his master's will, and is in the legal custody of his master. If he is secreted or carried away, that is not his own act, but the act of his master. . . . The offence is of mischievous tendency and avarice or indiscreet partiality present great temptations to its commission."

22. State v. Spencer, November 22, 1853, Chambers County Circuit Court Minutes, vol. 6., Chambers County Courthouse, Haynesville, Ala.

23. See, e.g., Commonwealth v. Blade Johnston, Hampton Jones, and Tom Baker, slaves, December 8, 1797, Commonwealth v. Charles, February 23, 1798, Commonwealth v. Billy, May 1, 1798, and Commonwealth v. Peter, November 29, 1799, Petersburg City Hustings Court Minute Book, 1797–1800, VSL.

24. Quoted in Dalton, *Countrey Justice*, 233–34.

25. Hawkins, *Treatise of the Pleas of the Crown*, 103–4; Hale, *History of the Pleas of the Crown*, 1:546; Blackstone, *Commentaries*, 4:220, 223–24.

26. Adam Smith, *Lectures on Jurisprudence*, 127–28.

27. Maxcy, *Laws of Maryland*, 1:190–91; Hening, *Statutes at Large*, 6:105–6.

28. Cushing, *First Laws of . . . Delaware*, 1:68–69, 237.

29. *Session Laws of Georgia, 1806*, 335; U. B. Phillips, *Revised Statutes of Louisiana*, 50; Hardin, *Revised Statutes of . . . Missouri*, 2:572–74. William C. Jones, *Revised Statutes of . . . Missouri*, 356–57. Burglary was conspicuously left off the list of capital crimes in Texas, a list that included murder, rape, robbery, and arson. Oldham and White, *Digest of the . . . Laws of . . . Texas*, Penal Code, Title III, chap. 1, art. 819.

30. William C. Jones, *Revised Statutes of . . . Missouri*, 357; Oldham and White, *Digest of the . . . Laws of Texas . . .*, Penal Code, Title III, chap 1, arts. 819, 821; Gould, *Digest of the Statutes of Arkansas*, 340; *Revised Statutes of Delaware, 1852*, 257; Thompson, *Manual and Digest of the Statute Law of . . . Florida*, 538.

31. Ormond, Bagley, and Goldthwaite, *Code of Alabama*, 594; *Revised Code of . . . Mississippi, 1857*, 248.

32. *Ex parte Vincent, (a slave)*, 26 Ala. 153 (1855).

33. Commonwealth v. Dick, 1824, Auditor's Item 153, Box 4, VSL.

34. Commonwealth v. John, August 13, 1860 (not guilty), and Commonwealth v. Emanuel, December 8, 1862 (guilty), Lunenburg County Minute Book, 1859–66, VSL; Commonwealth v. Neat, 1843 (guilty), Circuit Court Clerk, Circuit Court Indictments, Jessamine County, Box 9, 1842–49, KSA; State v. Sam, June 1, 1830 (not guilty), Anderson District Magistrate Freeholders' Trial Papers, SCDAH.

35. Hindus, *Prison and Plantation*, 146.

36. Schwarz, *Twice Condemned*, 123. The percentage of convictions was higher, but many were granted benefit of clergy. "Slave courts," Schwarz noted, "began to concentrate on burglary in the 1770s." The conviction rate was 59.9 percent from 1770 to 1774 and 55.1 percent from 1775 to 1779; in the first period 40 percent of those convicted were granted clergy, and in the second the percentage was 58.7. Schwarz defined burglary as "breaking and entering with intent to steal, especially at night." This is a common perception today, but it is not the correct definition of burglary under English law.

37. Trial of Will, November 9, 1761, July 14, 1762, Charles City County Orders, 1758–62, VSL.

38. State v. John, December 17, 1852–June 22, 1853, Wilkinson County Circuit Court Minute Book, vol. 13, 1851–56, 118, 162, 173, 184, 188, Wilkinson County Courthouse, Woodville, Miss.; State v. Guy, October 1844, Screven County, Docket for Trial of Slaves and Free Persons of Color, 1844–48, GDAH.

39. *State v. Ridgell*, 2 Bailey 560–61 (S.C., 1831).

40. State v. Phillip, May 18, 1854, Anderson District Magistrate Freeholders' Trial Papers, SCDAH.

41. Dalton, *Countrey Justice*, 245–46.

42. Hawkins, *Treatise of the Pleas of the Crown*, 105–6; Blackstone, *Commentaries*, 4:220–21.

43. Ibid., 222; Maxcy, *Laws of Maryland*, 1:190, 286.

44. Hening, *Statutes at Large*, 3:271.

45. Thomas Cooper and McCord, *Statutes at Large of South Carolina*, 7:345, 354, 373, 402.

46. Trial of Phill, December 19, 1743, Caroline County Order Book, 1741–46, and Case of Cook, April 2, 1729, Princess Anne County Minute Book 4, 1728–37, VSL.

47. *Maryland Gazette*, December 23, 1762, January 6, 1763. A piece of evidence to suggest that whites did not always see arson in a burning is an entry in the *Maryland Gazette* of December 27, 1759: "Last week a very large Fodder House, near *Severn* Ferry, with about 400 Bushels of Corn in it, belong to *John Brice*, Esq., was burnt by the Carelessness of his Negroes."

48. Lord Proprietary v. Abram, November 1762, and Lord Proprietary v. Tim, March Court 1763, Talbot County Court Criminal Judgments, 1761–67, MHR; Lord Proprietary v. Adam, Lord Proprietary v. Beck, and Lord Proprietary v. Jenny and Grace, *Maryland Archives*, 32:55, 125, 28:504.

49. *South Carolina Gazette*, July 30–August 15, 1741.

50. Hening, *Statutes at Large*, 13:31; Commonwealth v. Claiborne, November 18, 1797, January 1–13, 1798, Petersburg City Hustings Court Minute Book, 1797–1800, VSL; *Revised Code of . . . Virginia, 1819*, 587.

51. Petigru, *Portion of the Code of Statute Law of South Carolina*, 604 n *.

52. Ormond, Bagley, and Goldthwaite, *Code of Alabama*, 594; Oldham and White, *Digest of the . . . Laws of Texas . . .*, 543; Meigs and Cooper, *Code of Tennessee*, 509; William C. Jones, *Revised Statutes of . . . Missouri*, 354–55.

53. Trials for arson or burnings were conducted in the following sample counties for Mississippi, Alabama, Kentucky, Florida, Tennessee, and Louisiana: State v. Ann, April 21, 1863, Lowndes County File Papers, File 2200–2498, 1860–63, Case 2212, Lowndes County Department of Archives and History, Lowndes County Courthouse, Columbia, Miss.; State v. Huldy, Spring 1857, and State v. Tom, April 1861–April 1864, Chambers County Circuit Court Minutes, State Cases, vol. 9, 1856–70, 26, 51, 239, 242, 250, 257, 263–64, Chambers County Courthouse, Lafayette, Ala.; Commonwealth v. Jess, 1826, Circuit Court, Clerk, Circuit Court Indictments Box 4, 1824–26, Jessamine County, KSA; State v. Gloster, November 17–April 29, 1844, Leon County Circuit Court Minute Book, 93, 165, 196, and State v. Billy Hays alias William Hays, Slave, May 16, 1849, Leon County Circuit Court Minute Book, 1847–55, 203, Leon County Courthouse, Tallahassee, Fla.; State v. Lawson, May 2–12, 1837, Maury County Circuit Court, vol. 1834–37, 429, 434, 476, 496, State v. Simon, May 14–18, 1847, Maury County Circuit Court Minutes, 1844–51, 253, 255, 258–59, and State v. Henry, May 1854, Davidson County Circuit Court Minutes, 1852–56, TSLA; Patrick Woods to State of Louisiana, May 28, 1838, St. Landry Parish Conveyance Record (1836–41), I-1, J-1, 237, St. Landry Parish Courthouse, Opelousas, La.

54. See, e.g., Commonwealth v. Sally, January 19, 1826, Petersburg City Hustings Court Minute Books, 1827–32, and Commonwealth v. Simon, March 7, 1834, Petersburg City Hustings Court Minute Books, 1832–35, VSL.

55. Commonwealth v. Dennis and Isaac, February 22, 1793, Petersburg City Hustings Court Minute Books, 1791–97, and Commonwealth v. Claiborne, November 18, 1797–January 1–13, 1798, Petersburg City Hustings Court Minute Books, 1797–1800, VSL.

56. Commonwealth v. Frank and George, November 1858, and Commonwealth v. Victoria, November 1858, Richmond City Hustings Court Minutes No. 24, 1857–58, 134, 169–70, VSL; Commonwealth v. Lewis, March 1858, Richmond City Hustings Court Minutes No. 24, 1857–58, 341, VSL.

57. See, e.g., Commonwealth v. Reuben, July 16, 1818, Petersburg City Hustings Court Minute Book, 1816–19, VSL. Reuben was acquitted of "robbery & arson" of a store.

58. Commonwealth v. Malinda and Andrew, January 1861, Caroline County Minute Book, 1858–61, 199, 202, 412–14; Commonwealth v. Lewis and Caesar, March 5, 1801, Sussex County Order Book, 1795–1801; Commonwealth v. Fed, April 18, 1833, Charles City County Minute Book, 1830–37, 1150—all in VSL.

59. See, e.g., Commonwealth v. Nelson and Lewis, February 12 and 27, 1818, Lunenburg Minute Book, 1817–19; Commonwealth v. Thornton, January 23, 1854, Orange County Order Book (Minutes), 1852–56; and Commonwealth v. Sarah and Monmouth, January 11, 1808, King George County Order Book 7A, 1805–8—all in VSL.

60. Mary's Case, August 7, 1819, Auditor's Item 153, VSL; *Jesse, (a slave), v. State*, 28 Miss. 110 (1854).

61. See, e.g., State v. Peggy Coale, May Term 1830, Frederick County, Criminal Docket, and State v. Galloway Pice, November 1854, Talbot County Criminal Judgments, 1842–57, 233, MHR.

62. State v. Susan, January 22, 1821, Chatham County Inferior Court, Trial Docket, 1813–27; State v. Rodney, February 12, 1819, Baldwin County, Ordinary Inferior Court Minutes, 1812–29; State v. Adeline, May 16–28, 1849, Hancock County, Ordinary Inferior Court Minutes, Slave Trials, 1843–50—all in GDAH.

63. State v. Sandy and John, March 1843, New Hanover Minute Docket, Superior Court, 1843–48. Sandy was sentenced to hang after a motion for a new trial was rejected. In June 1843 the state supreme court overruled the judgment because of "error in the record and proceedings." *State v. Sandy, (a slave)*, 3 Iredell 570 (N.C., 1843). The opinion by Judge Ruffin is a good example of formalism: "There cannot be judgment on this indictment, because it concludes 'against the form of the statutes,' while the offence depends on but a single statute." There had been a confession in the case.

64. Hindus, *Prison and Plantation*, 141, 144.

65. State v. Jane, May 4, 1863, State v. Thornton, George, Pete, and Phil, November 20, 1860, State v. Ellen, March 27, 1846, and State v. John, June 18, 1855, Anderson District Magistrate Freeholders' Trial Papers, SCDAH. Counsel for John and for Thornton was James L. Orr, the future governor of South Carolina during the early years of Reconstruction.

66. State v. Alfred, October 6, 1860, State v. Adam, April 9, 1855, State v. Miles and others, November 19, 1864 (Harriet was sentenced to 600 lashes, Sandy to 300, and no disposition was recorded in Minerva's case), and State v. George, April 28, 1865, Spartanburg District Magistrate Freeholders' Trial Papers, SCDAH.

CHAPTER 16

1. Jordan, *White Over Black*, 109; Blackstone, *Commentaries*, 1:125, 130; T. R. R. Cobb, *Law of Negro Slavery*, 105.

2. Blackstone, *Commentaries*, 1:134.

3. Stroud, *Sketch of the Laws*, 29–30; T. R. R. Cobb, *Law of Negro Slavery*, 235; Stampp, *Peculiar Institution*, chap. entitled "Chattels Personal."

4. T. R. R. Cobb, *Law of Negro Slavery*, 107, 109.

5. Hening, *Statutes at Large*, 2:481; Thomas Cooper and McCord, *Statutes at Large of South Carolina*, 7:410; Bullard and Curry, *New Digest of the Statute Laws of Louisiana*, 53.

6. See, e.g., Ormond, Bagley, and Goldthwaite, *Code of Alabama*, 238; Hening, *Statutes at Large*, 12:182; Morehead and Brown, *Digest of the Statute Laws of Kentucky*, 2:1472; Thompson, *Manual and Digest of the Statute Law of . . . Florida*, 174; Cushing, *Laws of the Province of Maryland*, 119–20; Cushing, *Earliest Printed Laws of North Carolina*, 170.

7. Thomas Cooper and McCord, *Statutes at Large of South Carolina*, 7:413, 442; Thompson, *Manual and Digest of the Statute Law of . . . Florida*, 176; Howell Cobb, *Compilation of the . . . Statutes of . . . Georgia*, 618 (by this law of 1823 the number was set at ten slaves over sixteen years old); *Revised Code of . . . Mississippi, 1857*, 243 (it was unlawful to quarter over six slaves a mile or more away without a white present); Bullard and Curry, *New Digest of the*

Statute Laws of Louisiana, 1:65 (the law of 1814 required one overseer for every "thirty slaves working on said plantation"); *Session Laws of Alabama, 1856*, 18 (this law was the same as Mississippi's); State v. James Turner, Spring 1861–Spring 1864, Case 34, State v. Ananias Bell, Spring 1861–Spring 1864, Case #51, and State v. Francis A. Turner, Spring 1863, Case 54, Lowndes County Circuit Court, State Docket, 1861, Lowndes County Courthouse, Lafayette, Ala.; State v. Louis Marshall, November 1851, Adams County, State Docket, Summary 1841–52, and State v. Oran Metcalfe, November 1860, Adams County Circuit Court Minutes, 1856–61, 660, Adams County Courthouse, Natchez, Miss.; State v. George Sherman, April 1855, Lowndes County Department of Archives and History, Criminal Files, Box 1100–199 (1854–56), Case 1136, Lowndes County Courthouse, Columbia, Miss.

8. Blassingame, *Slave Testimony*, 457–58.

9. Thomas Cooper and McCord, *Statutes at Large of South Carolina*, 7:363.

10. Haywood, *Manual of the Laws of North Carolina*, 2:136–37, 145–46; *Revised Statutes of . . . North Carolina*, 580.

11. Hening, *Statutes at Large*, 11:57 (for missing text in Hening see *Revised Code of . . . Virginia, 1819*, 1:442); Thomas Cooper and McCord, *Statutes at Large of South Carolina*, 7:462.

12. See, e.g., Meigs and Cooper, *Code of Tennessee*, 518 (the master would be fined and the slave seized and hired out at hard labor for the use of the county for up to twenty days); Morehead and Brown, *Digest of the Statute Laws of Kentucky*, 2:1481 (law of 1802).

13. See, e.g., State v. David B. Gree, 1856, Pulaski County Records, Indictment Records Books "B–C," 1848–63, 406, AHC.

14. Examples of unlawful slave hires include several cases heard on April 26, 1809 (Fauquier County Minute Book, 1806–9, VSL), as well as Commonwealth v. Billy Barber, a slave, March 5, 1798, Petersburg City Hustings Court Minute Book, 1797–1800, VSL. Two North Carolina examples are Grand Jury Presentment v. Ben, slave of Burrell Branch, September 1796, Northampton County, Slave Records, 1785–1829, and State v. Demps, April 1836, New Hanover County Superior Court Minutes, 1835–42, NCDAH.

15. Peter H. Wood, *Black Majority*, 239; Thomas D. Morris, *Free Men All*.

16. *Prigg v. Pennsylvania*, 16 Peters 633 (1842).

17. Woodfin and Tinling, *Another Secret Diary*, 123; Edwin Adams Davis, *Diary of Bennett H. Barrow*, 154, 165, 205.

18. These are collected in Windley, *Runaway Slave Advertisements*. See also Meaders, "South Carolina Fugitives," and Philip D. Morgan, "Colonial South Carolina Runaways."

19. Windley, *Runaway Slave Advertisements*, 3:41, 63, 1:370–71. See Isaac, "Communication and Control." Carter's sense of himself as a benevolent patriarch is replete throughout his diary. Jack P. Greene, *Diary of Landon Carter*.

20. Peter H. Wood, *Black Majority*, 239; Schwarz, *Twice Condemned*, 135–36.

21. *Revised Code of . . . Mississippi, 1857*, 240–41; John Johnson, Missouri State Penitentiary, Register of Inmates, vol. B November 26, 1841–July 18, 1865, vol C December 25, 1854–April 29, 1871, 258, MoSA.

22. Jerome Hall, *Theft, Law, and Society*. A significant exception to the argument in the text is in civil law Louisiana, where slaves were seen as stealing themselves—a view that followed Roman law. Schafer, *Slavery, the Civil Law, and the Supreme Court*, 95, 115–16.

23. Hening, *Statutes at Large*, 3:86, 461; Edmund S. Morgan, *American Slavery American Freedom*, 313.

24. Maxcy, *Laws of Maryland*, 1:237–38.

25. Thomas Cooper and McCord, *Statutes at Large of South Carolina*, 7:359–60, 353, 376, 399.

26. Ibid., 352.

27. Ibid., 397.

28. For some all too typical eighteenth-century examples, see Windley, *Runaway Slave Advertisements*, 1:7, 42, 57, 65–66, 121–22, 134, 196, 281, 311.

29. Randall M. Miller and Smith, *Dictionary of Afro-American Slavery*, 652.

30. A typical law would be that of Mississippi, *Revised Code of . . . Mississippi, 1824*, 376–77.

31. As noted before, there is a useful but sometimes inaccurate checklist in SCDAH. Hindus (*Prison and Plantation*) has relied heavily on these records. See also Henderson, "Spartan Slaves: A Documentary Account." On police control in South Carolina more generally see Norrece Jones, *Born a Child of Freedom, Yet a Slave*. Very dated but still useful is Henry, *Police Control of the Slave in South Carolina*.

32. See, e.g., State v. Jim, October 19, 1826, and State v. Nelson, September 21, 1827, Anderson District Magistrate Freeholders Trial Papers, SCDAH.

33. *Revised Code of . . . Mississippi, 1824*, 380 (thirty-nine lashes); *Revised Code of . . . Mississippi, 1857*, 241 (fifty lashes); Thomas Cooper and McCord, *Statutes at Large of South Carolina*, 7:407.

34. Oldham and White, *Digest of the . . . Laws of . . . Texas*, 541; *Cook v. State*, 26 Ga. 597–98 (1858).

35. State v. Bob et al., May 19–20, 1854, Anderson District Magistrate Freeholders' Trial Papers, SCDAH. See also State v. Elijah, April 16, 1839, State v. John, Edmund, and Harvey, February 12, 1864, and State v. Dan, George, and Charles, January 10, 1849, ibid.

36. April 7, 1829 (the defendant was not named), Fairfield District: Office: Clerk of Court (General Sessions) Journal, 1825–29, 1840–63, 1863–68, SCDAH.

37. State v. Morgan Granet, May 1853, Adams County, State Docket Summary, 1841–52 (despite the dates, the cases go to 1854), Adams County Courthouse, Natchez, Miss.; St. John R. Liddell to Oran Mayo, September 4, 1849, Liddell Papers, Louisiana State University Archives, Baton Rouge.

38. Blackstone, *Commentaries*, 3:142.

39. Thomas Cooper and McCord, *Statutes at Large of South Carolina*, 7:357, 376, 390.

40. Hening, *Statutes at Large*, 6:369; Thomas Cooper and McCord, *Statutes at Large of South Carolina*, 7:426.

41. Cushing, *Earliest Printed Laws of North Carolina*, 166; Maxcy, *Laws of Maryland*, 1:238.

42. Howell Cobb, *Compilation of the . . . Statutes of . . . Georgia*, 610, 618.

43. *Revised Code of . . . Mississippi, 1857*, 240; Stanton, *Revised Statutes of Kentucky*, 370–71. To conceal or harbor brought two to five years.

44. *Crosby v. Hawthorn*, 25 Ala. 221–24 (1854).

45. State v. George W. Pulliam, November 25, 1863, Lowndes County State Docket, April Term 1863, Case 1839, Lowndes County Department of Archives and History, Lowndes County Courthouse, Columbia, Miss.; State v. Berryman Burge, April 13, 19, 1825, Fairfield District: Office: Clerk of Court (General Sessions) Journal, 1825–29, 1840–43, 1863–68, SCDAH; State v. Spencer Roach, November 1847–November 1848, Leon County Circuit Court Minute Book, vol. 5, 1847–55, Leon County Courthouse, Tallahassee, Fla.; Texas v. William E. Adams, March 1859, Harrison County District Court Civil Minutes, vol. H (1860), 252–53, 290–91, Harrison County Courthouse, Marshall, Tex.; State v. George Thomas, January 1861, Anne Arundel County Circuit Court Docket, October 1860, MHR.

46. Hale, *History of the Pleas of the Crown*, entry, "riot."

47. Thompson, *Manual and Digest of the Statute Law of . . . Florida*, 175.

48. Hawkins, *Treatise of the Pleas of the Crown*, 1:158.

49. *Revised Code of . . . Mississippi, 1857*, 247.

50. Thomas Cooper and McCord, *Statutes at Large of South Carolina*, 7:440–41, 448; O'Neall, *Negro Law of South Carolina*, 24; *Bell ads. Graham*, 1 N. and McC. 279–82 (S.C., 1818).

51. He added this comment at the end of a note appearing in a large scrapbook in the collection, Lieber on Slavery, in Lieber Papers, Huntington Library, San Marino, Calif.

52. Thomas Cooper and McCord, *Statutes at Large of South Carolina*, 7:413; Stroud, *Sketch of the Laws*, 61; Hardin, *Revised Statutes of . . . Missouri*, 2:1475; Howell Cobb, *Compilation of the . . . Statutes of . . . Georgia*, 603. The Louisiana law is noted in Stroud, *Sketch of the Laws*, 61; it is not in the "Black Code" in U. B. Phillips, *Revised Statutes of Louisiana*.

53. *Code of Virginia*, 1849, 747.

54. *Session Laws of North Carolina, 1830–1831*, 11. The law does not appear in the *Revised Statutes of . . . North Carolina*.

55. Mohr, *On the Threshold of Freedom*, 247–61.

56. O'Neall, *Negro Law of South Carolina*, 23.

57. Upton and Jennings, *Civil Code of . . . Louisiana*, 27.

58. Buckland, *Roman Law of Slavery*, 187, 201.

59. Watson, *Roman Slave Law*, 95.

60. Hening, *Statutes at Large*, 1:226.

61. Thompson, *Manual and Digest of the Statute Law of . . . Florida*, 541; Meigs and Cooper, *Code of Tennessee*, 506–7; State v. Anthony, October 15, 1856, April 15, 1857, and State v. Steve, April 14, 1857, Union County (Ark.) Circuit Court Records, Books F–G, 1854–67, 319, 366, 373–74.

62. Hening, *Statutes at Large*, 3:103.

63. Thomas Cooper and McCord, *Statutes at Large of South Carolina*, 7:409; O'Neall, *Negro Law of South Carolina*, 21.

64. State v. Frederick Watkins, State v. Thomas G. Frierson, State v. Francis Smith, and May 12, 1845; State v. John M. S. Mayes, May 15, 1845; and State v. Duncan Brown, September 1, 1845—all in Maury County Circuit Court Minutes, 1844–51, 362–63, 380, 451, TSLA.

65. State v. Mack and Robert Hardison, May 4, 1846, State v. Saban Jordan, September 9, 1848, State v. William H. Foster, September 3, 1849, and State v. Philip Osborne, August 30, 1852, Maury County Circuit Court Minutes, 1851–52, TSLA.

66. Berlin, *Freedom: A Documentary History*, 1:139, 297.

67. Philip D. Morgan, "Ownership of Property by Slaves," 409.

68. Woodward, *Mary Chesnut's Civil War* (March 19, 1861), 32.

69. Hening, *Statutes at Large*, 3:451–52.

70. *South Carolina Gazette*, October 29–November 5, 1737; Thomas Cooper and McCord, *Statutes at Large of South Carolina*, 7:409–10.

71. Philip D. Morgan, "Black Life in Eighteenth-Century Charleston"; *South Carolina Gazette*, January 23, 1770 (quotation); Thomas Cooper and McCord, *Statutes at Large of South Carolina*, 7:454.

72. Howell Cobb, *Compilation of the . . . Statutes of . . . Georgia*, 618; *Revised Code of . . . Mississippi, 1857*, 244; Bullard and Curry, *New Digest of the Statute Laws of Louisiana*, 55–56.

73. Texas v. John Brown, July 8, 1853, Texas v. Joseph S. Stewart, December 29, 1853, Texas v. James Dopplemayer, 1856, and Texas v. John Dial, September 5, 1856, Harrison County Criminal Docket, 1853, 26, 310, 388, 400, Harrison County Courthouse, Marshall, Tex.; State v. Caspar Michael, December 1856, West Feliciana Parish, Minutes, Seventh Judicial Circuit, 1854–59, St. Francisville, La.; State v. Mary Keene, slave, 1844, Circuit Court Clerk, Circuit Court Indictments, Jessamine County, Box 9, 1842–49, KSA.

74. For instance, when he discussed the death of his carpenter, Guy, in his diary for February 3, 1772, Carter referred to him as "of a drunken race always stupid." Jack P. Greene, *Diary of Landon Carter*, 2:648.

75. *Revised Code of . . . Virginia, 1819*, 1:426; Thomas Cooper and McCord, *Statutes at Large of South Carolina*, 7:467. The fines were up to $100.

76. See, e.g., Pulaski County Indictment Records, Books "B–C," 1848–63, 48, 120, 177, 283,

299, 368, 385, 422, AHC. The following were indicted for selling liquor to slaves: Caleb Will (1849), Horatio Aldrich (1851), Patrick Lee (1853), Joseph Schrader (1853), John Shemberger (1853), Samuel Lemons (1855), Louis Myers (1855), and John F. Tune (1856).

77. Commonwealth v. Billy Barber, Slave, March 5, 1798, Petersburg City Hustings Court Minute Books, 1797–1800, VSL; Commonwealth v. Arch, December 19, 1857, and Commonwealth v. Reuben, July 28, 1858, Warren County Circuit Court Minutes, 1856–60 (2 vols.), 1:515; 2:33, 106, KSA.

78. Handwritten piece, State v. John Wilson, Newberry, Indictment Larceny, Spring Term 1815, Case 3, O'Neall Papers, South Caroliniana, Columbia; O'Neall to Joseph Henry Lumpkin, October 17, 1849, and Theobald Mathew to Lumpkin, July 25, 1849, Box 2, MS 192, Lumpkin Papers, University of Georgia, Athens.

CHAPTER 17

1. *Cawthorn v. Deas*, 2 Port. 279 (Ala., 1835); *Gaillardet v. Demaries*, 18 La. 491 (1841).

2. Calabresi, *The Costs of Accidents*, 22–23; Morton Horwitz, *Transformation of American Law, 1780–1860*, 85–99 (quotation, p. 99); White, *Tort Law in America*; Gary Schwartz, "Tort Law and the Economy in Nineteenth-Century America."

3. White, *Tort Law in America*, 3.

4. Ibid., 14–15.

5. Tushnet, *American Law of Slavery*, 37.

6. See Chapter 2 above, where the sources of legal norms rooted in English common law are discussed.

7. Oliver Wendell Holmes, *Common Law*, 86; Reid, *Chief Justice*, 133–51; Stone, *Social Dimensions of Law and Justice*, 152 (Pound). See also White, *Tort Law in America*, 180.

8. Milsom, *Historical Foundations*, 266.

9. Prosser, *Handbook on the Law of Torts*, 506–10.

10. Morton Horwitz, *Transformation of American Law, 1780–1860*, 87; Blackstone, *Commentaries*, 1:431, 3:153, 211.

11. *Campbell v. Staiert*, 6 N.C. 286 (1818).

12. *Wright v. Weatherly*, 7 Yerg. 367 (Tenn., 1835); *Ewing v. Thompson*, 13 Mo. 132 (1850); *Brandon v. Planter's & Merchant's Bank*, 1 Stew. 320 (Ala., 1828).

13. *Snee v. Trice*, 1 Brevard 179 (S.C., 1802). There are two reports of this case.

14. Ibid.; Blackstone, *Commentaries*, 1:431.

15. *Snee v. Trice*, 2 Bay 349 (S.C., 1802).

16. *Wingis v. Smith*, 3 McCord 400 (S.C., 1825); Tushnet, *American Law of Slavery*, 37; *O'Connell v. Strong*, Dudley 267–68 (S.C., 1838).

17. *Cawthorn v. Deas*, 2 Port. 279 (Ala., 1835).

18. *Snee v. Trice*, 2 Bay 349 (S.C., 1802); *White v. Chambers*, 2 Bay 70 (S.C., 1796).

19. Morton Horwitz, *Transformation of American Law, 1780–1860*, 87.

20. Ibid., 93.

21. Blackstone, *Commentaries*, 1:419.

22. *Snee v. Trice*, 2 Bay 349 (S.C., 1802).

23. In Brevard's report of the case, the court defined the problem as "whether the mischief was occasioned by a want of ordinary care in keeping the fire, or to an extraordinary gust of wind, or some other unexpected and uncommon circumstance." The problem concerns the meaning of the phrase "want of ordinary care." Should it be seen as the modern standard of "due care"? Probably not, as Brevard added a lengthy footnote on the subject of the English rules in fire-spreading cases. It was only a summary of the law as it stood in the seventeenth century, when liability was strict.

24. *O'Connell v. Strong*, Dudley 267–68 (S.C., 1838).

25. *Garrett v. Freeman*, 50 N.C. 89 (1857); *Maille v. Blas*, 15 La. Ann. 100 (1860).

26. Modern tort language appeared in a Mississippi case, *Leggett v. Simmons*, 7 Smedes and M. 348 (Miss., 1846), but it failed to create a liability in the master. It was an action of trespass to recover damages from the owner of a slave who had killed the slave of another master. Judge J. S. B. Thacher ruled that the liability of the master "seems to depend upon the criminal knowledge or agency of that master." That was not shown. The facts were that the owner of the slave who killed the other not only allowed the slaves to have liquor but also knew they had fought. When the fight ended he went to bed, leaving the slaves still together, and woke up to find one of them dead. Thacher observed that "the defendant was doubtless censurable and blamable, for want of care, prudence, and resolute and sufficient interference between the slaves at the outset of the fatal difficulty, but his conduct seems hardly to warrant the finding of the jury, as such cases are contemplated by the law."

27. Morton Horwitz, *Transformation of American Law, 1780–1860*, 85–99.

28. Weber, *On Law in Economy and Society*, 15.

29. *Gaillardet v. Demaries*, 18 La. 491 (1841); Buckland, *Roman Law of Slavery*, 112–13.

30. Quoted in Tushnet, "American Law of Slavery," 182–83.

31. Upton and Jennings, *Civil Code of . . . Louisiana*, chap. 3, art. 180.

32. Ibid., art. 181.

33. *Gaillardet v. Demaries*, 18 La. 491 (1841).

34. *Boulard v. Calhoun*, 13 La. Ann. 100 (1858).

35. *Parham v. Blackwelder*, 30 N.C. 326 (1848).

36. *Wright v. Weatherly*, 7 Yerg. 67 (Tenn., 1835). There is a full examination of this and other Tennessee cases in Corré, "Thinking Property at Memphis."

37. Gould, *Digest of the Statutes of Arkansas*, 385.

38. *McConnell v. Hardeman*, 15 Ark. 157 (1854).

39. *Ewing v. Thompson*, 13 Mo. 132 (1850).

40. Ibid.

41. Helper, *Impending Crisis of the South*, 279; Blanche Henry Clark, *Tennessee Yeoman*; Shugg, *Origins of Class Struggle in Louisiana*; Weaver, *Mississippi Farmers*; Stampp, *Peculiar Institution*, chap. 3; Genovese, "Yeoman Farmers in a Slaveholders' Democracy," 341 (see, however, Durrill, *War of Another Kind*).

42. See, e.g., Hahn, *Roots of Southern Populism*; Inscoe, *Mountain Masters*; Burton and McMath, *Class, Conflict, and Consensus*; and Ford, *Origins of Southern Radicalism*.

43. *McConnell v. Hardeman*, 15 Ark. 157 (1854) (Watkins); Howington, " 'Not in the Condition of a Horse or an Ox,' " 249; *Wright v. Weatherly*, 7 Yerg. 367 (Tenn., 1835) (Green).

44. Mooney, *Slavery in Tennessee*, chap. 1.

45. Orville W. Taylor, *Negro Slavery in Arkansas*, 38.

46. Eaton, *History of the Southern Confederacy*, 47–48, 154–55; Barney, *Road to Secession*, 14–15, 101, 118, 124, 144.

47. Chused, "Married Women's Property Law."

48. *Parham v. Blackwelder*, 30 N.C. 326 (1848).

49. Channing, *Crisis of Fear*, 255–56.

CHAPTER 18

1. Patterson, *Slavery and Social Death*, 210–11; Buckland, *Roman Law of Slavery*, chap. 19, "Release from Slavery: Generalia"; Mauss, *The Gift*; Patterson, *Slavery and Social Death*, 294: David Brion Davis, *Slavery and Human Progress*, 17.

2. Atiyah, *Freedom of Contract*; A. W. B. Simpson, *History of Contract*; Morton Horwitz,

Transformation of American Law, 1780–1860; Watson, *Roman Slave Law*, 39; Moreau and Carleton, *Laws of Las Siete Partidas . . . in Force*, 594 (first quotation); *Coke on Littleton*, 137b.

3. *Bryan v. Walton*, 14 Ga. 198 (1853).

4. See, e.g., *Statutes at Large of Virginia, 1792–1806*, 2:252. The best overall study of the problem remains Berlin, *Slaves Without Masters*.

5. Commonwealth v. Patty Green and Betty, June 27, 1834, Charles City County Circuit Court Order Book, 1831–52, 75, VSL; Berlin, *Slaves Without Masters*.

6. *Cleland v. Waters*, 16 Ga. 505 (1854). See also *Knight v. Hardeman*, 17 Ga. 262 (1855).

7. Hurd, *Law of Freedom and Bondage*, 1:214 n. 2; *Coke on Littleton*, 137a; Buckland, *Roman Law of Slavery*, 438.

8. Thomas Cooper and McCord, *Statutes at Large of South Carolina*, 7:443; *Linam v. Johnson*, 2 Bailey 137–39, 141 (S.C., 1831). See also, *Fisher's Negroes v. Dabbs*, 12 Tenn. 126 (1834).

9. *State v. Dorsey*, 6 Gill 391 (Md., 1848); *Nancy v. Snell*, 6 Dana 149 (Ky., 1838); *Wood v. Humphreys*, 12 Grattan 339–41 (Va., 1855).

10. *Lenoir v. Sylvester*, 1 Bailey 642 (S.C., 1830).

11. *Bowers v. Newman*, 2 McMul. 472 (S.C., 1842).

12. *White v. Green*, 36 N.C. 35 (1840); *Wade v. American Colonization Society*, 7 Smedes and M. 694 (Miss., 1846), quoting an earlier Mississippi case, *Leach v. Cooley*, 6 Smedes and M. 93 (Miss., 1846). See also *Wade v. American Colonization Society*, 4 Smedes and M. 670 (Miss., 1845).

13. Gareth Jones, *History of the Law of Charity*, 3, 10, 22.

14. *Charles et al. v. Hunnicutt*, 5 Call 324–30 (Va., 1804).

15. *Haywood v. Craven's Ex'rs.*, 4 N.C. 281 n. * (1816).

16. *Cameron v. Commissioners*, 36 N.C. 357 (1841); *Haywood v. Craven's Ex'rs.*, 4 N.C. 281 (1816); O'Neall, *Negro Law of South Carolina*, 41–42; *Mitchell v. Wells*, 37 Miss. 235 (1859). An extensive discussion of this Mississippi case is in Finkelman, *An Imperfect Union*, 5–6, 183–84, 234, 287–95, 310–11.

17. *Hurdle v. Outlaw*, 55 N.C. 67 (1854).

18. *Thompson v. Newlin*, 38 N.C. 268 (1844). This case was before the court on two other occasions: *Thompson v. Newlin*, 41 N.C. 270 (1849), and *Thompson v. Newlin*, 43 N.C. 28 (1851).

19. *Lemmond v. Peoples*, 41 N.C. 109 (1848); *Thompson v. Newlin*, 41 N.C. 273 (1849).

20. *Ross v. Vertner*, 5 How. 323, 335–36, 357 (Miss., 1840).

21. *Hunter, guardian v. Bass, Ex'r.*, 18 Ga. 127 (1855): *Adams, guardian v. Bass, Ex'r.*, 18 Ga. 130 (1855).

22. *Hunter, guardian v. Bass, Ex'r.*, 18 Ga. 129 (1855).

23. *Adams, guardian v. Bass, Ex'r.*, 18 Ga. 135–36, 138–39 (1855).

24. *American Colonization Society v. Gartrell*, 23 Ga. 448 (1857).

25. *Frazier v. Frazier*, 2 Hill Eq. 304, 317 (S.C., 1835); *Bynum v. Bostick*, 4 DeSaussure 266 (S.C., 1812).

26. O'Neall, *Negro Law of South Carolina*, 11–12.

27. *Thompson v. Newlin*, 41 N.C. 273 (1349); *Sanders v. Ward*, 25 Ga. 121 (1858).

28. *Ross v. Vertner*, 5 How. 807 (Miss., 1840). See also *Ross v. Duncan*, Fr. Miss. Ch. 587 (Miss., 1840).

29. *Vance v. Crawford*, 4 Ga. 445, 460 (1848).

30. *Session Laws of Georgia, 1859*, 68.

31. *Hughes v. Negro Milly et al.*, 5 H. and J. 253 (Md., 1821).

32. Hening, *Statutes at Large*, 4:132, 11:39–40; Cushing, *Earliest Printed Laws of North Carolina*, 173; *Revised Statutes of . . . North Carolina*, 1:585.

33. Thomas Cooper and McCord, *Statutes at Large of South Carolina*, 7:442–43 (quota-

tion), 459; O'Neall, *Negro Law of South Carolina*, 11–12 (1841); Hutchinson, *Code of Mississippi, 1848*, 539.

34. *Trotter v. Blocker*, 6 Port. 291–92 (Ala. 1838); *Prater's Adm'r. v. Darby*, 24 Ala. 507 (1854) *Evans v. Kittrell*, 33 Ala. 453 (1859).

35. Rebecca J. Scott, *Slave Emancipation in Cuba*, 13–14, 74–75, 82.

36. Blassingame, *Slave Testimony*, 82 n. 49.

37. *Guardian of Sally, a Negro, v. Beaty*, 1 Bay 266 (S.C., 1792).

38. *Stevenson v. Singleton*, 1 Leigh 73 (Va., 1829). See also *Sawney v. Carter*, 6 Rand. 173 (Va., 1828)

39. *Ford v. Ford*, 7 Humphreys 95–96 (Tenn., 1846). The fullest account is Howington, "'Not in the Condition of a Horse or an Ox.'"

40. *Lewis v. Simonton*, 8 Humphreys 126–28 (Tenn., 1847).

41. Ibid., 128–29.

42. *Isaac v. Sliger*, 3 Head 161–63 (Tenn., 1859).

43. *Isaac v. Farnsworth*, 3 Head 208–10 (Tenn., 1859).

44. M. Burns to Robert L. Caruthers, March 6, 1852, Caruthers Papers, Southern Historical Collection, Chapel Hill, N.C.

45. *Isaac v. Farnsworth*, 3 Head 209–10 (Tenn., 1859).

46. Ibid., 210.

47. *McCloud and Karnes v. Chiles*, 1 Coldwell 251–52 (Tenn., 1860).

48. Howington, "'Not in the Condition of a Horse or an Ox,'" and works cited there.

49. *Beall v. Joseph (a negro)*, Hardin 56 (Ky., 1806). See also Post, "Kentucky Law concerning Emancipation or Freedom of Slaves."

50. *Thompson v. Wilmot*, 1 Bibb 422 (Ky., 1809).

51. Ibid., 422–24.

52. *Willis (of Color) v. Bruce and Warfield*, 8 B. Mon. 550–51 (Ky., 1848).

53. Upton and Jennings, *Civil Code of . . . Louisiana*, 27; Schafer, "The Long Arm of the Law," 281; *Victoire v. Dussuau*, 4 Mart. La. 212 (La., 1816).

54. *Carroll v. Brumby*, 13 Ala. 105 (1848).

55. *Elder v. Elder*, 4 Leigh 252, 254–55, 260–64 (Va., 1833). Judge Carr's opinion bypassed the issue by focusing on the intention of the testator, which he held was controlling.

56. *Forward's Adm'r. v. Thamer*, 9 Grattan 537–40 (Va., 1853).

57. *Osborne v. Taylor*, 12 Grattan 117, 128 (Va., 1855).

58. *Baily v. Poindexter*, 14 Grattan 139, 145–46 (Va., 1858).

59. *Bean v. Summers*, 13 Grattan 412 (Va., 1856).

60. *Baily v. Poindexter*, 14 Grattan 159, 197 (Va., 1858).

61. Ibid., 201, 204.

62. *Williamson v. Coalter*, 14 Grattan 395, 397, 403–4 (Va., 1858).

63. A. E. Keir Nash, "Reason of Slavery," 183.

64. *Cox v. Williams*, 39 N.C. 13–14 (1845).

65. *Redding v. Findley*, 4 Jones Eq. 218–19 (N.C., 1858).

66. Ibid., 219.

67. Stroud, *Sketch of the Laws*, 96. For the claims of widows see *Negro William v. Kelly*, 5 H. and J. 48 (Md., 1820).

68. Hening, *Statutes at Large*, 11:39–40.

69. *Woodley v. Abby*, 5 Call 336–37, 342 (Va., 1805).

70. Ibid., 349; *Statutes at Large of Virginia . . . 1792–1806*, 1:128.

71. *Woodley v. Abby*, 5 Call 348, 343, 347, 349–50 (Va., 1805).

72. *Dunn v. Amey*, 1 Leigh 471–72 (Va., 1829).

73. *Nicholas v. Burruss*, 4 Leigh 293–95 (Va., 1833).

74. *Negro George et al. v. Corse's Adm'r.*, 2 H. and G. 5–7 (Md., 1827).

75. *Fenwick v. Chapman*, 9 Peters 470–75 (1835). The Court also asked, "What is manumission?" Its answer was, "It is the giving of liberty to one who has been in just servitude, with the power of acting, except as retrained by law." Ibid., 472.

76. *Cornish v. Willson*, 6 Gill. 237, 246 (Md., 1848).

77. *Allein v. Sharp*, 7 G. and J. 77 (Md., 1835); *Thomas v. Wood*, 1 Md. Ch. 301 (1848).

78. *Harry v. Green*, 9 Humphreys 185 (Tenn., 1848).

79. *Ferguson v. Sarah*, 4 J. J. Marsh. 105 (Ky., 1830); *Nancy (a colored woman) v. Snell*, 6 Dana 149 (Ky., 1838).

80. *Caleb v. Fields*, 9 Dana 348 (Ky., 1840).

81. *Snead v. David*, 9 Dana 352, 355 (Ky., 1840).

82. Hening, *Statutes at Large*, 2:260, 3:460, 87.

83. McIlwaine, *Executive Journals*, 4:315, 366 (December 19, 1735).

82. Ibid., 5:60 (June 19, 1741), 193 (November 4, 1745), and 6:450–51 (March 21, 1771); Will of Joseph Walker, December 16, 1723, and Will of William Drury, July 18, 1726, York County Orders, Wills and Inventories, 1720–32, VSL; Petition of Josias, a Spanish Mulatto, February 5, 1728/9, Princess Anne County Minute Book 4, 1728–37, VSL.

85. Entry for January 8, 1778, Southampton County Court Order Book, 1778–84, VSL; Jordan, *White Over Black*; Mullin, *Flight and Rebellion*; Russell, *Free Negro in Virginia*; Albert, "Protean Institution," Part 2, "The Slavery Question: Agitation and Legislation."

86. Hening, *Statutes at Large*, 11:39–40 (first quotation); *Statutes at Large of Virginia, 1792–1806*, 2:252; *Code of Virginia, 1849*, 1:466; Thorpe, *Federal and State Constitutions*, 7:3840 (last quotation).

87. Russell, *Free Negro in Virginia*, 61; Jordan, *White Over Black*, 347; Gary B. Nash, *Race and Revolution*, 18, 43.

88. Bruns, *Am I Not a Man and a Brother*, 506–7; Morton, *Carter of Nomini Hall*, 251; Flexner, *Washington*, 39; Finkelman, "Jefferson and Slavery," 181–82; Schmidt and Wilhelm, "Early Proslavery Petitions in Virginia," 139.

89. Dunn, "Black Society in the Chesapeake" and "A Tale of Two Plantations"; Morton, *Carter of Nomini Hall*.

90. Will of Daniel Bailey, November 30, 1786, Westmoreland County Deeds and Wills, 1773–87, VSL; Will of Samuel Sanford, September 6, 1797, in *Wills of Westmoreland County, Virginia*, 200.

91. Will of Joseph Pierce, August 27, 1798, Westmoreland County Deeds and Wills, 1794–99, VSL.

92. Among those with close ties to Carter were Samuel Templeman, Moore Fauntleroy, Henry Toler, Benjamin Dawson, and Austin Brockenbrough. Morton, *Carter of Nomini Hall*, 153, 236, 238, 268–69, 291; Jack P. Greene, *Diary of Landon Carter*, 2:923.

93. See, e.g., Deed of Emancipation from William Jett to Ned, November 24, 1800, Westmoreland County Orders, 1799–1800, and Deed of Emancipation from Lewis Chastain, November 26, 1798, Westmoreland County Records and Inventories No. 7, 1790–98, VSL. Chastain's reason was that he did "believe that God created all men equally here and that Slavery with all its horrid Consequences to be a National, Political and Religious evil and do hereby Emancipate and set free . . ."

94. See, e.g., Deed of "Emanumission," February 28, 1792, from Carter, and Deed of Emancipation from Brinnon, May 29, 1792, Westmoreland County Orders, 1790–95, VSL.

95. Deed of Manumission to Frank from John Rowand, April 25, 1786, and Deed of Manumission for Florinda, Fanny, April 26, 1786, Westmoreland County Court Orders, 1776–86, VSL.

96. Deeds of Manumission to Sundry Slaves, February 28, 1792 (Carter), April 24, 1792 (Carter), May 29, 1792 (Brinnon), February 27, 1793 (Carter), February 28, 1793 (Carter), and June 24, 1794 (Carter), Westmoreland County Court Orders, 1790–95, VSL.

97. See n. 93 above.

98. Deed of Manumission to Sundry Slaves, June 1804, Westmoreland County Court Orders, 1801–4, VSL. Cf. Gary B. Nash, *Race and Revolution*, 2–30.

99. Albert, "Protean Institution," 279; Schwarz, "Emancipators, Protectors, and Anomalies."

100. Deed of Manumission to Harry et al., September 19, 1793, Charles City County Deed Book, 1789–1802, VSL.

101. Deeds of Manumission from Samuel Hargrave, January 20, 1791, January 15, 1795, January 21, 1796; Deed of Manumission from Charles Binns, December 19, 1793; and Deeds of Manumission from John Crew, January 17, September 17, 1798—all in Charles City County Deed Book, 1780–1802, VSL. See also Deed of Transfer, Crew to Hargrave, 1798 (a deed involving the transfer of land belonging to the Society of Friends). Ibid.

102. See, e.g., Will of Ann Minge, March 20, 1800, and Will of Richardson Walker, October 16, 1794, Charles City County Will Book, 1789–1808, VSL.

103. Will of Benjamin Harrison, June 16, 1791, ibid.

104. See Will of Lettice Ball, December 15, 1788, Lancaster County Wills, 1783–95, 193, VSL; Will of Fleming Bates, March 5, 1784, Will of John Lester, September 30, 1790, Will of Ann Ellis, September 15, 1794, Will of Mary Moss, June 17, 1799, Will of John Dickson, September 21, 1801, Will of John Robinson, February 18, 1795, and Will of William Cary, July 15, 1805, York County Wills and Inventories, 1783–1811, VSL.

105. Dunn, "A Tale of Two Plantations."

106. See, e.g., *Session Laws of Virginia, 1839*, 204. Other examples can be found easily in Finkelman, *State Slavery Statutes*.

107. Thomas D. Morris, *Free Men All*; Finkelman, *An Imperfect Union*; Litwack, *North of Slavery*.

108. *Session Laws of Arkansas, 1859*, 69; Scott and McCullough, *Maryland Code*, 1:458.

109. *Mitchell v. Wells*, 37 Miss. 250 (1859).

110. O'Neall, *Negro Law of South Carolina*, 12.

CHAPTER 19

1. Fitzhugh, *Cannibals All!*, 78.

2. Steinfeld, *Invention of Free Labor*.

3. *Trustees of the Quaker Society of Contentnea v. William Dickenson*, 12 N.C. 121–23 (1827).

4. Ibid., 125. See also *State v. Boon*, Taylor 246 (N.C., 1801).

5. *Thompson v. Newlin*, 38 N.C. 266–68 (1844).

6. *Huckaby v. Jones*, 2 Hawks 120 (N.C., 1822); *Stevens v. Ely*, 16 N.C. 295 (1830); *Sorry v. Bright*, 1 Dev. and Bat. Eq. 113 (N.C., 1835).

7. *Lemmond v. Peoples*, 41 N.C. 109–10 (1848).

8. *Lea v. Brown*, 5 Jones Eq. 145–47 (N.C., 1857).

9. *Cline v. Caldwell*, 1 Hill 274–77 (S.C., 1833).

10. Ibid., 276.

11. *Carmille v. Carmille's Adm'r.*, 2 McMul. 467–68 (S.C., 1842); 468–69; *McLeish v. Burch*, 3 Strob. Eq. 226 (S.C., 1849).

12. *Cleland v. Waters*, 16 Ga. 505 (1854); *Knight v. Hardeman*, 17 Ga. 262 (1855).

13. *Broughton v. Telfer*, 3 Rich. Eq. 436, 438–39 (S.C., 1851); *Ford v. Dangerfield*, 8 Rich. Eq. 100–101 (S.C., 1856).

14. *Pleasants v. Pleasants*, 2 Call 319, 323 (Va., 1799). What promises to be the definitive study of this crucial case (by James Kettner of the University of California, Berkeley) is in progress. See also Herbert A. Johnson, *Papers of John Marshall*, 5:541–49. Marshall was counsel for the emancipator Robert Pleasants. As the editors of his papers note, "in his

argument he seems to have deliberately eschewed the rhetoric of liberty in order to make the case on strict legal grounds" (p. 543).

15. *Pleasants v. Pleasants*, 2 Call 338–39 (Va., 1799).

16. Keith Hopkins, *Conquerors and Slaves*, 143; Stc. Croix, *Class Struggle in the Ancient World*, 135; Samuel, "Role of *Paramone* Clauses," 221–311.

17. *Pleasants v. Pleasants*, 2 Call 319 (Va., 1799).

18. Kent, *Commentaries on American Law*, 4:655.

19. *Pleasants v. Pleasants*, 2 Call 348–49 (Va., 1799).

20. Ibid., 348, 350, 352.

21. David Brion Davis, *Problem of Slavery in Western Culture*, 271.

22. Cover, *Justice Accused*, 74; A. E. Keir Nash, "Reason of Slavery," 152.

23. *Mayho v. Sears*, 25 N.C. 162 (1842); *Maria v. Surbaugh*, 2 Rand. 228 (Va., 1824).

24. Ibid., 229; *Pleasants v. Pleasants*, 2 Call 346 (Va., 1799).

25. *Maria v. Surbaugh*, 2 Rand. 229 (Va., 1824).

26. Ibid., 231.

27. Ibid., 230.

28. Ibid., 232–33, 240.

29. Ibid., 241, 234.

30. Ibid.

31. *Isaac v. West's Ex'r.*, 6 Rand. 652–53, 656 (Va., 1828).

32. Ibid., 657; Watson, *Roman Slave Law*, 39; Moreau and Carleton, *Laws of Las Siete Partidas . . . in Force*, 594.

33. *Isaac v. West's Ex'r.*, 6 Rand. 657 (Va., 1828).

34. A. E. Keir Nash, "Reason of Slavery," 152.

35. *Erskine v. Henry*, 9 Leigh 188, 193 (Va., 1838).

36. *Crawford v. Moses*, 10 Leigh 277 (Va., 1839).

37. *Anderson's Ex'rs. v. Anderson*, 11 Leigh 616–17, 621–23 n * (Va., 1841).

38. Ibid., 624.

39. *Code of Virginia, 1849*, 1:458–59.

40. *Wood v. Humphreys*, 12 Grattan 333–34 (Va., 1855).

41. Ibid., 338.

42. *Maria v. Surbaugh*, 2 Rand. 246 (Va., 1824); *Jones v. Wootten*, 1 Harr. 83 (Del., 1833); *Smith v. Milman*, 2 Harr. 498 (Del., 1839).

43. *Ned v. Beal*, 2 Bibb 299 (Ky., 1811); *Mayho v. Sears*, 25 N.C. 162 (1842); *Sidney v. White*, 12 Ala. 730 (1848); *Catin v. D'Orgenoy's Heirs*, 8 Mart. La. 218 (1820); Upton and Jennings, *Civil Code of . . . Louisiana*, 30.

44. *Campbell v. Street*, 23 N.C. 88 (1840).

45. *Caffey v. Davis*, 54 N.C. 13, 15 (1853); *Myers v. Williams*, 58 N.C. 290–91 (1860).

46. A. E. Keir Nash, "Reason of Slavery," 157; Howington, "Treatment of Slaves and Free Blacks," 13–14.

47. *Harris v. Clarissa*, 6 Yerg. 243–45 (Tenn., 1834).

48. Maxcy, *Laws of Maryland*, 3:493.

49. *Catin v. D'Orgenoy's Heirs*, 8 Mart. La. 219 (1820); Upton and Jennings, *Civil Code of . . . Louisiana*, 30; *Heirs of Henderson v. Rost & Montgomery*, 11 La. Ann. 542 (1856); *Session Laws of Louisiana, 1857*, 55; *Julienne (f. w. c.) v. Touriac*, 13 La. Ann. 599 (1858).

50. For the statute, see *Jones v. Wootten*, 1 Harr. 77 (Del., 1833).

51. Ibid., 80, 85.

52. *Revised Statutes of Kentucky, 1852*, 384; *Revised Code of North Carolina, 1854*, 574.

53. *Pleasants v. Pleasants*, 2 Call 339, 352 (Va., 1799); *Maria v. Surbaugh*, 2 Rand. 235 (Va., 1824).

54. *Hamilton v. Cragg*, 6 H. and J. 18 (Md., 1823); *Chew v. Gary*, 6 H. and J. 431 (Md., 1823).

55. *Sidney v. White*, 12 Ala. 730 (1848).

56. *Isaac v. West's Ex'r.*, 6 Rand. 656 (Va., 1828). On white servitude in colonial America, the classic work by Abbot Emerson Smith, *Colonists in Bondage*, remains of real value.

57. *Revised Code of Delaware, 1852*, 259.

58. *Jones v. Wootten*, 1 Harr. 84 (Del., 1833).

59. *Harris v. Clarissa*, 6 Yerg. 243–44 (Tenn., 1834).

60. *Hartsell v. George*, 3 Humphreys 259 (Tenn., 1842).

61. A. W. B. Simpson, *History of the Land Law*, 226; Blackstone, *Commentaries*, 2:174; Leach, "Perpetuities in a Nutshell," 640.

62. *Pleasants v. Pleasants*, 2 Call 325, 328–29 (Va., 1799).

63. Ibid., 331.

64. Herbert A. Johnson, *Papers of John Marshall*, 5:545.

65. *Pleasants v. Pleasants*, 2 Call 336, 339–40 (Va., 1799).

66. Ibid., 340.

67. Ibid., 349, 351.

68. *Wood v. Humphreys*, 12 Grattan 339 (Va., 1853).

69. Ibid., 340–41.

70. Ibid., 352, 356.

71. Ibid., 361–62.

72. *Harris v. Clarissa*, 6 Yerg. 241, 243 (Tenn., 1834).

73. *Ludwig, (of color), v. Combs*, 1 Met. Ky. 129–32 (Ky., 1858).

74. *Myers v. Williams*, 58 N.C. 291 (1860).

CONCLUSION

1. Buckland, *Roman Law of Slavery*, 2; Rice, *Rise and Fall of Black Slavery*, 22; Stampp, *Peculiar Institution*, 192–93; Owens, *This Species of Property*, 16–17; Fede, *People Without Rights*, 18–19; Finley, *Encyclopedia of the Social Sciences*, 14:307; Patterson, *Slavery and Social Death*, 9, 17–21; Meillassoux, *Anthropology of Slavery*, 11, 10.

2. McTyeire, Sturgis, and Holmes, *Duties of Masters to Servants*, 79.

3. Hegel, *Philosophy of Right*, 261; Buckland, *Roman Law of Slavery*, 3.

4. T. R. R. Cobb, *Law of Negro Slavery*, 3–4.

5. Buckland, *Roman Law of Slavery*, 10; *Revised Statutes of Delaware, 1852*, 259.

6. Elliott, *Cotton Is King*, vii.

7. Finley, *Ancient Slavery and Modern Ideology*, 126–27.

8. Ste. Croix, *Class Struggle in the Ancient World*, 462–63.

9. Bloch, *Feudal Society*, 257.

10. Krygier, "Law as Tradition," 242.

11. Bender, *Antislavery Debate*.

12. Eric Williams, *Capitalism and Slavery*; Solow and Engerman, *British Capitalism and Caribbean Slavery*; Drescher, *Econocide*; Fogel, *Without Consent or Contract*, 410; Fogel and Engerman, *Time on the Cross*.

13. Bender, *Antislavery Debate*.

14. Drescher, "Long Goodbye."

15. Oakes, *Slavery and Freedom*, 56–57, 68, 79.

16. Hurd, *Law of Freedom and Bondage*, 1:42; Oakes, *Slavery and Freedom*, 155, 159; Patterson, *Slavery and Social Death*, 22.

17. Tushnet, *American Law of Slavery*, 228; Fox-Genovese and Genovese, *Fruits of Merchant Capital*, 377. Fede (*People Without Rights*, 4) argued that Stroud was correct that the

slave was a thing at law, and essentially "all references to slave humanity and right obfuscate the real meaning of the slave law of the U.S. South."

18. Undated, untitled essay in folder 96, Gaston Papers, Southern Historical Collection, Chapel Hill, N.C.

19. Jack P. Greene, *Pursuits of Happiness.*

20. *State v. Mann*, 13 N.C. 170 (1829).

21. Baker, "Property in Chattels," 217.

22. Eltis, "Labour and Coercion in the English Atlantic World," 207–8.

23. On the pressures within the Federal Union see Fehrenbacher, *Dred Scott;* Finkelman, *An Imperfect Union;* and Thomas D. Morris, *Free Men All.*

24. Bestor, "State Sovereignty and Slavery"; Frederick Cooper, *From Slaves to Squatters;* Rodney, *History of the Guyanese Working People.*

25. Fogel, *Without Consent or Contract*, 411–12 (Potter).

26. Blackstone, *Commentaries,* 3:268; Morton Horwitz, *Transformation of American Law, 1870–1960,* 39–51.

27. *Polk v. Faris,* 9 Yerg. 233 (Tenn., 1836).

28. Genovese, *"Slavery Ordained of God,"* 14.

29. *Robinson v. McDonald,* 2 Ga. 123 (1847); Fox-Genovese and Genovese, "Slavery, Economic Development, and the Law," 26.

30. *Judge v. Wilkins,* 19 Ala. 770 (1851).

31. *Waddill v. Chamberlayn* (1735), in Barton, *Virginia Colonial Decisions,* 2:45–50; *Randolph v. Randolph,* 6 Rand. 197 (Va., 1828).

32. Patterson, *Slavery and Social Death,* 22.

33. *Smith v. M'Call,* 1 McCord 223 (S.C. 1821); *Caldwell v. Wallace,* 4 Stew. and P. 285 (Ala., 1833).

34. *Monday v. Wilson et al.,* 4 La. 341 (1832); Hening, *Statutes at Large,* 2:288; *Hicks v. Parham, Ex'r.,* 3 Haywood 225–27 (Tenn., 1827).

35. *Young v. Burton,* McMul. Eq. 161 (S.C., 1841). The practice was halted in *M'Dowell ads. Murdock,* 1 N. and McC. 144 (S.C., 1818).

36. Goodell, *American Slave Code,* 289–90.

37. For the arguments and tensions produced by the violent punishment of slaves see the discussion in Chapter 12.

38. *Bailey v. Poindexter,* 14 Grattan 139 (Va., 1858); *Cox v. Williams,* 39 N.C. 13–14 (1845).

39. See especially *Commonwealth v. Richard Booth,* 2 Va. Ca. 394 (1824), and *Commonwealth v. Richard Turner,* 5 Rand. 678 (Va., 1827).

40. *Gayle v. Cunningham,* Harp. Eq. 125 (S.C., 1824).

41. Lieberman, *Province of Legislation Determined;* Thomas Cooper and McCord, *Statutes at Large of South Carolina,* 7:411.

42. "Slave Marriages," *DeBow's Review,* July 1855, 130.

43. Quoted in Genovese, *Roll, Jordan, Roll,* 52–53.

44. T. R. R. Cobb, *Law of Negro Slavery,* 245–46; O'Neall, *Negro Law of South Carolina,* 18.

45. See, e.g., Howell Cobb, *Compilation of the . . . Statutes of . . . Georgia,* 709.

46. Genovese, *Roll, Jordan, Roll,* 53.

47. Kettner, *Development of American Citizenship,* 16–28.

48. Occasionally such responsibilities even extended to the hirer of the slave. An example is *Latimer v. Alexander,* 14 Ga. 259 (1853).

49. Fisher, "Ideology and Imagery in the Law of Slavery," 1080.

50. *Mitchell v. Wells,* 37 Miss. 235 (1859).

51. See the discussion of the options in Chapter 2.

52. Berlin, *Slaves Without Masters.*

53. See, however, Lumpkin's discussion in *Scudder v. Woodbridge,* 1 Ga. 195 (1846).

54. Oliver Wendell Holmes, *Common Law*, 56.

55. *State v. Caesar, (a slave)*, 31 N.C. 270–73 (1849).

56. *John, (a slave), v. State*, 16 Ga. 203 (1854); Tannenbaum, *Slave and Citizen*, 110.

57. *Gorman v. Campbell*, 14 Ga. 143 (1853).

58. *Commonwealth v. Richard Turner*, 5 Rand. 686–90 (Va., 1827).

59. Weber, *On Law in Economy and Society*, 35, 37.

60. Holt, *Problem of Freedom*; Brathwaite, *Development of Creole Society in Jamaica*; Craton, *Testing the Chains*; Dunn, *Sugar and Slaves*; Mintz, *Caribbean Transformations*; Patterson, *Sociology of Slavery*; Rodney, *History of the Guyanese Working People*; Beckles, *White Servitude and Black Slavery in Barbados*; Goveia, *Slave Society in the British Leeward Islands*; Handler and Lange, *Plantation Slavery in Barbados*; Rice, *Rise and Fall of Black Slavery*.

61. O'Neall, *Negro Law of South Carolina*, 12; Cobb to his daughter Cally, June 25, 1862, Cobb Papers, University of Georgia, Athens.

Bibliography

This bibliography is organized as follows:

Unpublished primary material: county records, manuscripts
Published primary material: newspapers and periodicals, legal treatises, statutes, appellate cases
Other published primary material
Secondary works: books, articles, dissertations

UNPUBLISHED PRIMARY MATERIAL

County Records

The records from the Southern counties vary in quality and accessibility. Some—either the originals or on microfilm—are available in the state archives. Those for Louisiana (except for some material transferred to the state archives from St. Landry Parish), Mississippi, Alabama, and Florida are presently in the county courthouses. In either case many county records have not survived. Some were not kept, and some were lost in ordinary courthouse fires. I have tried to assemble a representative sample from throughout the South. The sole exception is Delaware. For that state, with the smallest number of slaves anywhere in the South, I relied on published records and secondary studies. For the remainder of the region I used records from urban and rural counties scattered over time. In some cases the records used cover over half a century. In others it might be chunks of ten or more years. The minimum number of counties whose records were used for any state was two. This was dictated by accessibility and the limits of any one person's ability to examine these records.

The files include probate records, order books, minute books, criminal dockets, and trial papers. Because the nature of the property involved in most civil actions was rarely recorded, the county records are more valuable for insights into the criminal justice system, but some cases on the civil side are helpful as well. The material was rounded out for some counties with information in the manuscript census microfilms available from the National Archives. The county records used in this study come from the following counties:

Alabama: Chambers and Lowndes.
Arkansas: Arkansas, Crittenden, Jefferson, Pulaski, and Union.
Florida: Leon and Madison.
Georgia: Baldwin, Chatham, Elbert, Hancock, Jackson, Liberty, Lincoln, Putnam, and Screven.
Kentucky: Boyle, Jessamine, Mercer, Scott, and Warren.
Louisiana: Natchitoches, St. Landry, and West Feliciana.
Maryland: Anne Arundel, Frederick, Prince Georges, Queen Anne, Somerset, and Talbot.
Mississippi: Adams, Lowndes, and Wilkinson.
Missouri: Boone and Saline.
North Carolina: Edgecombe, Granville, New Hanover, and Northampton.
South Carolina: Fairfield, Greenville, Laurens, Marlborough, Spartanburg, and York.
Tennessee: Davidson and Maury.

Texas: Bastrop and Harrison.

Virginia: Caroline, Charles City County, Fauquier, Essex, Lancaster, Lunenburg, Orange, Petersburg City, Richmond City, Richmond County, Southampton, Sussex, Westmoreland, and York.

Manuscripts

Information from personal papers was generally disappointing as far as legal issues were concerned. There was some useful information in the following manuscript collections:

Athens, Georgia
  University of Georgia
    Thomas R. R. Cobb Papers
    Joseph Henry Lumpkin Papers
Baton Rouge, Louisiana
  Louisiana State University Archives
    Alexander Farrar Papers
    Liddell Papers
    Minor Papers
    Alonzo Snyder Papers
Chapel Hill, North Carolina
  Southern Historical Collection
    William H. Battle Papers
    Robert L. Caruthers Papers
    William Gaston Papers
    Richmond Pearson Papers
Columbia, Missouri
  Missouri Historical Society
    Abiel Leonard Papers
Columbia, South Carolina
  South Caroliniana
    John Belton O'Neall Papers
    James L. Petigru Papers
Frankfort, Kentucky
  Kentucky State Department of Libraries and Archives
    J. J. Crittenden Papers
    C. S. Morehead Papers
Jackson, Mississippi
  Mississippi Department of Archives and History
    Trypehna Holder Fox Collection
    James T. Harrison Notebook
San Marino, California
  Huntington Library
    Francis Lieber Papers

PUBLISHED PRIMARY MATERIAL

Newspapers and Periodicals

Advertiser and State Gazette (Montgomery, Alabama)
Charleston Mercury
DeBow's Review
Georgia Gazette

Kentucky Gazette
Maryland Gazette
Mississippi Free Trader (Natchez)
Nashville Gazette
New Orleans Times Picayune
North Carolina Gazette
Primitive Republican (Columbus, Mississippi)
Richmond Enquirer
South Carolina Gazette
South Carolina Gazette and Country Journal
South Carolina Gazette and General Advertiser
Southern Cultivator
Southern Law Journal
Virginia Gazette

Legal Treatises

Beccaria, Cesare. *On Crimes and Punishments.* Indianapolis: Bobbs-Merrill, 1963.

Bishop, Joel Prentiss. *New Commentaries on the Criminal Law upon a New System of Legal Exposition.* 8th ed. 2 vols. Chicago: T. H. Flood and Co., 1892.

Blackstone, Sir William. *Commentaries on the Laws of England.* 4 vols. Oxford: Clarendon Press, 1765–69.

Bouvier, John. *Institutes of American Law.* 2 vols. Boston: Little, Brown, 1880.

Chitty, Joseph. *A Practical Treatise on the Law of Contracts, Not under Seal.* London: S. Sweet, 1826.

——. *A Treatise on Pleading.* 7th ed. London: S. Sweet, 1844.

Cobb, T. R. R. *An Inquiry into the Law of Negro Slavery in the United States of America: To Which Is Prefixed, an Historical Sketch of Slavery.* 1858. Reprint, New York: Negro Universities Press, 1968.

Coke, Sir Edward. *The First Part of the Institutes of the Laws of England; or, A Commentary upon Littleton.* 1628. 18th ed., London: J. and W. T. Clarke, R. Pheney, and S. Brooke, 1823.

——. *The Third Part of the Institutes of the Laws of England: Concerning High Treason, and Other Pleas of the Crown, and Criminall Causes.* London: Printed by M. Flesher, 1644.

Cooper, Thomas, ed. *Institutes of Justinian, with Notes by Thomas Cooper.* Philadelphia: P. Byrne, 1812.

Corpus Juris: Being a Complete and Systematic Statement of the Whole Body of the Law. 72 vols. William Mack et al. New York: American Law Book Co., 1914–35.

Corpus Juris Secundum: A Complete Restatement of the Entire American Law as Developed by All Reported Cases. 101 vols. William Mack et al. St. Paul, Minn.: West Publishing Co., 1936–91.

Cowel, John. *The Institutes of the Lawes of England, Digested into the Method of the Civill or Imperiall Institutions.* London: Thomas Roycroft, 1651.

Dalton, Michael. *The Countrey Justice, Containing the Practise of the Justices of the Peace out of Their Sessions.* London: Printed for the Society of Stationers, 1622. See also the following editions: London: Printed by G. Sawbridge, T. Roycroft, and W. Rawlins, 1677, and a 1682 volume printed by the same firm. An edition of 1690 was published in London by Williams Rawlins and Samuel Roycroft.

Dane, Nathan. *A General Abridgement and Digest of American Law, with Occasional Notes and Comments.* 9 vols. Boston: Cummings, Hilliard and Co., 1823–29.

Domat, Jean. *The Civil Law in Its Natural Order.* 2d London ed. 2 vols. Boston: Little, Brown, 1850. The first London edition was published in 1720, the second in 1737.

Ely, Richard T. *Property and Contract in Their Relations to the Distribution of Wealth.* 2 vols. Port Washington, N.Y.: Kennikat Press, 1971.

Farnsworth, E. Allan. *Contracts.* Boston: Little, Brown, 1982.

Finch, Sir Henry. *Law; or, A Discourse Thereof.* London: Printed for the Society of Stationers, 1627.

Fonblonque, John. *A Treatise of Equity.* 3d ed. 2 vols. Philadelphia: P. Byrne, 1807.

Goodell, William. *The American Slave Code in Theory and Practice.* New York: American and Foreign Antislavery Society, 1853.

Greenleaf, Simon. *A Treatise on the Law of Evidence.* 4 vols. Boston: Little, Brown, 1842.

Grotius, Hugo. *De Jure Belli Ac Pacis Libri Tres.* Translated by Francis W. Kelsey, Arthur E. R. Boak, Henry A. Sanders, Jesse S. Reeves, and Herbert F. Wright. Oxford: Clarendon Press, 1925.

Hale, Sir Matthew. *De successionibus apud Anglos; or, A Treatise of Hereditary Descents.* London: A. Baldwin, 1699.

——. *Historia Placitorum Coronae: The History of the Pleas of the Crown.* Edited by W. A. Stokes and S. Ingersoll. 1st American ed. 2 vols. Philadelphia: R. H. Small, 1847.

——. *The History of the Common Law of England.* Edited by Charles M. Gray. Chicago: University of Chicago Press, 1971.

——. *Pleas of the Crown.* London: Richard Tonson, 1678.

Hall, Jerome. *General Principles of Criminal Law.* 2d ed. Indianapolis: Bobbs-Merrill, 1947.

Hawkins, Sir William. *A Treatise of the Pleas of the Crown.* 2 vols. London: Printed by E. and R. Nutt, 1724–26.

Hobbes, Thomas. *A Dialogue between a Philosopher and a Student of the Common Laws of England.* Edited by Joseph Cropsey. Chicago: University of Chicago Press, 1971.

Holmes, Oliver Wendell, Jr. *The Common Law.* Boston: Little, Brown, 1880.

Hurd, John Codman. *The Law of Freedom and Bondage in the United States.* 2 vols. New York: Negro Universities Press, 1968. Originally published by Little, Brown, 1858.

Jones, Sir William. *An Essay on the Law of Bailments.* From the last London ed. Philadelphia: Hogan and Thompson, 1836.

Kent, Chancellor James. *Commentaries on American Law.* 10th ed. 4 vols. Boston: Little, Brown, 1860.

Lambard, William. *Eirenarcha; or, Of the Office of Justices of Peace.* 2 books. London: R. Newbery, 1581.

Livingston, Edward. *A System of Penal Law, for the State of Louisiana.* Philadelphia: James Kay Jr. and Co., 1833.

McCloskey, Robert Green, ed. *The Works of James Wilson.* 2 vols. Cambridge: Harvard University Press, 1967.

Maine, Henry Sumner. *Ancient Law: Its Connection with the Early History of Society, and Its Relation to Modern Ideas.* London: John Murray, 1861.

Moreau, L. Lislet, and Henry Carleton. *The Laws of Las Siete Partidas Which Are Still in Force in the State of Louisiana.* 2 vols. New Orleans: J. M'Karaher, 1820.

Oldham, James, ed. *The Mansfield Manuscripts and the Growth of English Law in the Eighteenth Century.* 2 vols. Chapel Hill: University of North Carolina Press, 1992.

O'Neall, John Belton. *The Negro Law of South Carolina.* Columbia: John G. Bowman, 1848.

Parsons, Theophilus. *The Law of Contracts.* 2 vols. Boston: Little, Brown, 1852–55.

Pothier, Robert Joseph. *Traite du contrat e Louage, selon regles tont du for de la conscience, que du for extérieur par l'auteur du traite des obligation.* Paris: Chez les frerer Debure, 1778.

——. *A Treatise on Obligation, Considered in a Moral and Legal View.* 2 vols. in 1. New Bern, N.C.: Martin and Ogden, 1802.

Powell, John Joseph. *Essay upon the Law of Contracts and Agreements.* London: Dublin, Chamberlaine and Rice, 1790.

——. *A Treatise on the Law of Mortgages.* 2 vols. London: J. Butterworth, 1799.

Prosser, William. *Handbook on the Law of Torts.* St. Paul: West Publishing Co., 1964.

Reeve, Tapping. *The Law of Baron and Femme, of Parent and Child, Guardian and Ward, Master and Servant, and of the Powers of Courts of Chancery.* 2d ed. New York: Banks, Gould and Co., 1846.

Simes, Lewis M. *Handbook on the Law of Future Interests.* 2d ed. St. Paul: West Publishing Co., 1966.

Simpson, William. *The Practical Justice of the Peace and Parish-Officer, of His Majesty's Province of South Carolina.* Charlestown: Robert Wells, 1761.

Smith, Adam. *Lectures on Jurisprudence.* Edited by R. L. Meek, D. D. Raphael, and P. G. Stein. Oxford: Oxford University Press, 1978.

Story, Joseph. *Commentaries on Equity Jurisprudence.* 12th ed. 2 vols. Boston: Little, Brown, 1877.

——. *Commentaries on the Law of Agency.* Boston: Little, Brown, 1839.

——. *Commentaries on the Law of Bailments, with Illustrations from the Civil and the Foreign Law.* 9th ed. Boston: Little, Brown, 1878.

Story, William Wetmore. *A Treatise on the Law of Contracts Not under Seal.* 1844. Reprint, New York: Arno Press, 1972.

Stroud, George. *A Sketch of the Laws Relating to Slavery in the Several States of the United States of America.* 1827. Reprint, New York: Negro Universities Press, 1968.

Swinburne, Henry. *A Brief Treatise of Testaments and Last Willes.* London: J. Windet, 1590. Also, editions of 1611 by W. Stansby and 1677 by George Sawbridge, Thomas Raycroft, and William Rawlins.

Taylor, John. *Elements of the Civil Law.* London: Cambridge: Charles Bathurst, 1755.

Thayer, James Bradley. *A Preliminary Treatise on Evidence at the Common Law.* 1898. Reprint, New York: Augustus M. Kelley, 1969.

Tucker, St. George. *Blackstone's Commentaries: With Notes of Reference, to the Constitution and Laws, of the Federal Government of the United States, and of the Commonwealth of Virginia.* 5 vols. Philadelphia: William Young Burch and Abraham Small, 1803.

Vold, Lawrence. *Handbook of the Law of Sales.* 2d ed. St. Paul: West Publishing Co., 1959.

Waggoner, Lawrence. *Future Interests in a Nutshell.* St. Paul: West Publishing Co., 1981.

Walker, Timothy. *Introduction to American Law.* 1837. Reprint, New York: DaCapo Press, 1972.

Wheeler, Jacob D. *A Practical Treatise on the Law of Slavery.* 1837. Reprint, New York: Negro Universities Press, 1968.

Wooddeson, Richard. *A Systematical View of the Laws of England: As Treated of in a Course of Vinerian Lectures, Read at Oxford, During a Series of Years, Commencing in Michaelmas Term, 1777.* 3 vols. London: T. Payne, 1792.

Statutes

In addition to the session laws of the various states, I consulted a number of compilations, revisions, and digests for this study. Most were identifiable by compilers or editors, but some had no individual listed on the title page.

A useful guide to the session laws is Paul Finkelman, editorial adviser, *State Slavery Statutes* (Frederick, Md.: University Publications of America, 1989). By state, the compilations, revisions, and digests examined here are the following:

Alabama

Aikin, John D. *A Digest of the Laws of the State of Alabama.* 2d ed. Tuscaloosa: D. Woodruff, 1836.

Ormond, John J., Arthur P. Bagley, and George Goldthwaite. *The Code of Alabama.* Montgomery: Britain and DeWolf, State Printers, 1852.

Arkansas

English, E. H. *A Digest of the Statutes of Arkansas.* Little Rock: Reardon and Garritt, 1848.
Gould, Josiah. *A Digest of the Statutes of Arkansas.* Little Rock: Johnson and Yerkes, 1858.

Delaware

Cushing John D. *The Earliest Printed Laws of Delaware, 1704–1741.* Wilmington: Michael Glazier, Inc., 1978.
———. *First Laws of the State of Delaware.* 4 vols. Wilmington: Michael Glazier, Inc., 1981.
Revised Statutes of the State of Delaware. Dover: S. Kimmey, 1852.

Florida

Thompson, Leslie. *A Manual and Digest of the Statute Law of the State of Florida.* Boston: Little, Brown, 1847.

Georgia

Cobb, Howell. *A Compilation of the General and Public Statutes of the State of Georgia.* New York: E. O. Jenkins, 1859.
Cushing, John D. *The First Laws of the State of Georgia.* 2 vols. Wilmington: Michael Glazier, Inc., 1981.
Lamar, Lucius Q. C. *Laws of the State of Georgia.* Augusta: T. S. Hannon, 1821.
Prince, Oliver. *A Digest of the Laws of the State of Georgia.* 2d ed. Athens: Published by the Author, 1837.

Kentucky

Littell, William, and Jacob Swigert. *A Digest of the Statute Law of Kentucky.* 2 vols. Frankfort: Kendall and Russell, 1822.
Morehead, C. S., and Mason Brown. *A Digest of the Statute Laws of Kentucky.* 2 vols. Frankfort: A. G. Hodges, 1834.
Stanton, Richard H. *The Revised Statutes of Kentucky.* 2 vols. Cincinnati: R. Clarke and Co., 1860.

Louisiana

Bullard, Henry, and Thomas Curry. *A New Digest of the Statute Laws of Louisiana.* New Orleans: E. Johns, 1842.
Civil Code of the State of Louisiana. New Orleans: Published by a Citizen of Louisiana, 1825.
The Laws of the Territory of Louisiana. St. Louis: Joseph Charles, 1808.
Peirce, Levi, Miles Taylor, and William W. King. *The Consolidation and Revision of the Statutes of the State, of a General Nature.* New Orleans: Printed at the Bee Office, 1852.
Phillips, U. B. *The Revised Statutes of Louisiana.* New Orleans: J. Claiborne, 1856.
Upton, Wheelock S., and Needler R. Jennings. *The Civil Code of the State of Louisiana, with Annotations.* New Orleans: E. Johns and Co., 1838.

Maryland

Cushing, John D. *Laws of the Province of Maryland.* Wilmington: Michael Glazier, Inc., 1978.
Kilty, William, Thomas Harris, and John Watkins. *The Laws of Maryland, from the End of the Year 1799.* 7 vols. Annapolis: J. Green, 1819.
Maxcy, Virgil. *The Laws of Maryland.* 3 vols. Baltimore: Philip H. Nicklin and Co., 1811.

Scott, Otho, and Hiram McCullough. *The Maryland Code.* 2 vols. Baltimore: J. Murphey and Co., 1860.

Mississippi

Alden, T. J. Fox, and J. A. Van Hoesen. *A Digest of the Laws of Mississippi.* New York: Alexander S. Gould, 1839.

Hutchinson, A. *Code of Mississippi, from 1798 to 1848.* Jackson: Price and Hall, 1848.

The Revised Code of the Laws of Mississippi. Natchez: Francis Baker, 1824.

The Revised Code of the Statute Laws of the State of Mississippi. Jackson: E. Barksdale, 1857.

Missouri

Hardin, Charles. *The Revised Statutes of the State of Missouri.* 2 vols. Columbia: James Lusk, 1856.

Jones, William C. *The Revised Statutes of the State of Missouri.* St. Louis: J. W. Dougherty, 1845.

North Carolina

Cushing, John D. *The Earliest Printed Laws of North Carolina, 1669–1751.* 2 vols. Wilmington: Michael Glazier, Inc., 1977.

Haywood, John. *A Manual of the Laws of North Carolina.* 2 vols. Raleigh: J. Gales and W. Boylan, 1808.

Moore, Bartholemew F., and Asa Biggs. *Revised Code of North Carolina.* Boston: Little, Brown, 1855.

Revised Code of North Carolina. Raleigh, 1854.

Revised Statutes of the State of North Carolina. 2 vols. Raleigh: Turner and Hughes, 1837.

South Carolina

Cooper, Thomas, and David J. McCord. *Statutes at Large of South Carolina.* 10 vols. Columbia: A. S. Johnston, 1836–41.

Petigru, James L. *Portion of the Code of Statute Law of South Carolina.* Charleston: Evans and Cogswell, 1860–62.

Tennessee

Haywood, John, and Robert L. Cobbs. *The Statute Laws of the State of Tennessee.* 2 vols. Knoxville: F. S. Heiskell, 1831.

Meigs, Return J., and William F. Cooper. *The Code of Tennessee.* Nashville: E. G. Eastman and Co., 1858.

Scott, Edward. *Laws of the State of Tennessee.* 2 vols. Knoxville: Heiskell and Brown, 1821.

Texas

Hartley, Oliver C. *A Digest of the Laws of Texas.* Philadelphia: Thomas, Cowperthwait and Co., 1850.

Oldham, Williamson S., and George W. White. *A Digest of the General Statute Laws of the State of Texas.* Austin: J. Marshall and Co., 1859.

Virginia

The Code of Virginia. Richmond: W. F. Ritchie, 1849.

Hening, William Waller. *The Statutes at Large: Being a Collection of All the Laws of Virginia, from the First Session of the Legislature in the Year 1619.* 13 vols. Richmond: W. Gray Printers, 1819–23.

The Revised Code of the Laws of Virginia. 2 vols. Richmond: Thomas Ritchie, 1819.
The Statutes at Large of Virginia, from 1712 to 1806. 3 vols. Richmond: Samuel Shepard, 1835.

Appellate Cases

A valuable starting point is Helen Tunnicliff Catterall, ed., *Judicial Cases concerning American Slavery and the Negro.* 5 vols. (New York: Octagon Books, 1968), which was originally published by the Carnegie Institution of Washington in 1937. However, Catterall excerpted portions of cases and omitted the most notable parts of some. Moreover, she overlooked a number of important cases. Although she was a lawyer, her primary concern in this collection was with the social information that could be gleaned from law cases. There is no substitute, then, for reading the published higher court records, although Catterall is an adequate guide to the various law and equity reports for the Southern states.

There are hundred of volumes. Rather than list each (sometimes by the editor of the reports and sometimes by the state), I merely refer to the list of abbreviations at the beginning of the Notes. One exception is the collection of colonial legal records in Louisiana ranging from documents in the Cabildo Archives to the Records of the Superior Council of Louisiana. The collection is in volumes 1–15 of the *Louisiana Historical Quarterly,* 1917–32.

In citing the titles of legal cases, I have generally followed Catterall.

Other Published Primary Material

Adams, Lark Emerson, ed. *The State Records of South Carolina: Journals of the House of Representatives, 1785–1786.* Columbia: University of South Carolina Press, 1979.

Allain, Mathé, and Gerard L. St. Martin. "Notes and Documents: A Slave Trial in Colonial Natchitoches." *Louisiana History* 28 (1987): 57–91.

Ames, Susie M., ed. *County Court Records of Accomack-Northampton, Virginia, 1640–1645.* Charlottesville: University Press of Virginia, 1973.

Barnes, Thomas. *The Book of the General Lawes and Libertyes concerning the Inhabitants of the Massachusetts.* 1648. Reprint, San Marino, Calif.: Huntington Library, 1975.

Barton, R. T., ed. *Virginia Colonial Decisions: The Reports of Sir John Randolph and by Edward Barradall of Decisions of the General Court of Virginia.* 2 vols. Boston: Boston Book Co., 1909.

Berlin, Ira, Barbara J. Fields, Thavolia Glymph, Joseph P. Reidy, and Leslie S. Rowland, eds. *Freedom: A Documentary History of Emancipation, 1861–1867.* Ser. 1, vol. 1, *The Destruction of Slavery.* Cambridge: Cambridge University Press, 1985.

Billings, Warren M., ed. *The Old Dominion in the Seventeenth Century: A Documentary History of Virginia, 1606–1689.* Chapel Hill: University of North Carolina Press, 1975.

Black, Henry Campbell. *Black's Law Dictionary.* Revised 4th ed. St. Paul, Minn.: West Publishing Co., 1968.

Blassingame, John W., ed. *Slave Testimony: Two Centuries of Letters, Speeches, Interviews, and Autobiographies.* Baton Rouge: Louisiana State University Press, 1977.

Bledsoe, Albert Taylor. *An Essay on Liberty and Slavery.* Philadelphia: J. B. Lippincott and Co., 1856.

Boyd, Julian, Charles T. Cullen, and John Cantanzariti, eds. *The Papers of Thomas Jefferson.* 25 vols. to date. Princeton: Princeton University Press, 1950–92.

Boyd, William K. "Documents and Comments on Benefit of Clergy as Applied to Slaves." *Journal of Negro History* 8 (1923): 443–47.

Breeden, James O., ed. *Advice Among Masters: The Ideal in Slave Management in the Old South.* Westport, Conn.: Greenwood Press, 1980.

British Parliamentary Papers: Slave Trade. 94 vols. 1826–99. Reprint, Shannon, Ireland: Irish Universities Press, 1969.

Browne, William Hand, et al., eds. *Archives of Maryland.* 72 vols. Baltimore: Historical Society of Maryland, 1883–.

Bruns, Roger, ed. *Am I Not a Man and a Brother: The Antislavery Crusade of Revolutionary America, 1688–1788.* New York: Chelsea House Publishers, 1977.

Burtt, E. A., ed. *The English Philosophers from Bacon to Mill.* New York: Modern Library, 1939.

Cairnes, John Elliott. *The Slave Power.* With an introduction by Harold Woodman. 1862. Reprint, New York: Harper and Row, 1969.

Carter, Nathaniel, and William Stone, reporters. *Reports of the Proceedings and Debates of the Convention of 1821.* Albany: E. and E. Horsford, 1821.

Clay, Cassius. *The Writings of Cassius Marcellus Clay.* Edited by Horace Greeley. 1848. Reprint, New York: Negro University Press, 1969.

Conrad, Robert Edgar, ed. *Children of God's Fire: A Documentary History of Black Slavery in Brazil.* Princeton: Princeton University Press, 1983.

Cooper, Thomas. "Chancery Law," *American Quarterly Review* (1829): 358–87.

Craton, Michael, James Walvin, and David Wright, eds. *Slavery, Abolition, and Emancipation: Black Slaves and the British Empire.* London: Longman, 1976.

Davis, Edwin Adams, ed. *Plantation Life in the Florida Parishes of Louisiana, 1836–1846, as Reflected in the Diary of Bennett H. Barrow.* New York: AMS Press, 1967.

Dew, Thomas R. *Review of the Debate in the Virginia Legislature of 1831 and 1832.* Richmond: T. W. White, 1832.

Douglass, Frederick. *Life and Times of Frederick Douglass.* New York: Collier Books, 1962. From the 1892 revision.

———. *My Bondage and My Freedom.* 1855. Reprint, New York: Dover Publications, 1969.

———. *Narrative of the Life of Frederick Douglass: An American Slave.* New York: Penguin, 1986.

Durden, Robert F., ed. *The Gray and the Black: The Confederate Debate on Emancipation.* Baton Rouge: Louisiana University Press, 1972.

Elliott, E. N. *Cotton Is King, and Pro-Slavery Arguments.* 1860. Reprint, New York: Negro Universities Press, 1969.

Farish, Hunter Dickinson, ed. *Journal and Letters of Philip Vickers Fithian, 1773–1774: A Plantation Tutor of the Old Dominion.* Charlottesville: University Press of Virginia, 1968.

Faust, Drew Gilpin, ed. *The Ideology of Slavery: Proslavery Thought in the Antebellum South, 1830–1860.* Baton Rouge: Louisiana University Press, 1981.

Fielding, Henry. *Amelia.* 2 vols. London: Dent, 1966.

Finkelman, Paul, ed. *The Law of Freedom and Bondage: A Casebook.* New York: Oceana Publications, Inc., 1986.

Fitzhugh, George. *Cannibals All!; or, Slaves Without Masters.* Edited by C. Vann Woodward. Cambridge: Harvard University Press, 1960.

———. *Sociology for the South; or, The Failure of Free Society.* New York: Burt Franklin, 1854.

Fitzpatrick, John C. *The Writings of George Washington.* 39 vols. Westport, Conn.: Greenwood Press, 1970.

Godwyn, Morgan. *The Negro's & Indians Advocate.* London: Printed for the Author by J. D., 1680.

Greene, Jack P., ed. *The Diary of Landon Carter of Sabine Hall, 1752–1778.* 2 vols. Charlottesville: University Press of Virginia, 1965.

Grimké, Thomas S. *An Oration, on the Practicability and Expediency of Reducing the Whole Body of the Law to the Simplicity and Order of a Code.* Charleston: A. E. Miller, 1827.

Hall, Richard, comp. *Acts Passed in the Island of Barbados, from 1643 to 1762, Inclusive.* London: Printed for Richard Hall, 1764.

Hamilton, J. G. De Roulhac, ed. *The Papers of Thomas Ruffin.* 4 vols. Raleigh: North Carolina Historical Commission, 1918–20.

Hegel, Georg Wilhelm Friedrich. *Philosophy of Right.* Translated by T. M. Knox. London: Oxford University Press, 1952.

Helper, Hinton Rowan. *The Impending Crisis of the South: How to Meet It.* 1857. Reprint, Cambridge, Mass.: Belknap Press, 1968.

Hildreth, Richard. *Despotism in America: An Inquiry into the Nature, Results, and Legal Basis of the Slave-Holding System in the United States.* 1854. Reprint, New York: Negro Universities Press, 1968.

Hobbes, Thomas. *The English Works of Thomas Hobbes of Malmesbury.* 11 vols. London: John Bohn, 1966.

Hoffer, Peter Charles, and William B. Scott, eds. *Criminal Proceedings in Colonial Virginia: /Records of/Fines, Examination of Criminals, Trials of Slaves, etc., from March 1710/1711/to /1754/(Richmond County, Virginia).* American Legal Records, vol. 10. Athens: University of Georgia Press, 1984.

Hopkins, James F., et al., eds. *The Papers of Henry Clay.* 10 vols. Lexington: University Press of Kentucky, 1959–91.

Horsmanden, Daniel. *The New York Conspiracy.* Edited with an introduction by Thomas J. Davis. Boston: Beacon Press, 1971.

Hume, David. *A Treatise on Human Nature.* Edited by L. A. Selby-Bigge. Oxford: Oxford University Press, 1958.

Hundley, Daniel R. *Social Relations in Our Southern States.* Edited by William J. Cooper Jr. 1860. Reprint, Baton Rouge: Louisiana State University Press, 1979.

Jefferson, Thomas. *Notes on the State of Virginia.* With an introduction by Thomas Perkins Abernethy. New York: Harper and Row, 1964.

———. *Reports of Cases Determined in the General Court of Virginia, From 1730, to 1740; and From 1768, to 1772.* Charlottesville: F. Carr and Co., 1829.

Johnson, Herbert A. *Imported Eighteenth-Century Law Treatises in American Libraries, 1700–1799.* Knoxville: University of Tennessee Press, 1978.

Johnson, Herbert A., et al., eds. *The Papers of John Marshall.* 7 vols. Chapel Hill: University of North Carolina Press, 1974–93.

Johnson, Samuel. *A Dictionary of the English Language.* 4 vols. London: Longman, 1818.

Jones, Charles Colcock. *The Religious Instruction of the Negroes in the United States.* Savannah: Thomas Purse, 1842.

Kant, Immanuel. *The Metaphysical Elements of Justice.* Translated by John Ladd. Indianapolis: Bobbs-Merrill, 1965.

Kennedy, Lionel H., and Thomas Parker. *An Official Report of the Trials of Sundry Negroes, Charged with an attempt to Raise an Insurrection in the State of South Carolina.* Charleston: James R. Schenck, 1822.

Klingberg, Frank J., ed. *The Carolina Chronicle of Dr. Francis Le Jau, 1706–1717.* Berkeley: University of California Press, 1956.

Lipscomb, Andrew A., ed. *The Writings of Thomas Jefferson.* 20 vols. Washington, D.C.: Thomas Jefferson Memorial Association, 1903.

Locke, John. *Two Treatises of Government.* Edited by Peter Laslett. Cambridge: Cambridge University Press, 1960.

Loewald, Klaus, Beverly Starika, and Paul S. Taylor. "Notes and Documents: Johann Martin Bolzius Answers a Questionnaire on Carolina and Georgia." *William and Mary Quarterly,* 3d ser., 14 (1957): 217–61.

McCuen, Anne K. *Abstracts of Some Greenville County, South Carolina, Records concerning Black People Free and Slave, 1791–1865.* Spartanburg: Reprint Co., 1991.

McIlwaine, H. R., ed. *Minutes of the Council and General Court of Colonial Virginia.* 2d ed. Richmond: Virginia State Library, 1979.

McIlwaine, H. R., Wilmer L. Hall, and Benjamin J. Hillman, eds. *Executive Journals of the Council of Colonial Virginia.* 6 vols. Charlottesville: University Press of Virginia, 1925–66.

McTyeire, Holland N., C. F. Sturgis, and A. T. Holmes. *Duties of Masters to Servants: Three Premium Essays.* Charleston: Southern Baptist Publication Society, 1851.

Marx, Karl. *Capital: A Critique of Political Economy.* 3 vols. New York: International Publishers, 1967.

Mays, David John, ed. *The Letters and Papers of Edmund Pendleton, 1734–1803.* 2 vols. Charlottesville: University Press of Virginia, 1967.

Miller, Perry, ed. *The Legal Mind in America: From Independence to the Civil War.* New York: Anchor, 1962.

Montesquieu, Baron de. *The Spirit of the Laws.* New York: Hafner Publishing Co., 1966.

Myers, Robert Manson, ed. *The Children of Pride: A True Story of Georgia and the Civil War.* 3 vols. New York: Popular Library, 1972.

Northrup, Solomon. *Twelve Years a Slave.* Baton Rouge: Louisiana State University Press, 1968.

Olmsted, Frederick Law. *Slave States.* Edited by Harvey Wish. New York: Capricorn Books, 1959.

Paley, William. *The Principles of Moral and Political Philosophy.* 8th American ed. 1785. Reprint, Boston: West and Richardson, 1815.

Parker, Mattie Erma Edwards, ed. *North Carolina Higher-Court Records, 1670–1696.* Raleigh: Department of Cultural Resources, Division of Archives and History, 1968.

———, ed. *North Carolina Higher-Court Records, 1697–1701.* Raleigh: Department of Cultural Resources, Division of Archives and History, 1971.

Pease, William H., and Jane H. Pease, eds. *The Antislavery Argument.* Indianapolis: Bobbs-Merrill, 1965.

Porteous, Laura L., ed. "Official Investigation of the Murder of Juan Baptiste Cezaire Lebreton on the Night of May 31, 1771, Including the Trial, Condemnation and Execution of the Principals, and the Punishment of the Accessories Before the Fact." *Louisiana Historical Quarterly* 8 (1925): 6–22.

The Proslavery Argument, as Maintained by the Most Distinguished Writings of the Southern States, Containing the Several Essays on the Subject by Chancellor Harper, Governor Hammond, Dr. Simms, and Professor Dew. Charleston: Walker, Richards and Co., 1852.

Raphael, D. D., ed. *British Moralists, 1650–1800.* 2 vols. Oxford: Oxford University Press, 1969.

Rose, Willie Lee, ed. *A Documentary History of Slavery in North America.* New York: Oxford University Press, 1976.

Rosengarten, Theodore. *Tombee: Portrait of a Cotton Planter: With the Journal of Thomas B. Chaplin, 1822–1890.* New York: William Morrow and Co., 1986.

Rousseau, Jean Jacques. *The Social Contract and Discourses.* Translated by G. D. H. Cole. London: Dent, 1968.

Rutland, Robert A., ed. *The Papers of James Madison.* 17 vols. Charlottesville: University Press of Virginia, 1962–91.

Sawyer, George S. *Southern Institutes; or, An Inquiry into the Origins and Early Prevalence of Slavery and the Slave Trade.* Philadelphia: J. B. Lippincott, 1858.

Scott, S. P., C. S. Lohinger, and J. Vance. *Las Siete Partidas.* Chicago: University of Chicago Press, 1931.

Smedes, Susan Dabney. *Memorials of a Southern Planter.* Edited by Fletcher M. Green. Jackson: University Press of Mississippi, 1981.

Smith, Joseph Henry. *Appeals to the Privy Council from the American Plantations*. New York: Octagon Books, 1965.

Stowe, Harriet Beecher. *The Key to Uncle Tom's Cabin*. Boston: John P. Jewell and Co., 1854.

Thorpe, Francis Newton, comp. *The Federal and State Constitutions*. 7 vols. Washington, D.C.: U.S. Government Printing Office, 1909.

Tinling, Marion, ed. *The Correspondence of the Three William Byrds of Westover, Virginia, 1684–1776*. 2 vols. Charlottesville: University Press of Virginia, 1977.

Tocqueville, Alexis de. *Democracy in America*. Edited by Phillips Bradley. 2 vols. New York: Vintage Books, 1959.

Tragle, Henry Irving, ed. *The Southampton Slave Revolt of 1831: A Compilation of Source Material*. New York: Vintage Books, 1973.

Tyler, Lyon Gardiner, ed. *Narratives of Early Virginia, 1606–1625*. New York: Barnes and Noble, 1907.

Wiedemann, Thomas, ed. *Greek and Roman Slavery*. Baltimore: Johns Hopkins University Press, 1981.

Wills of Westmoreland County, Virginia, 1654–1800. Richmond: Appeals Press, 1935.

Wilson, Clyde, Robert L. Meriwether, and W. Edwin Hemphill. *The Papers of John C. Calhoun*. 21 vols. Columbia: University of South Carolina Press, 1959–93.

Wilson, John L. *Codification: Speech of the Hon. John L. Wilson on the Propriety and Expediency of Reducing the Laws of the State into a Code*. New York: Gray and Bunce, 1827.

Windley, Lathan A., ed. *Runaway Slave Advertisements: A Documentary History from the 1730s to 1790*. 4 vols. Westport, Conn.: Greenwood Press, 1983.

Woodfin, Maude H., and Marion Tinling, eds. *Another Secret Diary of William Byrd of Westover, 1739–1741*. Richmond: Dietz Press, 1942.

Woodward, C. Vann. *Mary Chesnut's Civil War*. New Haven: Yale University Press, 1981.

Wright, Louis B., and Marion Tinling, eds. *The Secret Diary of William Byrd of Westover, 1709–1712*. Richmond: Dietz Press, 1941.

Wythe, George. *Decisions of Cases in Virginia, by the High Court of Chancery: With Remarks upon Decrees by the Court of Appeals, Reversing Some of These Decisions*. Richmond: Thomas Nicholson, 1795.

SECONDARY WORKS

Books

Very useful bibliographic guides to the secondary literature are Joseph C. Miller, *Slavery: A Worldwide Bibliography, 1900–1982* (White Plains, New York: Kraus International, 1985), and John David Smith, *Black Slavery in the Americas: An Interdisciplinary Bibliography, 1865–1980*, 2 vols. (Westport, Conn.: Greenwood Press, 1982). Also of value are the annual bibliographic updates in the journal, *Slavery and Abolition*.

Abzug, Robert, and Stephen Maizlish, eds. *New Perspectives on Race and Slavery in America: Essays in Honor of Kenneth M. Stampp*. Lexington: University Press of Kentucky, 1986.

Ames, Susie. *Studies of the Virginia Eastern Shore in the Seventeenth Century*. Richmond: Dietz Press, 1940.

Andrews, K. R., N. P. Canny, and P. E. H. Hair, eds. *Westward Enterprise: English Activities in Ireland, the Atlantic, and America, 1480–1650*. Detroit: Wayne State University Press, 1979.

Anstey, Roger. *The Atlantic Slave Trade and British Abolition, 1760–1810*. Atlantic Highlands, N.J.: Humanities Press, 1975.

Appleby, Joyce. *Capitalism and a New Social Order: The Republican Vision of the 1790s.* New York: New York University Press, 1984.

Aptheker, Herbert. *American Negro Slave Revolts.* New York: Columbia University Press, 1943.

Archer, Leonie, ed. *Slavery and Other Forms of Unfree Labor.* London: Routledge, 1980.

Arnold, Morris S. *Unequal Laws unto a Savage Race: European Legal Traditions in Arkansas, 1686–1836.* Fayetteville: University of Arkansas Press, 1985.

Atiyah, Patrick S. *The Rise and Fall of Freedom of Contract.* Oxford: Oxford University Press, 1979.

Atiyah, Patrick S., and Robert S. Summers. *Form and Substance in Anglo-American Law: A Comparative Study of Legal Reasoning, Legal Theory, and Legal Institutions.* Oxford: Oxford University Press, 1987.

Ayers, Edward L. *Vengeance and Justice: Crime and Punishment in the 19th-Century American South.* New York: Oxford University Press, 1984.

Baker, J. H. *An Introduction to English Legal History.* 2d ed. London: Butterworths, 1979.

Ballagh, James Curtis. *A History of Slavery in Virginia.* Baltimore: Johns Hopkins University Press, 1902.

Bancroft, Frederic. *Slave Trading in the Old South.* New York: Frederic Unger Publishing, 1931.

Banton, Michael. *The Idea of Race.* Boulder, Col.: Westview Press, 1977.

Bateman, Fred, and Thomas Weiss. *A Deplorable Scarcity: The Failure of Industrialization in the Slave Economy.* Chapel Hill: University of North Carolina Press, 1981.

Barney, William L. *The Road to Secession: A New Perspective on the Old South.* New York: Praeger, 1972.

———. *The Secessionist Impulse: Alabama and Mississippi in 1860.* Princeton: Princeton University Press, 1974.

Beckles, Hilary McD. *White Servitude and Black Slavery in Barbados, 1627–1715.* Knoxville: University of Tennessee Press, 1989.

Beeman, Richard K. *The Evolution of the Southern Backcountry: A Case Study of Lunenburg County, Virginia, 1746–1832.* Philadelphia: University of Pennsylvania Press, 1984.

Bellamy, J. R. *The Law of Treason in England in the Later Middle Ages.* Cambridge: Cambridge University Press, 1970.

Bender, Thomas, ed. *The Antislavery Debate: Capitalism and Abolitionism as a Problem in Historical Interpretation.* Berkeley: University of California Press, 1992.

Berlin, Ira. *Slaves Without Masters: The Free Negro in the Antebellum South.* New York: Vintage Books, 1976.

Berlin, Ira, and Ronald Hoffman, eds. *Slavery and Freedom in the Age of the American Revolution.* Charlottesville: University Press of Virginia, 1983.

Berlin, Ira, and Philip D. Morgan, eds. *Cultivation and Culture: Labor and the Shaping of Slave Life in the Americas.* Charlottesville: University Press of Virginia, 1993.

Berman, Harold. *Law and Revolution: The Formation of the Western Legal Tradition.* Cambridge: Harvard University Press, 1983.

Blackburn, Robin. *The Overthrow of Colonial Slavery, 1776–1848.* London: Verso, 1988.

Blassingame, John. *The Slave Community.* New York: Oxford University Press, 1972.

Bloch, Marc. *Feudal Society.* Chicago: University of Chicago Press, 1962.

Bloomfield, Maxwell. *American Lawyers in a Changing Society, 1776–1876.* Cambridge: Harvard University Press, 1976.

Bodenhamer, David J., and James W. Ely Jr., eds. *Ambivalent Legacy: A Legal History of the South.* Jackson: University Press of Mississippi, 1984.

Boles, John B., ed. *Masters and Slaves in the House of the Lord: Race and Religion in the American South, 1740–1870.* Lexington: University Press of Kentucky, 1988.

Botein, Stephen. *Early American Law and Society.* New York: Alfred A. Knopf, 1983.

Bowman, Shearer Davis. *Masters and Lords: Mid-19th Century U.S. Planters and Prussian Junkers.* New York: Oxford University Press, 1993.

Bradley, F. H. *Ethical Studies (Selected Essays).* New York: Liberal Arts Press, 1951.

Brathwaite, Edward. *The Development of Creole Society in Jamaica, 1770–1820.* Oxford: Clarendon Press, 1971.

Breen, T. H. *Tobacco Culture: The Mentality of the Great Tidewater Planters on the Eve of Revolution.* Princeton: Princeton University Press, 1985.

Breen, T. H., and Stephen Innes. *"Myne Owne Ground": Race & Freedom on Virginia's Eastern Shore, 1640–1676.* New York: Oxford University Press, 1980.

Bridenbaugh, Carl. *Myths and Realities: Societies of the Colonial South.* Baton Rouge: Louisiana State University Press, 1952.

Brissaud, Jean. *A History of French Private Law.* 1915. Reprint, South Hackensack, N.J.: Rothman Reprints, 1968.

Brooks, U. R. *South Carolina Bench and Bar.* 2 vols. Columbia: The State Co., 1908.

Brown, Robert E., and Katherine B. Brown. *Virginia, 1705–1786: Democracy or Aristocracy?.* East Lansing: Michigan State University Press, 1964.

Buckland, W. W. *The Roman Law of Slavery: The Condition of the Slave in Private Law from Augustus to Justinian.* Cambridge: Cambridge University Press, 1908.

Burton, Orville Vernon. *In My Father's House Are Many Mansions: Family and Community in Edgefield, South Carolina.* Chapel Hill: University of North Carolina Press, 1985.

Burton, Orville Vernon, and Robert C. McMath Jr. *Class, Conflict, and Consensus: Antebellum Southern Community Studies.* Westport, Conn.: Greenwood Press, 1982.

Caenegem, R. C. Van. *Judges, Legislators, and Professors: Chapters in European Legal History.* Cambridge: Cambridge University Press, 1987.

Calabresi, Guido. *A Common Law for the Age of Statutes.* Cambridge: Harvard University Press, 1982.

——. *The Costs of Accidents: A Legal and Economic Analysis.* New Haven: Yale University Press, 1970.

Campbell, Randolph B. *An Empire for Slavery: The Peculiar Institution in Texas, 1821–1865.* Baton Rouge: Louisiana State University Press, 1989.

——. *A Southern Community in Crisis: Harrison County, Texas, 1850–1880.* Austin: Texas State Historical Association, 1983.

Cash, W. J. *The Mind of the South.* New York: Vintage, 1960.

Channing, Steven A. *Crisis of Fear: Secession in South Carolina.* New York: W. W. Norton, 1970.

Chapin, Bradley. *The American Law of Treason: Revolutionary and Early National Origins.* Seattle: University of Washington Press, 1964.

——. *Criminal Justice in Colonial America, 1606–1660.* Athens: University of Georgia Press, 1983.

Chipman, Donald E. *Spanish Texas, 1519–1821.* Austin: University of Texas Press, 1992.

Chitwood, O. P. *Justice in Colonial Virginia.* Baltimore: Johns Hopkins University Press, 1905.

Clark, Blanche Henry. *The Tennessee Yeoman, 1840–1860.* Nashville: Vanderbilt University Press, 1942.

Clark, Leroy D. *The Grand Jury: The Use and Abuse of Political Power.* New York: Quadrangle, 1975.

Cleaver, Eldridge. *Soul on Ice.* New York: McGraw-Hill, 1968.

Cobb, James C. *The Most Southern Place on Earth: The Mississippi Delta and the Roots of Regional Identity.* New York: Oxford University Press, 1992.

Cockburn, J. S., ed. *Crime in England, 1550–1800*. Princeton: Princeton University Press, 1977.

Coclanis, Peter A. *The Shadow of a Dream: Economic Life and Death in the South Carolina Low Country, 1670–1920*. New York: Oxford University Press, 1989.

Cohen, David, and Jack Greene, eds. *Neither Slave Nor Free: The Freedman of African Descent in the Slave Societies of the New World*. Baltimore: Johns Hopkins University Press, 1972.

Coleman, John W. *Slavery Times in Kentucky*. Chapel Hill: University of North Carolina Press, 1940.

Conrad, Robert. *The Destruction of Brazilian Slavery, 1850–1888*. Berkeley: University of California Press, 1972.

Cook, Charles M. *The American Codification Movement: A Study of Antebellum Legal Reform*. Westport, Conn.: Greenwood Press, 1981.

Cooper, Frederick. *From Slaves to Squatters: Plantation Labor & Agriculture in Zanzibar & Coastal Kenya, 1890–1925*. New Haven: Yale University Press, 1981.

———. *Plantation Slavery on the East Coast of Africa*. New Haven: Yale University Press, 1977.

Cooper, William J., Jr. *The South and the Politics of Slavery, 1828–1856*. Baton Rouge: Louisiana State University Press, 1978.

Cornish, W. R. *The Jury*. London: Allen Lane, 1968.

Cover, Robert M. *Justice Accused: Antislavery and the Judicial Process*. New Haven: Yale University Press, 1975.

Craton, Michael. *Sinews of Empire: A Short History of British Slavery*. Garden City: N.Y.: Anchor Press, 1974.

———. *Testing the Chains: Resistance to Slavery in the British West Indies*. Ithaca: Cornell University Press, 1982.

Craven, Wesley F. *White, Red, and Black*. New York: W. W. Norton, 1977.

Creel, Margaret Washington. *"A Peculiar People": Slave Religion and Community-Culture among the Gullahs*. New York: New York University Press, 1988.

Crofts, Daniel. *Old Southampton: Politics and Society in a Virginia County, 1834–1869*. Charlottesville: University Press of Virginia, 1992.

Crow, Jeffrey J. *The Black Experience in Revolutionary North Carolina*. Raleigh: Department of Cultural Resources, Division of Archives and History, 1977.

Cunliffe, Marcus. *Chattel Slavery and Wage Slavery: The Anglo-American Context, 1830–1860*. Athens: University of Georgia Press, 1979.

Dalzell, George W. *Benefit of Clergy in America & Related Matters*. Winston-Salem: John F. Blair, 1955.

Dargo, George. *Jefferson's Louisiana: Politics and the Clash of Legal Traditions*. Cambridge: Harvard University Press, 1975.

Davis, David Brion. *The Problem of Slavery in the Age of Revolution*. Ithaca: Cornell University Press, 1975.

———. *The Problem of Slavery in Western Culture*. Ithaca: Cornell University Press, 1966.

———. *Slavery and Human Progress*. New York: Oxford University Press, 1984.

Davis, Thomas J. *A Rumor of Revolt: The "Great Negro Plot" in Colonial New York*. Amherst, Mass.: Free Press, 1985.

Degler, Carl. *Neither Black Nor White: Slavery and Race Relations in Brazil and the United States*. New York: Macmillan, 1971.

———. *The Other South: Southern Dissenters in the Nineteenth Century*. New York: Harper and Row, 1974.

Demos, John Putnam. *Entertaining Satan: Witchcraft and the Culture of Early New England*. New York: Oxford University Press, 1982.

Dillon, Morton L. *Slavery Attacked: Southern Slaves and Their Allies, 1619–1865.* Baton Rouge: Louisiana State University Press, 1990.

Dodson, Leonidas. *Alexander Spotswood: Governor of Colonial Virginia.* New York: AMS Press, 1969.

Drake, Thomas E. *Quakers and Slavery in America.* Gloucester, Mass.: Patterson Smith, 1965.

Drescher, Seymour. *Econocide: British Slavery in the Era of Abolition.* Pittsburg: University of Pittsburg Press, 1977.

Dunn, Richard S. *Sugar and Slaves: The Rise of the Planter Class in the British West Indies, 1624–1713.* New York: W. W. Norton, 1973.

Dunne, Gerald T. *Justice Joseph Story and the Rise of the Supreme Court.* New York: Simon and Schuster, 1970.

Durrill, Wayne K. *War of Another Kind: A Southern Community in the Great Rebellion.* New York: Oxford University Press, 1990.

Dworkin, Ronald. *Taking Rights Seriously.* Cambridge: Harvard University Press, 1977.

Eaton, Clement. *A History of the Southern Confederacy.* New York: Macmillan, 1954.

Edsall, Nicholas C. *The Anti-Poor Law Movement, 1834–44.* Manchester: Manchester University Press, 1971.

Egerton, Douglas R. *Gabriel's Rebellion: The Virginia Slave Conspiracies of 1800 and 1802.* Chapel Hill: University of North Carolina Press, 1993.

Ehrlich, Walter. *They Have No Rights: Dred Scott's Struggle for Freedom.* Westport, Conn.: Greenwood Press, 1979.

Elkins, Stanley M. *Slavery: A Problem in American Institutional and Intellectual Life.* Chicago: University of Chicago Press, 1968.

Engerman, Stanley, and Eugene D. Genovese, eds. *Race and Slavery in the Western Hemisphere: Quantitative Studies.* Princeton: Princeton University Press, 1975.

Faust, Drew Gilpin. *James Henry Hammond and the Old South: A Design for Mastery.* Baton Rouge: Louisiana State University Press, 1982.

Fede, Andrew. *People Without Rights: An Interpretation of the Fundamentals of the Law of Slavery in the U.S. South.* New York: Garland Publishing, 1992.

Fehrenbacher, Don. *The Dred Scott Case: Its Significance in American Law & Politics.* New York: Oxford University Press, 1968.

Fields, Barbara Jeanne. *Slavery and Freedom on the Middle Ground: Maryland during the Nineteenth Century.* New Haven: Yale University Press, 1983.

Finkelman, Paul. *An Imperfect Union: Slavery, Federalism, and Comity.* Chapel Hill: University of North Carolina Press, 1981.

Finley, Moses I. *Ancient Slavery and Modern Ideology.* New York: Viking Press, 1980.

——. *The Use and Abuse of History: From the Myths of the Greeks to Levi-Strauss, the Past Alive and the Present Illumined.* New York: Penguin, 1987.

Flexner, James Thomas. *Washington: The Indispensable Man.* Boston: Little, Brown, 1974.

Fogel, Robert W. *Without Consent or Contract: The Rise and Fall of American Slavery.* New York: W. W. Norton, 1989.

Fogel, Robert W., and Stanley L. Engerman. *Time on the Cross: The Economics of American Negro Slavery.* 2 vols. New York: W. W. Norton, 1989.

Foner, Eric. *Free Soil, Free Labor, Free Men: The Ideology of the Republican Party before the Civil War.* New York: Oxford University Press, 1970.

Foner, Laura, and Eugene D. Genovese, eds. *Slavery in the New World: A Reader in Comparative History.* Englewood Cliffs, N.J.: Prentice-Hall, 1969.

Ford, Lacy K. *Origins of Southern Radicalism: The South Carolina Upcountry, 1800–1860.* New York: Oxford University Press, 1988.

Foucault, Michel. *Discipline and Punish: The Birth of the Prison.* New York: Pantheon, 1977.

Fox-Genovese, Elizabeth, and Eugene D. Genovese. *Fruits of Merchant Capital: Slavery and Bourgeois Property in the Rise and Expansion of Capitalism.* New York: Oxford University Press, 1983.

Frank, Jerome. *Law and the Modern Mind.* New York: Brentano's, 1930.

Frankel, Marvin E., and Gary P. Naftalis. *The Grand Jury: An Institution on Trial.* New York: Hill and Wang, 1977.

Fredrickson, George M. *The Arrogance of Race: Historical Perspectives on Slavery, Racism, and Social Inequality.* Middletown, Conn.: Wesleyan University Press, 1988.

——. *The Black Image in the White Mind: The Debate on Afro-American Character and Destiny, 1817–1914.* New York: Harper and Row, 1971.

——. *White Supremacy: A Comparative Study in American & South African History.* New York: Oxford University Press, 1981.

Freehling, Alison Goodyear. *Drift Toward Dissolution: The Virginia Slavery Debate of 1831–1832.* Baton Rouge: Louisiana State University Press, 1982.

Freehling, William W. *Prelude to Civil War: The Nullification Controversy in South Carolina, 1816–1836.* New York: Harper and Row, 1966.

——. *The Road to Disunion.* Vol. 1, *Secessionists at Bay, 1776–1854.* New York: Oxford University Press, 1990.

Freidel, Frank. *Francis Lieber: Nineteenth-Century Liberal.* Gloucester, Mass.: Patterson Smith, 1968.

Freyre, Gilberto. *The Masters and the Slaves: A Study in the Development of Brazilian Civilization.* New York: Alfred A. Knopf, 1946.

Friedman, Lawrence M. *A History of American Law.* New York: Simon and Schuster, 1973.

Fuller, Lon L. *Legal Fictions.* Stanford: Stanford University Press, 1967.

Galenson, David W. *Traders, Planters, and Slaves: Market Behavior in Early English America.* New York: Cambridge University Press, 1986.

Gaspar, David Barry. *Bondmen & Rebels: A Study of Master-Slave Relations in Antigua, with Implications for Colonial British America.* Baltimore: Johns Hopkins University Press, 1985.

Gay, Peter. *The Enlightenment: An Interpretation.* 2 vols. Vol. 2, *The Science of Freedom.* New York: Alfred A. Knopf, 1969.

Genovese, Eugene D. *From Rebellion to Revolution: Afro-American Slave Revolts in the Making of the New World.* New York: Vintage Books, 1981.

——. *In Red and Black: Marxian Explorations in Southern and Afro-American History.* New York: Pantheon, 1968.

——. *Roll, Jordan, Roll: The World the Slaves Made.* New York: Pantheon, 1974.

——. *The Slaveholders' Dilemma: Freedom and Progress in Southern Conservative Thought, 1820–1860.* Columbia: University of South Carolina Press, 1992.

——. *"Slavery Ordained of God": The Southern Slaveholders' View of Biblical History and Modern Politics.* Gettysburg, Pa.: Gettysburg College, 1985.

——. *The World the Slaveholders Made: Two Essays in Interpretation.* New York: Vintage Books, 1969.

Gewehr, Wesley M. *The Great Awakening in Virginia, 1740–1790.* Durham, N.C.: Duke University Press, 1930.

Gilmore, Grant. *The Ages of American Law.* New Haven: Yale University Press, 1977.

Gleason, J. H. *The Justices of the Peace in England, 1558 to 1640: A Later Eirenarcha.* Oxford: Oxford University Press, 1969.

Glenn, Myra. *Campaigns against Corporal Punishment: Prisoners, Sailors, Women, and Children in Antebellum America.* Albany: State University of New York Press, 1984.

Goebel, Julius, Jr., and Raymond T. Naughton. *Law Enforcement in Colonial New York.* Montclair, N.J.: Patterson Smith, 1970.

Goldin, Claudia Dale. *Urban Slavery in the American South, 1820–1860*. Chicago: University of Chicago Press, 1976.

Goveia, Elsa. *Slave Society in the British Leeward Islands at the End of the Eighteenth Century*. New Haven: Yale University Press, 1969.

———. *The West Indian Slave Laws of the 18th Century*. Lodge Hill, Barbados: Caribbean Universities Press, 1973.

Graveson, R. H. *Status in the Common Law*. London: Oxford University Press, 1953.

Green, Thomas A. *Verdict according to Conscience: Perspectives on the English Criminal Trial Jury, 1200–1800*. Chicago: University of Chicago Press, 1985.

Greenberg, Kenneth S. *Masters and Statesmen: The Political Culture of American Slavery*. Baltimore: Johns Hopkins University Press, 1985.

Greene, Evarts B., and Virginia Harrington. *American Population before the Federal Census of 1790*. Gloucester, Mass.: Patterson Smith, 1932.

Greene, Jack P. *Pursuits of Happiness: The Social Development of Early Modern British Colonies and the Formation of American Culture*. Chapel Hill: University of North Carolina Press, 1988.

Guest, A. G., ed. *Oxford Essays in Jurisprudence*. Oxford: Oxford University Press, 1961.

Gutman, Herbert. *The Black Family in Slavery and Freedom, 1750–1925*. New York: Pantheon, 1976.

———. *Slavery and the Numbers Game: A Critique of Time on the Cross*. Urbana: University of Illinois Press, 1975.

Haas, Edward F., ed. *Louisiana's Legal Heritage*. Pensacola: Perdido Bay Press, 1983.

Hahn, Steven. *The Roots of Southern Populism: Yeoman Farmers and the Transformation of the Georgia Upcountry, 1850–1890*. New York: Oxford University Press, 1983.

Hall, Gwendolyn Midlo. *Africans in Colonial Louisiana: The Development of Afro-Creole Culture in the Eighteenth Century*. Baton Rouge: Louisiana State University Press, 1992.

Hall, Jerome. *Theft, Law, and Society*. 2d ed. Indianapolis: Bobbs-Merrill, 1952.

Hall, Kermit L. *The Magic Mirror: Law in American History*. New York: Oxford University Press, 1989.

Handler, Jerome S., and Frederick W. Lange. *Plantation Slavery in Barbados: An Archaeological and Historical Investigation*. Cambridge: Harvard University Press, 1978.

Hanke, Lewis. *Aristotle and the American Indians: A Study in Race Prejudice in the Modern World*. Bloomington: Indiana University Press, 1975.

———. *The Spanish Struggle for Justice in the Conquest of America*. Boston: Little, Brown, 1965.

Harding, Alan. *A Social History of English Law*. Gloucester, Mass.: Peter Smith, 1973.

Harding, Vincent. *There Is a River: The Black Struggle for Freedom in America*. New York: Vintage Books, 1983.

Harris, J. William. *Plain Folk and Gentry in a Slave Society: White Liberty and Black Slavery in Augusta's Hinterlands*. Middletown, Conn.: Wesleyan University Press, 1985.

Hart, H. L. A. *The Concept of Law*. Oxford: Clarendon Press, 1961.

———. *Punishment and Responsibility: Essays in the Philosophy of Law*. New York: Oxford University Press, 1968.

Hay, Douglas, Peter Linebaugh, John G. Rule, E. P. Thompson, and Cal Winslow, eds. *Albion's Fatal Tree: Crime and Society in Eighteenth-Century England*. New York: Pantheon, 1975.

Hellie, Richard. *Slavery in Russia, 1450–1725*. Chicago: University of Chicago Press, 1985.

Henry, H. M. *The Police Control of the Slave in South Carolina*. 1914. Reprint, New York: Negro Universities Press, 1968.

Heuman, Gad J., ed. *Out of the House of Bondage: Runaways, Resistance, and Marronage in Africa and the New World*. New York: F. Cass Publishers, 1986.

Higginbotham, A. Leon, Jr. *In the Matter of Color: Race and the American Legal Process: The Colonial Period.* New York: Oxford University Press, 1978.

Hindus, Michael Stephen. *Prison and Plantation: Crime, Justice, and Authority in Massachusetts and South Carolina, 1767–1878.* Chapel Hill: University of North Carolina Press, 1980.

Historical Statistics of the United States: Colonial Times to 1970. 2 parts. Washington, D.C.: U.S. Government Printing Office, 1975.

Hobsbawm, E. J. *Primitive Rebels: Studies in Archaic Forms of Social Movement in the 19th and 20th Centuries.* New York: W. W. Norton, 1965.

Hoebel, E. Adamson. *The Law of Primitive Man: A Study in Comparative Legal Dynamics.* New York: Atheneum, 1972.

Hoetink, Harry. *Caribbean Race Relations: A Study of Two Variants.* London: Oxford University Press, 1967.

Hoffer, Peter Charles. *The Law's Conscience: Equitable Constitutionalism in America.* Chapel Hill: University of North Carolina Press, 1990.

Holdsworth, Sir William. *A History of English Law.* 16 vols. London: Methuen, Sweet and Maxwell, 1903–66.

——. *Some Makers of English Law.* Cambridge: Cambridge University Press, 1966.

Holmes, Oliver Wendell, Jr. *Collected Legal Papers.* New York: Harcourt, Brace and Co., 1920.

Holt, Thomas C. *The Problem of Freedom: Race, Labor, and Politics in Jamaica and Britain, 1832–1938.* Baltimore: Johns Hopkins University Press, 1992.

Hopkins, Keith. *Conquerors and Slaves.* Vol. 1, *Sociological Studies in Roman History.* Cambridge: Cambridge University Press, 1978.

Horwitz, Morton. *The Transformation of American Law, 1780–1860.* Cambridge: Harvard University Press, 1977.

——. *The Transformation of American Law, 1870–1960: The Crisis of Legal Orthodoxy.* New York: Oxford University Press, 1992.

Howington, Arthur F. *What Sayeth the Law: The Treatment of Slaves and Free Blacks in the State and Local Courts of Tennessee.* New York: Garland Publishing, 1986.

Huggins, Nathan. *Black Odyssey: The Afro-American Ordeal in Slavery.* New York: Vintage Books, 1979.

Hurst, James Willard. *Law and the Conditions of Freedom in the Nineteenth-Century United States.* Madison: University of Wisconsin Press, 1964.

Hurt, R. Douglas. *Agriculture and Slavery in Missouri's Little Dixie.* Columbia: University of Missouri Press, 1992.

Innes, Stephen, ed. *Work and Labor in Early America.* Chapel Hill: University of North Carolina Press, 1988.

Inscoe, John C. *Mountain Masters, Slavery, and the Sectional Crisis in Western North Carolina.* Knoxville: University of Tennessee Press, 1989.

Isaac, Rhys. *The Transformation of Virginia, 1740–1790.* Chapel Hill: University of North Carolina Press, 1982.

Jackson, Luther Porter. *Free Negro Labor and Property Holding in Virginia, 1830–1860.* New York: Atheneum, 1969.

James, C. L. R. *The Black Jacobins: Toussaint L'Ouverture and the San Domingo Revolution.* New York: Vintage Books, 1989.

Johnson, Allen, ed. *Dictionary of American Biography.* 20 vols. New York: Charles Scribner's Sons, 1946. 8 supplements, 1946–88.

Johnson, Michael P., and James L. Roark. *Black Masters: A Free Family of Color in the Old South.* New York: W. W. Norton, 1984.

Johnston, James Hugo. *Race Relations in Virginia & Miscegenation in the South, 1776–1860.* Amherst: University of Massachusetts Press, 1970.

Jones, Gareth. *History of the Law of Charity, 1532–1827*. Cambridge: Cambridge University Press, 1969.

Jones, Norrece, Jr. *Born a Child of Freedom, Yet a Slave: Mechanisms of Control and Strategies of Resistance in Antebellum South Carolina*. Hanover, N.H.: Wesleyan University Press, 1990.

Jordan, Winthrop. *Tumult and Silence at Second Creek: An Inquiry into a Civil War Slave Conspiracy*. Baton Rouge: Louisiana State University Press, 1993.

——. *White Over Black: American Attitudes toward the Negro, 1550–1812*. New York: W. W. Norton, 1968.

Jordan, Winthrop, and Sheila L. Skemp, eds. *Race and Family in the Colonial South*. Jackson: University Press of Mississippi, 1987.

Joyner, Charles. *Down by the Riverside: A South Carolina Slave Community*. Urbana: University of Illinois Press, 1984.

Kairys, David, ed. *The Politics of Law: A Progressive Critique*. New York: Pantheon, 1982.

Kammen, Michael. *A Machine That Would Go of Itself: The Constitution in American Culture*. New York: Alfred A. Knopf, 1986.

Kay, Marvin L. Michael, and Lorin Lee Cary. *Slavery in North Carolina, 1748–1775*. Chapel Hill: University of North Carolina Press, 1995.

Kettner, James. *The Development of American Citizenship, 1608–1870*. Chapel Hill: University of North Carolina Press, 1978.

Kilbourne, R. H., Jr. *A History of the Louisiana Civil Code: The Formative Years, 1803–1839*. Baton Rouge: Louisiana State University Press, 1975.

King, Peter J. *Utilitarian Jurisprudence in America: The Influence of Bentham and Austin on American Legal Thought in the Nineteenth Century*. New York: Garland Publishing, 1986.

Klein, Herbert S. *Slavery in the Americas: A Comparative Study of Virginia and Cuba*. Chicago: University of Chicago Press, 1967.

Klein, Rachel N. *Unification of a Slave State: The Rise of the Planter Class in the South Carolina Backcountry, 1760–1808*. Chapel Hill: University of North Carolina Press, 1990.

Knight, Franklin. *Slave Society in Cuba during the Nineteenth Century*. Madison: University of Wisconsin Press, 1970.

Kolchin, Peter. *American Slavery, 1619–1877*. New York: Hill and Wang, 1993.

——. *Unfree Labor: American Slavery and Russian Serfdom*. Cambridge: Belknap Press of Harvard University Press, 1987.

Kulikoff, Allan. *The Agrarian Origins of American Capitalism*. Charlottesville: University Press of Virginia, 1992.

——. *Tobacco and Slaves: The Development of Southern Cultures in the Chesapeake, 1680–1800*. Chapel Hill: University of North Carolina Press, 1986.

Landau, Norma. *The Justices of the Peace, 1679–1760*. Berkeley: University of California Press, 1984.

Lane, Ann J., ed. *The Debate over Slavery: Stanley Elkins and His Critics*. Urbana: University of Illinois Press, 1971.

Lebsock, Suzanne. *The Free Women of Petersburg: Status and Culture in a Southern Town, 1784–1860*. New York: W. W. Norton, 1985.

Levack, Brian P. *The Civil Lawyers in England, 1603–1641: A Political Study*. Oxford: Oxford University Press, 1973.

Levine, Lawrence. *Black Culture and Black Consciousness: Afro-American Folk Thought from Slavery to Freedom*. New York: Oxford University Press, 1977.

Lewis, Jan. *The Pursuit of Happiness: Family and Values in Jefferson's Virginia*. Cambridge: Cambridge University Press, 1985.

Lewis, Ronald L. *Coal, Iron, and Slaves: Industrial Slavery in Maryland and Virginia, 1715–1865*. Westport, Conn.: Greenwood Press, 1979.

Lieberman, David. *The Province of Legislation Determined: Legal Theory in Eighteenth-Century Britain.* Cambridge: Cambridge University Press, 1989.

Littlefield, Daniel C. *Rice and Slaves: Ethnicity and the Slave Trade in Colonial South Carolina.* Baton Rouge: Louisiana State University Press, 1981.

Litwack, Leon F. *North of Slavery: The Negro in the Free States, 1790–1860.* Chicago: University of Chicago Press, 1961.

Lofton, John. *Insurrection in South Carolina: The Turbulent World of Denmark Vesey.* Yellow Springs, Ohio: Antioch Press, 1964.

Lovejoy, Arthur O. *The Great Chain of Being: A Study of the History of an Idea.* New York: Harper and Row, 1965.

Lovejoy, Paul. *Transformations in Slavery: A History of Slavery in Africa.* Cambridge: Cambridge University Press, 1983.

McCash, William B. *Thomas R. R. Cobb, 1823–1862: The Making of a Southern Nationalist.* Macon, Ga.: Mercer University Press, 1983.

McCoy, Drew R. *The Last of the Fathers: James Madison and the Republican Legacy.* Cambridge: Cambridge University Press, 1989.

McDonald, Roderick A. *The Economy and Material Culture of Slaves: Goods and Chattels on the Sugar Plantations of Jamaica and Louisiana.* Baton Rouge: Louisiana State University Press, 1993.

McGovern, James R. *Anatomy of a Lynching: The Killing of Claude Neal.* Baton Rouge: Louisiana State University Press, 1982.

McLaurin, Melton A. *Celia: A Slave.* Athens: University of Georgia Press, 1991.

MacLeod, Duncan J. *Slavery, Race, and the American Revolution.* London: Cambridge University Press, 1974.

Macpherson, C. B. *The Political Theory of Possessive Individualism: Hobbes to Locke.* Oxford: Oxford University Press, 1962.

McPherson, James M. *Battle Cry of Freedom: The Civil War Era.* New York: Oxford University Press, 1988.

Main, Gloria L. *Tobacco Colony: Life in Early Maryland, 1650–1720.* Princeton: Princeton University Press, 1982.

Maitland, Frederic W. *Equity: A Course of Lectures.* Cambridge: Cambridge University Press, 1909.

——. *The Forms of Action at Common Law: A Course of Lectures.* Edited by A. H. Chaytor and W. J. Whittaker. Cambridge: Cambridge University Press, 1963.

Malone, Ann Patton. *Sweet Chariot: Slave Family and Household Structure in Nineteenth-Century Louisiana.* Chapel Hill: University of North Carolina Press, 1992.

Mann, Bruce H. *Neighbors and Strangers: Law and Community in Early Connecticut.* Chapel Hill: University of North Carolina Press, 1987.

Martinez-Alier, Verena. *Marriage, Class, and Colour in Nineteenth-Century Cuba: A Study of Racial Attitudes and Sexual Values in a Slave Society.* Cambridge: Cambridge University Press, 1973.

Masur, Louis P. *Rites of Execution: Capital Punishment and the Transformation of American Culture, 1776–1865.* New York: Oxford University Press, 1985.

Mathews, Donald G. *Religion in the Old South.* Chicago: University of Chicago Press, 1977.

——. *Slavery and Methodism: A Chapter in American Morality, 1780–1845.* Princeton: Princeton University Press, 1965.

Mathews, Mitford M., ed. *A Dictionary of Americanisms on Historical Principles.* Chicago: University of Chicago Press, 1951.

Mauss, Marcel. *The Gift: The Form and Reason for Exchange in Archaic Societies.* New York: W. W. Norton, 1989.

Mays, David John. *Edmund Pendleton, 1721–1803: A Biography.* 2 vols. Cambridge: Harvard University Press, 1984.

Meillassoux, Claude. *Anthropology of Slavery: The Womb of Iron and Gold.* Chicago: University of Chicago Press, 1991.

Menn, Joseph Karl. *The Large Slaveholders of Louisiana, 1860.* New Orleans: Pelican Publishing Co., 1964.

Merk, Frederick. *Slavery and the Annexation of Texas.* New York: Alfred A. Knopf, 1972.

Miers, Suxanne, and Igor Kopytoff, eds. *Slavery in Africa: Historical and Anthropological Perspectives.* Madison: University of Wisconsin Press, 1977.

Miller, Charles A. *The Supreme Court and the Uses of History.* Cambridge: Harvard University Press, 1969.

Miller, Elinor, and Eugene D. Genovese, eds. *Plantation Town and County: Essays on the Local History of American Slave Society.* Urbana: University of Illinois Press, 1974.

Miller, John Chester. *The Wolf by the Ears: Thomas Jefferson and Slavery.* New York: Meridian Press, 1977.

Miller, Randall M., and John David Smith, eds. *Dictionary of Afro-American Slavery.* New York: Greenwood Press, 1988.

Mills, Gary B. *The Forgotten People: Cane River's Creoles of Color.* Baton Rouge: Louisiana State University Press, 1977.

Milsom, S. F. C. *Historical Foundations of the Common Law.* 2d ed. London: Butterworths, 1981.

——. *Studies in the History of the Common Law.* London: Hambledon Press, 1985.

Milton, Frank. *The English Magistracy.* London: Oxford University Press, 1967.

Mintz, Sidney. *Caribbean Transformations.* Chicago: Aldine Publishing Co., 1974.

Mohr, Clarence L. *On the Threshold of Freedom: Masters and Slaves in Civil War Georgia.* Athens: University of Georgia Press, 1986.

Mooney, Chase C. *Slavery in Tennessee.* Bloomington: Indiana University Press, 1957.

Moore, Glover. *The Missouri Controversy, 1819–1821.* Lexington: University of Kentucky Press, 1953.

Moore, John Hebron. *The Emergence of the Cotton Kingdom in the Old Southwest: Mississippi, 1770–1860.* Baton Rouge: Louisiana State University Press, 1988.

Moore, Wilbert E. *American Negro Slavery and Abolition: A Sociological Study.* New York: Third Press, 1971.

Morgan, Edmund S. *American Slavery American Freedom: The Ordeal of Colonial Virginia.* New York: W. W. Norton, 1975.

Morgan, Gwenda. *The Hegemony of the Law: Richmond County, Virginia, 1692–1776.* New York: Garland Publishing, 1989.

Morris, Thomas D. *Free Men All: The Personal Liberty Laws of the North, 1780–1860.* Baltimore: Johns Hopkins University Press, 1974.

Morton, Louis. *Robert Carter of Nomini Hall: A Virginia Tobacco Planter of the Eighteenth Century.* Charlottesville: University Press of Virginia, 1945.

Mullin, Gerald W. *Flight and Rebellion: Slave Resistance in Eighteenth-Century Virginia.* London: Oxford University Press, 1972.

Mullin, Michael. *Africa in America: Slave Acculturation and Resistance in the American South and the British Caribbean, 1736–1831.* Urbana: University of Illinois Press, 1992.

Nash, Gary B. *Race and Revolution.* Madison: Madison House Publisher, 1990.

——. *Red, White, and Black: The Peoples of Early North America.* 3d ed. Englewood Cliffs, N.J.: Prentice Hall, 1992.

Negro Population in the United States, 1790–1915. New York: Arno Press, 1968.

Nelson, William E. *Americanization of the Common Law: The Impact of Legal Change on Massachusetts Society, 1760–1830.* Cambridge: Harvard University Press, 1975.

Newton, James S., and Ronald L. Lewis, eds. *The Other Slaves: Mechanics, Artisans, and Craftsmen.* Boston: G. K. Hall, 1978.

Nicholas, Barry. *An Introduction to Roman Law.* Oxford: Oxford University Press, 1962.

Noel, Donald L., ed. *The Origins of American Slavery and Racism.* Columbus, Ohio: Bobbs-Merrill, 1972.

Novick, Peter. *That Noble Dream: The "Objectivity Question" and the American Historical Profession.* New York: Cambridge University Press, 1988.

Oakes, James. *The Ruling Race: A History of American Slaveholders.* New York: Alfred A. Knopf, 1982.

——. *Slavery and Freedom: An Interpretation of the Old South.* New York: Alfred A. Knopf, 1990.

Oates, Stephen B. *The Fires of Jubilee: Nat Turner's Fierce Rebellion.* New York: Harper and Row, 1975.

Okihiro, Gary Y., ed. *In Resistance: Studies in African, Caribbean. and Afro-American History.* Amherst: University of Massachusetts Press, 1986.

Onuf, Peter S., ed. *Jeffersonian Legacies.* Charlottesville: University Press of Virginia, 1993.

Owens, Leslie Howard. *This Species of Property: Slave Life and Culture in the Old South.* New York: Oxford University Press, 1976.

Parish, Peter J. *Slavery: History and Historians.* New York: Harper and Row, 1989.

Patterson, Orlando. *Freedom.* Vol. 1, *Freedom in the Making of Western Culture.* New York: Basic Books, 1991.

——. *Slavery and Social Death: A Comparative Study.* Cambridge: Harvard University Press, 1982.

——. *The Sociology of Slavery: An Analysis of the Origins, Development, and Structure of Negro Slave Society in Jamaica.* London: Associated University Presses, 1967.

Phillips, Ulrich B. *American Negro Slavery.* 1918. Reprint, Baton Rouge: Louisiana State University Press, 1966.

Plucknett, Theodore F. T. *A Concise History of the Common Law.* 2d ed. Rochester, N.Y.: Lawyers Co-operative Publishing Co., 1936.

Pocock, J. G. A. *The Ancient Constitution and the Feudal Law: English Historical Thought in the Seventeenth Century.* New York: W. W. Norton, 1967.

——. *The Machiavellian Moment: Florentine Political Thought and the Atlantic Republican Tradition.* Princeton: Princeton University Press, 1975.

Pound, Roscoe. *Criminal Justice in America.* New York: DaCapo, 1975.

Quarles, Benjamin. *The Negro in the American Revolution.* Chapel Hill: University of North Carolina Press, 1961.

——. *The Negro in the Civil War.* Boston: Little, Brown, 1969.

Raboteau, Albert J. *Slave Religion: The "Invisible Institution" in the Antebellum South.* New York: Oxford University Press, 1978.

Rankin, Hugh F. *Criminal Trial Proceedings in the General Court of Colonial Virginia.* Williamsburg: Research Studies, a Colonial Williamsburg Publication, 1965.

Ransom, Roger L. *Conflict and Compromise: The Political Economy of Slavery, Emancipation, and the American Civil War.* Cambridge: Cambridge University Press, 1989.

Ransom, Roger L., and Richard Sutch. *One Kind of Freedom: The Economic Consequences of Emancipation.* Cambridge: Cambridge University Press, 1977.

Rawick, George P. *From Sundown to Sunup: The Making of the Black Community.* Westport, Conn.: Greenwood Press, 1972.

Reid, John Phillip. *Chief Justice: The Judicial World of Charles Doe.* Cambridge: Harvard University Press, 1967.

Rice, C. Duncan. *The Rise and Fall of Black Slavery.* Baton Rouge: Louisiana State University Press, 1975.

Robert, Joseph C. *The Road from Monticello: A Study of the Virginia Slavery Debate of 1832.* Durham, N.C.: Duke University Press, 1941.

Robinson, Donald. *Slavery in the Structure of American Politics, 1765–1820.* New York: W. W. Norton, 1979.

Rodney, Walter. *A History of the Guyanese Working People, 1881–1905.* Baltimore: Johns Hopkins University Press, 1981.

Roeber, A. G. *Faithful Magistrates and Republican Lawyers: Creators of Virginia Legal Culture, 1680–1810.* Chapel Hill: University of North Carolina Press, 1981.

Rogers, George C., Jr. *The History of Georgetown County, South Carolina.* Columbia: University of South Carolina Press, 1970.

Rose, Willie Lee. *Slavery and Freedom.* Oxford: Oxford University Press, 1982. Expanded edition edited by William Freehling.

Rubin, Vera, and Arthur Tuden, eds. *Comparative Perspectives on Slavery in New World Plantation Societies.* New York: New York Academy of Sciences, 1977.

Russell, John H. *The Free Negro in Virginia, 1619–1865.* New York: Dover Publications, 1969.

Rutman, Darret B., and Anita H. Rutman. *A Place in Time: Middlesex County, Virginia, 1650–1750.* New York: W. W. Norton, 1984.

Sartre, Jean Paul. *Critique of Dialectical Reason.* London: Verso, 1982.

Saunders, A. C. *A Social History of Black Slaves & Freedmen in Portugal, 1441–1555.* Cambridge: Cambridge University Press, 1982.

Savitt, Todd L. *Medicine and Slavery: The Diseases and Health Care of Slaves in Antebellum Virginia.* Urbana: University of Illinois Press, 1978.

Scarborough, William K. *The Overseer: Plantation Management in the Old South.* Baton Rouge: Louisiana State University Press, 1966.

Schafer, Judith Kelleher. *Slavery, the Civil Law, and the Supreme Court of Louisiana.* Baton Rouge: Louisiana State University Press, 1994.

Schwartz, Stuart B. *Sugar Plantations in the Formation of Brazilian Society.* Cambridge: Cambridge University Press, 1985.

Schwarz, Philip J. *Twice Condemned: Slaves and the Criminal Laws of Virginia, 1705–1865.* Baton Rouge: Louisiana State University Press, 1988.

Scott, Arthur P. *Criminal Law in Colonial Virginia.* Chicago: University of Chicago Press, 1930.

Scott, Rebecca J. *Slave Emancipation in Cuba: The Transition to Free Labor, 1860–1899.* Princeton: Princeton University Press, 1985.

Sellers, James B. *Slavery in Alabama.* Tuscaloosa: University of Alabama Press, 1950.

Semmes, Raphael. *Crime and Punishment in Early Maryland.* Montclair, N.J.: Patterson Smith, 1970.

Shammas, Carole, Marylynn Salmon, and Michel Dublin. *Inheritance in America from Colonial Times to the Present.* New Brunswick: Rutgers University Press, 1987.

Shapiro, Barbara J. *Beyond Reasonable Doubt and Probable Cause: Historical Perspectives on the Anglo-American Law of Evidence.* Berkeley: University of California Press, 1991.

Shugg, Roger. *Origins of Class Struggle in Louisiana: A Social History of White Farmers and Laborers during Slavery and After, 1840–1875.* Baton Rouge: Louisiana State University Press, 1939.

Shyllon, F. O. *Black Slaves in Britain.* London: Oxford University Press, 1974.

Simpson, A. W. B. *A History of the Common Law of Contract: The Rise of the Action of Assumpsit.* Oxford: Oxford University Press, 1975.

———. *A History of the Land Law.* 2d ed. Oxford: Oxford University Press, 1986.

———. *Legal Theory and Legal History: Essays on the Common Law.* London: Hambledon Press, 1987.

Sirmans, M. Eugene. *Colonial South Carolina: A Political History, 1663–1763*. Chapel Hill: University of North Carolina Press, 1966.

Smith, Abbot Emerson. *Colonists in Bondage: White Servitude and Convict Labor in America, 1607–1776*. New York: W. W. Norton, 1971.

Smith, Julia Floyd. *Slavery and Plantation Growth in Antebellum Florida, 1821–1860*. Gainesville: University of Florida Press, 1973.

——. *Slavery and Rice Culture in Low Country Georgia, 1750–1860*. Knoxville: University of Tennessee Press, 1985.

Sobel, Mechal. *The World They Made Together: Black and White Values in Eighteenth-Century Virginia*. Princeton: Princeton University Press, 1987.

Soderlund, Jean R. *Quakers and Slavery: A Divided Spirit*. Princeton: Princeton University Press, 1985.

Solow, Barbara L., ed. *Slavery and the Rise of the Atlantic System*. Cambridge: Cambridge University Press, 1991.

Solow, Barbara L., and Stanley L. Engerman, eds. *British Capitalism and Caribbean Slavery: The Legacy of Eric Williams*. Cambridge: Cambridge University Press, 1987.

Stampp, Kenneth. *The Peculiar Institution: Slavery in the Ante-Bellum South*. New York: Vintage Books, 1965.

Starobin, Robert S. *Industrial Slavery in the Old South*. New York: Oxford University Press, 1970.

Staudenraus, Philip J. *The African Colonization Movement, 1816–1865*. New York: Columbia University Press, 1961.

Ste. Croix, G. E. M. De. *The Class Struggle in the Ancient Greek World: From the Archaic Age to the Arab Conquests*. Ithaca: Cornell University Press, 1981.

Stein, Peter. *Legal Evolution: The Story of an Idea*. Cambridge: Cambridge University Press, 1960.

Stein, Stanley. *Vassouras: A Brazilian Coffee County, 1850–1900*. New York: Atheneum, 1972.

Steinfeld, Robert J. *The Invention of Free Labor: The Employment Relation in English and American Law and Culture, 1350–1870*. Chapel Hill: University of North Carolina Press, 1991.

Stone, Julius. *The Province and Function of Law: Law as Logic, Justice, and Social Control: A Study in Jurisprudence*. Cambridge: Harvard University Press, 1961.

——. *Social Dimensions of Law and Justice*. Stanford: Stanford University Press, 1966.

Stuckey, Sterling. *Slave Culture: Nationalist Theory and the Foundations of Black America*. New York: Oxford University Press, 1987.

Sydnor, Charles S. *American Revolutionaries in the Making: Political Practices in Washington's Virginia*. New York: Collier Books, 1965.

——. *Slavery in Mississippi*. Gloucester, Mass.: Peter Smith, 1965.

Tadman, Michael. *Speculators and Slaves; Masters, Traders, and Slaves in the Old South*. Madison: University of Wisconsin Press, 1989.

Tannenbaum, Frank. *Slave and Citizen: The Negro in the Americas*. New York: Vintage Books, 1946.

Tate, Thad W. *The Negro in Eighteenth-Century Williamsburg*. Charlottesville: University Press of Virginia, 1965.

Taylor, Joe Gray. *Negro Slavery in Louisiana*. Baton Rouge: Louisiana Historical Association, 1963.

Taylor, Orville W. *Negro Slavery in Arkansas*. Durham, N.C.: Duke University Press, 1958.

Thompson, E. P. *Whigs and Hunters: The Origins of the Black Act*. New York: Pantheon, 1975.

Thornton, J. Miles, III. *Politics and Power in a Slave Society: Alabama, 1800–1860*. Baton Rouge: Louisiana State University Press, 1978.

Tillson, Albert H., Jr. *Gentry and Common Folk: Political Culture on a Virginia Frontier, 1740–1789*. Lexington: University Press of Kentucky, 1991.

Tise, Larry E. *Proslavery: A History of the Defense of Slavery in America, 1701–1840*. Athens: University of Georgia Press, 1987.

Tomlins, Christopher L. *Law, Labor, and Ideology in the Early American Republic*. New York: Cambridge University Press, 1993.

Tushnet, Mark. *The American Law of Slavery, 1810–1860: Considerations of Humanity and Interest*. Princeton: Princeton University Press, 1981.

Veall, Donald. *The Popular Movement for Law Reform, 1640–1660*. Oxford: Oxford University Press, 1970.

Verlindin, Charles. *Beginnings of Modern Colonization: Eleven Essays with an Introduction*. Ithaca: Cornell University Press, 1970.

VerSteeg, Clarence L. *Origins of a Southern Mosaic: Studies of Early Carolina and Georgia*. Athens: University of Georgia Press, 1975.

Vinogradoff, Paul. *Villainage in England: Essays in English Medieval History*. Oxford: Oxford University Press, 1968.

Wade, Richard C. *Slavery in the Cities: The South, 1820–1860*. New York: Oxford University Press, 1964.

Waldron, Jeremy, ed. *Nonsense Upon Stilts: Bentham, Burke, and Marx, on the Rights of Man*. London: Routledge, Chapman and Hew, 1987.

——. *The Right of Private Property*. Oxford: Oxford University Press, 1988.

Ward, J. R. *British West Indian Slavery, 1750–1834: The Process of Amelioration*. Oxford: Oxford University Press, 1988.

Watson, Alan. *The Evolution of Law*. Baltimore: Johns Hopkins University Press, 1985.

——. *Failures of the Legal Imagination*. Philadelphia: University of Pennsylvania Press, 1988.

——. *Roman Slave Law*. Baltimore: Johns Hopkins University Press, 1987.

——. *Slave Law in the Americas*. Athens: University of Georgia Press, 1989.

——. *Sources of Law, Legal Change, and Ambiguity*. Philadelphia: University of Pennsylvania Press, 1984.

Weaver, Herbert. *Mississippi Farmers, 1850–1860*. Nashville: University of Tennessee Press, 1945.

Webber, Thomas S. *Deep Like the Rivers: Education in the Slave Quarter Community, 1831–1865*. New York: W. W. Norton, 1978.

Weber, Max. *On Law in Economy and Society*. Edited by Max Rheinstein. New York: Simon and Schuster, 1967.

West, Cornel. *Race Matters*. New York: Vintage Books, 1994.

White, G. Edward. *The American Judicial Tradition: Profiles of Leading American Judges*. New York: Oxford University Press, 1976.

——. *The Marshall Court and Cultural Change, 1815–1835*. 4 vols. New York: Macmillan, 1988. Volumes 3 and 4 are in the Holmes Devise History of the U.S. Supreme Court.

——. *Tort Law in America: An Intellectual History*. New York: Oxford University Press, 1980.

Wiecek, William. *The Sources of Antislavery Constitutionalism in America, 1760–1848*. Ithaca: Cornell University Press, 1977.

Wikramanayake, Marina. *A World in Shadow: The Free Black in Antebellum South Carolina*. Columbia: University of South Carolina Press, 1973.

Wilentz, Sean. *Chants Democratic: New York City & the Rise of the American Working Class, 1788–1850*. New York: Oxford University Press, 1984.

Williams, Eric. *Capitalism and Slavery*. New York: Capricorn Books, 1966.

Williams, Jack Kenny. *Vogues in Villainy: Crime and Retribution in Ante-Bellum South Car-olina.* Columbia: University of South Carolina Press, 1959.

Williamson, Joel. *New People: Miscegenation and Mulattoes in the United States.* New York: Free Press, 1980.

Winston, Kenneth I., ed. *The Principles of Social Order: Selected Essays of Lon L. Fuller.* Dur-ham, N.C.: Duke University Press, 1981.

Wood, Betty. *Slavery in Colonial Georgia, 1730–1775.* Athens: University of Georgia Press, 1984.

Wood, Gordon S. *The Creation of the American Republic, 1776–1787.* Chapel Hill: University of North Carolina Press, 1969.

Wood, Peter H. *Black Majority: Negroes in Colonial South Carolina from 1670 through the Stono Rebellion.* New York: Alfred A. Knopf, 1974.

Woodward, C. Vann. *American Counterpoint: Slavery and Racism in the North-South Di-alogue.* Boston: Little, Brown, 1971.

Wright, Gavin. *Old South, New South: Revolutions in the Southern Economy since the Civil War.* New York: Basic Books, 1986.

——. *Political Economy of the Cotton South: Households, Markets, and Wealth in the Nine-teenth Century.* New York: W. W. Norton, 1978.

Wyatt-Brown, Bertram. *Southern Honor: Ethics and Behavior in the Old South.* New York: Oxford University Press, 1982.

Younger, Richard D. *The People's Panel: The Grand Jury in the United States, 1643–1941.* Providence, R.I.: Brown University Press, 1963.

Articles

A number of the following articles have been reprinted. The most extensive collection is Paul Finkelman, ed., *Articles on American Slavery*, 18 vols. (New York: Garland, 1989).

Addington, Wendell G. "Slave Insurrections in Texas." *Journal of Negro History* 34 (1950): 408–34.

Alexander, Gregory, S. "The Dead Hand and the Law of Trusts in the Nineteenth Century." *Stanford Law Review* 37 (1985): 1189–1266.

Allain, Mathé. "Slave Policies in French Louisiana." *Louisiana History* 21 (1980): 127–37.

Allain, Mathé (introduction), and Gerard L. St. Martin (translation). "A Slave Trial in Colonial Natchitoches." *Louisiana History* 28 (1987): 57–91.

Alpert, Jonathan L. "The Origin of Slavery in the United States: The Maryland Precedent." *American Journal of Legal History* 14 (1970): 189–221.

Ames, Susie M. "Law-in-Action: The Court Records of Virginia's Eastern Shore." *William and Mary Quarterly*, 3d ser., 4 (1947): 177–91.

Anesko, Michael. "So Discreet a Zeal: Slavery and the Anglican Church in Virginia, 1680–1730." *Virginia Magazine of History and Biography* 93 (1985): 247–78.

Baade, Hans W. "The Law of Slavery in Spanish Luisiana, 1769–1803." In *Louisiana's Legal Heritage*, edited by Edward F. Haas. Pensacola: Perdido Bay Press, 1983.

Baker, J. H. "Criminal Courts and Procedure." In *Crime in England, 1550–1800*, edited by J. S. Cockburn. Princeton: Princeton University Press, 1977.

——. "Property in Chattels." *Selden Society* 94 (1978): 209–21.

Bardaglio, Peter W. "Rape and the Law in the Old South: 'Calculated to Excite Indignation in Every Heart.'" *Journal of Southern History* 60 (1994): 749–72.

Batiza, Rodolfo. "The Louisiana Civil Code of 1808: Its Actual Sources and Present Rele-vance." *Tulane Law Review* 46 (1971): 4–165.

——. "Sources of the Civil Code of 1808: Facts and Speculations: A Rejoinder." *Tulane Law Review* 46 (1972): 628–52.

Bauer, Raymond A., and Alice H. Bauer. "Day to Day Resistance to Slavery." *Journal of Negro History* 27 (1942): 388–419.

Berlin, Ira. "Time, Space, and the Evolution of Afro-American Society in British Mainland North America." *American Historical Review* 85 (1980): 44–78.

Berman, Harold J. "The Origins of Historical Jurisprudence: Coke, Selden, Hale." *Yale Law Journal* 103 (1994): 1651–1738.

Bestor, Arthur. "State Sovereignty and Slavery: A Reinterpretation of Proslavery Constitutional Doctrine, 1846–1860." *Journal of the Illinois State Historical Society* 54 (1961): 117–80.

Billings, Warren M. "The Cases of Fernando and Elizabeth Key: A Note on the Status of Blacks in Seventeenth-Century Virginia." *William and Mary Quarterly*, 3d ser., 30 (1973): 467–74.

———. "English Legal Literature as a Source of Law and Legal Practice for Seventeenth-Century Virginia." *Virginia Magazine of History and Biography* 87 (1979): 403–16.

———. "The Law of Servants and Slaves in Seventeenth-Century Virginia." *Virginia Magazine of History and Biography* 99 (1991): 45–62.

———. "Pleading, Procedure, and Practice: The Meaning of Due Process of Law in Seventeenth-Century Virginia." *Journal of Southern History* 47 (1981): 569–84.

———. "The Transfer of English Law to Virginia. In *Westward Enterprise: English Activities in Ireland, the Atlantic, and America, 1480–1650*, edited by K. R. Andrews, N. P. Canny, and P. E. H. Hair. Detroit: Wayne State University Press, 1979.

Brady, Patrick S. "Slavery, Race, and the Criminal Law in Antebellum North Carolina: A Reconsideration of the Thomas Ruffin Court." *North Carolina Central Law Journal* 10 (1978): 248–60.

Brasseaux, Carl A. "The Administration of Slave Regulations in French Louisiana, 1724–1766." *Louisiana History* 21 (1980): 139–58.

Bryson, W. Hamilton. "The Use of Roman Law in Virginia Courts." *American Journal of Legal History* 28 (1984): 135–46.

Burdick, Francis M. "Is Law the Expression of Class Selfishness?" *Harvard Law Review* 25 (1911–12): 349–71.

Burnham, Margaret A. "An Impossible Marriage: Slave Law and Family Law." *Law and Inequality* 5 (1987): 187–225.

Bush, Jonathan A. "Free to Enslave: The Foundations of Colonial American Slave Law." *Yale Journal of Law and the Humanities* 5 (1993): 417–70.

Chaplin, Joyce E. "Creating a Cotton South in Georgia and South Carolina, 1760–1815." *Journal of Southern History* 57 (1991): 171–200.

Chapman, Terry. "Crime in Eighteenth-Century England: E. P. Thompson and the Conflict Theory of Crime." *Criminal Justice History: An International Annual* 1 (1980): 139–56.

Chused, Richard. "Married Women's Property Law, 1800–1850." *Georgetown Law Journal* 71 (1983): 1359–1425.

Corré, Jacob I. "Thinking Property at Memphis: An Application of Watson." *Chicago-Kent Law Review* 68 (1993): 1373–90.

Cottroll, Robert J. "Liberalism and Paternalism: Ideology, Economic Interest, and the Business Law of Slavery." *American Journal of Legal History* 31 (1987): 359–73.

Crouch, Barry A. " 'Booty Capitalism' and Capitalism's Booty: Slaves and Slavery in Ancient Rome and the American South." *Slavery and Abolition* 6 (1985): 3–24.

Crow, Jeffrey J. "Slave Rebelliousness and Social Conflict in North Carolina, 1775 to 1802." *William and Mary Quarterly*, 3d ser., 37 (1980): 79–102.

Currie, James T. "From Slavery to Freedom in Mississippi's Legal System." *Journal of Negro History* 65 (1980): 112–25.

Davies, C. S. L. "Slavery and Protector Somerset: The Vagrancy Act of 1547." *Economic History Review* 19 (1966): 533–49.

Dew, Charles B. "Black Ironworkers and the Slave Insurrection Panic of 1856." *Journal of Southern History* 41 (1975): 321–38.

Drescher, Seymour. "British Way, French Way: Opinion Building and Revolution in the Second French Slave Emancipation." *American Historical Review* 96 (1991): 709–34.

——. "The Long Goodbye: Dutch Capitalism and Antislavery in Comparative Perspective." *American Historical Review* 99 (1994): 44–69.

Dunn, Richard S. "Black Society in the Chesapeake, 1776–1810." In *Slavery and Freedom in the Age of the American Revolution*, edited by Ira Berlin and Ronald Hoffman. Charlottesville: University Press of Virginia, 1983.

——. "A Tale of Two Plantations: Slave Life in Mesopotamia in Jamaica and Mount Airy in Virginia, 1799 to 1828." *William and Mary Quarterly*, 3d ser., 34 (1977): 32–65.

Edwards, John C. "Slave Justice in Four Middle Georgia Counties." *Georgia Historical Quarterly* 57 (1973): 265–73.

Eltis, David. "Europeans and the Rise and Fall of African Slavery in the Americas: An Interpretation." *American Historical Review* 98 (1993): 1399–1423.

——. "Labour and Coercion in the English Atlantic World from the Seventeenth to the Early Twentieth Century." *Slavery and Abolition* 14 (1993): 207–26.

Engerman, Stanley L. "Slavery and Emancipation in Comparative Perspective: A Look at Some Recent Debates." *Journal of Economic History* 46 (1986): 317–39.

Epstein, Richard A. "The Social Consequences of Common Law Rules." *Harvard Law Review* 95 (1982): 1717–51.

Evans, William McKee. "From the Land of Canaan to the Land of Guinea: The Strange Odyssey of the Sons of Ham." *American Historical Review* 85 (1980): 15–43.

"An Exchange on Critical Legal Studies between Robert W. Gordon and William Nelson." *Law and History Review* 6 (1988): 139–86.

Fede, Andrew. "Legal Protection for Slave Buyers in the U.S. South: A Caveat Concerning *Caveat Emptor*." *American Journal of Legal History* 31 (1987): 322–58.

——. "Legitimized Violent Slave Abuse in the American South, 1619–1865: A Case Study of Law and Social Change in Six Southern States." *American Journal of Legal History* 29 (1985): 93–150.

——. "Toward a Solution of the Slave Law Dilemma: A Critique of Tushnet's 'The American Law of Slavery.'" *Law and History Review* 2 (1984): 301–20.

Ferris, William R. "The Collection of Racial Lore: Approaches and Problems." *New York Folklore Quarterly* 27 (1971): 261–79.

Finkelman, Paul. "The Color of Law." *Northwestern University Law Review* 87 (1992–93): 937–91.

——. "The Crime of Color." *Tulane Law Review* 67 (1993): 2063–112.

——. "Jefferson and Slavery: 'Treason against the Hopes of the World.'" In *Jeffersonian Legacies*, edited by Peter S. Onuf. Charlottesville: University Press of Virginia, 1993.

——. "Prosecutions in Defense of the Cornerstone." *Reviews in American History* 17 (1989): 397–403.

——. "Slaves as Fellow Servants: Ideology, Law, and Industrialization." *American Journal of Legal History* 31 (1987): 269–305.

Finley, Moses I. "Slavery." *International Encyclopedia of the Social Sciences*, 14:307–13.

Finnie, Gordon E. "The Antislavery Movement in the Upper South before 1840." *Journal of Southern History* 35 (1969): 319–42.

Fisher, William W., III. "Ideology and Imagery in the Law of Slavery." *Chicago-Kent Law Review* 68 (1993): 1051–86.

Flanigan, Daniel J. "Criminal Procedure in Slave Trials in the Antebellum South." *Journal of Southern History* 40 (1974): 537–64.

Ford, Lacy K. "Republican Ideology in a Slave Society: The Political Economy of John C. Calhoun." *Journal of Southern History* 54 (1988): 405–24.

Fox-Genovese, Elizabeth, and Eugene D. Genovese. "Slavery, Economic Development, and the Law: The Dilemma of the Southern Political Economists, 1800–1860." *Washington and Lee Law Review* 41 (1984): 1–29.

Fuller, L. L., and William R. Perdue. "The Reliance Interest in Contract Damages." *Yale Law Journal* 46 (1936–37): 52–96, 373–420.

Gallay, Allan. "The Origins of Slaveholders' Paternalism: George Whitefield, the Bryan Family, and the Great Awakening in the South." *Journal of Southern History* 53 (1987): 369–94.

Genovese, Eugene D. "Slave States of North America." In *Neither Slave Nor Free: The Freedman of African Descent in the Slave Societies of the New World*, edited by David Cohen and Jack Greene. Baltimore: Johns Hopkins University Press, 1972.

——. "The Treatment of Slaves in Different Countries." In *Slavery in the New World: A Reader in Comparative History*, edited by Laura Foner and Genovese. Englewood Cliffs, N.J.: Prentice-Hall, 1969.

——. "Yeoman Farmers in a Slaveholders' Democracy." *Agricultural History* 47 (1974): 331–42.

Gordon, Robert. "Historicism in Legal Scholarship." *Yale Law Journal* 90 (1981): 1017–56.

Green, Rodney D. "Black Tobacco Factory Workers and Social Conflict in Antebellum Richmond: Were Slavery and Urban Industry Really Compatible?" *Slavery and Abolition* 8 (1987): 183–203.

Hallion, Marie. "Criminal Justice in the Province of Maryland." *Maryland Historian* 15 (1984): 6–18.

Hammond, James Henry. "Letter to an English Abolitionist." In *The Ideology of Slavery: Proslavery Thought in the Antebellum South, 1830–1860*, edited by Drew Gilpin Faust. Baton Rouge: Louisiana University Press, 1981.

Handler, Jerome S., and John T. Pohlmann. "Slave Manumissions and Freedmen in Seventeenth-Century Barbados." *William and Mary Quarterly*, 3d ser., 41 (1984): 390–408.

Handlin, Oscar, and Mary F. Handlin. "Origins of the Southern Labor System." *William and Mary Quarterly*, 3d ser., 7 (1950): 199–222.

Hardy, James D. "The Banality of Slavery." *Southern Studies* 25 (1986): 187–95.

Hardy, James D., and Robert B. Robinson. "The Roman Law and Louisiana Slavery: An Example of Mortgage." *Southern Studies*, new ser., 1 (1990): 355–69.

Harper, William. "Memoir on Slavery." In *The Ideology of Slavery: Proslavery Thought in the Antebellum South, 1830–1860*, edited by Drew Gilpin Faust. Baton Rouge: Louisiana University Press, 1981.

Harrold, Stanley. "Violence and Nonviolence in Kentucky Abolitionism." *Journal of Southern History* 62 (1991): 15–38.

Hartfield, Marianne. "New Thoughts on the Proslavery Natural Law Theory: The Importance of History and the Study of Ancient Slavery." *Southern Studies* 22 (1983): 244–59.

Haskell, Thomas L. "Capitalism and the Origins of the Humanitarian Sensibility." *American Historical Review* 90 (1985): 339–61, 547–66.

Hast, Adele. "The Legal Status of the Negro in Virginia, 1705–1765." *Journal of Negro History* 14 (1969): 217–39.

Hay, Douglas. "Property, Authority, and Criminal Law." In *Albion's Fatal Tree: Crime and Society in Eighteenth-Century England*, edited by Hay, Peter Linebaugh, John G. Rule, E. P. Thompson, and Cal Winslow. New York: Pantheon, 1975.

Higginbotham, A. Leon, Jr., and Anne F. Jacobs. "The 'Law Only as an Enemy': The Legitimization of Racial Powerlessness through the Colonial and Antebellum Criminal Laws of Virginia." *North Carolina Law Review* 70 (1992): 969–1070.

Higginbotham, A. Leon, Jr., and Barbara K. Kopytoff. "Property First, Humanity Second: The Recognition of the Slave's Human Nature in Virginia Civil Law." *Ohio State Law Journal* 50 (1989): 511–40.

Higginbotham, A. Leon, Jr., and Barbara K. Kopytoff. "Racial Purity and Interrracial Sex in the Law of Colonial and Antebellum Virginia." *Georgetown Law Journal* 77 (1989): 1967–2029.

Higginbotham, Don, and William S. Price Jr. "Was It Murder for a White Man to Kill a Slave? Chief Justice Martin Howard Condemns the Peculiar Institution in North Carolina." *William and Mary Quarterly*, 3d ser., 36 (1979): 593–601.

Hoetink, Harry. "Slavery and Race." *Historical Reflections: Reflexion historique* 9 (1979): 255–74.

———. "Surinam and Curaçao." In *Neither Slave Nor Free: The Freedman of African Descent in the Slave Societies of the New World*, edited by David Cohen and Jack Greene. Baltimore: Johns Hopkins University Press, 1972.

Holmes, Jack D. L. "The Abortive Revolt at Point Coupee, Louisiana, 1795." *Louisiana History* 11 (1970): 341–62.

Horwitz, Donald L. "Color Differentiation in the American Systems of Slavery." *Journal of Interdisciplinary History* 3 (1973): 509–41.

Horwitz, Morton J. "The Historical Contingency of the Role of History." *Yale Law Journal* 90 (1981): 1057–60.

Howington, Arthur, III. "'Not in the Condition of a Horse or an Ox': *Ford v. Ford*, the Law of Testamentary Manumission, and the Tennessee Courts' Recognition of Slave Humanity." *Tennessee Historical Quarterly* 34 (1975): 249–63.

Hughes, Sarah S. "Slaves for Hire: The Allocation of Black Labor in Elizabeth City County, Virginia, 1782 to 1810." *William and Mary Quarterly*, 3d ser., 35 (1978): 260–86.

Isaac, Rhys. "Communication and Control: Authority Metaphors and Power Contests on Colonel Landon Carter's Virginia Plantation, 1752–1778." In *Rites of Power: Symbolism, Ritual, and Politics since the Middle Ages*, edited by Sean Wilentz. Philadelphia: University of Pennsylvania Press, 1985.

Johnson, Whittington B. "The Origins and Nature of African Slavery in Seventeenth-Century Maryland." *Maryland Historical Magazine* 73 (1978): 236–45.

Jordan, Winthrop. "American Chiaroscuro: The Status and Definition of Mulattoes in the British Colonies." *William and Mary Quarterly*, 3d ser., 19 (1962): 183–200.

Katz, Stanley. "The Politics of Law in Colonial America: Controversies over Chancery Courts and Equity Law in the Eighteenth Century." In *Perspectives in American History*, edited by Donald Fleming and Bernard Bailyn. Cambridge: Harvard University Press, 1971.

———. "Republicanism and the Law of Inheritance in the American Revolutionary Era." *Michigan Law Review* 76 (1977): 1–29.

Kay, Marvin L. Michael, and Lorin Lee Cary. "'The Planters Suffer Little or Nothing': North Carolina Compensation for Executed Slaves, 1748–1772." *Science and Society* 40 (1976–77): 288–306.

Kay, Marvin L. Michael, and Lorin Lee Cary. "'They are Indeed the Constant Plague of Their Tyrants': Slave Defense of a Moral Economy in Colonial North Carolina, 1748–1772." *Science and Society* 6 (1985): 37–55.

Keim, C. Ray. "Primogeniture and Entail in Colonial Virginia." *William and Mary Quarterly*, 3d ser., 25 (1968): 544–86.

Kennedy, Duncan. "The Structure of Blackstone's Commentaries." *Buffalo Law Review* 28 (1979): 205–382.

Kiely, Terrance F. "The Hollow Words: An Experiment in Legal Historical Method as Applied to the Institution of Slavery." *De Paul Law Review* 25 (1976): 842–93.

Kilbride, Daniel. "Slavery and Utilitarianism: Thomas Cooper and the Mind of the Old South." *Journal of Southern History* 59 (1993): 469–86.

Knight, Franklin. "Slavery and Capitalism in the Spanish and Portuguese Empire." In *Slavery and the Rise of the Atlantic System*, edited by Barbara L. Solow. Cambridge: Cambridge University Press, 1991.

Konefsky, Alfred S. " 'As Best to Subserve Their Own Interests': Lemuel Shaw, Labor Conspiracy, and Fellow Servants." *Law and History Review* 7 (1989): 219–39.

Konig, David Thomas. " 'Dale's Laws' and the Non-Common Law Origins of Criminal Justice in Virginia." *American Journal of Legal History* 26 (1982): 354–75.

Kronman, Anthony. "Specific Performance." *University of Chicago Law Review* 45 (1978): 351–83.

Krygier, Martin. "Law as Tradition." *Law and Philosophy* 5 (1986): 237–62.

Kulikoff, Allan. "The Origins of Afro-American Society in Tidewater Maryland and Virginia, 1700 to 1790." *William and Mary Quarterly*, 3d ser., 35 (1978): 226–59.

Langbein, John H. "Albion's Fatal Flaws." *Past and Present* 98 (1983): 76–136.

——. "The Criminal Trial before the Lawyers." *University of Chicago Law Review* 45 (1978): 263–316.

Langum, David J. "The Role of Intellect and Fortuity in Legal Change: An Incident from the Law of Slavery." *American Journal of Legal History* 28 (1984): 1–16.

Leach, W. Barton. "Perpetuities in a Nutshell." *Harvard Law Review* 51 (1938): 638–71.

Lichtenstein, Alex. " 'That Disposition to Theft, with Which They Have Been Branded': Moral Economy, Slave Management, and the Law." *Journal of Social History* 22 (1988): 413–40.

Lobban, Michael. "Blackstone and the Science of Law." *Historical Journal* 30 (1987): 311–35.

Macauley, Stewart. "Non-contractual Relations in Business: A Preliminary Study." *American Sociological Review* 28 (1963): 55–66.

McClain, Emlin. "Implied Warranties in Sales." *Harvard Law Review* 7 (1894): 212–20.

McColley, Robert. "Slavery in Virginia, 1619–1660: A Reexamination." In *New Perspectives on Race and Slavery in America: Essays in Honor of Kenneth M. Stampp*, edited by Robert Abzug and Stephen Maizlish. Lexington: University Press of Kentucky, 1986.

McGettigan, James W., Jr. "Boone County Slaves: Sales, Estate Divisions, and Families, 1820–1865." *Missouri Historical Review* 72 (1978): 176–97, 271–95.

McKibben, Davidson B. "Negro Slave Insurrections in Mississippi, 1800–1865." *Journal of Negro History* 34 (1949): 73–94.

Meaders, Daniel E. "South Carolina Fugitives as Viewed through Local Colonial Newspapers with Emphasis on Runaway Notices, 1732–1801." *Journal of Negro History* 60 (1975): 288–319.

Menard, Russell. "From Servants to Slaves: The Transformation of the Chesapeake Labor System." *Southern Studies* (1974): 355–90.

——. "The Maryland Slave Population, 1658 to 1730: A Demographic Profile of Blacks in Four Counties." *William and Mary Quarterly*, 3d ser., 32 (1975): 29–54.

Moore, Wilbert E. "Slave Law and Social Structure." *Journal of Negro History* 26 (1941): 171–202.

Morgan, Gwenda. "Law and Social Change in Colonial Virginia: The Role of the Grand Jury in Richmond County, 1692–1776." *Virginia Magazine of History and Biography* 95 (1987): 453–80.

Morgan, Philip D. "Black Life in Eighteenth-Century Charleston." In *Perspectives in American History*, edited by Bernard Bailyn, Donald Fleming, and Stephen Thernstrons, eds. Cambridge: Harvard University Press, 1984.

——. "Colonial South Carolina Runaways." In *Out of the House of Bondage: Runaways, Resistance, and Marronage in Africa and the New World*, edited by Gad J. Heuman. New York: F. Cass Publishers, 1986.

——. "The Ownership of Property by Slaves in the Mid-Nineteenth Century Low Country." *Journal of Southern History* 49 (1983): 399–420.

——. "Three Planters and Their Slaves: Perspectives on Slavery in Virginia, South Carolina, and Jamaica, 1750–1790." In *Race and Family in the Colonial South*, edited by Winthrop Jordan and Sheila L. Skemp. Jackson: University Press of Mississippi, 1987.

Morgan, Philip D., and Michael L. Nicholls. "Slaves in Piedmont Virginia, 1720–1790." *William and Mary Quarterly*, 3d ser., 46 (1987): 211–51.

Morgan, Philip D., and George D. Terry. "Slavery in Microcosm: A Conspiracy Scare in Colonial South Carolina." *Southern Studies* 21 (1982): 121–45.

Morris, Christopher. "An Event in Community Organization: The Mississippi Slave Insurrection Scare of 1835." *Journal of Southern History* 22 (1988): 93–111.

Morris, Thomas D. " 'As If the Injury Was Effected by the Natural Elements of Air or Fire': Slave Wrongs and the Liability of Masters." *Law and Society Review* 16 (1981–82): 569–99.

——. "Slaves and the Rules of Evidence in Criminal Trials." *Chicago-Kent Law Review* 68 (1993): 1209–40.

——. " 'Society Is Not Marked by Punctuality in the Payment of Debts': The Chattel Mortgages of Slaves." In *Ambivalent Legacy: A Legal History of the South*, edited by David J. Bodenhamer and James W. Ely Jr. Jackson: University Press of Mississippi, 1984.

——. " 'Villeinage . . . as It Existed in England, Reflects but Little Light on Our Subject': The Problem of the Sources of Southern Slave Law." *American Journal of Legal History* 32 (1988): 95–137.

Nash, A. E. Keir. "Fairness and Formalism in the Trials of Blacks in the State Supreme Courts of the Old South." *Virginia Law Review* 56 (1970): 64–100.

——. "A More Equitable Past? Southern Supreme Courts and the Protection of the Antebellum Negro." *North Carolina Law Review* 48 (1970): 197–241.

——. "Negro Rights, Unionism, and Greatness on the South Carolina Court of Appeals: The Extraordinary Chief Justice John Belton O'Neall." *South Carolina Law Review* 21 (1969): 141–90.

——. "Reason of Slavery: Understanding the Judicial Role in the Peculiar Institution." *Vanderbilt Law Review* 32 (1979): 7–218.

——. "The Texas Supreme Court and the Trial Rights of Blacks, 1845–1860." *Journal of American History* 58 (1971): 622–42.

Nicholson, Bradley J. "Legal Borrowing and the Origins of Slave Law in the British Colonies." *American Journal of Legal History* 38 (1994): 38–55.

Note. "Common Law Crimes in the United States." *Columbia Law Review* 47 (1947): 1332–37.

Note. "Strict Liability in Hybrid Cases." *Stanford Law Review* 32 (1980): 391–408.

Oppenheim, Leonard. "The Law of Slaves—A Comparative Study of Roman and Louisiana Systems." *Tulane Law Review* 14 (1940): 384–406.

Palmer, Paul C. "Servant into Slave: The Evolution of the Legal Status of the Negro Laborer in Colonial Virginia." *South Atlantic Quarterly* 65 (1966): 355–70.

Pascal, Robert A. "Sources of the Digest of 1808: A Reply to Professor Bastiza." *Tulane Law Review* 46 (1972): 602–27.

Phillips, Ulrich B. "The Central Theme of Southern History." *American Historical Review* 34 (1928): 30–43.

Post, Edward M. "Kentucky Law concerning Emancipation or Freedom of Slaves." *Filson Club History Quarterly* 59 (1985): 344–67.

Preyer, Kathryn. "Crime, the Criminal Law, and Reform in Post-Revolutionary Virginia." *Law and History Review* 1 (1983): 53–85.

Quarles, Benjamin. "Lord Dunmore as Liberator." *William and Mary Quarterly*, 3d ser., 15 (1958): 494–507.

Rankin, David C. "The Tannenbaum Thesis Reconsidered: Slavery and Race Relations in Antebellum Louisiana." *Southern Studies* 18 (1979): 5–31.

Reid, John Phillip. "Lessons of Lumpkin: A Review of Recent Literature on Law, Comity, and the Impending Crisis." *William and Mary Law Review* 23 (1982): 571–624.

Rivers, Larry E. "Slavery in Microcosm: Leon County, Florida, 1824 to 1860." *Journal of Negro History* 66 (1981): 236–45.

Roeber, A. G. "Authority, Law, and Custom: The Rituals of Court Day in Tidewater Virginia, 1720 to 1750." *William and Mary Quarterly*, 3d ser., 37 (1980): 29–52.

Roover, Raymond de. "The Concept of the Just Price: Theory and Economic Policy." *Journal of Economic History* 18 (1958): 418–34.

Russell, Marion J. "American Slave Discontent in the Records of the High Courts." *Journal of Negro History* 31 (1946): 411–34.

Russell, Thomas D. "South Carolina's Largest Slave Auctioneering Firm." *Chicago-Kent Law Review* 68 (1993): 1241–82.

Samuel, Alan E. "The Role of *Paramone* Clauses in Ancient Documents." *Journal of Juristic Papyrology* 15–17 (1965–71): 221–311.

Savitt, Todd L. "Slave Life Insurance in Virginia and North Carolina." *Journal of Southern History* 43 (1977): 583–600.

Sawyer, Jeffrey K. " 'Benefit of Clergy' in Maryland and Virginia." *American Journal of Legal History* 34 (1990): 460–68.

Sayre, Francis. "Criminal Conspiracy." *Harvard Law Review* 35 (1922): 393–427.

Schafer, Judith K. " 'Details Are of a Most Revolting Character': Cruelty to Slaves as Seen in Appeals to the Supreme Court of Louisiana." *Chicago-Kent Law Review* 68 (1993): 1283–1312.

———. " 'Guaranteed against the Vices and Maladies Prescribed by Law': Consumer Protection, the Law of Slave Sales, and the Supreme Court of Antebellum Louisiana." *American Journal of Legal History* 31 (1987): 306–22.

———. "The Long Arm of the Law: Slave Criminals and the Supreme Court in Antebellum Louisiana." *Tulane Law Review* 60 (1986): 1247–68.

———. "Sexual Cruelty to Slaves: The Unreported Case of *Humphreys v. Utz.*" *Chicago-Kent Law Review* 68 (1993): 1212–42.

Schmidt, Fredrika Teute, and Barbara Ripel Wilhelm. "Early Proslavery Petitions in Virginia." *William and Mary Quarterly*, 3d ser., 30 (1973): 133–46.

Schwartz, Gary T. "Tort Law and the Economy in Nineteenth-Century America: A Reinterpretation." *Yale Law Journal* 90 (1981): 1717–75.

Schwarz, Philip J. "Emancipators, Protectors, and Anomalies: Free Black Slaveowners in Virginia." *Virginia Magazine of History and Biography* 95 (1987): 317–38.

———. "Forging the Shackles: The Development of Virginia's Criminal Code for Slaves." In *Ambivalent Legacy: A Legal History of the South*, edited by David J. Bodenhamer and James W. Ely Jr. Jackson: University Press of Mississippi, 1984.

———. "Gabriel's Challenge: Slaves and Crime in Late Eighteenth-Century Virginia." *Virginia Magazine of History and Biography* 90 (1982): 283–309.

———. "The Transportation of Slaves from Virginia, 1801–1865." *Virginia Magazine of History and Biography* 97 (1986): 215–40.

Shapiro, Barbara. "Law and Science in Seventeenth-Century England." *Stanford Law Review* 21 (1969): 727–66.

Sheldon, Marianne Buroff. "Black-White Relations in Richmond, Virginia, 1782–1820." *Journal of Southern History* 45 (1979): 27–44.

Shingleton, Royse Gordon. "The Trial and Punishment of Slaves in Baldwin County, Georgia, 1812–1826." *Southern Humanities Review* 8 (1974): 67–73.

Simpson, A. W. B. "Entails and Perpetuities." In *Legal Theory and Legal History: Essays on the Common Law*. London: Hambledon Press, 1987.

———. "The Horwitz Thesis and the History of Contracts." *University of Chicago Law Review* 46 (1979): 533–601.

———. "The Rise and Fall of the Legal Treatise: Legal Principles and the Forms of Legal Literature." *University of Chicago Law Review* 48 (1981): 632–80.

Sio, Arnold. "Commentary." In *Historical Reflections: Réflexion historique* 9, Waterloo, Ontario: History Department, University of Waterloo, 1979.

———. "Interpretations of Slavery: The Slave Status in the Americas." *Comparative Studies in Society and History* 7 (1965): 289–308.

Sirmans, M. Eugene. "The Legal Status of the Slave in South Carolina, 1670–1740." *Journal of Southern History* 28 (1962): 462–73.

Skilton, Robert H. "Developments in Mortgage Law and Practice." *Temple University Law Quarterly* 17 (1943): 315–84.

Skinner, Quentin. "The Idea of Negative Liberty: Philosophical and Historical Perspectives." In *Philosophy in History: Essays in the Historiography of Philosophy*, edited by Richard Rorty, J. C. Schneewind, and Skinner. Cambridge: Harvard University Press, 1984.

Smiddy, Linda O. "Judicial Nullification of State Statutes Restricting the Emancipation of Slaves: A Southern Court's Call for Reform." *South Carolina Law Review* 42 (1991): 589–655.

Sparks, Randy J. "Religion in Amite County, Mississippi." In *Masters and Slaves in the House of the Lord: Race and Religion in the American South, 1740–1870*, edited by John B. Boles. Lexington: University of Kentucky Press, 1988.

Stealey, John Edmund, III. "Responsibilities and Liabilities of the Bailee of Slave Labor in Virginia." *American Journal of Legal History* 12 (1968): 336–53.

Stephenson, Mason W., and D. Grier Stephenson Jr. " 'To Protect and Defend': Joseph Henry Lumpkin, the Supreme Court of Georgia, and Slavery." *Emory Law Journal* 25 (1976): 579–608.

Tansey, Richard. "Bernard Kendig and the New Orleans Slave Trade." *Louisiana History* 23 (1982): 159–78.

Temperley, Howard. "Capitalism, Slavery, and Ideology." *Past and Present* 75 (1977): 94–118.

Thompson, E. P. "The Moral Economy of the English Crowd in the Eighteenth Century." *Past and Present* 50 (1971): 76–136.

Toplin, Robert Brent. "Between Black and White: Attitudes toward Southern Mulattoes, 1830–1860." *Journal of Southern History* 45 (1979): 185–200.

Traynor, Roger J. "Fact Skepticism and the Judicial Process." *University of Pennsylvania Law Review* 106 (1958): 635–62.

Tushnet, Mark. "The American Law of Slavery, 1810–1860: A Study in the Persistence of Legal Autonomy." *Law and Society Review* 10 (1975): 119–84.

Vaughan, Alden T. "Blacks in Virginia: A Note on the First Decade." *William and Mary Quarterly*, 3d ser., 29 (1972): 469–78.

———. "The Origins Debate: Slavery and Racism in Seventeenth-Century Virginia." *Virginia Magazine of History and Biography* 97 (1989): 311–54.

Wade, Richard. "The Vesey Plot: A Reconsideration." *Journal of Southern History* 30 (1964): 143–61.

Wahl, Jenny Bourne. "The Bondsman's Burden: An Economic Analysis of the Jurisprudence of Slaves and Common Carriers." *Journal of Economic History* 53 (1993): 495–526.

Washburne, Wilcomb E. "Law and Authority in Colonial Virginia." In *Law and Authority in Colonial America*, edited by George Athan Billias. New York: Dover Publications, 1965.

Watson, Alan. "The Evolution of Law: Continued." *Law and History Review* 5 (198): 537–70.

———. "The Structure of Blackstone's Commentaries." *Yale Law Journal* 97 (1988): 795–822.

Watson, Alan D. "Impulse Toward Independence: Resistance and Rebellion among North Carolina Slaves, 1750–1775." *Journal of Negro History* 63 (1978): 317–28.

———. "North Carolina Slave Courts, 1715–1785." *North Carolina Historical Review* 60 (1983): 24–36.

Wax, Darold D. " 'The Great Risque We Run': The Aftermath of Slave Rebellion at Stono, South Carolina, 1739–1745." *Journal of Negro History* 67 (1982): 136–47.

Wayne, Michael. "An Old South Morality Play: Reconsidering the Social Underpinnings of the Proslavery Ideology." *Journal of American History* 77 (1990): 864–85.

Wertheim, Frederick. "Note: Slavery and the Fellow Servant Rule: An Antebellum Dilemma." *New York University Law Review* 61 (1986): 1112–48.

Wiecek, William M. "*Somerset*: Lord Mansfield and the Legitimacy of Slavery in the Anglo-American World." *University of Chicago Law Review* 42 (1974): 86–147.

———. "The Statutory Law of Slavery and Race in the Thirteen Mainland Colonies of British America." *William and Mary Quarterly*, 3d ser., 34 (1977): 58–80.

Wood, Betty. "Prisons, Workhouses, and the Control of Slave Labour in Low Country Georgia, 1763–1815." *Slavery and Abolition* 8 (1987): 247–71.

———. " 'Until He Shall Be Dead, Dead, Dead': The Judicial Treatment of Slaves in Eighteenth-Century Georgia." *Georgia Historical Quarterly* 71 (1987): 377–98.

Wren, J. Thomas. "A 'Two-Fold Character': The Slave as Person and Property in Virginia Court Cases, 1800–1860." *Southern Studies* 24 (1985): 417–31.

Yanuck, Julius. "Thomas Ruffin and North Carolina Slave Law." *Journal of Southern History* 21 (1955): 456–75.

Yetman, Norman R. "The Background of the Slave Narrative Collection." *American Quarterly* 19 (1967): 534–53.

Younger, Richard D. "Southern Grand Juries and Slavery." *Journal of Negro History* 40 (1955): 166–78.

Dissertations

Albert, Peter Joseph. "The Protean Institution: The Geography, Economy, and Ideology of Slavery in Post-Revolutionary Virginia." Ph.D. dissertation, University of Maryland, 1976.

Clark, Ernest James, Jr. "Slave Cases before the North Carolina Supreme Court, 1818–1858." Ph.D. dissertation, University of North Carolina, 1959.

Duncan, John Donald. "Servitude and Slavery in Colonial South Carolina, 1670–1776." Ph.D. dissertation, Emory University, 1972.

Essah, Patience. "Slavery and Freedom in the First State: The History of Blacks in Delaware from the Colonial Period to 1865." Ph.D. dissertation, University of California, Los Angeles, 1985.

Flanigan, Daniel. "The Criminal Law of Slavery and Freedom." Ph.D. dissertation, Rice University, 1973.

Henderson, William Cinque. "Spartan Slaves: A Documentary Account of Blacks on Trial in Spartanburg, South Carolina, 1830 to 1865." Ph.D. dissertation, Northwestern University, 1978.

Howington, Arthur, III. "The Treatment of Slaves and Free Blacks in the State and Local Courts of Tennessee." Ph.D. dissertation, Vanderbilt University, 1982.

Ingersoll, Thomas N. "Old New Orleans: Race, Class, Sex, and Order in the Early Deep South, 1718–1819." Ph.D. dissertation, University of California, Los Angeles, 1990.

Kerr, Derek. "Petty Felony, Slave Defiance, and Frontier Villainy: Crime and Criminal Justice in Spanish Louisiana, 1770–1803." Ph.D. dissertation, Tulane University, 1983.

McGowan, James Thomas. "Creation of a Slave Society: Louisiana Plantations in the Eighteenth Century." Ph.D. dissertation, University of Rochester, 1976.

Parent, Anthony S., Jr. " 'Either a Fool or a Fury': The Emergence of Paternalism in Colonial Virginia Slave Society." Ph.D. dissertation, University of California, Los Angeles, 1982.

Russell, Thomas R. "Sale Day in Antebellum South Carolina: Slavery, Law, Economy, and Court-Supervised Sales." Ph.D. dissertation, Stanford University, 1993.

Schafer, Judith K. "The Long Arm of the Law: Slavery and the Supreme Court in Antebellum Louisiana, 1809–1862." Ph.D. dissertation, Tulane University, 1985.

Schlotterbeck, John Thomas. "Plantation and Farm: Social and Economic Change in Orange and Greene Counties, Virginia, 1716 to 1860." Ph.D. dissertation, Johns Hopkins University, 1980.

Senese, Donald. "Legal Thought in South Carolina, 1800–1860." Ph.D. dissertation, University of South Carolina, 1970.

Index